Franklin D. Roosevelt and Foreign Affairs

VOLUME III: SEPTEMBER 1935–JANUARY 1937

Roosevelt with President Gabriel Terra of Uruguay in Montevideo.
December 3, 1936.

Franklin D. Roosevelt and Foreign Affairs

VOLUME III: SEPTEMBER 1935–JANUARY 1937

Edited by Edgar B. Nixon

Franklin D. Roosevelt Library

HYDE PARK, NEW YORK

The Belknap Press of Harvard University Press

Cambridge, Massachusetts   1969

Franklin D. Roosevelt and Foreign Affairs, an annotated collection of documents, will ultimately cover all of Roosevelt's terms as President. The first three volumes, being published simultaneously in 1969, cover the first term, 1933 to 1937. The documents are drawn from the Roosevelt papers in the Franklin D. Roosevelt Library, Hyde Park, New York.

Editorial Method

Annotation of the text is confined to identification of persons and explanation of events mentioned; there is no attempt to provide a narrative of the events of the period. It is assumed that users of the volumes will be familiar with the general history of the years covered. However, every effort has been made to explain in the notes obscure or incomplete references. Significant items not printed are cited to source and briefly described. Cross references to related documents "above" and "below" are provided, and running heads give dates of documents on the page for easy location of cross references. Enclosures are printed directly below a document, and when not reprinted their presence or absence in the Roosevelt papers is noted.

Texts are reproduced verbatim except that obvious typist's errors were corrected. Where letters are handwritten all eccentricities of spelling and punctuation are retained. Crossed-out words are printed with a line through them and words substituted for the crossed-out words are in italics. All parenthetical words in the press conference transcripts are by the reporter unless otherwise noted. Uniform style is used in rendering headings, salutations, closes, and signatures. Annotations on the document are reproduced, with a descriptive symbol (explained in the list following) and indication, when possible, of authorship. Marguerite LeHand, private secretary to President Roosevelt, is the LeHand who appears frequently on such notations. When it is apparent that a letter or other document was drafted for the President's signature, either the name of the drafter or that of the department in which it originated is indicated. Explanatory words inserted in the text by the editor appear in italics in brackets.

The different kinds of texts of President Roosevelt's speeches and messages to Congress are indicated in the notes. They may be drafts, the final copy or reading copy, the press release of the final copy, the stenographic transcript, or in the case of speeches a recording of the radio broadcast. The broadcast recording is used as the text when available and differences between this and other texts are noted.

The citation in brackets at the end of each document gives the particular section of the White House files in which the document is located, the subfile, and a descriptive symbol. These designations are explained in the list of abbreviations below. (The Roosevelt Library has in large part retained the White House filing system.) The documents printed are from the Roosevelt papers in the Library (the White House papers) or, in the case of one or two items, Group 14, Roosevelt family papers, or from their collections acquired by the Library. Of the latter, several items are from the papers of R. Walton Moore, Assistant Secretary of State and Counselor to the State Department, 1933–1937. Other collections in the Library from which a few items have been selected for publication are the papers of Louis McHenry Howe, President Roosevelt's personal secretary until his death in 1936, and the papers of Rear Admiral Wilson Brown, Naval Aide to President Roosevelt.

The index to the first three volumes is at the end of Volume III.

Abbreviations

File division

OF: Official File
PPF: President's Personal File
PSF: President's Secretary's File
RL Recordings: Roosevelt Library Recordings

Descriptive symbol

A: autograph, not signed
AS: autograph, signed
CT: carbon typescript, not signed
CTS: carbon typescript, signed
M: mimeographed
T: typescript, ribbon copy, not signed
TS: typescript, ribbon copy, signed

Contents

Franklin D. Roosevelt and Foreign Affairs

VOLUME III: SEPTEMBER 1935–JANUARY 1937

Press Conference, Hyde Park, New York, September 4, 1935, 11 A.M.

[*Excerpt*] Q: Is there anything you want to say further on this Ethiopian situation, that is, the cancellation of the oil leases?[1]

The President: No, I think it has got pretty full stories from Washington.

Q: It was a good piece of diplomacy.

The President: A good job. Of course you can—if I were writing the story, I would put it this way: that by no stretch of the imagination has the President or the Secretary of State ever been the least bit concerned over the possibility of this oil lease involving the United States, in any shape, manner or form in the Ethiopian or Italian problems. Nobody who knows the Administration policies could think for a minute that there could be involvement. The only danger lay in the effect of the oil lease on the negotiations between European powers and Ethiopia that are now going on in Geneva. And of course the result yesterday of the withdrawal from the concession has been a fine thing because it has cleared the air of those conferences. And then, if I were going to write one more paragraph, I would put it this way, "that this is another proof that since March 4th, 1933, dollar diplomacy is not recognized by the American Government."[2]

Q: May we quote that?

The President: I think you could quote that.

Mr. Early: Just that one sentence.

The President: Since the 4th of March, 1933, dollar diplomacy is no longer recognized by the United States Government.

Q: Are you sure that this was dollar diplomacy and that there were no other currencies involved?

The President: Off the record, I would say that that would depend on the rate of exchange.

Q: Would you be willing to answer the question that neither is the pound sterling diplomacy going to be recognized? (The President did not answer.)

Q: As I get it, Mr. President, this means we are not interested—

The President: Wait a minute—as you get it! Off the record, again, I had a very amusing time night before last. One of the more important people said, "You know, it is perfectly clear what it is. This fellow Rickett is an intimate friend"—this is off the record but it shows the flight of imagination people will take—"Rickett is an intimate friend of the Italian baron who shot himself out hunting the other day. And the Italian baron is the son-in-law of the British Minister to Ethiopia, so you get a perfect triangle, do you see?" And I said, "That is very ingenious. What is the next step?" "That is simple. The Italian baron has got hold of his intimate friend, Rickett, and he has told his father-in-law, the British Minister. Rickett comes in and gets the concession and then, when the time comes, he turns it over to the Italian baron, who turns it over to Mussolini. His face is saved and the baron has dropped out. You all fell down."

Q: This fellow Rickett did refer to his "old friend Mussolini" when he announced it.

The President: Yes.

[President's Press Conferences:T]

[1] On Aug. 30, 1935, Francis M. Rickett, a British promoter, announced that he had, on behalf of the Standard Vacuum Oil Company (U.S.), secured from the Ethiopian government the oil exploration concession to some 150,000 square miles in eastern Ethiopia (New York *Times*, Aug. 31, 1935, p. 1). Hull at once announced that the United States had no connection with the deal. Standard Oil officials expressed surprise at the world-wide publicity caused by what they termed a purely commercial transaction and asked the State Department's advice. They were advised to cancel the contract and this was done. Haile Selassie, however, expressed his regret at the cancellation and said he had intended the concession to be a proof of his friendly feelings toward the United States (*Foreign Relations, 1935*, I, 778–784).

[2] See Early to Hull, Sept. 4, 1935, below.

Stephen T. Early, Assistant Secretary to the President, to Cordell Hull, Secretary of State

[Hyde Park] 9/4/35

Memo for the Sec. of State: Att. Mr. McDermott: At his Conference with the newspaper men today, the President, commenting on the cancellation of the Oil Lease,[1] said:

"Since the 4th of March 1933 Dollar Diplomacy is no longer recognized by the United States Government."

The President authorized the newspapermen to use this statement in direct quotes.

This is for your information.

Stephen T. Early

[OF 20:CT]

[1] See above.

Breckinridge Long, Ambassador to Italy, to Roosevelt

Rome, September 6, 1935

My dear Chief: This may be entirely impertinent by the time it reaches you, but the Geneva session may be a long and drawn-out affair. The Italians now expect that the matter will not be decided by the Council and will be thrown over to the Assembly meeting, and it lasts for several weeks.

While the tone of the Italian diplomatic branch is moderate, their intentions are definite, and some of their other declarations more accurately express their purposes than do their expressions to diplomatic officers. They have worked themselves into a fury here. Every man, woman, and child in Italy today hates England. Even if this affair should be settled amicably, I am afraid it will leave its permanent impress upon international relations. It will take years, if they should start today, to change public sentiment in favor of England and to reestablish the cordial and almost historic relations between the two countries which existed up to four or five months ago. They have worked themselves into a state of self-adoration and self-consciousness which leads them to believe that they can meet any Power in battle with success.

The Italian propaganda in Egypt has been rather intense. They have a propaganda organization there and a large colony of citizens which are organized according to Fascist groups. With their air fleet they could make an enormous amount of trouble for England there, and I think could have some marked temporary success if they should come to the point of hostilities. Italy has a large air fleet, and it is all concentrated, or capable of being concentrated, around the Eastern Mediterranean. It is only two and a half hours by air from the bases in Sicily to the coast of Lybia. Lybia flanks Egypt and the Sudan on the west. Eritrea

3

flanks the Sudan on the east, and when they will have arrived in Ethiopia they will flank the Sudan on the south. The Suez Canal assumes a particular political importance for Italy today just as it has for England. With a large body of men in East Africa it will be necessary for Italy to have some communication between them and the home country. That communication can be established through Lybia and across the Sudan. It can be also established through the Suez Canal. The Canal route is more important than the other because of the transport of supplies. If they are brought to the point of hostility with England, they will attempt to take control of the Canal.

Of course this is a direct threat to the British Empire. Without the Canal England loses her route to India, Ceylon, Burma, the Straits Settlements, Australia, and New Zealand. With air bases on the west boundary of Egypt and the Sudan and with air bases on the eastern and southern borders of the Sudan and all communicating directly with supplies from Italy only two and a half hours from the coast of Lybia, it can be understood that their position is rather strategic.

Of course I do not believe they are going to have trouble with England, but the situation is such that England must feel the threat to her empire, and it is also such that Italy feels her power in connection with it. Consequently they are emboldened to rashness, and the high state of fanaticism to which they have been worked renders them a very dangerous people, particularly in view of the excellent organization which they support.

They are now in a state of excitement which might lead them to any rash act in case of hostility, and if they found that they could not take and use the Canal, they might, after the manner of Sampson, attempt to destroy the temple and themselves amongst the rest.

Provided, however, that they do not come to open hostilities with England, and provided also that they do proceed in Ethiopia to establish a military and political control over the country, it will not mean that their objective has been reached. I am conscious that I am walking on delicate ground, but it is my firm belief that the success which probably awaits them in their first venture from home will only lead them on to other fields.

They will be trouble-makers in Africa and will attempt to connect Lybia and Ethiopia. Across the Red Sea they will try to reinforce their friendly relations with the Iman of Yemen and fortify him in his opposition to Ibn Saud, the King of Arabia with the object of controlling that at present unoccupied and independent country. This will not happen in the immediate future. They will entrench themselves in Ethiopia before they venture to other fields. But I have not the slightest doubt in my mind that they have intentions on the eastern side of the Red Sea.

Their declarations to the effect that they had no hostile intentions toward any British province are hardly to be taken at their face value considering their present and recent activities in Egypt and their incitement in the Italian press to Egypt to assume its independence.

So that whatever the outcome of the present difficulties being thrashed out at Geneva we are going to be confronted with a continuing source of trouble in the future—and that on several accounts. First, the threat to the British Empire in the east; second, the failure of the League of Nations to be useful for anything outside of Europe with the possible dropping of the League as an instrument of policy by England; third, a reversion to the pre-League theory of practical politics and alliances; and fourth, the distrust which will exist in the future between Italy and England and will serve to disrupt the solidarity of the three western Powers. The result of this last will be an aggrandizement of the power and importance of Germany and an extension, perhaps stealthily, of her influence southerly and easterly.

There is a report in circulation that Mussolini is mad—that he has lost his reason. He has not. He is just as cool and calm and deliberate and has prepared for this present situation through the last year and a half in a stealthy but deliberate manner. Each economic and financial move, attributed at the time to the pressure of economic necessity, is now revealed as a part of his military preparations. It is quite possible that they have been hurried because of the economic conditions that existed, by its need for expansion and the necessity to show that they are a world power and their fanatical belief in the power of their own organization and in the efficacy of that thing they call Fascism which has led them on and which is today driving them. They are not mad. They are deliberate, determined, obdurate, ruthless, and almost vicious. The whole organization is as one man. The efficiency of the army has been increased enormously till it is not recognizable as the same military organization, and the whole civil and military elements of the population are moving as pieces of a single organism, spurred on by the thought that failure means utter collapse and that they must succeed.

So whichever way Geneva goes there is trouble on our hands in Europe for years to come. A new order is in the making, and the results of it cannot yet be foreseen.

I hurry this off to catch you before you leave on your western trip. I am talking to the British Ambassador this evening, but it will be after the pouch closes, and I want to put this in this pouch, because I am not sure that it will reach you before you get away.

You may be interested to know that my health is much better and that after several weeks in hospitals that I am looking forward to a real return to health. The ulcer has gone, but my stomach is still suffering from some of its effects.

I hope you are well and that you will have a wonderful trip and get some rest and recreation, which you so fully deserve and need.

With every good wish and expressions of affectionate regard I am, Yours as ever,

Breckinridge Long[1]

[PSF:Italy:TS]

[1] In Roosevelt's reply of Sept. 19, 1935 (*Personal Letters, 1928–1945*, I, 508), he said that Long and Dodd had been far more accurate in their pessimism than any of his other friends in Europe; however, even if hostilities started he believed he could take the cruise he had planned. He left Washington on September 26 for the West Coast, boarded the *Houston* at San Diego on October 2, and returned to Washington on October 24 (PPF 1-0).

Roosevelt to R. Walton Moore, Assistant Secretary of State

Hyde Park, N. Y., September 11, 1935

Memorandum for Hon. R. Walton Moore: I entirely approve the suggested leave for Ambassador Dodd, and I also agree with you that he should not extend the ninety days' leave, which will be due him, to much longer than that period—perhaps one hundred days over here in all would be a good arrangement.

You should tell him I think that in the event of war in which Germany engages, our Embassy would probably be asked to look after the citizens and property of belligerents and that in that event he would, of course, have to stay at his post. However, if things are peaceful, I do not see any reason why he should not carry out his idea.

In any event, we most certainly do not want him to consider resigning. I need him in Berlin.

F.D.R.

[OF 523:CT]

Press Conference, Hyde Park, New York, September 13, 1935, 11 A.M.

[*Excerpt*] The President: There again is a complete lack of news value.[1] The real news value today is the foreign situation.

Q: What can you say on that?

The President: Well, that is the real news of course. We are all watching it. The Secretary of State in his very excellent statement in the papers this morning seemed to put the situation very well and there isn't anything further that we are doing at the present time.[2] We were all very much concerned over it.

Q: Does that imply—

The President: No, it does not imply. We are not going to get into the war.

Q: It might be a question of judgment but, as I read one of these sentences and as an implication based on what you said, "That you are not doing anything more at the present time," does that imply that you might at a certain time participate in sanctions?

The President: If the war breaks out we have perfectly definite legislation covering the subject. Simply a question of following legislation. Nothing further, not even by a stretch of the imagination.

Q: That legislation is subject to your interpretation.

The President: As to whether a state of war exists.

Q: Mr. President, would you state what constitutes implements of war?

The President: That question is being studied by the State Department at the present time.

[President's Press Conferences:T]

[1] The President had just been asked about his talks on the day before with WPA Administrator Hopkins and Secretary of the Interior Ickes.

[2] Hull, in a statement dated Sept. 13, 1935, had called on Italy and Ethiopia to observe their obligations under the Kellogg Pact and to solve their differences peaceably (State Department, *Press Releases,* Sept. 14, 1935, pp. 194–196).

Roosevelt to James W. Gerard, New York

Hyde Park, N.Y., September 13, 1935

Dear Jimmy: That is a grand speech and I wish more of them like that could be made in London and on the Continent. Why is it that so many Americans spend their time when visiting Europe in running down or apologizing for their own nation. I sometimes wish that we could have a check-up made and then let them know that for their sins they could not return to the United States for a year or two.[1]

Keep up the good work.

As ever yours,

[PPF 977:CT]

[1] Gerard had spoken at a luncheon given in his honor by The Pilgrims at the Hotel Victoria in London on July 12, 1935 (Gerard to Roosevelt, Sept. 12, 1935, PPF 977). In his speech (printed in a program of the proceedings), he defended the Administration's policies and the "bold and resolute measures" taken by Roosevelt in 1933.

Roosevelt to Cordell Hull, Secretary of State, and Henry A. Wallace, Secretary of Agriculture

Hyde Park, N.Y., September 13, 1935

Memorandum for the Secretary of State and the Secretary of Agriculture: What would you think of restoring the tariff on Canadian hay? As I remember it this was reduced last because of the shortage. The price was then $22.00 a ton. Today, with excellent crops, western hay has come back and eastern farmers are suffering from a low price, $16.00 to $17.00 a ton.[1]

F.D.R.

[OF 1412:CT]

[1] No further reference to this proposal has been found.

James Harvey Rogers to Roosevelt

Paris, September 17, 1935

My dear Mr. President: After sitting through the sessions of the Economic Committee of the League of Nations, I have come to certain conclusions which I have decided to write to you.

In my opinion, no international agreement on monetary stabilization will bring any worthwhile assurance of actual stability on the continent of Europe. Until the gold-bloc and pseudo-gold-bloc countries are prepared to devalue their currencies to more realistic levels, few believe that, even if entered into, such an agreement could be kept. On the other hand, the complete stability of the dollar and the relatively narrow fluctuations of the sterling group currencies are leading to the impression that a de facto stabilization may be in sight. In my opinion, such a stabilization is all that can be hoped for in the near future and I believe that it would be a mistake to attempt anything further.

The Dutch florin is again under pressure and should it break within the next few months this pressure is almost sure to be transferred in turn to the Swiss and French francs.

With the outbreak of war in Africa and the succeeding wrangle over sanctions, there is a clear expectation in Paris that a larger and more persistent flow of funds to the United States will be precipitated—with a resultant further gold drain from Europe.

Confidence in the dollar has increased greatly in the past few months—largely, I think, because of its complete stability since January 1934, and because of a growing belief that it will not be further devalued. Also the extent of our recovery has made a great impression all over Europe, and many express the opinion that at last America will pull the world out of depression.

I shall arrive on the *Normandie* on September 23, and, if you wish, I shall be delighted to talk with you about European conditions at your convenience.[1]

With kindest regards and trusting that you are getting a real vacation,

Yours very sincerely,

James Harvey Rogers

[PPF 3038:TS]

[1] Rogers, professor of political economy at Yale, and American representative on the League of Nations Economic Committee, had been in Geneva since April 29, assisting the committee in the drafting of a report on economic obstructions to world trade. He had a half-hour appointment with Roosevelt on Nov. 12, 1935 (New York *Times*, April 30, p. 10; Sept. 25, 1935, p. 16; PPF 1-0). Roosevelt replied Sept. 28, 1935, below.

Press Conference, Hyde Park, New York, September 18, 1935, 10:45 A.M.

[*Excerpt*] Q: Mr. President, is there any late news from Europe?

The President: Nothing. I talked yesterday afternoon and the thing is absolutely the same.

Q: The Associated Press reports today that Italy is looking for a compromise, or is ready to talk turkey anyway.[1]

The President: I cannot comment on it because, off the record, I do think, from the newspaper stories this morning, that it is beginning to look as though there is a ray of hope.

Q: That is off the record?

The President: I have had nothing from the State Department up to today at noon. I have had no cheering news.

Q: As a matter of fact, rather careful reading of those dispatches this morning indicated that all Italy has agreed to do is to consider substantial proposals, if made, and no suggestion that they have been made.

Q: It shows that the British Empire is a more powerful agency of peace than the League of Nations.

The President: Yes.

[President's Press Conferences:T]

[1] Cf. Clarence K. Streit's dispatch of September 17 from Geneva in the New York *Times* of Sept. 18, 1935, pp. 1–2.

Roosevelt to Nicholas Roosevelt, New York

Hyde Park, N.Y., September 19, 1935

Dear Nick: I have not had a chance before this to answer yours of September third.[1] The general feeling is that much will be gained in the long run by giving to the Service men some Consular e..perience at one time or another. Moffat was delighted to go to what amounts to almost a Ministerial post. No other shifts have been made as yet among those you mention—nor will they be in the present emergency.

Always sincerely,

[PPF 1431:CT]

[1] Roosevelt, of the editorial staff of the New York *Herald-Tribune*, had questioned the wisdom of certain proposed transfers in the Foreign Service, including that of Pierrepont Moffat, chief of the Division of Western European Affairs, transferred to Sydney as consul general (Sept. 21, 1935, PPF 1431).

Cordell Hull, Secretary of State, to Roosevelt

Washington [September 25, 1935]

My dear Mr. President: Section 2 of the Joint Resolution of Congress which you approved August 31, 1935, contains the following provision:

The President is hereby authorized to proclaim upon recommendation of the Board from time to time a list of articles which shall be considered arms, ammunition, and implements of war for the purposes of this section.

In order that the administrative machinery required by Section 2 may be set up with the least possible delay and in order that the required registration of manufacturers, exporters and importers of arms may be completed before the provisions in regard to licenses become effective on November 29, it has seemed advisable that a proclamation enumerating the arms, ammunition and implements of war considered to be such for the purposes of Section 2 be issued immediately. I, therefore, enclose for your consideration and, if you approve, your signature, a draft of a proclamation which was prepared by officers of the Department in consultation with officers of the Department of the Treasury, the War Department, the Navy Department and the Department of Commerce. The enumeration of arms, ammunition and implements of war contained therein is, I believe, satisfactory both from the technical point of view and from the point of view of efficient administration.

This draft is submitted to you upon the recommendation of the National Munitions Control Board which approved it at a meeting held in my office on September 24.[1]

Faithfully yours,

Cordell Hull

[OF 178-A:TS]

[1] The draft proclamation enclosed was issued Sept. 25, 1935; it is printed in *Public Papers*, IV, 373–375. This version was based on a draft prepared by Joseph C. Green, chief of the Office of Arms and Munitions Control in the State Department, who sent it to Hull with a long letter of comment dated Sept. 14, 1935 (Moore Papers). Green noted that it "was certainly the intent of Congress that the President should be obliged to proclaim an embargo upon the exportation of arms, ammunition and implements of war to any foreign country as soon as it became involved in hostilities with any other country"; also, the country had certainly been led to believe that the joint resolution would bar the exportation of arms "to any country engaged in armed hostility against any other country."

Green noted further that this conclusion did not necessarily follow: the President could, under the language of the resolution, wait until the last day of hostilities before invoking the law. However, the pressure of public opinion would probably cause him to invoke it immediately after the declaration of war. Assistant Secretary of State Moore agreed that under the letter of the law the President could delay an arms embargo proclamation "until the last hour of the war before its termination." But he also agreed that the pressure of public opinion would make this unlikely (Moore to Hull, Oct. 3, 1935, Moore Papers). The first meeting of the National Munitions Control Board (established by S.J.R. 173) was held Sept. 24, 1935; on the meeting see Hull, *Memoirs*, I, 416.

Roosevelt to James Harvey Rogers, Yale University, New Haven, Connecticut

[Grand Island, Nebraska] September 28, 1935

Dear Jim: That is an exceedingly interesting note of yours of September seventeenth.[1] It has just come to me at Grand Island, Nebraska.

What you say coincides very definitely with the conclusions I had come to.

I shall hope to see you very soon after I get back, about October twenty-second.[2]

Always sincerely,

[PPF 3038:CT]

[1] Above.
[2] Rogers saw Roosevelt on November 12 (PPF 1-0).

Roosevelt to Cordell Hull, Secretary of State

[En route to San Diego] October 1, 1935

[*Telegram*] The last third of my speech at Exposition Wednesday referring to foreign matters will interest you and our missions abroad. You can get it from Associated Press first thing in morning.[1] All well. Most successful trip. Expect to sail Wednesday afternoon. Warm regards.

Franklin D. Roosevelt

[OF 1561:CT]

[1] See below.

Speech by Roosevelt at the San Diego Exposition, San Diego, California, Oct. 2, 1935

[*Excerpt*][1] Several centuries ago the greatest writer in our history described the two most menacing clouds that hang over human government and human society as "malice domestic and fierce foreign war." We are not rid of those dangers but we can summon our intelligence to meet them.

Never was there more genuine reason for Americans to face down these two causes of fear. "Malice domestic" from time to time will come to you in the shape of those who would raise false issues, pervert facts, preach the gospel of hate, and minimize the importance of public action to secure human rights or spiritual ideals. There are those today who would sow these seeds, but your answer to them is in the possession of the plain facts of our present condition.

The second cloud—"foreign war"—is more real—a more potent danger at this moment to the future of civilization. It is not surprising that many of our citizens feel a deep sense of apprehension lest some of the nations of the world repeat the folly of twenty years ago and drag civilization to a level from which world-wide recovery may be all but impossible.

In the face of this apprehension the American people can have but one concern—the American people can speak but one sentiment: despite what happens in continents overseas, the United States of America shall and must remain, as long ago the Father of our Country prayed that it might remain—unentangled and free.

This country seeks no conquest. We have no imperial designs. From day to day and year to year, we are establishing a more perfect assurance of peace with our neighbors. We rejoice especially in the prosperity, the stability and the independence of all of the American republics. We not only earnestly desire peace, but we are moved by a stern determination to avoid those perils that will endanger our peace with the world.

Our national determination to keep free of foreign wars and foreign entanglements cannot prevent us from feeling deep concern when ideals and principles that we have cherished are challenged. In the United States we regard it as axiomatic that every person shall enjoy the free exercise of his religion according to the dictates of his conscience. Our flag for a century and a half has been the symbol of the principle of liberty of conscience, of religious freedom and equality before the law; and these concepts are deeply ingrained in our national character.

It is true that other nations may, as they do, enforce contrary rules of conscience and conduct. It is true that policies may be pursued under flags other than our own, and those policies are beyond our jurisdiction. Yet in our inner individual lives we can never be indifferent, and we assert for ourselves complete freedom to embrace, to profess and to observe the principles for which our flag has so long been the lofty symbol. As it was so well said by James Madison, long over a century ago, "We hold it for a fundamental and inalienable truth that religion and the manner of discharging it can be directed only by reason and conviction, not by force or violence."

My friends, as President of the United States I say to you most earnestly once more that the people of America and the Government of those people intend and expect to remain at peace with the world. In the two years and a half of my Presidency, this Government has remained constant in following this policy of our own choice. At home we have preached, and will continue to preach, the gospel of the good neighbor. I hope from the bottom of my heart that as the years go on, nation will follow nation in proving by deed as well as by word their adherence to the ideal of the Americas—I am a Good Neighbor.[2]

[Speech File:T]

[1] This speech was delivered at 2 P.M. in the San Diego high school stadium before a crowd of 45,000 people. Governor Frank Merriam of California presented the President and Mrs. Roosevelt. After leaving Washington late in the evening of September 26, the President had spoken briefly at several stops on the trip and had made major addresses at Fremont, Nebraska, on September 28; at the dedication of Boulder Dam in Nevada on September 30; and at Los Angeles on October 1. At San Diego the President boarded the U.S.S. *Houston* for the return to Washington via the Panama Canal.

[2] This text is that of the stenographic transcript. Roosevelt made a number of changes in the reading copy (Speech File), all unimportant except a revision of this last sentence, which read originally: " . . . nation will follow nation in subscribing to the ideal of the Americas—I am a good neighbor." The entire speech is printed in *Public Papers,* IV, 405–412.

Stephen T. Early, Assistant Secretary to the President, to Frederick A. Storm, Edward L. Roddan, and Francis M. Stephenson, Aboard the U.S.S. *Portland*

[Aboard the U.S.S. *Houston,* October 4, 1935]

[*Radiogram*] For Storm, Roddan and Stevenson[1]

The President suggests the following for your stories quote

The President is receiving almost hourly bulletins from Washington covering the foreign situation. Even while fishing from a small boat he can receive information by signal from the *Houston*. He is thus in complete contact with the situation. As a matter of fact the complete freedom from a constant stream of callers and telephone messages enables him for the first time in six months to get relaxation while at the same time he can have opportunities to give quiet consideration to the nation's foreign and domestic policies. It is clear that he is satisfied as definitely stated in his San Diego speech that the European situation will not involve the U.S. in any possibility of war.[2]

[Wilson Brown Papers:FDR:A][3]

[1] Frederick A. Storm of the United Press, Edward L. Roddan of Universal News Service, and Francis M. Stephenson of the Associated Press, aboard the U.S.S. *Portland,* which served as the base of operations for some two dozen reporters, photographers, and newsreel men. Procedure in the handling of official dispatches was prescribed in a letter from Capt. G. J. Rowcliff, director of Naval Communications, to Rudolph Forster, executive clerk of the White House, Sept. 28, 1935 (OF 200-L). No dispatches were to be sent from Washington to the President without the approval of Forster or Maurice Latta, Forster's assistant, except those sent by the State Department. Confidential messages should be marked "confidential"; for these the Navy had prepared a special cipher. Rowcliff asked, however, that if possible the confidential system not be used for messages that contained quotations from the press or information that would be made public in the future, "or for messages which have been received or will be sent in plain language by telegraph or telephone." Such use would jeopardize the security of all other messages sent in the cipher. He also asked that dispatches that were not confidential but contained information not to be made public immediately be marked "restricted"; these messages would also be sent in cipher.
[2] Oct. 2, 1935, above. The President's suggestion respecting news stories was followed: see New York *Times,* Oct. 5, 1935, p. 6.
[3] This copy of the radiogram is Roosevelt's autograph draft.

Cordell Hull, Secretary of State, to Roosevelt, Aboard the U.S.S. *Houston*

[Washington, October 4, 1935]

Secret

[*Radiogram*] Replying to your telegram of today,[1] we are expecting further and official proofs of state of war tomorrow morning and will at once communicate with you. The proposed proclamations are two in number, the first applying to section one of the Neutrality Act, and we hope to make public this proclamation under section one tomorrow, Saturday, assuming adequate official information to warrant doing so is then in our hands. This, the Munitions Embargo Proclamation, contains the reasons and the policy so fully that we think the following brief statement to accompany will be sufficient:

In view of the situation which has unfortunately developed in relations between Ethiopia and Italy, it has become my duty toward carrying out the spirit and intent of the Joint Resolution of Congress, approved 31 August 1935, to issue, and I am today issuing, a Proclamation prohibiting the exportation to Ethiopia and Italy from this country of arms, ammunition and implements of war.

It is our opinion that your Proclamation under section six, requiring passengers to travel at their own risk on belligerent vessels, should be held in reserve since Ethiopia has no vessels and Italy is not at war with any other country. We are giving careful consideration to the suggestions contained in your last paragraph and will send you our views.[2]

[OF 200-L:T]

[1] Roosevelt said that as soon as Hull received official confirmation of Italian hostilities within Ethiopia he would issue a neutrality proclamation, and he asked Hull to draft an accompanying statement (*Foreign Relations, 1935,* I, 794).

[2] Roosevelt had asked Hull (*ibid.*) to consider giving publicity (after the proclamation was issued) to the names of Americans sailing from the United States on Italian ships, and making public the cargo manifests of all American goods "destined for either belligerent including those goods all raw materials which do not fall into munitions classification." The next day the President radioed Hull that the facts appeared to establish the commencement of hostilities and authorized him to take action (*ibid.,* pp. 797–798).

Statement by Roosevelt on the Arms Embargo Proclamation

[Washington, October 5, 1935]

In view of the situation which has unhappily developed between Ethiopia and Italy, it has become my duty under the provisions of the Joint Resolution of Congress approved August 31, 1935, to issue, and I am today issuing, my Proclamation making effective an embargo on the exportation from this country to Ethiopia and Italy of arms, ammunition and implements of war.[1] Notwithstanding the hope we entertained that war would be avoided, and the exertion of our influence in that direction, we are now compelled to recognize the simple and indisputable fact that Ethiopian and Italian armed forces are engaged in combat, thus creating a state of war within the intent and meaning of the Joint Resolution.

In these specific circumstances I desire it to be understood that any of our people who voluntarily engage in transactions of any character with either of the belligerents do so at their own risk.[2]

[OF 200-L:T]

[1] Printed in *Public Papers,* IV, 412–415, and widely published in the newspapers of October 6.

[2] This statement (also printed *ibid.,* 417–418) was drafted in the State Department. Hull's accompanying message noted that the statement did not include references to measures as drastic as those proposed by the President in case the proclamation were violated. Hull thought that the statement went about as far as was advisable at the time; if necessary, further steps could be taken later (OF 200-L). Asked about the last sentence at his October 10 press conference, Hull read a prepared statement that, while technically there was nothing to prevent American citizens from doing business with either of the belligerents (other than the exporting of arms and munitions), the President's warning was part of his policy of trying to keep the United States out of war (New York *Times,* Oct. 11, 1935, p. 11; *Foreign Relations, 1935,* I, 803–804). Ambassador Long cabled Hull on Oct. 10, 1935 (*ibid.,* p. 804), that Italian reaction to the proclamation was "quite mild."

The Federal Council of the Churches of Christ in America to Roosevelt, Aboard the U.S.S. *Houston*

New York, N.Y., Oct. 5 [1935]

The President of the United States, U.S.S. *Houston,* San Francisco Radio

Sir: The Federal Council of Churches stands squarely behind you in your declared purpose to keep the United States from becoming involved in war. We believe that the churches belonging to the Council will uphold you in your determination to remain at peace with all the world. We are confident that the people of our churches will pray unitedly that divine guidance may be yours in the solemn hour of the world's history.

Samuel McCrea Cavert, General Secretary, Federal Council of the Churches of Christ in America

[OF 200-L:CT]

Roosevelt to Cordell Hull, Secretary of State

[Aboard U.S.S. *Houston,* October 10, 1935][1]

[*Radiogram*] For Hull—I approve your Black One Hundred Four.[2] Period In regard general policy at this time I suggest for your study the following outline colon

First: U.S.A. position is clear in that it is bound by the Neutrality Act and President has no authority to enter into embargo or import or export agreements affecting belligerents outside the scope of that Act.

Second: The Act itself allows two matters of latitude which are subject to the President's interpretation (a) what constitutes munitions of war and (b) what constitutes export of such munitions to neutral nations but for transhipment to a belligerent.

Paragraph. In regard to (a) the list of munitions contained in proclamation should stand for the present at least.[3] Period. We should study carefully possible future additions to the list including such things as processed copper and steel, so as to be ready to make decision in case League or Great Britain and France add articles of commerce not on our present munitions list. In making this study try to find out what orders of all kinds are being placed with us by Italian government or firms. Period. In any event I am opposed to any quota system of exports to Italy. Period. We must either allow an export item or disallow it as a munition.

Paragraph As to (b) This will depend on what nations apply sanctions. Period To those which do it is obvious that we can continue to export everything with certainty such exports will not go to belligerents Period From those which do not apply sanctions we can require such drastic proof of nontranshipment that in effect such exports by us will be negligible.

Paragraph Third: I am a great believer in the good effect of making public names of those who trade even at their own risk with belligerents. Period. This information is easily obtainable through Treasury and Commerce Departments and I believe there is no law to prevent making this information public. Period. The same principle applies to names of Americans travelling at own risk on belligerent ships [.]

Paragraph Fourth It can and should be made clear at Geneva and in Washington that United States cannot and will not join other nation or nations in sanctions but will go as far as laws allow to avoid giving material assistance to belligerents to further their conducting what we have already officially declared to be a war.[4] End

Roosevelt

[Wilson Brown Papers:AS]

[1] Neither this text (Roosevelt's autograph original) nor the typed copy (OF 200-L) is dated; this date is derived from Hull, *Memoirs*, I, 432.

[2] ("Black" denotes the particular code being used.) This cable is not in the Roosevelt

papers; however, it appears to have been sent by Hull on October 9 or 10 and was a summary of his cable to Wilson in Geneva of October 9 (Hull, *Memoirs*, I, 432). In the latter cable Hull told the minister that it should be made clear to the League that the United States was acting independently and could not join in any League action (*Foreign Relations, 1935*, I, 843).

[3] Proclamation of Oct. 5, 1934 (*Public Papers*, IV, 412–415).

[4] Hull acknowledged this radiogram in a cable of Oct. 11, 1935 (OF 200-L), and replied at greater length below.

Cordell Hull, Secretary of State, to Roosevelt, Aboard the U.S.S. *Houston*

Washington, 11 Oct. [1935]

Secret

[*Radiogram*] With regard to your first suggestion,[1] I have already before me a carefully considered study of the legal aspect of your thought. Certain raw materials or partly processed products might eventually be added to the list of arms, ammunition and implements of war enumerated in your Embargo Proclamation. It is our opinion that the Joint Resolution does not give authority for such additions to the list as you suggest and that additional legislation would be necessary to warrant any additions of that nature. I invite your attention to the fact that the Joint Resolution uses the expression "arms, ammunition and implements of war" and not, repeat not, "munitions of war," which is a broader term. The courts would almost undoubtedly interpret the words "arms, ammunition and implements of war" according to their commonly recognized definition and hold that to do otherwise would be contrary to the intent of Congress. Should the courts entertain doubt on the question, they would turn to the history of the legislation and scrutinize the reports of the committees and what was stated by the members in charge of the legislation at the time it was presented and considered. They would find that the following question was addressed to Senator Pittman on the floor, "Mr. President, may I inquire of the Senator whether the articles mentioned, implements of war, etc., include such commodities as wheat, corn, cotton and other food products?" To that question Senator Pittman replied in the negative, stating that the definition of arms, ammunition and implements of war is well recognized in international law and referring to the list in the Arms Traffic Convention of 1925 to which the Senate gave its advice and consent to ratification during the session.

19

The enumeration in your Proclamation follows in general the enumeration in the Arms Traffic Convention of 1925 and the enumeration in the draft convention now under negotiation in Geneva. These constitute the most generally recognized definitions of the terms used. Influential section of the press has been urging that the enumeration be extended to include certain raw materials. In order to put an end to this agitation, I propose, if you concur in this suggestion, to issue a statement to the press setting forth the legal status of the question along the lines of the exposition in this telegram. With regard to your third suggestion,[2] early this week we arranged with Departments of Treasury and Commerce to have daily confidential reports on import and export trade with belligerents in such considerable detail as their standing methods of reporting make possible. I expect to have the first of such reports shortly and will advise you as soon as details become operative. Secretary Roper and I both feel that in the present situation it would be better to withhold publicity with regard to the details of trading with belligerents until we see whether or not our present efforts of cooperation with the American public are effective. As to the publication of names, I feel it would be wiser to proceed slowly and to avoid incurring the criticism and the certain antagonism of traders and travelers when it is not yet evident that they are failing to support our program. It would seem to me that a cooperative method with our public at the moment might probably have more beneficial results. Furthermore, if the policy of publishing names should be adopted, it would be a simple matter for traders to have their export declarations filed in the names of customs brokers, agents, etc., and so conceal their own identity. I am venturing these personal observations with a view merely to be of help to you.[3]

Hull

[OF 200-L:T]

[1] See above.

[2] Apparently no statement was issued. On this question, see two memoranda by Joseph C. Green of the Office of Arms and Munitions Control of the State Department, Oct. 7 and 9, 1935, in *Foreign Relations, 1935,* I, 801–802, 802–803; and cf. Roosevelt's statement of Oct. 30, 1935, quoted in the press conference of that date, below.

[3] This text is that of the unpunctuated copy of the radiogram; capitals and punctuation have been supplied.

John Cudahy, Ambassador to Poland, to Roosevelt

Warsaw, Poland, October 11, 1935

Confidential

My dear Mr. President: The situation I found in England is a striking illustration of the fact that it is impossible to predict six months in advance the course of events in Europe. When I was in London at the end of May I heard from our Ambassador, and from other reliable, authentic sources, that any government which attempted to lead the British people into war would be overthrown. Now, four months afterwards, there is a complete reversal of sentiment and the recent vote of the trade unions, overwhelmingly in favor of sustaining the League of Nations and the imposition of sanctions, even though this vote was admittedly prejudiced, because of the opposition of organized labor, to Italian Fascism, is taken as a clear index of public opinion.

This about face is not explained by any leadership but is due, so I was informed, to a realization of England's position by reason of the rearmament of Germany and the belligerent attitude of Italy. The average man in the street shows an extraordinary knowledge of political events on the continent and is thoroughly alarmed at the defenselessness of the British Isles, their vulnerability to air attacks, and their complete isolation from food supplies in the event of an effective blockade. Instead of leading popular sentiment the Government is attempting to restrain the demand for more aggressive action, but it is certain that the British are thoroughly alarmed and have scrapped all notion of disarmament.

The entire home fleet is concentrated in the Mediterranean and about one-fourth of the military planes. It is quite apparent that the British regard Italy's ambitions in Africa as a menace to the security of the Empire and will make every effort to prevent Italy from winning the Abyssinian war. The military people are of the opinion that this war should last two years, and when one looks at the map and is told of the vulnerability of Malta from the air, the concentration of Italian war planes in Sicily, only a few miles away, and that large military forces are being kept in Italy because of the British threat in the Mediterranean, it is a pessimistic outlook. A single incident, such as the blowing up of the *Mainè*, might well bring about hostilities, and the possibility of such an incident in the Mediterranean, if the Abyssinian war continues for any length of time, is very apparent.

Popular opinion in France is to stay out of any war at any cost and the position of Laval is a very difficult one. If he follows British leader-

21

ship in demanding severe sanctions under Article 16 of the League he will probably undertake a commitment that will meet with the opposition of the majority, but if he fails to sustain the League he will fatally weaken what France has regarded as the greatest instrumentality against revision of the Versailles Treaty. I heard the opinion expressed by competent observers in Paris that the Prime Minister would probably go down in the coming elections, but bankers and business men say that they think the Laval Government will continue because after Laval there is no one to look to for leadership. They deprecated the opinion which I heard expressed on several sides—that after the downfall of the present Government the future of France would be fought out on the streets. But there is no question but what the economic situation is a trying one. The franc is entirely overvalued and must be lowered for the purposes of international trade. There is no hope of wiping out the deficit in spite of the unpopular economies of the Government. The cost of living is mounting and unemployment is increasing.

In Germany it is surprising but there is no elation over the situation arising from Italy's commitment in Africa and the differences between France and Great Britain. The sentiment expressed in all quarters was that Germany was not ready for war and would not be ready until the end of another two years. The army has been expanded to 600,000 but with expansion it has ceased to be the close-knit, well-functioning political organization that it was when confined to a smaller number and it is agreed that there is a striking shortage of trained officers. One gets the impression that Germany is unmoved by the war in Abyssinia and the potentialities it presents, but intends to continue along the course charted when rearmament was decided.

The economic policy of the country must, before a very long period, lead to impoverishment and a lowering of the living standard. There is a good deal of underground complaint now against the shortage of butter and other food supplies. Germany is very deficient in animal fats, must import 90 per cent of its wool, and all cotton and iron. Exports have been forced and are on an artificial basis to compensate for the great imports of war materials. Competent and conservative opinion express the belief that 60 per cent of all industrial activities are engaged in war preparation and, while no one cared to estimate the number of persons employed in war industries, it was stated that these certainly would be not less than 3,000,000. This non-productive economy must mean a diminution of national wealth with a consequent reduction of the basis upon which taxes can be levied. But the military preparation must go on for any cessation would mean an increase of unemployment with resulting opposition to the Government. It is very clear that either the present policy must culminate in war or else the present Government must be overthrown and this war preparation brought to a stop.

With the permission of the Ambassador, I saw a man closely associated with Hitler, who told me that the final stage of the Nazi program would be started in 1936 and finished in 1938, the two years necessary for the completion of the military program expressed by the military people.

The Nazi Government is most probably a minority one although Hitler personally has a great following throughout the country. The opposition among all religious people, even the Lutherans, is very emphatic. But all opposition lacks unity, can present no effective front and, therefore, will probably continue to have little or no influence. The internal stability of the mark is a continuing mystery but the national debt continues to mount with no apparent possibility of eventual settlement and, while the volume of currency has been kept constant, there is a great credit inflation which is the basis of all governmental financing. The disastrous consequences of inflation may be abruptly felt over night.

Here in Poland there are no radical changes to record and the Government continues under President Mościcki much as it did under the direction of the late Marshal Pilsudski. Foreign policy will no doubt continue friendly but alert vis-á-vis Germany.

I am glad Joe Kennedy is over here and he will, I am sure, give you a very informative report of the countries he visits. He is sound and sensible and a discriminating observer. I hope he will keep his promise to come to Poland as I am anxious to show him living conditions here so that he may take back his first-hand impressions for the people back home who are the most spoiled people in the world.[1]

Respectfully yours,

John Cudahy

[PSF:Poland:TS]

[1] Answered Oct. 28, 1935, below.

Samuel R. Fuller, Jr., to Roosevelt

New York, 11 October 1935

Dear Mr. President: Subject: European trends. Reference: My letter even date, same subject.[1]

Supplementing above reference may the liberty be taken please of adding some personal impressions and a thought with the belief that they are within the scope of the European work you kindly gave me? Attention is respectfully invited that not only were conversations had with foreign Government officials as recorded, but with our own Legation and Embassy people in Holland, Germany and England and with many business friends in these countries.

These impressions are as follows:

1. That a Germany and an Italy armed under dictatorships, with a population of some 105 millions within an area of approximately 303,000 square miles with great basic raw material shortages and little foreign exchange, present a day to day menace to the peace of all nations.

2. That if the League and powers outside the League act reasonably in unison, the Italian-Abyssinian matter soon will be resolved; but that otherwise danger exists of an imminent general European war, because other dictators might be induced thereby to seize territory.

3. That Germany, unless the Italian matter brings on an immediate war, is the greatest European danger; because, in addition to her dictatorship, compactness and economic necessities, her people possess such great virility and fervor for collective obedience to Government.

4. That neither the German nor English peoples want war if it can be avoided; but both would follow their leaders to fight for what they may believe are their economic and/or political necessities.

5. That Hoare does not want war now; and that Schacht probably does not want war now.

6. That Hitler will remain for some time at least (a year or so anyway) as head of the German State regardless of the political character of the regime which may surround him.

7. That Germany and England might readily agree in matters vitally important to the maintenance of peace but that they have not yet got together satisfactorily: For example: Schacht wants stabilization and threatens war for colonies but believes England opposes the former, and apparently has no real knowledge of England's attitude toward the latter; while Hoare told me for you that England will stabilize when the present crisis is over and that she is ready to attempt to give territory to Germany.

8. That peace of considerable duration might be assured should Germany and England reach territorial agreements, and the principal countries of the world conclude stabilization.

9. That although Germany and England have not got together, each individually spoke freely to me as your friend regarding these above

mentioned matters which are of vital importance to their relations with each other and to our peace.

From the above cited impressions and because in a general European conflict it seems logical to assume that we probably would be forced into it, the thought arises: Is there not merit in considering, as an advantage to us, the further use of the kind of forehandedness which calls for discussions (perhaps frequent ones) with the heads of the principal European Governments in the manner of and at least to the same general ends as my mission? While the thought is presented as a possible aid for the maintenance of our peace, it is presented with the greatest of diffidence; partly on account of the personal angle which unavoidably appears in it but mainly on account of my complete inexperience in such matters and lack of all knowledge of our recent diplomatic history.

May I repeat my deep gratitude to you for the opportunity of these visits and the profound hope that they may be of some little good to you? It was a very great honor you were good enough to give me; and as such is unforgettable.[2]

With kindest wishes always, believe me, Faithfully yours,

S. R. Fuller, jr.

[PPF 2616:TS]

[1] A very long report of Fuller's talks with Hendrik Colijn, Prime Minister of The Netherlands, Hjalmar Schacht, president of the Reichsbank, Stanley Baldwin, British Prime Minister, Sir Samuel Hoare, British Foreign Secretary, and F. H. F. van Vlissingen, president of the International Chamber of Commerce (PPF 2616). His report of his interview with Schacht is printed in *Foreign Relations, 1935*, II, 282–286.

[2] Fuller saw the President for half an hour at the White House on Oct. 25, 1935 (PPF 1-0); presumably it was to this conversation that the latter referred in his letter to Fuller of Nov. 14, 1935 (PPF 2616): "May I tell you again how very grateful I was to you for that tremendously interesting report you brought back. Be sure to let me know if and when you plan another trip!"

Roosevelt to Cordell Hull, Secretary of State

[Aboard U.S.S. *Houston,* October 13, 1935]

Secret

[*Radiogram*] Your black one seventy-five.[1] I have not a complete copy of Kellogg-Briand Pact on board. Can you let me have language under which it can be "invoked." I recollect no clause under which any positive action can be taken by signatories against a violating nation except possibly a pro forma protest or a request by one or more signatories that an offending nation ought to conform to arbitration or peaceful means to avert war. This seems somewhat far fetched after the horse is out of the stable. Just what does Hoare suggest?[2]

[OF 200-L:T]

[1] Not present.

[2] Hull's "black one seventy-five" apparently referred to Bingham's dispatch to him of October 11 (*Foreign Relations, 1935,* I, 772–773). In this dispatch Hoare had outlined several possible courses of action under the Kellogg-Briand Pact, including a conference of the signatories or action initiated by the President of the United States. To Roosevelt, Hull replied (Oct. 13, 1935, *ibid.,* pp. 773–775) that there was "no provision and no language" prescribing any method for invocation of the pact. If, however, it should be invoked it should be by the South American governments rather than by the League of Nations or the United States. He submitted a proposed dispatch to be sent by him (Hull) to Bingham; this was approved and sent October 14. Bingham was directed to inform Hoare that the United States position was that the opportunity for invocation of the pact, or for some action such as a conference, had gone by. However, the United States would not oppose a proposal for a "simultaneous utterance" by the signatories (*ibid.,* pp. 775–776). Hull notes in his *Memoirs,* I, 434, that the question of action under the Kellogg-Briand Pact did not again arise.

Lincoln MacVeagh, Minister to Greece, to Roosevelt

Athens, October 15, 1935

Personal

Dear Franklin: Having in mind your admonition to write to you, I am going to send a few words in the present pouch, since a good deal has been going on around here since I saw you in Washington.

The Anglo-Italian situation continues loaded with dynamite in this part of the world, while war vessels of both navies prowl around fully equipped for any emergency. The British Minister here, who recently returned from London, tells me he thinks the danger of conflict is less than it was a while ago, but with so many people carrying weapons and nervously wrought up, we can never exclude the possibility of an "incident." The Greeks are acutely conscious of their exposed position, and the temptation which their many excellent harbors would be to both belligerents in time of war. The Italians have already anchored repeatedly in these harbors without asking the Greek Government's permission beforehand—a high-handed policy which they seem now to have abandoned under Greek protest, but which has inflamed the Greek press against them, and increased the normal dislike here, and distrust of

Fascist Italy. Consequently Greece may be said to be, at the present moment, not pro-British certainly, but less disposed to criticize England than Italy in the situation which has arisen between them. She is desperately anxious to preserve her neutrality, and quite baffled as to how she is going to be able to do it, if war comes. The Turks seem to be very much in the same quandary. The Turkish Minister here came to see me the other day and bewailed the difficulty of his country's situation.

England has a great fleet, but Italy has converted the Islands of the Dodecanese into a powerful base only a few miles from the Turkish Coast. It did not seem to console him to think that Italy is already using up a lot of money and men in Abyssinia. Incidentally, the British out here have quite frankly given Malta up for lost should hostilities break out with Mussolini. On account of the airplane and the submarine, there is a general feeling that Italian lines of communication will be preserved to a greater degree than British, at least at the outset, so that if any of the Near Eastern States join England at the start of an Anglo-Italian war they will risk receiving paralyzing damage before they can make their assistance felt to any great degree. Consequently we should expect them to do their best to remain neutral, at least till some decisive actions had been fought, or until time had made it possible to make a good guess as to the ultimate victor.

The Greeks are, characteristically, much excited over their own internal affairs, despite the World situation. The question of the restoration of the monarchy became a burning one when the small group which has been agitating for the King's recall for some time with little success secured the adherence of the Minister of War, during the summer. Last month these people, mostly in Athens society and in the Army, forced the moderate and reluctant Premier to embrace their cause also. A few days ago, because his support seemed too lukewarm, and in order to make the recall of the King a certainty, they overthrew the Government and set up a Regency under the Minister of War. The Royalist Constitution of 1911 is again in force, and a plebiscite will be held November 3rd, the result of which is almost a foregone conclusion. The best observers here maintain, however, that the country is predominantly Republican. Contrary to popular report it seems that the British are not favoring the Restoration. The British Minister told me that he is advising the Foreign Office that the return of the King would be a "calamity." He also said he had talked with the King of England about the matter and that the King said he was trying to persuade George of Greece not to be foolish and get himself into difficulties. Meanwhile, the Republicans, though suppressed, are many of them in an ugly mood.[1]

Affectionately as always,

Lincoln MacVeagh

[PSF:Greece:TS]

[1] Answered Nov. 2, 1935, below.

Louis M. Howe, Personal Secretary to the President, to Roosevelt, Aboard the U.S.S. *Houston*

[Washington] 18 October [1935]

Secret

[*Radiogram*] Long has been hypnotized by Mussolini. Is sending five or six cables a day little short of absolute Italian propaganda.[1] Has given one interview which was highly indiscreet.[2] Hull tells me confidentially Long considers himself only under your authority and does not pay any attention to what he suggests. Knowing Long as we do think you can see danger if this goes unchecked. Think you should tactfully urge him first to keep an open mind and even keel and be absolutely neutral in all he says and does; second, to keep Hull in closest touch as you are relying entirely on Hull to handle this thing and that he has your fullest confidence in the matter. I think there is possibility of coup d'etat at Abyssinian Capitol and replacement of Emperor by man bought or coaxed to favor Italians and after that a deal between Abyssinia and the Italians. Present Emperor has little real authority and it is a loose confederation of scheming local chiefs that needs either a Menelik or a Lawrence to keep quiet. This will account for the continued postponement of Abyssinian attacks which is contrary to their natural desire to fight and one chief has already been won over. Italian minister may be staying on to manage the Capitol end of the deal. Think it over.

[OF 200-L:T]

[1] For the period October 1 to 18 there are no communications from Long to Roosevelt in the Roosevelt papers. For the same period, four telegrams from Long to Hull are printed in *Foreign Relations, 1935,* I, 667–669, 675, 792–793, 804. However, information from the National Archives indicates that during this period Long sent from two to fourteen telegrams and dispatches daily to the State Department or 140 telegrams and dispatches in all.

[2] Apparently an interview given to the editor of the *Tribuna* of Rome, reported by Long to Hull, Oct. 15, 1935, and quoted by Wallace Murray, chief of the Division of Near Eastern Affairs, in a memorandum of the same date, in *Foreign Relations, 1935,* I, 805–806. See Long to Hull, October 9 and Hull to Long, Oct. 16, 1935, *ibid.,* pp. 667–669, 806–807.

Press Conference Aboard the U.S.S. *Houston,* Charleston Navy Yard, Charleston, South Carolina, October 23, 1935, 2:15 P.M.

[*Excerpt*] Q: Have complaints of the exporters been forwarded to you in connection with the embargo on Italy?

The President: I do not think I got that. I think it went to Washington. I saw all of the dispatches that came to us aboard ship but I did not get that.

Mr. McIntyre: What was that?

The President: The protest of the export group on the Neutrality Proclamation.[1]

Mr. McIntyre: I do not think it was forwarded to you.

The President: I do not think it was forwarded to me.

Q: There was a direct statement from the State Department that if anything was said, you would say it.

Q: Is there to be a big political discussion on the way north? (Referring to the President and Postmaster General Farley.)

The President: Not yet. I doubt very much if we will have a big political discussion.

Q: Is there any need for one?

The President: No.

Q: You said you would talk principally with Secretary Hull. Any new move?

The President: Oh, no, just to bring me up to date.

Q: Have we been sounded out by the League of Nations yet?

The President: No.

Q: On economic sanctions?

The President: No.

Q: The State Department has some letter for you.

The President: When did it come?

Q: Yesterday.

The President: I have not got it.[2]

Q: They say we should act in the Kellogg Pact because we got under it in Manchukuo.

The President: We have acted, all right, under the Kellogg Pact, about two months ago.

Q: Any hint of what our policy is?

The President: I think we did it twice.

Q: You mean by the declaration of the Secretary of State suggesting that the world—[3]

The President: (Interposing) Yes. I think I said something about it too. Didn't I? I don't know whether I did or not.

Q: You said that it should be preserved.[4]

The President: Yes.

[President's Press Conferences:T]

[1] Not found in the Roosevelt papers.

[2] See Wilson to Hull, Oct. 21, 1935 (*Foreign Relations, 1935,* I, 849); see also Hull, *Memoirs,* I, 434.

[3] Presumably Hull's statement of July 12, 1935, reaffirming American support of the Pact of Paris. The text is quoted in Phillips to Dodd, July 13, 1935 (*Foreign Relations,* I, 731–732), and is printed in the New York *Times,* July 13, 1935, p. 1. In a statement of September 19 made on the radio in connection with a World Peaceways program, Hull said he wished to emphasize again the deep interest of the United States in the preservation of peace and its belief in the Pact of Paris (*ibid.,* Sept. 20, 1935, p. 8).

[4] See statement of Aug. 1, 1935, expressing hope that the League Council would find a solution to the controversy (*Public Papers,* IV, 315).

Fred Morris Dearing, Ambassador to Peru, to Roosevelt

Lima, October 23, 1935

Strictly Confidential

My dear Mr. President: Although Peru is pretty far away from Italy and Ethiopia, I have just had an opportunity for a glance behind the scenes and believe you may be interested in having a brief report of what I saw. The State Department, of course, keeps you informed of the reports from our missions in the principal capitals in Europe, but what I shall say may, nevertheless, be of some value as a check on your other information.

I had an opportunity yesterday to read a number of the original despatches from the British representatives at these capitals to the Foreign Office in London, which were written not much more than a month ago, and I thought you might be interested in hearing something of the tenor of these reports and of the main points brought out in them.

Sir Robert Vansittart,[1] in replying to the British Ambassador in Paris,[2] reports a conversation with Corbin,[3] the French Ambassador in London, in which he emphasizes the points made not so long ago by Sir Samuel Hoare in his speech to Parliament. Sir Robert makes it quite apparent to Sir George Clerk that the British Government stands squarely back of the League and for collective action, but lets it be seen that he made it clear to the French Ambassador that unless the French Government would do the same, the necessity would arise for the British Government to reconsider its whole position. He reports the French Ambassador as saying nothing in rebuttal to this statement and as simply receiving it in noncommittal silence.

Clerk, the British Ambassador in Paris, wrote to Hoare expressing himself with the greatest frankness about Laval's personal characteristics and French policy. He thinks the fundamental fact in the whole situation is the arrangement made between Laval and Mussolini in January last, which resulted in the removal of any Italian threat towards Tunis and towards the French frontier, and permitted the French Government to move a number of its military units from the Italian frontier to the German frontier. The British Ambassador feels certain that for these considerations Laval has promised Mussolini a completely free hand in Ethiopia and that this explains all of his subsequent actions.

I gather that the British Government has not yet obtained complete confirmation of its surmises as to just what took place between Laval and Mussolini, and has had no copy of their agreement in the doubtful case that it was ever reduced to written form.

The British Ambassador declares that Laval is always a man of "negotiation and compromise" and that he is so much for immediate expediency that he will not hesitate to sacrifice principles if necessary. On the other hand he states that Laval will do anything to keep peace as that is most in accord with his French bourgeois character and desires. The Ambassador feels that Laval will avoid commitments until the last possible moment and will temporize in every conceivable way rather than take a position favoring sanctions against Italy. And it would seem that subsequent events have borne out the justice of this opinion.

Clerk reports that the chief offset to Laval in government circles is Herriot. He states that the Left parties have been increasing in influence and that the "common front" is now the most powerful element in French political life. Nevertheless, he states that Laval needs Herriot's

Right and radical following on account of his fiscal measures and other economy acts and must, therefore, compromise.

Herriot is reported by the Ambassador as being opposed to Laval's commitments to Mussolini and to feel that it will be suicidal for France to cast her fortune with Italy rather than with Great Britain and the League. And the Ambassador tells his Chief in London that he has it on excellent authority that in a cabinet meeting Herriot came out quite bluntly and stated his position. Laval hedged and managed to get out of the session still uncommitted and with his hands untied.

The upshot of the Ambassador's report is that Laval is not to be trusted; he must be understood to act in accordance with his characteristics; that Laval will avoid, in every possible way, taking a strong stand against the Italians, primarily on account of his January agreements with Mussolini, but that in the last analysis his determination to preserve the peace may make it possible to get a certain measure of support and cooperation from him.

The Ambassador then goes into the intricacies of French policy in Europe, but as the general outlines of that policy must be fairly well known to you, I do not attempt to give you from memory what I could only glance at in a somewhat hurried manner.

Ambassador Drummond in Rome, in his reports, brings out a statement frequently repeated in the reports of the other representatives, namely, that the Italians feel the British are too weak to do very much in case there is an outbreak of hostilities and that, therefore, the British will not act. This rather surprising opinion (in view of the character of the British navy in the Mediterranean) is repeated several times.

The Ambassador in Rome also stresses the fact—as does Clerk in Paris—that there is no real comprehension on the Continent of the British temper or attitude, which is ascribed entirely to direct material interests, and states that no one will believe that Great Britain cares anything about the League or its principles except as a cat's paw!

The British Ambassador at Rome makes it plain that the Italians are counting confidently upon the French as a result of Mussolini's understanding of last January with Laval. He then says that there is no doubt about the entire Italian nation being back of Mussolini in his enterprise, but he states that it is a qualified backing and not exactly one of wild and fanatical enthusiasm. He repeats, however, that the entire nation is with its Chief and then makes an interesting analysis of Italian opinion. The Facisti, he states, are chiefly the young hotheads, and other extremists, who are not notable for thoughtfulness but who follow their chief blindly in everything, believing that whatever Italy desires is right and that morals are not to be considered in carrying out the aggrandizement of the country, and that even Machiavelli is of no use unless he serves Facisti purposes. There is none of Machiavelli's cool foresightedness in the attitude of the body of the Facisti, Ambassador Drummond declares. From them he expects nothing but pressure for a war of conquest, regardless of consequences.

The Ambassador next speaks of the middle classes and the nobility in Italy, among whom the British have heretofore found their best friends and have made their most intimate connections. These people, he says, have been very much influenced by what they see in the press and he remarks, with regret, that the more flamboyant English press—aided, of course, by the Italian press—have placed them behind Mussolini where, however, they must place themselves if they are freely to continue their lives in Italy.

Finally, the Ambassador refers to the peasantry which he estimates, comprises about sixty percent or more of the country. He said that they have been so filled with tales of unlimited lands in Ethiopia and a free and successful career for everybody, that this, in comparison with their restricted life at home, and the constantly dropping scale of living, makes them prefer the war. On the other hand, the Ambassador feels that they do not wish to get themselves into any more difficulties than possible and that memories of the last war are somewhat too recent.

The Ambassador here mentions one of the basic facts in the entire situation to which nobody ever seems to pay much attention, namely, the pressure of population and the effect it is having upon the standard of life in Italy and the political objectives of the government. It is apparent from what the Ambassador says that this is the prime cause— whether it is consciously realized or not—for the Italian enterprise, and yet nothing seems to be even contemplated in the way of population control. The pressure gradually results in conditions of peace which are so terrible that war is a preferable alternative.

An interesting despatch from Newton,[4] the Chargé in Berlin (Phipps, apparently, is away) indicates a considerable understanding between the British and German governments, an anti-Italian attitude on the part of Germany and a policy of quiet but great alertness on the part of the Nazi government. The Chargé reports that he has it on the best of authority that Germany does not intend to do anything whatever to alienate Great Britain; that the Nazi government feels resentful towards Mussolini, is very suspicious of the provisions of the agreement between

Laval and Mussolini and was particularly bored by Mussolini's grandiose gesture and mobilization along the Brenner.[5]

I gather from other papers that the British are not happy about their association with the French and are also considerably irked by the League but support it as the best means for obtaining collective action, preserving peace, curbing Italy and upholding civilized ideals. I also gather that our policies are considered to be justified and are quite understood.

I saw one paper from Sir Gerald Campbell[6] reporting on the negro riots in Harlem, but it had no particular significance.

I wondered, as I read some of the papers and recalled former French efforts to span Africa from east to west as these efforts came into conflict with the British band of continuous territory from north to south, whether the French were not remembering Fashoda in much the same way that the Italians have been recalling Adowa.

Here in Peru, due to a number of causes, there seems to be a movement towards Italy and against sanctions and what sanctions may involve, primarily for reasons of self interest. Peruvian respect for League principles has always been rather academic except where her own interests have been directly concerned and when she felt some advantageous use might be made of the League. But as the present situation deepens, the Government evidently finds its obligations as a member of the League irksome and embarrassing and would like very much to avoid them. Racially, culturally, religiously and in a good many other ways the Peruvians are sympathetic to the Italians and they like to see a Latin nation asserting itself as Mussolini is doing. As I have already reported, however, there are a number of the more thoughtful Peruvians who feel that if Mussolini is able to accomplish his aggrandizement and then force other nations to accept it as a fait accompli and thus consolidate his predatory gains, the day may come when Peru, as a smaller nation coveted by some greater one, will also be the victim of equally cynical aggression.

I trust this report will be of some use to you, and beg you to believe me, Yours most sincerely,

Fred Morris Dearing

P.S. I have also reported what you have found herein to the Secretary in a personal and strictly confidential letter. F.M.D.[7]

[PSF:Peru:TS]

34

[1] Permanent Under Secretary in the British Foreign Office.
[2] Sir George Clerk.
[3] Charles Corbin.
[4] Basil C. Newton.
[5] In July 1934, to bolster Austria against German threats.
[6] British consul general in New York.
[7] Not present; see Roosevelt's reply, Nov. 5, 1935, below.

Press Conference, Executive Offices of the White House, October 25, 1935, 10:40 A.M.

[*Excerpt*] Q: Do you think that the farm program is having any effect on our foreign markets abroad, cutting down our exports?

The President: That is a pretty general question. Let me put it this way for background. We would sell more cotton abroad if we sold it at 6 cents, some more, but what would happen to the cotton growers of this country? We would not sell anything like enough to make up the difference between 6 cents and 12 cents. Therefore, the purchasing power of the Southern cotton farmers would be so drastically cut that we would have the same troubles in the South we had before. That is the simple example. Now you can multiply that ten times. If we would sell below the cost of production in this country, of course we will increase our markets. That is another way of putting it.

Q: This program isn't stimulating production in competitive countries?

The President: That is a very definite world trend, and was a definite world trend before we did anything. You will find that Brazil was raising more cotton starting back in 1921 and 1922 with a fairly constant increase up to 1929 and 1930 and a comparatively small increase since then. Germany started ten years ago to increase their food production so as to become self-sustaining. France the same way. The British on their Islands, raise more and more of their own foodstuffs. That goes on all over the world. That has been a nationalistic tendency in every country, so far as I know. And that is what the Eastern managing editors do not understand. That is off the record, too.

Q: Is that statement to be connected with the corn-hog program or not?

The President: Oh, no. That has been preparing for a long time.

Q: Are you planning any new statements on neutrality in connection with our reply to the League?

The President: No. I think there will be something soon—not from me—that would be just the reply.

Q: Could you tell us, if the League actually should impose economic sanctions against Italy, would you do what you could to restrain American trade from interfering with the effectiveness of the sanctions?

The President: All you could do is read the law.

Q: Could you give us your interpretation of that law? Is it such that it would be possible to extend such embargoes to oil or copper?

The President: I think that question would have to be taken up when it arose. It has not arisen up to the present time.

Q: Wasn't there a Standard Oil announcement saying they would send oil to Italy regardless of the law?

The President: I don't think so. They have a subsidiary over there which is conducting its normal business and nothing more, so far as I know.

Q: Do you expect to see Mr. Teagle about that?[1]

The President: No.

Q: Could you tell us whether Admiral Standley will be the chief American delegate to the Naval Conference?

The President: We haven't got as far as that. We haven't done more than say that we would send some people over there . . .

Q: Mr. President, will you add anything to what Chester Davis said the other day as to what is being tried on the boosting of exports by the use of tariff revenues under the present Agricultural Act?

The President: I did not see it.

Q: He spoke of the difficulties in selling—

The President: Of course the situation on that is very different from what it was, even when the old McNary-Haugen Bill was passed and vetoed, as I remember it, by President Coolidge, largely on the recommendation of Secretary of Commerce Hoover. It was vetoed at that time, but the conditions then were very different from what they are today. Foreign countries, away back in President Coolidge's Administration, did not have the same kind of embargoes on agricultural imports into those countries as they have today. For example, today Great Britain gives a very, very strong preference to British colonies. On wheat, Great Britain prefers to buy from Canada and Australia and not from us. France has a strong embargo on the importation of foodstuffs. Germany has certain embargoes and also great difficulty in paying in cash for what she does import.

Almost every country today has embargoes on the importation of foodstuffs. There has been a great change in the last six years, since 1929.

Q: And all of those things operate against the effectiveness of any exports?

The President: One of the great difficulties is to get those people to tear down their barriers so as to permit us to export more foodstuffs of all kinds.

Q: Has Secretary Morgenthau made any report?

The President: I have not had a chance to more than shake him by the hand yesterday at the train.

Q: What is he going to do with all the gold coming in here?

The President: That is a great problem. Like some other things, we cannot eat it.

Q: In your admonition to American citizens not to trade with belligerents, you advised them if they did trade or attempt to trade, they did so at their own risk.[2] What about American ships that call at Italian ports, particularly where the American Government has a mortgage and holds the investment?

The President: That is a nice one. I cannot give you an offhand reply to that.

[President's Press Conferences:T]

[1] Walter C. Teagle, president of the Standard Oil Company.
[2] Statement by Roosevelt on the Arms Embargo Proclamation, Oct. 5, 1935, above.

Roosevelt to John Cudahy, Ambassador to Poland, Warsaw

[Washington] October 28, 1935

Dear John: I am delighted to find yours of October eleventh[1] on my return from a grand trip from San Diego back through the Canal.

What you tell me checks up very well with things that I hear from our own and special sources. Things are moving so fast that I feel that my opinion of the situation today may have to be completely changed tomorrow. We are certainly living on a day to day basis.

Keep me in touch.

Always sincerely,

[PSF:Poland:CT]

[1] Above.

Roosevelt to Cordell Hull, Secretary of State

Washington, October 28, 1935

Confidential

Memorandum for the Secretary of State: If you have not read these I think you will find them of great interest. Will you let me have them back?[1]

FDR

[PPF 2616:TS]

[1] Reports of Fuller's talks with Schacht and other European statesmen, in Fuller's letter to Roosevelt of Oct. 11, 1935, above. Hull said he had read them with a great deal of interest (McBride to McIntyre, Oct. 30, 1935, PPF 2616).

Roosevelt to Philip C. Jessup, School of Law, Columbia University, New York

[Washington] October 28, 1935

My dear Dr. Jessup: Many thanks for your letter of October fourteenth,[1] which I found upon my return to Washington. It is gratifying to know that you approve our course and very good of you to tell me so.

Very sincerely yours,

[OF 1561:CT]

[1] Jessup expressed his appreciation of Roosevelt's neutrality policy (OF 1561). "I happen to have been devoting a number of years to the study of this general question and while I believe that Congress has not yet even approached a satisfactory solution of the whole problem, I believe that the present course of your administration is the most satisfactory which could be followed under the circumstances."

The Secretaries of Commerce, State, Agriculture, and Labor to Roosevelt

Washington, October 28, 1935

My dear Mr. President: You will recall that in the report of the Cabinet Committee on Cotton Textiles submitted to you on August 20,

1935, we referred to the increasing importations into this country of certain types of textiles from Japan and expressed the opinion that since Section 3(e) of the National Industrial Recovery Act was no longer operative, the most desirable and expedient course of action now available for securing an effective adjudgment of the situation created by such importations would be through informal conference with the Japanese Government with respect to those textile products which have been the subject of complaint to this government. It was felt that as the result of such discussions a voluntary agreement might be reached as to the volume and terms under which imports of cotton cloth and other cotton products enter this country from Japan. This method had been employed with respect to other Japanese products and at that time conversations were in progress with representatives of the Japanese Government regarding shipments of Japanese cotton cloth into the Philippine Islands.

On October 11, after lengthy negotiations with the Japanese Government, a final agreement was reached providing for the voluntary limitation, by Japanese textile exporters, of importations into the Philippine Islands of Japanese cotton piece goods. This arrangement, it is anticipated, will materially improve the position for American cotton textiles in the Philippine Islands without adversely affecting the interests of the Filipino people, and at the same time it should stabilize the Philippine market for cotton goods. The Governments of both the United States and Japan found themselves in entire agreement upon this method of dealing with a situation which might otherwise lead to increasing conflict between their competing commercial interests.

Within the last few weeks the Cotton Textile Institute and other domestic textile interests have urged this Government to take early action to regulate or restrict textile imports from Japan, either in accordance with the Cabinet Committee's recommendation or in pursuance of the authority which they maintain is vested in you by Section 22(a) of the Agricultural Adjustment Act, as amended.

In view of the successful completion of negotiations with the Japanese concerning the Philippine market for cotton textiles and the renewed drive on the part of the domestic industry for some definite action with respect to importations of textiles into this country, it is the opinion of the members of the Cabinet Committee that the present affords a propitious time for initiating conferences with the Japanese Government with respect to shipments of certain textiles into the United States, if it is your desire to seek an adjustment along these lines before giving serious consideration to the possibility or desirability of employing more direct means of controlling such imports. In the event that an agreement with the Japanese along these lines is to be sought, it would appear to be advisable to undertake the discussions as soon as possible, inasmuch as negotiations of this character usually take considerable time.

In order to save time, the Executive Committee on Commercial Policy, which has helped to formulate the recent agreement with Japan with respect to Philippine importations, have directed their attention recently to the principal textiles imported into the United States from Japan against which complaint has been made, namely, cotton cloth, cotton rugs, cotton velveteens, woolen gloves and mittens, and cotton fish netting. It has appointed a sub-committee to gather all pertinent facts relating to these commodities and to study the direction which negotiations should take in the event that it is your desire to proceed with negotiations. As a result of this study the Executive Committee on Commercial Policy will therefore shortly be in a position to advise with respect to these matters.

It is our considered opinion that the fear of sharply increasing importations at very low prices of Japanese textile products, rather than the actual amount, has been a disturbing element in the domestic textile situation. Prompt action by this Government, therefore, in seeking a solution of this aspect of the general textile problem may prove of considerable assistance to the industry in continuing the present improvement trend and in safeguarding wages and labor conditions first established in the industry under Code No. 1 of the National Industrial Recovery Act.

Faithfully yours,

(s) Daniel C. Roper, Secretary of Commerce, Chairman
(s) Cordell Hull, Secretary of State
(s) Henry A. Wallace, Secretary of Agriculture
(s) Frances Perkins, Secretary of Labor

[*Notation*:T] President's handwriting: "D.C.R. I approve—go ahead FDR."

[OF 355:T]

Press Conference, Executive Offices of the White House, October 30, 1935, 4:05 P.M.

[*Excerpt*] Q: Mr. President, Secretary Hull, in his statement on neutrality today, said it is now the definite policy of the Government to discourage trade with belligerents.[1] Does that mean that you are contemplating possibly stronger measures to restrain trade?

The President: I thought you were going to ask that question. Since it relates to foreign affairs, I dictated something in reply to that question and Steve (Early) will have it for you. This is not—don't use it as a statement by the President. I have to be very careful to use correct language on foreign affairs. It is just headed as a statement because we want to be sure to use the proper language. (Reading)

In dealing with the conflict between Ethiopia and Italy, I have carried into effect the will and intent of the Neutrality Resolution recently enacted by Congress. We have prohibited all shipments of arms, ammunition, and implements of war to the belligerent governments. By my public statement of October fifth, which was emphasized by the Secretary of State on October tenth, we have warned American citizens against transactions of any character with either of the belligerent nations except at their own risk.

This Government is determined not to become involved in the controversy and is anxious for the restoration and maintenance of peace.

However, in the course of war, tempting trade opportunities may be offered to our people to supply materials which would prolong the war. I do not believe that the American people will wish for abnormally increased profits that temporarily might be secured by greatly extending our trade in such materials; nor would they wish the struggles on the battlefield to be prolonged because of profits accruing to a comparatively small number of American citizens.

Accordingly, the American Government is keeping informed as to all shipments consigned for export to both belligerents.[2]

Mr. Early: I think, Mr. President, you will have to make that a statement.

The President: That is all right, you can use it as a statement, if you want.

Q: That statement is not to be quoted?

The President: Yes, that can be quoted.

Q: This Government is keeping informed, sir, to what end? (Laughter)

The President: That is all for today.

Q: Mr. President, is any liberalization of the regulations governing information as to exports to be made? At present the Treasury regulations do not allow the name of the exporters to be made public.

The President: That is putting, in other language, what Fred (Mr. Essary) just asked. (Laughter) . . .

Q: On the neutrality thing, would it be a correct statement to say, on our authority, that it is the policy of the Government to discourage extraordinary trade with the belligerents?

The President: No, I am not saying anything about that further than the statement.

Q: Is the Government interested in shipments of such things as oil to neutral powers for trans-shipment to belligerents? I understand that Germany is being—

The President: (interposing) I take it that that would be taken into consideration in exactly the same way that I said that anything going to belligerent governments would be checked up on. Of course, in the case of proscribed articles—arms, implements of war, munitions—it prohibits their shipments either to belligerent countries or to a neutral country for trans-shipment.

Q: Can you tell us anything about some of the temptations that have been presented so far? (Laughter)

The President: Well, yes. I will tell you a story on that and it is rather an interesting one. I see no reason why you should not use it. When I was at Hyde Park a very splendid old gentleman came to see me, Mr. Johnson of the Endicott-Johnson Shoe Company. Mind you, that was before hostilities had started. It was about the 19th or 20th of September. Mr. Johnson said to me at length, "I would like to ask your advice. I have had an order from the Italian Government for a very large number of pairs of shoes." I said, "What are they, ladies' slippers?" He said, "No, they were heavy shoes." I said, "Shoes that could have been worn by soldiers?" He said, "Yes, I'd say so." I said, "Well, what is the question?" He said, "Would you fill the order if you were the Endicott-Johnson Company?" I said, "No, I would not." He said, "All right, I won't."

Q: Hasn't that order been filled? (Laughter) Hasn't some other American firm filled that order?

The President: I don't know. All I know is this story I told you. I have been away over a month since then, but that is what Mr. Johnson told me.

Q: Would your prohibitions include such commodities as wheat or cotton, or just those implements of war?

The President: Nothing further than stated.

[President's Press Conferences:T]

[1] Printed in *Foreign Relations, 1935,* I, 813.
[2] This statement is printed *ibid.,* pp. 812–813, and in *Public Papers,* IV, 440.

Roosevelt to the Reverend W. Russell Bowie, New York

[Washington] October 30, 1935

Confidential

Dear Russell: Thank you for that clipping from the *Times.* The difficulty is that under ordinary and normal circumstances wheat, cotton and copper ingots are not implements of war. The letter of the law does not say so and the trouble is that the spirit of the law, as shown by the debates during its passage, does not allow me to stretch it that far out—no matter how worthy the cause.[1]

As ever yours,

[PPF 44:CT]

[1] Bowie, rector of Grace Church, enclosed the leading editorial from the New York *Times* of Oct. 24, 1935, p. 20; in his covering note he said that he hoped it reflected Roosevelt's opinion. The editorial urged him to accept the League's list of contraband, "even should these include food, copper, chemicals, oil and cotton."

William E. Dodd, Ambassador to Germany, to Roosevelt

Berlin, October 31, 1935

Dear Mr. President: There is no real change of policy here since I wrote you some months ago.[1] While Hitler has not said a word publicly since last May on German foreign policy, Goebbels and Göring have frequently made statements as belligerent as ever. Göring's boast at Breslau October 26 about rapid re-armament and re-employment in arms factories was so challenging that parts of his speech were not published here. A vast army and annexations on the northern and eastern fronts are commonly accepted as quite as definite a program as Mussolini's Julius Caesar idea. I am informed today reliably, I believe, that 26 aircraft officers leave for Japan this week-end. There were already 70 Japanese officers at German military barracks. The Russian Ambassador says he is fairly certain of German-Japanese alliance. This tends to show there has been no change.

Your proclamation of October 5[2] and the Secretary's speech of October 10[3] produced a lot of sympathetic feeling here, the newspapers even printing the most significant passages. But during the last two weeks there has been a reversion of attitude, especially since the American influence seems to give the League actual power to stop Italy. Dr. Schacht a few days ago almost denounced the English-League demand that Italy be barred from taking colonial area. There have been as much exports to Italy as possible since September 1. The financial positions of both countries are such that exchange of goods, barter, is the chief method: economic nationalism, urged in the United States. One thing is certain here: the early defeat or forced withdrawal of Italy from Ethiopia would be considered a serious set-back for German autocratic-military procedure. If Italy succeeds, it is the common feeling that the two dictatorships would unite upon a policy of aggression.

This brings to my mind again the conviction that the Senate minority attitude last February was favorable to war. That is, we did as much to encourage German and Italian aggressions on weaker neighbors as either Germany or Italy had done up to October 1. I offered my resignation as a protest against minority dictation in our country. Judge Moore and the Secretary thought such a protest would be unwise, so the matter never came to your attention. I am not blaming the Department. Its leaders know domestic politics better than I; but I still think I made a mistake in not simply handing you my protest resignation. However, our country may still bring the "civilized" world to pursue peace policies, if it can stop all shipments of arms material as you and Secretary Hull intimated October 31. While the domestic situation must be your fundamental problem, world peace is not less important. If Italy, Germany and Japan at some critical moment move at the same time in their spheres, I cannot see any way to stop dictatorships. One of the Ministers here said to me today: "In that case I would commit suicide; your country alone can save civilization."[4]

Sincerely yours,

William E. Dodd

[PSF:Germany:TS]

[1] July 29, 1933, above.

[2] Printed in *Public Papers,* IV, 412–415, and widely published in the newspapers of October 6. See Roosevelt's statement on the proclamation, Oct. 5, 1935, above.

[3] Presumably Hull's statement to the press of Oct. 10, 1935, is meant; see Roosevelt's statement of Oct. 5, 1935, n. 2, above.

[4] Answered Dec. 2, 1935, below.

Cordell Hull, Secretary of State, to Roosevelt

Washington, October 31, 1935

My dear Mr. President: I am enclosing herewith a draft of a telegram to Judge Bingham which I have received from Norman Davis. I have made a few minor changes in his draft and I feel that it would be entirely appropriate for you to send it in its present form, if you chose to do so.

Faithfully yours,

Cordell Hull

[*Notation*:AS] Sec. State or Under Secretary   OK—Send   FDR   One added word on last page

[PSF:London Naval Conference:TS]

[*Enclosure*] Roosevelt to Robert W. Bingham, Ambassador to Great Britain, London

The question of our representation in the forth-coming naval conference[1] must be determined largely by how seriously the conference is to be taken by the British and ourselves, as well as the other governments concerned, and by what the aims and scope of the negotiations are to be and also the desire and prospects for ultimate agreement.

If the conference is being called by the British at this time mainly as a matter of strategy and in order to comply formally with provisions in the present treaties, but without much expectation of success or a determined effort to reach agreement on a new naval treaty to replace existing treaties, I agree that it would be unnecessary and perhaps inadvisable to send a special mission to London for this purpose. I also question the advisability in such a case of sending our highest ranking naval officers as advisers. On the other hand, if there is to be a serious effort on the part of the British as well as ourselves to negotiate and

45

enter into a new naval treaty with Japan, and if possible other naval powers, which is most important in order to avoid a disastrous naval race, there are controlling reasons for designating a special national delegation to negotiate and execute a multilateral treaty of such a nature.

I realize, of course, that there are certain disadvantages and embarrassments inherent in a formal Conference. I do not feel, however, that these difficulties can be avoided by calling a conference and then trying to make it appear as something else, and particularly if it is to result in a new multilateral treaty.

We have understood from your previous despatches[2] that, while the British think there is little chance of agreement on quantitative limitation, they do state they intend at least to make an attempt in that direction and they do think there is a good chance of reaching agreements such as qualitative limitation and possibly building programs and various other problems involved. If they do not think this is possible and do not intend to make every effort to that end, it is difficult to understand why they would have assumed the responsibility of calling such a conference and why they would have indicated the possibility of extending the conference to include other naval powers. Moreover, I understand the Japanese are sending a special delegation.

I feel that we must not only make the greatest possible effort to negotiate a new naval treaty, but that we should in every way make our desire to do so manifest. While it is important that our public must not be led to expect too much from such a conference, it is equally important for us to do nothing that would make it appear that we are taking this naval conference casually and less seriously than we have taken previous naval conferences and thus run the risk of being blamed for failure.

In view of all the circumstances my judgment is that as a matter of principle and policy it is advisable to follow the well established precedent of appointing a special delegation to attend the conference and negotiate a treaty. From your own standpoint I frankly feel that it would be inadvisable for you to assume, in addition to your many exacting duties and responsibilities as our accredited representative to Great Britain, the *sole*[3] responsibility and burden of conducting the naval negotiations with all of the naval powers.[4]

[PSF:London Naval Conference:T]

[1] The British government, acting under provisions of the Washington and London naval treaties, had invited the United States to resume discussions with the French,

Italians, and Japanese in London on December 2. The United States accepted, the date being subsequently changed to December 9 (*Foreign Relations, 1935*, I, 129, 130).

[2] See *ibid.,* pp. 64ff.

[3] "Sole" was inserted by Roosevelt.

[4] This draft, with the addition mentioned, was sent Nov. 1, 1935 (*ibid.,* pp. 136–138). In his reply of November 5, Bingham again asked to be allowed to head the delegation; Roosevelt, however, cabled him on November 18 that he had decided to continue Norman Davis as head, with Admiral Standley and William Phillips as the other delegates (*ibid.,* pp. 139–141, 143–144). See Roosevelt to Bingham, Nov. 23, 1935, below.

G. Ashton Oldham, Bishop, Diocese of Albany, to Roosevelt

Albany, New York, October 31, 1935

An Open Letter

My dear Mr. President: With multitudes of fellow citizens, I want to thank you for your strong statement reported in today's press,[1] regarding trade with belligerents, and to express the ardent hope that this step will be followed by others making for full cooperation with the agencies working for peace. For some time past the question has been running through my mind—"Will America let the world down?" and it has received new emphasis from an editorial in the New York *Times* of October 28, which states, in effect, that Mussolini had interpreted the high sounding but noncommital note of this country as meaning that we would not support in any whole hearted way the action of the League of Nations, in case it should apply economic sanctions against Italy in the present conflict and that, accordingly, he has taken new heart in the promotion of the war. The *Times* further draws the conclusion that, by withholding such support, "We shall have assumed first responsibility for the failure of those sanctions, if they fail, and the application of dangerous military measures, such as a naval blockade." Do we, Mr. President, really want to assume such a responsibility?

It seems the tragedy of tragedies that, with all our ardent and genuine love of peace, we should be prevented by political or other considerations from rendering adequate help to the world in its present crisis. I know full well that there are other than idealistic motives at work in Europe, as also here. It may even be, as asserted, that England's policy is in part dictated by her own interests, because in this case her interests and her duty happen to coincide. But this is of trifling importance as compared with the fact that she is rendering invaluable service to the cause of peace, while we, from equally selfish motives, are refusing the help so desperately needed. The real issue, which must be kept clear and not befogged by irrelevant criticism, is simply whether the collective forces of peace shall be supported as against an aggressor.

The League of Nations at the moment is in the most critical position of its entire existence. If it fails in its present effort, we shall be back again in the old system of armed alliances, each nation for itself, with a result no thinking man dare contemplate without dismay. If, however, it should succeed in effectively expressing the voice of the bulk of mankind in this instance, it would be well launched on the path which spells the end of the old war system and the beginning of a new method of settling international disputes.

Admittedly the United States is the most powerful nation in the world, and its attitude in this crisis will be a determining factor. Whole hearted support of the League would seem both in accord with our duty and self-interest. Of course we don't want our boys to be sacrificed in Europe, but neither the present neutrality legislation nor any other will give any positive assurance that that will not be. No realist, no honest and well informed person, believes otherwise. The only sure way for us to keep out of war is to have no war anywhere, just as the only assurance that your own house will not go down in the conflagration is to take effective steps to prevent all fires. Our own self-interest, therefore, coincides with our duty to mankind, of which we cannot be wholly neglectful, to throw our whole weight into the scales on the side of collective security.

Again and again have we asserted willingness to do all in our power for the cause of peace, though insisting that we must be free to act in our own way. Abstaining from the League has conserved this freedom of action. No one is attempting to coerce us. But the important question remains: How are we going to use this freedom? The present issue presents an acid test of the sincerity of our assertions of devotion to the cause of peace.

From the standpoint of practical politics, it would seem certain that, if Mussolini knew the whole moral and economic force of America was back of the League and against him, he would take quick steps to terminate the war. Fifty-two nations of the world are trying their best to do this, but their efforts may come to naught if the United States stands aloof. If she does, she cannot escape responsibility for the continuance of the war and any other direful consequences that may result. It is inconceivable that, if the American people could see the issue clearly, they would not want to have the mighty moral influence of their country behind the collective forces of peace. If we fail at this juncture, history will have some sad and bitter things to say about us. I therefore ask the question, "Will America let the world down?"

I address this question to you knowing it will receive sympathetic consideration. You were not only the friend but are the heir of Wilson's policies and ideals. You once believed in the thing for which he gave his life, and I cannot believe that you have so changed your mind as to consider the League of Nations a thing so evil that we cannot give it our full support even when it is so manifestly right and when such tremendous issues are in the balance.

You will, I am sure, meet the ardent wishes and aspirations and hopes of multitudes of your own people as well as multitudes of the peoples of the world if you take a definite and unequivocal stand on the moral issues involved and line up this great country with those that are working and striving for a peaceful and ordered world. I trust with all my heart, my dear Mr. President, future historians may never be able to say that under your administration "America let the world down."

Faithfully yours,

G. Ashton Oldham

[*Notation*:A] Mac   Prep reply[2]
[PPF 418:TS]

[1] See press conference of October 30, above.

[2] Answered Nov. 14, 1935 (*Public Papers,* IV, 452–453). Roosevelt said that, rather than standing aloof, the United States had done its share toward the restoration of peace, and, in a number of respects, more than other nations. Oldham asked permission to release Roosevelt's letter to the press and this was given (Oldham to Roosevelt, Nov. 20; Early to Oldham, Nov. 25, 1935, PPF 418).

Ray Stannard Baker to Roosevelt

Amherst, Mass., November 1, 1935

My dear President Roosevelt: I feel sure that you will be interested in the volume of *The Life and Letters of Woodrow Wilson*—[1] just from the press—which deals with his struggle with the problems of American neutrality at the beginning of the World War. They are so much like your own!

I am venturing to send you a copy in advance of publication.

Since it is based upon the original letters and papers of President

Wilson I believe this narrative to be the first complete and accurate account of the period. I have done my best to make it honestly objective, and if it can be widely read, I feel sure it will have a powerful effect in formulating public opinion alike as to the difficulties and necessities which now confront you in dealing with much the same issues. It is a tremendous object lesson—if America will only take it to heart!

When I talked with you in April,[2] you made a remark to the effect that foreign affairs in the near future might become more important in our public thought than our domestic problems. I remember doubting it at the time, but it was true prophecy. And America is now looking to you for leadership in world affairs as it looked to Woodrow Wilson in 1914 and 1915. If only people could know the backgrounds of the neutrality problem, your difficulties would certainly be much simplified!

Incidentally, you may be interested to know that I quote a beautiful letter written by Woodrow Wilson to you in June 1915 (on page 359), responding to an equally beautiful expression of your own loyalty and devotion.

With the warmest assurances of my own confidence and support, I am, Sincerely yours,

Ray Stannard Baker

It seems of such importance to get these facts before the people that if you could and think it warranted give us a few words of comment or approval I think it would help greatly in securing a wider reading & discussion. I should not venture to ask such a thing, if it did not seem so important.[3]

[PPF 2332:TS]

[1] *Woodrow Wilson: Life and Letters,* 8 vols. (New York: Doubleday, 1927–1939); the volume here mentioned is volume V, *Neutrality: 1914–1915,* published in 1935. Baker sent all the volumes as published to Roosevelt.
[2] Baker had tea with Roosevelt on April 18.
[3] Answered Nov. 13, 1935, below.

Governor Herbert H. Lehman of New York to Roosevelt

Albany, November 1, 1935

My dear Mr. President: I am sending you herewith letter received by Mr. Felix M. Warburg from Professor James G. McDonald, High

Commissioner for Refugees coming from Germany.[1] I know that you are well acquainted with Professor McDonald and know how reliable he is.

The situation which Mr. Warburg has asked me to take up with you is as follows: The present immigration quota from Germany is, I believe, 25,000. This quota has never been availed of and immigration has in the recent past been limited to about 2,500. Because of conditions in Germany with which you are familiar and which appear to be getting worse continually, it is imperative that the opportunity for immigration be given to as many of the persecuted Jewish citizens of that country as is possible.

The type of immigration from Germany is of the highest. I have met many of those who have come over here in recent months and they have impressed me as very much the type of men like my father, Carl Schurz, and other Germans who came over here in the days of 1848 and who later were among our best citizens. Mr. Warburg and those associated with him in caring for the unfortunate refugees are very desirous of having the very stringent regulations with regard to the immigration quota from Germany liberalized to some extent by the State Department. They would greatly appreciate it if you would ask the Secretary of State to make certain that our diplomatic and consular representatives show sympathetic interest in permitting immigration of German Jews into this country, providing, of course, they fulfill the immigration requirements in every particular. They ask that the immigration quota of German Jews to this country be increased from 2,500 to 5,000. This, of course, is almost a negligible number.

As I have said, because of conditions the type of immigration is different from that I have known for many years. They are men and women of the highest character and many of them have attained positions of great distinction in their own country. I therefore can very strongly endorse the request of Commissioner McDonald and Mr. Warburg. The matter is of such importance that I feel justified in taking it up directly with you. I hope that it will receive your personal consideration and favorable action.[2]

With kind personal regards, I remain, Yours very sincerely,

Herbert H. Lehman

[OF 133:TS]

[1] McDonald wrote (Oct. 10, 1935, OF 133), that he feared nothing could be done to mitigate the severity of the Nazi anti-Semitic program; nevertheless, he thought

certain of the governments, particularly the United States and Great Britain, should make informal representations to the Reich. In the probable event that such representations would be unavailing the need for relief measures "on a scale heretofore not undertaken and except in very few quarters envisaged" seemed clear. McDonald had written to Mrs. Roosevelt on July 24, 1935 (OF 198-A) to the same effect. He raised the question whether the time had not come when "the American Government should take the initiative in protesting against the prevailing violations of elementary civil and religious rights in Germany." Mrs. Roosevelt replied Aug. 2, 1935 (OF 198-A), that she had given the letter to her husband.

[2] Answered Nov. 13, 1935, below.

Roosevelt to Lincoln MacVeagh, Minister to Greece, Athens

Hyde Park, N.Y., November 2, 1935

Dear Lincoln: It is good to get your interesting letter of October fifteenth.[1] You are very clearly in one of the most interesting spots in Europe just now. Cannon to right of you, cannon to left of you, and apparently quite a lot of potential cannon right next door in Athens!

Things move so fast that no one can tell what will be the story a month from now. Meanwhile, as you know, we are really keeping our skirts pretty clear of any involvements.

Always sincerely,

[PSF:Greece:CT]

[1] Above.

Roosevelt to W. D. Griffith, Executive Vice President, New York Board of Trade, Inc., New York

[Washington] November 4, 1935

My dear Mr. Griffith: I have your letter of October twenty-third telling me that newspaper accounts reporting the New York Board of Trade as opposed to the Neutrality Proclamation were erroneous.[1] I am, of course, very glad to know this.

I know you will not mind my saying that, in my opinion, many persons throughout the country have drawn the conclusion from this and other published statements that your organization is, broadly speaking, opposed to most of the acts and policies of the United States Government. Therefore, your statement that the Board has not officially opposed the Proclamation of Neutrality is welcome.

I shall be very glad if you care to read this letter at the luncheon on November thirteenth.[2]

Very sincerely yours,

[PPF 2978:CT]

[1] Griffith had enclosed a news release to the effect that the New York Board of Trade had taken no action on the President's neutrality proclamation (PPF 2978).

[2] Drafted by McIntyre from a State Department draft (Moore to McIntyre, Nov. 1, 1935; McIntyre to Early, Nov. 4, 1935, PPF 2978).

Roosevelt to Fred Morris Dearing, Ambassador to Peru

Hyde Park, N.Y., November 5, 1935

Dear Fred: Many thanks for that interesting letter of yours.[1] I am particularly glad to get the slant on the British news service.

Yesterday your good wife came in to Tea and it was delightful to see her again. I am so glad that she has recuperated so well from her operation and illness. Apparently your youngster is getting on well at Williams.[2]

My warm regards, Always sincerely,

[PSF:Peru:CT]

[1] Oct. 23, 1935, above.
[2] See Dearing to Roosevelt, Dec. 2, 1935, below.

Harold J. Laski, London School of Economics and Political Science, University of London, to Roosevelt

London, 5th November, 1935

Personal

Dear Mr. President: I think you may like to know the view taken by the Labour Party of the situation that will arise at the Naval Conference next month. We all feel that it is governed by two considerations:

(1) The determination of the Government to go in if at all possible for a greatly enlarged naval programme.

(2) The existence of widespread popular opinion that resents any increases which might jeopardise our keeping in step with the United States and its desire to arrive at some formula which permits decreases generally applied.

We feel quite certain that if your delegates were to come here in the spirit of the opening speech of the Washington Conference, that is, with an agreed and dramatic programme for a drastic reduction of expenditure, public opinion in this country would rally widely to it, and there would be a real prospect of forcing this Government to be on the side of disarmament.

This would have important ramifications in relation both to military and air expenditure and might easily alter a good deal of the direction of British foreign policy.

I do not of course know what you feel yourself about the situation. We are gravely alarmed by the temper of the Admiralty and we feel that the only prospect of curbing its exuberance lies in Washington and not in London. We believe that the elections will give us such an increased representation in the House of Commons as to assure a very formidable backing for proposals from America of this kind and we believe that such co-operation would awaken an amazing response in the country at large.

The alternative seems to us so dangerous that we think it important to put this before you.[1]

With warm regard, Yours ever,

Harold J. Laski

[PPF 3014:TS]

[1] Answered Nov. 18, 1935, below.

Press Conference, Hyde Park, November 6, 1935, 11 A.M.

[*Excerpt*] Q: Can you tell us any developments on the foreign situation with respect to the visit of Mr. Baruch yesterday?

The President: He was over there twice this summer and he told me about his general observations—the difficulties in Europe. It is not encouraging. Nothing that comes over is particularly encouraging. That is why I am spending such an awful lot of time on the foreign situation. It is a good deal more worry to me personally than the domestic situation.[1]

[President's Press Conferences:T]

[1] Baruch was a luncheon guest on November 5.

Press Conference, Executive Offices of the White House, November 8, 1935, 4:18 P.M.

[*Excerpt*] Q: Anything on Canadian negotiations?

The President: I talked over with the State Department this morning the progress that had been made up to date in discussing the trade agreement.[1]

Q: Have they given you a list of the commodities you might talk about?

The President: Oh, we have been talking about it—how long has it been going—three months?

Q: It started since last January?

The President: They have had all that time a list of commodities as long as your arm—both sides.

Q: Have you agreed on any exchange?

The President: Still in the discussion stage.

Q: Is it likely that the discussion with Mr. King[2] may also cover the St. Lawrence Waterway Project?

The President: We may mention it; I don't know yet.

Q: Have you decided on who will go to London for the Naval Conference?

The President: Not yet. The actual date of its opening is not yet definitely determined because the Japanese delegation can't get there on the second and I understand it will be postponed; probably only for a short time.

Q: Even if it is for December fifth, those people will have to leave on November twenty-fifth.

The President: That is plenty of time . . .

Q: Have you any further moves on the neutrality question, particularly with regard to trade with belligerent countries?

The President: I have not had a chance to talk to the State Department about it.

Q: Have you had any reports on exports for the month of October to Italy, on oil or any other commodities?

The President: I think the Department of Commerce and the Treasury have those ready today. I have not seen them complete for the month of October yet.

Q: Are they being put out publicly or privately?

The President: I don't know; I hope so.[3]

Q: Can we induce you to speak about the increased export of oil?

The President: I haven't seen that . . .

Q: Do you expect to strike a bargain with Mackenzie King while he is here?

The President: What?

Q: Do you expect to trade?

The President: I hope these negotiations will result in a trade agreement. They have been under way for some time. I hope they will be concluded soon.

Q: In that connection, is there any possibility of them being extended to include some of the articles covered by the so-called Ottawa Agreements?

The President: I do not know, for the reason that I do not know what articles are included in the Ottawa Agreements.

Q: Some of the important ones are autos and motor machinery and some of the things we are particularly interested in.

The President: Of course I should like to see the agreement as broad as it can be made. The whole purpose is to increase trade back and forth between Canada and the United States in as many articles as possible.

Q: Mr. President, have the Canadian wheat reserves figured in the discussion?

The President: No, not yet. They may. I don't know; they haven't come up yet.[4]

[President's Press Conferences:T]

---

[1] Hull and Phillips were at the White House from 10:30 to 11:30 A.M.
[2] Prime Minister Mackenzie King of Canada.
[3] The President apparently misunderstood the question.
[4] See telegram following.

Roosevelt to Senator L. B. Schwellenbach of Washington, Seattle

Washington, November 12, 1935

[*Telegram*] I have received your telegram of November eleventh[1] relative to the negotiation of a trade agreement with Canada and assure you that I would indeed be glad did circumstances permit to postpone or cause to be postponed any action in this matter pending the discussion of it with you which you have suggested. You have however doubtless noted the reference in my Armistice Day address[2] to the reaching of agreement with the Canadian Prime Minister. This agreement is the culmination of detailed and careful negotiations which have been proceeding for some time and which have been based upon exhaustive preparations in which all aspects of our trade relations with Canada were very fully considered. In these preparations the statements received from interested parties, which these parties were given full opportunity to submit following the announcement on January twenty-first last of our intention to negotiate a trade agreement with Canada and including very full and repeated expressions of the views and position of our lumbering interests in the Northwest, have been the subject of most detailed and attentive consideration.[3] I am convinced that when the terms of this agreement are published, its value as a means of increasing the trade between the two countries and thus stimulating the revival and maintenance of employment and production as well as solidifying our peaceful and friendly relations with Canada will be recognized and that the agreement will be received with widespread public satisfaction and approval.[4]

Franklin D. Roosevelt

[PPF 2754:T]

[1] Schwellenbach asked (OF 61-L) that no changes in the tariff on Canadian lumber imports be made under the new treaty. He said British Columbia lumber already had the advantage of lower wages and a longer work week and greater imports would further depress the Pacific Northwest.

[2] *Public Papers,* IV, 441–444.

[3] Notice of intention to negotiate a trade agreement with Canada, signed by Hull, issued by the State Department on Jan. 21, 1935, and accompanied with a statement and tables showing the extent and character of United States-Canadian trade; published in State Department, *Press Releases,* Jan. 26, 1935, pp. 44–45. The agreement was signed Nov. 15, 1935 (49 *Stat.* 3960), and ratification was completed May 14, 1936.

⁴ The same telegram was sent to Senator Charles L. McNary of Oregon in response to his telegram of Nov. 12, 1936 (PPF 2677). See also Roosevelt to Governor Charles H. Martin of Oregon, Nov. 15, 1935, in *Public Papers*, IV, 457–458, and press conference of November 17, below.

Press Conference, Executive Offices of the White House, November 13, 1935, 10:45 A.M.

[*Excerpt*] The President: I don't think I could invent any news for you if I tried. I don't know a thing.

Q: Mr. President, can you tell us anything about the Canadian Treaty?

The President: No.

Q: I mean, as to when it will be released?

The President: I don't know. I just signed the usual authority to have it signed but I do not know when it is to be signed.

Q: Mr. President, would you care to say anything about the inauguration of the Philippine Commonwealth on Friday?

The President: I am giving out a statement and a telegram, et cetera. You are a little ahead of time. It is coming tomorrow.

Q: What is that authority, for the Secretary of State to sign the treaty?

The President: I do not know what the technical name of it is. It is a proclamation, to which I sign my name and they put the seal of the United States on it.[1]

Q: Is there any likelihood that the Argentine Trade Agreement will be consummated in the near future?

The President: I don't know; I have not heard about it for a long time.

Q: I understand plans for its consummation have about been abandoned.

The President: I haven't seen anything about it since I came back from the cruise.[2]

Q: Can you tell us anything about the conversations with (Asst. Sec.) Roosevelt and Admiral Standley yesterday?[3]

The President: Yes, I have to develop the story. We talked about the total personnel, first of the Navy, to go into the budget and secondly of the Marine Corps. We went, with a great deal of detail, into the problems of manning the new ships to be put into commission, also of maintaining the Marine Corps up to a reasonable strength in comparison with the Navy. Nothing was decided. I won't take it up until I get to the Navy bill and the Navy budget bill won't be ready—it will be one of the last two, Bell told me yesterday.[4]

Q: Did they indicate what our total personnel in the fleet would have to be by the end of 1937, when we have the new ships?

The President: It will probably come to—it is now I think 93,500 and the question is how close we can bring it this coming year to 100,000. That, of course, is the 100,000 maximum. If Congress is asked for and authorizes 100,000, it means an average in the service during the year of 96,500. I haven't decided whether I will ask for the whole 100,000 or not.

Q: That is both Navy and Marine Corps?

The President: No, just Navy.

Q: Did you discuss the possibility of a new battleship?

The President: For about a minute and a half. In other words, we decided not to make any final decision until a little later.

Q: A hypothetical question seems to have arisen on our neutrality order and the Executive Orders following it.[5] In the event Great Britain were to enter a war with any power, not necessarily Italy, what would that do to our trade with Britain's colonies?

The President: I don't know. It is too hypothetical. I have never thought of it. Of course the general rule—it would be leaving out the question of Great Britain—the general rule would be that any other nation entering the war—I have discretionary power in that case to apply the Arms, Ammunition and Implement Section to that nation.

Q: Mr. President, will the request for the new battleship rest on the outcome of the Naval Conference?

The President: That is going too far ahead. I just said we are not making any decision now.

Q: Have you made any decision as to whom you are going to send to the Naval Conference?

The President: No, because we do not know the date of it yet . . .

Q: Have you discussed the St. Lawrence Waterway Treaty with Mackenzie King?

The President: There isn't any news on that at all. I am looking into a thing that both the Prime Minister and I were very much interested in and that is the Niagara Falls problem, the problem of the Falls being cut back year after year, and I have asked for a report of a study that was being made jointly by, I think, the Federal Power Commission, the

New York State Power Authority and the Army Engineers. I have asked for that report.

Q: Any further study being made as to possible amendments to the Treaty requiring re-negotiation?

The President: Not at the present time.

Q: You have mentioned that you have discretionary power to apply the arms embargo to any other nation engaged in war. I wondered if that meant any other nation engaged in the Italian-Ethiopian conflict or any other war that breaks out in any way?

The President: War. In other words, what I said the other day—"War is war."

Q: War is hell. (Laughter)

[President's Press Conferences: T]

[1] See Roosevelt's proclamation of Nov. 14, 1935, and his cable to President Quezon, same date, in *Public Papers,* IV, 455–457.

[2] See Weddell to Hull, Sept. 27, 1935, in *Foreign Relations, 1935,* IV, 278–280.

[3] Standley and Assistant Secretary of the Navy Roosevelt were at the White House the preceding morning (PPF 1-0).

[4] Acting Director of the Budget Daniel W. Bell and Secretary of the Treasury Morgenthau were at the White House from 2:30 to 4:30 in the afternoon (PPF 1-0).

[5] See the two proclamations of Oct. 5, 1935, prohibiting the export of arms and munitions to Italy and Ethiopia, and warning against travel on ships of belligerents, in *Public Papers,* IV, 412–415, 416–417, and Roosevelt's statement accompanying them, of the same date, above.

Roosevelt to Ray Stannard Baker, Amherst, Massachusetts

[Washington] November 13, 1935

My dear Ray: It was most thoughtful and therefore characteristic of you to send me a copy of the volume of *The Life and Letters of Woodrow Wilson* in advance of publication.[1] I shall read every line of it with interest because, as you aptly observe, the problems of American neutrality which confronted Woodrow Wilson at the beginning of the World War were very much like the problems which face the Administration today and are likely to assume increasing gravity in the period just ahead of us.

The publication of the volume just now is indeed timely and all friends of our late leader will be grateful that the task of preparing it was committed to your capable hands. This work, supplementing your previous labors in the same field, will be invaluable, not only to contemporary readers but in preserving in permanent form the record of a great figure in a momentous period of world affairs.[2]

Very sincerely yours,

[PPF 2332:CT]

[1] Nov. 1, 1935, above.
[2] Drafted by William D. Hassett, assistant to Early.

Roosevelt to Martin H. Carmody, Supreme Knight, Knights of Columbus, New Haven, Connecticut

[Washington, November 13, 1935]

My dear Mr. Carmody: I have received your letter of October 25th.[1]

Without commenting upon the language of your communication under acknowledgment, and without reference to the accuracy of the statements or conclusions which you advance, I shall inform you once more of the attitude of this Administration in the matter of the policy pursued by the Government of Mexico towards religious activities in that Republic.

The right of United States citizens resident or traveling in foreign countries to worship freely, to conduct services within their houses, or within appropriate buildings maintained for that purpose, is desired by this Government. There has not been brought to this Government during the past year a single complaint by any United States citizen that such opportunities in Mexico have been refused him.

In respect to the rights enjoyed by Mexican citizens living in Mexico, it has been the policy of this Administration to refrain from intervening in such direct concerns of the Mexican Government. That policy of non-intervention I shall continue to pursue.

While this Government does not assume to undertake any accurate determination of what the facts in such domestic concerns of other Governments may be, this policy of non-intervention, however, can in no sense be construed as indifference on our part. I repeat what I stated publicly in San Diego, California, on October 2nd, last:

Our national determination to keep free of foreign wars and foreign entanglements cannot prevent us from feeling deep concern when ideals and principles that we have cherished are challenged. In the United States we regard it as axiomatic that every person shall enjoy the free exercise of his religion according to the dictates of his conscience. Our flag for a century and a half has been the symbol of the principles of liberty of conscience, of religious freedom and equality before the law; and these concepts are deeply ingrained in our national character.

It is true that other Nations may, as they do, enforce contrary rules of conscience and conduct. It is true that policies that may be pursued under flags other than our own are beyond our jurisdiction. Yet in our inner individual lives we can never be indifferent, and we assert for ourselves complete freedom to embrace, to profess and to observe the principles for which our flag has so long been the lofty symbol. As it was so well said by James Madison, "We hold it for a fundamental and inalienable truth that religion and the manner of discharging it can be directed only by reason and conviction, not by force or violence."[2]

This statement, I now reiterate to you. Inasmuch as you have referred in your letter under acknowledgment to the policy pursued in such matters as this by previous Administrations and have mentioned specifically the Administration of President Theodore Roosevelt, it may not be inappropriate to call to your attention the statement of former President Theodore Roosevelt contained in his Annual Message to the Congress of December 6, 1904:

... Ordinarily it is very much wiser and more useful for us to concern ourselves with striving for our own moral and material betterment here at home than to concern ourselves with trying to better the conditions of things in other Nations. We have plenty of sins of our own to war against, and under ordinary circumstances we can do more for the general uplifting of humanity by striving with heart and soul to put a stop to civic corruption, to brutal lawlessness and violent race prejudices here at home than by passing resolutions about wrongdoing elsewhere.

You and I abhor equally, I trust, religious intolerance, whether at home or abroad. For my own part, however, I decline to permit this Government to undertake a policy of interference in the domestic concerns of foreign Governments and thereby jeopardize the maintenance of peaceful conditions.[3]

Sincerely yours,

[OF 28:CT]

---

[1] In this long letter (over 2,000 words), Carmody referred to the meeting he and other officials of the Knights of Columbus had had with Roosevelt on July 8, 1935: "Before

the conference ended, you advised our committee that in your opinion a public statement by you, expressing the attitude of our government concerning conditions in Mexico, would help to bring about a change in those conditions and that the time was now opportune for you to make such a statement, and thereupon you assured our committee that you would take advantage of your first public address for that purpose." Carmody said the President's San Diego speech of Oct. 2, 1935, could not be accepted in fulfillment of this promise because he had made no mention of Mexico. (Roosevelt had there made brief reference to the American belief in freedom of religion and it was suggested at the time by the press that the reference was aimed at the Mexican situation. See excerpt, above.)

Carmody concluded his letter with the charge that responsibility for the situation was solely the President's: "You cannot escape responsibility for throttling the Borah Resolution. You cannot escape responsibility for the endorsement given to the Mexican Government and its policies by your Ambassador to that country . . . You cannot escape responsibility for non-action on behalf of bleeding and oppressed Mexico."

McIntyre sent Carmody's letter to Under Secretary of State Phillips for draft of reply; in his covering note (Nov. 1, 1935, OF 28) he said he thought it might be better to send only a brief, courteous acknowledgment "without going into any argument or discussion." He added: "After you have talked with 'Burke' would you be kind enough to give me a ring." (The Reverend John J. Burke was a prominent Catholic churchman frequently called upon to give advice on Catholic issues; see Roosevelt to Noll, May 23, 1935, above, n. 1.

Roosevelt was in Hyde Park from October 31 to November 7; from Washington McIntyre wired that a reply had been drafted but that he and Welles thought it advisable to delay sending it until the President returned, "especially in view Thursday's program" (McIntyre to Early, Nov. 5, 1935, OF 28). This program was Roosevelt's attendance on November 7 at a ceremony in Masonic Hall in New York where his sons James and Franklin, Jr., received the third degree in Freemasonry from Architect Lodge and where Roosevelt made a brief speech on the principles of the order (Speech File). In Washington Roosevelt made certain revisions in the draft reply; these were discussed with Sumner Welles at lunch at the White House on November 8 (Welles to Roosevelt, Nov. 11, 1935, PSF:Mexico).

[2] The entire speech is printed in *Public Papers,* IV, 405–412.

[3] Carmody gave this letter to the press on Nov. 17, 1935 (New York *Times,* Nov. 18, 1935, p. 1). He had given out his letter of October 25 on October 27 (*ibid.,* Oct. 28, 1935, p. 3). On Dec. 16, 1935, he repeated his charges and demands in a ten-page letter to Roosevelt, which was sent to the State Department for draft of reply (OF 28). Welles, however, returned Carmody's letter with a note of December 21 (OF 28), in which he said: "I had assumed that in view of the nature of the letter addressed by you to Mr. Carmody on November 13th, you would not desire, nor indeed find it necessary, to address any further communication to Mr. Carmody with regard to the religious question in Mexico. Mr. Carmody's most recent letter to you raises no new questions which, in my judgment, seem to warrant any further comment from the President of the United States."

On this letter appears this note: "STE Tell Sumner Welles that his suggestion is correct. FDR." Early so informed Welles in a note of December 26 and added that the White House considered the subject closed (OF 28). Letters to the White House inspired by the publication of the Carmody letter and the President's reply (OF 28; OF 146-A) without exception supported the President's position. See Daniels to Roosevelt, Nov. 18, 1935, below.

Roosevelt to Governor Herbert H. Lehman of New York, Albany

[Washington] November 13, 1935

My dear Governor Lehman: I have your letter of November 1, 1935, with its enclosed letter of October 10, 1935, from Professor James G. McDonald, High Commissioner for Refugees (Jewish and Other) coming from Germany, to Mr. Felix M. Warburg with reference to the question of the immigration of German Jews into the United States.[1]

I have brought your letter to the particular attention of the Department of State in view of the responsibility placed by law upon its consular officers abroad for the issuance or refusal of immigration visas. In connection with my reference of this important matter to the competent officers of the Department of State, I am informed that the situation as regards the points you have raised is briefly as follows:

With regard to your request that the quota for German Jews be increased from 2,500 to 5,000 per annum, there is no immigration quota fixed for persons in the class described, nor has there been any arbitrary limitation set upon the number of visas to be issued to natives of Germany other than the maximum quota fixed by law, which is 25,957. Consular officers must issue immigration visas, within quota limitations, to all quota applicants who qualify under the law to receive such visas. They cannot of course issue visas to applicants who are found to be inadmissible under the public charge clause or any other restrictive limitation set by existing law.

I am informed that nearly all immigration quotas have been considerably under-issued during the past four years. Although the German quota comprises only 16.9 per cent of the total of all quotas, immigration visas issued under it now represent 26.9 of the visas issued under all quotas. While estimates on this point vary somewhat, it is understood that a very large majority of immigration visas under the German quota are issued to Jewish applicants. Since there is also a considerable number of aliens chargeable, because of their birthplace, to the Polish and other quotas who have lived in Germany and who immigrate into the United States, it is reasonable to take the number of immigration visas issued to natives of Germany as approximating numerically the total of the classes to which your letter refers.

The following figures, showing the issuance of immigration visas to natives of Germany are therefore of particular interest in relation to your inquiry.

Fiscal year (ending June 30)	Immigration visas issued (exclusive of students and returning residents of the United States)
1932	2,571
1933	1,798
1934	4,715
1935	5,117

As regards your wish that it be made certain that our consular representatives show sympathetic interest in permitting immigration of German Jews into this country, the Department of State has issued instructions to its consular officers, which are now in effect, that persons who are obliged to leave the country of their regular residence, and who seek to escape from the conditions in that country by coming to the United States, should receive, on the part of American consular officers, the most considerate attention and the most generous and favorable treatment possible under the laws of this country.

In addition to the above, consular officers have been instructed that in cases where it is found that an immigration visa applicant cannot obtain a supporting document normally required by the Immigration Act of 1924 without the peculiar delay and embarrassment that might attend a request of a political or religious refugee, the requirement of such document may be waived on the basis of its being not "available."

Furthermore, the principal consular officers stationed at Berlin, Hamburg and Stuttgart, which are the only three consular offices in Germany which now issue immigration visas, have all visited the Department of State during recent months and the problems in which you are interested have been discussed verbally and sympathetically with them at the time of their visits. The recently appointed Consul General at Berlin, Mr. Douglas Jenkins, who is the supervising consular officer for Germany, spent a number of days at the Department before proceeding to his new post, and these matters were discussed particularly with him.

I note that you have made the request to which I have referred above on the condition that these prospective immigrants "fulfill the immigration requirements in every particular." I believe that the Department of State and its consular officers abroad have had no other desire than to carry out the immigration duties placed upon them by the Immigration Act of 1924 in a considerate and humane manner, consistent with a faithful discharge of their responsibilities under the law. I understand that the percentage of immigration visa refusals in Germany has recently been considerably below the average for all countries.

I appreciate your action in bringing these matters to my attention and I can assure you that it is my earnest desire that all consideration and justice shall continue to be shown to the type of immigrants in whom you are interested.[2]

Very sincerely yours,

[OF 133:CT]

[1] Above.

[2] Drafted in the State Department (Hull to Roosevelt, Nov. 13, 1935, OF 133). Lehman acknowledged the letter November 18, 1935, (OF 133), and said he would send a copy to McDonald. In the meantime, McDonald had again written to Warburg who in turn wrote to Lehman; Lehman sent the letters (October 29, November 8) to Roosevelt on Nov. 15, 1935 (OF 133). McDonald said he had received the impression from the British Foreign Office that the British would go no further than to direct their ambassador to cooperate with Dodd in making representations against the German government's intensified anti-Semitism policy. He hoped that if the President was unwilling to make strong representations he would at least authorize Dodd to go along with the British. The President could also help by directing American consuls in Germany to be more lenient in their interpretation of their instructions respecting issuance of visas. Roosevelt acknowledged Lehman's second letter on Dec. 10, 1933 (OF 133), noting merely that he wished to repeat his "earnest desire that all consideration and justice . . . continue to be shown to the type of immigrants in whom you are interested." See Lehman to Roosevelt, June 15, 1936, below.

Cordell Hull, Secretary of State, to Roosevelt

Washington, November 13, 1935

My dear Mr. President: The Peace Conference in Plenary Session at Buenos Aires formally adopted, on October 28, 1935, a resolution declaring that the war between Bolivia and Paraguay had come to an end. In these circumstances I suggest that the time has come for you to revoke your Proclamation of May 28, 1934, prohibiting the sale of arms and munitions to those countries.[1] I submit therefore for your consideration and, if you approve, your signature, a draft of a Proclamation revoking your former Proclamation.[2]

I invite your attention to the fact that this draft is so worded that your action is predicated upon the action of the Peace Conference and also upon the agreement between Bolivia and Paraguay that, pending the conclusion of the Treaty of Peace, they will not import war material beyond what is indispensable for replacement. I invite your attention further to the fact that the draft is so worded that the revocation will become effective on November 29 and that the right of the Government to prosecute violations of your Proclamation of May 28, 1934, is safeguarded. The date November 29 was selected because on that date the system of licenses for all exports of arms, provided for in Section 2 of the Neutrality Act, becomes operative. The language intended to safeguard the right of the Government to prosecute persons who have sold arms to Bolivia or Paraguay in violation of your Proclamation was suggested by Mr. Martin Conboy, Special Assistant to the Attorney General, in charge of the investigation and the prosecution of such cases.

Faithfully yours,

Cordell Hull

[OF 338-C:TS]

[1] Printed in *Public Papers,* III, 268–269.
[2] Issued under date of Nov. 14, 1935, *ibid.,* IV, 453–455.

Cordell Hull, Secretary of State, to Roosevelt

Washington, Nov. 13, 1935

Dear Mr. President: I herewith attach a proposed statement for you to consider giving to the press. My individual view would be to omit the last paragraph in this proposed statement, because it has been previously stated, in substance, by you.

I also enclose table showing considerable recent increases of exports of the war materials mentioned in the proposed statement.[1] You will observe that the increase in machinery and vehicles relates to Italian Africa rather than to Italy.

You will observe that the proposed statement is made to relate back immediately to our policy primarily of keeping out of the war and also not to do anything to prolong the war, but without repeating any portion of either of your past statements or either of mine, setting forth the steps we were undertaking and the policy underlying them.

You will observe from these former statements that we definitely stated that the policy of the neutrality act as extended and applied by us to war materials was intended to discourage trade especially in war materials with either of the belligerent countries. Your last statement dwelt on this phase and closed with the sentence: "Accordingly, the American Government is keeping informed as to all shipments consigned for export to both belligerents."

You will observe that the present proposed statement carries you one step further in applying this same policy which we have pursued from the beginning, and that step places a ban on any further shipments of "oils, copper, trucks, tractors, scrap iron and scrap steel" to the belligerents. Affirmative action could not fairly be attributed to any agreement with Geneva or London or Paris, but solely in accordance with our separate independent course from the outset, under our own policy already referred to.[2]

Faithfully yours,

Cordell Hull

[*Notation*:A:FDR] File[3]
[OF 547-A:TS]

---

[1] The table is present.
[2] The proposed statement was not issued.
[3] This appears in the upper right-hand corner of the first page and was underscored twice by Roosevelt.

[*Enclosure*] Proposed Statement by the President

The recent foreign trade statistics show that such essential war materials as oils, copper, trucks, tractors, scrap iron and scrap steel are being exported, presumably for war purposes, in amounts considerably larger than similar exports for any corresponding recent period.

This class of trade is directly contrary to the already declared policy of this Government as contained in the recent neutrality act and the official statements of myself and the Secretary of State extending the application of this policy.

With deep conviction of the responsibilities of our country in the present specific circumstances, I now appeal to our citizens to enter into no new transactions to furnish the materials above named to the belligerents.

I am aware that this may mean some immediate economic sacrifice to a few of our citizens or groups of citizens. It should be recognized, however, that the apparent temporary benefits of trade created by war are apt to prove unsound, and may even in their final outcome endanger the much greater possible benefits of the normal permanent trade that peace alone affords.

[OF 547-A:T]

Roosevelt to Samuel R. Fuller, Jr., New York

[Washington] November 14, 1935

Dear Dick: That is a mighty nice note of yours. May I tell you again how very grateful I was to you for that tremendously interesting report you brought back. Be sure to let me know if and when you plan any other trip![1]

As ever yours,

[PPF 2616:CT]

[1] Fuller had written Nov. 12, 1935 (PPF 2616), congratulating Roosevelt on his Armistice Day speech (*Public Papers*, IV, 441–444). Concerning Fuller's report, see his letter of Oct. 11, 1935, above.

Press Conference, Executive Offices of the White House, November 15, 1935, 4 P.M.

[*Excerpt*] Q: Do you approve of the change in PWA on buying of foreign materials?

The President: A change in PWA?

Q: As announced yesterday?

The President: What paper do you read? (Laughter)

Q: He announced it himself in his letter to Mr. Green as a change in policy.[1]

The President: He said that?

Q: Yes, sir; he said, "Accordingly I am changing the policy of PWA." Those are the exact words.

The President: Suppose you give the whole thing. I don't remember it except as I read it in the paper. Let us get this straight. When a newspaper says to the public that any department of the Government is changing its policy in regard to the purchase of foreign materials, that is a deliberate misrepresentation. Let that stand. The reason is this: The

Secretary definitely stated that the policy of the Government was not to buy foreign materials, never was, and for that reason they had put on, in addition to the tariff, a percentage which was supposed to keep foreign materials out. As soon as it became apparent in these two cases, after many, many months that the percentage was not high enough, then we changed the percentage, but the policy remained the same.

Q: Has the percentage been changed?

The President: Yes, it will be changed. And with that goes, of course, the supplementary part of the statement that in the future where a foreign bid is lower, we will find out first, whether it was a subsidized bid and, secondly, whether there was collusion on the part of American bidders as occurred in one of those two cases on the face of things.

Q: Are you going to investigate the alleged collusion?

The President: Oh, yes.

Q: The Federal Trade Commission?

The President: Yes.

Q: Is the Treasury Department going to investigate the possibility of dumping in this connection?

The President: Yes. There are various methods by which, in some nations, they are able to assist exporters through various kinds of ways.

Q: Is it a fair inference that if foreign exporters have been found to send materials here and are selling them cheaper because of government subsidies in their own countries, that purchases of those materials would not be allowed?

The President: Obviously because, after all, if you once admit the subsidized goods, they could subsidize manufacturers 100 per cent and the manufacturer could sell things for one per cent of the cost of manufacture.

Q: Under the amended AAA subsidy, subsidies will be granted on our agricultural products. Would that, perhaps, constitute dumping abroad?

The President: You are talking about an export debenture plan?

Q: Something of that sort. It applies to the export of agricultural products.

The President: It is essentially the same principle.

Q: Senator Lonergan, I believe, wants you to subsidize cotton exports.

The President: It is essentially the same principle. In other words, it is something contrary to the free flow of trade. It is an artificial stimulation to trade which ends in cut-throat competition . . .

Q: Is it possible for you to make any announcement of American participation in the Naval Conference?

The President: I have to have it in the next two days. We have not heard from London on the date. We telegraphed and have not had any reply yet . . .

Q: Mr. President, is there a possibility that the German order may be stopped in case dumping is found?

The President: I do not believe it can. How much was it—$19,000 out of a $42,000,000 project?

Q: Anything new on the neutrality situation?

The President: No.

Q: The Secretary of State reported today that the figures show some increases since those of October fifth?

The President: I do not think so.

Q: Would you care to say anything for quotation on the general policy of the Administration with respect to dumping foreign materials on relief or P.W.A. projects?

The President: The Secretary's letter gave the full story.

[President's Press Conferences:T]

[1] "He" is not identified in the preceding part of the press conference (devoted to George W. Norris' possible retirement from the Senate and Roosevelt's coming trip to Warm Springs); the reference, however, is to Ickes. As head of the Public Works Administration Ickes had directed that all proposed purchases of foreign-made materials intended for P.W.A. projects be first submitted to him for approval. He had so informed William Green, president of the American Federation of Labor, in a letter of Nov. 13, 1935, published in the New York *Times* of Nov. 15, 1935, p. 4. The purchase of German-made steel for the Tri-Borough Bridge in New York and the Ocean Terminal in Morehead City, N.C., had aroused wide criticism from both business and labor groups (*ibid.*, Nov. 14, p. 6; Nov. 15, 1935, p. 1).

Roosevelt to Henry Morgenthau, Sr., New York

[Washington] November 15, 1935

Dear Uncle Henry: I wish you would tell Doctor Trexler that I wish much that I could help the candidacy of Doctor Morehead for the Nobel Prize.[1] He is a splendid person but my difficulty is that ever since I became Governor of New York, I have had to decline, every year, to make recommendations on account of my official position. I know you will understand.

As ever yours,

[OF 518:CT]

[1] Morgenthau had written to Roosevelt Nov. 13, 1935 (OF 518), enclosing a letter of Nov. 12, 1935, from Samuel Trexler, president of the United Lutheran Synod of New York. Trexler presented the endorsement of the recent world convention of the Lutheran Church on behalf of John A. Morehead, also a prominent Lutheran clergyman, who had worked for the rehabilitation of European Lutherans from 1919 to 1923 as chairman of the European Commission of the National Lutheran Council. Morgenthau said that from his conversation with Trexler he believed Morehead was deserving of the Nobel prize.

Roosevelt to L. S. Rowe, Director General, Pan American Union, Washington

[Washington] November 16, 1935

My dear Dr. Rowe: Thanks much for your letter of November thirteenth.

I do not think we can ever place too much stress on the "good neighbor" policy.

I look forward to seeing you and having a real talk after my return from Warm Springs.[1]

Very sincerely yours,

[OF 480:CT]

[1] Rowe said (OF 480) that because of Roosevelt's Good Neighbor policies the confidence of Latin American countries in the policies of the United States was the highest it had been in forty years. (This letter was drafted by McIntyre.)

Press Conference, The White House, November 17 (Sunday), 1935, 2 P.M.

(This Press Conference held in the State Dining Room. There were present, in addition to the Press, Secretary Hull, Secretary Wallace, Under Secretary Phillips, Assistant Secretary Sayre, and several others.)

The President: Good afternoon. I am glad I do not have to read your story. (Laughter)

I am very glad to welcome this new class in Advanced Economics. As to some of you, I have had the privilege of having you in my course before this year, but I see however a number of freshmen. The copies of the State Department release have run out, but there will be some more in about ten minutes and I appreciate what a difficult story this is to write because it has so much in it.[1] I will do my best, and I thought that possibly by using this copy I could go over somewhat hurriedly the paragraphs which I have marked and which I think are the more important paragraphs for you to read. Afterwards, when we get through with this, for I suppose it will take half an hour, go ahead and ask questions. I have asked the good people who are experts in this matter to come here and they will be able to answer, I think, any questions you may ask.

The salient thing, when you come down to it, is the very interesting fact that a territory that adjoins us, which has in relation to us a very small population—what is the population?—10 or 11, about $10\frac{1}{2}$ million people or in other words a couple of million people fewer than there are in the State of New York—that that country, small in population, prior to 1929 bought from the United States more goods of all kinds than all of Latin America put together. Or, for that matter, all of Asia put together. They were buying nearly a billion dollars worth of our products—about 900 million—and since that time our trade with Canada has dropped about 66 per cent, all in the last five or six years.

Now, that being so, because they are a nation adjoining us—same general stock—same general conditions of life—we see no reason why we should not try to build our trade back, and we hope as a result of this step which has been taken that we will build our trade with Canada back to what it was before. It means putting a very, very large number of people to work. It seems perfectly obvious that we should think in terms of trading, not on the bilateral angle, but on the triangular methods—the more trade you have between countries, the more people are at work in both countries, the less unemployment there is in both countries. That is a perfectly obvious thing, therefore we are trying to visualize this as the sole purpose and we expect that, as a result of this trade agreement, our trade with Canada is going to double in the course of the next year or two years. I hope and I really believe that it will.

Now, let us get down to this written story that some or most of you have. The trade negotiations were initiated in 1934 and have culminated on Friday[2] in the signing, but the actual agreement was made a week ago Friday . . .[3]

Q: Is this a statement by you or by the State Department?

The President: Oh, no. By right, I am not in this picture any more than I am on the third day of January, when we have a family gathering and try to explain the mysteries of the Budget. I am only doing this to be helpful and if anybody wants to ask any questions, if I can answer them I will, or else I will get somebody else to answer them.

Q: On page 9, that item with regard to Canada, will they give an assurance that they will permit Canadians to carry back into Canada $100 in American goods? Is there any limitation?

The President: I think the American rule is once a month.

Mr. Sayre: There will be limitations on it.

Q: What is the present American rule?

The President: $100 once a month. You cannot do it every day.

Q: Mr. President, this whiskey concession is given only as to whiskey and not all distilled spirits?

The President: Only whiskey; that is right.

Q: Can it be applied to Canuck Brandy?

The President: Only whiskey.

Q: On that whiskey matter, does that apply to re-exports?

The President: Or whiskey over four years old from any country, provided the other country has a most-favored-nation clause.

Q: Does that, in effect, write a new product into the Tariff Act?

The President: It is a new classification or subclassification.

Q: In several places you have mentioned "during the life of the agreement." This has no specific limit.

The President: No, but it can be revised every three years.

Q: What is the total amount of cattle of all kinds permitted to come into the country under the agreement?

The President: Beef type cattle—155,000 head, which is about one per cent of the total slaughtered in this country—no, three-quarters of one per cent of the total slaughter of these cattle in this country in a year?

Q: That is beef cattle?

The President: That is all cattle slaughtered.

Q: 155,000 head?

The President: 155,000 head which is three-quarters of one per cent of all cattle slaughtered in this country. They have to weigh over 700 pounds apiece.

Q: Is that to keep out the Mexican cattle—the 700-pound provision?

The President: Yes.

Q: You refer to these as "slaughter cattle." Is there any distinction for feeder and stockyard cattle or are they included in these 155,000?

The President: They are included—all lumped together.

Q: What is the provision for cows?

The President: On dairy cows, this lets 20,000 head come in, which is again a fraction of one per cent of the total number of cows that freshen in this country every year. That may be compared, incidentally, with 800,000 dairy cattle that we slaughtered—the States and the Federal Government slaughtered last year because of T.B. or other disease.

Q: Is there any possibility for the raising of those quotas?

The President: No.

Q: Is it correct to say that that limitation takes the particular item out of the operation of the most-favored-nation clause?

The President: No, but we do not bring in any from other places. These quotas cover imports from all countries.

Q: How much cream is included in this?

The President: 1,500,000 gallons, which sounded to me like an awful lot of cream, but it is less than one per cent of the cream consumed in this country.

Secretary Wallace: It is 8/10ths of 1 per cent of the production in the Atlantic States.

The President: It represents one pint a year for every fifteen people in our population.

Q: Mr. President, under the most-favored-nation clause, could another million and a half gallons of cream come in from New Zealand?

The President: No, the million and a half includes all countries.

Q: But, under the practical operation, it would be Canada?

The President: Yes; it is the only country that ever sent fresh cream to us.

Q: When does this become effective?

The President: January first next.

Q: How many beef cattle have been imported so far this year from Canada?

The President: At the rate of 140,000 a year.

Q: Mr. President, what is the anticipated effect of the agreement on American branch plants in Canada, if any?

The President: I don't think we know yet. I think every industry will have to study how it is going to affect them. Of course, they do not know yet because they have not seen this. I will give you something but you cannot use it. I was talking to Myron Taylor, head of U.S. Steel

Corporation. He said that they were very much interested in this, because they have a branch steel plant in Canada and also, of course, since the Ottawa Agreement, the American plants in Canada have been using mostly British steel. He is very much interested and all their people are to see whether this means that American semi-manufactured steel can go over into those plants in Canada that are owned by American capital. They do not know yet because they have not seen the agreement. Of course, on the general theory of increased business in both countries, it will start up a good many plants here and on the other side.

Q: Does it affect any of the requirements with respect to medicines and pharmaceuticals?

The President: They have sent us a note that in this coming session of Parliament they are going to define those more clearly than now.

Q: Is Canadian legislation needed to effect the general reduction?

The President: No. I think most of the cases will not require legislation, except for special things. For example, I think they will have to have legislation on the $100 a month that individuals can take in.

Q: Does this require ratification by Parliament?

The President: All the rate reductions can be done by orders immediately—the first of January—and they go into effect by the first of January, but eventually it will have to have general ratification.

Q: There is an item here "motor vehicles," does that include automobiles?

The President: They get a reduction of one-sixth. There is a table you will all get that goes with this to cover each specific item.

Q: That is one-sixth—a reduction from 30 to 25?

The President: That is right.

Q: Have the experts feared what effect on American butter markets this exportation of cream will have?

The President: I don't think it can be measured. Probably no effect at all.

Q: Mr. President, several times you have mentioned transferring articles to the free list. I thought that the present Trade Agreements Bill did not give you that power?

The President: I never mentioned transferring articles to the free list. Canada does that, we do not. I cannot put an article on the free list. I can cut the duty in half but we put no articles on the free list.

Q: How do these tariff rates compare with the British preferential rates?

The President: It varies so greatly that you have to take it up by specific items.

Q: How much does this cost in tariff duties a year?

The President: It will probably increase our tariff receipts and Canada's as well.

Q: Increase the receipts because of more imports?

The President: Yes.

Q: About what would the limitation be on calves?

The President: One-forth of one per cent.

Q: Has that been figured?

The President: Roughly, 50,000 head.

Q: As to most of the dutiable articles from Canada, would you say that this is merely taking off the duties imposed by the Smoot-Hawley Bill and putting them back to the rates previously existing?

The President: In a great many cases, yes, but you cannot say, strictly speaking, that it is doing that because there are a great many variations.

Q: You mentioned that our exports to Canada have dropped by 66 per cent. What is the general decline of Canadian exports or imports from all countries?

The President: It is less than that 66 per cent decline. We have suffered more than all the rest of the trade has suffered.

Q: Mr. President, can you explain to us more clearly the matter of putting articles on the free list?

The President: I tried to explain it before. It is this: Suppose I am a manufacturer dependent for my raw materials on Canada—say that it is some kind of metal which is the basis of my particular product. I may want to put an addition on to my factory, but I can never tell today whether or not there is going to be a duty, one way or the other. By putting it on the free list, I know that for three years at least I can proceed with my business on the present basis as to my raw materials.

Q: That means that Congress cannot hamper the free list without upsetting the whole agreement?

The President: That is right.

Q: You said that this could be diagnosed after the end of three years. Does that mean that no action can be taken by Congress that would upset this in less than three years? Does it have the status, in other words, of a treaty?

The President: Only if we did it by mutual consent and there isn't much difficulty in that at the present time. For example, if some great inequity appears in here, under the present friendly relations existing between the countries, we probably can get an agreement without very much difficulty.

Q: For example, one representative of the cream interest said that they would have a bill in the next Congress forbidding the importation of cream from any country where the herds are not examined for tuberculosis or something of that kind.

The President: We think they examine them in Canada.

Q: I was wondering as to the possibility of Congressional sniping at this?

The President: I suppose that somebody who is concerned about some particular item or other may present a bill—there may be 50 bills presented.

Q: I was wondering whether the three-year provision virtually precluded any action by Congress.

The President: I don't think we will have any trouble because if any substantial unfairness from the standpoint of either country results, we can get together and rectify it. I don't think Congressional action would be necessary.

Q: Referring again to the binding proposition, can you go any further than declaring that as a policy? Can you bind Congress not to take something off the free list and put a duty on it?

The President: It has the weight of a treaty with another country.

Q: The distillers that have testified said that if you would reduce the duty here—the duty on whiskey—to two dollars and a half a gallon that that would result in a decrease in retail prices of around ten dollars. Did that enter into the negotiations in any way?

The President: I don't think so. Of course it depends a little bit. In other words, on this question of liquor prices at the present time, let us say that on whiskey there is a spread in there, because of the existing tariff, of twenty-one dollars a case on any imported whiskey. That is a spread, in a sense an operating spread primarily for the bootlegger. That is, the bootlegger has a twenty-one dollar advantage a case when he starts off his operations today, and in my own personal opinion this provision is going to do as much as anything else to cut down bootlegging in this country.

Q: Can you say approximately how many beef cattle were slaughtered last year on account of the drought?

The President: There were around 7 or 8 million that would have died on the range and they were brought in on board trains and turned into food.

Q: Was the bootlegging aspect entered into in including Scotch and Irish types of whiskies?

The President: It did not enter into it but that would be a result.

Q: The idea or principle involved was to grant reductions to countries where they are principal suppliers?

The President: Canada is the largest supplier.

Q: Under the previous trade agreements thus far negotiated, have we utilized the quota system?

The President: Yes.

Q: Which ones were they?

The President: Cuba, for example.

Q: There is a quota stated here for lumber, fir and hemlock, from Canada. Can that quantity be compared with what the imports were when the lumber was on the free list?

The President: Somewhere between a third and a half. In other words, the new quota will put it to about a third or a half of what used to be imported.

Q: Are all cattle weighing less than 700 pounds classified as calves?

The President: No; only under 175 pounds. There is no reduction involved in this agreement.

Q: Can you clarify what you said about the Congressional aspect of it? If Congress should adopt a rate on some commodity which was bound by the free list, wouldn't that hold? Would not an Act of Congress hold?

The President: It would be a violation of the agreement.

Q: Then Congress—

The President: (interposing) Congress gives to the President a great many rights to make certain kinds of agreements with foreign nations, not only in this Act but in a great many prior acts. We have the right to make international agreements relating to all kinds of things without going through a treaty. This falls into that category of agreements between nations. However, where Congress does not give that grant, it has to be carried through in the form of a treaty and ratified by the Senate.

Q: The hypothetical question is: Suppose the McCarran Bill had carried, what then would have been the effect?

The President: It would mean that we could not make any more.

Q: It would not affect this treaty?

The President: No.

Q: These rates would stand?

The President: Yes.

Q: The authority to make them ends next year, does it not?

The President: 1937.

Q: Is three years the period on which the other trade agreements with Cuba and Brazil were negotiated?

The President: I think the same in all of them.

Mr. Young: Thank you, Mr. President.[4]

[President's Press Conferences:T]

[1] The press release was published in State Department, *Press Releases,* Nov. 23, 1935, pp. 388–442. For text of the treaty and articles concerning it, see the New York *Times,* Nov. 18, 1935.

[2] November 15.

[3] The President here read the greater part of the press release cited above.

[4] Some American lumber and dairy interests objected to the treaty but its reception was mostly favorable; see New York *Times,* Nov. 19, 1935, p. 18. Prime Minister King, who was a guest at the White House when the treaty was signed on November 15, wrote to Roosevelt on Nov. 25, 1935 (PSF:Canada): "I am glad that the agreement has been so sympathetically received in both the United States and Canada not by Government supporters only, but by many who are of the opposition."

Roosevelt to Harold J. Laski, London School of Economics and Political Science, University of London

[Washington] November 18, 1935

My dear Laski: Many thanks for your nice note.[1] I think we can all count on a continuance of a general American effort since 1921 to work, first, for further reduction and, second, if that is unattainable, to work to prevent increases.

I do hope you will come over here sometime this winter.

With warm regards, Very sincerely yours,

[PPF 3014:CT]

[1] Nov. 5, 1935, above.

Josephus Daniels, Ambassador to Mexico, to Roosevelt

Mexico, November 18, 1935

Personal and Confidential

Dear Franklin: I have just read your letter replying to one from Mr. Martin H. Carmody, head of the Knights of Columbus, which was couched in terms more offensive than I supposed the head of any important organization would employ.[1] When I finished reading your answer aloud to my wife, we both said "Bravo." It was complete and effective—"a hit, a palpable hit," and left Mr. Carmody not an inch of ground to stand upon. A friend of mine writes me that in a radio address in New York the Secretary of the Knights of Columbus demanded, in addition to what was printed in the papers quoting the address, that the embargo on arms should be lifted so that Catholics could arm themselves for war in Mexico. When I was at home last summer, talking with a Catholic Bishop, the prelate said that it was a shame that our government put an embargo on arms so that no effective resistance could be made by the Catholics in Mexico. These gentlemen are laboring under the erroneous impression that such an embargo exists by direction of the American government, whereas the only deterrent for individuals or would-be revolutionists here in obtaining arms is the vigilance of the Mexican government against the importation of arms. They evidently think the Wilson and Coolidge embargoes, limited as to time, in special emergencies still exist. In spite of the efforts of the Mexican government, some arms have been smuggled into Mexico and it is believed were used by opponents of the government in the recent disturbances in Sonora.

Last summer a committee of Americans—Dr. Brown, a Protestant, of Princeton, who was in the diplomatic service in one of the Central American countries under Coolidge, Mr. Carl Sherman, a Jew, who was Attorney General during Governor Smith's term of office; and Mr. William Franklin Sands, a Catholic who teaches in Georgetown University—called, or calling themselves, the American Committee on the Rights of Religious Minorities, spent several weeks in Mexico. Upon their return they made a report to those responsible for their mission, in which they reached the conclusion that they were confirmed in the opinion that the Government desires "not merely the correction of alleged abuses in any Church but the extirpation of all religion in the country."[2]

I do not think that sweeping conclusion is justified by the situation here, though the action of a number of States in closing all churches is as indefensible as it is indicative of the continued fight upon the Roman Catholic Church by some of the revolutionists. Since that time churches have been opened in Querétaro and services have been renewed in other States. The fight is not against religion as such; it is more a hang-over of the fight between the revolutionists and Catholic priests which blazed out in the revolution of 1910 and afterwards. Mr. Sands was here in August 1929 and upon his return to the United States wrote a long letter to Col. Patrick H. Callahan giving his impressions. In the course of the letter Mr. Sands says: "Archbishop Díaz was asked if it is true that 'the church' in Mexico is in politics. He answered: 'In politics? I am in politics up to my neck and intend to stay there! How do you suppose we are to get anti-religious laws repealed except by politics?'"

Catholic church leaders today deny they are in politics, and, even when admitting that this is true, the Government officials say that they are ready to return to their old activities if they were not restrained by the Government's measures.

Several individuals have been here this year to investigate the religious situation, among them Dr. McFarland, who wrote a book that has been widely circulated.[3] I do not think he can be relied upon, and Mr. Hull could give you some information showing him guilty of an effort to involve the State Department and the Embassy here in his flagrant use of material I am sure consisting of forged documents.

In one respect the letter of Mr. Sands, written in 1929, shows he was something of a prophet. He wrote:

"The revolutionary government has developed a program of education with particular attention to the Indian. The Church and State struggle will concentrate on educational work in the future." That is the nub of the present conflict. When Article 3 of the Constitution was adopted last year (every State ratified it) it was decreed that there should be no schools controlled by religious organizations, and that every school should impart "socialistic education." All private schools must employ a large proportion of Mexican teachers and must impart "socialistic education." The Catholics, who had largely directed education in Mexico, declared war on the new school system, asserting that it was atheistic. That war has gone on since. Only last week five public school teachers were murdered in the State of Puebla and early in the month several Mayors in the North were murdered by those who opposed "socialistic education." The Government believes this is the method of militant Catholics to try to prevent this character of public education. Certainly the Catholics are in opposition to the public educational policy and the Government is determined at any cost to carry it out.

The Government, as I have unofficially pointed out to leaders in the administration, is following an antiquated policy, born out of past differences, when it denies full liberty as to churches and priests and preachers. This policy, pursued in a number of States, stands in the way of national prestige. Some of them see this. Some, like Calles, see the religious situation as injuring the standing of the country, but say "we will have to endure it because the priests if unrestrained would again dominate politics." President Cárdenas, while unwilling to suggest any change in the laws, is believed to be desirous of a better situation by which religious practices will not be restricted or unduly limited. But if so, the school question is the lion in the path. The Catholic Church puts the right to have schools conducted by priests of equal importance with free church worship. This is the impasse. I do not know how long it will last. I have done all I can to point out that religious freedom is essential to a modern free government and must come. I shall, wholly unofficially, seek to impress upon those with whom I am in contact, that upon their own initiative Mexico should have churches open and priests and preachers functioning without restraint in every part of the republic. I am sure this will come, and that its forerunner is an educated population. Thirty years ago eighty per cent of the people in Mexico were illiterate. That proportion has been decreased to fifty per cent. Another generation will see a large majority able to read and write. With knowledge will come a demand for religious liberty and freedom from any connection between Church and State.

Mexico is more super-national than most countries even in an age when super-nationalism is a world curse. Our example and such expressions and quotations as contained in your letter, and the diffusion of knowledge will tend toward preventing restrictions upon religious freedom. Outside attempts to investigate or dictate will harden ancient conflicts and delay the coming of the better day. I hope our Catholic friends will see that the high ideals of our government cannot be imparted or advanced by outside pressure. The improvement must come from within.

Nothing distresses me here more than the attitude of residents here of so-called Christian countries. Very few of them go to church or seem at all interested in religion. There are two English speaking Protestant churches here—one Episcopal and one Union composed of all denominations except the Episcopalians. With an English speaking population of several thousand, a mere handful attend these two churches. I doubt if on an average as many as one hundred attend the services of both those churches. Our example is not helpful.

With my affectionate regards to you and Mrs. Roosevelt, in which my wife joins, I am, Faithfully yours,

Josephus Daniels

P.S. The papers here all printed your letter to Mr. Carmody. I am enclosing a clipping from *Excelsior* so you can see how they handled the letter.[4] JD

[PSF:Mexico:TS]

[1] Nov. 13, 1935, above.
[2] This report, to the Institute of Human Relations at Williams College on Aug. 27, 1935, charged the Mexican government with religious persecution. The charge was denied in a speech to the Institute by Ramón Beteta of the Mexican Department of Economy (New York *Times,* Aug. 28, 1935, p. 15).
[3] Charles S. Macfarland, *Chaos in Mexico; the Conflict of Church and State* (New York: Harper, 1935).
[4] The clipping, from the issue of Aug. 17, 1935, and apparently from the first page, is of the text of the letter, without comment.

Senator Hiram W. Johnson of California to Roosevelt

San Francisco, California, November 18, 1935

My dear Mr. President: What a kind note it was you sent me under date of November 14th.[1] I marvel at your wonderful memory. I recall very distinctly our last conversation in the White House before our departure for the west when my Boss made a most peculiar request of you, and that you should have remembered it in the multiplicity of your duties and the onerous things with which you are burdened, is to me most remarkable.[2] Thank you so very much for writing me.

Will you pardon me for what I am sure is an utterly unnecessary suggestion; but I happen to know that certain gentlemen are on tenterhooks, hoping and praying that in the present world crisis something will be done which may be distorted into an endeavor on the part of our country to be a part of the League of Nations or of England's policy. It will enable them to make an issue of internationalism next year, and while I feel sure that they are bound to be disappointed, nevertheless I felt that you would not take amiss this well-meant word of mine.[3]

My Boss joins me in affectionate regards.

Sincerely yours,

Hiram W. Johnson

[PPF 1134:TS]

[1] Roosevelt asked Johnson (PPF 1134) to return to Washington well in advance of the next session, referred to Johnson's study of public utility issues, and asked him to persuade Norris to run again.

[2] This reference is not explained in the letter just cited; presumably Roosevelt added a postscript that does not appear on the carbon copy.

[3] Another reference to foreign relations as a possible 1936 political issue is found in a letter from Assistant Secretary of State Moore to John Cudahy, ambassador to Poland, Nov. 7, 1935 (OF 20): "There has been a remarkable unanimity of approval of the course of the Administration relative to the Italian-Ethiopian broil. We are now in an excellent position, and will go along very cautiously so as not to make any mistake that would cause our foreign relations to become an issue next year."

Press Conference, Executive Offices of the White House, November 19, 1935, 4:10 P.M.

[*Excerpt*] The President: I think the only news I have is that the American delegation to the Naval Conference will be Mr. Norman Davis, as chairman, and the Under Secretary of State, Mr. Phillips, and Admiral Standley.

Mr. Phillips will go over with them but come back after a few weeks. The objective is, of course, to give him personal familiarity with the situation in the Conference so that, when he returns here, we will have a more intelligent liaison with the Conference than if we had nobody here who had attended. I think that is about all there is.

Q: When does the delegation sail, Mr. President?

The President: I don't know. The Conference is for the sixth of December and the chief problem is what kind of boat they can get to get there in time.

Q: What technical experts will they take with them, do you know?

The President: Oh, the usual staff.

Q: Did the imposing delegation which Japan is sending have any bearing on the decision to send Phillips?

The President: Who—

Q: (Interposing) Japan is sending a large delegation, one of the largest they have ever sent.

The President: I don't know.

Q: Do we have an American program to put before them?

The President: I do not think there is any news on that. If I were writing the story, I think the American position will be the same as it was in the beginning.

Q: That means no change?

The President: We oppose navies that cost nations more money than they cost—

Q: (Interposing) A little louder.

The President: We oppose navies that will cost peoples of the various nations more monies than they cost today . . .

Q: Anything you can tell us on new developments in China?

The President: No; I haven't got a thing except what I read in the papers.

Q: You mentioned that the position would be to oppose larger navies. The British have made it known publicly, or at least they have let us know they wanted twenty more cruisers. I wonder how emphatic our opposition to that would be?

The President: I just stated the general principle. I cannot go into details.

Q: What would be the position of Ambassador Bingham with reference to our delegation in the Conference?

The President: He will be Ambassador to Great Britain, just as he was before. In other words—this is just for background—the situation in Europe is such, as you all know, that the Ambassador to Great Britain ought to be foot-loose over there to attend to the many European problems from his post in London.

Q: Mr. President, do you regard the officials of the United States Lines responsible for failure of the shipyards to build new ships?

The President: No.

Q: The London papers are carrying a dispatch from Ottawa that you have accepted the invitation from Premier King to visit Canada?

The President: Nothing more than I have hoped to do for the last three years, which was some day to go up and see them up there. No date, no promise, just a hope.

Q: Some of us have long telegrams from some Chamber of Commerce of Nova Scotia saying you are coming up there to catch fish but we have not been able to check on it at all.

The President: I hope they are right. It is the first I had heard of it.

Q: Mr. President, what have you been hearing from the country on the agreement with Canada?

The President: I have not heard a thing except what I read in the papers.

Q: Mr. President, Italy has threatened to cut off our export trade with her if we refuse to permit her to buy oil here. Can we induce you to comment on that?

The President: Has she?

Q: According to dispatches from Rome.

The President: Has she? Has the State Department received any protest?

Q: I do not believe so.

Q: There has been an indication that the Postmaster General is going to resign sometime in January or February. Can you clear us on that?

The President: (Laughing) That is just the same old story.

Q: Can you tell us anything about your conference with George Peek?[1]

The President: We talked about quite a lot of things he is studying for me. He is going to have some reports for me either while I am at Warm Springs or as soon as I get back.

Q: Can you tell us what any of them were?

The President: No.

Q: Can you tell us what any of the reports would concern?

The President: All kinds of things—foreign trade.

Q: You indicated he was making a study of the Canadian Treaty.

The President: Yes; that and also the effect of the Canadian Treaty on imports from and exports to other nations.

[President's Press Conferences:T]

[1] On Nov. 19, 1935, from 12:30 to 1 P.M. (PPF 1-0).

Roosevelt to Thomas G. Chamberlain, New York

[Washington] November 20, 1935

My dear Mr. Chamberlain: I acknowledge with appreciation the receipt of your letter of November 1, 1935, in regard to the policy of this Government in respect to commercial transactions with Ethiopia and Italy.[1]

The policy which we have adopted has been based upon the Neutrality Act of August 31[2] and the measures which we have taken have been taken independently and on our own initiative. At the same time we view "with sympathetic interest the individual or concerted efforts of other nations to preserve peace or to localize and shorten the duration of war," as the Secretary of State declared in his note of October 26, addressed to Doctor Augusto de Vasconcellos, President of the Committee of Coordination of the League of Nations.[3]

I enclose, as of interest in this connection, a copy of a statement which Mr. Hull made on November 15, in regard to the purpose and policy of this Government in respect to commercial transactions with the belligerents.[4]

Sincerely yours,

[PPF 3015:CT]

---

[1] Chamberlain, a New York lawyer, a prominent Republican, and a director of the League of Nations Association, had written to commend Roosevelt's statement of Oct. 30, 1935 (PPF 3015). He said that the action of the League in the Italo-Ethiopian conflict was in effect an international police action and to interfere with that action "would be to assay the role of the gangster."

[2] 49 *Stat.* 1081.

[3] Printed in *Foreign Relations, 1935,* I, 852–854, and in the New York *Times,* Oct. 27, 1935, p. 34.

[4] Hull's statement was a review and further explanation of Roosevelt's statements of Oct. 5 and 30, 1935 (above). At the end Hull said: "The administration is closely observing the trend and volume of exports to those countries, and within a few days the Department of Commerce expects to have complete detailed lists of all commodities exported to the belligerents which will enable exact comparison with lists for the same period last year." The statement was published in the newspapers of Nov. 16, 1935. The New York *Times* commented in its issue of that date (p. 6) that "The warning was the only recourse open to discourage the war trade, inasmuch as the neutrality resolution is restricted to 'arms, ammunition and implements of war' and does not permit the imposition of embargoes on the broader field of 'munitions of war.'"

Roosevelt to Robert W. Bingham, Ambassador to Great Britain, London

[Warm Springs] November 23, 1935

My dear Bob: I know that in your highly important post located in the center of many of the most interesting and serious world political and economic discussions as they relate to international relationships, you are having your trials and tribulations, and I can fully sympathize with you. I only hope that they may not prove burdensome, as I know you will bear up under them with ability and fortitude. Naturally, I am also heir to manifold problems and difficulties of a somewhat burdensome nature.

Some phases of the pending Naval Conference situation offer a disagreeable illustration. I refer especially to the personnel question. I may preface what I have in mind with the remark that I have really been under not the slightest pressure here in regard to the set-up for the coming conversations at London. On the other hand, Norman Davis has repeatedly indicated a definite disposition to get back and gather up the threads of his business affairs, which he has neglected for some three years while undertaking to represent this Government abroad on military and naval disarmament problems.

The Navy has very earnestly urged the retention of Davis on the American delegation practically as it was constituted back last year for the purpose of the preliminary London naval conversations. This urging by the Navy was entirely impersonal, and based upon the belief that the increasing number of highly technical naval questions and delicate political questions renders it exceedingly important that one of the experience and familiarity of Davis with these questions and conditions should be in attendance. Frankly, with information on each of these classes of problems and conditions, which I think reaches me here from wider sources than they probably reach you in London, coupled with my special personal knowledge of naval problems in particular, I am constrained to agree with the views of the Navy as to the personnel.

This is not intended to and does not remotely reflect upon you, occupying as you do the premier position of all the notable Americans stationed abroad. I think you know the extent and nature of my friendship, not to say affection, for you. It is difficult also drastically to reorganize the delegation without occasioning wide-spread comment of a more or less confusing and possibly undesirable nature. In these extreme exigencies I am simply obliged to appeal to you to come to my relief by cooperating in your usual effective manner with the organization as originally constituted.

Mr. Phillips, as stated, will drop over for a few weeks in order to come back and talk with me at first hand about some phases of international affairs about which I desire him to confer specially with you.

In regard to the Italian situation, I wish you would write me personally concerning 3 points:

1. Do you think the British and French Governments really expect that the Ethiopians will hold together and continue to effect and organize resistance until the rainy season begins, even if the Italians continue their advance?

2. Do you think the British and French Governments expect the Sanctions to be so effective that Italy will succumb or begin to crack up within three or four months?

3. Do you think, from what you hear in London, that Mussolini, if things begin to go badly for him in Ethiopia or at home, will decide

to pull the whole building about his ears by picking a definite quarrel with England and attacking the British in the Mediterranean?[1]

With warm personal regards, Always sincerely,

[PPF 716:CT]

[1] Answered Dec. 24, 1935, below.

Roosevelt to Frederic R. Coudert, New York

At Warm Springs, Ga., November 23, 1935

Dear Fred: Many thanks for that nice note of yours.[1] I really believe that this method of correcting tariff ills, piece by piece through Executive action, will work more fairly and more intelligently than the form of log-rolling, catch as catch can, general tariff law hitherto used.

I suppose, however, that some of your New York friends and mine will set this down as another communistic decree of a Brain Trust ruled Dictator!

I do hope to see you one of these days soon.

As ever yours,

[PPF 269:CT]

[1] Coudert had written Nov. 21, 1935 (PPF 269), to congratulate Roosevelt on the Canadian treaty which, he said, had repaired the errors of a quarter of a century. Among those who took a contrary view of the treaty was Raymond Moley, editor of *Today;* see Roosevelt's letter to him of Nov. 23, 1935, in *Personal Letters, 1928–1945,* I, 523–524. Coudert was a prominent New York lawyer who had been special assistant attorney general of the United States from 1913 to 1914, and had been legal adviser to the British Embassy from 1915 to 1920. He wrote frequently to Roosevelt on various domestic and foreign issues (PPF 269).

Roosevelt to Cordell Hull, Secretary of State

At Warm Springs, Ga., November 23, 1935

Memorandum for the Secretary of State: Please ask the Standard Oil of New York, Standard Oil of New Jersey and Standard Oil of California if this is true, and why the Standard Oil Company of Switzerland has been organized. If it is for the facilitating of exports of oil from this country to Italy, I strongly recommend that you tell the story to the Press.

F.D.R.

[*Notation*:T] Copy of communication from Skinner, Istanbul, to Secy. of State, 11/21, advising of organization of Standard Oil Co. of Switzerland.[1]

[OF 663:CT]

[1] Ambassador Skinner's dispatch was returned to the State Department; Hull replied to Roosevelt's note on Nov. 27, 1935 (OF 663), to say that Skinner must have been misinformed.

Roosevelt to Eliot Wadsworth, President's Office, Boston Chamber of Commerce, Boston

Warm Springs, November 25, 1935

Dear Eliot: Many thanks for that nice note of yours.[1] I think the International Chamber has been doing excellent work. The Government, as you know, is at last succeeding in improving our foreign trade by considering the broad, national effects of agreements. This seems, on the whole, more wise than the older method of passing a general tariff law by the process of log-rolling, political give-and-take, and domination by vociferous minorities. However, I suppose that the "powers that be" in New England will not agree.

I do hope to see you one of these days.

Always sincerely,

[PPF 1335:CT]

[1] Nov. 22, 1935 (PPF 1335), to congratulate Roosevelt on the Canadian treaty and to thank him for his letter to the National Foreign Trade Council of Nov. 19, 1935 (*Public Papers*, IV, 462–465). Wadsworth was American member of the Committee on Resolutions of the International Chamber of Commerce at its meeting in Paris in June 1935; in his letter to the Foreign Trade Council Roosevelt had noted a resolution of the Council supporting bilateral trade agreements with strict observance of the unconditional most-favored-nation clause. Wadsworth said: "That resolution was only passed after very full consideration by the delegates. The American delegation of about 70 approved it by a formal vote. As the American member of the Committee on Resolutions, I can assure you that there was no lack of discussion and perspiration within that body before final action was taken. In the Final Plenary Session there was not a dissenting voice."

Norman H. Davis, Chairman, American Delegation, London Naval Conference, to Roosevelt

New York, November 25, 1935

Dear Mr. President: I am enclosing draft of my speech to be made at the opening of the Naval Conference. On account of the shortness of time, as we are sailing Friday and the speech must be cabled over beforehand, I would appreciate it if you could call me by telephone with regard to any suggested changes in the speech. My office telephone number is Hanover 2-5695 and my residence number is Butterfield 8-1395.

I suggest that it would be worth your while to take the time to read the article in the Magazine Section of last Sunday's New York *Times*, by Hugh Bayas, from Tokio.[1] He is the ablest and most reliable correspondent in the Far East and in this article he gives what I think is the best analysis of the Far Eastern question I have read.

With warmest personal regards and hoping that you are having a good rest, I am, as ever, Faithfully yours,

Norman H. Davis

P.S. Since the British Government practically received a mandate in the last election to increase cruiser tonnage they may consider my speech as rather antagonistic.[2]

[PSF:London Naval Conference:TS]

[1] "'Manifest Destiny' Stirs Japan."

[2] Davis' speech was not revised; it is quoted in Hull's cable to Bingham of Nov. 30, 1935 (*Foreign Relations, Japan, 1931–1941*, I, 281–284). Davis first quoted in its entirety Roosevelt's letter of instructions to him of Oct. 5, 1934. The United States, he said, would still like to see the objectives therein stated achieved but it was recognized that Japan's denunciation of the Washington Treaty had changed the situation. He urged a renewal of existing treaties, with such modifications as circumstances might require.

George N. Peek, President, Export-Import Bank of Washington, to Roosevelt

Washington, November 26, 1935

Dear Mr. President: I have your letter of November 22.[1] The memorandum to which you refer, "America's Choice," was part of a short speech I gave at the luncheon of the War Industries Board Association on November 11. I sent a copy of the full text of my remarks on that occasion to Mr. Early on November 13, but enclose another copy in case it has not come to your direct attention. The authorship is mine and mine alone. I neither conferred nor advised with anyone at any time about it. This memorandum represents my considered views.

In contrasting American and internationalist policy in the various fields I mentioned, I referred, of course, to trends, and accordingly I should be extremely sorry if my memorandum were to be construed by you or anyone else as a categoric attack upon your Administration. As I observed in my November 11 speech, the question is not a partisan one as our political parties are now constituted. Both parties have wavered indecisively between the two points of view. Neither of them can point to a clear cut record or program. The issue cuts across party lines.

Nevertheless the issue is there. Its presence is amply evidenced in the numerous public statements relating to these matters by persons of importance in or out of the Government; in the many acts and decisions of public officials and private individuals; in the extensive discussions in the press and elsewhere. All of these make it plainly apparent that there are certain conflicting trends in the fields of policy I have mentioned. I have tried to present them as clearly and objectively as I knew how. I feel that my presentation is essentially a fair one. I gather from your letter that you do not.

In the face of so fundamental a difference of opinion as to policy my course is plain. I am therefore referring to our correspondence of last July and am resigning as President and Trustee of the Export-Import Banks, and as Special Adviser, effective today.[2]

In severing my connection with your Administration I wish to express my high appreciation of your personal and official courtesies and consideration. You have as always my most sincere good wishes.[3]

Sincerely yours,

George N. Peek

[PSF:Agriculture:TS]

[1] Printed in *Personal Letters, 1928–1945*, I, 518–522, with the memorandum mentioned in the next sentence. Under "A Policy for Internationalists," Peek listed relaxation of immigration laws, reduction of tariffs, a foreign-controlled gold standard, naval strength determined by other powers, dependence on foreign shipping, submission of disputes to the World Court, and intervention in foreign disputes. Under "A Policy for America," he urged the tightening of immigration laws, tariff reductions for specific advantage

only, stabilization of the dollar at the American price level, control of capital exports, a navy designed for American requirements, development of American shipping, and neutrality in foreign wars.

Peek presented "America's Choice" in a talk before the War Industries Board Association in New York on Armistice Day, 1935, and it was widely published in the newspapers. (It is also printed in Peek's *Why Quit Our Own*, pp. 36–37.) Roosevelt in his letter of November 22 disputed Peek's proposals point by point, concluding: "In other words, this kind of statement amounts to nothing more than the setting up deliberately of straw men, who do not exist in reality, and then making a great show of knocking them over with a firing of salutes and a fan-fare of trumpets."

[2] Peek's last task as special adviser was to report on the Canadian reciprocal trade agreement, which he had discussed with Roosevelt on November 19 (PPF 1-0). In a memorandum on the agreement dated December 6 (PSF:Agriculture), he told the President that it was a direct reversal of the Democratic party's position of 1932 that duties on imports of agricultural commodities should not be lowered. He said the lowering of these duties was a matter of national policy that Congress had not passed upon when it passed the Reciprocal Trade Agreements Act, and he recommended the ending of the agreement.

[3] Roosevelt prepared a reply (Dec. 11, 1935, below) to this letter but it was not sent.

J. David Stern, Publisher, The New York *Post*, to Roosevelt

New York, November 27, 1935

Dear Mr. President: When I saw you last Wednesday, you mentioned that Hutton's expression "ganging up on the Government" was a good break.[1] Your hunch was right. Even though he has recanted I have heard more comment on this attack than on any other of the many which have been made by big business recently.

I enclose one of many letters we have received on the subject.[2] I am suggesting to Charlie Michelson and Jim Farley that the expression be kept alive. I think that it exactly describes the destructive, unfair attitude of reactionaries.

But there is another line of comment on your administration which is giving me grave concern. That is criticism of your foreign policy. I believe that an overwhelming majority of Americans care more about keeping out of war than about any other one thing. If the average citizen suspects, rightfully or wrongfully, that your administration is backing up the League or Great Britain, it would cause a most unfavorable reaction.

If you had declared oil contraband under the Nye resolution, I think it would have been popular, but the way the matter is being handled is creating the impression that you are taking sides with Italy. I don't say that this is so. I am only telling you the impression that I believe prevails with the average citizen.

You may call me a "hair shirt," but from now until the election, I am anxious to keep my criticism of your administration to a minimum. If I am thinking wrongly on this subject, I would appreciate it if you or one of your staff would put me right.

I hope you are enjoying your stay at Warm Springs.[3]

Sincerely yours,

J. David Stern

[PPF 1039:TS]

[1] Stern was at the White House from 12:45 to 1 P.M. on Nov. 20, 1935 (PPF 1-0). Edward F. Hutton, chairman of the board of General Foods Corporation, in an article in the *Public Utilities Fortnightly Magazine* on the effect of utility holding company legislation, had said he was in favor of industry "ganging up" on the government and forming a powerful lobby to combat collectivism. He later said he used the expression merely in the sense of "let's get together" (New York *Times,* Nov. 20, 1935, p. 19; Nov. 22, 1935, p. 17).

[2] Paul Davis of Paul Davis, Inc., New York, to Stern, Nov. 25, 1935. Davis called attention to the great increase in the value of certain stocks since 1933.

[3] Answered Dec. 11, 1935, below.

Roosevelt to Marvin H. McIntyre, Assistant Secretary to the President

Washington, November 28, 1935

Memo for Mac: Will you get in touch with Giannini and tell him that there is no relationship or connection between American action in regard to belligerent trade and that of the League; that under the law, we have forbidden shipments of arms, ammunition and implements of war to both sides and that we are discouraging shipments of articles which could be regarded as munitions in quantities over and above the normal amount of such shipments for the past few years?[1]

F.D.R.

[OF 547-A:TS]

[1] A. P. Giannini, head of the Bank of America, had written to McIntyre Nov. 25, 1935 (OF 547-A), enclosing a telegram from a friend, Ettore Patrizi, publisher of *L'Italia* of San Francisco, at this time in Italy. In the telegram (undated), Patrizi asked Giannini to use his influence against League of Nations pressure aimed at getting the United

States to embargo oil shipments to Italy, thus impairing the "traditional beautiful friendship between our two countries." McIntyre wrote to Giannini on Dec. 3, 1935 (OF 547-A): " . . . there is no relationship or connection between American action in regard to belligerent trade and that of the League. Under the law as passed in the last session of Congress, we have forbidden shipments of arms, ammunition and implements of war to both sides and, likewise, are discouraging shipments of articles which could be regarded as munitions in quantities over and above the normal amount of such shipments for the past few years."

R. Walton Moore, Assistant Secretary of State, to Roosevelt

Washington, November 29, 1935

My dear Mr. President: Some time before mentioning to you the other day the opportunity that certain of the Western European nations now have to afford an outlet to such pent-in nations as Germany and Italy, I requested the Geographer of this Department to make an investigation of the situation in Africa relative to the present ownership, population and development of that Continent, and as a result he has furnished me a quite elaborate memorandum which I am enclosing herewith.[1] When Sir Ronald Lindsay was in my office an hour or so last Monday, and various subjects were touched on, I casually suggested to him that Sir Samuel Hoare might add to his recent statement that the demands of such nations as Italy and Germany should be met by affording them access to food and raw materials, a consideration of the possibility of satisfying their land hunger by concessions in Africa. While of course not expressing any opinion, Sir Ronald did not put aside the suggestion as impractical, when Article XIX of the Covenant was mentioned.

The Ambassador came in again Wednesday to explain that his Government is in no way responsible for the League's delay in extending its sanction policy. In attributing the delay altogether to the failure of the French Prime Minister to go to Geneva, I thought he talked rather gloomily about what the League may do, and what its future will be.

Ambassador Rosso called this morning to talk of the owner of the steamer *San Diego* being prevented from complying with a contract which he says had the approval of the Shipping Board, for its sale to an Italian firm. What was intended was that the vessel should take a cargo of scrap iron to Italy and itself be scrapped on reaching there.[2] He discussed the general situation, and was not strong in combatting the suggestion that his Government, instead of warring on Ethiopia, might have resorted for relief to Article XIX of the League Covenant, which reads as follows, and was one of the provisions insisted on by President Wilson as of major importance:

The assembly may from time to time advise the reconsideration by Members of the League of treaties which have become imapplicable, and the consideration of international conditions whose continuance might endanger the peace of the world.

You may find of interest the enclosed letter from Ambassador Dodd.[3]

I have a note from Mr. Peek, asking that his resignation as President of the Export-Import Banks be brought to the attention of the Banks' Boards.[4] As Chairman of the Boards I feel a good deal of responsibility for the activities of the Banks, and on your return would like to talk with you about the appointment of his successor. In this connection, enclosed is copy of a memorandum relative to the business of the Banks, which you will perhaps have a better opportunity of reading while you are away than after your return.[5]

Yours very sincerely,

R. Walton Moore

[PSF:State:TS]

[1] The memorandum, prepared by S. W. Boggs, and dated Nov. 26, 1935, is present. Boggs concluded that "The geographical factors, chiefly climate and soil productivity, make it clear that Africa can not be expected to provide an outlet for any great surplus populations in Europe."

[2] The Shipping Board had ruled against this practice.

[3] Dodd to Moore, Nov. 17, 1935 (Moore Papers), on Germany's preparations for war, the effect of her withdrawal from the League, and the position of England.

[4] Peek had resigned Nov. 26, 1935.

[5] Not present.

Roosevelt to Senator Homer T. Bone of Washington

Warm Springs, Georgia, November 30, 1935

My dear Senator: I have your note of November eighth.[1] I can assure you that the possible effects of the reductions of the lumber tariff on limited quantities of Douglas fir and hemlock were very carefully considered by me during the treaty negotiations. I realize the dependency of the people of Washington and other nearby states on the lumber industry. But I also considered the dependency of that lumber industry for its markets on the possible general improvement of our other industries. I look to see a widespread improvement result from this treaty, one which will strengthen our economic fabric and thus benefit the lumber industry to a far greater extent that will be involved in the possible importation of 250,000,000 board feet of lumber.

In spite of serious strike handicaps, there has been a forty per cent increase in lumber cut of Washington and Oregon in 1934 compared with 1932. The annual lumber production in these states is now about twenty times the amount of Douglas fir and hemlock involved in the treaty. It was my conclusion that, in view of the necessity for giving the Canadians some reciprocal markets in the United States, the benefits from the treaty as a whole would be reflected in the Pacific Northwest to a far greater degree than would any injury due to the importation of lumber from Canada in the limited quantity specified. The primary objective of the treaty is to improve general conditions so that increases in consumption and demand will follow. I know that the lumber industry of your region is equipped to take advantage of any general improvement in demand from other parts of the country.

Very sincerely yours,

[OF 61-L:CT]

[1] Bone's letter (OF 61-L) protesting a proposed reduction in duty on British Columbian lumber was referred to Secretary of Agriculture Wallace for draft of reply; Roosevelt's note to Wallace (Nov. 12, 1935, OF 61-L), reads: "Can you get me figures from the Forestry Service to show the situation in regard to the annual cut of Oregon lumber, the original amount before lumbering began, the present amount that is left, the excess of annual cut over annual growth, and any other data to prove that Oregon lumber should be cut more slowly than it is being cut at the present time? It seems to me that we might just as well face this problem in Washington, Oregon, Idaho and California . . ."

Wallace returned the reply here printed, with a similar draft for Governor Martin of Oregon, who had also protested the proposed duty reduction. Martin's reply of Dec. 20, 1935 (OF 61-L), called attention to the loss of former important export markets within the British Empire "because of preferential trade agreements discriminatory against the lumber of Washington and Oregon." He urged that this be kept in mind in making trade agreements with Australia, New Zealand, and other British Empire countries.

Roosevelt to Senator John H. Bankhead of Alabama

Warm Springs, Georgia, December 2, 1935

My dear Senator Bankhead: I have received your letter of November eighth, in which you refer to our conversation about the importance of providing foreign commercial credits for the purchase of our cotton.[1]

As indicated to you during our conversation, I have given consideration to the possibilities of credit extension through the medium of the Export-Import Bank.

I have noted the trend of cotton exports with which you are so familiar, and with a view to exploring possibilities for the provision of foreign commercial credits for the purchase of our cotton I have transmitted your valuable comments to the Export-Import Bank with a special request that a report be submitted to me covering the subject of the Export-Import Bank and foreign credits for the purchase of American raw cotton.

Enclosed is a copy of the memorandum of November fourteenth in reply to this request. You will observe that the Export-Import Bank is constantly confronted with a variety of obstacles preventing the effective establishment of foreign credits due to circumstances which appear to be wholly outside its control. Also, you will observe with interest that the Export-Import Bank approved two deals for Hungarian cotton purchases and one transaction for the Latvian market. However, due mainly to a severe shortage of dollar and other free exchange, no cotton moved under these commitments through inability of the principals satisfactorily to conclude negotiations with respect to the price of cotton and other details independent of the Bank's terms and conditions. In the case of Poland and Roumania, which countries figured in proposals of a long-term financial character, investigation convinced the Bank that Poland's real purpose was to acquire working capital for general industrial economy at cheap rates, and in connection with the Roumanian proposals the Bank could find no adequate means to secure advances due to extremely bad exchange conditions in that country. You will note that a small amount of cotton has already been exported to Czechoslovakia as a result of short-term credits arranged by the Export-Import Bank.

I fully appreciate the outstanding importance of the cotton problem in our national economic life which you so aptly call to my attention, and it is my wish to cooperate with you wholeheartedly in the development of a constructive formula for the betterment of our cotton export conditions.[2]

Very sincerely yours,

[OF 258:CT]

[1] Bankhead said (OF 258) that authority existed and funds were available to provide foreign commercial credits for the purchase of cotton, but there seemed to be no agency that was prepared to prepare a plan and put it into effect.

[2] Drafted in the Agriculture Department (Wallace to Roosevelt, Nov. 30, 1935, OF 258).

[*Enclosure*] Memorandum

November 14, 1935

Subject: The Export-Import Bank and Foreign Credits for the Purchase of American Raw Cotton

In its constant attempts to aid cotton exports through credits the Bank has been and continues to be faced with a variety of circumstances wholly outside its control. The Bank is not a sales or production agent and therefore has no control over the price of the commodity to be financed. The monetary, currency, exchange, economic or political conditions in the countries of destination are factual circumstances over which the Bank is powerless to effect any change. The Bank's freedom of action in any cotton deal is confined to length of terms, security and/or collateral offered, and the range of costs that should be imposed for its services. Even on these self-determinates there immediately appear various limitations, if the Bank is to serve all parties at interest in an equitable fashion. In consequence thereof the Bank has found it impossible to evolve a definite formula for all cotton credits that are proposed to it, although some achievement has been made as to those credits that obviously can be called "commercial" as distinguished from those of a purely "financial" nature.

Proposed cotton credits that call for terms of six months or less the Bank classifies (in the case of cotton) as commercial, mainly because in most foreign markets the processing and distribution period is more nearly six months than three months.

In the absence of any unusual conditions credit proposals on cotton are compressed to six months as to terms and to regular commercial banking practice as to charges. Such a formula utilizes the commercial banking machinery and money market, substitutes the foreign consumer's own bank as security, and permits any American shipper to procure available business on equal terms independent of their size or financial strength. This method has been utilized in three specific instances, two deals with Czechoslovakian banks and one with a Polish bank. So far only a small amount of cotton has moved, and then only to Czechoslovakia. Generally the Bank is prepared to extend this method to selected countries (possibly including Spain, Portugal, Belgium, Switzerland, Holland, Scandinavian countries, and others) providing the leading bankers in such selected countries have or can qualify to obtain ninety-day reimbursement credits with commercial banks in this country.

Obviously such a method is not suitable for countries having stringent exchange restrictions or where a dearth of means of payment exists. Likewise it will not be satisfactory for a market that needs working capital for its industrial economy.

In other cases the proposals must be considered on their merits and the unusual circumstances presented. Of course the Bank has not considered proposals involving Russia, as such proposals are barred by virtue of the Board of Trustees' resolution under date of March 16, 1934. Also, the belligerent status of Italy and Ethiopia eliminates these two countries, although prior to Italo-Ethiopian conflict the Bank had under consideration proposals involving Italy.

Of the proposals of a financial character (i.e. longer terms than six months) the Bank approved two deals for Hungarian cotton purchases and one transaction to the Latvian market. Here special circumstances were encountered due to exchange difficulties and particularly a severe shortage of dollar or other free exchange. Under suitable guaranties and security terms up to 15 months were granted. No cotton moved under these commitments, through inability of principals to satisfactorily conclude negotiations on price of cotton and other details independent of the Bank's terms and conditions.

Two other countries have figured in proposals of a like character in length of terms; namely, Roumania and Poland. In the former the Bank could find no adequate means to secure the advances due to the extremely bad exchange conditions in Roumania. As for Poland, the request was on a two to three year basis. Investigation convinced the Bank that the real purpose was to acquire working capital for Poland's general industrial economy at cheap rates and not necessarily to continued purchases of American cotton. Non-utilization of the commercial credit approved, as related in a previous paragraph, more than substantiates this conclusion.

Lastly, the Bank has given its greatest efforts to consideration of the German market. There have been any number of proposals submitted, amounting to several hundred millions of dollars, but for practical purposes the possible amount that could be involved would not exceed $60,000,000 for one year's shipments. Here the Bank has been confronted with a maze of difficulties. After considerable probing the Bank is now endeavoring to consummate the transaction on the basis of collateral security either in securities or commodity form deposited outside of Germany. Terms of presumably one year or longer will be necessary in view of exchange situation while rates of interest must be kept low in order to encourage acceptance and adequate fulfillment of collateral deposit.

From all of the foregoing it must be evident that, considering the limited framework within which the Bank must work, every possible avenue of approach to the problem is explored in the desire to be of the greatest assistance in cotton exports.[1]

[OF 258:T]

[1] This memorandum was sent to Secretary of Agriculture Wallace by John T. Harding, assistant secretary of the Export-Import Bank, in a note of Nov. 18, 1935 (OF 258).

Roosevelt to William E. Dodd, Ambassador to Germany, Berlin

At Warm Springs, Ga., December 2, 1935

My dear Dodd: I am glad to know from yours of October thirty-first that I was right in assuming that there had been no real change in German policy for the last few months.[1] It seems clear that from the point of view of the group which now controls the destinies of the German people, their policy is succeeding admirably. Germany got an acceptance, passive though it may have been, of her rearmament by land and sea. Germany has kept out of the Italian situation by resigning from Geneva. Germany seems to be staving off actual bankruptcy through the tricky Schacht policies which win him the admiration of the international bankers.

I wish I could talk with you at length in regard to the Neutrality situation. If you had been here I do not think that you would have felt the Senate Bill last August was an unmitigated evil. The crux of the matter lies in the deep question of allowing some discretion to the Chief Executive. Quite aside from any connection with the League, the President should have some discretion. For example, if some European power were to seek, by force of arms, a raw material source in South America, we should have to take sides and might, without going to war ourselves, assist the South American nation with supplies of one kind or another. Complete stoppage of all arms material in the broadest sense in the case of a European conflict can be attained, and last summer's law tends in that direction. Meanwhile, the country is being fairly well educated, and I hope that next January I can get an even stronger law, leaving, however, some authority to the President.

I do not know that the United States can save civilization but at least by our example we can make people think and give them the opportunity of saving themselves. The trouble is that the people of Germany, Italy and Japan are not given the privilege of thinking.[2]

As ever yours,

[PSF:Germany:CT]

[1] Above.
[2] Also printed in *Personal Letters, 1928–1945*, I, 530–531.

Fred Morris Dearing, Ambassador to Peru, to Roosevelt

Lima, December 2, 1935

Personal and Strictly Confidential

[*Excerpt*][1] My dear Mr. President: I have had again an opportunity to read in somewhat hurried fashion (I have *not* broken into any one's strong box) a number of the official communications exchanged between the British Foreign Minister and his agents at various foreign capitals. They are dated from about October 7th to about October 20th. That is now about a month and a half behind us, but the communications are sufficiently recent, and report so directly what is taking place in Europe, bear so immediately upon your own attitude towards events in the Mediterranean quarter, that again they may serve you as a check upon your reports from other sources, though they may convey nothing more than a certain confirmation. There are also indications of personal characteristics which may also be of interest to you.

I shall particularly appreciate it if you will let me know if you would like to have further reports of the same nature in case I find myself in a position to make them now and then.

Ricketts Concession. The first communication is an extensive report from Barton, the British representative at Addis Ababa,[2] to Hoare, with regard to the Ricketts oil concession. According to Barton, the secret of the concession was so well kept that no one in Abyssinia, except the Negus[3] and Ricketts, knew anything about it until it was suddenly sprung upon the world. The news came through first in the form of a flash from the Home office in New York to the correspondent of the

New York *Times* or of the Associated Press—I do not recall just which—
and from the New York office of the London *Times* to its correspondent,
both getting their messages at about the same moment.

The correspondents apparently then informed the British and the
American legations, and the story immediately got out. Ricketts was
reproached by Barton for not having said anything about the matter—
especially since he was a British subject—either to the British representatives at Cairo or to himself. Ricketts replied he thought it would be
best to leave the British representatives in a position to say they knew
nothing about the matter. It would appear from Barton's report that
the British Government really did not know anything about the concession previously and had been left completely in the dark.

Barton argues pointedly that when grave political considerations are
so much to the fore, it is highly important for any British subject engaged
in enterprises of this kind to share his information with the Legation;
much more important than merely to leave the Legation the moral right
to disclaim fore knowledge.

Barton expresses a good deal of skepticism—although confessing his
ignorance about such matters—as to the absolute bonafides of the concession. He says he understands such enterprises are preceded by geolog-
ical survey which is followed up by the drilling of test wells, and that
very little of the former and practically nothing of the latter was carried
out. He also expresses, with emphasis, his surprise that the concession-
aires—meaning the Standard Oil Company of New York—should have
yielded so quickly to the pressure brought upon them by Secretary Hull.

American Government's Policy. The next communications are of
particular interest to our own Government, that is, to you and to the
Secretary. They are dated October 8th, 11th and 17th, and addressed
by Hoare to the British Chargé in Washington, Osborne. In the first
he tells of a conversation with Atherton, and in the next two of two
conversations with Bingham. Hoare gives, in considerable detail, the
substance of the conversations and the character of the deliberations
within the Foreign Office which preceded what he said to Atherton and
Bingham.

I pause here to say that it would seem that your own and the Secretary's most intimate communications are made a matter of record in
the Foreign Office as soon as received, and immediately distributed to
the entire British Foreign Service. Your own foreign service officers
throughout the world, not having been similarly informed, are, therefore,
always in the position of knowing less—and sometimes nothing at all—

about what has been done by our Government even in matters of major policy, than their British colleagues. It is true, perhaps, that this state of affairs may make it easier for American representatives not to be indiscreet, but it does not help much towards their understanding of policies and the lines that are being followed in carrying them out. In many instances absence of information among our men may be of no importance, but I can imagine situations in which the American representative would be at a distinct disadvantage in emergencies in which he might have to compete with his British colleagues.

The first thing that appears in these communications is your own eagerness—as the British understand it—to back up the League and the British position, and this is emphasized in such a way as to make it seem as if you regard that as almost more important than the fulfilment of our neutrality law or the preservation of peace.

Hoare states that in all the remarks he made to Atherton, and particularly in those made to Bingham, he had been guided almost completely by the advice of Lindsay, who apparently was at the Foreign Office. He therefore told Bingham the British Government had noted with the greatest satisfaction your attitude towards the situation developing in connection with the Italian-Ethiopian war, specifically your acts in establishing an embargo on war material under the neutrality act, and particularly your additional measure warning Americans they would sail on Italian ships and do business with Italians at their own risk.[4]

Hoare also expressed a satisfaction he restrained with difficulty that a message he had just received from Washington indicated that Secretary Hull was contemplating the extension of the embargo to petroleum, cotton, copper, steel and other products.

Hoare would make it appear, in writing to Osborne, that you would go even further, and further than the Secretary if you were perfectly sure of the reaction of American opinion. This opinion, he gathered, you thought to be almost unanimously against Italy in the present circumstances. He said you were represented as being especially sensitive to this condition of the American mind and desirous of being especially careful not to exceed what Americans in general would seem likely to sanction, whatever your own feelings might be.

The question of the mobilization of the signatories to the Kellogg pact was carefully considered by the Foreign Minister and his advisers, and after reflecting as to how the matter might best be initiated (it was assumed that you and the Secretary were quite anxious to act but were uncertain as to just how you should do so) three alternatives were listed:

First: initiation by the League;

Second: initiation by Great Britain, and

Third: initiation by our own Government.

One was rejected because it was felt it might be interpreted by the American public as drawing our Government too much into the sphere of League influence. Two was rejected because it was felt this also would excite American prejudice and make it appear that we were being subtly influenced to play Great Britain's game, and so, Osborne is informed, Bingham is told that in the view of the British Government, it would be best for you, the President of the United States, untrammeled and of your own will and judgement, to take the initiative in calling upon the Kellogg signatories for a declaration against the course that has been taken by Italy and in support of the League and of sanctions.

The report then states that Secretary Hull felt this third course would not be the best one, but preferred that some one of the Kellogg pact signatories, as distinct from Great Britain and the League as an organization, should start the ball rolling.

Here the correspondence on this phase of the matter stopped.

The important thing seems to be: that you are understood to be quite ardently pro-League and pro-British and intent upon doing something to make sanctions so effective that Italy will be rapidly and actually stopped. You are regarded, it seems to me, as committed rather more to stopping the war than to keeping us out of war. There is a clear indication that you would like to do more if you only had the latitude to do so and were sure of American opinion; that your neutral position and your desire to keep our Government absolutely unentangled marches, not much perhaps, but slightly to the rear.

Incidentally it is mentioned, in connection with American policy, that the line you are understood to favor may serve to bring the Germans out into the open so their real attitude will become clear, and that it is hoped the American policy will have its effect also upon any undue ambitions on the part of Germany and on the part of Japan.

Again, incidentally, it would appear that Hoare and Bingham discussed the approaching Naval Conference and that Bingham informed Hoare he hoped very much that only he and Admiral Standley would compose the American delegation as he wished to handle the conversations himself. Bingham said he expected to leave London about the middle of December and would be unable to return until February and expressed the hope that Hoare would postpone the opening of the naval conversations until that date. Hoare informs Osborne it would be impossible to wait so long and indicated he would not be affected by the Ambassador's suggestions.

I have the feeling it may be rather unsportsmanlike to report this, but I also feel my loyalty to the interests of the Country, to you, to the Secretary, to Billy Phillips and to Norman Davis take precedence . . .

It is revealing to read these despatches and to realize that although the British are accused, even by ourselves, of being adepts at clothing their selfish purposes with the most grandiose and impressive of moral principles, there is no conscious hypocrisy apparently in what is sent out from the Foreign Office as instructions to officers in the field or what is sent back to London as reports to the Foreign Minister. There is, indeed, even more disinterestedness and a further view into the future than would have seemed possible, in view of the fact that as between themselves, the British have no propaganda interests to serve. They are either quite sincere or have most effectively hypnotized themselves or are subtle and dissembling beyond the bounds of imagination.

It appears—chiefly from Drummond's reports—that at present Great Britain is playing for time and has not yet abandoned this policy, whereas both the French and the Italians, with the possible exception of Mussolini himself, seem bent upon the earliest possible settlement, even though incomplete and unsatisfactory, which will save Italy's face and prevent a debacle of the Fascist regime which the French and Italian spokesmen named above insist they fear.

Under the sanctions theory it looks as if fate and events were going to place the effective decision in this war in the hands of our own Government, and unless we choose to ignore Italian animosity towards us as being the authors of their misfortune on the one hand, and the frustration of the League's peace efforts and its resentment on the other, we shall have many things to consider in making such a decision. We shall in any event. At this moment it would seem a pity that our recent legislation did not give you greater latitude, as you desired at the time, so that from the start and prior to the League's action, the embargo could have been extended to oil, copper, cotton, iron, steel, etc., thus avoiding the placing of our Government in the invidious position of being the nation which must give the coup de grace to the Mussolini adventure . . .

I beg to add a remark or two of a general character which may make the foregoing documents somewhat more significant:

General. The unity and power of the manner in which the policy of the British Government is being carried out by the Foreign Office and its Foreign Service is extremely impressive. There is a minimum of confusion and contradiction, although it is evident that the various officers cannot be always in the closest of touch with each other. However, so well is the basic policy understood that in their separate conversations the Foreign Office officers and the representatives abroad rarely err in giving disparate statements or misinterpretations.

It is again noteworthy that the British insist their major purpose—they even insist strenuously at times their sole purpose—is to support the League and the collective system and wherever this is not admitted, they claim there is a complete failure to comprehend the British point of view.

I wonder if you have read the "International Conciliation," Document No. 314 of November, 1935? It publishes an article entitled "Abyssinia," taken from *The New Statesman and Nation* of September 7, 1935, said to be written by a "group of expert students of international affairs," which criticizes severely and searchingly the policy followed by the British Government since the early autumn of 1934.

This rather impassioned document would have it that precisely what the British mean to do and must do is to smash Fascism. And yet Hoare and Van Sittart go out of their way to say that precisely what Great Britain does not intend to do is that, and whether the Italians really believe this is the British purpose or not, they have been busy telling the Germans that it is and that the Nazis will come next.

So far as it is based on hind-sight, this article seems to me to underestimate the crude difficulties the Government has actually to deal with in carrying out its foreign policy, and that even though much of the criticism is justified, the assured statements that certain consequences would have followed a different course of action are predictions extremely difficult to prove valid. The writers, who remain anonymous, are chiefly concerned with the preservation of the League—just as the British Government is, to be sure—but argue it could have been, and should be done by a different course of conduct. They impress me, however, despite the penetration of their analysis and their boldness in presenting their constructive suggestions, as being the kind of people who stay at Capitals and juggle with international affairs on paper and know but little about the actual face of such affairs as they occur out on the fringes of the world and away from the center of policy and its execution.

I note once more—and with amazement—the absence of a single word regarding any control whatsoever of population, despite the fact that the pressure surplus numbers create is the basic fact in all this present trouble. The idea that something should be done about it never seems to enter the mental horizon of any of the responsible statesmen.

Here in Peru the Italians continue to spread their propaganda and it is having its effect. There is no doubt that opinion in general, on account of racial sympathies and because of this propaganda, is veering towards Italy. Mussolini's aggression has been displaced by other considerations and almost forgotten. Peruvians do not think about the present struggle. They merely feel about it. Moral aspects, legal rights, political and economic considerations weigh for very little. League obligations are irksome in this instance as they have proven to be before—during the Leticia struggle, for example—and Peruvians in general would like to escape them.

The extremely evasive and noncommittal reply to the Italian Government regarding sanctions, which is tantamount to a communication to the League, is therefore generally approved and Peru seems likely to avoid taking a stand any more definite for as long as possible.

I cannot discover that the French are doing much here. The British are more active but less effective than the Italians, which is not surprising in view of the power of the Italian Bank, the Italian character of the church, the numerous Italian colony, the wide ramifications of Italian business within the country, and above all, Latin and racial sympathies.

My British colleague occupies himself with ascertaining the actualities. He tells me a story is current that Great Britain failed to warn Italy in time of the serious consequences that would result from the initiation of a war in Africa. He says he has papers to show that Italy was warned repeatedly and in the most solemn manner and cannot allege the contrary or that they would not have gone to war if they had known how seriously the British would take it.

Reports concerning Canada's retention of a free hand so far as a petroleum embargo is concerned have attracted considerable attention, but for the most part Peru waits upon events and will move but slowly, I believe, observing, meanwhile, the letter rather than the substance of her League obligations.

May I lighten this report for you at the close—if you have come this far—by repeating for you Dorothy's verse on: "The Fascisti": "The boys from Italy, O! what a pitaly."

With warmest good wishes as always, Yours sincerely,

Fred Morris Dearing

P.S. Dorothy disclaims authorship. Says her's was about the Nazis: "Nutting but Nazis, Nazing but Nuts."

P.P.S. The Italian Bank here is lending money to the Government for public works and has just loaned a second sum of 500,000 soles at 7 percent. F.M.D.[5]

[PSF:Peru:TS]

[1] This excerpt constitutes about a third of the original letter. Omitted are summaries of telegrams exchanged between Sir Samuel Hoare, Secretary of State for Foreign Affairs, and British ministers and ambassadors, much of it dealing with British-Italian relations and the Italo-Ethiopian War. Relations with France, Austria, Germany, Hungary, Chile, and Argentina are also discussed in the correspondence, frequently in the form of reports by Sir Eric Drummond, ambassador to Italy, to Hoare in London.
[2] Sir Sidney Barton; see press conference of Sept. 4, 1935, above.
[3] Emperor Haile Selassie.
[4] Proclamation of Oct. 5, 1935 (*Public Papers*, IV, 416–417).
[5] Answered Dec. 20, 1935, below.

Roosevelt to Fred B. Griffin, New England Tobacco Growers Association, Hartford, Connecticut

Warm Springs, Georgia, December 3, 1935

My dear Mr. Griffin: I have your letter of November twentieth,[1] stating that you and many other tobacco producers of New England are disturbed over the possibility that provision will be made in the proposed reciprocal trade agreement with the Netherlands for a reduction in the present import duty on Sumatra tobacco, and expressing your views with respect to the position of the tobacco growers in your section. Your statements concerning these matters and the operation of the Agricultural Adjustment Act are appreciated.

I am informed that the brief submitted on behalf of the members of the New England Tobacco Growers Association to the Departments of State and Agriculture, protesting against any reduction in the present import duty on tobacco, has been brought to the attention of the Committee for Reciprocity Information. This Committee was established for the purpose of receiving relevant information and making it available to all officials concerned in the negotiation of reciprocal trade agreements. The facts presented by your Association will, I feel sure, receive every consideration by those charged with the negotiation of the Nether-lands agreement.[2]

Very sincerely yours,

[OF 61-T:CT]

[1] Griffin said (OF 61-T) that the Connecticut Valley tobacco growers were disturbed over the fact that Sumatra tobacco, produced by coolie labor, could be delivered in Amsterdam for sale for about what it cost American growers to sort and pack their crop. He said the tariff reduction would aid a few rich Holland firms and a few large American importers and manufacturers but not the growers: "it does not seem to us that it is in keeping with the intent of the AAA Act, which I feel is a sound proposition and has been of great benefit in teaching the farmers to conduct their farms more on a business basis."

[2] Drafted in the Agricultural Adjustment Administration.

Roosevelt to Judge Julian W. Mack, New York

At Warm Springs, Ga., December 4, 1935

Dear Julian: Thank you much for the copy of that excellent letter from George Messersmith.[1] He is one of the best men we have in the whole Service and I count greatly on his judgment.

I do hope to see you soon.

Always sincerely,

[PPF 2211:CT]

[1] Messersmith had written to Mack on Nov. 13, 1935, expressing opposition to United States participation in the 1936 Olympics because of the certainty that the Germans would use them for propaganda purposes. Mack sent this letter to Roosevelt on Dec. 2, 1935 (PPF 2211).

Robert P. Skinner, Ambassador to Turkey, to Roosevelt

Istanbul, Turkey, December 5, 1935

Dear Mr. President: Dr. Aras,[1] our Foreign Minister, represents Tur-key in the Council of the League of Nations and is a member of the Committee of Five. As you may not see the communications which I have made to the Department of State on this matter, I should like to inform you that Dr. Aras told me the other day that the new proposals which Great Britain and France are supposed to have submitted to Italy differ in form, but only slightly in substance, from the proposals of several months ago.[2] For the public, much is to be made of territorial adjustments under which Italy would be given a generous slice of the Ogaden and Ethiopia would have a narrow strip of land running to the sea. The essential portion of the arrangement has to do with mineral rights. Ethiopia is to "ask" that these be brought under foreign control and this foreign control is to be completely exercised by a bank to which Ethiopia would transfer all her mineral resources. As Great Britain, France, and Italy (without Ethiopia's consent) have already a treaty which divides the country into three parts, it is a fair guess to suppose that the proposed bank would be controlled by them in like proportions. Dr. Aras did not put it that way, but not being completely blind, it seems to me that if this arrangement goes through the effect is that Italy, which wants the whole of Ethiopia, will have to divide with Great Britain and France. Thus Ethiopia is to be saved.

The Ethiopians, being badly scared, and a simple people, are said, as I have mentioned, to have "asked" for something of this sort. Very likely. Having to choose between being executed by the Italians or skinned alive by the Great Powers, they may have elected for the latter!

You will recall that a clamor arose a short time ago when the celebrated Mr. Ricketts announced a petroleum concession for the Standard Oil Company of New York, which the Standard first denied, then admitted, and from which it finally retreated somewhat ingloriously. The morality of the Europeans was shocked that these audacious Americans should try to get a commercial concession for one form of mineral wealth in Ethiopia when, as now seems reasonably clear, they intended all the time to get the whole of it for themselves. It is not our affair to become unpleasantly involved in European politics, but I suppose we may contemplate events with an unprejudiced eye.

Poor old Ethiopia—she is trying to fight her enemies, but can she escape from her "friends"?

You may infer from the foregoing that I am not profoundly impressed with European ideology.

I am not.[3]

I am, dear Mr. President, respectfully and Sincerely yours,

Robert P. Skinner

[OF 502:TS]

[1] Tevfik Rüstü Aras was Minister of Foreign Affairs from 1925 to 1938.

[2] Ambassador Straus in Paris described this proposal in a dispatch to Hull of Dec. 9, 1935 (*Foreign Relations, 1935*, I, 699–700). The Hoare-Laval plan was made public on Dec. 11, 1935.

[3] Answered Dec. 19, 1935, below.

Robert W. Bingham, Ambassador to Great Britain, to Roosevelt

[London] December 6, 1935

Dear Mr. President: Your letter of November 23rd has just reached me, and I thank you heartily for it.[1] I had already sent a letter both through the State Department for you, and a copy directly to you, explaining the reasons which impelled me to take the position I took in connection with the Naval Conference. I felt both my loyalty to you as my Commander in Chief, and my deep and abiding personal loyalty to you, made it imperative for me to tell you the truth as I saw it. This I have always done and this I shall always do, as a matter of course.

This also makes it equally imperative and certain that I shall give the best I have in me in trying to carry out any purpose or plan which you may have decided upon, and that I shall give this naval delegation whatever aid it is possible for me to give.

What I particularly want you to understand is that my position was wholly impersonal and based upon my belief as to the method by which the best results could be secured. My personal relations with Norman Davis are, and have always been, entirely friendly, and in his work heretofore I have supported him to the best of my ability in every phase and all the time, and I shall proceed now in exactly the same spirit and to the same end.

As the pouch goes tomorrow, I shall not attempt to answer your three questions upon the Italian situation in this letter, but shall write you fully by the next ship thereafter.

As always, Sincerely yours,

Robert W. Bingham

[PSF:London Naval Conference:TS]

[1] Above.

Breckinridge Long, Ambassador to Italy, to Roosevelt

Rome, December 6, 1935

My dear Chief: This may be known in history as the "oil war"—or "no oil war"—depending on which side you are on or what the future historian may think about it all. It certainly to my mind is demonstrating one thing—that under the conditions in the world as now organized and mechanized nobody can make war unless he has an oil well. On that thesis there are only three Governments in the world that can successfully wage war—the United States, England, and Russia. And even England is dependent upon the carriage of oil and the protection of the seas in order to insure that she will have oil. Other places, such as Mexico, Venezuela, and Rumania, have oil wells, but that is about all they have got in the way of war industry.

On that predicate, I think it would be a very wise thing for you to set up some unannounced and confidential committee—if one does not already exist—to consider the very great power which the United States has over and above that of any other Government in the world in these circumstances and to consider how that power might be further developed and how it might be exercised for the best interests of the United States. Such an inquiry might develop that it would be wise to encourage American oil production outside of the United States and that the Government itself might be interested in having American oil companies exercising exclusive rights in such countries as Mexico, Venezuela, Columbia and Bolivia.

I hope the policy to prevent war will not react in favor of British oil companies by permitting them to extend their influence and become more widely and securely entrenched. There is no doubt that English companies are preparing to sell oil to Italy through Germany. I telegraphed that to the Department as having been obtained from official sources in connection with the activities in Rome of an American who was selling oil to Italy. He had in his pockets contracts with British companies for future delivery to be imported into Italy through Germany. It is of course known to you that the British oil companies at Suez are selling oil and loading it directly into the bunkers of Italian ships on their way to and from Italian East Africa. The British do not miss one chance to "earn an honest penny."

But there are several possibilities, not only through the ownership, but through the well-directed control of oil in the Caribbean area and in the United States, to exercise an enormous influence in the world. I don't see how Japan is going to get very far in a war without oil. She must confine herself to neighboring lands in China and eastern Siberia. If all flow of oil could be stopped toward Japan, she would find herself in the same position that France would find herself if an embargo were placed on oil to France.

The practical lessons involved in this small war may be very far-reaching, and I am only wondering whether the possibility that the Congress might place oil on the embargo list might not interfere with the use of the power of the United States in some future situation which might be much more important to us than the present.[1]

Affectionately and respectfully,

Breckinridge Long

[PSF:Italy:TS]

[1] Long had written to Roosevelt on Nov. 29, 1935 (PSF:Italy), urging him not to embargo oil shipments to Italy because of Mussolini's desperate frame of mind. Long suggested that the United States sell to Italy only as much oil as she had been buying regularly in normal times. No action was taken on this suggestion and no reply to this letter has been found. Roosevelt's next letter to Long was that of Feb. 22, 1936 (*Personal Letters, 1928–1945*, I, 560).

Speech by Roosevelt to the American Farm Bureau Convention, Chicago, December 9, 1935

[*Excerpt*][1] Some of the same type of individuals and groups are also trying to stir up the farm population of America against other phases of the broad recovery program. Dispensers of discord are saying that farmers have been victimized by the new Reciprocal Trade Agreement with Canada and they are painting pictures of a great flood of imports of farm products rushing across the border. But, just as I am confident that the great masses of city people are fair-minded, so I am equally sure that the great majority of American farmers will be fair in their judgment of the new Trade Agreement. Let us put it this way: If the calamity howlers should happen to be right, you have every assurance that Canada and the United States will join in correcting inequalities as good neighbors will do. But I, for one, do not believe for a single moment that the calamity howlers are right.

No, agriculture, far from being crucified by this Agreement, as some have told you, actually gains from it. We export more agricultural products to Canada than we have imported from her. We shall continue to do so, for the very simple reason that the United States, with its larger area of agricultural land, its more varied climate, its vastly greater population, produces far more of most products, including animal products, vegetable and fruits, than does Canada. In the case of the few reductions that have been made, quota limitations are set on the amount that may be brought in at the lower rates.

On the other side of the picture we believe, and most unbiased men believe, that the general increase in our trade with Canada, including the exports of our factories, will so add to the purchasing power of hundreds of thousands of wage earners that they will be able to spend far more than they do today for the products of our own farms, our own forests and our own fisheries. We have heard before and we hear every week the simple statement that greater trade is merely another word for more production and more employment, and that statement ought to be understood in every farmhouse of the country. The proof of this particular pudding is in the eating and the best way to judge the new accord is to see how it works out. Analyze, my friends, the sources of the objections, analyze the motives of the objectors. Remember too the old saying, "It all depends on whose baby has the measles."[2]

[Speech File:T]

---

[1] Roosevelt had just referred to "political advantage seekers" and "profiteers." The whole speech is printed in *Public Papers,* IV, 483–491.

[2] The excerpt here printed was based on a draft prepared by Secretary of Agriculture Wallace and Agricultural Adjustment Administrator Chester Davis (Wallace to Roosevelt, Nov. 30, 1935, Speech File). Wallace said that their version was "intentionally a general statement" of Roosevelt's position on the Canadian trade agreement; he proposed to cover the agreement in detail in his own speech to the Farm Bureau meeting on the next day. (His speech is summarized in the New York *Times* of Dec. 11, 1935, p. 8). Moley prepared a draft of the speech as a whole, based on contributions by Wallace, Davis, and Tugwell (Moley to Roosevelt, Dec. 4, 1935, Speech File); Roosevelt's draft is, however, almost entirely in his own language ("Draft for Chicago, Dec. 9, 1935," Speech File).

The President's reference to the Canadian trade treaty and Wallace's lengthier comments of the following day were carefully weighed in the drafting of the two speeches. Early had been collecting trade treaty data for the Chicago speech; on Nov. 29, 1935, he telegraphed the President in Warm Springs (Speech File): "This material of course will be shaped in the light of developments which have taken place since the Treaty was first announced. It will not be defensive. Chester Davis tells me in this connection the Treaty is not satisfactorily understood by the farmers of the West. They need further enlightenment and if that is given he thinks they will accept the Treaty and many who are still doubtful will approve it." Before leaving Chicago, Roosevelt spoke briefly to the Saddle and Sirloin Club; in this speech he said the United States had "no intention of getting mixed up in the wars of the rest of the world" (*Public Papers*, IV, 491–493).

Speech by Roosevelt at Notre Dame University, Notre Dame, Indiana, December 9, 1935

[*Excerpt*] And I am especially happy to take part in this special convocation called to honor the new Commonwealth of the Philippines. And I am especially privileged to have heard that brilliant address of Mr. Romulo, who so well represents his Commonwealth.[1]

It cannot seem so long because even I remember it and yet it is forty years since the United States took over the sovereignty of the Philippine Islands, nearly forty years. The acceptance of sovereignty was but an obligation to serve the people of the Philippines until the day they might themselves be independent and take their own place among the nations of the world.

We are here to welcome the Commonwealth. I consider it one of the happiest events in my office as President of the United States to have signed in the name of the United States the instrument which will give national freedom to the Philippine people.

The time is not given to me to recite the history of these forty years. That history reveals one of the most extraordinary examples of national cooperation, national adjustment and national independence that the world has ever witnessed. It is a tribute to the genius of the Philippine people. Subject to the government of a country other than their own, they generously adjusted themselves to conditions often not to their liking; they patiently waited; they forfeited none of that freedom, that essential freedom, which is natively theirs as a people, a freedom which they have so definitely expressed with due regard for fundamental human rights in their new constitution.

We have a clear right also to congratulate ourselves, in our country, as a people, because in the long run we have chosen the right course with respect to the Philippine Islands. Through our power we have not sought our power.[2] Through our power we have sought to benefit others.

That both nations kept to the policy of leading to this most happy event is due to the fact that both nations have the deepest respect for the inalienable rights of man. These rights were specifically championed more than a century and a half ago in our own Declaration of Independence. And again they have been championed within a few months in the new Constitution of the Philippine Commonwealth, a constitution which I would like to have read and learned about in every school and college of the United States.

No, there can be no true national life either within a nation itself or between that nation and other nations unless there be the specific acknowledgment of, and the support of the organic law to, the rights of man. Supreme among those rights we, and now the Philippine Commonwealth, hold to be the rights of freedom of education and freedom of religious worship.[3]

[RL Recordings]

[1] This speech (printed in its entirety in *Public Papers*, IV, 493–496) followed the conferring of the honorary degree LL.D. on President Roosevelt and Carlos P. Romulo. (Romulo, at this time prominent in the Philippines as educator, editor, and publisher, distinguished himself during World War II as aid-de-camp to General MacArthur and later as ambassador to the United States and in other posts in the Philippine government.) Roosevelt was introduced by his friend, George Cardinal Mundelein, archbishop of Chicago. Special significance attached to the cardinal's words because of the strong feelings that had been aroused in some Catholic circles because of the Administration's refusal to take overt diplomatic action in the religious controversy in Mexico. Mundelein said he wanted the President to feel that he had come into the house of his friends. "We are not in politics, neither the Church nor I, no individual Cardinal, Bishop or priest, no organization of laymen or Catholic newspaper has the right to speak for the twenty million Catholics in this country in matters of politics; only the Bishops of the country together, in conference or in council, and they have not done so, and so we do not wish our words to be interpreted in that sense" (from a copy of Mundelein's remarks sent to the White House by the National Catholic Welfare Conference News Service of Washington, PPF 321; cf. New York *Times*, Dec. 10, 1935, p. 12, which did not print this particular sentence).

[2] The reading copy has, "Through our power we have not sought our own." In delivering the speech, Roosevelt read this as, "Through our power we have not sought our power." The text as printed in *Public Papers*, IV, 494, reads, "Through our power we have not sought more power," and very likely this is what he intended to say. However, the President gave it as here printed; the recording is distinct. He made a number of other changes in reading the speech, none important.

[3] In addition to the recording from which this text is taken, the Roosevelt Library has a draft, with revisions in Roosevelt's hand; the reading copy; the press release with shorthand notes of the changes made in reading the speech; and a transcript showing the revisions. The drafting was assigned to William D. Hassett but Father John J. Burke of Washington, D.C., whom Hassett consulted, was apparently responsible for the greater part (LeHand to Early, no date, PPF 2329; Early to Roosevelt, Dec. 7, 1935, Speech File). Moley supplied a section, the reference to freedom of conscience in the Virginia Declaration of Rights, not included in this excerpt (Moley to Roosevelt, Dec. 6, 1935, PPF 2329).

Moley recommended against trying to approach the Mexican situation from a new angle: "You have already indicated that as a government we cannot take effective action of any sort. It is unnecessary to repeat that now, because it would add to the irritation, however unjustifiable, that certain Catholic organs have expressed." The invitation to receive the degree was extended in a letter of Nov. 7, 1935, from the Reverend John F. O'Hara, president of Notre Dame (PPF 2329). O'Hara spent an hour with the President on November 14 planning the arrangements (PPF 1-0).

Roosevelt to George N. Peek

Washington, December 11, 1935[1]

Personal

Dear George: When I wrote you before in regard to the unsigned memorandum you handed me, I honestly had no idea that you were the author of it.[2] If I had known that you were, I should not have been so rude as to call it silly or to say that it was setting up a purely imaginary straw man in order to prove certain obvious points, nearly all of which you and I, and I think everybody else, agree on.

Nevertheless, having written you frankly in regard to it, I must, even if you are the author, stick very firmly to my guns.

I say this with a further feeling of some disappointment because I now find that before you resigned, and while you were still a member of the Administration, your memorandum was not only given in the form of a speech on November eleventh,[3] but that the Hearst papers used it on November twenty-sixth as the subject of their leading editorial. This editorial, evidently in pursuance of your thought, for you must have furnished the memorandum to the Hearst papers, states unequivocally that the policy of this Administration is the same as what you label "A Policy for Internationalists."[4]

I know you will not mind my being frank in telling you that I am disappointed for the very simple reason that some modicum of loyalty and some modicum of honor are involved.

In your letter to me of November twenty-sixth you say that you referred to trends and that you would be sorry if the memorandum were construed as a categoric attack upon my Administration. It was so used while you were still the President of the Export-Import Bank and a Special Advisor to the President.

May I ask you to read once more my last letter to you? You will see that I subscribe very nearly one hundred per cent to what you call "A Policy for America." I hope much that, for your own sake, you will not align yourself with those unfortunate Americans like Hearst who for many years have thriven by deliberate and wholly unprincipled misrepresentation.

People in public life, people who use various vehicles of publicity, and people who discuss public questions of all kinds still have an obligation to maintain their honor and to be scrupulously careful not to misrepresent facts.

Also because I have always liked you and because we have worked so long together, I hope for your own sake that you will not put yourself, in the estimation of the American public, in the class either of unscrupulous publishers or of those few persons who have, on leaving the Administration, used every opportunity to stab their erstwhile friends in the back.

I do not know if you have seen this particular gossip sheet which I enclose.[5] I am confident you are not responsible for it but it is an illustration of what happens.

Just before leaving Warm Springs I received your letter of December sixth with the memorandum on the Canadian Trade Agreement.[6] As you will remember, I asked your opinion of this Agreement on November nineteenth,[7] not knowing at that time that you were going to resign. I do not know whether you have given this memorandum to the public or the press since your resignation but, of course, you will realize that as I asked it of you in your capacity as Special Advisor, it became a wholly confidential communication to me and subject to my release only.

I expect to be here from now on and perhaps you will care to run in some day and see me.

Very sincerely yours,

[PSF:Agriculture:T]

---

[1] This letter was not sent; see Peek to Roosevelt, Nov. 26, 1935, above, n. 1.

[2] This memorandum is printed in *Personal Letters, 1928–1945*, I, 520–522.

[3] Before the War Industries Board Association on Nov. 11, 1935.

[4] A copy of the editorial is filed with this letter.

[5] Not identified.

[6] See Peek to Roosevelt, Nov. 26, 1935, n. 2, above.

[7] Peek talked with Roosevelt at the White House from 12:30 to 1 P.M. on this date (PPF 1-0).

Roosevelt to J. David Stern, Publisher, The New York *Post*, New York

[Washington] December 11, 1935

Personal

Dear David: That suggestion of yours in regard to retailers is an interesting one and I am following it up.[1]

Come down and see me some day soon. The oil situation was as usual misrepresented. I could not declare oil contraband under the Nye resolution. Whether we like it or not neither it, nor cotton, nor copper, nor scrap iron are "implements of war." The Senate debates brought this out very clearly. Hence the policy of using any and every honorable Administration pressure we can to limit the export of these articles to normal quantities. This action neither had nor has the slightest connection with League action or British action. By checking the dates you will see that, as a matter of fact, we have preceded Great Britain and the League in every move made. Perhaps in January Congress will give me a little more power which I do not need to say will be exercised for the primary objective of keeping us out of this or any other war!

As ever yours,

[PPF 1039:CT]

[1] Nov. 27, 1935, above.

Press Conference, Executive Offices of the White House, December 13, 1935, 10:30 A.M.

[*Excerpt*] Q: Is it your intention to seek neutrality legislation in relation with the steps which have already been taken to discourage war profits?

The President: I cannot answer that intelligently yet. We will have to wait about two weeks.

Q: Will you make that the subject of a Message to Congress?

The President: Make what?

Q: New and permanent neutrality legislation?

The President: We have to have something before the first of February, obviously. The old Act runs out. Whether we are going after new neutrality legislation, I don't know. Obviously, we will try to get something before the first of February.

Q: Will it involve a Message to Congress?

The President: I don't know; I have no idea . . .

Q: Mr. President, is there any present intention to extend the neutrality legislation to include raw materials?

The President: I can't discuss it because Congress has not gotten here yet.

[President's Press Conferences:T]

William E. Dodd, Ambassador to Germany, to Roosevelt

Berlin, December 15, 1935

Personal

Dear Mr. President: Let me return the hearty thanks of us all here for your kind letter of November 27.[1] I wish to add our best wishes to you and yours for a Merry Christmas and Happy New Year, the more since problems both at home and abroad are such that a happy new year would be almost miraculous.

I have thought from month to month, since we came here: "Now we shall have a quiet time"; and the silence and avowed neutrality the last two months looked a little that way. But now we are in an atmosphere of strain and anxiety quite as great as last March. The English have put themselves in the worst plight they have been in since the war with all the minor states: the Balkan zone, Sweden, Norway, Denmark, Holland and Belgium. I have seen Ministers of these countries the last twenty-four hours, and they talk of withdrawing from the League if England and France do not put the clamps on Italy. There is an intense fear of war and the likelihood of these little states losing their independence. One of these men, who is generally well-informed, insisted last night that Hitler replied to the British proposal on the 13th for arms limitation: We must go to war on the Soviets, and talked excitedly for minutes upon the necessity, therefore, of the immense armament here. Much as one may be annoyed at the foolish Soviet propaganda, it seems to me increasingly necessary for democratic peoples to avoid breaks with Russia. With Japan attacking Vladivostok, and Germany breaking into Leningrad, we should have such horrors that one can hardly imagine the consequences.

What a world we live in! Industrial civilization having reached a state where it can hardly go on without regulation, insists upon the right to arm to the limit—when majorities of peoples are concentrated in vast cities, inviting air attacks. One of our aircraft firms recently made a deal here for selling, through a German firm, 100 up-to-date war planes to Italy, the man coming to me and talking as if no such thing were thought of. Last evening an eminent German connected with the old regime said: "Now that old men are twice as numerous as before the war and young men being limited more and more in all the greater countries, we are about to start another war. Think of killing off all the young men."

This started again the urge of unofficial Germany against Mussolini. I believe two-thirds of the German people (in spite of army popularity) are now entirely in sympathy with the reported United States oil boycott of Italy—and hopeful that this would limit Hitler's crazy war activity. Perhaps this is enough; but we cannot overlook the fact that our country has immense moral influence all over the world. But can anybody convince Congressmen, who always think of their district's advantage, of the real significance of things? We think permanent prosperity is coming when the machine age needs fewer workers every year. We believe a hundred billion dollars of "watered securities" can be made valid when population is relatively declining, and apt to cease increasing altogether about 1960, when few people are willing to earn their livings in the normal way. Thus war, armaments, trade barriers and declining populations mean nothing to many governments and less to vast industrial corporations.

I hope you may be able to arouse our people to the dangers that lie ahead—next year perhaps a decisive year in many parts of the world.[2]

Sincerely yours,

William E. Dodd

[PSF:Germany:TS]

[1] Christmas greetings to Dodd and his staff (PSF:Germany).

[2] In his reply of Jan. 6, 1936 (*Personal Letters, 1928–1945*, I, 543), Roosevelt said that Dodd had confirmed his feelings about the extreme gravity of European and Asiatic affairs. Dodd's letter was also discussed at the Dec. 27, 1935, Cabinet meeting (Ickes, *Diary*, I, 494).

Roosevelt to Henry A. Wallace, Secretary of Agriculture

Washington, December 16, 1935

Memorandum for the Secretary of Agriculture: This is very interesting. Perhaps you will speak with the Postmaster General about the New

Caledonia Island and the possibility of starting some conversations with the French just to get in ahead of anybody else.

F.D.R.

[OF 19-Misc.:CT]

[Enclosure] F. D. Richey, Chief, Bureau of Plant Industry, to Henry A. Wallace

December 10, 1935

Dear Mr. Secretary: The successful inauguration of regularly scheduled commercial air service across the Pacific Ocean to the Philippines and China, with its promise of strengthening commercial relations between the United States and the Far East, brings within the realm of possibility another forward-looking development in strengthening by similar means our trade relations with Australia and New Zealand. We have under the American flag three of the four necessary stations forming practically a Great Circle Route from San Francisco to Sidney, namely, the Hawaiian Islands, where regular service with the West Coast was established this month, Palmyra Island (or Christmas Island claimed by both the United States and Great Britain), and American Samoa. All of these stations have harbors or lagoons suitable for landing seaplanes. The fourth station necessary for daylight flying is the Island of New Caledonia, a French possession, which, with its dependencies, the Loyalty Islands, is situated almost exactly midway between Samoa and Sidney. New Caledonia is a rich but undeveloped tropical island nearly 250 miles long and from 30 to 40 miles wide with only 50,000 inhabitants, about 5,000 of whom are French or of French descent. The island has important agricultural and mineral resources which only require close connection with a country such as ours to provide the stimulus for development. Present communication with the mother country, France, is by the Messageries Maritimes Service from Dunkirk and Marseilles, and because this requires two months the island is, according to influential citizens there, a neglected stepchild of France. The Messageries Maritimes with government subsidy has been maintaining two services to New Caledonia, one westward through the Panama Canal, touching at the French West Indies and Tahiti; the other eastward through the Suez Canal, touching at French Indo-China and the New Hebrides. Within the past two months announcement has been made that the latter service would be discontinued because of termination of the subsidy.

More or less responsible people have suggested that France partly liquidate her debt to the United States by transfer of certain of her island possessions to the United States. In general, these suggestions have very little to recommend them. They would simply add to the administrative problems of the United States with no adequate compensation. New Caledonia, which, so far as I know, has never been specifically mentioned by proponents of this method of debt settlement, has, on the other hand, definite promise of playing a large part in planning for our future relations with Australia and New Zealand. These countries are bound to support large English speaking, white populations in the future, which will no doubt afford the opportunity for absorption of our products in increasing amounts. An indispensable requisite for gaining and holding a share of this market in competition with Japan and European countries will be improvement in mail service and transportation. By present airmail routes, it requires nine days from Europe to Sidney and by airmail and steamship routes a minimum of two weeks from Europe to New Caledonia. The route from the United States here suggested would require less than half that time.

With the view of stimulating trade between Japan and the Commonwealth of Australia and New Zealand, the Japanese Government this year sent a "trading ship" to those countries, and a trading commission which by displays and contacts with importing houses was able to promote in some degree objectives of the Japanese Government. In the past few years Japan has become one of the largest buyers of Australian wool, and there is certainly justification for such efforts. It can be said, however, that Australians and New Zealanders definitely prefer to do business with Americans. Because of superior quality of products and more familiar business methods the people of the Antipodes have, in general, a high regard for Americans and American products. Looking ahead it seems worth while to preserve this valuable asset of good will against what is quite obviously the beginning of a sustained effort on the part of the Japanese to capture these markets.

Dr. E. W. Brandes, who has just returned from New Caledonia and is responsible for bringing to attention the facts and possible usefulness of them, is in a position to give information on the agricultural possibilities of that island, if desired. In a trip of nearly 2,000 miles around the coast and through the mountains, in which practically every district was visited, a large amount of data and photographs were accumulated on

125

the agricultural and pastoral industries, which, together with notes of general interest, would be of value in presenting a reconnaissance of the country's resources, population, climate, and other physical features.

Sincerely yours,

F. D. Richey

[OF 19-Misc.:CT:Photostat]

Roosevelt to Cordell Hull, Secretary of State

Washington, December 17, 1935

Memorandum for the Secretary of State: This article in the October *Atlantic Monthly* "Worse Than Arnold"[1] is of extraordinary interest and teaches a real lesson to all American Diplomatic officers abroad. It is so good in fact that I am inclined to think it would be a very excellent and inexpensive object lesson if the State Department would have it mimeographed and sent to all Embassies and major Consulates, with the request that it be read by Diplomatic and Consular officers.

I say this because I am more and more fearful that a large percentage of our so-called confidential matters, relating to foreign affairs, come into the possession of foreign nations almost as soon as we get them ourselves. The very fact of sending this article broadcast to all of our people would make them think more seriously than if we send them a whole series of regulations.

F.D.R.

[OF 20:T]

[1] Burton J. Hendrick, "Worse Than Arnold," *The Atlantic,* vol. 156 (October 1935), pp. 385–395, an account of the machinations of Dr. Edward Bancroft, an American on Franklin's staff in Paris during the Revolution who was in the pay of the British.

Roosevelt to William J. Reagan, Principal, Oakwood School, Poughkeepsie, New York

[Washington] December 17, 1935

Personal and Confidential

My dear Mr. Reagan: I am marking this letter "Personal and Confidential" because the last thing in the world that I want to do is to enter into any kind of a public controversy with my real friends of the Society of Friends, with many of whose leaders I have worked shoulder to shoulder on so many occasions.[1]

I have no objection to your telling the members of the Faculty of Oakwood School verbally the gist of what I am writing you but, of course, it should not be used in any way by you for quotation.

If you knew Secretary Dern I am confident that you would not place the construction you did on his statement that "all citizens, except a few who despise our form of government and seek its overthrow, think the United States worth fighting for." I am very certain that he did not mean "fighting for" in the sense of bearing arms. He is completely in harmony, as you and I are, with the basic principle of religious liberty.

It is because I was personally familiar with the splendid work of the American Friends Service Committee in Europe during and following the World War that I feel they were most nobly supporting the great humanitarian objectives of their country even if they did not bear arms.

The last thing in the world that the Secretary and I would have in mind would be classifying the Society of Friends with "those who despise our form of government and seek its overthrow." Your whole history stands for loyalty to the government, and in time of war you have shown that loyalty by the splendid work you have done for the sick, the wounded and the destitute.

Today, for example, the Society of Friends, through their many fine activities, are "fighting for the United States" and I am proud of this work.

Very sincerely yours,

[PPF 3068:CT]

---

[1] Reagan had written Dec. 13, 1935 (PPF 3068), in behalf of the faculty of Oakwood School (which was under the control of the Society of Friends of the New York Yearly Meeting) to protest a statement in Secretary of War Dern's annual report that, "We must assume that all citizens, except a few who despise our form of government and seek its overthrow, think the United States worth fighting for." He said that he and the school faculty considered this an affront to the whole Society of Friends who throughout their history had been convinced that war was both futile and unchristian. He called attention to the work of the American Friends Service Committee in Europe during and after the World War.

M. Llewellyn Raney, Director, University Libraries, University of Chicago, to Roosevelt

[Chicago] December 19, 1935

Mr. President: My thanks for your fine courtesy. It was good to share some minutes with you.[1]

Here, as requested, is a resumé of the proposed plan for copyright action:

1. Bring the Berne Convention to early Senate vote.

2. Postpone proclamation of adherence till Congress acts on appropriate amendatory legislation or adjourns.

3. Urge passage of such attendant legislation at the coming session. Brief comment on the above:

The Convention. Sent to Senate, February 19, 1934; reported out by Senator Duffy, April 18, 1935; ratified without objection, April 19; restored to calendar, April 22, at Senator Duffy's instance.[2] This reversal is understood to have been due to the Senator's promise given the magazine publishers to hold back the treaty until his S. 3047, the amendatory bill, had been disposed of.

Thus, we are back at scratch, with only one session of Congress before the close of your first term. Left to old momentum, the instrument will never reach ratification. A new push is needed. An effective way is open, thus:

Ask Senators Pittman and Duffy to bring the Convention again to vote. Stress the moral argument as compelling. Secretary Hull's letter which you transmitted with the text of the Convention cited the undoubted economic advantages of membership in the International Copyright Union, but the abatement of an ancient national scandal is far more important. We have always been wrong on copyright, because, unlike patents, to which anyone is eligible, we began by limiting recognition of an author's exclusive title to citizens and residents here. This threw the outside world's literature open to piracy, and for a hundred years we assiduously practiced the ugly art. Even now, with the public conscience more sensitive, and legislative improvements effected by the revisions of 1891 and 1909, it is still true that our law sanctions piracy of any work in English, if manufactured abroad.

This is an indefensible position. Campaign after campaign in and out of Congress has been waged against it since the days of Clay. Its maintenance bars us from the Union, and brings another mortifying experience. It is this: The British allow an American book, despite its American manufacture, to count as British and, therefore, Union, if the (6) deposited copies carry a British title page. This is an unrequired and entirely unrequited courtesy. We should be too proud to use the back door. There are now unmistakable signs of slamming that door shut in retaliation. The British can hurt us a lot if they choose to and we could not open our mouths in protest. Let's beat the Tory Government to it. Complete the task begun by President Cleveland and advanced by President Wilson in proclaiming adherence to the Pan American Copyright Convention, and get for your term and country the high honor of clearing from the national escutcheon a stain of 145 years' standing. The Senate and the nation cannot withstand such an argument.

The Proclamation. The Convention is not effective till proclaimed. This provides the way out for Senator Duffy. Agree to withhold proclamation till the end of the coming session or the action of Congress on S. 3047 if earlier. The ratification will act as a spur to compromise differences and secure enactment of appropriate supplemental legislation. For fourteen years now only stalemate has been scored. Virtually all interests agree on the ultimate propriety of membership in the Union. The two chief critics of the pending bill, the authors and musicians, assure me of their desire to see the Convention ratified first.

The Bill. The main purpose of any attendant bill must be to bring the statute into harmony with the Convention, though the latter is presumably self executive. Good manners demand positive amendment. But the necessary amendments need not cover one page, while the bill has thirty-one pages. The reason is that the occasion for presenting these amendments is seized on as one for adding a great many revisions of the Act of 1909, suggested by the experience of a quarter century and by invention. These ancillary provisions are highly controversial, but they are sure of adjudication if a kind of time limit, as above suggested, is set to debate.

The Administration's position should remain one concerned with ratification of the treaty, and enactment of the statutory amendments therewith immediately co-ordinate, on the grounds of economic justice, but especially of moral obligation.[3]

Respectfully submitted,

M. L. Raney

The Season's good wishes.

[OF 699:TS]

[1]After the House failed to act on the Duffy copyright bill, Raney asked for an appointment with the President to restate the case for the Copyright Treaty (to McIntyre, Nov. 12, 1935, OF 699). His letter came to the attention of Assistant Secretary of State Moore who urged that the appointment be made; he told McIntyre that the Department was "strongly desirous" of obtaining action on the treaty (Nov. 27, 1935, OF 699). Raney saw Roosevelt for fifteen minutes on December 16 (PPF 1-0) and talked with McIntyre afterward.

[2]*Cong. Rec.,* vol. 78, p. 2768; vol. 79, pp. 5921, 6032, 6099.

[3]See Hull to Roosevelt, Dec. 31, 1935, below.

Roosevelt to Robert P. Skinner, Ambassador to Turkey, Istanbul

[Washington] December 19, 1935

My dear Skinner: Thank you very much for that nice note of yours of December fifth.[1] I feel just the way you do. What a commentary on world ethics these past weeks have shown. I wonder whether, if these methods are applied to Ethiopia, they cannot at some later date be applied to Turkey as well. If I were a Turk it would give me some concern.

Very sincerely yours,

[OF 502:CT]

[1]Above.

Roosevelt to Fred Morris Dearing, Ambassador to Peru, Lima

[Washington] December 20, 1935

Dear Fred: That is a grand report of yours[1] and I am very glad to get this triangular type of information. Also I love the Italian and Nazi verses. Do give me one on the Ethiops.

The latest one here is that the King of Italy said to an American the other day, "If this fellow Mussolini wins this war I shall be Emperor of Ethiopia and if he loses I shall be King of Italy."

Sincerely yours,

[PPF 1210:CT]

[1]Dec. 2, 1935, above.

Norman H. Davis, Chairman, American Delegation to the London Naval Conference, to Roosevelt

London, December 20, 1935

Dear Mr. President: I have endeavored, in the rush of our work here, to keep the State Department fully informed by cable as to the developments from day to day.[1] There are, however, certain matters which can not be covered well by cable and which will, I think, be of interest to you.

In the first place, there is every indication that the pro-Japanese group here, who were routed last year, have been unable to mobilize their forces again, and there seems to be no tendency in that direction. On the contrary British cooperation has so far been one hundred percent. Instead of trying to put the onus of disagreement with Japan upon us, they have been taking a positive stand against Japanese contentions; and the Admiralty tells us they are convinced that, while it is important to be patient and tactful with Japan in order to try not to give them an occasion to run out, it would be a mistake even to flirt with the idea of making any concessions as to principle. The Japanese apparently had the idea that they might tempt the British by taking the position that, because of their far flung Empire, they were justified in having the largest navy but that this did not apply as between Japan and the United States. The British did not take the bait. My contention has been that the question of parity between the British Empire and the United States has already been settled, that each one feels that this gives it equal security, and that each one of us is convinced that with a ratio of 3 to 5 Japan unquestionably has equal security and an equal power of defense. The British have definitely committed themselves to this thesis.

In our last talk with the Japanese, Admiral Nagano told us that there was a feeling of apprehension in Japan because of our superior naval strength and resources and that if they had an equal navy it would remove all fear of menace. We pointed out to him that, because of our long coast lines, the Panama Canal, and our possessions in both the Atlantic and the Pacific, we were exceedingly more vulnerable than Japan and had far greater needs and responsibilities which necessitated a larger navy for purely defensive purposes; and that, if such an unfortunate contingency should ever arise as that of conflict between us and Japan, he knew perfectly well that, even assuming we could employ all of our navy in an attack on Japan, we would be at a distinct disadvantage because of the distances from which we would have to operate. We furthermore pointed out that an acceptance by us of the Japanese proposal for a common upper limit would be tantamount to a surrender of our ability even to defend Alaska, which is nearer to Japan than to us, to say nothing of the Philippines and other possessions in the Pacific, or of our necessity of protecting our interests in the Atlantic.

In substance, we told Nagano that we could not afford to and would not agree to any material alteration in our naval strength as related to England and Japan. However, we recognized that because of the state of mind in Japan with regard to the ratio the word "ratio" has become an anathema, and that it was probably politically impossible for the Japanese now to commit themselves in principle to a continuation of the ratio system. Furthermore, since we would not accept the common upper limit and they could not commit themselves to a continuance of the ratio, and since it is not possible with the present political instability in the world to get any nation to weaken its power of defense, it would be the part of wisdom to admit these facts frankly and agree upon a modus vivendi for a few years, which would prevent a naval race and any effort to alter the status quo until there is more of an atmosphere of good will and confidence. I pointed out to Nagano that with Italy invading Abyssinia—involving a threat of European war—and with the Japanese armies penetrating China, it was absolutely impossible, as he must realize, to get either the United States or England to reduce their relative naval strength and their power of defense. I pointed out that all we wanted was to increase our friendship with Japan and our mutually beneficial trade with one another, and that we had given every evidence that we have no other desire or intention. Nagano admitted that in the last two or three years our relations had improved and I suggested that, under these circumstances, it would be a mistake for us to try to alter our relative naval positions, particularly at a time when Japan is going through a very important process of evolution. I said we should try to find some way to bridge over the present situation and to continue to improve our relations until it is possible to find a more permanent and mutually satisfactory basis for naval limitation. The Japanese seem somewhat inclined to accept such an idea and at least said they would think it over. Our feeling, however, is that they have come with very strict instructions and limited authority and that they have not disclosed what is in their minds.

So far the Japanese have not receded from their position of refusing to accept or discuss qualitative without quantitative limitation, or to agree to quantitative limitation only on the basis of the common upper limit. They have, however, gotten themselves in a very untenable position. They first say they will not agree to a ratio system any longer but then they have to admit that a common upper limit or naval parity would merely be a change in the ratio from 5-5-3 to 5-5-5. When they insist upon equal naval armaments or parity they have to admit that there are different degrees of vulnerability and of needs and that there can only be equal security by adjusting relative naval strengths accordingly.

We adjourned today in a friendly way but without having done more than to bring out clearly the unsoundness and inconsistency of the Japanese proposals and admissions, and without any more promise of agreement when we reconvene than there was at the beginning. The Japanese are now fully aware of the fact that there is no chance of acceptance of anything approaching their proposals and within a few days after we reconvene we will unquestionably reach a crisis when the Japanese will either have to agree to qualitative limitation with advance notice of building programs or leave the Conference. I imagine that this will be decided in consultation with Tokyo during the holiday. The British are telling the Japanese that if there is no naval agreement, even as to qualitative, the United States could outbuild any of the other naval powers and that it would be a suicidal mistake not to take advantage now of our willingness and desire to reach an agreement that will avoid a naval race.

The British attitude towards Japan is not only stiffer than it was a year ago and distinctly more friendly to us and, while they are anxious to avoid giving Japan a good excuse to run out, they seem less concerned about that possibility than heretofore. In fact, the British, French and Italians all seem more concerned now about an agreement as between themselves, and ultimately Germany, and some of them have suggested the advisability of the rest of us entering into a naval agreement without Japan, but with a provision that would permit Japan to become a party if she so desires.

We all feel here now that our position is more satisfactory and less embarrassing than that of any of the other powers and apparently our own press has been acting very well up to the present. Our job is to keep the situation in hand as well as possible without taking the initiative away from the British. So far even Craigie seems to have gotten religion and I hope he will keep it.[2]

With warmest regards and best wishes, I am as ever, Sincerely yours,

Norman H. Davis[3]

[PSF:London Naval Conference:TS]

[1] The Conference opened Dec. 9, 1935. Minutes of the meetings are printed in Department of State, *The London Naval Conference, 1935,* Conference Series, No. 24 (Washington, 1936).

[2] Robert L. Craigie, assistant under secretary of state in the Foreign Office, was special adviser to the British delegation. In 1937 he was named ambassador to Japan.

[3] In his reply (Jan. 14, 1936, *Personal Letters, 1928–1945,* I, 544–545), Roosevelt said that press dispatches continued to give the impression that Japan was solely responsible for blocking the way to an agreement. See below.

William Phillips, Under Secretary of State, to Roosevelt

London, December 20, 1935

Dear Mr. President: Two weeks ago today we arrived in London and there has been ample time to take stock of the situation as between the Embassy and the Delegation.[1] In the circumstances, as you can readily imagine, I have kept an eye open for trouble and I have been equally watchful with regard to our relations with the British Delegation. On the way up from Southampton to London I went over the situation very frankly with Ray Atherton.[2] The Ambassador and Mrs. Bingham met us at the station on our arrival in London and your three Delegates called upon them at the Embassy within an hour after we had reached the hotel. Both Mr. and Mrs. Bingham were most cordial and there was not the slightest trace of a lack of friendliness on either side. Since then Atherton has been with us constantly, attending most of the full meetings of the Conference and seems to me to have done everything that he could to be of help, both officially and socially. The Ambassador had planned to give a large reception in honor of the Delegation, but, as you know, this had to be cancelled on account of Court mourning. Whether it is cancelled or merely postponed, I do not yet know, but, at any rate, Bingham is giving a luncheon today at the Embassy for our Delegation.

More important, however, than our relations with the Embassy is the decidedly cooperative spirit on behalf of the British Delegation. From the moment of our first call at Admiralty House upon Lord Monsell, Admiral Chatfield and Craigie[3] there has been nothing but the closest collaboration. In fact, the British do not make a move without talking it over with Norman, by telephone or otherwise. Vincent Massey[4] remarked last night at the Pilgrims Dinner that the evident understanding and cooperative spirit between the Americans and British was the outstanding and most satisfactory part of the Conference so far.

While actual accomplishments up-to-date are nil, owing to the adamant position of the Japanese with respect to the "common upper limit," the general atmosphere of the Conference could not, in my opinion, be improved upon.

I want to say a word about Norman. I have never before seen him in action, but only when he had not made up his mind about this or that and was, therefore, unnecessarily worried and in consequence, perhaps, unnecessarily worried others. In action all that disappears and I never cease to admire the way in which he handles himself in and out of the conferences. It may be his southern drawl, his slowness of speech or his innate courtesy, but the result is that he is able to say to the Japanese, as well as to anyone else, the most direct and unvarnished truths without incurring the slightest resentment. His knowledge, of course, of the technicalities makes it possible for him to rebut instantly any argument that is weak and without foundation in fact. Without disparaging in any way the Ambassador, it would have been quite impossible, as you so fully realized, for him to conduct the affairs of our Delegation. Moreover, no other ambassador has attended the meetings, except for the opening ceremony in the Locarno Room, when certain ambassadors were present and read formal statements on behalf of their respective delegations.

As for myself, I do not feel that I have added anything to our Delegation, although I have been immensely interested in everything that has been going on, not only within the Conference, but in the extraordinary political situation which has culminated in the resignation of Sir Samuel Hoare.[5] The Davises and I have adjoining apartments at Claridges and I have been with Norman constantly until the last day or two, when I have been laid up with a mild attack of the well-known "London flu." During the Christmas recess, I am planning to make a brief visit to Berlin and Paris, which I know will be of help to me in the Department. I shall have another ten days after the reassembling of the Conference to watch what we all hope will be some tangible developments. Unless something unforeseen happens, I am expecting to sail from here on the SS *Manhattan* on the 16th.

May I say again how grateful I am to you for sending me over here?

It has been a highly instructive experience and has opened my eyes to many situations which are difficult to see from the Washington angle.

Hoping that you are continuing in the best of health and are having a happy Christmas, surrounded by all the members of your family.

Very sincerely,

William Phillips

[PSF:London Naval Conference:TS]

[1] This remark refers to Bingham's efforts to be named head of the American delegation to the Naval Conference.

[2] United States counselor of embassy.

[3] B. M. E. Monsell, First Lord of the Admiralty, was the principal British delegate, Fleet Admiral Alfred E. Chatfield and Craigie (identified in note to letter above) were his advisers.

[4] Massey was Canadian representative at the Conference.

[5] Hoare resigned following public protest at the Hoare-Laval plan for the dismemberment of Ethiopia. He was succeeded by Anthony Eden.

Norman H. Davis, Chairman, American Delegation, London Naval Conference, to Roosevelt

London, December 21, 1935

Personal

My dear Mr. President: With regard to the situation here that concerned us so much, there is not much to say except that so far it has been working out as satisfactorily as could be expected. Our friends here seem to have accepted the inevitable and to be reconciled to it as much as it is humanly possible to be. I understand that Bill Phillips, who has had various talks with Atherton, has written fully to Cordell.[1]

With all of the excitement over the Ethiopian situation it has been very interesting here. The facts, as nearly as I can gather, are, in substance, that Laval told the British that, in view of the state of mind in France, they could not be relied upon to help in case of retaliation by Italy, and that Mussolini had threatened both England and France in case oil sanctions were imposed; also that Van Sittart, who has become obsessed with a fear of Germany and who has never cared much for the League but favors an Anglo-French alliance and if possible a combined agreement with Germany to maintain peace in Europe, helped to persuade Hoare to take the course that led to his downfall. The remarkable and encouraging thing has been the extent to which the moral consciousness of England has been aroused and made itself felt. Hoare strengthened himself by the manly way in which he acted and Baldwin weakened himself. As between the possibilities of a successor for Hoare I hope that it will be Eden because he is really more friendly to the United States than the others.

Bill Phillips has been in bed for a few days threatened with bronchial pneumonia but he is now recovering. My wife has also had a severe cold and the three of us have about decided to go to Switzerland to Gstaad for the holidays in order to get up into the sunshine.

I hope you and your family all have a very Merry Christmas and every possible happiness in the New Year.[2]

With affectionate regards, I am, as ever, Faithfully yours,

Norman H. Davis

[PSF:London Naval Conference:TS]

---

[1] See memorandum of Dec. 8, 1935, in *Foreign Relations, 1935*, I, 156–158, and the dispatches following.

[2] Answered Jan. 14, 1936 (*Personal Letters, 1928–1945*, I, 544–545).

R. Walton Moore, Assistant Secretary of State, to Roosevelt

Washington, December 21, 1935

Dear Mr. President: Before the Secretary left here last night, he requested Mr. Hackworth and myself to submit for your consideration what may be said in your message on international affairs. I submit with real diffidence the draft attached hereto, which has been dictated, and which I have read to Messrs. Hackworth and Green, who have stated their approval of it. Of course, I do not know whether you will wish to say that you intend to suggest neutrality legislation to Congress, or whether, on the other hand, you expect to refrain from any such suggestion until the situation in Congress develops to some extent, nor do I know whether you will wish to say anything on the religious subject.

I enclose a draft by Frank Sayre which relates particularly to the matters under his immediate supervision.

I also enclose notes by Messrs. Dunn, Hornbeck and Murray.[1]

Copies of everything covered by this envelope have been sent to Secretary Hull.

If I can be of any further service, I know you will tell me.

Yours very sincerely,

R. Walton Moore

[PPF 1820:International Relations:TS]

[1] The enclosures are present. In his own draft, Moore proposed the enlargement of the government's neutrality legislation, deprecated the "vast and expensive preparation for war" going on in some areas of the world, and deplored the "repression by some nations of religious freedom." Assistant Secretary of State Sayre emphasized the importance of the trade agreements program. James C. Dunn, special assistant to Hull, reviewed the accomplishments of the Administration's Good Neighbor policy in Latin America. Stanley K. Hornbeck, chief of the Division of Far Eastern Affairs, called attention to the inauguration of the commonwealth government of the Philippines and to the disturbing political developments in north China. Wallace Murray, chief of the Division of Near Eastern Affairs, called attention to the trade agreements policy as an instrument of peace and to the national policy of neutrality as exhibited in the Neutrality Act of 1935. None of this material was, however, used in Roosevelt's message to Congress of Jan. 3, 1936, below.

Roosevelt to Cordell Hull, Secretary of State

[Washington] December 23, 1935

Memorandum to the Secretary of State: I wish you personally would read this joint report of the Vice-Chairman of the Federal Power Commission and the Chairman of the Power Authority in the State of New York.[1]

On the whole, I agree with their conclusion. In view of this and of the fact that the so-called Preservation of Niagara Falls Convention and Protocol has been pending in the Senate since 1929, I believe that you and I should withdraw this Convention from the Senate. Of course, if we do this we should notify the Prime Minister. When Mr. Mackenzie King was here we discussed the whole subject of the Preservation of the scenery of Niagara Falls, and it is my thought that I would like to approach the whole subject anew.[2]

At the same time, I think we should take up with Mr. Mackenzie King the advisability of withdrawing from the Senate the St. Lawrence Treaty of 1932 which failed of ratification last spring. Mr. Mackenzie King may feel that it will be better to start fresh with the new treaty.

I am not convinced of this and would like to have your opinion on this latter suggestion.

I should like to have your slant on the recommendation for setting up a special Joint Commission to cover the whole subject, including investigation, scenery, power etc.

F.D.R.

[PPF 3089:CT]

[1] Basil Manly and Frank P. Walsh. This report was not returned to the White House.
[2] See Phillips to Roosevelt, Feb. 17, 1936, below.

Roosevelt to Samuel R. Fuller, Jr., New York

[Washington] December 23, 1935

Dear Dick: I am glad you are going over again in early February or the end of March. I think this is time enough because things are moving so fast at this minute that conversations are not of much practical use. Be sure to come down here before you go.[1]

Very sincerely yours,

[PPF 2616:CT]

[1] Fuller had asked, in a letter to Roosevelt of Dec. 19, 1935 (PPF 2616), if he should not make an attempt, on his coming trip to Europe, to discover the German reaction to Franco-British opposition toward a compromise with Mussolini. Fuller thought this might be a good time to negotiate a settlement with Germany; Schacht had spoken freely to him before and undoubtedly would again.

R. Walton Moore, Assistant Secretary of State, to Roosevelt

Washington, December 23, 1935

Dear Mr. President: You may not regard the matter mentioned in the notes herewith as of sufficient importance to warrant any statement about it at this time.

Should you wish me to take back the papers I sent you Saturday and write a comprehensive statement to include the substance of Mr. Sayre's memorandum, I will be glad to try my hand at it.[1]

I know that one idea I had in mind in writing my own statement was not really expressed by what I said, namely, the reference to our action in the Philippines and what other Governments might do to afford the opportunity for expansion to such nations as Italy and Germany. I of course had in mind the fact that much of the thinly settled and developed African area is held by the British, Portuguese and Belgians.

Yours very sincerely,

R. Walton Moore

[PPF 1820:International Relations:TS]

[1] See Moore to Roosevelt, Dec. 21, 1935, above.

[*Enclosure 1*] Wilbur J. Carr, Assistant Secretary of State, to R. Walton Moore

December 23, 1935

Dear Judge Moore: Inasmuch as there was a certain amount of misguided agitation in Congress last winter about placing quotas on immigration from the countries of the western hemisphere, particularly Mexico and Canada, and is likely to be renewed again in the coming winter, the President might find it useful to include such a paragraph as Mr. Simmons has drafted in his message.

W.J.C.

[PPF 1820:International Relations:TS]

[*Enclosure 2*] J. F. Simmons, Chief, Visa Division, to Wilbur J. Carr

December 20, 1935

Dear Mr. Carr: With reference to your telephone call of yesterday, I have attempted the preparation of the following paragraph for possible use in the President's forthcoming message should he desire to include therein a brief discussion of immigration.

As to immigration matters, the wage earners of this country are entitled to all the protection which the law can afford against an influx of competing foreigners.

Immigration into the United States has continued at a very low figure, chiefly due to the necessarily restrictive effect, under abnormal employment conditions, of the public charge clause of our immigration laws. As regards countries having immigration quotas, the issuance of visas thereunder for the past fiscal year was only eleven per cent of the total quotas. As regards the non-quota Western Hemisphere countries, immigration has been reduced to an even lower figure than in previous years, without any necessity for the imposition of immigration quotas on our neighbors of the American continents.

J. F. Simmons

[PPF 1820:International Relations:TS]

Robert W. Bingham, Ambassador to Great Britain, to Roosevelt

London, December 24, 1935

Dear Mr. President: I have not attempted to reply by letter to the questions with reference to the Italian situation in your recent letter because conditions were changing so rapidly from day to day I felt I could give you better information through my daily despatches.[1]

I heard the debate in the House of Commons on Thursday, the 19th, in connection with Sir Samuel Hoare's resignation. The peace proposal he made was made with the full knowledge and approval of the entire Cabinet, with the possible exception of Anthony Eden. The British Government adopted this policy because they were convinced they were on the eve of a war with Italy, with no assurance of real support from any quarter. They believed the moment hostilities began between England and Italy, this would so play into Germany's hands the result might mean a general war in Europe. In addition, they were confident Japan would take advantage of the situation to take at least all North China. It was on the basis of these beliefs they made the peace proposal. They had expected to break the news of the proposal to the British public in their own way; but the leak came from Paris, as they might have known it would come, and such a storm of opposition arose they concluded that they would have to back down.

In my opinion, the only member of the Government who came out of this situation untarnished was Sir Samuel Hoare. His statement in the House of Commons was definite, sincere and strong. He made no attack on his colleagues and no effort to shift the blame but definitely refused to recant. Mr. Baldwin's statement was weak and unconvincing, and the fact that he and his colleagues made a scapegoat of Hoare has damaged Baldwin's prestige greatly. There is a widespread belief that Hoare will come back in some capacity, though not as Foreign Secretary, and that Baldwin will go, within the next year or two.[2]

Eden's appointment has been well received, and it is generally believed that he was the only member of the Cabinet who took a position against the so-called Hoare-Laval peace proposals. In my own opinion, the Government would be in a stronger position if they had taken the public into their confidence as to their reasons for making this proposal, and had supported Hoare instead of deserting him. Eden's appointment has, as I have stated, been well received and it is generally believed here that there is a better prospect now of actual collective action than has existed heretofore. The better informed people here regard Germany as the real menace but there is much pro-German sentiment in the country and widespread criticism of France, and some actual feel of antagonism and hostility. The Prince of Wales has become the German protagonist. Some months ago he proposed fraternizing between the British and German ex-Service men, which caused much criticism in many quarters and resulted in a statement by Hoare to the French Ambassador that he had made this proposal on his own initiative and not only without the knowledge of the Government, but that the Government had informed him of its disapproval. Quite recently, at a large public dinner, he made another pro-German statement, which was not well received by the audience and which was hushed up in the newspapers.

In my opinion, the British Government will not attempt to press sanctions further, especially oil sanctions, without definite commitments of a military character, not only from France but from other members of the League.

Meanwhile, there is much apprehension that if and when things begin to go really badly for Italy, Mussolini will conclude that he cannot afford to lose to Abyssinia, and will provoke a war with England, on the theory that while he cannot afford to lose to Abyssinia he might maintain his position at the head of his own country if he loses to England.

Sincerely yours,

Robert W. Bingham

Webb Miller, head of United Press here has just returned from Italian front and reports morale of Italian troops excellent, that they are only two, or three weeks behind their schedule, have vast reserves of camels in case oil sanctions are put into effect, are confident of success even if war with England results.

[PSF:Great Britain:TS]

[1] Nov. 23, 1935, above.
[2] Hoare became First Lord of the Admiralty June 5, 1936, and Baldwin resigned as Prime Minister on May 28, 1937.

Marvin H. McIntyre, Assistant Secretary to the President, to Roosevelt

Washington, 12–26–35

Memorandum for the President: Secretary Moore said he hoped you would not see the Nye Committee until he, Secretary Moore, has talked with you.

He thinks we might very easily have trouble with Pittman, or one or two others, but believes it is working itself out naturally to a logical conclusion.

I assured him you would see him before you did anything with the Committee.[1]

M. H. M.

[*Notation*:A] Mac OK
[OF 1561:T]

[1] Roosevelt met with Moore, Hull, and Pittman on December 31 (PPF 1-0). For the State Department's relations with the Nye Committee at this time, see Hull, *Memoirs*, I, 403–404.

R. Walton Moore, Acting Secretary of State, to Roosevelt

Washington, December 27, 1935

Dear Mr. President: The Secretary, with whom I have just had a telephone conversation, wishes you to know that he is keeping closely in touch with the business of this Department.[1]

He thinks a view important to be stressed in any statement made is that the primary purpose of our policy is to prevent this country from being involved in war, but a very definite secondary purpose is for our Government to aid, as far as it legitimately can, in preventing the spread or protracting the duration of any war that may occur.[2]

There is no reason to hurry about discussing Bullitt's future,[3] but I will ask Colonel McIntyre this afternoon to have you advise me what is your thought in respect to a question raised in a telephone communication from Bullitt, and another question raised when this morning I discussed neutrality legislation at length with Senator Pittman.

I dislike very much to trouble you, even to read brief notes, when I know you are so busy with subjects of extreme importance.

Yours very sincerely,

R. Walton Moore

[PPF 1820:International Relations:TS]

[1] Hull was vacationing in Winter Park, Florida.
[2] Moore had sent Hull copies of drafts prepared by State Department officers for the President's state of the union message to Congress of Jan. 3, 1936, below.
[3] Bullitt was unhappy at his Moscow post but he remained there until the spring of 1936.

Cordell Hull, Secretary of State, to Roosevelt

[Washington] December 31, 1935

My dear Mr. President: I am returning, with the draft of a reply, the letter of December 19, 1935, which was addressed to you by Dr. M. L. Raney, Director of the University Libraries, University of Chicago.[1] I feel strongly that the action which Dr. Raney urges should be considered one of the measures that must be completed during the 1936 session of Congress. In order to accomplish this, prompt and sustained effort seems to be necessary.

The program suggested by Dr. Raney consists chiefly in immediate approval of the copyright treaty by the Senate with the statement by you that you will not perfect the adherence of the United States to it until appropriate accompanying legislation has been enacted or the current session of Congress had adjourned without taking such action.

Essentially this same attitude has long been that of the Department. Nearly two years ago Wallace McClure, the Departmental officer to whom I have assigned the task of presenting this matter to Congressional committees, urged the Committee on Foreign Relations of the Senate to recommend approval of the treaty with the understanding that it would be held in the Department of State for a reasonable time pending Congressional action amending the copyright law. The reason was that urged by Dr. Raney, namely, that, if the treaty were certain to come into force, the various interests concerned with copyright would settle their differences and unite upon a program of legislative reform.

Nearly all of these interests opposed action upon the treaty until after the statute should have been amended and, as a result, the treaty remains upon the executive calendar of the Senate, which has now passed the bill introduced by Senator Duffy as an accompanying measure. This bill is pending in the Committee on Patents of the House of Representatives.

I still feel that it would be desirable to obtain immediate favorable action upon the treaty and that to do so would expedite the adoption of a wise and just copyright statute. As this may not be practically possible, however, I also urge that every effort be made to obtain the prompt passage of the Duffy Bill by the House of Representatives, after the deletion of certain objectionable features in the bill as amended on the floor and passed by the Senate. I am attaching hereto a memorandum, prepared by McClure, for the purpose of setting forth the present situation in more detail.

Faithfully yours,

Cordell Hull

[OF 699:CT]

[1] Raney's letter is printed above; the reply, Jan. 7, 1936, is printed below.

[*Enclosure*] The Present Situation With Respect to the Pending Copyright Treaty

Dr. M. L. Raney, Director of the Libraries of the University of Chicago, after preliminary correspondence, had an interview with the President on December 16, 1935. Thereafter, on December 19, 1935, he addressed a letter to the President in which he urged immediate action upon the convention for the protection of literary and artistic works, commonly known as the copyright treaty, which has been favorably reported by the Committee on Foreign Relations and now stands upon the executive calendar of the Senate.[1] The facts set forth in Dr. Raney's letter, including the adoption of the treaty by the Senate on April 19, 1935, and the subsequent action rescinding this action and restoring the treaty to the calendar, are in substance correct.

Dr. Raney does not seem to overstate the situation from the point of view of the ethical untenability of the present attitude of the United States towards copyright in so far as other countries are concerned. The continued representations of the British Government in regard to the matter show all too clearly the likelihood of disastrous retaliation unless the United States shall accord to British authors the full privileges of protection in this country.

The National Association of Book Publishers, keenly alive to the dangers of retaliation, are exerting great efforts to obtain action to adopt and enforce the treaty.

During the 73rd Congress, bills were pending in both Houses for the purpose of amending the present law of the United States so as to conform to the obligations of the treaty. The treaty is, it is believed, self-executing and hence capable of overruling conflicting statutory law, but, as a matter of sound policy, the appropriate course would seem to be the alteration of existing legislation by amending legislation. The Department of State urged favorable action on the treaty at that time. Opposition developed because of the demand, on the part of most of the interests affected by copyright legislation, for a bill designed to go much further than merely to bring the statutory law into conformity with the treaty.

Thereafter the Interdepartmental Committee on Copyright was set up to draft such a bill. In consultation with the interests referred to, the committee prepared the early drafts of the bill which was completed under the direction of Senator F. Ryan Duffy, who introduced it. All of the interests not satisfied with the Duffy Bill were given a hearing by the Senate Committee on Patents, which extensively amended the bill before reporting it to the Senate. The bill passed the Senate on August 7, 1935.

In considering the present status of the bill which was prepared and guided through the Senate by Mr. Duffy, and which is pending in the Committee on Patents of the House of Representatives, initial attention should be given to certain amendments which, though with Senator Duffy's nominal consent, were against his will tacked on during the debate on the bill in the Senate. The effect of these amendments would be to continue in force the provision of the present law which makes the manufacture in the United States of books and other literary material in the English language a condition precedent to the enjoyment of American copyright protection. Such a provision is not only contrary to the treaty, and consequently must be overruled by the treaty or by statute before the United States can live up to the obligations of the treaty, but it is also contrary to every concept of reciprocity and good-neighborliness.

The House of Representatives should certainly delete it.

It would seem also to be desirable for the House of Representatives to delete from the bill as amended on the floor of the Senate, and to consider whether it will put into a separate bill, certain amendments which bring into the copyright law of the United States the wholly new concept of protection of commercial designs. The appropriate place for the consideration of such a far-reaching novelty in American law would seem to be in a separate measure, not in a measure designed primarily to pave the way for the adherence of the United States to a treaty which is in no wise concerned with design copyright. The question of design copyright is extremely controversial and its continuance in the Duffy Bill might seriously endanger passage. This matter was not before the Senate Committee on Patents and was not debated on the floor.

With these two amendments deleted, the bill as it passed the Senate would seem to be appropriate for enactment by the House of Representatives.

It is freely said that opponents of the measure are going to make every effort to defeat it through delay. Therefore immediate action should be taken if it is the desire of the administration to be assured of its passage at the session beginning in January, 1936.

Nearly all of the interests concerned with copyright are in favor of the Duffy Bill. These include the book publishers, the periodical publishers, the broadcasters, the hotel operators, certainly most and probably all of the motion picture producers and exhibitors, and a host of American educators, librarians and authors whose opinion may correctly be construed as impartial and public spirited.

From the practical point of view the opposition consists of the American Society of Composers, Authors and Publishers, and the Authors' League of America. Both of these interests are in favor of, and would benefit by, the treaty, but both are opposed to certain features of the bill.

The most controverted of the features of the bill is probably the one which repeals the present provision of law that grants a fixed minimum damage fee collectible from anyone who is proven to have infringed a copyright, regardless of injury to the copyright owner or benefit to himself. In most cases, this fee is fixed at $250. The American Society of Composers, Authors and Publishers is not particularly interested in collecting a fee of $250, but uses this provision of law as a threat or bargaining point for the sale of licenses for others to utilize the performing rights it owns in copyrighted music. Without the provision of law granting this heavy penalty, it claims that it would be unable to sell its licenses in a way that would be sufficiently profitable. The bill, however, definitely requires the courts, in case of infringement where damages are not proved, to award damages sufficient to stop infringement. This provision was drafted in consultation with officials of the Department of Justice and is believed to be an effective safeguard.

Careful consideration was given to this matter by the Senate Committee and it was particularly the subject of debate on the floor of the Senate, which brought out widespread opposition to the continuance of the minimum damage fee of $250. The fact that the bill passed the Senate without a record vote shows clearly enough the attitude of that branch of the Congress toward the minimum damage question and the other objections.

The Authors' League has been shown clearly to be the recipient of a long list of advantages in the bill as compared with the present law and its pleas for changes in the bill, after careful consideration in the Senate Committee, were overruled. Among the chief of these is the demand for copyright without registration. Such demand has much in its favor, but is with equal reasonableness opposed by other interests. Opinion in Congress is believed to be strongly against it.

It would seem reasonable for the Administration to continue to give its support to the Duffy bill. That support was freely given while the measure was before the Senate. Mr. Charles West, the personal representative of the President in liaison with Congress, worked for the bill and it was known in Congress as an administration measure. In order to obtain its passage over the objection of certain members of the House of Representatives, who happen to occupy strategic committee positions with reference to copyright legislation, it is believed that the administration must exercise some very real persuasive influence.

The failure of the United States to become a party to the convention for the protection of literary and artistic works at this time would be not only to continue to occupy an unethical position and to forego very real advantages for American authors and musicians, as well as many other American interests, but, as above set forth, would invite immediate retaliation. Such retaliation might be extremely injurious over a much wider area than merely the fields of literature and art. Failure of the House to enact legislation at this time would, of course, mean that it would have to be passed by the Senate as well as by the House in a future Congress. The loss of what has already been gained might mean setback in copyright reform for a period of many years. The losses to interests concerned with copyright during such a period might be very great indeed. Not improbably those who are at present opposed to the Duffy Bill would be the heaviest of the losers.

Approval of the treaty by the Senate, with or without accompanying legislation, is altogether desirable. But in view of the history of the case, such approval prior to the passage of a bill may not be practicable. The safest and most satisfactory course is to obtain both approval and enactment as soon as possible.

[OF 699:CT]

[1] Raney to Roosevelt, Dec. 19, 1935, above.

R. Walton Moore, Assistant Secretary of State, to Roosevelt

Washington, December 31, 1935

Dear Mr. President: There are one or two points with reference to the Neutrality Bill which I think you will wish to consider in advance of the conference this afternoon.[1]

Enclosed is a printed copy of the existing law.[2] The more the matter has been thought about here, the more we are inclined to believe that the law is sufficiently flexible in declaring that a proclamation shall be made and the embargo become effective "upon the outbreak or *during the progress of war*[3] between or among two or more foreign states." My belief is that the Senate will insist on that provision or a provision of that character being retained. But also enclosed is a redraft of the section which would make it more flexible, and which in all probability the Senate would reject.

A new section has to be considered pertaining to the executive authority relative to articles such as oil, copper, steel, and iron that can be readily used or converted for use in conducting war. The question will be raised as to whether the Executive should be given authority to *embargo* the export of such articles or simply restrict their export to a normal quantity, say based on the average for five preceding years. You may expect a great deal to be said on this subject.

Yours very sincerely,

R. Walton Moore

[PSF:Neutrality:TS]

[1] Administration agreement on a neutrality bill to replace the joint resolution approved Aug. 31, 1935 (49 *Stat.* 1081), was reached at a White House conference on the afternoon of Dec. 31, 1935, attended by the President, Secretary of State Hull, Assistant Secretary of State Moore, Senator Pittman, Representative McReynolds, and Representative John J. O'Connor, chairman of the House Rules Committee (Hull, *Memoirs,* I, 462). This bill, intended to forestall a more drastic measure sponsored by Senator Nye, and Senator Bennett Champ Clark, was based on a State Department revision of the 1935 law. The prohibition on trade in arms, munitions, and implements of war of the existing law was extended to materials that might be used for war purposes, such as oil and steel (other than normal commerce in such items), but excepting food and medical supplies. The President was required to apply all embargoes equally to all belligerents; however, he was given discretion to determine what was "normal commerce." American citizens would conduct business and travel on ships of belligerents at their own risk. American ports were barred for use as bases of supply by the war vessels of belligerents (text as printed in the New York *Times,* Jan. 4, 1936, p. 6). The measure was introduced in the Senate by Pittman on Jan. 3, 1936, as S. 3474, "The Neutrality Act of 1936," and referred to the Committee on Foreign Relations.

The companion House bill, H.J.R. 422, was introduced on the same day by McReynolds (*Cong. Rec.,* vol. 80, pp. 5, 34). On January 6, Senators Nye and Clark introduced S. 3478; the bill was introduced in the House by Maury Maverick as H.R. 9668. This bill went beyond the Administration bill in these respects: (1) the President was required to apply the embargo at once and was not given the alternative, "or during the progress of the war"; (2) he was given no discretion in determining what constituted normal trade in war materials other than arms and munitions; (3) commercial credits were much more restricted; (4) American vessels were barred from war zones; and (5) all goods were to be shipped at risk of the purchaser (*ibid.,* pp. 47, 119; committee print, Jan. 6, 1935, Moore Papers).

Those backing this bill planned, if it was not reported, to add these features to the Administration's bill by amendment (New York *Times,* Jan. 5, 1936, p. 34). Other neutrality bills introduced in the House between January 3 and January 20 were H.R. 9482, by H. P. Kopplemann; H.R. 9492 and H.R. 10304, by Ludlow; and H.R. 10361, by James A. Shanley. Representative Arthur D. Healey introduced H.R. 10400, to extend the 1935 act, and Senator Thomas (Utah) introduced S.J.R. 198 to the same end (*Cong. Rec.,* vol. 80, pp. 33, 462, 548, 632, 770). Of this group, only the last named was reported.

[2] Present.

[3] Italics here and below indicate underscoring.

[*Enclosure*] Revised Draft of Section 3 of Draft No. 4 of December 12, 1935

Sec. 3. Export of Arms, Ammunition and Implements of War.

(a) Whenever during any war in which the United States is neutral, the President shall find that the prohibition of the shipment of arms, ammunition or implements of war from the United States will serve to maintain peace and discourage war, or to protect the commercial and economic interests of the United States and its nationals, or to promote the security or preserve the neutrality of the United States and shall so proclaim, it shall thereafter be unlawful to export, or attempt to export, or cause to be exported, or sell for export, any such articles from any place in the United States to any belligerent country, named in the proclamation, or to any neutral country for transshipment to or for the use of any such belligerent country: Provided, That any prohibition of export shall apply equally to all belligerents, including those subsequently entering the war, the names of which shall be proclaimed by the President as and when they so enter.

(b) The President shall, by proclamation, definitely enumerate the arms, ammunition and implements of war, the export of which is prohibited by this act.

(c) When in the judgment of the President the conditions which have caused him to issue a proclamation have ceased to exist, he shall revoke the same and the provisions of this section shall thereupon cease to apply.[1]

[PSF:Neutrality:T]

[1] This draft became section 3 of the bill and, as introduced Jan. 3, 1936, read as follows (text from the New York *Times,* Jan. 4, 1936, p. 6):

"Section 3. Export of Articles and Materials Used for War Purposes—(a) Whenever during any war in which the United States is neutral the President shall find that the placing of restrictions on the shipment from the United States to belligerent countries of certain articles or materials used in the manufacture of arms, ammunition or implements of war, or in the conduct of war, will serve to promote the security and preserve the neutrality of the United States or to protect the lives and commerce of nationals of the United States, or that to refrain from placing such restriction would contribute to a prolongation or expansion of the war, he shall so proclaim, and it shall thereafter be unlawful to export, or attempt to export, or cause to be exported, or sell for export, such articles or materials from any place in the United States to any belligerent country named in the proclamation, or to any neutral country for transshipment to or for the use of any such belligerent country in excess of a normal amount in quantity and kind of exports from the United States to the respective belligerent countries prior to the

151

date of the proclamation, such normal amount to constitute the average of shipments during a previous period of years to be determined by the President:

"*Provided* that no restriction or prohibition imposed under this section shall under any circumstances be applied to food or medical supplies.

"(b) The President shall, by proclamation, definitely enumerate the articles or materials the exportation of which is to be restricted, and he may, from time to time, modify or revoke in whole or in part any proclamation issued by him under this section when he shall find that the conditions which caused him to issue his proclamation have ceased to exist or have so changed as to justify in his opinion such modification or revocation.

"(c) The President shall, from time to time, by proclamation, extend such restrictions as are imposed under this section to other countries as and when they may become involved in such war."

Further revisions were made by the Senate Committee on Foreign Relations meeting Jan. 10 and 22, 1934; see New York *Times,* Jan. 11, p. 6, and Jan. 23, 1936, p. 11; Hull, *Memoirs,* I, 463–466. See Moore to Roosevelt, Jan 13, 1936, below.

Roosevelt to the Congress, January 3, 1936

[*Excerpt*] Mr. President, Mr. Speaker, Members of the Senate and of the House of Representatives: We are about to enter upon another year of the responsibility which the electorate of the United States has placed in our hands. Having come thus far, it is fitting that we should pause to survey the ground which we have covered and the path which lies ahead.

On the fourth day of March, 1933, on the occasion of taking the oath of office as President of the United States, I addressed the people of our country. Need I recall either the scene or the national circumstances attending the occasion? The crisis of that moment was almost exclusively a national one. And in recognition of that fact, so obvious to the millions in the streets and in the homes of America, I devoted by far the greater part of that address to what I called, and the Nation called, critical days within our own borders.

You will remember that on that 4th of March, 1933, the world picture was an image of substantial peace. International consultation and widespread hope for the bettering of relations between the nations gave to all of us a reasonable expectation that the barriers to mutual confidence, to increased trade, and to the peaceful settlement of disputes could be progressively removed. In fact my only reference to the field of world policy in that address was in these words—"I would dedicate this Nation to the policy of the good neighbor—the neighbor who resolutely respects himself, and because he does so, respects the rights of others—a neighbor who respects his obligations and respects the sanctity of his agreements in and with a world of neighbors."

In the years that have followed, that sentiment has remained the dedication of this Nation. Among the nations of the great Western Hemisphere the policy of the good neighbor has happily prevailed. At no time in the four and a half centuries of modern civilization in the Americas has there existed—in any year, in any decade, in any generation in all that time—a greater spirit of mutual understanding, of common helpfulness, and of devotion to the ideals of self-government than exists today in the twenty-one American Republics and their neighbor, the Dominion of Canada. This policy of the good neighbor among the Americas is no longer a hope—no longer an objective remaining to be accomplished—it is a fact, active, present, pertinent and effective. In this achievement every American Nation takes an understanding part. There is neither war, nor rumor of war, nor desire for war. The inhabitants of this vast area, two hundred and fifty million strong, spreading more than eight thousand miles from the Arctic to the Antarctic, believe in, and propose to follow, the policy of the good neighbor. And they wish with all their hearts that the rest of the world might do likewise.

The rest of the world—Ah! there's the rub.

Were I today to deliver an Inaugural Address to the people of the United States, I could not limit my comments on world affairs to one paragraph. With much regret I should be compelled to devote the greater part to world affairs. Since the summer of that same year of 1933, the temper and the purposes of the rulers of many of the great populations in Europe and Asia have not pointed the way either to peace or to good-will among men. Not only have peace and good-will among men grown more remote in those areas of the earth during this period, but a point has been reached where the people of the Americas must take cognizance of growing ill-will, of marked trends towards aggression, of increasing armaments, of shortening tempers—a situation which has in it many of the elements that lead to the tragedy of general war.

On those other continents many nations, principally the smaller peoples, if left to themselves, would be content with their boundaries and willing to solve within themselves and in cooperation with their neighbors their individual problems, both economic and social. The rulers of those nations, deep in their hearts, follow these peaceful and reasonable aspirations of their peoples. These rulers must remain ever vigilant against the possibility today or tomorrow of invasion, of attack by the rulers of other peoples who fail to subscribe to the principles of bettering the human race by peaceful means.

And within those other nations—those which today must bear the primary, definite responsibility for jeopardizing world peace—what hope lies? To say the least, there are grounds for pessimism. It is idle for us or for others to preach that the masses of the people who constitute these nations are dominated by the twin spirits of autocracy and aggression, are out of sympathy with their rulers, that they are allowed no opportunity to express themselves, that they would change things if they could.

That, unfortunately, is not so clear. It might be true that the masses of the people in those nations would change the policies of their governments if they could be allowed full freedom, full access to the processes of Democratic government as we understand them. But they do not have that access; lacking it, they follow blindly and fervently the lead of those who seek autocratic power.

Nations, seeking expansion, seeking the rectification of injustice springing from former wars, seeking outlets for trade, for population or even for their own peaceful contributions to the progress of civilization, fail to demonstrate that patience necessary to attain reasonable and legitimate objectives by peaceful negotiation or by an appeal to the finer instincts of world justice.

They have therefore impatiently reverted to the old belief in the law of the sword, or to the fantastic conception that they, and they alone, are chosen to fulfill a mission and that all the others among the billion and a half of human beings in the world must and shall learn from and be subject to them.

I recognize and you will recognize that these words which I have chosen with deliberation will not prove popular in any nation that chooses to fit this shoe to its foot. Such sentiments, however, will find sympathy and understanding in those nations where the people themselves are honestly desirous of peace but must constantly align themselves on one side or the other in the kaleidoscopic jockeying for position that is characteristic of European and Asiatic relations today. For the peace-loving nations, and there are many of them, find that their very identity depends on their moving and moving again on the chess board of international politics.

I suggested in the spring of 1933 that eighty-five or ninety per cent of all the people in the world were content with the territorial limits of their respective nations and were willing further to reduce their armed forces if every other nation in the world would agree to do likewise.

That is equally true today, and it is even more true today that world peace and world good-will are blocked by only ten or fifteen per cent of the world's population. That is why efforts to reduce armies have thus far not only failed but have been met by vastly increased armaments on land and in the air. And that is why even efforts to continue the existing limits on Naval armaments into the years to come show such little current success.

But the policy of the United States has been clear and consistent. We have sought with earnestness in every possible way to limit world armaments and to attain the peaceful evolution, the peaceful solution of disputes among nations.

We have sought by every legitimate means to exert our moral influence against repression, against intolerance, against autocracy and in favor of freedom of expression, equality before the law, religious tolerance and popular rule.

In the field of commerce we have undertaken to encourage a more reasonable interchange of the world's goods. In the field of international finance we have, so far as we are concerned, put an end to dollar diplomacy, to money grabbing, to speculation for the benefit of the powerful and the rich, at the expense of the small and the poor.

As a consistent part of a clear policy, the United States is following a two fold neutrality towards any and all nations which engage in wars that are not of immediate concern to the Americas. First, we decline to encourage the prosecution of war by permitting belligerents to obtain arms, ammunition or implements of war from the United States. Second, we seek to discourage the use by belligerent nations of any and all American products calculated to facilitate the prosecution of a war in quantities over and above our normal exports of them in time of peace.

I trust that these clear objectives, thus unequivocally stated, will be carried forward by cooperation between this Congress and the President.

I realize that I have emphasized to you the gravity of the situation which confronts the people of the world. This emphasis is justified because of its importance to civilization and therefore to the United States. Peace is jeopardized by the few and not by the many. Peace is threatened by those who seek selfish power. The world has witnessed similar eras—as in the days when petty kings and feudal barons were changing the map of Europe every fortnight, or when great emperors and great kings were engaged in a mad scramble for colonial empire.

We hope that we are not again at the threshold of such an era. But if face it we must, then the United States and the rest of the Americas can play but one role: through a well-ordered neutrality to do naught to encourage the contest, through adequate defense to save ourselves from

embroilment and attack, and through example and all legitimate encouragement and assistance to persuade other nations to return to the
days of peace and good-will.

The evidence before us clearly proves that autocracy in world affairs
endangers peace and that such threats do not spring from those nations
devoted to the democratic ideal. If this be true in world affairs, it should
have the greatest weight in the determination of domestic policy.[1]

[RL Recordings]

[1] This annual message on the state of the union was read by Roosevelt before the
Congress on the evening of January 3. The message was broadcast; this text (about
half the speech) is from the recording made at the time. Roosevelt used as his reading
copy a typescript that bears some revisions in his hand (Speech File); these changes
were incorporated in the press release issued before the address. No earlier drafts have
been found (excepting those sent to the White House by Moore, Dec. 21, 1935, above,
which were not used). The official stenographic transcript shows many changes of words
and phrases made by Roosevelt when he read the message; however, not all of these
last-minute changes were caught by the stenographer. (The punctuation is that of the
stenographic transcript except where the President plainly changed it in his reading.)
The entire message is printed in Rosenman, *Public Papers*, V, 8–18; this version combines
parts of both the reading copy and the stenographic transcript. The message is also
printed in the *Congressional Record*, vol. 80, pp. 27–30. This version includes some of the
changes made when the message was read.

Frederick H. Allen to Roosevelt

Charleston, S.C., January 3, 1936

My dear President: I have read with care the draft of the Neutrality
proposal, made by the National Peace group, headed by Dr. Shotwell,
as it appeared in the New York *Times* of December 26th.[1] This Neutrality
proposal provides in Section 3 that upon the outbreak of war between
foreign states, that the President, "shall proclaim the existence of a state
of war," and shall put an embargo on the "export of arms, ammunition
or implements of war," to the belligerent States. And further that
"during the course of the war" he can prohibit the export to the belligerent States "of other articles or commodities essential to the continuing
conduct of the war," if such exports "would endanger the maintenance
of peace between the United States and foreign nations." But in article
7 of the proposal there is an escape clause and it is provided that if
"one or more" of the belligerent countries is attacked in contravention
of the provisions of the Pact of Paris (i.e. is the victim of aggression)
he may revoke the embargo proclamation issued under section 3 of the

proposal as against the victim or victims of the aggressor. But this he can only do in case a majority of the non-belligerent countries, parties to the Pact, shall decide there has been a contravention of the Pact (i.e. an aggression). After this has been obtained the President "shall so advise the Congress and with its consent he may revoke the embargo proclamation issued under section 3," in respect to the victim or victims of the attack. But this proviso takes no account of the time element which is of the utmost importance in any future war. The aggressor has the advantage of being able to choose the moment for his attack and would attack with a swiftness unknown in the last war, made possible by the remarkable development of the airplane and the different kinds of tanks that have been invented, and the infantry would not be very far behind because of their movement by motor trucks. If the President has to wait and see the position taken by the majority of the neutral nations under the Pact of Paris which may take place somewhat rapidly at Geneva, and then get the consent of Congress, which might not be in session, the victim or victims of the aggression might have been rendered helpless by this time. Many of its cities and towns might have been badly damaged, and many of its factories for the supply of war materials might have been destroyed. This provision of section 7 is so weak and piffling as to be an absurdity. As I have said above, rapidity would be the crux of any future war.

Is it not better to prevent a fire in a neighbor's house than to try to prevent the fire, after it has started, from spreading to one's own house? Likewise in the case of a neutrality resolution, is it not better to give power to the President to try to prevent a war, than to give him the right to exercise certain powers to prevent the war from spreading to our own shores and so disturbing our peace and safety?

The issue of neutrality comes down to this, do we wish to prevent a war from breaking out, or do we wish to prevent it from spreading to us after it has broken out. It would be better frankly to stick our heads in the sand, or like the Pharisee to pass by on the other side than to pass such a piddling clause as is contained in article 7 of the proposed neutrality act. It would be merely a pretense on the side of righteousness and would deceive nobody.

If however the President were to be given the power to declare a state of war, and to name the aggressor when the aggression is perfectly plain, as in the present Italo-Ethiopian war, and that he be given the power in such case to allow the export of arms, munitions and implements of war and other material necessary in the conduct of a war, such a power would be more effective to prevent the outbreak of a war than could be secured in any other way. We are the most powerful nation in the world today in efficient man power (Russia has the man power but not the efficiency) and in resources, such a power as is suggested above if put in the hands of the President, would make any nation hesitate before rushing into the arbitrament of war. It will be said how can the President tell who is the aggressor. This may not always be clear, but if it is not clear the President can prohibit the export of arms etc. etc. to both the parties, but when the case is clear, as in the present African war, the suggestion I have made would be a powerful deterrent against starting a war. If Great Britain had made it clear to Mussolini beforehand what would be it's attitude in case he started a war in Ethiopia, or had begun sending his soldiers there, there is little doubt that Mussolini would have refrained from doing so. And in the same way should we make our position clear in advance as to what we would do in the case of a war of aggression, it would have a powerful influence in preventing it.[2]

I beg to remain with high regard, Respectfully yours,

Frederick H. Allen

[OF 1561:TS]

[1] This "national peace group" was the National Peace Conference, an organization of thirty societies that had recently been placed on a permanent basis through a grant from the Carnegie Endowment for International Peace. Walter Van Kirk, secretary of the Department of International Justice and Good-Will of the Federal Council of Churches, was the director. The Conference had appointed a committee under James T. Shotwell, president of the League of Nations Association, to draft legislation to extend the Neutrality Act of 1935, due to expire Feb. 29, 1936; this proposed law was made public on Dec. 25, 1935 (New York *Times,* Dec. 26, 1935, pp. 1, 10–11). It would have renewed the obligation of the President to embargo arms to belligerents and would have made such embargoes applicable to all parties to the dispute. One section (which Allen here criticizes) provided that the President could lift an embargo against the nation attacked, following consent of Congress; the Conference had not, however, reached agreement on this section. The text is printed *ibid.,* Dec. 26, 1935, pp. 10–11.

[2] Answered Jan. 16, 1936, below.

John Cudahy, Ambassador to Poland, to Roosevelt

Warsaw, Poland, January 3, 1936

Confidential

Dear Mr. President: The significant phase of recent developments in Europe is the effect as a precedent upon an armed, aggressive Germany two years from now.

The rejection of the Hoare-Laval Proposals instead of indicating the futility of the League reveals the universal sentiment for the necessity of collective action. The dismissal of Hoare and the selection of Eden as Foreign Minister is, in the opinion of the best advised of my colleagues, an intelligent appraisal of public opinion in Great Britain which is insistent upon rigorous adherence to the League. The indications are that sanctions will now pass to a decisive stage, for the assurance of military assistance on the part of Turkey, Yugoslavia, and Greece, has given Great Britain the moral endorsement it has from the beginning demanded as a necessary condition for forceful coercive measures that may result in war with Italy.

Step by step Laval should be forced to take a more cooperative position. Otherwise he may find that he has been the instrument of creating a most hazardous League precedent for France in 1938 face to face with a prepared Germany.

The position you have taken under the Neutrality Act has been a great gratification to us in the active Foreign Service. Your utterance, amplified by that of the Secretary of State, has given us an enviable moral leadership in Europe. But it cannot be emphasized too often that the position of the United States is an entirely independent one, based solely upon American principles and the controlling purpose to preserve the peace for our own country. Unless the independent character of our neutrality measures is reiterated most emphatically on many occasions the argument will be made and will find credence that the United States is following the League.

An extension of further embargoes before the League acts on the question of further sanctions, would demonstrate our independent action beyond all equivocation. But in considering such an enlargement of the scope of the Neutrality Act there is a heavy responsibility for you must bear in mind not only the possibility but the probability of an extension to Europe of the Abyssinian War. A limitation upon exports to Italy might be countenanced without too great a protest but if such limitation were imposed upon shipments to Great Britain and possibly other countries in Europe there would be violent hostile criticism from many quarters in the United States. Yet I am satisfied the overwhelming weight of American public opinion will sustain you in deciding against such material considerations of selfish interests.

But the decision must be made deliberately with a view of far-reaching consequences.

Already under the Neutrality Act we are charting a course which is an abrupt departure and decisions further broadening this course will inaugurate a foreign policy for unborn generations.

I am writing you these impressions for what they are worth, confident that you will be glad to have them from one who is at an outpost in Europe and therefore conversant with sentiments with which those at home are further removed.[1]

Very respectfully,

John Cudahy

[PSF:Poland:TS]

[1] Referring to this letter two weeks later (Jan. 16, 1936, PSF:Poland), Cudahy told Roosevelt that the objectives outlined would be accomplished if Congress followed his recommendation that the United States follow a foreign policy entirely independent of the League "and one that assures us a high moral leadership, most important of all which guarantees peace as far as it can be guaranteed." Roosevelt replied to both letters on Jan. 21, 1936; he said everywhere people asked him if he could keep them out of a European war and that he told them he could and would if the nation backed him up (*Personal Letters, 1928–1945,* I, 547).

Roosevelt to Thorvald Solberg

[Washington] January 7, 1936

My dear Mr. Solberg: Thanks much for your letter of January second which set forth so completely the copyright situation.[1] I hope much that something can be worked out to take care of the points you raise.

With kind personal regards, Very sincerely yours,

[OF 699:CT]

[1] Reviewing the arguments in favor of the proposed copyright convention. See below.

Roosevelt to M. L. Raney, Director, University Libraries, University of Chicago, Chicago

[Washington, January 7, 1936][1]

My dear Dr. Raney: This is to acknowledge, and to express appreciation for, your letter of December 19, 1935, regarding the pending convention on copyright.[2]

I want to assure you, as I did during our recent conversation, that it is my very earnest desire to see this treaty approved by the Senate, with resulting adherence by the United States, at the earliest practicable moment.[3]

Sincerely yours,

[OF 699:CT]

[1] A supplied date.

[2] Above.

[3] Roosevelt sent the Raney-Solberg correspondence to Hull with a note of Jan. 7, 1936 (OF 699): "Will you speak to the Senate Committee people in regard to getting action on the copyright treaty?" On February 12 the House voted to discharge the Committee on Patents from consideration of H.R. 8557 to amend the copyright laws so that the Senate bill, S. 3047, could be taken up; no action on this was taken, however (*Cong. Rec.*, vol. 80, pp. 1942–1943). The Senate committee report on S. 3047 is printed *ibid.*, pp. 1943–1944.

Joseph C. Grew, Ambassador to Japan, to Cordell Hull, Secretary of State

Tokyo, Dated January 7, 1936

Strictly Confidential

[*Telegram*] Fleisher informs me that the resumé of Japanese reaction to the President's message to Congress which he cabled to the *Herald Tribune* was entirely fictitious having been compiled only from his own ideas of what the Japanese would think.[1] He has been unable to obtain any opinion from Japanese sources and the Foreign Office officials take refuge in the statement that they have not read the message.

There has been no editorial comment whatever in the Japanese press in regard to the message except an editorial in the *Japan Times and Mail* (Japanese owned English language newspaper) of January 6 which criticizes the bold wording of the message but points out that the message was intended primarily for domestic consumption with a view to insuring the passage of further neutrality legislation.[2]

Grew

[OF 197:M]

[1] Benjamin Fleisher, editor of the Tokyo *Japan Advertiser* from 1908 to 1940 and at various times a correspondent in the Orient for several American newspapers and periodicals. The message to Congress was that of Jan. 3, 1936, above.

[2] See Roosevelt to Hull, Jan. 14, 1936, below.

Cordell Hull, Secretary of State, to Roosevelt

Washington, January 7, 1936

My dear Mr. President: With reference to your recent request for further information regarding the military situation in Ethiopia, I enclose a copy of a telegram received today from Mr. Engert, our Chargé d'Affaires at Addis Ababa.[1] In this telegram Mr. Engert stresses the difficulty of obtaining reliable military information at Addis Ababa, particularly since the departure of the Emperor for his military headquarters at Dessye. However, Mr. Engert points out that the newly appointed Military Attaché, Captain Meade,[2] who arrived at Addis Ababa on December 10 and left for Dessye by mule caravan on December 26, will doubtless report from there in the near future. Meanwhile, the Chargé d'Affaires will send forward within the next few days his own personal impressions of the military situation.

In view of the absence of adequate means of communication between the war zones and the capital, I appreciate that it is not an easy matter for Mr. Engert to obtain reliable information at Addis Ababa. I feel confident, however, that he is doing his utmost in the matter, for he has all along done splendid work under most difficult and trying circumstances.

Faithfully yours,

Cordell Hull

[PSF:Ethiopia:TS]

[1] Cornelius Engert had been chargé d'affaires at Addis Ababa since July 22, 1935; on Jan. 23, 1936, he was named minister (Hull to Roosevelt, Jan. 23, 1936, OF 1922). In his telegram of Jan. 5, 1936 (PSF:Ethiopia), Engert complained that "75 per cent of the newspaper reports which have gone out from here regarding military events have been pure guesswork and padding."
[2] Capt. John Meade.

Stephen T. Early, Assistant Secretary to the President, to Roosevelt

Washington, January 13, 1936

Memorandum for the President: Here is the copy of the *Congressional Record* for January sixth, 1936, containing an extension of remarks by Senator Pittman, beginning on Page 50.[1] Under the title of "The Maintenance of Peace" the Senator discusses the Japanese situation and embodies in his remarks a radio interview which he granted to William K. Hutchinson of the International News Service.

Senator Pittman makes these points:

1. Treaty violation by Japan is a threat to the United States.

2. Present course of Japan in China threatens American interests and influence in the Pacific.

3. Setting up of the puppet government of Manchoukuo is a threat against the rights and peace of American citizens. It has already practically destroyed our trade in Manchuria.

4. Replying to a question whether Japanese action means war between Japan and the United States, Senator Pittman said that the aspirations of the present military government of Japan may make it the moral duty of the United States to take action.

5. Senator Pittman asked that this be called to your attention.

S.E.

[PPF 745:TS]

[1] In the bound edition, vol. 80, p. 56. Pittman was interviewed by Hutchinson in a radio broadcast of Jan. 4, 1936, and the interview is reprinted in the *Record* in its entirety.

R. Walton Moore, Assistant Secretary of State, to Roosevelt

Washington, January 13, 1936

Dear Mr. President: Last week I appeared at two or three sessions of the House Committee on Foreign Affairs while the neutrality bill was being considered, and Friday and today I appeared with the Secretary before the Senate Committee on Foreign Relations.

Friday one member of the Senate Committee raised the question as to the expediency of excepting the Latin American nations from the operation of the bill, but apparently he had no support, and I would feel no concern whatever on that point but for the fact that Judge McReynolds seems determined to urge his Committee in the House to make that exception. It strikes me as wholly unnecessary, since, first, it can hardly be supposed that any Old World naval power will venture to attack a Latin American country, and, second, any threat of such an attack would give Congress full opportunity to modify the legislation. Furthermore, the proposal appears to be undesirable because its adoption would renew the discussion of the Monroe Doctrine by our Latin American friends. Of course I agree with you that their criticism of the doctrine is "silly," but people cannot be prevented from doing silly things.

I enclose an article that was printed in the Washington *Star* yesterday, which was not instigated by this Department, and I feel certain was not instigated by Senator Pittman.[1] It states in a pretty emphatic way the objection to the desirability of incorporating in the bill the "Latin American clause." I have talked with Secretary Hull, and we think that you may possibly believe it well to call McReynolds and ask him to lay off on that matter.[2]

Although it would seem that Senators Johnson and Lewis would prefer that no legislation shall be enacted, I am sure that the other members of the Senate Committee, and all the members of the House Committee, favor legislation, though there are inevitable differences of opinion on specific provisions. For example, Senator Borah, who desires legislation, is very much disturbed by the provisions that will allow normal exports under the American flag, but authorize the shippers to be informed that they are to carry on at their own risk.[3]

Yours very sincerely,

R. Walton Moore

[PSF:Neutrality:TS]

[1] By Gaston Nerval, "Latin American Clause Regarded Unnecessary."

[2] Moore had earlier stated the State Department's opposition to excepting Latin American countries in a memorandum to Hull stamped "noted, Jan. 4, 1936" (Moore Papers). Moore said that the Senate would "almost certainly" object to raising the aggressor question, "and a detrimental issue [would] be brought into the next campaign." In the unlikely event that a European power should attack a Latin American country Congress could at once take necessary action. He concluded: "Perhaps it is not desirable to do more than extend the present Act, but public opinion and the Congressional attitude is such that there can be no doubt that legislation will be enacted, and we are now at the stage where it must be decided whether it will be Administration proposals or the Nye Committee proposals."

[3] Senator Hiram W. Johnson and Senator J. Hamilton Lewis were members of the Foreign Relations Committee. Johnson insisted that the United States should maintain its traditional "freedom of the seas" policy; he and others of like mind on the committee secured further revision of the Neutrality Bill to make more emphatic the assertion in section 15 (b) that the United States reserved all its rights under international law as it existed prior to Aug. 1, 1914 (New York *Times,* Jan. 14, p. 3; Jan. 16, 1936, p. 1). See Hull to Roosevelt, Jan. 22, 1936, below.

Roosevelt to Cordell Hull, Secretary of State

[Washington] January 14, 1936

Memorandum for the Secretary of State: I am inclined to think that the *Herald Tribune* should be officially informed of Fleisher's statement to Grew that his cabled resumé of Japan's reaction to the President's message was entirely fictitious.[1]

Please let me have a copy of the *Tribune* story, of your telegram to Grew and his reply for my personal files.

F.D.R.

[OF 197:CT]

[1] See Grew to Hull, Jan. 7, 1936, above.

Roosevelt to Marvin H. McIntyre, Assistant Secretary to the President

Washington, January 14, 1936

Memo for Mac: Will you tell him that I cannot take any position on this Bill and suggest that he check with the Secretary of State and the Secretary of Commerce?[1]

F.D.R.

[OF 614-A:T]

[1] Roosevelt here referred to a memorandum from McIntyre of Jan. 10, 1936 (OF 614-A), enclosing a typed copy of a bill introduced in the previous session by Rep. John R. Mitchell, H.R. 7838, "to promote the foreign trade of the United States, to authorize the creation of foreign trade promotion corporations, and for other purposes." The bill would have created a government board to set up exhibits or trade marts in foreign countries, showing American-made goods, with provision for financing sale of the goods. McIntyre said he had promised Mitchell he would call the bill to the President's attention; Mitchell said that in the previous session "he had approval all along the line." The bill had not, however, been reported in the 1935 session, and a similar bill, H.R. 11949, introduced by Mitchell on March 20, 1936, also died in committee (*Cong. Rec.,* vol. 79, pp. 6746, 14347; vol. 80, p. 4145).

Roosevelt to Frederick H. Allen, Charleston, South Carolina

[Washington] January 16, 1936

Dear Mr. Allen: Thank you very much for your letter of January 3 in which you set out your views on neutrality. I have found your remarks very interesting and shall pass them along to others interested in this subject.[1]

Sincerely yours,

[OF 1561:CT]

[1] Above. This reply was drafted in the State Department.

Jesse Isidor Straus, Ambassador to France, to Roosevelt

Paris January 20th 1936

Very personal and private

My dear Mr. President—I do not often write you because I realize that you have little time for chatter. For some weeks, however, I have been turning over in my mind the advisability of giving you my impressions of France after 2½ years residence, and visits to about one half of the consular districts, in each of which I had opportunity for conversation with leading industrialists, officials, and representatives of American business, as well, of course, as personal contact with our consular officials. This letter was, in fact drafted over two weeks ago, since which time I have vacillated as to whether I should or should not mail it. The draft was composed after the two year-end sessions of the Chamber of Deputies, at which I listened to the debate on the government's foreign policy. The Government during those debates was under severe, acrimonious, vituperative and unwarranted attack, in many respects for purely personal satisfaction and aggrandisement of the attacker and his party.

One must always remember that, if rumor and innuendo are to be believed, there is little honesty intellectual or moral among the politicians in France. Whether they are as dishonest as is reported, whether most of them are purchasable, as is reported, I can of course not assert. The press is said to be, almost without exception, venal. Italian money is said to flow into some coffers in large amounts, Russian, German &

Japanese into others. The signed articles of comment, criticism and opinion are in many instances said to be yieldful of munificent subsidies to the writers, of whom there are dozens in the many dailies and weeklies published in France. The papers themselves, due to lack of advertising, are in the main unprofitable, and with few exceptions like the *Figaro, Petit Parisien* and *Intransigeant,* whose owners are very rich and who need no subsidies, whatever profit accrues is the result of selling out to some "cause." In the case of the three above mentioned, and perhaps a few others, the owners have their own interests to present. In some cases domestic money is used to forward some political or industrial interest. It is a dirty picture, and as I see it, portends no very brilliant future for France.

Business here is rotten. Prices are high; the franc is overvalued, and though there is a fairish and I think a growing sentiment in favor of devaluation, led by Reynaud, former finance minister, there is also for obvious reasons, a strong opposition to what is realized and admitted to be the only way out. Invisible exports so much needed in France's economy are continuing to decrease. There is a surly attitude towards foreigners; one of injured innocence, strikingly apparent. There is an unwillingness to admit internal error and to seek to correct it. The fêtes, the 1937 exposition and other similar efforts like the establishment of a Bureau of French Information in New York, are the feeble attempts to counteract what seems to me to be a fundamental misconception or misunderstanding of a pernicious anaemia that cannot be cured by application of salves and other external medicaments.

There is constant dread of Germany, no doubt warranted. Fabry[1] the war minister, on the Friday before New Year plead for a temporary increase in military effectives, basing his plea on Germany's 800,000 men under arms against France's 400,000. The Cabinet would have fallen on that question had it not been for Laval's parliamentary sagacity. France's air force is insignificant, poorly equipped and unprepared with modern machines, compared to Germany. Her budget continues unbalanced, and will in my opinion continue so despite the goverment's representations to the contrary, unless they collect taxes in conformity with tax laws. Tax evasion, because of lack of proper audit, dishonest and bribable agents, and general unwillingness on the part of the average Frenchman, rich or moderately so, is, if one can believe what one hears on all sides, widespread. For the coming year it is claimed there will be a small surplus. Expenditures are shown on paper to be reduced to

167

40 billions. I do not believe the figures. They are so confused and confusing, and there is so much finagling, shuffling from one pocket to another, that I doubt whether the treasury itself knows what's what.

The Chamber of Deputies with its' 600 and odd members is a poor looking and bad acting national assembly. The members behave like a lot of naughty children in a nursery. In an important debate the various parties shout at one another, interrupt and revile an opposing speaker, and twice during the closing days of the last session, the chairman left the rostrum, thus recessing the seance until the rough necks calmed themselves in the lobbies, and would let the proceedings continue. There has been a recent movement to cut down by about ⅓ the number of deputies by a redistricting, and proportional representation, but few of them want to let go of their meal tickets. I'm reminded constantly of what my father used to say of our House when he was a member in '93 & '94; that most of our congressmen were country lawyers, that the salary (then $5000) was more than they ever before expected to have, more than they could earn practising law in the "sticks," and they risked their lives to hang on to their jobs. That goes double for these birds. Many of the deputies hold four or five jobs, and I believe that each job, (1) Mayor of their town, (2) Member of the Municipal Council, (3) Member of the General Council, (4) Member of Parliament (5) Member of the Cabinet—has some salary, honorarium or perquisites attached to it. Cumulatively it's a cinch.

From all the above diatribe you may conclude that I'm depressed. Not personally, but for France's future. This job is fascinatingly interesting and instructive—the latter largely in what not to do politically, financially or industrially. There is a lack of courageous, vital, disinterested, resourceful and imaginative leadership. Where we would have landed in 1933 under similar political direction is too painful to contemplate. They have a vague feeling here that as we pull out of the "crise," as they call it, we'll help them to pull out. I don't believe it. They need a Franklin D. as surgeon and everyone admits there ain't none in sight.

The atmosphere in Paris and in France is doleful. They are looking for a miracle to happen, but they have no miracle man. The same old political hacks revolve in different jobs in successive cabinets, many of them not knowing what it's all about, like Regnier,[2] for instance, the present finance minister, who is said recently to have been forbidden to open his mouth in Parliament until he has submitted his remarks to Laval and the Banque de France. Even in the shops and on the streets one observes a lackadaisicalness and absence of snap or élan. The police, the shop attendants, the street sweepers, the soldiers, the mechanics one employs, building laborers—they've all been stung by a wasp from the same hive.

What does the future hold in store for France? It's anyone's guess. The French still proclaim their inventiveness, their ingenuity, their artistic sense, (you should have seen the annual exhibition of paintings at the Grand Palais) and their leadership in this, that and the other. They're enveloped in a fog of fear of Germany, and they are justified. Whether they will end up as vassals, or whether they can form some kind of effective military coalition—who knows. Something is bound to happen in the next 10, 15 or 25 years, unless they can by the introduction of new blood, not only increase, but change the stature & character and mental make-up of the population.

All of the foregoing may be of no value to you whatsoever; may be utter drivel—but I had it on my chest and I had to get it off.

My best wishes to you and yours for a perfect '36. All the reports from home are cheery and hopeful—due to you.

Sincerely & cordially—

Jesse Isidor Straus

P.S. Since writing the above, for the length of which I apologise, I must now "extend my remarks." Some days ago there appeared in the London *Post* the first of a series of articles the rights to which for France had been secured by the Paris *Figaro*. I was shocked at what appeared to me to be excessively ill-advised and in bad taste. (I enclose the article)[3] In speaking to a British friend she agreed with me, and wrote to a mutual friend of ours, a London barrister, who is an intimate friend of Lord Tyrrel's, former British Ambassador to France, and who is furthermore very much in the political know. His reply arrived this evening, and I am enclosing it, thinking it may be of interest to you.[4]

I am also enclosing the daily "review of the press" prepared in the office of First Secretary Tuck[5] in charge of press relations &c, which summarizes the opinions of the leading political writers yesterday & today.

On re-reading the foregoing I am fearful that I may give you a false impression of my mental state. Personally my relations with French officialdom and with my diplomatic colleagues are most pleasant and agreeable. Also my wife's and my relations with French and American unofficial circles. As you might say "We're having a grand time!"[6]

Three enclosures—

1—Letter from British friend

2—Resumé of Paris press

3—Article from *Morning Post*

[PSF:France:AS]

[1] Jean Fabry.

[2] Marcel Régnier, reappointed Finance Minister Jan. 24, 1936.

[3] The article, unsigned, from the Jan. 16, 1936, issue of the *Morning Post*, was a review of British foreign policy from the Ethiopian crisis on; it was strongly critical of the government for supporting the Hoare-Laval proposal. (The *Post* was a "high Tory" paper.)

[4] This autograph letter of six sheets, addressed to "Dear Mrs. Charlton," dated Jan. 18, 1936, is incomplete and the writer has not been identified.

[5] S. Pinkney Tuck, first secretary of the Paris Embassy.

[6] In his reply of Feb. 13, 1936 (*Personal Letters, 1928–1945*, I, 555–556), Roosevelt said the "whole European panorama" seemed blacker than at any time in his life.

Cordell Hull, Secretary of State, to Roosevelt

Washington [January 22, 1936][1]

Memorandum for the President: I am informed that the House Committee on Foreign Affairs this morning adopted the following amendment to the pending Pittman-McReynolds neutrality bill:

(g) No American republic shall be considered a belligerent or a belligerent country or nation within the meaning of this act if such Republic is engaged in war against any country not an American Republic.

It is believed that this provision would except from the operation of the Act each and all of the 21 Latin American countries. I am of opinion that this amendment contains language about as desirable as could well be selected, in the light of all phases of the situation. This amendment, as stated makes an *exception*[2] of the Latin American nations from the operation of the act. Other proposed drafts would make a *reservation* as to the policy of our Government, such as the following draft of the original purposes of the Monroe Doctrine:

Nothing in this Act shall be construed as an abandonment or abridgment of the policy of the Government of the United States to oppose the acquisition or control of additional territory in this hemisphere by any non-American power, or the encroachment of any non-American power upon the political independence of any American state.

I think the former provision as adopted by the House Committee this morning, which by the way was framed by Mr. Hackworth, if my information is correct, is much more preferable of the two drafts.

It would seem to me that the draft which was to-day made an amendment to the McReynolds bill, as above stated, would serve every purpose in connection with neutrality legislation and policies that a recital of the Monroe Doctrine itself would serve, while avoiding the misunderstanding and controversy which the latter might create in Latin America.[3]

Hull

[PSF:Neutrality:TS]

[1] A supplied date derived from a statement in the New York *Times,* Jan. 23, 1936, p. 11.
[2] Italics, here and below, indicate underscoring.
[3] See Hull, *Memoirs,* I, 464ff.

R. Walton Moore, Assistant Secretary of State, to Roosevelt

Washington, January 23, 1936

Dear Mr. President: I think you may like to see the enclosed letter from Mr. Cudahy.[1]

With reference to the proposed neutrality legislation,[2] I trust that the House Committee may this week, and perhaps even today, report the bill without any very objectionable amendments, and that there will not be very much delay in the Senate Committee acting unless it should determine to have open hearings and permit people entertaining all sorts of views to appear. On the basis of what has occurred in the Senate hearings, which Secretary Hull and I have regularly attended, I incline to believe that the Committee will reach fairly satisfactory conclusions. The Chairman, Senator Pittman, anticipates a good deal of a struggle, but he appears to be likewise hopeful. The Senators with whom we have had most of the talking across the table are Borah, who I believe is going to support the bill in most of its features, and Johnson, who does not seem to be able to get rid of the idea that in some sort of fashion, if enacted, it might tend to link us up with the League of Nations. You know how extreme is his hostility to the League. He has, however, softened a little, and yesterday said that he expected to come to the State Department and discuss one feature of the measure. There has been a good deal of discussion of the bearing of the Italian treaty of 1871 on our domestic legislation, but I rather think that the majority of the Committee takes the view of the Department that if the pending bill becomes a law it will not breach any provision of the treaty. But there are treaties with other nations which would be breached by such legislation, and what the Department is now doing is to try to have those treaties modified so as to except from their operation any legislation that Congress may enact for the purpose of maintaining our neutrality in any war that may occur. The Secretary and I go before the Senate Committee again tomorrow, and that session may wind up the presentation of what is called the State Department testimony. Your talk with Senator Pittman seems to have put him in a better frame of mind.[3]

Thomas, of Utah, who is regarded as one of the very able members of the Senate Committee, has introduced a bill proposing to extend the present legislation for a period, so as to give more time for considering the pending bill, but we have urged that there is an insistent public demand for legislation, and Senator Pittman told me yesterday that he will talk with Senator Thomas, and does not think the latter will urge his proposal.[4]

There has developed very considerable opposition to the bill by the hyphenated Italians in this country, which evidently disturbs some members of the Senate and House. Yesterday Senator Wagner spoke of the desire of such people in New York to be heard, but agreed with me, in talking privately, that this Italian propaganda effort could be easily paralleled by having negroes in Harlem and elsewhere asking that the bill include a declaration that Italy is an aggressor nation. You can easily imagine how the Italian effort was propagated. I haven't the slightest doubt that the Italian Embassy could give us the whole story.[5]

Yours very sincerely,

R. Walton Moore

[*Notation*:A:Tully] Missy to thank for & return letter from Mr Cudahy—
[OF 1561:TS]

[1] Jan. 3, 1936 (Moore Papers), expressing interest in the neutrality debate and wishing he were in Washington to be nearer the scene of events.

[2] Discussed above.
[3] On Jan. 21, 1936 (PPF 1-0).
[4] Thomas introduced S.J.R. 198 on Jan. 16, 1936 (*Cong. Rec.,* vol. 80, p. 462).
[5] See below.

Marvin H. McIntyre, Secretary to the President, to Roosevelt

Washington, 1/23/36, 1:30 P

Mr. McIntyre dictated the following Memo for the President:

You have a memo on your desk about Congr. Lambeth. I told him there was no possibility of you seeing him right away. I promised him that if possible you would talk to him on the 'phone at 2 o'clock.

Right after that, Congr. Lambeth 'phoned again and said:

Some of our Democrats on the Committee (Foreign Affairs) wavered this morning and supported a motion by Tinkham of Mass.[1] All the Republicans are lined up against us.

I have been in touch with Sec. Hull and Judge Moore and I think I know their views. There are 4 or 5 men wavering and I don't think they see what it means politically and from the standpoint of foreign policy if any of these amendments prevail.

It may be desirable for the President to speak to one or two men on the 'phone and tell them to stand by. We are going to have plenty of fight on the floor, but we should come out of the Committee with a solid front.

When I asked for an appt. originally I knew the situation was bad, but it got so bad this morning that McReynolds and I beat our fists on the table.

I can't mention their names unless I talk to the President, because it might put them in the wrong light—I don't think they are deliberately doing it. Some of them have heavy foreign populations * * * the amendments offered would greatly circumscribe and limit the President's power.[2]

[OF 1561:T]

[1] (George H. Tinkham.) Apparently this was a motion to exempt Italy and Ethiopia from provisions of the pending Pittman-McReynolds Neutrality Bill, an action that would have been all to the advantage of Italy and one that was being urged by certain Italian-American groups. The move was, however, rejected by the committee (New York *Times,* Jan. 24, 1936, p. 4).

[2] The House bill (H.J.R. 422), was reported Jan. 28, 1936 (*Cong. Rec.,* vol. 80, p. 1143); a copy is present (OF 1561). It was reported with revision of section 16, which originally

provided that if the President should find that the neutrality act if applied would contravene treaty provisions in force with other countries, he might negotiate for changes in the treaty. If such negotiations failed he could, "in his discretion," give notice of the termination of the treaty. As revised, this section required him, under similar conditions, to terminate the treaty "in accordance with the terms thereof." The section in question was revised in Roosevelt's hand to change, "he may enter into negotiations . . . for the purpose of effecting such modification of the treaty provisions as may be necessary," to, "he shall enter into negotiations."

An accompanying memorandum by Kannee, Jan. 23, 1936, states that the President had asked him to telephone Hull to ask him to try to straighten the matter out. Kannee said he had read the memorandum (the one here printed) to Hull and that Hull had said he would handle it. See below.

Senator Key Pittman of Nevada to Roosevelt

[Washington] January 23, 1936

My dear Mr. President: I have suggested to the Secretary of State, and to Mr. Moore, the Assistant Secretary, a substitute for Sec. 4 (a) of the Neutrality Bill to read as follows:

Sec. 4. (a) Whenever during any war in which the United States is neutral, the President shall find that the placing of restrictions on the shipment from the United States to belligerent countries of certain articles or materials used in the manufacture of arms, ammunition or implements of war, and fuels, is necessary to the preservation of the peace of the United States, he shall so proclaim, and it shall thereafter be unlawful to export, or attempt to export, or cause to be exported, or sell for export, such articles or materials from any place in the United States to any belligerent country named in the proclamation, or to any neutral country for transshipment to any such belligerent country in excess of a normal amount, in quantity and kind, of exports from the United States to the respective belligerent countries prior to the date of the proclamation, such normal amount to constitute the average of shipments during a previous period of years to be determined by the President: Provided, That no restriction or prohibition imposed under this section shall under any circumstances be applied to foodstuffs or medical or surgical supplies.

It is evident that the purpose of the change is to relieve you of the moral obligation to restrict all of our commerce, with the exception of foodstuffs and medical and surgical supplies, to belligerents.

The section, as at present written in line 8, has this language, "or in the conduct of war." It must be obvious that a military population uses everything that a civil population uses, and therefore, under such language, all commerce to a belligerent country must be considered as used in the conduct of war. The section, in such form, would, in my opinion, be mandatory upon your conscience. The language in the present section which says, "will serve to promote the security and preserve the neutrality of the United States, or to protect the lives and commerce of the nationals of the United States," is also a mandate upon your conscience; and very probably no shipments at all would serve to promote the security and preserve the neutrality of the United States. Such being the case, you would have the mandate to reduce all shipments to normal.

The form in which I have redrafted the section for your consideration does not so strictly limit your discretion. You must find such restrictions are necessary to the preservation of the peace of the United States. That is a definite condition. The other provisions in the bill are too broad; too uncertain and indefinite. The freedom of the seas, as defined by Grotius and other international writers since his time, is not law, but is an expression as to what should be law. We have common law and statutory law. We have no treaties defining the freedom of the seas, or contraband of war. If we resort to the common law, which is based upon accepted customs, then we find that these customs have [not][1] been uniform; that the customs have varied with the radius and power of the navies, and the extent of the conflict. If we resort to the last customs which were established during the World War, we discover that the governments having control of the seas abolished all just conceptions of the freedom of the sea, and designated every article and material of commerce, even including foodstuffs, as contraband of war. When we entered the war, we adopted and promulgated this same law with regard to the freedom of the sea and contraband of war. We may only assert as a neutral our broadest demand for the freedom of the sea. We may, of course, follow the just principle laid down by Grotius and other writers that neutral governments should be disturbed as little as possible by a war being carried on by belligerents. I should say that this will be the opinion adopted by Congress when these issues are submitted.

While we assert this principle, we do it with a full realization that we can only enforce it through acts of war. Our people today are bitterly opposed to our entry into any foreign war in defense of commerce. The section that I have rewritten is not based on the undefined question of neutrality, but is based on peace. You are granted the discretion to restrict our commerce only to the extent that it is necessary to keep us out of war.

The Committee upon my suggestion, and with the approval of the Secretary of State, who was present, struck out paragraph (b) in Sec.

16, page 18 of the bill, because it admitted the abandonment of some of our rights under international law. The Committee added a proviso to Sec. 9 on page 9, taking a part of the language out of said paragraph (b). The proviso is as follows:

"Provided, That the United States reserves and reaffirms its rights under international law as it existed prior to August 1, 1914."

I desire to add to this proviso the following:

"And the issuance of the proclamation provided for in this section shall not be deemed or construed to waive, modify or abandon any of such rights."

This additional language will clearly give to foreign countries notice that our restraint upon our citizens shall not be considered as any grant of right to foreign belligerent governments.

I have taken the liberty to modify your language with regard to American Republics, so that it will read as follows:

I have dropped the word "Republic," as it might be interpreted as excluding Canada.[2]

Sincerely yours,

Key Pittman

[OF 1561:TS]

[1] "Not" has been supplied for what is obviously a typographical omission.

[2] "Your language" presumably refers to a draft by Roosevelt, although none is present. Pittman's typist apparently omitted the revision he here refers to.

R. Walton Moore, Assistant Secretary of State, to Roosevelt

Washington, January 24 [1936]

Dear Mr. President: Attached is the draft of a letter you may think it desirable to send Senator Pittman.[1] It has the Secretary's approval, both of us believing it highly important to show how confidently the Senator is relied on to lead what promises to be a bitter fight.

In order that you may know that our views upon the two points mentioned have been specifically expressed to the Senator, I am handing you a copy of my letter to him of January 24.

Yours very sincerely,

[OF 1561:T]

[1] See below.

[*Enclosure*] R. Walton Moore to Senator Key Pittman of Nevada

[Washington] January 24, 1936

Dear Senator Pittman: I am returning herewith the copy of your letter to the President which you handed me this morning.[1]

It seems to me that it would be better, instead of saying "is necessary to the preservation of the *peace*[2] of the United States" to use some such language as the following: "is necessary to the preservation of the *neutrality* of the United States" as the great purpose of the legislation is to insure our neutrality.

Apparently there is a question as to whether the language you use is sufficiently inclusive, in view of the fact that there are several articles, as for instance automobiles, trucks, tractors and tanks, that are almost as important as fuels in carrying on war. Someone has suggested that the word "munitions" might be used in addition to "articles and materials used in the manufacture of arms, ammunition or implements of war." But about this I am doubtful. As to this point please look at the copy of Attorney General Wickersham's opinion. His definition of munitions may be too broad for your purpose, and, on the other hand, a court might not only condemn its accuracy, but give the term an unduly narrow construction. Of course I recognize the great importance of the question you are considering.

With reference to the point mentioned in the last paragraph of your letter, I think you will wish to bear in mind the fact that not only is Canada a British dominion, but that the British, French and Dutch have possessions to the south of us in this hemisphere.

Yours very sincerely,

[OF 1561:CT]

[1] Jan. 23, 1936, above.
[2] The italicized words in this sentence were underscored in the original.

Roosevelt to Senator Key Pittman of Nevada

[Washington] January 29, 1936

Dear Key: This has reference to your letter to me of January 23 relative to the proposed neutrality legislation.[1] •

I have seen a copy of Mr. Moore's letter to you of January 24,[2] written with Secretary Hull's approval, after you had furnished Moore a copy of your letter to me.

Knowing your familiarity with the subject in all its aspects and having the utmost confidence in your judgment, I am glad to leave to you the determination of the two questions you raise, namely, as to how Section 4 should be amended to meet the general purpose we all have in view, and as to how the countries are to be described that may be exempted from the operation of the Act.[3]

Sincerely yours,

[OF 1561:CT]

[1] Above.

[2] Above.

[3] The House Committee on Foreign Affairs reported H.J.R. 422 on Jan. 28, 1936 (*Cong. Rec.*, vol. 80, p. 1143), but by this time the Senate Foreign Relations Committee was deadlocked over S. 3474. The chief issue was that of empowering the President to embargo materials used for war purposes (other than arms and munitions) and the extent of the authority to be given him to define the kind and quantity of such materials. The impasse was largely a result of the opposition of isolationist groups headed by Senators Johnson and Borah, sentiment in favor of the more drastic Nye-Clark bill (S. 3478), opposition by Italian-American organizations, and criticism by organizations such as the Foreign Policy Association and international lawyers, of whom Edwin M. Borchard and John Bassett Moore were most influential (Hull, *Memoirs*, I, 464–466; New York *Times*, Jan. 30, 1936, p. 13).

Administration leaders thereupon agreed to give up efforts to enact new legislation and decided to try to get agreement on an extension of the 1935 act. The decision was made at a White House conference mentioned by Moore in a letter to Bullitt of Feb. 25, 1936 (Moore Papers). Moore gives no date for this conference but it must have taken place about the end of January. After describing the deadlock on the bill in committee, Moore said: "This being the situation, there was a night conference at the White House, and a decision made to support the passage of a bill extending the life of the present law until May 1, 1937, with an addition pertaining to loans and credits to belligerents, and another addition exempting American Republics from the operation of the law. This was the best that could be done, and it has been done in such a way, I am satisfied, as to minimize the neutrality question as a campaign issue. The President agreed with me on this point."

On February 12, the Senate Foreign Relations Committee reported S.J.R. 198, providing for such extension; this resolution had been introduced by Thomas (Utah) on January 16. A similar bill, H.J.R. 491, was introduced in the House the next day by Kloeb. The Senate bill was debated at length on February 17; it introduced some changes in the 1935 act. That law gave the President an option to extend or not to extend the embargo to new conflicts arising after the initial one; the new version stated that the President "shall . . . extend such embargo." Also, the existing prohibition against the extension of credits or loans to belligerents by the government was extended to private persons, banks, and corporations. The act was not to apply to an American republic at war with a non-American state. H.J.R. 491, with much the same provisions, was debated in the House on February 17 under suspension of the rules, passed (by a vote of 353 to 27), and sent to the Senate. There, Pittman moved that the House bill be considered in lieu of S.J.R. 198 and it was passed February 18, without a record vote (*Cong. Rec.,* vol. 80, pp. 462, 1860, 2013, 2123, 2175–2189, 2239–2253, 2286–2288, 2288–2292, 2292–2306; 49 *Stat.* 1152). On Feb. 29, 1936, Roosevelt issued a proclamation forbidding the export of arms, ammunition, and implements of war to Italy and Ethiopia (*Public Papers,* V, 92–94). See his statement of the same date, below.

Norman H. Davis, Chairman, American Delegation, London Naval Conference, to Roosevelt

London, January 30, 1936

Personal and Confidential

My dear Mr. President: I am pleased to receive your letter of January 14th[1] but cannot account for the delay in my letters to you.

Once it became a foregone conclusion that the Japanese would leave the Conference it was better to have them do so with the full onus upon themselves and with the united rejection by the other Powers of the unreasonable Japanese proposals.

I must say that our relations with the British have improved remarkably since last year. They have stood with us, taking their full share of responsibility without any attempt to pass the buck to us. Whatever tendency there was before to coddle Japan, in the hope of thus placating her, has disappeared. At one time Craigie did want to postpone coming to grips with the fundamental principles raised by Japan, in the hope that we could play along and ultimately get Japan to agree to qualitative limitation. I was convinced that this would be construed by Japan as a weakening on our part, and would only serve to make her sorer than ever once her proposals were rejected, as they inevitably would be. I also felt that any further flirting with the matter would make us look ridiculous. Accordingly, I had a frank talk with my friend Eden, who, by the way, is a real friend of ours. He agreed entirely with my views and overruled Craigie. Monsell, the First Lord of the Admiralty also agreed with me.

We have had some differences recently with the British with regard to the effect which the Japanese withdrawal may have had upon the preliminary understandings which we reached last fall with regard to qualitative limitation as to cruisers, battleships and calibre guns and about which we have cabled fully. This, however, is primarily a difference of view as to approach and will, I am satisfied, be cleared up.

I was at first afraid that when we got into the Four Power discussions, there would be an effort to bring in European political questions but such has not been the case. The only European question so far raised has been between England and France as to the advisability of bringing Germany ultimately into the negotiations. The indications are now that they will compromise on this by dealing with Germany and perhaps Russia in the same way that they do Japan, namely, that if and when the Four Powers reach an agreement, these other Powers will be informed of it and will be invited to adhere before the end of this year. I question whether it will be politically possible for the Japanese Government to become a party to such treaty but the British feel confident that they can get Germany and Russia to accept such a treaty, which will have considerable effect on Japan and that after the Japanese elections next May, the Japanese point of view will change somewhat and that before the end of the year if Great Britain and the United States together approach Japan on the subject, the possibilities are that she will accept or at least that she would not attempt to go counter to the provisions of the treaty or to alter the existing status quo.

When I read your message to Congress[2] and your tribute to dictators with aggressive designs, I wanted to hug you. It was an excellent and wise thing to do.

I was also very proud of your veto of the bonus, although I presume it will be passed over your veto.

I have just read Al Smith's outburst before the Liberty League, which I think was a shameful performance.[3] Of course, the fact is that Al's attitude today is just the same as it was at the time of the convention and before there had been any New Deal legislation whatsoever. From this distance, it seems to me, however, that he will be unable to affect a single vote and that you have been gaining ground of late. Certainly I must say that it seems to me you have acted very wisely and courageously under the circumstances. I am proud of you. Your prestige in Europe is tremendous.

I presume we will be here about two weeks longer because if we can agree we ought to get through very quickly.

With warm regards and best wishes, I am as ever, Sincerely yours,

Norman H. Davis

[PSF:London Naval Conference:TS]

[1] *Personal Letters, 1928–1945,* I, 544–545, saying that Davis' letters of Dec. 20 and 21, 1935, had just been received. He approved his patience in the Conference negotiations "but without any thought as to making concessions as to principle."

180

[2] Jan. 3, 1936, above.

[3] Davis refers to Smith's speech at the American Liberty League annual dinner in Washington on Jan. 25, 1936, in which he attacked the New Deal as socialistic and called for a return of the Democratic party to the principles of its 1932 platform.

Roosevelt to Rabbi Stephen S. Wise, Chairman, United Palestine Appeal, Washington

[Washington] February 1, 1936

Dear Dr. Wise: I am glad to greet the National Conference for Palestine which is meeting in Washington to mobilize American Jewry behind a constructive effort to further the rebuilding of the Jewish homeland in Palestine.

Every American knows of the love of Jews for the land associated with the great beginnings of their history and every Jew must rejoice that this undying loyalty has been crowned by the establishment of a Jewish National Home resting upon the sure foundations of Justice and well-being for all the residents thereof.

The American people which has, by the action of Presidents and a joint resolution of Congress, attested its sympathy with the great purpose of a national Jewish home in Palestine will, I am persuaded, be ready to cooperate generously with the United Palestine Appeal which aims to provide a home for homeless Jews. I confidently hope that the cooperation of the American people will contribute to the further progress of the Holy Land, which, I am sure, will continue to give light and leading to all the world.[1]

Very sincerely yours,

[PPF 601:CT]

[1] Wise was founder of the Zionist Organization of America and had long been president of the American Jewish Congress. The United Palestine Conference was held in Washington, Feb. 1–2, 1936, to raise funds to enable Jews to emigrate to Palestine from Germany and other countries threatened by Nazi anti-Semitism. This message was sent just after Wise and Roosevelt had met at the White House on January 11 following an estrangement of several years. The meeting was arranged by M. Maldwin Fertig, a New York lawyer who had been delegated by the Zionists to secure Roosevelt's message to the conference (Fertig to Roosevelt, Jan. 6, 14, 25, 1936, PPF 601; McIntyre to Roosevelt, Jan. 10, 1936, PPF 3292). Wise describes his meeting with the President in *The Personal Letters of Stephen Wise* (Boston: Beacon Press, 1956), pp. 232–234. On the estrangement between Roosevelt and Wise mentioned above, see *ibid.*, p. 232, n. 7, and the latter's book, *Challenging Years: The Autobiography of Stephen Wise* (New York: Putnam, 1949).

Cordell Hull, Secretary of State, to Roosevelt

Washington, February 1, 1936

Confidential

My dear Mr. President: Upon looking into the matter of the possibility of having the instrument which might result from the deliberations now going on at the Naval Conference at London made in the form of an Executive Agreement, I find that it would be entirely proper for some matters now under discussion there to be incorporated in the form of an Executive Agreement to cover such points as might lie entirely within the executive power to carry out. There are, of course, other points under discussion, control over which would not lie exclusively within the executive power.

My own feeling is that at this stage of the negotiations it is not advisable to take any definite stand with regard to the form in which the final agreements will be drawn up, as any definite indication of a hesitancy to enter into a formal treaty on points upon which agreement might be reached in a form which would correspond to positions we have definitely been in favor of might very easily be misinterpreted as a change of attitude on the part of this Government toward positions we have been maintaining up to the present. The delegation is keeping us currently informed of developments and we are following closely the progress of the negotiations and particularly the suggested drafts of the agreements as the discussion goes forward. Before the treaty is ready to be put into final form, we will thus be in a position to suggest the eventual form into which we would desire the various agreements to be incorporated. We might find it possible and advisable to have those matters coming within the jurisdiction and authority of the Executive to be put in the form of Executive Agreements, leaving the other matters in which Congress also exercises authority to be put in a formal treaty, or we might desire to have all the agreements incorporated in one instrument on the understanding that if it is not possible to present this entire instrument to the Senate for ratification at the present short session that the Executive will undertake to carry out those parts of the treaty which come within your exclusive jurisdiction, such as the notification of building construction and the general exchange of information and any other agreements of a similar character.

If you concur in this method of handling the situation, it will not be necessary to give Mr. Davis any new instructions on the subject. I make this suggestion because, if the matter can be handled here as it develops in a way which would meet with your wishes, we would not have to disturb Mr. Davis in his plan of negotiation at the present time.[1]

Faithfully yours,

Cordell Hull

[*Notation*:A:FDR] File Confidential
[PSF:London Naval Conference:TS]

[1] Japan withdrew from the naval conference on Jan. 15, 1936; see *Foreign Relations, 1936,* I, 35ff. Hull felt that the American delegates should, in future, avoid taking a leading part in conference activities because of the strong sentiment at home against European involvement. He hoped, however, that the four remaining powers could agree to keep tonnage limits at existing levels (Hull to Davis, Jan. 18, 1936, *ibid.,* p. 38).

Norman H. Davis, Chairman, American Delegation, London Naval Conference, to Roosevelt

London, February 3, 1936

Personal and Confidential

My dear Mr. President: In conversation with King Edward on the night of January 28 when he received at Buckingham Palace the heads of the visiting delegations to the funeral of King George, he asked me particularly to tell you that he had been deeply touched by the manifestation of sympathy in the United States over his father's death and also to tell you that you could not have appointed as your personal representative at the funeral anyone that would have been more acceptable.[1]

In referring to a talk which he and I had at the Guildhall Reception only a few days before his father's death, he said, "how little did we know when we last met how soon this great tragedy and sorrow could come." He said he had been particularly impressed at the feeling shown to his father in the United States because his father had never even visited America.

He then abruptly asked me when can the United States and Great Britain get definitely together. I replied that while we were getting closer together, it was not possible to get together by one particular act or agreement; that it was more a matter of the spirit which had to be nurtured; but that two things had happened recently which had done more to bring us together than any agreements could do, namely, the way we had stood together in the Naval Conference and the spontaneous sympathy and sorrow manifested by the American people over the death of his father. He said that was encouraging but that the only hope for us and for the world was to stand together. He then remarked that Great Britain is facing some very difficult problems and situations. He intimated something about his own responsibility. I told him that while I sympathized with him in his deep sorrow and the great responsibility that had fallen upon him, I felt assured that he would discharge it with great credit to himself and with great benefit to his Empire and to the world as a whole. He said it was encouraging to him to have me say that, that his responsibility was indeed a heavy one but fortunately he had three brothers with whom he was very close and who would counsel with him and support him in every possible way. He then said he wanted me to know his brother, the Duke of York, who was standing near and whom he brought into the conversation and to whom he remarked that I was a very good friend and he wanted his brother and me to know each other. After a few moments of general conversation, I said goodnight and left.

As ever, Faithfully yours,

Norman H. Davis

[PSF:Great Britain:TS]

[1] Davis was referring to himself.

William Phillips, Under Secretary of State, to Roosevelt

Washington, February 5, 1936

My dear Mr. President: You will recall that recent telegrams from the Naval Delegation in London have brought up the British proposal for a holiday in the building of 10,000 ton cruisers carrying 8-inch guns and 10,000 ton cruisers mounting 6-inch guns. We have discussed this matter very fully with the Navy Department and have requested and obtained additional information on the subject from the Delegation at London. I am attaching hereto copies of two pertinent telegrams[1] from London on the subject, but I am quoting the last two paragraphs of Mr. Davis' No. 83 of February 3, as this, in my opinion, presents the nucleus of the question:

The question at issue is whether or not a treaty for qualitative limitation is of sufficient value to the United States for it to accept a building holiday in category A and 10,000 ton category B cruisers for a period of years. A decision on this question must be reached without definite assurance from the British either as to the ultimate tonnage of the light surface vessel category or as to the ultimate tonnage of any other category.

In view of the fact that we have eighteen category "A" and nine 10,000 ton category "B" cruisers built or building, Admiral Standley and I agree that we can afford to forego for a period of five or six years further construction of those two types with the treaty reservations, of course, that there is no (repeat no) agreement implied or expressed either to continue the holiday beyond five or six years or to abolish these types, and upon the assumption that a qualitative agreement upon these terms is advantageous, we had been proceeding.[2]

The Navy Department and ourselves have now reached the conclusion that we could very well acquiesce in the naval holiday on 10,000 ton cruisers and also accept the reclassification of light surface vessels, which in effect will be an amalgamation of destroyers and cruisers into one class which would comprise surface vessels from 100 tons to 8,000 tons.

Before communicating with the Delegation, however, I feel that we should have your considered decision in the matter as it is of course a step of rather considerable importance. I am therefore submitting herewith a draft of an instruction to the Delegation in London upon which I would be very grateful to have your comment.

Faithfully yours,

[*Notation*:T] February 6, 1936 Memorandum for the Under Secretary of State: Will you speak to me about this? FDR[3]

[PSF:London Naval Conference:CT]

[1] Only one telegram from London is present: Davis to Hull, Feb. 1, 1936, in reply to Hull's of Jan. 31, 1936 (*Foreign Relations, 1936*, I, 52–53, 53–54). Hull had sent a request of the Navy's General Board for more information on the British proposal for a holiday in the building of 10,000-ton cruisers.

[2] Printed *ibid.*, pp. 55–56.

[3] Phillips saw Roosevelt on Feb. 6, 1936 (PPF 1-0).

[Enclosure] Cordell Hull, Secretary of State, to Norman H. Davis, Chairman, American Delegation, London Naval Conference (draft)

[Washington] February 5, 1936

Your 81, February 1, 7 P.M. and 83, February 3, 10 P.M.

Upon the basis of the information and conditions contained in the above two telegrams, the Navy and State Departments agree that you may proceed with the discussion of a holiday for a period of five or six years in building Category A and 10,000-ton Category B cruisers with the reservation that there is no agreement, express or implied, either to abolish these types or continue the holiday period beyond five or six years.

On the basis of the information there is no objection to the reclassification of light surface vessels proposed by the British as reported in your 81, February 1, 7 P.M.

We are very anxious to receive even proposed tentative drafts of phraseology of provisions for a holiday as well as any other draft proposals as soon as they may be available.[1]

[PSF:London Naval Conference:T]

[1] As sent (*Foreign Relations, 1936*, I, 57–58), the telegram contained the following added paragraph:

"When the foregoing was brought to the attention of the President he approved it. However he asked that your attention and that of Admiral Standley should be called to the fact that by this agreement we would revert in new cruiser construction to 6-inch gun cruisers of less than 8,000 tons displacement. He does not object if the Navy approves reverting to the smaller tonnage type of cruiser, but he points out that any large increase of such type by Great Britain or other powers would have to be matched by us and the total cost of a large number of such ships will be very high in the United States."

Roosevelt to Cordell Hull, Secretary of State

Washington, February 6, 1936

Memorandum for the Secretary of State: You are splendid in what you said to the British Ambassador.[1] Incidentally, I get it from a number of sources in England and Europe that your policy and mine, working toward the long view program of general increase in trade, is beginning to get under their skins and that they are getting heartily sick of mere bilateral agreements. Keep up the good work!

F.D.R.

[OF 20:CT]

---

[1] Roosevelt refers to Hull's memorandum of his talk with Lindsay on Jan. 22, 1936 (*Foreign Relations, 1936,* I, 629–632). Hull had attempted to convince the ambassador that improvement of trade relations through measures such as the reciprocal trade agreements program was essential to the removal of international tensions caused by unemployment and depressed economies in countries like Germany and Italy. If the British did not join in this effort their responsibility would be great. Hull discusses this meeting in his *Memoirs,* I, 520–522; see also his memorandum of Feb. 5, 1936, of another meeting on the same subject in *Foreign Relations, 1936,* I, 633–635.

Roosevelt to John Bassett Moore, New York

[Washington] February 6, 1936

My dear Judge Moore: It is because of our old association at the Columbia Law School[1] and later in Washington that I venture to write to you directly to ask you quite simply and frankly a somewhat personal question. Of course, if you do not feel that it is right for you to answer it, I will perfectly understand.

It has been alleged to me by one who in the past has been reliable that for many years you have been in the service or on the payrolls of, or in receipt of retainers or other emoluments from the Standard Oil Company.[2] This, I am told, does not refer of necessity to the Standard Oil Company of New York or that of New Jersey, but might refer to any one of their many subsidiaries or to other companies controlled or owned by what might be called the Standard Oil group of individuals.

So many stories turn up in Washington, as you know, that I usually take the course of directly asking the person concerned. That is why I hope you will not mind my sending you this letter.

One of these days I shall hope to have the pleasure of seeing you again.[3]

Very sincerely yours,

[OF 1561:CT]

---

[1] Moore was professor of international law and diplomacy at Columbia University when Roosevelt was studying law there (1904–1907).

[2] Roosevelt's information came from a letter Horace G. Knowles, a prominent Wilmington, Delaware, lawyer and publisher, had sent to Mrs. Roosevelt. In his letter of Feb. 3, 1936 (OF 1561), Knowles indicated that he had known Moore all his life. He suggested that Moore's attack on Roosevelt's neutrality policy in his statement to the Senate Foreign Relations Committee on Jan. 29, 1936, might have had some connection with the fact that for twenty-five years he had been counsel for the Standard Oil Company of New Jersey.

[3] Answered Feb. 11, 1936, below.

Roosevelt to Lady Victoria Wester Wemyss, Cannes, France

[Washington] February 8, 1936

My dear Lady Wemyss: I was most happy to receive your kind letter of January fourteenth.[1] It is a pleasure to know that one's efforts for lasting world peace are being watched with interest and appreciation by friends beyond the seas.

I so well remember my delightful association with Lord Wemyss in the war days.

Very sincerely yours,

[PPF 3265:CT]

[1] Roosevelt had known Lady Wemyss and her late husband since the World War when he visited them in London. In her letter (PPF 3265), she expressed her admiration for Roosevelt's "courageous attitude towards the armament trusts." She said her husband had been convinced that the armament manufacturers had had no small part in the outbreak of the Great War. He had attempted to bring a proposal for nationalization of armaments before the Peace Conference but had received no help from the Admiralty and others in authority.

Cordell Hull, Secretary of State, to Roosevelt

Washington, February 10, 1936

My dear Mr. President: Norman Davis called us on the telephone this morning from London and said that as the work of the Naval Conference was developing now it is very possible that within a very short time they would proceed to the drafting of a treaty. He stated that he thought it would be advisable to send a lawyer from the State Department to assist them as legal adviser in the drafting. It seems to me that it probably would be advisable to send one of the Department's legal advisers over for this purpose, particularly in view of your suggestion that the instrument resulting from the Naval Conference be drawn up insofar as possible in the form of an Executive Agreement. The lawyer going from here could be given your instructions along these lines and thus could assist in the effort to follow out your suggestion as far as it may be possible.

As a means of refreshing your memory on the subject, I give here briefly the points upon which agreement has either been already reached or upon which there is likelihood of reaching an agreement:

1. Advance notification and exchange of information with regard to naval construction.

2. Limitation of unit tonnage of capital ships.

3. Agreement on caliber of guns mounted on capital ships.

4. Limitation on unit tonnage of aircraft carriers and guns mounted on aircraft carriers.

5. Suspension of new building for a five or six year period of 10,000 ton cruisers.

6. Establishment of new category of "light surface vessels" including all vessels from 100 tons to 8,000 tons, except certain exempt and auxiliary vessels. Limitation of gun caliber to 6.1 inches on all new construction in this category.

7. Limitation of unit tonnage of new submarines to 2,000 tons.

8. Provision for no building between 10,000 and 20,000 tons (or at least a suspension of building within these limitations for the period of the treaty).

9. A specific "escape clause" in connection with the suspension of building of 10,000 ton cruisers.

10. A general "escape clause" in case any power did not abide by the qualitative limitation to be fixed by the new treaty.

If it should meet with your approval to send a legal expert from the Department, I would suggest that Mr. Jacob A. Metzger, Assistant to the Legal Adviser of the Department of State, be designated for this duty. Mr. Davis further suggested that in order that he be available as soon as possible whoever is ordered to this duty sail from New York on the Steamship *Washington* on Wednesday, February 12. I should be grateful, therefore, to have your comment on this suggestion at your convenience.[1]

Faithfully yours,

Cordell Hull

[*Notation:*AS] CH   OK   FDR
[PSF:London Naval Conference:TS]

---

[1] Richard W. Flournoy, of the Office of the Legal Adviser of the State Department, was sent instead of Metzger (State Department, *London Naval Conference, 1935*, p. 23).

Press Conference, Executive Offices of the White House, February 11, 1936, 4 P.M.

[*Excerpt*] Q: Mr. President, our Canadian clients are asking whether you are likely to invite Canada to participate in the proposed Pan-American Peace Conference?

The President: I don't know. You will have to ask the State Department about that. I think they will probably say "No."

Q: Is anything being done on the Niagara Falls Treaty now?

The President: Not at the present time. There is a lot of correspondence going on about it . . .

Q: Will you issue an invitation to the Conference, or will that be left up to the State Department?

The President: I think we can say now—has the letter been given out?

Q: No.

The President: Well, the first thing to be done is to get the letter. Well, a letter has been signed and the only reason for not saying anything about it at the present time is a matter of courtesy to allow enough time for the letter to be received by all the heads of governments.

Mr. Early: Which is this afternoon.

The President: Steve says it is today.

Q: A letter to the Peace Conference?

The President: To all heads of governments . . .

Q: In the letter coming out today, could you comment on the ideas of the Conference?

The President: No. I think the letter is a story in itself. Don't put too much in one paper.

Q: We would like to be clear on one point: The letter was to be to the heads of the governments. I did not understand that the Conference was for the heads of governments.

The President: You had better see the letter. We are not going beyond the letter at this time.

Q: Have you a copy of it, sir? (Laughter)[1]

[President's Press Conferences:T]

---

[1] The letter of invitation dated Jan. 30, 1936, is printed in *Public Papers*, V, 72–73, with a note by Roosevelt on the reasons for his action. The Inter-American Conference for the Maintenance of Peace was held in Buenos Aires, Dec. 1, to 23, 1936.

John Bassett Moore to Roosevelt

New York, N.Y., February 11, 1936

My dear Mr. President: Your letter of February 6, addressed to 993 Park Avenue, has just come into my hands.[1] While the letter does not so state, your inquiry evidently is prompted by an insinuation from some quarter that my recent statement to the Committee on Foreign Relations concerning the pending so-called "neutrality" bill was influenced by some professional employment, and therefore was not made candidly and in good faith, but with a view to further some private interest.[2] I naturally resent such an insinuation, because it reflects on the motives that have impelled me, at no small sacrifice, to discharge what I deemed to be a service to my country, to which, and to which alone, I owe allegiance.

When I became a Judge of the Permanent Court of International Justice at the beginning of 1922, I went beyond what the statute of the court required, and thereafter refused to take any kind of professional business; and since my resignation from the court in 1928, in order to devote myself to a work supposed to be of some benefit to the world, I have given professional opinions in only two cases, neither of which had the remotest relation to the "neutrality" bill. My position on the pending bill is exactly the same as that which I took on the embargo bill three years ago, when I drew an amendment requiring the application of any embargo to be impartial; and this amendment was, as I am told, unanimously adopted at that time by the Committee on Foreign Affairs of the House and the Committee on Foreign Relations of the Senate.

As I consider the pending bill to be indefensible, I was sorry to be unable to appear in person before the Committee on Foreign Relations. But I wrote my statement at the instance of Senator Johnson, whose course in the present matter, as well as in other matters in which I have had occasion to cooperate with him in the past, has shown how deeply he has the interests of the country at heart. I am sending him a copy of this correspondence for his information.

Your statement that you will perfectly understand, should I not feel that it is right for me to answer your letter, is not fully understood by me. I do not readily conceive how I could leave unanswered a communication from the President of the United States conveying an insinuation as to the motives with which I performed what I felt to be an important public duty.[3]

Very respectfully yours,

John Bassett Moore

[OF 1561:TS]

[1] Above.

[2] Moore's statement opposing the neutrality bill was read to the Foreign Relations Committee on Jan. 29, 1936, by Professor Edwin Borchard of Yale, and appeared in the New York *Times* of Feb. 3, 1936, p. 12. On February 7, Borchard wrote to Assistant Secretary of State R. Walton Moore and referred to reports that the State Department was "quietly checking up on all the international lawyers" who opposed the proposed revisions in the 1935 neutrality law. He protested such activity. The Assistant Secretary replied Feb. 11, 1936, and referred to the contention of the Moore-Borchard group that reliance could safely be placed on international law, and that when the war ended methods would be found for the consideration of the claims of those who had sustained loss and damage.

Moore added: "This being the contention, it is easy to understand how there should have been more or less talk about your well known professional connection with very many claims consequent on the World War." He noted that John Bassett Moore had had long professional relations as a lawyer with the Standard Oil Company of New Jersey and the fact that oil was one of the war materials affected by the pending legislation. He did not imply that either Borchard or Moore was "consciously affected" by this; nevertheless, men were frequently swayed by the bias they received from their various activities (Moore Papers).

[3] An attached memorandum, Roosevelt to McIntyre, Feb. 14, 1936, reads: "Don't you think we can just file this?"

William Phillips, Under Secretary of State, to Roosevelt

Washington, February 12, 1936

Dear Mr. President: I did not fail to communicate with Norman Armour[1] the suggestion which you made to me the other day regarding your visit to Ottawa.

This morning Armour telephoned to me to say that the Governor General is enthusiastic over the idea of your visit and has already written to you to express the hope that you could make a longer stay than you originally contemplated. And, furthermore, Lord Tweedsmuir[2] sees no possible objection to your plan to visit the international section of the river during the afternoon.

Mr. Armour tells me, however, that he has not yet had an opportunity to consult with the Prime Minister, but expects an appointment at an early date. Armour appears a little doubtful as to Mr. King's attitude towards the joint visit to the St. Lawrence, more especially because Mr. Hepburn, the Liberal Prime Minister of Ontario,[3] is apparently definitely opposed to the power development in the international section. However, we shall know his attitude more fully in a few days.[4]

Faithfully yours,

William Phillips

[PSF:Canada:TS]

[1] Norman Armour, a career service officer, had been named minister to Canada on May 29, 1935.
[2] John Buchan, first Baron Tweedsmuir, governor general of Canada.
[3] Mitchell F. Hepburn.
[4] See Phillips to Roosevelt, Feb. 17, 1936, below.

Rabbi Stephen S. Wise, Chairman, United Palestine Appeal, to Roosevelt

New York, Feb. 13, 1936

Dear Mr. President: As chairman of the United Palestine Drive, which is about to be launched pursuant to the resolution adopted at the Convention in Washington a few days ago, I am deeply concerned, together with some of my friends such as Judge Julian Mack, over a telegram which has come from our News Agency to the effect that Consul Ely Palmer has been transferred to Ottawa, and that George Wadsworth has been appointed his successor.[1] If this appointment has not finally been made, may I urge that it be withheld until we may have the opportunity to obtain by cable, and in turn to forward to you, information in addition to that which came to some of us last October. This information caused Judge Mack to write to Mr. Phillips requesting the opportunity of discussing the matter with him or with Secretary Hull if the appointment had not then definitely been made.

We had and have no candidate for the place. As Judge Mack then wrote to Mr. Phillips, we desire only that the American representative at Jerusalem should have an understanding of and a real sympathy with the work of re-establishing the Jewish National Homeland. At the time,

Mr. Phillips advised Judge Mack that the transfer of Mr. Palmer would not take place in the then near future, and that he would remain on in Jerusalem indefinitely. He further stated that "When the question of appointing a successor to Mr. Palmer arises, the fullest possible consideration will be given to all the details in the rather complicated situation existing in Palestine, including of course the one to which you particularly refer in your letter."

The advice that we received in October in regard to Mr. Wadsworth was distinctly to the effect that he did not meet the above requirements.[2]

I am, my dear Mr. President, with most hearty greetings, Yours,

Stephen S. Wise

[OF 1978:TS]

[1] Palmer, who had been consul general at Jerusalem since Nov. 7, 1933, was transferred to Ottawa on Aug. 28, 1935. Wadsworth had been first secretary of the American legation in Bucharest from Aug. 26, 1933; on Aug. 22, 1935, he was made consul general in Bucharest and was transferred to the Jerusalem post on Dec. 10, 1935. He remained there until Nov. 16, 1939.

[2] Answered Feb. 21, 1936, below.

Roosevelt to Charles Lyon Chandler, Corn Exchange National Bank and Trust Company, Philadelphia

[Washington] February 15, 1936

Dear Chandler: Many thanks for that nice note of yours. I am glad to have the quotation from the Poinsett report. The time seems to be excellent for promoting close relations with Latin America.[1]

Always sincerely yours,

[PPF 659:CT]

[1] Chandler, in a letter of Feb. 13, 1936 (PPF 659), had referred to Roosevelt's efforts to promote friendly relations with Latin American countries through multilateral treaties. He noted that the President's idea went back 125 years to Joel Roberts Poinsett, first official United States representative in Buenos Aires. He quoted from Poinsett's report to Secretary of State Monroe of Oct. 24, 1811: "I have suggested to them (the Buenos Aires authorities) as the only means of opposing an effectual barrier to the ambitious views of the European Powers an alliance of all Spanish America engaged in the same cause, or that might under the auspices of such a confederation declare themselves, then to solicit the aid and protection of the United States and make one great simultaneous movement of the whole continent."

Roosevelt to Samuel R. Fuller, Jr., New York

[Washington] February 15, 1936

Memorandum for S. R. Fuller, Jr.: I enclose the three notes for you to bear with you on the trip and I have also sent three letters of which I enclose copies.

F.D.R.

[*Notation*:CT] 3 copies of letters to Dodd, Atherton, and Emmet, also three originals to Dodd, Atherton, and Emmet for him to present.[1]

[PPF 2616:CT]

---

[1] Brief notes of introduction, all dated Feb. 15, 1936, in each of which Roosevelt referred to Fuller as "a very old friend of mine" and asked that arrangements be made to enable him to see certain highly placed people. Fuller and his wife had tea at the White House on March 6 and sailed later in the month. In Europe he had conferences with Schacht, Hitler, Edward VIII, Sir Warren Fisher, Prime Minister Colijn of the Netherlands, and F. H. van Vlissingen, a Dutchman who was president of the International Chamber of Commerce. Fuller took detailed notes of these conversations, held between March 24 and April 13, and sent them to Roosevelt with his report of May 1, 1936 (PPF 2616). He saw Roosevelt briefly in Washington on May 6, 1936.

Representative Maury Maverick of Texas to Roosevelt

Washington, D.C., February 16, 1936

[*Telegram*] The President: Announcement has been made that Neutrality will be taken up Monday[1] under suspension of rules. This is the cruelest type of gag rule and it will leave sore spots that will hurt. It may help in a few districts like New York City, Boston, and San Francisco but it will definitely hurt politically in all agricultural districts. I respectfully request you to consider the grave inadvisability of this and if possible use your influence against it. An ordinary rule will effectuate the purpose without hard feelings.[2]

Maury Maverick, M.C.

[OF 1561:T]

---

[1] February 17.

[2] An attached note, Roosevelt to McIntyre, reads: "MC: Call up Maury Maverick and tell him quite frankly that I cannot and will not take part in legislative procedure.

I think it would be very improper if I did so." Maverick had supported the original bill but opposed the compromise bill to extend the 1935 act; see his remarks, *Cong. Rec.*, vol. 80, pp. 2240–2241.

William Phillips, Under Secretary of State, to Roosevelt

[Washington] February 17, 1936

My dear Mr. President: In accordance with the conclusions reached in our conversation of February 6th,[1] on the subject of the St. Lawrence Waterway Treaty and the Niagara Falls Convention, I called on Senator Pittman on the afternoon of February 13th and acquainted him with the substance of Mr. Walsh's letter to you of January 30th.[2] I pointed out Mr. Walsh's principal recommendations with respect to the proposed conference of Governors and Mayors and to the negotiation of a new treaty, covering both the St. Lawrence and Niagara developments. I also told the Senator of the possibility that Mr. Mackenzie King might not now be anxious to negotiate a new treaty, owing to the political situation in Canada, particularly the well-known positions of Premier Hepburn of Ontario and Premier Taschereau of Quebec.[3] On the other hand, I said that Mr. King, having been personally a strong supporter of the St. Lawrence project, might be willing to discuss it further.

Senator Pittman agreed that it would be best for us to withdraw the two treaties now before the Senate, the Niagara Falls Convention of 1929 and the St. Lawrence Treaty of 1932. He thought that it would be a good plan to say to the Canadian Government that we favored a modification of the two treaties and their combination into one instrument, as well as the appointment of a joint commission for the specific purpose of formulating the terms of the new treaty. Senator Pittman elaborated on the important work which such a commission could accomplish and said that it should be composed on our part—and presumably on the part of the Canadian Government—of an engineer, a traffic man, a power expert, an economist, and representatives of both Governments. He felt that it would be important to take as a basis the speeches and hearings in the Senate on the St. Lawrence Waterway Treaty and prepare answers to all the inquiries made therein in a scientific manner. Such a report, he believed, would be exceedingly helpful when it came to reintroducing the subject in the Senate.

The Senator was opposed to the conference of Governors and Mayors suggested by Mr. Walsh, his thought being that no useful purpose would be served by such a meeting and that it would be a mistake to call it. Finally, he was of the opinion that, in approaching the Canadian Government, we should do so officially in order that there would be a record of the State Department's continued interest in the entire project; he seemed to think that it might not be inappropriate if the fact that representations were being made became known publicly.

I think we are all now agreed that both the St. Lawrence Treaty and the Niagara Falls Convention should be withdrawn from the Senate, and I, therefore, recommend that this be done if we learn that the Canadian Government is prepared to reopen the St. Lawrence negotiations. We are also agreed that it would be desirable now to approach the Canadian authorities with a view to obtaining their reaction to the proposal that the St. Lawrence Waterway project and the Niagara Falls project be combined in a new instrument. With your approval, I shall, therefore, see that necessary instructions to this effect are drafted for the guidance of our Minister at Ottawa. I am inclined to feel that we should first obtain Mr. Mackenzie King's views informally, as this procedure is much more conducive to a full and frank exchange. If he agrees that our suggestion is feasible, there would then probably be no objection to having a formal and public exchange of views between the two governments.[4]

I still question the usefulness of the appointment of a joint commission to negotiate the treaty. It seems to me that the State Department and the Canadian Department of External Affaires are best qualified to do the negotiating of any new instrument. On the other hand, a national committee, appointed after the negotiation of the treaty, might be of immense help to Senator Pittman in coordinating favorable public opinion in this country and possibly in influencing votes in the Senate. Looking at the matter from another angle, would it not be more helpful to have the considered opinion of a national committee which had no part in the negotiation of a treaty rather than the opinion of a joint American-Canadian body?

In these circumstances, I recommend that you give consideration at a later date (after the signature of a new treaty or after we find that a new treaty is not possible at this time) to the appointment of an outstanding Committee, representing all affected interests, such as navigation, power, railways, Atlantic ports, etc., to report on the project. The advantages of having a purely national Committee appointed after a new treaty is signed are obvious.

With regard to the proposed meeting of interested Governors and

Mayors, I think that this is a matter which might advantageously wait upon the results of our informal representations to Mr. Mackenzie King. Should he agree to our proposal and be prepared to enter into negotiations in the near future, it might then be useful to call the suggested meeting, with a view to renewing public interest in areas to be affected by the project. If, on the other hand, he prefers not to proceed with negotiations, you may think it wiser not to hold the meeting.[5]

Faithfully yours,

[OF 156:CT]

[1] At the White House, from 10:45 to 11 A.M. (PPF 1-0).

[2] Frank P. Walsh was chairman of the New York State Power Authority. A file memorandum of Jan. 30, 1936 (OF 156), indicates that Walsh's letter was sent to Phillips Feb. 3, 1936, with Roosevelt's notation: "To speak to me about." The letter was apparently not returned to the White House; according to the memorandum, Walsh suggested that the governors and mayors of states and cities committed to the seaway proposal confer with Roosevelt at an early date to make plans for resubmitting the St. Lawrence Treaty to the Senate, or to present the facts for a new treaty. Walsh conferred with Hull and Phillips about the seaway negotiations on Feb. 17, 1936 (Walsh to Roosevelt, Feb. 25, 1936, OF 156).

[3] Louis A. Taschereau was Premier from 1920 to June 1936 when he and his cabinet resigned.

[4] On this see Armour to Hull, Feb. 26, 1936, in *Foreign Relations, 1936,* I, 838–839. King thought that raising the issue at the time would be embarrassing to him.

[5] Answered Feb. 24, 1936, below.

Mary E. Woolley, President, Mount Holyoke College, to Roosevelt

South Hadley, Massachusetts, February 17, 1936

Dear Mr. President: Realizing how many "freak" letters you must receive, I hesitate to run the risk of adding to them! My excuse must be that I am haunted by a suggestion and am convinced that the only thing to do is to hand it on to the person who can consider whether it has validity.

I have been thinking of the "Truce of God" of the Middle Ages and have wondered whether we of the modern world are not behind the Mediaeval period in that respect. Would it not be possible for the world to agree upon a "Truce" of five or ten years—a truce which would mean a cessation of war and the preparation for wars and as far as that is humanly possible, of intrigues? Such a Truce would give to the world statesmen an opportunity to consider the puzzling questions, which lie at the root of war. I am not an "alarmist" but if in human affairs the important thing is the direction in which one is moving, certainly the present world direction is ominous.

Very often during the months at Geneva in 1932,[1] the remark was made to me by Arthur Henderson and by representatives of other countries: "The United States is in a position to take the lead in world peace as no other country can." Your proposal of a "Parley on Pan-American Peace" which must be a joy to every "world citizen" strengthens my courage to send this letter.

Believe me, with appreciation of what you are doing for the "Good Neighbor Policy,"[2]

Very sincerely yours,

Mary E. Woolley

[PPF 537:TS]

[1] Miss Woolley had been one of the American delegates to the 1932 Disarmament Conference.
[2] Answered Feb. 25, 1936, below.

Press Conference, Executive Offices of the White House, February 18, 1936, 4 P.M.

[*Excerpt*] Q: In view of the passage of the Neutrality Bill by both Houses, are you planning any action on your Executive Order withdrawing protection from Americans traveling abroad?[1]

The President: It has not come to me yet.

Q: That is not included in the Neutrality Bill.

The President: I cannot discuss that until it comes down. Were there any changes? Was the House bill substituted?

Q: I do not think so; it was almost the same.

Q: Can you tell us anything of your talk with Sumner Welles today?

The President: No, just a lot of general matters. Nothing in particular.

Q: Any responses, sir, to your letter to South and Central American Presidents?

The President: I think a few have come in and the State Department is holding them all until they all come in. I suppose it will be some time before they all get up here; I suppose another ten days.

Q: In that connection, is Secretary Hull likely to head the American delegation?

The President: There is no conference yet. You are very, very previous.

[President's Press Conferences:T]

---

[1] The House approved the compromise Neutrality Bill on February 17 and the Senate on February 18. Roosevelt signed it Feb. 29, 1936; see his statement of that date, below.

Norman H. Davis, Chairman, American Delegation, London Naval Conference, to Roosevelt

London, February 18, 1936

My dear Mr. President: I realize, of course, that there are reasons why you should desire to avoid just now raising the question of battleship construction. However, my opinion is that it may be necessary and also expedient to do so before the adjournment of Congress. The British inform us confidentially that they intend to lay down two or three battleships this year and a corresponding number for each of the next four years. If therefore we do not make provision to lay down at least two this year, the first thing we know the British will be way ahead of us and then it will look as if we are building to catch up with the British. It seems to me therefore that once the British announce their building program, which they will probably do within the next thirty days, you would then be justified in asking Congress for an appropriation. While we have now tentatively agreed to increase the age of battleships to twenty-six years, you would have the justification by explaining that even if we should build two battleships a year for the next few years some of our battleships would be thirty years old before their replacements are completed.

As ever, faithfully yours,

Norman H. Davis

[PSF:London Naval Conference:TS]

Norman H. Davis, Chairman, American Delegation, London Naval Conference, to Roosevelt

London, February 18, 1936

My dear Mr. President: As I have explained in recent dispatches, the chief remaining obstacle to naval agreement is the question of German participation. The Anglo-German naval agreement[1] has a hole in it in that while it binds Germany to a maximum fleet of thirty-five percent of the British, it only obligates the Germans to maintain the same types as the British provided there is a general naval agreement limiting types. For the British as well as for the French it is most important to get Germany tied into a general agreement but our French friends, for political and other reasons, wish to trade on the British desire to tie Germany into a general agreement. The danger of the situation is that the Germans and the French are both in a position to hold a hammer over the British, the Germans refusing to go in unless they are original parties to a treaty, and the French refusing to go in if the Germans are original parties. The British, however, are becoming irritated, particularly at the French and I am inclined to believe they will find some way to break the impasse.

The British claim that the French are largely to blame for the growing menace of German rearmament and that it could have been prevented had the French not been so unwise and unreasonable as to refuse to accept the British Draft Disarmament Convention in the spring of 1933, which the Germans had agreed to as a basis for negotiations. The British also point out to the French that they missed another chance to hold Germany in line when they refused to accept the proposal, which Eden brought back from his visit to Hitler a year and a half ago, to limit the German air force to fifty percent of the French, with the result that the situation is now reversed. The British also defend their naval agreement with Germany on the ground that, in view of German air and land rearmament, the military clauses of the Treaty of Versailles had become a fiction and they did not propose to miss the opportunity so offered by the Germans for limiting German naval rearmament. In addition the British claim that this naval agreement was distinctly advantageous to France, which the French admit is true. The crux of the difference between the two of them is that the French want the British to commit themselves so definitely with France for the maintenance of the status quo in Europe as to close the door to any possible appeasement with Germany. The British, on the other hand, feel that while they must increase their own armaments as a protection against Germany, they should not overlook the possibility of exercising a moral influence over Germany to bring about an appeasement which would avert an ultimate war and which is all to the advantage of France as well as themselves. They furthermore contend that the French should know that in the last analysis Great Britain has to defend France, and that the French should realize that it is not in their own interests to have the British so tie themselves up as to leave only the alternative of war.

Unfortunately, nearly all of the political leaders in Europe and even here are now thinking of how best to prepare for the war which they think Germany is going to force upon them and giving no thought to how to avert such a war. Anthony Eden is one of the few who seems to have the vision to realize that while it is necessary to be prepared for any eventuality, it is vitally important to consider constructive ways and means to prevent war. Eden has told me in great confidence that while it is necessary to be well armed in order to exercise any influence over Germany, he is giving considerable thought to what might be done in a big and constructive way to give a sufficient measure of satisfaction to Germany to curb the war spirit and to avert war. He recognizes, however, that a sop will not be sufficient and that it has to be something big and comprehensive. If he should be able to work out such a solution, it would be in connection with the real reduction and limitation in armaments. Eden therefore thinks that a naval agreement is of vital importance, not only in order to avoid a naval race, but also in order that this may help pave the way to subsequent agreements as to land and air armaments. He is accordingly very averse to the French desire to make a naval agreement conditional upon a general political settlement.[2]

With warm regards and best wishes, I am, as ever, Faithfully yours,

Norman H. Davis

[*Notation*:A] file confidential
[PSF:London Naval Conference:TS]

[1] Signed June 18, 1935.
[2] See Phillips to Roosevelt, Feb. 25, 1936, below.

Roosevelt to Cordell Hull, Secretary of State

Washington, February 19, 1936

Memorandum for the Secretary of State: I entirely approve an Executive Order placing these Islands under the Interior Department. Will you speak with the Secretary of the Interior about it and have the necessary Order prepared?[1]

F.D.R.

[OF 6-V:CT]

[1] Roosevelt referred to Howland, Baker, and Jarvis islands in the central Pacific. See his letter to Ickes, May 4, 1936, below.

White House Memorandum

Washington, 2/20 [1936]

[*Excerpt*] 2. Rep. McReynolds 'phoned. Said that Sen. Pittman, he and a member of his Committee, want to be present when the President signs the Neutrality Bill. *No.*[1]

He would like to know whether this can be arranged.

3. Sec. Phillips: The French Govt. has instructed the French Amb. here to make a certain proposal to us with regard to the Naval Conference. Been quite a lot about it in the papers. The Amb. had instructions to take the matter up with the President.

The Amb. does not feel it is necessary and I have discouraged him from doing it.

On the other hand, we are sending a message back to the French Govt., through their Amb., and I have a feeling that I ought to go through the form of letting the President see it, otherwise it would get out that the President didn't know anything about this.

I can do it over the 'phone very well; on the other hand, the President may want to know the whole story as it is rather an intrigue on the part of the French to go over the heads of our delegation in London. What we have to do is the courteous thing, yet get it through our people in London.

I have to send the message over to the French Amb. today.[2]

[OF 203:T]

[1] "No?" is written in what appears to be Early's hand. This memorandum was probably from Early to McIntyre.

[2] Phillips followed this telephone call with a note to the same effect, Feb. 20, 1936, enclosing a proposed cable of instructions to Davis. This cable was approved by the President and sent under date of Feb. 20, 1936 (*Foreign Relations, 1936,* I, 65–67). See Phillips to Roosevelt, Feb. 25, 1936, below.

Roosevelt to Rabbi Stephen S. Wise, New York

[Washington] February 21, 1936

My dear Rabbi Wise: I have received your letter of February 13[1] concerning the appointment of Mr. George Wadsworth as Consul General at Jerusalem and have given it my very careful consideration.

I find, upon consulting with Secretary Hull, that Mr. Wadsworth was not selected for the position of Consul General at Jerusalem until after the fullest possible consideration of the facts available at the time the selection was made. If you have information affecting his suitability for the post I should be very glad indeed to receive it, because Mr. Wadsworth is a career Foreign Service officer who has the full confidence of the Department he serves. He has had twenty years' experience as an officer of the Foreign Service, most of which has been acquired in the Near East where he has served at Beirut, Istanbul, Sofia, Alexandria, Cairo, Teheran, and Bucharest. From 1924 to 1928 he was assigned to the Department of State in the Division of Near Eastern Affairs and was charged with responsibilities in the first instance for matters concerning Palestine.

I realize that there is probably no post in the Foreign Service where an understanding of the background of the situation is more essential and desirable than at Jerusalem and I am anxious that the officer selected for it shall be specially adapted to it. The records of the Department of State indicate that Mr. Wadsworth possesses to an unusual degree the knowledge and qualifications necessary to a successful administration of that post. In view of these facts your letter has been a complete surprise to me, and, unless you are in a position to give me in greater detail your reasons for the objection to Mr. Wadsworth, I am inclined to believe the assignment should stand.[2]

With kindest regards, Faithfully yours,

(S) Franklin D. Roosevelt

[OF 1978:CT]

[1] Above.
[2] Drafted in the State Department.

William C. Bullitt, Ambassador to the Union of Soviet Socialist Republics, to Roosevelt

Moscow, February 22, 1936

Personal and Confidential

Dear Mr. President: In order to spare you a solemn Cook's tour across Europe, I am going to confine this letter to disjointed fragments.[1]

1. London. . . . There is something like a wilful hysteria in London. In order to make sure that the increased military and naval estimates will encounter no opposition, the fear of Germany is being played up deliberately and the most commonplace remark at every lunch and dinner table is to the effect that within three years England will have to choose between making war on Germany or permitting Germany to dominate Czechoslovakia, Austria, Hungary, and Rumania preparatory to an attack on the Soviet Union. Strangely enough, all the old anti-Bolshevik fanatics like Winston Churchill are trumpeting this Bolshevik thesis and are advocating an entente with the Soviet Union!

2. Paris. There is a rising wave of feeling that France should not go to war with Germany to save either Czechoslovakia or the Soviet Union: Hence the stubborn opposition to ratification of the Franco-Soviet Treaty of Mutual Assistance.

Jesse Straus was not in Paris as he had gone to Vienna with poor Mrs. Straus, who is suffering severely from urticaria which is, I believe, a disease that makes one itch.

3. Brussels. I spoke to Van Zeeland, the Belgian Prime Minister, about the matter in which he was interested. He seemed pleased by the few amiable words I uttered and said he quite understood.

Dave and Mrs. Morris were both in prime form and I am sure that you can call on Dave for any campaign work that you may want him to do.

4. Berlin. I stopped in Berlin only between trains and had a talk with Dodd, who is still somewhat under the weather.

As you know, my close friend, Attolico, is now Italian Ambassador in Berlin.[2] He had just come from Rome where he had seen a great deal of Mussolini. I therefore pricked up my ears considerably when he suggested most seriously, as I cabled the Department, that the time was approaching when you might intervene with a "Hoare-Laval proposal with modifications favorable to Italy." I have no doubt that the Foreign Offices of both Britain and France, as well as Mussolini, would be delighted to have you take the onus of proposing such a settlement. The English could then throw up their hands in holy horror and say that you had forced them to accept an immoral compromise. I felt so sure that you would not rise to that bait—and hook—that I did not pursue Attolico's suggestion. But I warn you it was serious and you may hear more of it.

5. Warsaw. I saw a large number of Poles in Warsaw, including Beck, the Foreign Minister, with whom I had a long and intimate conversation. The Poles have not deviated from their determination not to allow a single Russian or German soldier to set foot on Polish soil. But, on the other hand, I gathered from Beck that Poland would offer no resistance, either physical or diplomatic, to a German attack on Czechoslovakia. Beck emphasized the closeness of the relations between Poland and Hungary and I gathered the impression that he would be glad, rather than otherwise, to see Germany control Austria and Bohemia, and to see Hungary walk off with Slovakia, while Poland got "frontier rectifications" in the Teschen district.

Needless to say, all the way from London to Moscow the chief topic of conversation was the dangerous situation of Czechoslovakia. The Czechoslovak position is made somewhat more desperate by the fact that nobody in Europe likes Czechs, to say nothing of Czechesses, whose piano legs and aversion to soap are notorious from one end of the continent to the other.

Cudahy was in Paradise when I told him that D.V. the Auld Sod was his.[3] He is eager to come home to campaign and promises 3,000,000 Polish votes.

6. Moscow. Russia, as usual, is looking up. The improvement in physical conditions is striking even after so short an absence as mine. The people are certainly better fed and clothed than at any time since the Revolution. And the Moscow Street Cleaning Department today puts that of New York to shame. In spite of the perpetual snows, you can see the asphalt on every street.

Litvinov greeted me in an unusually amiable manner. The day of my arrival I had an ordinary tea and movie at my house, and both he and Madame Litvinov, Marshal Budenny,[4] and a host of army officers and government officials turned up to bid me welcome. It means absolutely nothing from the political point of view but it does mean, I believe, that Stalin has told Litvinov to be more polite to this Mission.

Stalin's latest imitation of Le Roi Soleil is to dictate in the field of music and drama. Recently he went to see a modern Soviet opera and a modern ballet which had been praised by the critics as the supreme achievements of the human race. In the ballet Georgians were shown to be comic, in the opera Russians were shown to be drunk. Stalin at once caused ukases to be issued damning all the musicians and producers who have been heralded for the past few years by the Soviet press as demi-gods. The result is that half the artists and musicians in Moscow are engaged in having nervous prostration and the others are trying to imagine how to write and compose in a manner to please Stalin.

7. The Home Front. That osteopath I saw in New York worked so effectively that the pains have left my shoulders and arms and I feel ready for anything in the way of work.

By the time you get this letter I shall be engaged in waiting for that cryptic telegram from you. I warn you that from the 15th of March to the first of April, I shall be at the office each day from 7:30 A.M. forward to open personally all messages.[5]

Bless you and good luck, Yours always,

Bill

[PSF:Russia:TS]

[1] Bullitt, who had been home on leave, returned to Moscow on February 16.
[2] Bernardo Attolico had been director of the Reduction of Armaments section of the League of Nations and for a time ambassador to Russia.
[3] John Cudahy, ambassador to Poland, was transferred to Dublin in May 1937.
[4] Semen M. Budenny had been made a marshal of the Soviet Union the previous year.
[5] Answered March 16, 1936, below.

Roosevelt to William Phillips, Under Secretary of State

Hyde Park, N.Y., February 24, 1936

Memorandum for the Under Secretary of State: If this is satisfactory to the Secretary of State, go ahead along these lines.[1] If the Canadian Government is prepared to reopen negotiations, we can make an announcement to that effect and then withdraw the Treaties. In regard to a National Committee, I suggest that the actual negotiations of the

Treaty or Treaties be conducted by the State Department and the Canadian Department of External Affairs and that while negotiations are in progress a National Committee could simultaneously conduct the study.

Keep me in touch.[2]

F.D.R.

[OF 156:CT]

[1] The reference is to Phillips' letter of Feb. 17, 1936, above. Other correspondence on the proposal to negotiate a new treaty is printed in *Foreign Relations, 1936,* I, 834–846.
[2] See Roosevelt to Pittman, March 9, 1936, below.

Anthony J. Drexel Biddle, Jr., Minister to Norway, to Roosevelt

Oslo, Norway, February 24th, 1936

My dear Mr. President: I greatly appreciate your kind letter of January 8th, in acknowledgement of my cable of congratulations[1] on your magnificent speech at the opening of Congress. Realising how occupied you are, I was greatly touched by your writing me.

I cannot tell you how delighted I am over the current announcement of the Supreme Court's decision favoring the T.V.A. This is indeed a great victory, and I congratulate you from the bottom of my heart.

Margaret and I are so proud and happy that Philadelphia has been selected for the Democratic Convention, and I have already written to the Secretary of State requesting leave of absence, in order to be in Philadelphia at that time. For we want to do everything in our power towards helping to make the Convention a success.

During the past few months, I have been extremely interested in conversations with the leaders of the Norwegian Government Party, and in particular with Mr. Halvdan Koht, Minister for Foreign Affairs, about you and your policies. Only last night, at dinner here in the Legation, Mr. Koht told me that he and his associates in the Government, followed each and every move of yours with interest and study.

May I now take this opportunity to congratulate you heartily upon your highly constructive conception of a conference between the United States and the Latin American States, towards furthering peace in our own hemisphere. This is a tremendous step forward, a move of the most vital importance, which commands the attention and respect of the whole world.

The conservative press of Norway, which I feel has in the past been "Republican-minded," is now showing signs of appreciating the bigness, fairness, and humanitarianism of your policies. Special writers are more and more contributing articles favorably bearing on various phases of your program—special attention is given the trade agreement policy. For example, on March 22nd, *Morgenbladet* (regarded as Norway's most conservative newspaper) carried a signed article contributed by a well informed Oslo business man. This article referred most complimentarily to the trade agreement policy, and deals at some length with its far reaching benefits and its value towards creating a more solid and lasting basis for world peace. Especially it refers to the blessings acruable therefrom to Norway, a country limited industrially, and in its foreign trade. Since appearance of this article, I have talked with the writer. He said that he intended this article to be forwarded to Norwegian newspapers in the United States, in order to inform the readers of such publications of your Administration's fairness to their former native land, or country of their ancestors, as the case may be. I assure you, that I have been doing everything possible to encourage public expression of such views, for I myself appreciate the constructive value to the world at large in such a broad policy. The writer further maintains, that because of the love which every naturalised American citizen still carries for his native country, they will appreciate in the best interests thereof, the significance of our Administration's policy, as against the policy of a tariff wall.

It might interest you furthermore, to learn that Mr. Carl Hambro, President of the Storting, whom you so graciously received during his visit to America,[2] to a large extent dictates the *Morgenbladet's* policy, and frequently contributes to its editorials. Mr. Hambro has on many occasions warmly expressed his appreciation of your having received him. At the time of his departure for the United States, he was known to hold decided views as regards the relative merits of the policies of the political parties at home. In this regard it is significant that he is leader of the ultra-conservative group in the Storting. Hence it is interesting that his visit with you has resulted in moderating materially his previous antipathy towards our Party in general. I am convinced that his visit with you was not only an honor and pleasure to him, but also a highly constructive move in the interests of our two countries.

As of possible further interest to you, I have learned, in conversation with several special writers, well informed on the relations between the United States and Norway, that there has been considerable discussion here lately, to the effect, that yours and Secretary Hull's efforts to reach a more lasting world peace, by encouraging nations to enter into reciprocal trade pacts, sooner or later will result in your both receiving the Nobel Peace Prize.[3]

Oslo has recently been swarming with bankers from New York, Stockholm, London, and Paris. They have been bidding for the conversion of the Norwegian 6% dollar loan. Lazard Frères, of New York, London, and Paris, succeeded in getting the business with a high bid of 97⅜, and will shortly issue the bonds on a 4½% basis.

Each banker's eagerness to acquire the business, was most apparent. If this conversion goes over "big," there will probably be an additional amount of 30 million dollars in bonds, open for conversion this year. While the prospect of this additional business is undoubtedly partly responsible for the bankers' keenness for the current conversion, they have at the same time substantially demonstrated their interest and faith in this country.

Between conversations with these visiting bankers, and with Norwegian shipowners, who, through their many business connections throughout the world, are necessarily well informed in international affairs, I have learned much interesting information bearing on the international situation. Therefore, for your information, I take the liberty of setting forth an outline of what I have heard, in memorandum form, and am attaching it hereto.

Margaret joins me in affectionate regards, and every good wish for continued success and happiness.[4]

Faithfully yours,

Tony Biddle Jr.

[PSF:Norway:TS]

[1] Neither is present.

[2] On Nov. 19, 1935 (PPF 1-0).

[3] Hull eventually received the Nobel Prize for Peace in 1945, after he had left the State Department.

[4] Roosevelt replied March 12, 1936 (*Personal Letters, 1928–1945,* I, 569), that he was glad "to have the picture of the European scene" as Biddle saw it.

[*Enclosure*] Anthony J. Drexel Biddle, Jr. to Roosevelt

Memorandum

February 27th, 1936

General Picture. Realignment of major Powers taking place. At the present moment, the scene on this side of the Atlantic may be described as a mad scramble for position, in view of the major regroupings.

In order to forestall further ambitious attempts on the part of the expansionists, Germany, Japan, and Italy, it would appear, for the time being at any rate, that England and France might look to Russia for the balance of power. Pending such re-groupings' taking definite form, Poland is on the fence as regards definite position. In her desire to take a position in the realignments from which she can derive the greatest advantages, she has remained to date, noncommittal. It is considered that, so far she has been able to maintain, so-to-speak, an even balance between Russia and Germany. Though it is felt by foes of the Soviet here that Poland would naturally join the Italo-German group, were it to take definite form, nevertheless, the keenest, and less prejudiced observers believe that Poland must eventually fall in line with the British-French-Soviet combination.

Several nights ago, the Soviet Minister told me confidentially, that it was essential for his country to arm to the teeth, even though it was extremely expensive for them at this time, for they fully recognized the combined threat of Germany on one side, and Japan on the other.

Threat of Germany's Armed Position. As regards the recognized threat of Germany's heavily armed position, England's and Russia's recently announced armament programs, and England's recent friendly gestures to Russia, together with the pending ratification of the Franco-Soviet pact, have had a dampening effect on German confidence. It has given inner Government circles a jolt, and forced them to realize that others could and would match their armed strength. Perhaps it has caused even the Führer to stop and reconsider his position. In the early stages of his deliberate steps to rearm Germany on a gigantic scale, he was known to have remarked to a friend of the Press, that public opinion was bankrupt—that in the final analysis, effective collective action was out of the question. Even before the recent announcement of the British and Russian armament programs, the German General Staff, exemplified by their strongest and ablest member, General von Fritsch,[1] was recognized by foreign observers as the most conservative element in Germany, and probably the one element which does not believe in seeking trouble at this time. It is felt, the General Staff do not consider that Germany will be ready to fight for at least two years. On the other hand, there are those here who feel that Germany's huge investment in armament was not necessarily effected for the purpose of actually waging war, but to augment her trading position when the Government might deem it the psychological moment to insist on territory for expansion, or return of colonies.

Franco-Soviet Pact. Even amongst these Frenchmen who favor the Soviet pact, there is a certain apprehension over closer dealings with the Soviet, due to past disagreeable experience; encountered not only by France, but also by other nations. They feel that there is no real assurance that the Soviet will refrain from repeating her subversive propaganda through the same old channels, the Third International. Hence, future closer dealings would best be handled with "asbestos gloves."

Italo-Ethiopian Conflict. From shipowners here, and visiting bankers, I learn the following information: It is confidently expected that these hostilities will have come to a close by early fall.[2] England will have acquitted herself gracefully in the eyes of the black races of her Empire, as the protector of their rights, without so materially assisting the Ethiopians as to lead to the defeat of the white forces. It is felt that at the close of the conflict, England will accommodate Italy with refinancing in return for certain revisions in Italian Mediterranean bases which are today deemed a threat to British trade routes in that area.

Peace Will Be Expensive. It is felt here now, that to maintain peace in Europe will be expensive to those powers possessing credit and natural resources, whether the demands of the expansionist countries will have to be met eventually, or not. These countries will ultimately require refinancing, not only for the territories within their present borders, but also for any territories which might accrue to them through possible future trading. On the one hand, Germany will eventually require refinancing on an extensive scale, as will Italy; win or lose. Europe cannot afford to have a bankrupt Germany, or a bankrupt Italy.

French Devaluation in Prospect. As regards the political situation in France, and its bearing on eventual devaluation, it is confidently expected by several of the well informed continental bankers, recently here, that a 25% devaluation in the French franc will take place under the guidance of M. Paul Reynaud (several times Minister of Finance) shortly after the next election in the latter half of April or early May.[3] In such event, Switzerland and Holland will follow suit. As to what effect on forestalling devaluation will be caused by the recent 40 million pound sterling loan from London to Paris, Norwegian observers feel that, whereas it will temporarily alleviate the situation, it will not indefinitely stave off devaluation.

Moreover, in pointing to the clause in the loan providing for repayment in sterling, they observe that repayment on such basis in the event of a depreciated franc would create considerable difficulty in France.

British Political Picture. As regards the British political picture, it is expected here that Mr. Winston Churchill will eventually replace Mr. Baldwin.[4]

[PSF:Norway:T]

[1] Baron Werner von Fritsch was chief of staff of the German Army.

[2] The war ended with the fall of Addis Ababa on May 5, 1936, and Italy declared Ethiopia part of her empire on the next day.

[3] France devalued the franc on Sept. 25, 1936; see press conference of that date, below.

[4] Baldwin was succeeded by Neville Chamberlain on May 28, 1937.

Norman H. Davis, Chairman, American Delegation, London Naval Conference, to Roosevelt

London, February 24, 1936

My dear Mr. President: At a luncheon on Friday I had a rather interesting talk with Grandi[1] (with whom I have been on very friendly terms for several years) which I think will be of interest to you. Grandi, who was called to Rome recently for a meeting of the Council of State, showed concern about what the present situation may lead to. He intimated that he is not particularly in Mussolini's good graces. Being more of a Liberal, he realizes the dangers of dictatorship, but he is nevertheless a patriot and loyal to Mussolini. He said that he knew Mussolini most intimately and for that reason he was quite concerned about the future; that while Mussolini is not a statesman, he said that he is essentially a genius and a poet which leads him to do things at times which may not be good statesmanship. He said that he was particularly anxious to have the Abyssinian question settled quickly because otherwise it would lead to disastrous results. In substance he says that Mussolini will not give in and that he can see three possible

213

alternatives: first, combine with Germany; second, lead a Communist revolution in Italy, or third, a 50–50 settlement of the Abyssinian question. Either of the first two, as Grandi sees it, would be disastrous and the only hope is the 50–50 settlement. Grandi said that in his opinion such a settlement should be brought about by direct negotiations between England and Italy without the intervention of France but with the full cooperation of the League itself and that he felt it was greatly in the interests of Italy to remain in the League and to help strengthen the League.

As I cabled to Washington, Grandi also told me he doubted if Mussolini would commit himself definitely to a naval agreement until the Abyssinian question is settled.[2] My distinct impression was that Grandi and possibly Mussolini are most eager for a settlement but that if he should settle the naval question without any quid pro quo it would be difficult to explain to the Italian people and he would be giving up a card that might help him bring about a general settlement.

With best wishes, I am, as ever, Faithfully yours,

Norman H. Davis

[PSF:London Naval Conference:TS]

[1] Dino Grandi, Italian ambassador to Great Britain, 1932–1939.
[2] Davis to Hull, Feb. 21, 1936, printed in *Foreign Relations, 1936,* I, 69–70.

Roosevelt to Mary E. Woolley, President, Mount Holyoke College, South Hadley, Massachusetts

[Washington] February 25, 1936

My dear Dr. Woolley: I have received and thank you for your letter of February seventeenth, in which you suggest the possibility of a world "truce" for a period of five or ten years, such a truce as would give to statesmen an opportunity to consider the complicated questions which lie at the root of war.[1]

Your suggestion is extremely interesting. I shall see that it is brought to the attention of the Secretary of State. As you know, I am hopeful that the nations in this hemisphere can work out their destinies in peace, and I am trying to use every effective means to keep this ideal actively and constructively in the thoughts of the Governments and peoples of these nations.

With genuine appreciation of your interest, I am, my dear Dr. Woolley,

Very sincerely yours,

[PPF 537:CT]

[1] Above.

William Phillips, Under Secretary of State, to Roosevelt

Washington, February 25, 1936

Dear Mr. President: May I call your attention to the telegram just
received from Norman Davis?[1] You will note that the British have asked
Davis whether, if France and Italy continue to oppose conditions and
to put an impossible price on their adherence, we would be disposed
to enter into a naval agreement with Great Britain and Germany to
which the other powers would be invited to adhere. To this Davis
said that he was inclined to believe that there might be serious objections.

The British then suggested that, if we object to an American Anglo-
German treaty, we might be willing to sign an Anglo-American agreement, thus permitting England to undertake bilateral agreements with
Germany and possibly with France and thereafter that, acting together,
the British and American Governments might be able to bring Japan
into such an agreement.

Davis has very properly held that it would be better to have one treaty,
to which everyone would be invited to adhere, instead of a series of
bilateral agreements. Thereupon he has suggested the drafting of a naval
treaty to be initialed by Great Britain and the United States and then,
by an exchange of notes, agree to invite the other naval powers to adhere.
If, therefore, we follow Davis' thought in this connection, we would find
ourselves, together with Great Britain, obliged to appeal to the principal
naval powers to forget their political difficulties and differences and sign
up with us.

We in the Department feel that this might be unfortunate and that
it might be wiser for us to throw the burden on the British Government,
as the inviting power to the conference, to obtain, if she can, the other
signatures. With this in mind, we have drafted a brief instruction to

215

London, which expresses our viewpoint, but which we naturally shall not send without your approval.

Faithfully yours,

William Phillips

[*Notation*:A] Seen and approved by the President and draft telegram also approved by the President Feb 25 1936[2]

[PSF:London Naval Conference:TS]

---

[1] Davis to Hull, Feb. 25, 1936, in *Foreign Relations, 1936*, I, 71–72.
[2] *Ibid.,* pp. 72–73.

Grenville T. Emmet, Minister to The Netherlands, to Roosevelt

The Hague, Netherlands, February 26, 1936

My dear Mr. President: I am sending you some data on the Dutch origin of the Roosevelt family which I hope will interest you.

About six weeks ago an article appeared in the London *Telegraph* concerning the Dutch ancestry of the Roosevelts in Holland. I enclose you the article in question and also a photograph of the overmantel in the town hall of Vossemeer, in Zeeland, where the Roosevelt coat of arms appears and where also they point out a house in which one of your ancestors lived. The photograph is quite clear and you will see on it the arms of a number of well-known Dutch families of the present day; Snouck Hurgronje, for instance, whose arms appear twice, once on each side of the picture, is one of the best known Dutch families. Arnold Snouck Hurgronje is at present Secretary General of the Ministry of Foreign Affairs. His position somewhat resembles that held by Bill Phillips in our State Department.

I also enclose you a photograph of the Roosevelt coat of arms by itself; I wonder if it is correct. Also a picture of the town hall at Vossemeer, bearing date of Anno 1775, in which the Roosevelt arms appear and also a photograph of the house in Vossemeer supposed to have been occupied by one of your ancestors. It occurred to me that these might be of interest to some genealogically-minded member of the family, and so I am sending them on to you. Also a copy of an article appearing in the Dutch paper, *De Telegraaf,* of January 1, 1936, in which there is an account of the fame your family name has brought to Vossemeer, which I have had translated and send to you herewith.

The activities of armament building and war preparation continue unabated in Europe. I have kept the State Department fully advised as to what is happening in this country which is, of course, of significance in view of its geographical position. Belgium and France, in cooperation, have reinforced and built up their fortifications to a point where Germany, if she ever went in the same direction as she did in 1914, would probably be forced to go across that narrow peninsula-shaped point of Holland comprising a portion of the Province of Limburg. At one part it is only about three miles wide. The result has been that Holland has commenced with energy and speed to build up and reinforce its defenses so that it will be in a position to contest the advance of any invader. Neither the newspapers nor the public officials make any secret of it. In view of what Germany has done in building up her army and what Belgium in connection with France is doing in building up her army and strengthening her defenses, the Dutch frankly say that they are going to do the same. In addition to the annual budgetary allowance for the army, the Second Chamber recently passed a bill authorizing the expenditure of fifty-three million florins, a large sum for this country, for the strengthening and upbuilding of the army and navy. A considerable portion of it will be used in the Dutch East Indies. Already seven bombing planes for service in Dutch India have been ordered from the Glenn Martin Company in the United States, and it is expected that orders for about twenty–thirty more will be placed in the next year or so.

With the danger signal flying in the shape of military preparations in the making on all sides, and of course England is in it on a big scale, you naturally wonder where the trouble is going to begin, and when. That is not so easy to put your finger on at the moment. I think one of the things for which you must give Hitler credit (and there are not many in that category) is that he has perceptibly eased the anti-French feeling in Germany. In some way he has turned the nation's swivel, and the front of bitter German hatred of France, which always was so much in evidence, seems to have been turned in some other direction. It seems to me that fear of Russia is more pronounced. My feeling is that Hitler really has not at the moment deep designs against the French. He is more concerned with what Russia and Poland are doing and also Czechoslovakia. Perhaps, to be fair, one should give Laval some credit for this too. Now that the latter is out,[1] there may be a change, partic-

217

ularly as the Franco-Soviet Pact is up for debate in France and is backed by Flandin.

Accept my heartiest congratulations on the fine move you made in Pan-America.[2] It came at a most opportune time and will have good results. On Washington's birthday I had, as usual, a luncheon for all the Pan-American diplomats in service here, including two Judges from the Court of International Justice—from Salvador and Colombia. Everyone spoke in the highest terms of what you have done towards solidifying and unifying Pan-American relations and setting an example to the rest of the world for correct behavior in international affairs. Your call for a conference to consolidate peace in North and South America met with an enthusiastic response.

The Italian-Ethiopian war seems to be going more in favor of Italy. Taliani, the Italian Minister here, whom I see a good deal, tells me that he thinks the League of Nations is over and that England is in an embarrassing situation. Taliani is undoubtedly very clever. He has just written an excellent book on Russia,—notes of a diary he kept when he was on post in Russia at the time of the revolution. It had a great success in Italy and France and will be translated into English. I will send you a copy when it comes out.[3]

As I told you when I saw you in Washington last November, I want to do what I can to help this summer and I expect to come to America for six weeks or so. You told me that I might be able to help you in New York and I will, of course, be delighted to do any kind of speech making or missionary work that Jim Farley or Forbes Morgan think desirable. As to the best time to come, I had rather figured on August and the first half of September, although if you think any other time would be better, I can make my plans accordingly. The impression I get over here is that you will be reelected without much difficulty. I suppose there are certain spots where there may be defections, but that is natural enough and they do not cause me much concern. The news I get from New York is satisfactory; there is to be expected some uphill work there—but Al Smith seems to have been a flop[4] and the opposition will melt under the sun of returning prosperity.

Please forgive this long letter, and with affectionate remembrances to Eleanor, believe me to be,

As ever, Faithfully yours,

Grenville T. Emmet[5]

P.S. I was sorry to see in the paper yesterday the death of your cousin,

Henry L. Roosevelt, the Assistant Secretary of the Navy. Although I had not met him, he was doing a fine job in your old shoes and everyone spoke highly of him.

[PSF:Netherlands:TS]

[1] Laval resigned as Premier on Jan. 22, 1936, following a vote of no confidence on the Hoare-Laval proposal.

[2] Roosevelt's proposal to the American republics to hold the Inter-American Conference for the Maintenance of Peace.

[3] Francesco Maria Taliani di Marchio, *Pietrogrado 1917* (Milan, 1935).

[4] A reference to Smith's speech before the American Liberty League on Jan. 25, 1936, in which he suggested that anti-administration proponents "take a walk" from the Roosevelt leadership.

[5] Roosevelt replied, March 7, 1936 (*Personal Letters, 1928–1945,* I, 567–568). Mostly about the Roosevelt ancestry, the letter concluded with: "All you say about the general European situation is most interesting and is complicated by news this morning that Germany is taking some step in regard to Locarno."

Cordell Hull, Secretary of State, to Roosevelt

Washington, February 26, 1936

My dear Mr. President: I transmit herewith, for your consideration and, if you approve, your signature, a draft of a proclamation pursuant to Section 1 of the new Neutrality Bill. I suggest that, if you approve of this draft, you may wish to sign it at the time you sign the bill.[1]

Faithfully yours,

Cordell Hull

[OF 1561:TS]

[1] Issued Feb. 29, 1936, as proclamation 2159, prohibiting the export of arms and ammunition to Italy and Ethiopia, printed in *Public Papers,* V, 92–94. For the act (approved Feb. 29, 1936), see 49 *Stat.* 1152.

William Phillips, Under Secretary of State, to Roosevelt

Washington, February 27, 1936

Dear Mr. President: A further telegram from Norman Davis[1] just received requires new instructions, and I should be grateful if you would kindly indicate whether the proposed draft reply meets with your approval.[2]

You will note that the Italians will not now join in any naval agreement. In these circumstances Davis suggests three alternatives: First, an agreement to be signed by England, France and the United States (Germany to be brought in later); second, in case France should refuse to sign now, the suggestion is that we and Great Britain initial a treaty to which all the naval powers would be invited to adhere. Davis's third alternative is not clear to me, but it is possible that it refers to our No. 46, of February 25th, in which we offer to leave with the British Government a memorandum of the type of treaty we could accept, providing it is accepted by the principal naval powers.[3]

As a matter of fact all of Davis' inquiries have already been answered by us except authorizing him to sign a three power agreement (England, France and the United States). But that point also was disposed of in our original instructions to the American Delegation, authorizing the signature of a three power treaty in the event that there could not be a five power signature or a four power signature.[4]

Faithfully yours,

William Phillips

[*Notation*:AS] WP OK FDR
[PSF:London Naval Conference:TS]

[1] Feb. 27, 1936 (*Foreign Relations, 1936*, I, 76).
[2] Sent as Hull to Davis, Feb. 27, 1936 (*ibid.*, p. 77).
[3] *Ibid.*, pp. 72–73.
[4] Answered below.

Roosevelt to William Phillips, Under Secretary of State

Washington, February 28, 1936

Memorandum for the Under Secretary of State: What would you think of sending a telegram to Davis asking him to try to get even a gentleman's agreement from Great Britain, France, Italy (and through England from Germany) whereby each nation would agree to notify the other of every decision to lay down Naval vessels of any size over one hundred tons?

If such a gentleman's agreement could be obtained these four or five powers could then jointly or severally invite Japan to do the same thing.[1]

F.D.R.

[PSF:London Naval Conference:CT]

[1] Roosevelt's suggestion was cabled by Hull to Davis on the same day (*Foreign Relations, 1936*, I, 78–79). A dispatch from Davis to Hull (also of February 28 but not in reply) suggested that Germany might not wish to be the only power besides Great Britain and the United States to agree to sign the proposed treaty (*ibid.*, pp. 79–81). To this Hull replied February 29 (*ibid.*, pp. 82–83); the last paragraph of his cable was supplied by Roosevelt (PSF:London Naval Conference). This paragraph suggested that the British be informed "that in view of the essentially European aspects of the German Navy and the fact that the German Navy . . . would not exceed more than approximately a third of the total British naval force, the United States would greatly prefer a bilateral British-German arrangement if based essentially on their ratios as at present agreed on."

R. Walton Moore, Assistant Secretary of State, to Marvin H. McIntyre, Assistant Secretary to the President

Washington, February 28, 1936

Dear Colonel McIntyre: At the Secretary's request I am handing you such a statement as the President may consider making when he signs the neutrality resolution.[1] As the August resolution expires tomorrow, the resolution recently passed by Congress should be signed not later than tomorrow, and then immediately the new proclamation which I left with the President the other day should be signed.

I have attached to the statement copies of the two resolutions for convenient reference.[2]

Yours very sincerely,

R. Walton Moore

[OF 1561:TS]

[1] The draft is present. After further revision by Moore it was issued as the statement printed below (Moore to Roosevelt, Feb. 29, 1936, OF 1561).
[2] S.J.R. 173, approved Aug. 31, 1935, and H.J.R. 491, approved Feb. 29, 1936; the copies are present.

Statement by Roosevelt on Signing House Joint Resolution 491, February 29, 1936

By the Resolution approved August 31, 1935,[1] a definite step was taken towards enabling this country to maintain its neutrality and avoid being drawn into wars involving other nations. It provided that in the event of the Executive proclaiming the existence of such a war, thereupon an embargo would attach to the exportation of arms, ammunition and implements of war destined to any belligerent country. It also authorized the Executive to warn citizens of this country against traveling as passengers on the vessels of any belligerent except at their own risk.

By the Resolution I have just signed[2] the operation of the August Resolution is extended and strengthened until May 1, 1937. A new and definite step is taken by providing in substance that, when an embargo becomes effective, obligations of any belligerent government issued after the date of the proclamation shall not be purchased or sold in this country, and no loan or credit extended to such government, but with authority to the Executive, if our interests require, to except from the prohibition commercial credits and short time loans in aid of legal transactions. In addition, it in general exempts the other Republics of this hemisphere from the operation of the law.

Following the August enactment promptly on October 5, 1935, I issued a proclamation which made effective the embargo with respect to exportations to Italy and Ethiopia, and I have now issued a new proclamation in order to meet the requirements of the new enactment.[3]

The policies announced by the Secretary of State and myself at the time of and subsequent to the issuance of the original proclamation will be maintained in effect. It is true that the high moral duty I have urged on our people of restricting their exports of essential war materials to either belligerent to approximately the normal peace time basis has not been the subject of legislation. Nevertheless, it is clear to me that greatly to exceed that basis, with the result of earning profits not possible during peace, and especially with the result of giving actual assistance to the carrying on of war, would serve to magnify the very evil of war which we seek to prevent. This being my view, I renew the appeal made last October to the American people that they so conduct their trade with belligerent nations that it cannot be said that they are seizing new opportunities for profit or that by changing their peace time trade they give aid to the continuation of war.[4]

[White House Press Releases:M]

[1] 49 *Stat.* 1081.
[2] 49 *Stat.* 1152.
[3] See *Public Papers*, V, 92–94.
[4] Also printed in *Public Papers*, V, 89–91.

Lincoln MacVeagh, Minister to Greece, to Roosevelt

Athens, February 29, 1936

Personal

Dear Franklin: I was much cheered by hearing from you in answer to my letter of last Thanksgiving Day,[1] and I have only been waiting to continue my story of Greece until there should be a turn in affairs to give me a starting point. But the road has been long and still no turning is in sight, so I shall write you, anyhow, about the impasse into which the Greek internal situation has fallen, and which is in itself perhaps as remarkable as one of the local revolutions, if not more so. And I will add some words about the foreign situation, and about the Greek debt to us.

You will remember that the King came back on the strength of a revolution supported by a bogus plebiscite. The British, whom he most admires (he told me himself that "We need more Anglo-Saxon ideas in this country") are undoubtedly, as I wrote you, taking advantage of his being here for what it may be worth. But it can't be said to be worth much as yet. For in spite of newspaper correspondents, who see the restoration, à la E. Phillips Oppenheim, as a move in the British-Italian chess game, it was really, as I wrote you, a development of local politics, with its roots deep in the soil of recent Greek history, and only incidentally connected with foreign affairs. And it is because of the character of its local origin that it has been teetering on the verge between success and failure for months.

Whatever may have been the motives which led the King to accept the call of the plebiscite, the nature of which he probably understood then and certainly understands now, he has shown himself to be a serious-minded and genuine person determined to do his best as Monarch of the entire country and not simply of one party. He showed his attitude in this regard immediately on his return to Athens, when he insisted on amnesty and pardon for all persons, civil and military, who had been condemned for participation in the Veniselist revolt of last March.[2] At the same time he himself has not gone over to the Veniselists, as his enemies say. He has criticized Mr. Veniselos to me personally, and his aides have gone even further, so that I know where he stands. He is trying to be a non-partisan Greek. And it is precisely for this reason, which does him honor, that he has so far failed to achieve that prestige with the country which, among other things, would make him

223

an asset rather than a liability to interested foreign friends. There is still a good likelihood that he will remain here. It would probably mean the ruin of any political leader to be implicated just now in a move to get rid of him. But I have yet to find a politician who will say he is satisfied with his attitude, and all the party chiefs without exception have openly ignored his personal appeal to their patriotism to bury the hatchet and get together. His program of uniting the Veniselist and anti-Veniselist factions and ruling over a pacified people has shown no signs to date of even beginning to work.

As soon as he was settled on his throne he dismissed General Condylis,[3] and others who had helped to effect his restoration, and who desired to run him in their own interests, and set up a temporary government of non-political personages, headed by a university professor. With this body of men in power he then proceeded to hold honest elections in the hope that the example set by him and Mr. Veniselos in composing their differences would appeal to the people and be reflected at the polls. Honest elections were indeed held, but the result was far from what the King anticipated. The proportion of Veniselist and anti-Veniselist votes was almost exactly what it was three years ago, approximately 50-50. All that had happened in the interval, including two armed revolts, with their aftermath of courts-martial, one bloodless revolution, and a restoration—not counting the reconciliation of King and Cretan—had changed the opinions of hardly a single Greek! One ray of hope, however, seemed to exist in the fact that while the Veniselist front was strongly united about the nucleus of one party, the Liberal, which obtained a large plurality of seats in the Assembly, the anti-Veniselists were broken into several groups along apparently irreconcilable party lines. It was therefore thought that the King might call on the Liberal leader to form a coalition government. The adhesion of only one of the anti-Veniselist groups was, in fact, all that was necessary to that end. But the danger of control by the hated Veniselists promptly drew the anti-Veniselist factions together, and over a month of parleying has done no more than emphasize the essential antagonism existing between the two fronts. Now, the not very hopeful expedient of convoking the Assembly and letting it thrash the matter out itself seems about to be tried. If, as is likely, the deputies reach the same impasse as exists at present between the party leaders, then it would seem we must go on with a government such as the existing one, which is at best a temporary make-shift, and satisfactory to nobody in a country where politics is one and the same thing with government.

Such is the situation. Naturally, the root of the whole trouble lies in fear. A coalition government might be possible if only a government did not necessarily control the army, navy and police! Neither side dares trust the other, even in a sworn cabinet, with these important portfolios—and particularly, it seems, with the portfolio of the Interior. For it is this last which has jurisdiction not only over the police and the gendarmarie, but over the election machinery of the country as well, and matters being what they are, new general elections are already being mooted. The fear, of course, concerns the future consequences of past actions. There is hardly a politician in Greece who has not been exiled or condemned to death, or had friends and relatives executed at the instigation of rivals, or has not done these things to others. And the same thing is true of all the higher officers of the Army and Navy. Such people do not imagine that just because the King, presumably in his own interests, has made it up with Veniselos, their own political enemies will follow suit and forgive past injuries. "Do not trust the false promises of the Veniselists!" cried Mr. Tsaldaris,[4] the most moderate of the Antis, publicly in the last campaign. And so it goes.

As a result of this situation, and of the King's attitude, the erstwhile extreme Royalists are now the Crown's most bitter critics. Before his sudden death, which mercifully relieved the country of its greatest potential trouble-maker, General Condylis publicly exclaimed that the King should be King of all the Greeks and not only of the Veniselists. On the other hand, Mr. Cafandaris,[5] the veteran Republican ex-Premier and Minister of Finance, complained to me only the other night that the King was not acting properly. He was, so Mr. Cafandaris said, not taking a firm enough stand in opposing the absurd pretensions of the anti-Veniselists. When I said I supposed the King wished to stay apart and above party considerations, he remarked: "But he must take a stand somewhere!" And this, I think, shows where the present situation is really critical for the King. Willy-nilly, and by hook or by crook, the Greeks are trying to make a party man of him, and if they succeed in spite of his intentions, they will cook his goose for years in a repetition of King Constantine's fiasco.[6] He is fighting his battle now to avoid such a fate, and the battle is not going very well.

From the point of view of foreign affairs, Greece has been acting normally—though I would not imply by this that her troubled internal state is abnormal; far from it! Like all the little nations of the Near East and the Balkans, she sets great store by the League of Nations, which has helped her compose her difficulties with her neighbors time and again. In her view, she has simply got to stand by the League, and for that reason she subscribed to the sanctions against Italy, though she has hurt her trade thereby and has as yet received no compensation. For the same reason she answered England affirmatively when asked if she would live up to her military obligations under the Covenant if Italy attacked England as a result of the Sanctions. It is supposed that she has conferred with England as to what support she might render in such an eventuality. Indeed, the British Minister confidentially explained the recent visit of British destroyers here by saying that he had requested it for the purpose of exploring the possibilities of naval cooperation. But there seems to be no grounds for the story that some dicker has been made between the two nations—such as the cession of Cyprus in exchange for the use of Greece's western harbors. The British Minister has denied this to me, and besides there is no necessity for such action on England's part. The Greeks are strongly anti-Italian on the Abyssinian question, and do not forget what the Great War taught them in regard to their dependence on the power which controls the seas.

The recent revival in France of the policy, so actively pursued under Barthou, of encircling Germany with pacts, is causing some interest here, on account of the visit of King Carol to Yugoslavia after his conversations in Paris. It is felt that there may be a move on foot to get Bulgaria to join the Balkan Entente, two members of which, Rumania and Yugoslavia, are also members of the Petite Entente. Inasmuch as Bulgaria is suspected of still cherishing territorial designs, at the expense of Greece, by way of an outlet to the Aegean, Greek public opinion is somewhat restively awaiting clarification of this diplomatic activity. The German threat to the peace of Europe is so great in connection with the already critical Anglo-Italian situation that it is felt France may turn on considerable pressure to make her protective encirclement as complete as possible.

I was pleased and amused when the Greeks came forward the other day with another payment on account of interest on our Refugee Loan of 1929, which they persist in calling a War Loan. They insist that 35 per cent of the interest is all they can pay on any of their foreign debt just now, and there may be some merit in the claim. The question is by no means clear. Certainly it would be political suicide for any government here to pay much more. What really counts in the circumstances is the continued recognition of at least one of their obligations. But I was amused because of the kudos they have received. Apparently they figured correctly that most people would misunderstand the payment as being on account of war debts, on which Greece is actually in default, and thus she would share in some of the glory that has gone to Finland. Representative Shanley,[7] of my State of Connecticut, waxed truly rhapsodical on the floor of the House in his eulogy of Solon, Pericles, Aristotle, Plato and Socrates. And it wasn't so long ago that we were lambasting the Greeks over the Insull affair! They certainly have a kind of small cleverness which it is hard to beat. But in doing what I believe to be the best they can to keep some shreds of credit, they show an appreciation of their situation which is gratifying. Hundreds of years of oppression have made them, as a people, prone to take quick profits at the expense of credit, and I am always trying to make them see that this is bad business, particularly in international relations with a great friendly country whose past benefits to Greece are as nothing to what the future may hold if they will play the game right.

With all best wishes for your health and success at all times, I am, Affectionately yours,

Lincoln MacVeagh

[PSF:Greece:TS]

[1] Nov. 28, 1935 (PSF:Greece), a very long letter on the restoration of George II to the throne of Greece in November 1935; Roosevelt's reply, Dec. 20, 1935, is printed in *Personal Letters, 1928–1945*, I, 535.

[2] A revolt led by the Cretan politician Eleutherios Venizelos, head of the Liberal party. The revolt failed and Venizelos was exiled.

[3] Georgios Kondylis, Minister of War in the coalition government, 1932–1935, was for a time Prime Minister after the restoration of George II.

[4] Panayiotis Tsaldaris, leader of the Popular party and Prime Minister from 1933 to 1935.

[5] An old follower of Venizelos, Prime Minister for a short time in 1922–1923.

[6] Constantine I, father of George II, who was forced to abdicate during the Turkish War of 1922–1923.

[7] James A. Shanley.

Roosevelt to Fred Morris Dearing, Ambassador to Peru

[Washington] March 3, 1936

Dear Fred: Many thanks for that most interesting catalogue of Peruvian stamp issues. My Spanish is rather crude but I can understand most of it.

Thank you so much for making the Ourslers' visit so pleasant. We have heard that they were thrilled by all you did for them. I am glad you were in an armored automobile when the bull charged you. Lima sounds like a somewhat exciting spot![1]

Always sincerely,

[PSF:Peru:CT]

[1] This note is in reply to Dearing's letter of Feb. 8, 1936 (PSF:Peru), in which he described a visit from Charles Fulton Oursler and his wife. Oursler, as editor of *Liberty Magazine* in 1931–32, had helped Roosevelt prepare the *Liberty* articles later published as *Government—Not Politics* (New York: Covici, Friede, 1932).

Roosevelt to the Right Reverend G. Ashton Oldham, Bishop of Albany

[Washington] March 3, 1936

Personal

My dear Bishop: I have not had a chance before this to thank you for your letter of February twenty-first.[1] I, too, wish I had had a chance to talk with you about foreign policy and national defense. The difficulty, as I see it, is that so few people really understand what defense means. Necessarily it is a technical subject on which there is a vast amount of misinformation, which goes all the way to the theory of Mr. Bryan, that this Nation would be secure against attack because "a million men would spring to arms overnight."

I know you will not mind if I give you personally a practical example: We have two coasts to defend against Naval attack and communication between the two must be kept open through adequate defense of the Panama Canal. If, for example, the attack comes from the western Pacific, the key to the whole defense is Hawaii, for the very simple reason that if Hawaii were in the possession of an enemy fleet that fleet could act either in a Naval attack or to cover an actual invasion against any point on the whole length of our Pacific Coast from Puget Sound to San Diego, or against the Panama Canal itself. This being so, it is necessary to have in Hawaii a very costly defense system for both Naval operations and land protection.

Some day I shall be glad to talk with you in regard to the whole subject. The main point to be made, however, is that all of our defense costs are strictly for defense and follow foreign armament. They do not precede nor do they go along simultaneously with foreign armaments.

Always sincerely,

[PPF 418:CT]

[1] Oldham referred (PPF 418) to a recent talk with Roosevelt at the White House; this is not noted in the appointments list. In his letter he protested the increases in military and naval appropriations and thought them unnecessary if United States policy aimed only at defense.

William E. Dodd, Ambassador to Germany, to Roosevelt

[Berlin] March 3, 1936

Dear Mr. President: It seems to me the location of all offices of the Service here would be most advantageous; and to that end an enormous palace was bought some years ago.[1] But this building is now in such condition that it would cost over a million dollars to put it in order; and the consequences of building of a subway under one corner of it are such that I have urged upon the Department the exchange of the palace for another place. If this could be approved this spring, I think we could get a far better bargain than we could hope for later. In case you can give the matter a moment's consideration, I wish you might see Mr. Phillips who was here January 1 and looked into the matter carefully. Carr and Merrill[2] of the Department are still using every influence they have to get more than a million dollars added to the million seven hundred thousand already invested; their attitudes are personal I fear, rather than national.

How many mistakes our greater nations have made since 1920! We refused to give the League of Nations a trial, though we might have withdrawn in case we became convinced membership meant nothing. Then we put through two tariff laws which made the payment of debts impossible, nearly everybody talking about paying in gold! Those two acts did more to set up the barriers to commerce than anything else, and reduced our standard of living sadly. Then France insisted upon armaments to the limit and caused Hitler to be able to seize control of the German nation. And England refused to support us when we tried to stop Japan's imperialism in China! Last November–December Hoare and Laval defeated the first real League movement to stop war at a moment when two-thirds of the German people were hoping to see Mussolini stopped because it would mean later a stoppage here. That was a blunder which now leads to the necessity of alliances; and alliances are only repetitions of 1879 to 1914. I hardly know which people have acted more stupidly; and all this armament business now reaches five billion dollars cost a year—all nations bankrupt!

I had a long talk last Saturday with Secretary von Neurath, 29th of February, who revealed his great anxiety, though he insisted Hitler is really getting uneasy and listens more to the Foreign Office. He agreed as to the terrible blunder of last November[3] and added that the hope of Europe now depends on a restoration of the League and Germany's joining. Then he added, "but your country is forming a League which will have the effect of making our League European and then of creating an Asiatic League: certain war." Well, I could only say "No" with some doubt.

Yours sincerely,

William E. Dodd

You see how poor a typist I am.[4]

[PSF:Germany:TS]

[1] The Blücher Palace, bought from the German government in 1931 for $1,700,000. A fire had destroyed part of the building; Dodd estimated that it would cost $1,000,000 to repair it. The American Embassy at this time was on the Tiergarten Strasse (*Diary*, pp. 15, 324).

[2] Wilbur J. Carr, an assistant secretary of state, was also budget officer of the State Department at this time; Keith Merrill was his executive assistant.

[3] Presumably the Hoare-Laval proposal for settling the Italo-Ethiopian crisis, made public on Dec. 7, 1935.

[4] Roosevelt replied March 16, 1936 (*Personal Letters, 1928–1945*, I, 571), that he agreed with Dodd and had so informed Hull, Phillips, and Moore. He added that if the situation should ever warrant a gesture or offer from him that would make for peace he should at once be informed.

Walter W. Van Kirk, Director, National Peace Conference, to Roosevelt

New York, N.Y., March 3, 1936

Dear Mr. President: I am enclosing herewith an "Appeal to the President and Congress of the United States," regarding military and naval expenditures, which has been signed by more than 450 prominent citizens, including many college presidents, business men, educators and churchmen. These persons unite in protesting against the ever increasing expenditures of the army and navy. With equal emphasis, the signatories urge "that our national defense policies be brought into harmony with the declared purpose of the United States to act the part of the 'good neighbor'; that our military and naval expenditures be fixed on the basis of the defense of our soil; that our army and navy be limited in accordance with this conception."

This Appeal has been given to the press for release Thursday morning, March 5.

Respectfully yours,

Walter W. Van Kirk

[OF 2020:TS]

[*Enclosure*] An Appeal to the President and Congress of the United States

The undersigned, deeply disturbed by the tremendous increase in military and naval expenditures, call your earnest attention to the increasing percentage of the country's annual expenditure now being devoted to national defense. In two years' time the figures for the army and navy in the regular budget have risen from $533,597,243 in 1935 to $744,839,588 in 1936 and now to no less than $937,791,966 in the estimated budget submitted to Congress on January 6 last—an increase of no less than seventy-five percent. But this tells only a part of the story because of the allotment to both the services of huge sums from relief and employment appropriations, conservatively estimated to be approximately $200,000,000 in the current year, which would bring the total military and naval expense for the present fiscal year to nearly one billion dollars. Should a similar sum be allotted next year from sums given to other departments for relief or employment purposes the total would come to $1,137,791,966, almost exactly as much as the total cost of the Civil War in the year 1865 when our war expenditures were at their maximum. The total army and navy expense for the current fiscal year already approximates the total cost of the Federal Government for all purposes in the year 1916.

No explanation of this arming, unprecedented in all our peace-time history, has been forthcoming. The American people have not been told where the danger lies or against whom we are arming. But that is not all. There is no evidence that any far-reaching defense policy has been

231

settled upon, save as one is outlined in the National Defense Act. The country has not heard whether this armament is predicated upon the policy of again throwing some millions of men across the seas, or whether the policy is to be only one of defense against attack. The country has a right to know, therefore, if so large a part of its regular budget is essential to the protection of our coasts and our boundaries when no such vast precautions have ever been deemed necessary in the previous 147 years of our national existence.

If our peace and security are threatened, the country is entitled to that knowledge, and to a statement of what the government of the United States is doing to prevent such a calamity. Common sense and fidelity to the interests of the American people demand the immediate projection of a basic policy of national defense, the answering of the question of defensive or offensive armaments, to which the entire defense program must be subordinated with the complete coordination and cooperation of army and navy and the aviation forces, which cooperation is not now existent.

The United States is a signatory of the Kellogg-Briand Pact, under the terms of which our government is pledged to seek the settlement of international disputes only by pacific means. In his address to the Woodrow Wilson Foundation on December 30, 1933,[1] President Roosevelt pointed to the correct policy for the United States when he recommended that all nations pledge themselves never to send their armies and navies beyond their own frontiers. Moreover, the President has repeatedly asserted, as at the grave of the Unknown Soldier on Armistice Day, 1935, that this country was wholly without thoughts of aggression.

We respectfully submit that our expanding military and naval establishments are wholly contrary to the foreign policy embodied in the Kellogg-Briand Pact and in the repeated declaration of the President regarding our relations with other nations. We urge that our national defense policies be brought into harmony with the declared purpose of the United States to act the part of the "good neighbor"; that our military and naval expenditures be fixed on the basis of the defense of our soil; that our army and navy be limited in accordance with this conception.

Respectfully submitted,

Mildred A. Ailman
Librarian, Westminster College,
New Wilmington, Pa. . . .[2]

[OF 2020:TS]

[1] Dec. 28, 1933, above.

[2] Among the almost five hundred other signers were President James R. Angell of Yale, Charles L. Carhart, secretary of the Council of International Relations, Henry Goddard Leach, editor of the *Forum*, Judge Joseph H. Proskauer of New York, Charles P. Taft of Cincinnati, and William Allen White of Emporia, Kansas. Early placed the statement on the President's desk with a note of March 4, 1936 (OF 2020): ". . . Stanley High has contacts with this group. He suggests that it would be 'good ball' for you to invite and confer with not more than a half dozen of their leaders. Stanley High says the attitude of those selected will be both friendly and reasonable. I, too, believe that it would be worthwhile to see such a small group. Through them, your beliefs and policies can be passed on to the other petitioners and peace organizations."

Roosevelt told Early to arrange a meeting; Early then asked High if Van Kirk should have a free hand in selecting those to come with him. High assured Early that he himself would see to it that Van Kirk chose "the right people." High also thought that if the President would see them for about an hour's informal talk, "it would do immeasurable good throughout the whole peace group." (Roosevelt to Early, March 5; Early to High, March 6; "memorandum for Mr. Early," March 7, 1936, OF 2020). See Roosevelt to Van Kirk, March 9, 1936, below.

William C. Bullitt, Ambassador to the Union of Soviet Socialist Republics, to Roosevelt

Moscow, March 4, 1936

Personal and Confidential

Dear Mr. President: Roy Howard has just blown through Moscow like a healthy wind and I hope that when he calls on you in Washington you will tell him what a great little fellow he is.[1]

Before he arrived I had arranged for him to interview Stalin and on the night of his arrival he was given a dinner by Doletsky, the head of *Tass*, at which a lot of prominent Bolsheviks were present. When he rose to reply to a toast he made a speech which was so perfect that it might have been made by yourself.

This is the first time within my knowledge that any prominent American has talked like an American to the Bolsheviks. The usual run of business men who come here think that they will get somewhere by licking the Bolshevik boots. Howard, on the contrary, told the Bolsheviks that while there had been no country in the world that had regarded their experiment with more sympathy than the United States, they could not expect our friendship so long as they continued to interfere in our internal affairs. He did it politely and beautifully and it would have done you good to have seen the shocked expressions on the faces of the more fanatical Bolsheviks—like Radek and that filthy little squirt, Umansky, who is about to go to America to replace Skvirsky.[2]

In the course of Howard's conversation with Stalin, which lasted three and one-half hours, he told the Dictator that he was certain, as a newspaper man, that any repetition of Soviet interference in American internal affairs would produce a break in diplomatic relations. Umansky was interpreting and Howard said that when Umansky had to translate that remark his face looked "like a spanked baby's butt."

Howard is really a great fellow and it pleased me immensely to discover that his support of you was based on real friendship.

Incidentally, Howard would make a startling but superb Ambassador of the United States to Great Britain. The King, at least, would love him. You will recall the King's thrice repeated remark to me (apropos of Atherton)[3] about his wish to see America represented in London by Americans, not imitation Englishmen.

The chief excitement of the week in Moscow, however, was not provided by Howard but by the Tokyo assassins. As I cabled the Department, the Bolsheviks were at first extremely apprehensive, fearing that General Mazaki was about to achieve control of the government and that a vigorous advance into Outer Mongolia would follow his appointment.[4] As soon as the Bolsheviks discovered that Prince Saionji had advised the Emperor to treat the mutineers with the greatest severity possible and that it was improbable that the government would fall into the hands of the extreme militarists, they calmed down and began to feel that the mutiny had been a very good thing for the Soviet Union. Their belief now is that the mutineers destroyed whatever respect might still exist in foreign countries for the Japanese Government, made Japan ridiculous by killing Okada's brother-in-law instead of Okada,[5] and created such a condition of internal tension in Japan that it would not be possible for Japan to follow any strong policy for some time.

I felt sure that Stalin's readiness to receive Howard was not due primarily to any love for my beautiful eyes or his desire to improve relations with the United States, but because he wished to make an announcement about Outer Mongolia. I told Howard that before he saw Stalin and Howard asked the appropriate question. Stalin came out with the blunt announcement that the Soviet Union would fight if the Japanese should invade Outer Mongolia.

The Bolsheviks at the moment are extremely confident about their position in the world. Their most recent information from Paris indicates that the Franco-Soviet Pact will be ratified by the French Senate.[6] The Soviet-Czech Pact which, as you know, does not come into effect until the Franco-Soviet Pact has been ratified will then exist also; and they expect confidently that a Soviet-Rumanian Pact will then be concluded.

I have got to the bottom of the delay in the conclusion of the Soviet-Rumanian Pact. There is no serious dispute; but both Titulescu and Litvinov are oriental bargainers of the Levantine-rug-vendor type and each one feels it is his duty to haggle until the customer leaves the shop. They understand each other perfectly, however, and each one knows that the rug is going to be sold.

The Bolsheviks are still engaged in talking about the imminence of German aggression against the Soviet Union, and their present disposal of their military forces on the western frontier gives a clear indication of the line of German advance they fear. I have been informed most confidentially that they have now sixteen divisions in the Kiev-Odessa military district; that is to say, the Rumanian border; six in the White Russian district and only three in the Leningrad area.

There are, in addition, six divisions in the triangle, Moscow-Kiev-Kharkov, for support of the sixteen that are closer to the Rumanian border.

This distribution of forces indicates clearly that the Council of Peoples Commissars is of the opinion that if German attack is to be expected it is to be expected by way of the line Czechoslovakia, Hungary and Rumania.

I can not find anyone in Moscow who believes any longer that the Germans may try to march on the Soviet Union by way of Lithuania and Latvia although Stalin made a remark about attack via the Baltic States to Howard. In that region the railroad communications would be so poor and the front so narrow that it would be impossible for the Germans to maneuver any great force. In order to deploy, it would be necessary for the Germans to follow the classic route of invasion via Vilna. As Vilna is in the hands of the Poles and as Pilsudski had the political cleverness to have his heart buried there, it is almost impossible for the Poles to let the Germans through by that route.

German communications to Rumania via Czechoslovakia, even if Austria were included, would be so inadequate that it would be most difficult for them to maintain a big army on the Rumanian frontier of Russia unless they had permission of the Poles to use the main line which runs from Breslau through Cracow and Lemberg.

It is, therefore, clear that unless the Germans have the cooperation of the Poles they can not make an attack on the Soviet Union with any hopes of success. I am absolutely convinced that the Poles today will not permit the Germans to send an army through Poland. This Polish attitude might conceivably change if the Germans should be able to annex Austria and overwhelm Czechoslovakia, but I believe that even in that case the Poles would refuse to allow the foot of a German soldier to be placed on Polish soil. They would be damned fools if they did allow that and they are no longer such idiots as they were in the 18th century.

The Bolsheviks will continue to emit loud cries about the Japanese and German militarists but in reality they will have little to fear unless some incident changes the international situation.

As I said to you in Washington, we are, in my opinion, back where we were before 1914 when the familiar and true remark was, "Peace is at the mercy of an incident." The recent Japanese incident might have touched off war. It appears, on the contrary, to have strengthened the possibility of peace; but a new incident in Europe or Asia can loose the whirlwind.

I was delighted by your proposal for an Inter-American Conference. There is constructive work to be done in the Americas but there is little that we can do in the rest of the world except get ourselves mixed up in a hopeless mess.

Before you get this letter I hope I shall have received that wire from you. In any event, the Lord be with you and good luck.

Yours affectionately,

Bill

[PSF:Russia:TS]

[1] Howard was editor and president of the New York *World-Telegram* and editorial director of the Scripps-Howard newspaper chain. His interview with Stalin, March 4, 1936, is printed in Stephen Heald, ed., *Documents On International Affairs: 1936* (London: Oxford University Press, 1937), pp. 464–472.

[2] Karl B. Radek, prominent in the early years of the Bolshevik revolution and a leading Trotskyite, was tried on charges of treason in 1937 and sentenced to ten years imprisonment. Konstantin Umanski, formerly chief censor of the U.S.S.R. Commissariat of Foreign Affairs, had not long before replaced Boris E. Skvirsky as counselor of the Russian Embassy.

[3] Ray Atherton, counselor of embassy in London, was acting as adviser to the American delegation at the London Naval Conference. He was named consul general on May 14, 1936.

[4] General Jinzaburo Mazaki, a member of the Supreme War Council, was accused of having been sympathetic with the aims of the disgruntled extremist Japanese army officers who had staged the recent abortive revolt against what they regarded as the anti-imperialist policies of the government. Many high-ranking army officers were involved in what became known as the "February 26 incident." Mazaki resigned his military posts shortly after the revolt.

[5] Prime Minister Keisuke Okada's government was formed in July 1934; he escaped

death in the February 26 uprising when his brother-in-law was mistaken for him and was murdered instead.

[6] Hitler used the French Senate's prospective ratification of this pact as his excuse for occupying the Rhineland on March 9, 1936. See Heald, *Documents,* pp. 15ff and *Foreign Relations, 1936,* I, 207ff.

Roosevelt to Senator Key Pittman of Nevada

[Washington] March 9, 1936

My dear Key: I am glad you are going out to Detroit for the St. Lawrence Conference and I am enclosing a message which I will appreciate very much if you will deliver personally to the Conference for me.[1]

Confidentially, let's don't any of us make any reference at all to any inquiry sent to the Canadian Government at this time.

I want to talk this over with you when I have a chance but for the present it can't even be mentioned. I am wondering also if it wouldn't be awfully good ball for you to have a talk with Mr. Hickerson of the State Department,[2] and check up on what you are going to say in your speech with the material that they have, so that everybody will be talking along the same line.

For your information, that is exactly what I did with the message I am asking you to deliver for me.

Very sincerely yours,

[*Notation*:CT] Copy for Frank Walsh. For your confidential information. [OF 156-A:CT]

[1] The message to the Seaway and Power Conference was read on March 11, 1936, by Pittman; it is printed in *Public Papers,* V, 117–121, with a long note by Roosevelt on the history of the project following defeat of the St. Lawrence Waterway treaty in 1934.

[2] John Hickerson, assistant chief of the Division of European Affairs.

Roosevelt to Walter W. Van Kirk, Director, National Peace Conference, New York

[Washington] March 9, 1936

Dear Mr. Van Kirk: I very much appreciate the frankness of the communication recently addressed to me by the National Peace Conference on the subject of military and naval expenditures.[1] Because I desire to be equally frank in regard to the Administration's policy on this important issue I should be glad to meet with you and four or five other representatives of your organization whom you may choose for an informal discussion of this problem.

Should you desire a conference of this sort, I wish you would communicate with Assistant Secretary McIntyre, who then will arrange the appointment. As you probably know, I expect to leave Washington, if possible, about March nineteenth, for a fishing trip in Florida waters. If you care to confer with me before then or after I return to Washington, about April third, please let Mr. McIntyre know.[2]

Very sincerely yours,

[OF 2020:CT]

[1] March 3, 1936, above.

[2] Stanley High and representatives of the peace group were invited to a tea and conference at the White House on March 13: Walter Van Kirk; William P. Merrill, pastor of Brick Presbyterian Church, New York; James T. Shotwell of Columbia University; Josephine Schain, chairman of the Committee for the Cause and Cure of War; Dorothy Detzer, Women's International League for Peace and Freedom; Mrs. Estelle Sternberger of World Peaceways; William Stone of the Foreign Policy Association; and John N. Sayre, president of the National Peace Conference (OF 2020). In a letter to the President of March 17, 1936, Van Kirk expressed the appreciation of the peace delegation for having been received but said the members were still not convinced that huge military and naval expenditures were necessary for defense purposes (OF 2020). He added: "We were very pleased to learn from you that the administration had repudiated the speech of Senator Pittman in which provocative references were made to Japan. Would it be agreeable with you if we quoted you to this effect?" No other mention of what took place has been found.

The Pittman speech was made in the Senate on Feb. 10, 1936; in it Pittman declared that the only answer to Japan was overwhelmingly strong naval and air power on the part of the United States (*Cong. Rec.*, vol. 80, pp. 1703-1708). In his reply to Van Kirk, March 21, 1936 (OF 2020), Early asked that the conference be treated as "an informal, off the record meeting." He said it was hoped that the meeting might be followed by other similar ones and for that reason it was preferable that "they be regarded as off the record rather than to be made a matter of publicity."

Fred Morris Dearing, Ambassador to Peru, to Roosevelt

Lima, March 10, 1936

Personal

My dear Mr. President: It is about time, I expect, to give you another brief resumé of what is happening in this part of the world:

Secretary Morgenthau's decision to buy the Peruvian silver output has just been announced and may have more effects than one. An immediate result, however, may be that of taking some of the tension out of the situation at the Cerro de Pasco Copper Corporation mines where we hear that, on account of the drop in price to around forty-two cents, the management has cut wages by ten per cent.[1] The cut represents an increase of ten per cent which was voluntarily accorded some months ago when the price of silver got above seventy cents. However, the intelligence of most of the miners will not take this price fluctuation into account, and up to a few days ago some trouble was expected and troops, I understand, were sent up the Hill to be in readiness for it. I don't know what price Mr. Morgenthau is going to pay or whether it will prevent the salary cut from being carried out, but I hope it will somewhat soften the resentment of the miners as we have a great many Americans up in the central part of the country where the mines are situated and I do not want them to be placed in danger as they have been in previous years. Moreover, the "good-neighbor" policy is making so much good will for us that I do not like to see our companies associated with wage cuts which must necessarily cause resentment.

I fancy that by now it is only the situation in Paraguay that prevents you from going rapidly forward with the Inter-American Peace Conference.[2] I do not, of course, wish to appear too wise, but it seems to me it was a mistake to enter into any sort of an agreement, even though it was tacit, to take action similar to that of all the nations participating in the Buenos Aires Conference in the matter of the recognition of the new Paraguayan government. It seems to me that states of actuality ought to be recognized immediately and as rapidly as they pop up. In that way a new government is placed in responsible relationship to the recognizing government, and such advantages and engagements as can be obtained are obtained in the best of circumstances. Not to recognize immediately implies that recognition is to be traded for something; this sort of pressure is always resented and this attitude always misses the main and important fact which is that it is the de facto situation with which we have to deal and that every step possible ought to be taken to deal with it in a regular and efficient manner. Non-recognition merely blockades all efforts, whereas recognition makes it possible to obtain everything that could be obtained in any other way and in the best possible atmosphere to boot.

We have just had another incident in the Zarumilla region on the Ecuadoran frontier and tension between the two governments is rapidly increasing. Peru has sent two warships to the north and one of them has soldiers on board. The two foreign offices are issuing communiqués and the language of these communiqués is not helping matters much, although I am convinced that the foreign ministers themselves are sincerely endeavoring to prevent the situation from becoming aggravated. We cannot say just now what will happen and today the situation is easier. But I am afraid these incidents are going to continue to occur until one bright day the two countries will be at each others' throats and there will be more war and loss of life and treasure, all of which is, of course, another reason for speeding the proposed Peace Conference.

I suppose you have noticed that our communist friends have been active again in South America. The newspapers carried the news of the outbreak in Brazil and they also have reported the recent flurry in Chile.[3] But unless you have seen our recent despatches, you have heard nothing of the fact that a similar movement was scotched opportunely and vigorously here in Peru. The government received word a few weeks ago through one of its secret agencies (we hear incidentally that the government is paying a pretty penny for as many as four secret organizations) that some ten or more Russian agents had worked their way into the country through the south. With this information seven of them were nabbed at once and the rest seem to have slipped away. For four or five days a large number of arrests were made here in Lima, and then finally the excitement died down and the danger, for the moment, seems to have passed. The Foreign Minister told me that the government had no particular fear of what the malcontents might do as the army is quite loyal. The objective, he said, was to prevent reports from going abroad and appearing in the press which would be detrimental to the recovery and progress now going on in Peru.

Our last reports are to the effect that Peru is continuing conversations, begun some time ago, with Argentina, Chile, Bolivia, Uruguay and possibly with Brazil, for a common understanding so that any further plans of communist revolutionaries can be frustrated.

The question of the treaty with Panama used to draw from Peruvian commentators condemnation of the severest kind, in which would peep forth the old prejudices and animosities against us. Since that time, under the good-neighbor policy, an enormous amount has been done to remove the old rancor, but traces of it still exist, indicating that we must persevere in the good work you, the Secretary and Sumner have initiated.

I have an article in front of me now stating that the treaty is only a first step towards the removal of many objectionable circumstances and that only "a sincere spirit of cordiality and collaboration and equality can dispel the justified distrust which is felt towards Yankee policy whose absorbing imperialism has left so deep a mark upon the Panamanian Republic." Of course we shall never be entirely free from ill-willed and suspicious critics, but I have mentioned this expression so we shall both be reminded of the actualities, be made conscious of what has been gained, and realize that we have to go straight ahead along the present lines in order to bring about an even more complete realization of the good-neighbor policy.

The present Peruvian congress is also a Constituent Assembly and the one which established the present Peruvian constitution. The members of this body, therefore, feel that they can alter the aspects of this creature of theirs in any way they wish. When they were setting up the constitution several years ago, the fact that they might wish to continue in office was somewhat remote and accordingly provision was made for elections and the creation of a bi-cameral congress composed of senate and chamber. The date for presidential and congressional elections is not now far away; they are to take place at about the same time that ours take place in the States. The deputies have now discovered, however, that it may be more conducive to their personal interests merely to continue as a Constituent Assembly than to go to the trouble of being elected either deputies or senators; and, accordingly, tampering with various provisions of the constitution has begun.

It is impossible to say just what will occur, and if anything too raw is attempted there may be a somewhat violent reaction. At times it looks as if elections might be deferred indefinitely through the expedient of altering the electoral law. At other times it seems more likely that the elections will be held and that everything will take place as the constitution provides. The general situation, however, is confused and the outlook is uncertain. A number of candidates are coming into the field, the right and center parties continue to pull in all directions, and the left parties are virtually smothered under.

One of the wisest of the local observers tells me that this sort of thing will go on until just a week or two before the elections, when the most powerful of the right and center parties will coalesce and virtually impose a new government. He thinks it certain that President Benavides will go out of office and almost equally certain that someone equally able and conservative will be put in his place—but so far this someone has been difficult to identify.[4]

Our Japanese friends continue to work steadily to improve their position all through South America, and of course in Peru. They push their trade all they can, they recede when they must and then they come back to the attack; they are quiet but they are industrious. Labor circles here have become alarmed and a continual attack in the lesser newspapers goes on. This is composed of violent diatribes and a good deal of misinformation; but sometimes the actual aspects of the situation are, to a certain extent, revealed. Our Naval Attaché is following it closely.

You have doubtless heard already of the visit of a Japanese mother ship and some submarines to the Galapagos Islands, and you know of our own Navy's recently announced visit to the West Coast. It will be a good thing for our men to become acquainted with its geographical features. Meanwhile, I understand that Vincent Astor is going back to the Galapagos Islands again with a few visitors, but I expect he might pick up some scraps of information for you while he is there.

Bill Phillips made a good speech in Chicago, and he has had a very good press on it here.[5] His, of course, was one of the first confirmations of the calling of the Inter-American Conference, and I am glad to see in today's papers that Sumner has announced that all the nations have now accepted except Paraguay.

I am even happier to note that recognition of the Franco regime will be forthcoming almost at once. I have written Sumner it seems to me it is always a fundamental error to trade recognition for anything one desires from the new government. Recognition should be accorded, as I see it, to any government—no matter how weak or wicked—the minute it becomes actual, and if another government succeeds it the following day, I would recognize that one. The great need is to put the new and shaky organization into a definite relationship to the recognizing government as soon as possible. That creates the most advantageous situation in which to get anything out of the new people. And, as I see it, it was also a mistake for us to make our own action in the matter of recognition contingent in any way upon what the other countries might do. I believe we should have kept a complete independence and have recognized the Franco regime at once. However, if recognition now comes along immediately, we shall have nothing to regret and I believe the Paraguayans will perform as desired and the Conference can go forward.

There has been an immense amount of speculation as to the significance and the importance of the Conference and it has fired men's imaginations. The last developments in Europe and in Japan throw the meaning of the meeting into even higher and sharper relief. It seems to be regarded here now not only as a most excellent thing from the Inter-American point of view, but a positive protection of the most vital character against any rampant imperialist in Europe and against any ultimate design on the part of the Asiatics. In between, possibilities of enormous economic development and strength are perceived; and finally, the possibility of performing like a great balance-wheel in case the European, Asiatic and African world should further disintegrate under the pressure of on-rushing populations and of war. The beneficent possibilities, however, have only been glimpsed and I fancy the practical difficulty will be to confine the Conference to accomplishments which can be made real while not dimming the greater possibilities so many people in this part of the world perceive.

I hope you have noticed that at last the Peruvian government has squarely taken the position that its obligations to our American holders of Peruvian bonds are sacred and honorable and the Government must make every effort to discharge them. The recent budget carried an item of four million soles as a practical expression of the new attitude which was written into the record by speeches made by the Ministers of Foreign Affairs and of Finance and Deputy Badani of Loreto, all of whom made excellent presentations in the Constituent Assembly of the case for the bondholders and the duty of the Peruvian Government. Our hope is that next year Peru will—as we believe it can—do even better, and if it does, Peruvian credit and American trade will be benefited no less than those holders of bonds who will receive larger interest payments.

The case of the Condor planes remains just about where it was. We do not yet know exactly to whom the planes belong; they have not yet a license to do anything more than a little freight work in a private capacity for some of the mining companies who are backing the Condor Company. Occasionally, as the developments slowly take place, we hear in the newspapers of Mr. Conboy's successive steps in the prosecution. I fancy that some day we shall have the whole story, but that Mr. Conboy will not be hurried since the developments in Ethiopia and now in Germany make it peculiarly important not to make a mistake and to do thoroughly and well what Mr. Conboy has set out to do in this prosecution.[6]

I believe we have moved the famous Lee-Yurimaguas case forward towards a solution.[7] This involves great potential oil reserves in the northern part of Peru which may be of some interest to our navy. On

243

February 28th the Foreign Minister formally notified me that the Peruvian Government was willing to arbitrate the matter in the way requested by the State Department, and at present we are awaiting a written confirmation of this notification.

In other respects the Government has been showing a certain stiffening all through the administration. I see nothing particularly inimical in it, but chiefly a desire to bring about a more efficient administration of public affairs. However, it has affected our business in a number of ways and under the impulse of standing up straight, the Government has leaned over a little backward in some cases.

One of our mining men, Clarence Woods, who bought and has been developing a property here in a way which seemed to me must be beneficial to the country, is now called upon, under a rather dubious technical set-up, to pay an inheritance tax on the estate of the former owner of the mines. It looks as if it were going to be a long drawn out question into which we shall have to go.

Gold mining is increasing enormously throughout the country. The effects have not yet been seen to any great extent in the output because the preliminary work and first installation is slow and costly, but within the next few months some of the newly developed properties should be going into production and Peru's gold output should then steadily increase.

I wonder if you are still enthusiastically interested in the development of the Pan-American Highway. I feel sure you are. In that case I enclose a copy of a personal letter I recently wrote to Secretary Ickes which will disclose to you an initiation I took recently in the conviction that it was worth while to do so and that our Government would be really interested in having the Peruvian section of the Highway completed.[8] Should you feel that you can give me any direct expression of your interest, I should be very glad indeed to have it as I could then probably use it as a leverage on appropriate occasions to get the officials here to do something definite.

I notice that your soil conservation measure has passed.[9] Should you wish any warrant for it you might find it in the following: The pastor of his flock walked up to the fence where one of the members of his congregation was working in the field. "Well, my good man," he said benignly, "I see that God has helped you and that you have prospered." "Yes," the farmer replied, "but you just ought to have seen this place when God was doing it by himself."

With my warmest good wishes, and Dorothy's too, and our remembrances to Mrs. Roosevelt, Yours most sincerely,

Fred Morris Dearing

[PSF:Peru:TS]

[1] On March 5, 1936, Morgenthau announced that the Treasury would buy the entire production of silver of certain South American mines (New York *Times,* March 6, 1936, p. 38). Peru was the fourth largest silver producer in the world; 62 per cent of her output was mined by Cerro de Pasco, an American corporation.

[2] The revolution of Feb. 17–18, 1936, which ousted Eusebio Ayala and supplanted him with Rafael Franco.

[3] Anti-communist measures in Brazil were taken by the government of Getulio Vargas in late 1935 and early 1936, resulting in the imprisonment and exile of several Americans who were accused of communist activity against the government. In Chile an abortive revolt of retired army officers against the government was crushed in February 1936.

[4] President Óscar Raimundo Benavides remained in office until 1939.

[5] On Feb. 15, 1936, to the Chicago Council of Foreign Relations (New York *Times,* Feb. 16, 1936, p. 30).

[6] Martin Conboy, a United States attorney, was appointed in 1935 to investigate the grounding by Peru of four Condor planes that had been sold to Chile by an American company.

[7] Bertram L. Lee was an American who had been granted extensive oil concessions in the Yurimaguas, in northeastern Peru.

[8] March 3, 1936 (present) urging Ickes' support for the highway.

[9] The Soil Conservation and Domestic Allotment Act, approved Feb. 29, 1936 (49 *Stat.* 1148).

William Phillips, Under Secretary of State, to Roosevelt

Washington, March 11, 1936

Confidential

My dear Mr. President: Senator Trammell,[1] Chairman of the Naval Affairs Committee in the Senate, has asked the Department, for use in connection with draft legislation on the subject, whether it will be necessary for the United States to scrap its excess tonnage in each category of naval vessels in excess of the limits set forth in the London Treaty before December 31, 1936, and, further, whether the State Department has any information or assurances which would indicate that Japan and Great Britain interpret the treaty in the same way, and whether they intend to scrap their excess tonnage also.

We have drawn up a letter to Senator Trammell, copy of which I enclose herewith, stating the position of this Government as we see it in the matter, and I might say, also, that this letter has been shown informally to the Navy Department and has received their approval.

In order that you may be fully informed of all developments in connection with the naval situation, the Secretary has asked me to lay this letter before you for any comment you may care to make before it is sent forward to Senator Trammell.

Faithfully yours,

William Phillips

[*Notation*:AS] WP   OK   FDR
[PSF:London Naval Conference:TS]

<hr>

[1] Park Trammell of Florida.

[*Enclosure*] Cordell Hull, Secretary of State, to Senator Park Trammell of Florida (draft)

Strictly Confidential

My dear Senator Trammell: I refer to your letter of February 21, 1936, and to my preliminary reply of February 27, 1936,[1] with regard to the intentions and obligations of the United States, Great Britain and Japan under the Treaty for the Limitation and Reduction of Naval Armament signed at London, April 22, 1930, with respect to the scrapping of excess naval tonnage. You request on behalf of the Committee on Naval Affairs this Department's interpretation of certain provisions of the London Naval Treaty. You inquire specifically (1) whether it will be necessary for the United States to scrap the tonnage in each category in excess of the limits set forth in the London Treaty by December 31, 1936; (2) whether this Department has any information or assurance which would indicate that Japan and Great Britain interpret the treaty in the same way and that they intend to scrap their excess tonnage in like manner.

The obligation regarding the scrapping of tonnage under the London Naval Treaty of April 22, 1930, is set forth in Part III, Article 16. I enclose for convenient reference a copy of the Treaty. The article referred to will be found on page 23. It will be noted that this article states that the completed tonnage in the cruiser, destroyer and submarine categories as given in a table embodied therein "is not to be exceeded on the 31st December, 1936" and, furthermore, that "Vessels which cause the total tonnage in any category to exceed the figures given in the foregoing table shall be disposed of gradually during the period ending on the 31st December, 1936."

This Department believes that the intent of the foregoing provision is unmistakable and that under it the process of scrapping tonnage in excess of the amounts given must be completed by December 31, 1936.

This Government has no specific information as to the interpretation placed upon Article 16 of the treaty by the other signatories thereto. It has, however, no reason to doubt, in view of the unequivocal language of the provision cited, that their interpretation corresponds with its own.

This provision, however, is subject to an exception. Should any contracting power desire to retain tonnage in excess of the figures embodied in the table given in Article 16, it may do so under the terms of Article 21. (See page 26 of the enclosed copy of the treaty.) In such event "that High Contracting Party will notify the other Parties to Part III as to the increase required to be made in its own tonnages within one or more of the categories of such vessels of war, specifying particularly the proposed increases and the reasons therefor, and shall be entitled to make such increase. Thereupon the other Parties to Part III of this Treaty shall be entitled to make a proportionate increase in the category or categories specified * * *."

Up to the present this Government has received no formal notification that one or other of the parties to Part III of the London Treaty intends to invoke Article 21. However, one of the technical advisers to the British delegation at the Naval Conference now in progress at London has informally indicated to the chief American delegate to the Conference that the British intend to scrap all cruisers in excess of the 339,000 tons permitted by treaty by December 31, 1936, and to invoke the "escalator clause" (Article 21) in order to retain 40,000 tons in destroyers which would otherwise have to be scrapped.

No information regarding the intentions of the Japanese Government with respect to the scrapping of excess tonnage has come to the attention of this Government.

I would reiterate that this Government has no evidence which would indicate that the interpretation placed on the provisions by the other signatories to the treaty differ from its own. I feel confident that in the event that one or the other country decides to invoke the "escalator clause" and retain any excess tonnage it will duly inform the other signatories to Part III of the London Treaty. Finally, I see no reason to doubt that such scrapping as may be obligatory upon the signatories to Part III of the London Treaty will be accomplished in accord with the terms of Article 16, which require that the scrapping shall be effected "during the period ending on the 31st December, 1936."

In view of the confidential character of this letter I shall be grateful if the Committee will take precautions to safeguard its contents from becoming public.[2]

Sincerely yours,

[PSF:London Naval Conference:T]

---

[1] Neither is present.

[2] There is no indication whether Trammell replied to Hull, but presumably his death on May, 8, 1936, put an end to the matter.

Roosevelt to the People's Mandate to End War Committee, Executive Offices of the White House, March 12, 1936, 11 A.M.

(The Chairman introduced the members of the Committee to the President and expressed to the President the appreciation of the Committee for his courtesy in seeing them. He also expressed the appreciation of his organization for the work being done by the President in promoting the Pan-American Conferences and told the President of the very favorable reaction throughout the country.)[1]

I am glad to know about that because I was wondering whether our own country is as conscious of it as other countries in Central and South America which are particularly appreciative of it.

(The Chairman of the Committee expressed to the President his thought that the entire country was conscious of the good work being done and that they further hoped that the United States would be sympathetic with the policy being sponsored by their organization which was to stop the construction of armaments immediately and thereafter go on with the machinery for peace, such as disarmament conferences, etc.)

I am very, very sympathetic, of course from a personal point of view although, of course, we always have to be practical.

Examples are important and that is what we are trying to do, to set an example. The difficulty is to get the example known in every part of the world. About a year ago I considered making a radio appeal to the people of Europe. I, fortunately, talk French and German, I talked it when I was a small boy, and I conceived the idea of a short address of perhaps fifteen minutes, first in English on a radio world hook-up and then in French and then in German. I could not do it in Italian and I could not do it in Czecho or Russian or other languages, but those three would have been fairly effective and would have covered a great many homes.

We even went so far as to get the radio stations in Europe that have very, very high power and could send all over Europe. Then we discovered, we discovered what President Wilson discovered when he attempted to appeal to the peoples over the heads of their rulers, we discovered that while in England they have radios in a great many homes, in France they only have on a per capita basis about one per cent of the radios we have got. We discovered in Italy that they have practically no radios in their homes and we discovered that in Germany, while they have a good many radios, they can only listen in through a single station twenty-five miles from them and could not get any reception from high-powered stations. That is by Government decree.

So, we are up against that problem—we cannot get information to most of the people.

I can give you a good example: somebody here went over there in the late summer of 1934. She went to stay with a Professor in Germany and she found the Professor's house, the whole top story, being rebuilt. She asked whether he was putting on an additional story and he said, "No, we are taking advantage of the Fuehrer's magnificent offer. We won't have to pay taxes this year if we make the top story of our houses fireproof and proof against bombs and also put a bomb proof in the cellar." She said, "What for? It is hundreds of miles from the French frontier."

He said, "The Fuehrer has said that every house must be made bomb proof against airplanes, that they are doing it in France. And they are doing it in England, too." Then the German Professor went on to say, "Furthermore, we are told, and the information we have is correct, that in the United States, in every seaport city, the Government is making homes flame proof and bomb proof."

Of course that is not true but the German people believe it.

Of course, the chief thing we are up against, as you know, is the problem of the living up to the written compact, in other words the treaties. That is the thing we have to concentrate on more than anything else. This has to be off the record, of course. Suppose some nation comes to us and asks us to make a treaty. Now what is the use of making a treaty if they break it tomorrow if they find it convenient to do so. Now, that is the state of the world in the Far East and in Europe today. The result is that all we can do is work with the people who respect their written word.

However, I am not worried about our foreign affairs, not the least bit. At present, all we can do is show by example.

On the armament question, it is a perfectly simple thing. We worked toward disarmament and they said, "We will not arm unless the other fellow makes it necessary for us to do so."

We are way behind. The army has only eight hundred planes, England has twenty-five hundred, France four thousand, Germany is working up to five thousand and Russia has six thousand.

(Somebody in the audience asked, "Do you think Europe feels it would be to their interest to attack us?")

That is a problem we have to think about. Are we going to stand for European nations coming in and attacking independent countries on this hemisphere in order to get raw materials. We cannot permit that. We have had one hundred years of opinion on that.

In South America, for example, there has been in the past twenty-five years a tremendous increase in the democratic form of government. They are having an election in Panama. Twenty or twenty-five years ago that election would have been decided in a junta meeting in the city of Panama. We know that. Today, what happens? You have four candidates in Panama that are stumping the country. Isn't that grand? They are going before the electors of Panama and are stumping the country, showing themselves. You cannot guarantee the kind of election you have here but, on the whole, it will be an expression of popular choice. And they are going back to the democratic ideal of Central and South America. It has been a grand advance. That is why, if the world is to continue in the democratic form of government, we have to encourage democracy.

On coast defense, I had a very delightful chat the other day with a gentleman who came in and said that perhaps we ought to go back to the idea of coast defenses. I told him a story. The story is well worth while and well worth remembering because it shows a type of thinking.

In 1898 we got into the Spanish War. That was in April. About the first of May, there appeared in all our papers, under great, big headlines, a story from the French side of Spain to the effect that news had come from Spain that Spanish cruisers had left Spain to bombard the American coast, that there were four cruisers. They were the cruisers which were afterwards destroyed in the Battle of Santiago. But the story was that they had started for the American coast.

Well, the Secretary of the Navy was waited upon by the Congressional delegation from the state of Maine. They said, "Here is this dispatch and it mentions Portland, Maine as the point of attack. And here is all of the American navy down in the West Indies. You have to give us some ironclads." So Secretary Long said, "I haven't got any ironclads. They are down around Cuba."

"Well," they said, "You must protect Portland, Maine and all the good people of Portland, Maine. We must have ironclads in Portland, Maine." And Secretary Long said, "I think I will go back to my office and see what I can do."

So, he called up the Philadelphia navy yard where there were a number of Civil War merchanteers made of iron, each one carrying two fifteen-inch guns that would throw a great, round ball almost a mile. However, they were ironclads. He had them pulled off the mud flat and painted and then he had them pulled by a tug up to the mouth of the harbor of Portland and anchored them there. Everybody was perfectly assured and happy and the men, women and children who had been drawing their bank deposits and going up country went back to Portland.

("Did the Spanish warships ever come?")

If they had come, they would have anchored a little more than a mile from the ironclads and would have shelled Portland, Maine. But there was the population, perfectly satisfied because the ironclads were anchored at the mouth of the harbor.

(Members of the Committee then spoke to the President on behalf of the group in the organization represented by them. They pointed out that laboring people in the Bethlehem and U.S. Steel plant were members of their organization, also people in the ship-building plant. A member representing the Churches spoke at some length. The President again pointed out the necessity of working toward living up to agreements. One member, who said she represented sixty thousand business and professional women, pointed out the economic loss occasioned by the construction of arms, to which the President replied:)

They have to be paid for in the long run. Along that line, probably most of the European nations today would be in serious trouble, economically, if it were not for the fact that they are employed on armaments. There is no one unemployed in Italy, they are in the munitions factories. There is no one unemployed in Germany, they are all working on war orders. Eventually, of course, they will have to pay.

(The Chairman of the Committee again thanked the President and the Committee left the President's office.)[2]

[Speech File:T]

[1] The members of the committee were introduced to the President by Rep. Caroline O'Day of New York, long active in peace movements (New York *Times,* March 13, 1936, p. 11). Mary E. Woolley headed the delegation; the identity of the "chairman" is not known.

[2] The "Mandate to Governments to End War" was a petition circulated during 1936 in the hope of securing 12,000,000 signatures as an anti-war protest. By Feb. 27, 1936, when the committee met in New York, about 1,000,000 signatures had been obtained (New York *Times,* Feb. 28, 1936, p. 17). The intent behind the "mandate" was to force the American government to live up to its Kellogg-Briand Pact obligations by discontinuing immediately all armament and armed forces increases; by using existing machinery, such as the World Court, to settle international conflicts; by securing a "World Treaty" for immediate arms reduction; and by securing international agreements founded on recognition of world interdependence.

Jeannette Rankin to Roosevelt

Bogart, Georgia, March 12, 1936

Dear Mr. President: As a candidate for the nomination as President at the Democratic Convention, I wish to inquire your stand on the question of war.

Since the pledge given in the General Pact for the Renunciation of War, do you feel that war is a legitimate method for settling international disputes?

Under what circumstances would you ask this country to go to war?

Would you advocate a reorganized, unified military system to protect our shores from invasion as a substitute for the army and navy designed for fighting foreign wars?

Where would you put the emphasis in governmental considerations on property rights or on the rights of the individual?

It will be necessary for me to have an understanding of your attitude toward these questions if I am to cast an intelligent vote.[1]

Sincerely yours,

Jeannette Rankin

[PPF 120:TS]

[1] Miss Rankin, a former suffragette leader and the first woman to be elected to Congress, had voted against declaring war on Germany in 1917. McIntyre replied to

her letter on March 19, 1936 (PPF 120), suggesting that she read Roosevelt's speeches and messages to Congress since his inauguration, adding that these "set forth very clearly the President's sincere efforts to prevent war and to discourage armaments."

Press Conference, Executive Offices of the White House, March 13, 1936, 10:40 A.M.

[*Excerpt*] Q: Is there any way in which the St. Lawrence can be handled, either as a power or navigation project, without ratification of a treaty with Canada?

The President: I had never thought of it. I do not believe there is, offhand.

Q: The reason I asked was that Frank Walsh said in Detroit that we should not overlook the fact that a majority of Congress voted for the St. Lawrence Treaty, but that, lacking two-thirds, the Treaty was defeated. I thought perhaps that was a hint that you might do this on a majority.

The President: No, I had not thought of it. That is a new one to me.

Q: There was some indication in your Message, read at that meeting, that conveyed the same idea. I have not got it with me but I know several people got the same impression.[1]

The President: I am afraid it is just fine imagination. I never thought of it.

Q: Are you going to seek a new treaty with Canada on the St. Lawrence?

The President: Oh, yes. That is not news. You have known it for a long time. There will be negotiations undertaken sometime, but I do not know when.

Q: Does this contemplate the Niagara Falls thing at the same time?[2]

The President: I think it would be better to clean up the whole thing at one time, as far as we can go . . .

Q: Is there anything new to say on the Pan-American Conference?

The President: No, I suppose the State Department will be ready with some kind of a statement pretty soon. I think all the replies, except one, have come in.

Q: Are you inclined to recognize the new Fascist Government of Paraguay?

The President: You will have to ask the State Department . . .

Q: Getting back to the St. Lawrence, do your remarks indicate that a treaty will be sent to the Senate for ratification this session?

The President: Oh, my, no; not a chance.

[President's Press Conferences:T]

[1] Roosevelt's message to the Great Lakes–St. Lawrence Seaway and Power Conference in Detroit, read by Pittman on March 11, is printed in *Public Papers*, V, 117–121.

[2] The 1929 convention with Canada for the preservation of Niagara Falls.

Breckinridge Long, Ambassador to Italy, to Roosevelt

Rome, March 13, 1936

My dear Chief: I have your letter of February 22 and gladly follow your suggestion.[1] My "tummy" is gladder. I am planning to leave in May and by that time hope to have the war debts question definitely settled one way or the other.

Since the date of your letter the situation in Europe has assumed an entirely different phase. Germany's action in the Rhineland has produced a crisis which may not be so easily settled. By the time you receive this you will know whether you want me to come home now—even under the circumstances of an upheaval here—or would rather I postpone my departure a while. In case you think I ought to stay longer, of course I can do it. I cannot be of much practical assistance to you before or during the Convention, because nomination is only a formal matter and the Campaign will not really begin until August.

One other thing I think you ought to consider is the possible political effect upon you of letting a number of men from key posts in Europe return to participate in political activities during a period which is more dangerous than any since 1918.

However—I am not arguing the question. I am simply expressing things which are in my mind and which you may want to consider before I leave here and which are not susceptible of determination today.

There are certain formalities which will have to be complied with here and which you will want me to comply with before I leave, and I think the courtesies involved prior to my departure would be much easier if you would have me telegraphed to proceed to Washington for consultation via Paris. The "via Paris" will eliminate the question of traveling on an Italian ship and the order to return for consultation will afford the basis to do the proper things before I leave, and which I would not do if just going on leave.

Can we not leave it this way? I will plan to proceed to the United States in May on receipt of orders, unless you want me earlier. If you see any reason to change your mind so that I should postpone my return, you could telegraph and simply mention the date of this letter which I will understand to mean that I will postpone my return until I receive further orders. If I hear nothing I will return in May.

I will be very glad to be back in the States and do what I can to see that the things you have been fighting for are confirmed in November. This being Friday, the thirteenth, the omen is good. I am always lucky on that coincidence. The last one—last December—I got $2,000 refund unexpectedly.

Affectionately and respectfully,

Breckinridge Long

[*Notation*:A] Sec of State   Please speak to President about this at Cabinet—[2]

[PSF:Italy:TS]

[1] Suggesting that he return home to take part in the coming campaign (*Personal Letters, 1928–1945*, I, 560).
[2] No reply to this letter has been found. See Long to Roosevelt, June 15, 1936, below.

William Phillips, Under Secretary of State, to Roosevelt

Washington, March 14, 1936

My dear Mr. President: I am enclosing copies of Norman Davis' telegrams, No. 137, March 13, and 138 of March 14,[1] with regard to the question of our delegation's initialing or signing the naval treaty in London now, and the possibility of ratification being required at the present session of the Senate. I am also enclosing a draft of a telegram which I would suggest sending to the delegation with a view to having them so arrange the initialing or signing of the treaty as far as we are concerned in a manner which will not commit us to the presentation of the treaty for ratification before the adjournment of Congress, as I understand it is your desire not to have the treaty presented for ratification at this session.[2]

I would be very grateful if you would give me your comment as to whether this draft telegram would meet with your approval.

Faithfully yours,

William Phillips

[*Notation*:AS] W.P.   OK   FDR

[PSF:London Naval Conference:TS]

---

[1] *Foreign Relations, 1936,* I, 89–91, 91–92.

[2] March 14, 1936, *ibid.,* pp. 92–93. Phillips said that the President considered it "extremely inadvisable" to commit himself to asking for ratification in the current session, and urged that the effective date of the treaty be changed from Jan. 1, 1937, to April or May of that year.

Marvin H. McIntyre, Assistant Secretary to the President, to Roosevelt

Washington, March 16, 1936

Memorandum for the President: Secretary Phillips called up and dictated the following: In regard to legislation proposed by the Treasury covering the export of liquor from the United States, the State Department has been in very close touch with the Treasury for the last three or four days in an effort to reach a compromise agreement. So far they have been unable to arrive at any such agreement, for the reason that the Treasury is insistent on maintaining the principle that the Government cannot embargo goods coming in from abroad owned by foreigners unless they meet certain conditions set out by the Secretary of the Treasury. This we feel very strongly is a new departure in international relations.[1] A form of compulsion against foreigners, in order to compel them to come into our courts which has never been exercised before. Acting on the President's suggestion, Phillips went before Senators Harrison and King on Friday last. They were very sympathetic to the State Department's point of view and they held up action of the Finance Committee. They said that they hoped before the next meeting that the two Departments could straighten it out. The next meeting is tomorrow morning. Phillips has been asked by Harrison to appear before that Committee unless they can reach an agreement with the Treasury, which seems doubtful. In that event no legislation would be necessary. Because of the President, Phillips does not like the idea of going before the full Committee and expressing views contrary to those of the Treasury Department. The important part of this whole legislation is that this principle will be applied against Americans in compelling our exporters to come into foreign courts.

Phillips and Judge Moore or Phillips or Judge Moore would like to come over this afternoon. They think it is very important.

Phillips has spoken to the Secretary of State over the telephone and the Secretary also feels very strongly that the State Department should not present a case in which they are in disagreement with the Treasury before the Committee. Also he says that the principle involved is of considerable importance and he, the Secretary, hopes the President will see them this afternoon.[2]

[PSF:State Department:T]

[1] The Treasury Department bill, H.R. 9185, "to insure the collection of the revenue on intoxicating liquor," had been passed by the House in the previous session and was before the Senate Finance Committee (*Cong. Rec.,* vol. 79, pp. 13928, 14113, 14120; vol. 80, p. 7360). Section 403 of the bill empowered the Secretary of the Treasury to embargo imports from any individual manufacturer against whom the American government had a prior claim for unpaid excise or income taxes. Canadian whiskey had been granted special consideration under the 1935 Reciprocal Trade Treaty and the distillers argued that efforts to collect millions of dollars in claims dating back to the prohibition era before 1930 (when Canada forbade liquor smuggling to the United States) were discriminatory and illegal. The State Department and the Treasury disputed each other's rights and jurisdiction in the case (see *Foreign Relations, 1936,* I, 796–825), and Canada threatened to withdraw from the trade treaty if the United States persisted in efforts to collect the full extent of the claims against the distillers.

[2] There is no indication that Roosevelt saw Phillips or any other State Department official on this date. Evidently the matter was handled by telephone; see below.

Roosevelt to William Phillips, Under Secretary of State

Washington, March 16, 1936

Message telephoned to Secretary Phillips: This is a matter solely for the Committee.[1] You and the Treasury should appear before the Committee in Executive session. Bear in mind the fact that the Canadian distillers owe the United States Government $40,000,000 and as a matter of justice they should not be allowed to continue to do business in the U.S. without paying all or part of what they owe. The pressure by these distillers on the Canadian Government might become a matter of notoriety.[2]

[PSF:State:T]

[1] See above.
[2] See Moore to Roosevelt, March 20, 1936, below.

Roosevelt to William C. Bullitt, Ambassador to the Union of Soviet Socialist Republics

[Washington] March 16, 1936

Dear Bill: It is good to get yours written on Washington's Birthday.[1] I am glad you were able at least to stop in so many Capitols.

Meanwhile, since a week ago, the fat is in the fire again.[2] What a thoroughly disgusting spectacle so-called civilized man in Europe can make himself!

I fear I cannot send you any message until I get back April fourth. The Secretary has left and I go on the nineteenth.[3] Many foundations have been laid.

Our all American conference is coming well and I think it will be held in September. The Secretary stands so well in South America that already they are talking of erecting statues to him. Pretty good for a Democratic Administration and a great fellow!

As ever yours,

[PSF:Russia:CT]

[1] Above.
[2] Occupation of the Rhineland.
[3] Roosevelt actually left for his Florida vacation on March 22, 1936.

Senator Key Pittman of Nevada, Chairman, Senate Committee on Foreign Relations, to Roosevelt

Washington, D.C., March 16, 1936

My dear Mr. President: [*Excerpt*][1] Just one other subject that I wish to lay before you: I fully realize that the conference which you have called to be held at Buenos Aires is for the sole purpose of bringing about cooperation between the Americas in the matter of preservation of their peace.

I can not, however, dismiss from my mind a number of informal conferences with delegates from South America to the London Conference. Those discussions were relative to a closer economic tie-up between the United States and South American republics. These conferences were due to the fact that all of us realized that economic agreements with Europe were impossible at that time by reason of both the economic and political situations there. Cordell is doing a good work through his bilateral treaties, and, yet, I believe that the monetary and exchange situation will greatly handicap him and make it quite difficult for us to compete with Great Britain by reason of the exchange preferences she is creating.

I talked a number of times with the recent dementia of Jimmy Warburg with regard to these matters.[2] He suggested that we could utilize a number of economic systems of countries of South America. He said there were some, however, that would have to start over now. He favored the central bank idea, with us lending credit in stimulation of the currencies issued by such banks. I was very much impressed with Jimmy's suggestions. We have the gold and silver reserves upon which to base such credits. Such a program seems worthy of consideration.

Would it be advisable that some of your monetary and banking experts accompany our delegation to Buenos Aires, not for the purpose of injecting the question into the convention, but for the purpose of feeling out such Latin-American monetary experts as might be in Buenos Aires at that time? It would seem that this question must be taken up at some time, and the longer it is put off the more uncertain its success. It does not seem that these matters can be consummated through conferences with Ambassadors or Ministers or through correspondence. Such informal conferences might decide whether you deem it advisable subsequently to call another conference to deal with the monetary question. I hope that you will pardon me for this intrusion.

I may not see you before your vacation, and I, therefore, at this time express my pleasure that you have made the opportunity for recreation, which everyone knows you so well deserve.[3]

With best wishes, I am, Sincerely,

Key Pittman

[PPF 745:TS]

[1] The first part of this letter has to do with rivers and harbors development.

[2] So in the original; the sentence has obviously been garbled in the typing.

[3] This letter was sent to Hull for his information; see his letter of March 28, 1936, below.

Press Conference, Executive Offices of the White House, March 17, 1936, 4:10 P.M.

[*Excerpt*] The President: Steve has a memorandum for you afterwards on the Pan-American Conference that will be held some time in Buenos

Aires.[1] It explains itself and shows that we have had letters of acceptance and replies from all the American Republics except Paraguay, and that is on its way. There was a change of government down there while my letter[2] was on its way to the President of Paraguay and the new President will reply as soon as he gets my invitation.[3] The important thing is that the substantial accord of every one of the American Republics to this suggestion and the real hope we have is that it is going to be not only of practical use but will also cement the real friendship existing between the Republics at the present time.

Every reply goes along with the suggestion of Buenos Aires as the place of meeting and the President of Argentina says, "I take pleasure in offering Buenos Aires as the seat of the proposed conference, accepting the suggestion which your Excellency formulated of holding the conference in its midst. I esteem it as a great honor, for which I am deeply grateful."[4]

As to the date of the conference, that has to be talked over the next two or three weeks through diplomatic channels and I won't know until we have had those conversations.

Q: It has been definitely decided that it will be held in Buenos Aires?

The President: Yes.

Q: Has the agenda been worked out for the conference?

The President: No, that also has to be discussed.

[President's Press Conferences:T]

---

[1] Printed as a press release under date of March 17, 1936, in *Public Papers,* V, 124–125. Welles (drafter of the statement) had written to Early on March 16 (OF 1970) that it would be "particularly helpful" if the President were to talk about the Inter-American Conference at his March 17 press conference, as he said he had noted "some feeling of chagrin" among Latin American representatives because no comment had been made by the President regarding the letters he had received.

[2] Roosevelt to Ayala, Jan. 29, 1936 (OF 338). President Eusebio Ayala of Paraguay was turned out of office on Feb. 18, 1936, by the forces of Rafael Franco, who took the oath as provisional president on Feb. 20, 1936 (*Foreign Relations, 1936,* V, 858ff).

[3] Franco cabled Roosevelt on March 5, 1936, that his government intended to honor its international obligations; Roosevelt recognized his regime in a telegram of March 14, 1936 (*ibid.,* pp. 878–879, 891).

[4] Roosevelt read the quotation from the press release.

Anthony J. Drexel Biddle, Jr., Minister to Norway, to Roosevelt

Oslo, Norway, March 18th, 1936

My dear Mr. President: As Norway's merchant fleet plays such an important part in world commerce, the shipowners here are, as I have written you before, well posted on international affairs bearing directly or indirectly on their business. Likewise are the bankers for these shipping interests, well informed. Through my constant contact with these men, and others who represent Norwegian business with important international connections, I am able to keep very close touch with what transpires internationally—especially when matters have a bearing on business here.

Although Norway has fulfilled her obligations to the League as regards sanctions against Italy, the imposition thereof, have caused detrimental repercussions in the Norwegian economic structure. The fishing districts of the northern part of this country supplied Italy with about 46% of their annual catch of stockfish. Now that they no longer ship to Italy, they have been unable as yet to find another market; this however, is just one instance.

It is interesting in this connection, that Dr. Munch, Danish Minister for Foreign Affairs, and representing the Scandinavian countries at the recent London Conference, stated flatly, that the Northern States were opposed to the imposition of sanctions against Germany, on the grounds that they were not signators of the Locarno Pact.[1] Hence it would seem that the question of sanctions has become a vital one to the Scandinavian group.

As regards Norway, officials, as well as shipping men, were seriously concerned over the proposal to include shipping transportation in sanctions.

As regards sanctions, I learn from well informed circles, that we are about to enter a stage wherein a breakdown in sanctions will take place, and a subsequent cessation of the Italo-Abyssinian hostilities, with a realistic settlement of their differences.

It seems that Mr. Runciman, head of the British Board of Trade, several days ago circulated a memorandum among the Cabinet officers, pointing out the inadequacy of current sanctions, and urging that they be dispensed with on account of the unfavorable repercussions they were effecting, not only on British trade, but on that of other countries as well.

For your information, I am attaching hereto, a memorandum containing information gathered from well informed sources today. The information portrays a vast scheme proposed to be enacted over the next twelve months, towards a definite objective of bringing about a peaceful solution of current European difficulties. It calls for a New Deal for international relationships in Europe, with the British taking the lead. I deemed this information so important, that I am today cabling the substance of the attached memorandum to the Department of State.

My most sincere wishes for your continued success, and good health.

With warmest regards, I am, Faithfully yours,

Tony Biddle Jr.

[PSF:Norway:TS]

---

[1] Dr. Peter Munch's statement was reported in the New York *Times,* March 19, 1936, p. 10.

[*Enclosure*] Anthony J. Drexel Biddle, Jr., to Roosevelt

I am led to believe that we are about to enter upon an era where we may watch for vast peace proposals on the part of Great Britain. From various authoritative sources I am informed that the British have conceived a new policy involving a vast scheme of peace proposals to be put forward by stages over the next twelve months. The definite objective of this course is to bring about a "New Deal" in Europe in which Germany must have a part. There must be security for Belgium and France and equality and security for Germany. The main stages through which this is planned to be brought about are as follows:

I. To relieve the tension brought about by the present situation.

II. To suggest a new Locarno Pact for Western Europe to include an international force to patrol the Rhineland.

III. Other peace suggestions along lines of Hitler's proposals and some other proposals of the British. In other words a series of pacification pacts between Western European countries.

IV. To call a disarmament conference to be conducted along the lines of the recent Naval Conference. The policy underlying this conference will *not be to reduce armaments*[1] but rather simply to state what armaments each nation has as of that instant. It will be assumed by the meeting that whatever armaments exist at that time will have been essential for each country. Thereupon each nation will be requested to report its proposed program for the ensuing year, *in order to eliminate the element of surprise.*

It is thought that in the event of a conference along such lines the United States might be persuaded to attend. This newly proposed course on the part of the British entails a realistic diplomatic policy calling for a New Deal in Europe with the objective of arriving at realistic settlements. Therefore, I believe we may look for diplomatic maneuvers to be conducted along the foregoing lines for the next twelve months. Mainly responsible for the new British policy is Neville Chamberlain.

In its bearing on the Italy-Abyssinian conflict, I understand that the foregoing policy will entail an even more strenuous effort to bring about a cessation of hostilities and a realistic settlement. Meanwhile, serious consideration is being given to the elimination of existent sanctions, for the British will take the lead in endeavoring to eliminate everything which would give rise to tension and intrigues.

Regarding the Franco-Soviet Pact, I understand that it will be referred to The Hague Tribunal in due course.

We are entering a stage of breaking down of sanctions and of settlement of an Italian Ethiopian conflict.[2]

AJDB Jr.

[PSF:Norway:TS]

---

[1] Italics, here and below, indicate underscoring in the original.
[2] See Biddle to Hull, March 18, 1936, in *Foreign Relations, 1936,* I, 254. Roosevelt replied April 15, 1936 (*Personal Letters, 1928–1945,* I, 576), that the situation in Europe seemed "not only chaotic but much in need of some new plan and new leadership. Perhaps the time is not ripe but it is at least worthwhile pointing towards it."

Roosevelt to Cordell Hull, Secretary of State

[Washington, March 19, 1936]

My dear Mr. Secretary: Receipt is acknowledged of your letter dated March 18, with enclosures,[1] all referring to the request of the Secretary of Agriculture dated November 19, 1935,[2] approved by the Department of State, for the transfer of one hundred thousand dollars to the Bureau of Public Roads, of the Department of Agriculture, from the appropriation of one million dollars made by the Act of June 19, 1934 (48 *Stat.* 1042), to enable the United States to cooperate further with several governments, members of the Pan American Union, in connection with the survey and construction of the proposed Inter-American highway.

In reply you are informed that the statements which you refer to and quote in your letter, from the Governments of Honduras, Guatemala, Panama, Nicaragua, Mexico, Salvador, and Costa Rica, are considered to be satisfactory assurances that the several governments involved will cooperate in the construction of the projected Inter-American highway.

The request of the Secretary of Agriculture, dated November, 1935, is therefore hereby approved.

Very sincerely yours,

[*Notation*:A] 3/19/36
[OF 608:CT]

[1] OF 608; the enclosed correspondence has to do with the legality of building certain bridges along the route of the proposed Inter-American Highway under the enabling statute (48 *Stat.* 1042).

[2] Not present.

Roosevelt to Frank P. Walsh, Chairman, Power Authority of the State of New York

[Washington] March 19, 1936

Dear Frank: Many thanks for your letter and for the splendid presentation at Detroit.[1]

I will see you when I get back.

Always sincerely,

[OF 156-A:CT]

[1] March 16, 1936 (OF 156-A), enclosing a copy of the resolutions adopted by the Great Lakes-St. Lawrence Seaway and Power Conference held at Detroit, March 11–12, 1936. The resolutions affirmed the support of the participating organizations in the President's efforts in behalf of the seaway and urged the formation of a central body to further the plan. Walsh also enclosed a copy of his address before the Conference on March 11 and copies of press comments.

William Phillips, Under Secretary of State, to Roosevelt

Washington, March 19, 1936

My dear Mr. President: We have just received from the delegation in London the complete draft of the naval treaty, copy of which I am enclosing herewith.[1]

Of course, most of the clauses have come to your attention as the work of the Conference has progressed, and it remains only for a final check to be given to the complete treaty by the Navy Department and by this Department, provided it meets with your approval. The clauses which have not come to your attention before are particularly articles 23, 24 and 25, which are the escape clauses to be resorted to in the event of one of the parties to the treaty becoming involved in a war or in the event of excessive building by nations not parties to the treaty.[2] As far as I can see at the moment, the treaty is acceptable to us. Of course, as I said before, I would want to have a final check on this draft made by the Navy Department, in order to make certain that it is acceptable to the Navy.

Norman Davis has informed us that it is now anticipated that the text of the treaty will be approved by the First Committee tomorrow and that a plenary session will be held on Tuesday, March 24, to proceed with the signature of the treaty.[3] I would be very grateful, therefore, if we could have your comment on the text as it now stands as soon as convenient, in order that we may accordingly notify the delegation.[4]

Faithfully yours,

William Phillips

[PSF:London Naval Conference:TS]

---

[1] For text see State Department, *The London Naval Conference, 1935,* pp. 27–43, or 50 *Stat.* 1363.

[2] On the escape clauses, see Davis to Hull, March 19, 1936, in *Foreign Relations, 1936,* I, 96.

[3] The treaty was signed March 25, 1936.

[4] Answered March 21, 1936 (*Foreign Relations, 1936,* I, 96–97). Roosevelt said that one point should be made clear: if the treaty should be ratified by July 1, 1937, and if by then one of the signators should have started to build a number of light cruisers, the United States should have the right to make up such deficiencies. See Phillips to Roosevelt, March 20, 1936, below.

William Phillips, Under Secretary of State, to Roosevelt

Washington, March 19, 1936

My dear Mr. President: Norman Davis has just sent us a telegram, No. 146, a copy of which I enclose,[1] suggesting that a declaration of policy be agreed to as between the United States and Great Britain to the effect that, notwithstanding that the new naval treaty has no provision for quantitative limitation, the Governments of the United States and Great Britain intend to avoid at least as between themselves competition in naval construction, that parity as between their naval requirements has become an established principle acceptable to both Governments and countries, and that adherence to this principle will contribute to the furtherance of friendly relations between them.

I am not at all sure that it is advisable that this question arise at all at this moment, as I believe both Governments have been acting on the supposition that parity was an established principle between them. However, as the matter has come up, I have drafted a reply[2] to Mr. Davis which agrees with his suggestion, but asks that the arranging of such a declaration by our two Governments be made in a manner which will avoid any appearance of an agreement between the two countries which might raise the question of ratification on our part, and also that there appears to be no need for any undue publicity with regard to such an arrangement.

I would be grateful to have an expression of your opinion on this question.

Faithfully yours,

William Phillips

[*Notation*:T] Enclosure: Telegram 146, March 19, 4 P.M. from Amdelgat, London. Draft reply.

[*Notation*:AS] Instructions along lines of President's direction telephoned to Mr. Davis at 7:30 P.M. March 20, 1936. File J[3]

[*Notation*:AS] W. P. Will you change in accordance with our conversation? FDR

[PSF:London Naval Conference:TS]

[1] Davis to Roosevelt and Hull, March 19, 1936, printed in *Foreign Relations, 1936*, I, 95–96. (Not present with the letter here printed.)
[2] Not present.
[3] No memorandum of this telephone call has been found.

John Cudahy, Ambassador to Poland, to Roosevelt

Warsaw, March 20, 1936

Strictly Confidential

Dear Mr. President: This has been an exciting week and I hope you are being kept thoroughly in touch from London.

It is clear that the French, driven by panic, are standing firm while the British, faced by the reality of their lack of preparation for war, and by the resentment they feel towards France because of its failure to support them against Italy, are attempting to work out some sort of compromise.

The outstanding thing is that the principle involved in Germany's violation of the treaties has been completely lost in the tumult, and Austen Chamberlain's protest is like a voice crying in the wilderness.

This principle is no juridical nicety or matter of sentiment. It is the plain common working-day sense base of security in any stabilized social organization. It is exactly the same motive which prompted our Vigilantes to string up the outlaws in Montana fifty years ago.

The past week has demonstrated very clearly that this principle has crashed in European international affairs and that the League of Nations and collective action are all illusory. Only a miracle can preclude a war in Europe. After the meetings in London are over every country will settle down to a realization of war and to prepare accordingly. The catastrophe may be averted for a time but if the Hitler Government is not overthrown a war in Europe is as certain as the rising sun. It may be a matter of a year, two years, five years. But that another contest with Germany is coming is universally conceded now even by the most conservative.

This certainty of war we must recognize and accept as an established fact. I am sure you are aware of the situation but it is disturbing to get petitions from peace societies, one of them signed by prominent college Presidents and a retired Major General, protesting against the National Defense appropriations of the present Congress. I suppose that even if these well-meaning people were to visit Europe at the present time they would remain unconvinced.

I am thoroughly sorry Congress did not pass a Neutrality Act giving you discretion to include materials other than war munitions in an embargo. Arguments opposed to this have not changed my viewpoint that it would give us a powerful weapon in a warring world.

An observation of the German Ambassador might be worth passing on to Mr. Hopkins. He said that it was far better that the unemployed in Germany should be kept busy making ammunition and war materials than that they should receive relief in the way of a dole.[1]

Very respectfully yours,

John Cudahy

[PSF:Poland:TS]

[1] In his reply of April 15, 1936 (*Personal Letters, 1928–1945,* I, 577), Roosevelt said merely that the situation seemed to change daily.

R. Walton Moore, Assistant Secretary of State, to Roosevelt

Washington, March 20, 1936

Dear Mr. President: I hope you will think I am not going too far in venturing to write you about the liquor legislation now being considered by the Senate Finance Committee, to which the Prime Minister of Canada has presented publicly and privately his very strenuous objection. As you know, he has frankly stated in the Canadian House of Commons that should legislation of such character be enacted he will probably find it necessary to discard the trade agreement you recently approved. He is evidently under strong political pressure, which is, however, simply in line with his own personal opinion.

Mr. Phillips and I, assisted by Mr. Hackworth, this Department's legal adviser, have talked for hours, not with Secretary Morgenthau, or with Mr. Oliphant, but with a group of subordinate officials of the Treasury, but apparently have not been able to make them understand the extent to which the legislation would endanger our friendly relations with Canada, and the comparatively small amount that might perhaps be recovered on the claims that grew out of alleged bootlegging operations prior to the repeal of prohibition. The fact that in the prohibition period the Canadian Government very generously adopted a policy helpful to us, which involved it in a considerable loss of revenue seems to make no impression, nor do they seem to take into account the fact that to endeavor to coerce the payment of claims by an embargo of importations is a novel rule of international action, furnishing a precedent to other governments to be used against us. At this very moment, there are some

European Governments that are urging us to pay large claims and conceivably they might enact corresponding legislation.

The best we have been able to do is to persuade the Treasury officials to approve some such substitute draft as that herewith enclosed. That draft was talked over with the Canadian Chargé here, who, after communicating with the Prime Minister, handed us a statement, a copy of which Mr. Phillips has furnished you.

Following all of this, Mr. Phillips and I went to the Capitol yesterday to confer with Senator King, who is Chairman of the sub-committee which has been considering the legislation, and discussed the matter at length with him, and with Senators George and Barkley, who are also members of the sub-committee, Senator Harrison, Chairman of the Committee, being so occupied in the Senate as to not find it possible to do more than spend a few minutes with us. Without assuming to speak for any of the Senators mentioned, we got the idea that the proposed legislation is rather distasteful to all of them. When it was suggested that some way should be found to require payment of the old claims, there was almost as a matter of course reference made to the fact that many governments are in default to our Government, and that countless American citizens have claims against other governments, as for instance several of the Latin American Governments, and the Soviet, which they are utterly unable to collect, and that it has never been suggested that the effort should be made to coerce payment by a resort to an embargo of imports. Furthermore, it was recognized that the political effect during the campaign would be injurious, should legislation be enacted that would result in the much lauded trade agreement with Canada being scrapped. The Senators seemed to think that the only method of disposing of the problem so as to avoid a controversy between two of our departments would be for you to make a final decision. A controversy could not be privately aired in a meeting of the Finance Committee, because Senator Couzens, who is a member of that Committee, insists on his right to disregard any order of secrecy that may be adopted.

A glance at the enclosed draft will, I think convince you that aside from the objectionable embargo feature, there is another most extraordinary provision, namely, that if the Treasury finds that *some person*[1] who violates our law and is sued, has a *substantial interest* in a distillery corporation, thereupon a wholesale embargo shall attach to the importation into this country of the product of that corporation.[2] You will notice that the Secretary of the Treasury is left free to say what is a substantial interest. He may say that it consists of the ownership of one hundred shares of stock, or one thousand shares of stock, or any number of shares of stock of the corporation. I do not believe that in your experience as a lawyer you ever heard of such a basis of drastic action against a producing concern being adopted. When I asked Senator George whether in his long experience as a lawyer and judge he had heard of any such thing, he answered in the negative.

During the two years and a half that I have been in the Department, it has been necessary for me to consider almost innumerable matters of importance, but not one of them has given me so much trouble and anxiety as the one in question. As Secretary Hull will return here Monday, the Senators with whom we conferred determined to postpone until Tuesday the meeting of the Finance Committee which was to be held this morning.

I hope you will pardon me for troubling you in this way just as you are about to leave on vacation.[3]

Yours very sincerely,

R. Walton Moore

[PSF:Canada:TS]

[1] Italics indicate underscoring in the original.

[2] The section (402-A) to which Moore objected (present) was removed from the act as approved June 26, 1936 (49 *Stat.* 1939).

[3] Roosevelt then talked with Oliphant and proposed to Phillips that if the Canadian companies would give assurance that they would come into court and pay such judgment as would be obtained against them, the United States would press no legislation. On March 30 representatives of State and Treasury met with representatives of the distillers and eventually agreement was reached to settle the claims out of court at greatly reduced figures (*Foreign Relations, 1936,* I, 803–804, 810–813; Hull, *Memoirs,* I, 206–207; Blum, *From the Morgenthau Diaries,* I, pp. 112–119). See Phillips to Roosevelt, May 14, 1936, below.

William Phillips, Under Secretary of State, to Roosevelt

Washington, March 20, 1936

My dear Mr. President: I am enclosing a copy of a telegram from Norman Davis which is in two sections.[1] The first section of this telegram describes the reasons for a protocol of signature to be entered into by France, Great Britain and ourselves at the time of signing the naval treaty. This protocol provides for exchange of information on any construction which might take place in the interval between January 1 and the coming into force of the treaty, and permits of consultation between the signatories in the event of the construction of any other power at any time before the treaty comes into force rendering it desirable that the treaty be changed before coming into force. Section 2 of Mr. Davis' telegram gives the actual text of the protocol of signature.[2] It appears advisable to us to enter into this arrangement to take care of the gap between the 1st of January and the date of the treaty coming into force, which will, of course, be delayed as far as we are concerned by the necessity for ratification by the Senate.

I might say that this protocol of signature is not in a form which would require the ratification of the Senate, but calls only for action which probably comes within the jurisdiction of the Executive.

If this protocol of signature meets with your approval, I shall be very glad so to inform Mr. Davis.

Faithfully yours,

William Phillips

[*Notation*:AS] W.P.   OK   FDR
[PSF:London Naval Conference:TS]

---

[1] Not present.

[2] The protocol of signature is printed in Department of State, *The London Naval Conference, 1935: Report of the Delegates of the United States of America. Text of the London Naval Treaty of 1936 and Other Documents.* Conference Series No. 24 (Washington, 1936), pp. 42–43. It was signed March 25, 1936.

Roosevelt to the Reverend Arthur M. Stevenson, First Presbyterian Church, Ellwood City, Pennsylvania

[Washington] March 21, 1936

Dear Mr. Stevenson: I am happy to inform you that the appropriations for the War and Navy Departments now being considered by Congress have for their purpose only the maintenance of our national peace and security.[1]

Our nation has no aggressive designs against any other nation. It seeks merely to provide a state of defense that will permit us to remain at peace with all nations. Under no circumstances will this policy of self protection go to lengths beyond self protection. Aggression on the part of the United States is an impossibility insofar as the present administration is concerned. Defense against aggression by others is our accepted policy and the measure of that defense will be solely the amount necessary to safeguard us against the armaments of others. The more greatly they decrease their armaments, the more quickly and surely shall we decrease ours.

Your letter indicates you believe that the appropriations for military purposes are greatly in excess of those authorized last year. I can assure you that is not the case. If you will examine the War Department Appropriation Bill, recently passed by the House of Representatives, you will find that the increase in funds is very largely for non-military purposes, such as river and harbor improvements and flood control projects. Of the total in the bill non-military items, such as public works projects and the operation of the Panama Canal, amount to approximately $174,000,000, none of which is devoted to national defense. The increase in military items amounts to about $25,000,000, which is primarily due to a greater strength in enlisted men in the Regular Army and National Guard, as authorized by the last session of Congress, to the enrollment of more cadets at the Military Academy, to the training of additional reserve officers, to higher costs of food, clothing and shelter, and above all to the necessity of procuring substantial numbers of new and improved aircraft to replace worn-out and obsolescent airplanes and to augment slightly our strength in this important arm.

I appreciate your interest in the vital question of national defense and hope that this rather brief answer to your inquiry will serve to convince you that our policy has for its purpose only the continued maintenance of peace and security.[2]

Sincerely yours,

[OF 335:CT]

[1] Stevenson had asked the President what the purpose was of such large military appropriations and said he was led to believe it was for foreign war (Feb. 27, 1936, OF 335).

[2] Drafted in the War Department.

Roosevelt to Representative John J. McSwain of South Carolina, Chairman, Committee on Military Affairs, House of Representatives

En Route Miami, Florida, March 23, 1936

My dear Mr. McSwain: I have been giving consideration to the matter we discussed recently.[1]

I agree with you that wrong interpretations have from time to time been put on the letter which I wrote you, as Chairman of the Committee on Military Affairs, on April 29, 1935.[2]

As you know, my purpose in writing that letter was to call to the attention not only of your Committee but other congressional committees, the urgent necessity for the greatest caution in connection with testimony submitted to them, the publication of which might have an effect on our international relations. In the case of your Committee specifically, it is quite obvious that any testimony revealing war plans or military secrets may have serious repercussions in our international dealings.

I feel very deeply that when executive sessions are held the testimony should be held in the strictest confidence by committee members. At the instance referred to last year, I want to assure you that I never for a moment thought that publication of the testimony given your Committee in executive session by ranking officers of the Army and Navy was made public intentionally. Your prompt and immediate reply to my letter was complete assurance of this. I have every confidence that you, as you said in your letter last May, make every effort to keep confidential testimony on matters referred to above. I think your suggestion that such testimony be not even taken down stenographically will go far toward preventing premature or unauthorized publication.[3]

Very sincerely yours,

[OF 25:T]

[1] At the White House on March 20 (PPF 1-0).
[2] Printed in *Public Papers,* IV, 141–142; see Bingham to Roosevelt, May 10, 1935, above.
[3] This letter was prepared by McSwain, according to an accompanying draft. The draft was revised in the White House, by whom is not clear.

Sumner Welles, Assistant Secretary of State, to Roosevelt

Washington, March 25, 1936

My dear Mr. President: I hate to trouble you on your vacation with any matter of official business, but I thought the following information would be of interest to you and that you might want to consider it during the time you are away. You may remember that in my last talk with you before you left,[1] you referred to the cable which we had received from our Ambassador in Argentina indicating apparently some disquiet on the part of the Argentine Government because of the reports it had received of the possibility that this Government might dispose of ten of its cruisers of the *Omaha* class over a period of ten years to the Government of Brazil.[2]

Yesterday, the Argentine Ambassador came in to see me with a confidential message from his Government to the effect that if the Ambassador ascertained that this was correct, he was to make immediate representations to this Government urging that we agree to sell five of the suggested ten cruisers on similar terms to the Argentine Government. The opinion expressed by the Argentine Government for the Ambassador's personal information was: that such a solution would be "highly desirable, as well as economical."

In other words, this Government would have, in my belief, the chance, which might never be repeated, to obtain unification of standards between the Argentine, Brazilian, and United States navies, and through this step, to consolidate for a long time the position we now temporarily enjoy, of having our own naval instructors in both Argentina and Brazil. If the step could be taken, neither Argentina nor Brazil would require new units for a considerable number of years, and pressure by our British friends both for the replacement of our instructors by British instructors and for the building of warships for those two Republics in British shipyards would be quashed.

I have, of course, told the Ambassador that under present conditions we have been unable to agree to the Brazilian proposal, and that we never would have agreed to such a proposal unless we had first made known our consideration of such proposal to the other Governments of South America and had offered them similar accommodation on equal terms.[3]

I feel so keenly about the importance to the United States of this opportunity that I trust you may feel able to authorize further consideration of a project in this new light in the event that the London naval agreement can later be amended.

I hope you are having a highly successful fishing trip and that you are enjoying the best kind of a real vacation.

Believe me, always, Faithfully yours,

Sumner Welles

[OF 366:TS]

[1] The President talked with Welles on March 11 and left for a Florida fishing vacation on March 22, 1936.
[2] Weddell to Hull, March 18, 1936, printed in *Foreign Relations, 1936,* V, 299, with

Phillips' reply of March 19 (*ibid.*, pp. 299–300) and other correspondence on this subject. Roosevelt wrote to President Vargas on July 6, 1936 (*ibid.*, pp. 300–301).

[3] The cruisers were promised to Brazil in the summer of 1937, after protracted negotiations (*Foreign Relations, 1937*, V, 149–174), but protests from Great Britain and from Argentina finally blocked the plan.

Cordell Hull, Secretary of State, to Roosevelt

[Washington, March 28, 1936]

[*Radiogram*] The Mexican ambassador has communicated to us confidentially the text of a telegram he received yesterday from the Mexican Secretary of the Treasury. It reads as follows:

Please consult Secretary Morgenthau whether it would be in accordance with his plans regarding silver for Mexico to suggest as a question to be discussed in the approaching Inter-American Conference convoked by President Roosevelt the subject of the use of silver as a part of banking reserves in the payment of international balances and the stimulation of the coinage of silver for fiduciary currency.[1]

The ambassador states that it is his own belief and that he is disposed so to recommend to his Government that this subject is completely outside the range of the topics which should be appropriately discussed at the Inter-American Peace Conference suggested by yourself. He has however desired confidentially to ascertain whether by any chance this Government would favor his adopting a different course. Please advise what your desires may be. You will of course recall that an inter-American financial congress has already been convoked to meet in Santiago, Chile, during the course of the coming year.[2]

[OF 200-W:CT]

[1] After negotiations over silver purchases during much of 1935, Morgenthau concluded an agreement with Mexico on Jan. 6, 1936, which provided for the monthly purchase from Mexico of 5,000,000 ounces of silver, the agreement subject to monthly renewal (Allan S. Everest, *Morgenthau, the New Deal, and Silver* [New York: King's Crown Press, 1950], pp. 83–84; New York *Times*, Jan. 7, 1936, p. 31). "Stimulation of the coinage of silver for fiduciary currency" refers to Morgenthau's efforts to convince the Mexicans that they should coin and use more of their silver domestically.

[2] Upon receipt of Hull's telegram, Roosevelt wired Morgenthau immediately: "Please let me have your views Mexican suggestion. To discuss finances at what is primarily a peace conference seems to me somewhat out of place. It might be possible however to discuss the general subject informally and wholly outside of the official agenda."

Morgenthau replied on March 30: "Inasmuch as South American Conference is primarily to discuss peace, would greatly prefer that all monetary questions be left out of both official and unofficial discussions. I have been able to survey best by discussing monetary problems with one country at a time in Washington where I always have your most helpful advice and guidance" (OF 200-W).

Roosevelt to Cordell Hull, Secretary of State

U.S.S. *Dickerson*, 29 March 1936

[*Radiogram*] Please tell Secretary of War and Acting Secretary Navy confidentially from me that the position of both Services in appearance before Senate Committee on Panama Treaty should be as follows: They should maintain military necessity of exercising troops in Panama territory, of full freedom of action in event of war or threat of war and of prevention of ship to shore radio except through United States or Panama control. On the other hand, it is my belief and that of the State Department that the wording of the Treaty provides adequately for these contingencies. Therefore War and Navy should not question effect of language which diplomatic usage makes perfectly clear to the foreign affairs departments of both governments. It is highly important to the relations of this Government with all the other American Republics that this treaty be ratified.[1]

[OF 200-W:CT]

[1] This message was in response to Hull's radiogram of March 28, 1936 (OF 20), reporting that Senator Johnson had asked that representatives of the War and Navy Departments be present at the next meeting of the Foreign Relations Committee to get their views on the Panama treaties. Hull wanted to know what views Roosevelt wished to send through the department representatives.

William E. Dodd, Ambassador to Germany, to Roosevelt

Berlin, April 1, 1936

Dear Mr. President: At this critical moment, I venture a summary of conditions and blunders which have brought the more democratic peoples of Europe into their present dangerous status, perhaps repeating some things I have written before.

I cabled from Basle late in August the anxieties of different nations about Mussolini's expected break into Ethiopia. From that date to December 10, I watched popular and official attitudes here. There was no question in my mind that two-thirds of the German people hoped and prayed for prompt application of sanctions, including oil, upon Italy. Germans of semi-official, University, religious and royalist relations were unanimous in their hope that one dictatorship would be broken down, especially through the cooperation of the United States. If that happened, these people thought their own miserable position would be improved, even corrected. If I were to give the names of the people who showed great concern and talked freely, you could hardly doubt my conclusions. From September till the Hoare-Laval blunder even the triumvirate criticized the Duce; they would be neutral and not help him kill Ethiopians.

But as soon as the Hoare-Laval announcement was made, clever leaders like Goebbels began to speak in favor of Italian "colonial needs." Then the remilitarization of the Rhineland zone was talked seriously, but always under cover. About January 1, there was a conference of the generals of the army. They voted unanimously against sending troops into the Rhine zone and also against lending any aid to Nazis who might break into Austria. Conferences and discussions were held frequently between January 1 and March 7. On the 6th of March all opposition ceased; the Führer was in close relations with Mussolini; and the Foreign Office was ready to approve drastic action and criticism of France and Russia. I sent a telegram on February 29 giving positive avowal of Secretary von Neurath's opposition to doing or proposing what was proclaimed on March 7, but on that date he shouted approval. What was the cause of this?

The French had promised their support to Mussolini in January 1935 in case he annexed Ethiopia. This was a violation of the League's solemn agreement. When England became aware of Mussolini's purpose to control the Nile and annex Egypt itself, she called upon France and the League. France defeated England and gave Hitler the best opportunity he had had, since he came to power, to take the lead in European affairs. Before December 15 Mussolini was in grave danger of being overthrown, and influential groups in Italy were working toward that end, even the Pope was lending aid and the King of Italy hopeful of a restoration of the throne he had lost. Frenchmen here and in Paris seemed to have no real understanding of their own blunders. I had a long talk with the French Ambassador on December 12. He could not foresee consequences.

As to the Franco-Soviet pact, nobody here considered it serious before January 1. Von Neurath said to me February 29 it was only a defense agreement and that the Russians had no idea of making war beyond their western boundaries. Even Dr. Schacht, most influential man here after Hitler, said there was no danger in that direction. But Hitler-Goebbels were ready March 1 to use Franco-Soviet pact for propaganda; they were approving Mussolini's right to annex Ethiopia and putting forward Germany's right to having her colonies restored; and making ready secretly to send troops into the Rhine zone. It was the best chance imaginable. Hitler even quoted Woodrow Wilson more than once. How could France reply to these charges, having violated the League agreement in January 1933? If she approved the Italian seizure of territory how could she complain if Germany re-seized her historic Rhine country?

Illogical as it was, the French Ambassador here and his superiors in Paris showed great excitement March 7 to 29, called off invitations to parties and talked of sending their army into the German Rhine area. When France then turned to England just as England had turned to her in December preceding, she was terribly angry to learn that England would treat Germany just as France had treated Italy. There had been a slight danger of war in the Mediterranean in December, for a week or two; there was greater danger of war on the Rhine in March. The outcome, as we all know, was German success. Nothing else could have been expected.

In conclusion, the French nation is now on a definite decline toward the position of Spain, her population at a standstill. Although she has her peace pact with Russia, it means little. The Balkan states could hardly be assisted from either direction if Hitler's Rhine peace idea be applied—these states disposed now to line up with Germany or Italy. The English nation, having failed to cooperate with the United States in 1931 and failed in December to balk Mussolini, is beginning a similar decline, her population at a standstill and her relations with her colonies weakening. Will she parallel the history of the Netherlands after 1713?

But Germany's dictatorship is now stronger than ever. If she keeps the pace three more years she can beat the whole of Europe in a war. No man, no newspaper here is permitted to talk pacifism, except Hitler. Protestants and Catholics, regardless of many imprisonments, all shout and vote hurrah for their second "Jesu Christu" and the population is increasing as no other in western Europe. The 67,000,000 is expected to be 80,000,000 when Austria (including part of Czechoslovakia) is annexed. With universal service, both in aircraft and on land, and with a solid front never before enjoyed here or elsewhere, Europe can hardly escape domination: Italy taking control of the Mediterranean and Germany the Balkan zone. It looks as if our blunders 1920–1933 and English and French blunders 1920–26 and 1931–36 have given us a new and dangerous world situation: Germany dominating Europe, Japan dominating the Far East and the United States dominating both Americas.

If Woodrow Wilson's bones do not turn in the Cathedral grave, then bones never turn in graves. Possibly you can do something, but from reports of Congressmen's attitudes, I have grave doubts. So many men, including my friend Beard, think absolute isolation a coming paradise.[1]

Sincerely yours,

William E. Dodd

[PSF:Germany:TS]

[1] Charles A. Beard.

Raymond Moley to Marguerite LeHand, Private Secretary to the President

New York, April 4, 1936

Dear Missy: I have received the following letter from Felix.[1]

What follows is also in your field of knowledge and interest, and so I write you in the hope that, if you concur with what I propose, you will pass it on to Missy for F.D.R. as our joint view:

1. Early in July next there is to be an inter-governmental conference in Geneva to fix the legal status of the German refugees.

2. On the assumption that our government will be invited to send representatives, I suggest that Rabbi Wise be designated as one of them, and for the following reasons:

a. He really knows the Jewish problem the world over as probably not another American;

b. He has probably a greater sway over the great Jewish masses—I say the masses and not the Jimmie Warburgs—than any other person, barring only Brandeis, and such an appointment would hearten them as a symbol of interest and sympathy;

c. Wise himself would, I am sure, be greatly moved by such a designation, and he is a whole-souled, unselfish supporter of the President's, and will be one of the most powerful advocates of the New Deal (I have seen him in action—I know) in the months to come;

d. It's a purely honorific post, and great good can be achieved, in various quarters, without any countervailing cost.

I hope much that you concur and will pass this on.

I do concur and I want to pass on the suggestion.[2]
Cordially yours,

R.M.

[OF 20:TS]

[1] Felix Frankfurter.
[2] When the President returned from his cruise he sent Moley's letter to Hull with a memorandum asking that Hull speak to him about it (April 20, 1936, OF 20). In the meantime, however, Hull had notified Prentiss Gilbert and the Secretary General of the League of Nations, in messages of April 6 and 7, 1936, respectively, that the United States did not plan to take part in the conference and would not be a party to any convention it might adopt (*Foreign Relations, 1936*, II, 207). Curtis T. Everett, consul in Geneva, was, however, sent as an observer (Hull to Gilbert, June 6, 1936, *ibid.*, pp. 208–209). See Hull to Roosevelt, April 21, 1936, below.

Roosevelt to Harry Martens, Bethel College, Newton, Kansas

[Washington] April 10, 1936

Dear Mr. Martens: In the promotion of peace and good will among nations no less than among individuals the churches ought to be, and I believe they are, the greatest harmonizing influence in the world. They embody the very spirit and teaching of Him who came into the world as the Prince of Peace and gave to all mankind a new commandment of love.

The way will be made easy for statesmen to set up the machinery of peace between nations if we as individuals cultivate a strong and virile "will to peace" in our everyday relations one with another. In other words we must cultivate the spirit of neighborliness. I have previously given voice to this thought in a public utterance in which I said:

As President of the United States I say to you most earnestly once more that the people of America and the Government of those people intend and expect to remain at peace with all the world. In the . . . years . . . of my Presidency, this Government has remained constant in following this policy of our own choice. At home we have preached, and will continue to preach, the gospel of the good neighbor. I hope from the bottom of my heart that as the years go on, in every continent and in every clime, nation will follow nation in proving by deed as well as by word their adherence to the ideal of the Americas—I am a good neighbor.[1]

Very sincerely yours,

[PPF 120:CT]

[1] Martens, a student at Bethel College, had asked Roosevelt in a letter of April 3, 1936 (PPF 120), for a message to be used in a speech celebrating the sixtieth anniversary of the founding of a Mennonite church in Kansas. The message sent was the final paragraph of Roosevelt's San Diego speech of Oct. 2, 1935, above.

Prime Minister William L. Mackenzie King of Canada to Roosevelt

Ottawa, 19–4–36.

Personal

My dear Mr. President: I was delighted to receive yesterday your very kind letter of the 16th inst.[1] I need no assurances concerning your heart being in the right place as respects either Canada or myself. The latest expression of its generosity is nonetheless most welcome.

The Governor General and I are wholly of your view that the more "natural" in all respects visits between the White House, Washington, and Rideau Hall, Ottawa, can be made the more pleasurable they are certain to be, and the more frequent. Lord Tweedsmuir and I may be counted upon to further your own wishes; also to understand the difficulties which may beset your path in seeking to further them yourself. We both much hope that Congress may not sit too long to prevent your getting away at the time at present in mind, but we shall understand any postponement that may be necessary. A visit to Ottawa by yourself would, I believe, not only mean very much to our respective countries, and to relations which were never more friendly, but might have a quieting effect upon the situation in Europe, where international friendliness and good-will seem to have lost their footing altogether.

I am greatly pleased at the outcome, thus far, of our agreement. I never doubted but that once in effect, opposition to a measure of this kind would soon give place to wide spread appreciation of its benefits. I much hope that we may yet have opportunity greatly to enlarge the latter.

My visit to the White House continues to afford me the happiest memories official and personal alike. Please let this acknowledgement of your kind letter bring my best of regards and wishes to Mrs. Roosevelt and yourself.

Yours very sincerely,

W. L. Mackenzie King

[PSF:Canada:AS]

[1] Roosevelt said he hoped to visit Ottawa on June 8 unless Congress should still be in session, in which event he would come later in the summer (*Personal Letters, 1928–1945,* I, 578–579). He had told Norman Armour that he should like to visit Canada and Tweedsmuir had extended a cordial invitation which the President had accepted (Tweedsmuir to Roosevelt, Feb. 10, 1936, PPF 3396; Phillips to Roosevelt, Feb. 12, 1936, PSF:Canada; Roosevelt to Tweedsmuir, Feb. 15, 1936, *Personal Letters, 1928–1945,* I, 556–557).

Cordell Hull, Secretary of State, to Roosevelt

[Washington] April 21, 1936

My dear Mr. President: With regard to the Inter-Governmental Conference on Jewish and Non-Jewish Refugees coming from Germany, referred to in Mr. Frankfurter's letter to Mr. Moley, and the latter's letter which you sent to me by confidential memorandum of April 20th,[1] I should perhaps state that the Council of the League of Nations has called a conference of the States members of the League, as well as the United States of America and the United States of Brazil, to meet at Geneva on July 2, next. The provisional program of this conference (a copy of which I am appending hereto) contains the following items of discussion:

1. Framing of provisional arrangements concerning the legal status of German refugees.

2. Drafting of a convention determining the status of refugees.

3. Examination of methods of obtaining facilities for the delivery of civil status and other papers by the authorities of the country of origin.

As you will see, the agenda of the conference calls for discussion only of matters pertaining to the legal status of German and other refugees. As far as this country is concerned, the status of all aliens is determined by law and there is no latitude left to the Executive to discuss questions concerning the legal status of aliens. It does not appear advisable, therefore, for this Government to place itself in the position of even appearing to have any authority or discretion in connection with the status of other than American citizens. We have, in consequence, already informed the Secretary General of the League that this Government does not contemplate participating actively in the conference or in becoming a party to any convention which it may draw up, but will be very glad to have the American Consul in Geneva, or a member of his staff, attend the meetings as an observer.[2]

In response to an inquiry on his part, we have informed Professor Joseph P. Chamberlain, who was the American representative on the Governing Body of the High Commission for Refugees from Germany until the recent dissolution of that Body, of our intention to have an observer from the American Consulate in Geneva attend the conference. Professor Chamberlain, in acknowledging the Department's letter, stated that he understood the position of this Government and that he was glad to learn that the American Consul would attend the conference as an observer.[3]

Faithfully yours,

[*Notation*:AS] C.H.   OK   FDR
[OF 3186:T]

[1] See Moley's letter of April 4, 1936, addressed to Marguerite LeHand, above.
[2] Hull to Avenol, April 7, 1936, *Foreign Relations, 1936*, II, 207.
[3] Curtis T. Everett.

Roosevelt to Charles G. Fenwick, President, The Catholic Association for International Peace, Washington

[Washington] April 28, 1936

My dear Doctor Fenwick: I was gratified to learn by your letter of April 11, 1936,[1] of your deep interest in the proposed Inter-American Conference. As you say, the world today is in a very troubled state. Respect for treaties and other international commitments has been undermined and healthy economic relations have been impaired by the extreme forms of economic nationalism. Perhaps the most encouraging sign in this otherwise discouraging situation is the marked improvement in the general relations between the American Republics. The maintenance of the peace of this continent is becoming to an increasing extent the joint responsibility of the American Republics, and the restoration of trade is recognized as a necessity to recovery. It is for these reasons that I addressed the other Chiefs of State, suggesting that an inter-American conference be convened. I feel confident that such a conference is not only timely but can give a practical demonstration to the rest of the world of the mutual benefits to be derived from international cooperation.

It is very heartening, therefore, to learn that the Conference has the support of The Catholic Association for International Peace, and that the Association, through its publications and by such conferences as that held in Washington on April thirteenth and fourteenth, is laying the groundwork for an intelligent understanding by the people of this country of the problems confronting the American Republics.

I shall be glad to bear in mind your suggestion that a delegate be appointed, representative of the principles for which the organization of which you are the President stands, and when the time comes to give attention to the appointment of a delegation, will give every consideration to your suggestion.

Very sincerely yours,

[PPF 3486:CT]

[1] Fenwick had asked (PPF 3486) that one of the delegates to the Inter-American Conference be representative of the principles of the Catholic Association for International Peace. He was confident that the Latin American states would be particularly responsive to the appeals for peace contained in the various papal encyclicals. Roosevelt had himself raised the question of a representative of the peace groups; see his memorandum to Hull of April 18, 1936, in *Personal Letters, 1928–1945*, I, 579.

Lincoln MacVeagh, Minister to Greece, to Roosevelt

[Athens] April 30, 1936

Dear Franklin: I see that the clans are gathering and from what Smouch[1] says in a recent letter I hope very soon to hear whether you want me to come home and when. If you think I can be of any help to you, I shall certainly do my best, and am in fact ready to go at the drop of the hat.

Since I last wrote,[2] things have moved along here at a merry rate. You will remember that I described to you the difficulties besetting the King in his attempt to unite the country under his leadership as a constitutional monarchy. Shortly after I wrote, a group of the highest officers in the army, navy and aviation, hearing that a continuation of the King's conciliatory policy would result in reintegration in the army forces of the seditious officers whom they themselves exiled or condemned to death last year, called on the King, and demanded a dictatorship. The sequel shows pretty well the King's calibre. He had no time to ask advice of those who are supposed to be his mentors, such as the British Minister. He replied at once: "Who will be the Dictator?" "You will be," they said, "if you will stand with us."

You may remember what I said in my last letter about the King's greatest difficulty being to remain non-partisan. Here he was faced with it in an acute form.

"Let me think over your proposition, Gentlemen," he said. "Give me twenty-four hours." They agreed and withdrew. Whereupon the King immediately seized the telephone and called up Professor Demertzis,[3] the Premier, and ordered him to secure at once the resignation of General Papagos,[4] the Minister of War, and General Platis,[5] the Under-Minister. The truth was that both these men really belonged to the Condylis faction of die-hard anti-Veniselists (which the King had turned out at the time of his restoration) but had played a double game, pretending to be the King's men while preparing the way to force him to be their partisan. It was this fact to which the King now suddenly woke up, and they and their bold officers found themselves figuratively in the street. "Send General Metaxas to me," went on the King, and in a jiffy Greece had a new Minister of War and Vice President of the Council; and very shortly thereafter this man became Minister of Marine, and temporary Minister of Aviation, as well.

One might describe the above as a coup d'état with a reverse English on it. The ball was struck but went the other way. General Metaxas was formerly King Constantine's Chief of Staff. Latterly he has been only one of the smaller political figures in Greece, eclipsed first by Veniselos and then by Tsaldaris. He has a following of only six deputies in the Chamber. But when the King, in order to come back made it up with the exiled but powerful Veniselos, Metaxas alone among the old Royalists jumped with him. He has proved himself indeed the King's man and has reaped his reward. He is a good soldier and a disciplinarian, and seems now to have the army in his fist. His assumption of the War and other Ministries greatly strengthened the King's non-partisan government. And when Professor Demertzis died suddenly on Easter Monday, General Metaxas took over the Premiership and the Ministry for Foreign Affairs as good measure—and running over!

At that time, the King's plan was to have his non-partisan government receive a vote of confidence from the Chamber, which would thereafter adjourn till the fall. The inability of the various party-leaders either to form a one-party government or a coalition made this program advisable if not, indeed, inevitable, while the death of Mr. Veniselos seemed to herald considerable political changes, the extent of which cannot be immediately foretold. General Metaxas took over this program, and while he has received rather a vote of tolerance than of confidence— owing to the fact that he is himself a politician and therefore hardly to be called "non-partisan"—he may, according to present indications, run Greece until the first of October, when new elections will be in order. Of course, the Chamber may try to tie some strings to his power before it finally adjourns, but if it gets too rambunctious the King may dissolve it altogether.

In the realm of foreign affairs, Greece is still, so far as Italy is concerned, in England's boat. The King has actually admitted as much to a friend of mine, but the fact is evident and inevitable as long as England controls the sea. Germany's action in flouting the treaties of Locarno and Versailles, has, on the other hand, complicated the general situation immensely. It has caused Turkey to ask permission to refortify the Dardanelles, aroused revisionist ambitions in Bulgaria, and brought sharply to the fore again, in Greek foreign policy, the question of the Balkan Pact.

As you will remember, that pact, signed by Rumania, Turkey, Yugoslavia and Greece, guarantees the status quo of Balkan boundaries.[6] It was conceived originally as an extension of Titulesco's francophile policy and aimed to isolate Bulgaria. On account, however, of the possibility of Italian aid to Bulgaria should the latter attempt to break her bonds, a secret military protocol seems to have been attached to the pact, according to article 3 of which the signatory powers are bound to make war on a non-Balkan power should such a power aid a Balkan power in an attempt to change the boundaries guaranteed.

The existence of this secret protocol, which seems to have been signed in Geneva in June, 1934, has long been regarded among us foreigners as an open secret, and recently the Greek Government in official communiqués has actually referred to it and to article 3 (though the Turkish Minister here looked me in the eye and said he couldn't imagine what was meant!) There are soi-disant copies of it in our files here and in Washington. It seems to have been this protocol, rather than the Pact itself, which led Veniselos, who dreaded anything tending to embroil Greece with Italy, to launch a terrific attack on the ratification of the

Pact by Greece two years ago, forcing the Foreign Minister, Mr. Maximos, to make a declaration before the Chamber to the effect that nothing in the Pact obligated Greece to make war on a non-Balkan State. And it was only on the strength of that declaration that the Government secured ratification.

Recently, only a short time before he died, Mr. Veniselos returned to the question and charged, what has not been denied by the Government, not only that Mr. Maximos signed a document (the secret protocol) at Geneva in contravention of his statement before the Chamber, but that he made no written reservations in keeping with that statement, and that therefore Greece stands committed under certain conditions to fight a non-Balkan power under the provisions of the Balkan Pact. Mr. Maximos replied, rather weakly, that he made "verbal reservations" as to article 3 and so reported by telegram to his Government. But no copy of his telegram exists in the government's files, the Veniselist press has branded him as a traitor, and altogether there has been a sweet to-do! A secret meeting of the Government and the Party-leaders has now resulted in the publication of a statement that all is well, and that Greece stands by the Pact and is not committed in the sense indicated by paragraph 3 (which is often referred to but never quoted!) and the up-shot is that Greece's allies are puzzled as to how one can sign and not sign at the same time, and Mr. Metaxas, the present Premier, is going to attend the meeting of the representatives of the Balkan Entente at Belgrade next week and try to explain his country's position—if he can!

The situation is indeed ticklish for Greece. To have the Balkan Pact dissolve away would be a calamity for her, vulnerable as she is not only by sea but along her northern border. Yet she cannot support a policy which may lead her to cross swords with Italy, if she has only Balkan States to back her. Thus in the face of renewed Bulgarian hopes of eventually reaching the Aegean, which have been stirred up by what is going on in Central Europe, she is trying to have her cake and eat it too, to enjoy the secure possession of Greek Macedonia and Thrace by the help of allies whom she herself is not willing to support wholeheartedly.

All this might conceivably be called a tempest in a teapot. But the Balkan Entente is, as you know, tied in with the Little Entente by the participation of Yugoslavia and Rumania, and the above represents the progress of one of those cross-currents which seem threatening the whole structure of French-inspired regional pacts encircling the danger zone of German ambitions. That the current sets from the direction of Italy may be a sign of the times. Perhaps Greece should be forgiven if her foreign policy seems a bit erratic just now. As I wrote before, it is necessarily anchored to England on the one hand and the status quo on the other, and one if not both of these rocks would appear to have come somewhat unstuck. One remembers the wobbliness, and importance, of Greek foreign policy in the first years of the World War.

The Greco-Turkish treaty of friendship does not at present show the same shakiness as the Balkan Pact.[7] As peoples, the Greeks and Turks don't love each other. They could hardly be expected to. But economically the two countries are rather complementary than otherwise, Turkey being more of a producer and Greece controlling the carrying trade. Also both countries fear Italy and Bulgaria. Consequently when Turkey the other day, in gentlemanly fashion (compared with Germany) asked permission to refortify the Straits, the Greek Government immediately expressed its sympathy with the Turkish point of view. The general assent to the Turkish proposition is another sign of the times. Turkish feelers in that direction were not similarly encouraged a year ago. Europe seems rapidly reaching a sort of "scrap-of-paper" stage by mutual consent (or necessity?), and allies are being sought on the basis of "what armaments have you got?" rather than "what have you signed?" Observers here feel that Mussolini has bluffed England out on the Abyssinian question and that the next war will at least not start in that quarter. Eyes are rather on Germany and Central and Eastern Europe.

Economically and financially, Greece is in pretty good condition. Too much of her population is concentrated in Athens, and the housing boom is a cause for uneasiness. But in general she is doing well. The Finance Minister is going to London shortly to discuss with the English Committee of the holders of Greek bonds the possibility of increasing the present percentage of payment. His main argument against doing so is likely to be the necessity of increasing the appropriation for national defense. At the same time, the Greeks don't want to be too intransigent, as they undoubtedly wish to work along gradually towards a general reconsideration, and writing down, of their whole foreign debt. Perhaps the most outstanding recent development of their economic and financial situation, however, is the extent to which they have fallen into the hands of the Germans, through the working of the 100% clearing arrangement between the two countries. Germany has for the past year and a half been buying Macedonian tobacco of even the poorest grades (we take the best) at fantastic prices. The Bank of Greece pays the producers in drachmas and gets credit in Berlin in blocked Reichsmarks. This enables Germany to bring pressure on the Greek import trade and flood the country with a lot of poor stuff at high prices, and still, in spite of all Greece can do, the amount of her credits in Germany increases. The Bank of Greece recently tried to take measures to correct the situation, but political pressure from the tobacco regions put a stop to that, and as a result the Government has had to step in and take the responsibility; borrowing the Bank's credits in Berlin and promising to do something to ameliorate the situation when present crops are exhausted!

I have already written too much, and I will spare you other details, such as how the past months of uncertainty have encouraged the Communists, and the great number of strikes which we have had in consequence. In general, we cannot say that the country is badly off, and it plays no observable part in causing the present troubles, but it is so placed that it reacts in some way or other to nearly every current of unrest in Europe today, and as you know there are a lot of these.

Smouch seems to have seen something of you and Eleanor recently. He writes a good letter about politics, but says nothing about his own activities. I must find out about them when I get home! It seems that little Eleanor has been with you too. We miss her a lot this year.[8]

Affectionately yours,

Lincoln MacVeagh[9]

[PSF:Greece:TS]

[1] G. Hall Roosevelt, a friend of MacVeagh since Groton.

[2] Feb. 29, 1936, above.

[3] Constantine B. Demertjis, professor of jurisprudence at the University of Athens, had resigned as premier on Jan. 29, 1936, but had been asked by King George to form a nonpartisan cabinet and had taken his oath of office on March 15, 1936. He died of a heart attack on April 13, 1936 (New York *Times*, April 14, 1936, p. 17). He was succeeded by General John Metaxas, Minister of War.

[4] Alexander Papagos.

[5] General M. Platis.

[6] Signed Feb. 9, 1934.

[7] The Treaty of Ankara, Oct. 30, 1930.

[8] Eleanor Roosevelt, daughter of G. Hall Roosevelt ("Smouch"), had spent the previous winter with the MacVeaghs.

[9] Roosevelt replied May 23 (*Personal Letters, 1928–1945,* I, 592). He said MacVeagh should not return to the United States unless the situation in the Balkans became more quiet.

R. Walton Moore, Assistant Secretary of State, to Roosevelt

[Washington] May 1, 1936

For the President: I have just received this letter from Dr. Dodd, who will reach his farm in Loudoun County, Virginia, today, and probably shortly be in Washington. The zeppelin in charge of Dr. Eckener is expected to reach Lakehurst, New Jersey, next week.

R. Walton Moore

[Notation:A:LeHand]   Mac   Will you take care of this?
[OF 523:TS]

[Enclosure] William E. Dodd, Ambassador to Germany, to R. Walton Moore

Berlin, April 18, 1936

Personal and Confidential

Dear Judge Moore: Dr. Hugo Eckener, the one outstanding authority for Zeppelin aircraft, refused to engage in propaganda on March 28 and 29, i.e., refused to make public statements about people's voting.[1] He did fly his machines over the big cities and let people consider that as a demonstration for the Führer, but he would not go further. He wrote a very polite and kindly note excusing himself. In reply, the Führer ordered Goebbels, first, to put him out of the business. That was impossible, and Goebbels gave the press orders not to mention his name or to pay any tribute in any way to him in the future, and the press was perfectly obedient to this order, although Eckener went to Brazil and back and had an accident, though not serious, on the way back. The masses of German people, in so far as I have been able to contact with them, are very displeased, but not able to say a word.

As Dr. Eckener is planning to fly to the United States about the middle of May,[2] I think it would be nothing but appropriate for our Government to give him a hearty reception as he lands in New Jersey and, if possible, for the President to give him some attention when he goes to Washington. The whole outside world respects Eckener, and it would seem to me to be nothing but fair if our Washington authorities could even give him a luncheon and allow the press people to know it. In case you think this sort of thing ought to be done, I wish you would mention it to the President. The whole thing ought to be a tribute to Eckener's ability and genius, not so much to the mere matter of flying machines.[3]

Sincerely yours,

William E. Dodd

[OF 523:TS]

[1] Hitler dissolved the Reichstag on March 28 and new elections were held the next day. Eckener's refusal to aid the Nazi party angered the Goebbels propaganda offices and all mention of him in the press was forbidden for a time.

[2] This was the maiden trip of the *Hindenburg*.

[3] On recommendation of the State Department's Division of Protocol and Conferences, Eckener was invited to lunch at the White House on May 11. He was received by the President on that day but his schedule of public appearances did not permit him to stay for lunch (Kannee to McIntyre, May 5, 1936, OF 198-A).

Samuel R. Fuller, Jr., to Roosevelt

New York, 1 May 1936

Dear Mr. President: Subject: European and particularly German trends.

Enclosures: Memoranda of interviews as follows:

a. Dr. Hjalmar Schacht, Berlin, 27–30 March 1936;

b. Adolf Hitler, Berlin, 1 April 1936;

c. Dr. Hjalmar Schacht, Berlin, 1 April 1936;

d. King Edward VIII, Buckingham Palace, London, 3 April 1936;

e. Sir Warren Fisher, Permanent Under Secretary of Treasury, London, 7 April 1936;

f. Dr. H. Colijn, P.M. Holland, The Hague, 13 April 1936;

g. F. H. Fentener van Vlissingen, Dutch business colleague of mine who is President of International Chamber of Commerce, Paris, 24 March 1936.

Reference: Our conversations 13 February 1936 and 6 March 1936.[1]

In accordance with the above reference, an attempt was made by me during my recent European trip (19 March–21 April 1936) to ascertain European and particularly German trends, through conversations recorded in the above enclosures.[2]

The transcriptions of the conversations recorded in enclosures are not word for word accurate: but they are made from long-hand notes written by me soon after the conversations; and are substantially word for word accurate and are exactly accurate as to meaning.

Inasmuch as my mission was to gain information, the recorded conversations do not necessarily reflect personal opinions regarding the subjects covered.

Supplementing the above enclosures may the liberty be taken please of adding some personal impressions and thoughts with the belief that they are within the scope of the work you so kindly gave me? They are as follows:

1. That there will be no immediate European war.

2. That we should keep clear of the European political cobweb.

3. That unless some change occurs in the present course of events, war in Europe seems inevitable within a year or so.

4. That the averting of war for a time at least, it would seem, can be greatly helped by an announcement of a continuation of the present de facto stabilized relation between the dollar and the pound for a year or so, or by the announcement that either the dollar or the pound will remain at its present value during this time for the reason that this will reduce the strain on Germany, France, et al.; and that the prolongation of peace further will be vastly aided by the adoption among peoples of reciprocal trade treaties of the most favored nation plan as propounded by the Secretary of State. And that very possibly these are the only means now at our command to aid practically in this matter, because they do not involve us in political entanglements.

5. That the prolongation of European peace, it appears logical to believe, will help us; while a European war undoubtedly would hurt us vastly, because of the real danger that we would be drawn into it.

6. That Hitler appears to be at his highest point of popularity because of the military occupation of the Rhineland, though some fear of him undoubtedly exists.

7. That a definite impression taken from the Hitler interview was that he would negotiate for his desires, but that his deep belief for attainment of them lay in armament; and that the cost of this armament was secondary with him; and that the present need for foreign exchange is vital to the Germans.

8. Therefore, may the following not be worthy of thought: that consideration be given here as soon as possible to the advisability of an arrangement for a continuation of the de facto stabilization between the dollar and the pound for perhaps a year, with the retainment, meantime, of freedom of action against the eventuality of war or assaults upon such

stabilization; determining at the same time whether it would be better to announce the continuation of the present stabilization, or merely to announce that either the dollar or the pound would continue to remain at its present value for perhaps a year. The result upon the so-called gold bloc in Europe in either case, it seems proper to believe, would be favorable, but here is it not possible to conceive that the result might be better should the latter step be adopted?

That if it should be decided to enter upon such a consideration and the result is favorable to a continuation of the present relation between the dollar and the pound and to some sort of announcement, might not the question then properly be asked direct of the English Prime Minister whether or not, as a matter of English National policy, such a program would be considered by the English as satisfactory? If the answer is affirmative, might not thereupon conferences take place with him or with such English Government ministers as he might designate with the end in view of concluding the matter?

It was a great honor to have been permitted to make these visits as your friend; and I shall never forget it. I thank you from the depths of my heart and hope most sincerely that the information gained will be of some little service to you.[3]

With warmest regard always, believe me Faithfully yours,

S. R. Fuller, Jr.

[PPF 2616:TS]

[1] For half an hour on February 13 and at tea on March 6.

[2] The transcripts of Fuller's conversations with Schacht, Hitler, and the others occupy twenty-eight single-spaced typed pages, enclosed with the letter here printed. The most important of the conversations were those with Schacht in Berlin. Fuller saw Schacht on five separate occasions and Schacht was with him on April 1, 1936, when Fuller talked with Hitler, Schacht acting as translator. The talks with Schacht covered Germany's financial and economic status, trade relations, the need for colonies, and currency stabilization.

Fuller suggested to Schacht, after the talk with Hitler, that Germany consider the idea of "leasing" colonies, which he said Roosevelt had proposed: "The President's idea is as follows: The question of sovereignty likely would be the most controversial. Germany needs raw materials. For example, let us use as illustrations copper, cotton and rubber. Supposing a copper mine in the Belgian Congo, for instance, could be leased to Germany and with it land were leased sufficient to support a population of, say, five thousand people and this land were marked off for Germany to cover this copper mine, say, twenty-five miles each way; and a railroad were built and leased to Germany from the copper mine to the seaboard, and this lease were guaranteed her: might not this satisfy Germany so far as copper is concerned?" (interview of April 1, 1936).

Fuller also asked Schacht where Germany might find her needed raw materials all in one spot, and was told that she wanted the Kameroons. In Fuller's talk with Prime

Minister Colijn of the Netherlands, Colijn asked the American to thank Roosevelt for Hull's reciprocal trade treaties, and also added: "Tell him to keep the Philippines, though I know his difficulties in this matter. Japan will try to overwhelm them some day" (interview of April 13, 1936).

[3] Fuller saw Roosevelt for fifteen minutes on May 6, 1936, at which time he gave the President the letter here printed. See Fuller to Roosevelt, Oct. 22, 1936, below.

Roosevelt to Harold L. Ickes, Secretary of the Interior

Washington, May 4, 1936

Confidential

Memorandum for the Secretary of the Interior: In regard to the removal of guano phosphate or other minerals from Howland, Baker and Jarvis Islands, and in regard to the broader subject of civilian use of these Islands by non-government individuals or corporations for any purpose, I wish you would have a conference with the Secretary of State, the Attorney General and the Acting Secretary of the Navy and let me have a recommendation in regard to the departmental jurisdiction.

It is obvious that the Islands have several uses—(a) for Naval Defense (b) for commercial aviation (c) for private agricultural, industrial or mineral business.

It would be easy to say that the Navy Department should have jurisdiction, as in the case of Guam or Samoa, but this raises the question of what authority the Navy Department would have to grant licenses or leases for aviation or business purposes.

While it is recognized, of course, that Naval and commercial aviation base uses are at present the most important, it is my thought that we should not turn down commercial or mineral development by private capital, for the very good reason that such use would enhance and fortify any future question of sovereignty which might arise.

Please let me have a joint recommendation in full.[1]

F.D.R.

[*Notation*:T] Copy to: The Secretary of State, The Attorney General, The Acting Secretary of the Navy

[OF 6-V:CT]

[1] Roosevelt here refers to a memorandum of April 28, 1936, from Assistant Secretary of the Interior Walters enclosing correspondence from the Oceanic Nitrates Corporation of New York seeking to lease Howland, Baker, and Jarvis Islands for exploitation of

their nitrate deposits (OF 6-V). Roosevelt had approved placing the islands under the Department of the Interior as part of Hawaii but the proclamation so doing (No. 7368) did not issue until May 13, 1936. See Kannee to McIntyre, June 18, 1936, below.

Roosevelt to Walter Runciman, President, British Board of Trade

Washington [May 4, 1936][1]

My dear Mr. Runciman: Col. Murray who has been visiting us tells me that there is a chance that you may be coming over here some time in the autumn.

Should this be I hope much that you will come and stay with me, not only because I have looked forward to meeting you for many years, but also because I should much like to talk with you about various things I am doing on which your experience would be very valuable to me personally.

It would be great pleasure to see you.[2]

[PPF 4322:A:FDR]

[1] A supplied and approximate date (this copy is a draft).

[2] Arthur Murray and his wife, close friends of Runciman, were White House guests from April 30 to May 4, 1936; presumably this note was written near the end of their visit. Runciman had been in the United States in April 1936, but had not seen the President (New York *Times,* March 30, 1936, p. 39). See Runciman's reply, June 30, 1936, below.

Press Conference, Executive Offices of the White House, May 5, 1936, 4:12 P.M.

[*Excerpt*] The President: I don't think there is any particular news today. I suppose you have all been in touch with this Ethiopian situation. It is one of the most dramatic things, I think, that has happened in most recent history. Here were two Legations, four and a half or five miles apart, with this whole mob in the middle, between, and they cannot communicate with each other.[1] Our Naval radio people in our location got a radio through to Washington, D.C., saying that they are in need of help but they are holding out all right but they would very much like to have some of their people evacuated by the British who have a large force of Sikhs. The State Department telephoned it to London and the relief takes place. The messages had to travel about fifteen thousand miles in order to get help from five miles away. I think it is a perfectly amazing story.

I just got the last dispatch. The Italian forces have entered Addis Ababa about four o'clock and we have re-occupied the American Legation. We evacuated it at nine o'clock this morning and re-occupied it at five o'clock. So it looks as though the danger to the lives of Americans there is pretty well over.

Q: How will our policy of non-recognition of territory occupied by force take place? (The President did not answer.) . . .

Q: Is this Government taking any steps to fore-arm itself against possible monetary action in Europe?

The President: Yes, on a 24-hour basis. We re-arm ourselves every morning.

[President's Press Conferences:T]

[1] The American and British legations in Addis Ababa were under siege for several days before the Italians took the city on May 5. The dispatches of the American minister, Cornelius Van H. Engert, are printed in *Foreign Relations, 1936,* III, 254–266. Engert was congratulated by the President for his conduct and that of his staff during the period and was promoted (Roosevelt to Engert, May 9, and the latter's reply, May 10, 1936, OF 1922). Engert's reply contains a brief account of the siege.

Anthony J. Drexel Biddle, Jr., Minister to Norway, to Roosevelt

Oslo, Norway, May 7th, 1936

My dear Mr. President: I greatly appreciate your thoughtful and welcome letter of April 15th[1] in kind acknowledgement of mine of March 18th.[2]

Just recently, during conversations with the head of the important munitions interests of this country, I came across some information in which I thought you might be interested. I learned that the German sales of Toluene, an important ingredient for T.N.T., have been of sufficient volume during the past 30 days to indicate to authoritative munitions circles, that the Germans do not intend to initiate war for at least two years. It is felt accordingly, that Germany could not spare the amounts she is now selling, and offering, were she contemplating war within that time. Munitions interests feel, that Germany would undoubtedly prohibit exports of Toluene in the event of definite war plans.

My attention was furthermore drawn to the munitions manufacturers' barometer for gauging war tendencies: namely, a chart showing the price trend for glycerine from 1884 up to the present month. For your information, and of possible interest, I am enclosing herewith a copy of such chart, showing the price range in terms of Norwegian øre per kilogram.[3]

It was confidentially pointed out to me, with particular regard to the trend in price of the immediate past and present, that one year and a half ago, the price had reached 60 øre per kilogram, constituting a sub-normal level. Thereafter, the price advanced to 160 øre per kilogram, as of December 1935; an exceedingly high level, indicating imminent war tendencies. Thereafter, the price gradually declined to the current level of 135 øre; indicating in turn, a diminution of war tendencies. Munitions interests accordingly believe that the likelihood of war in the near future has materially lessened.

This "barometer" interested me so much, that I have drawn up the accompanying chart with the tracing paper laid over, containing an explanatory outline of major historical events leading up to, and culminating in, the corresponding important swings in the trend of glycerine prices.

For the sake of brevity, and in order to point out an interesting example as to how the chart works, I should like to draw your attention to the causes motivating the major swings in the price trend after 1905. It is interesting to observe the gradual incline from 1906 to 1908—then the more abrupt ascendant course which took place between that year and 1911; during the latter period, there was growing international unrest leading to important Franco-German crisis in 1911 (Agadir affair). This resulted in a period of tension when war seemed imminent between these countries. Differences were adjusted, and it will be noted that the glycerine price consequently dropped abruptly from 1911 to 1912; whereupon it started again on a gradual ascendant course to the outbreak of the war in 1914. It can be noted from the outline of events (on tracing paper cover) that from 1911 to 1914 was a period indicated by growing unrest, increasing tension, extensive expansion of military and naval establishments on the part of Germany, first and second Balkan Wars; all finally leading to the World War.

In 1919, the price level reached its lowest since the commencement of hostilities in the Great War. Thereupon followed an up-swing in glycerine prices from 1919 to 1920, during which period there was a succession of more or less serious crises resulting from tension during peace negotiations, which led to re-accumulation of glycerine.

Another high was reached in 1927, which was due to the crisis between China and Japan, resulting in international occupation of Shanghai. Once this situation was adjusted, the price fell and continued along a fairly even course until 1932.

It is then interesting to note, that from 1932, which year marks Hitler's commencement of power in Germany, the price has swung rather steadily up to a new recent high in December 1935, indicating Germany's rearmament and preparation for war. This was augmented of course by activities in the Far East, and France's and Russia's armament expansion. Finally we find the price trend dropping from December 1935 to the present month, a fact which indicates to the munitions manufacturers that the likelihood of war in the immediate future has somewhat lessened during the past five months.

This particular subject interested me and I thought that it would likewise prove of interest to you.

I am in the course of preparing a report on this subject to the State Department.

Margaret and I are so happy over and proud of your outstanding success indicated by the results of the primaries.

According to present plans, we expect to arrive in Washington the middle part of June, and I am looking forward to the honor and pleasure of seeing you during our stay in America.

With warmest regards from us both.

Faithfully yours,

Tony Biddle, Jr.

P.S. I am attaching hereto a list of important events from 1884 to 1923 for convenient reference.[4]

[PSF:Norway:TS]

[1] *Personal Letters, 1928–1945,* I, 576.
[2] Above.
[3] Present.
[4] Present. Answered May 20, 1936, below.

Henry Morgenthau, Jr., Secretary of the Treasury, to Roosevelt

Washington, May 12, 1936

My dear Mr. President: Enclosed herewith is a draft of the proposed agreement furnished us by the Chinese. I hope that you will find time to read it and advise me whether there is anything in this proposed agreement that you feel is not in the best interests of the United States government.[1]

Faithfully yours,

H. Morgenthau Jr.

[PSF:China:TS]

[1] Not present; issued as a press release by the Treasury Department on May 18, 1936, and quoted in full in Hull to Ambassador Johnson in China, May 19, 1936, *Foreign Relations, 1936,* IV, 482–483. China, in 1935, had nationalized silver and had abandoned the silver standard. Under the terms of the agreement, the United States agreed to buy some 75,000,000 ounces of Chinese silver between June 15, 1936, and June 15, 1937, at the world price, paying for it in gold. With the letter here printed is a Treasury Department memorandum, "Memorandum on Increasing the Use of Silver in China," undated, apparently prepared for the President's information. See press conference of May 19, 1936, below.

William Phillips, Under Secretary of State, to Roosevelt

Washington, May 14, 1936

Dear Mr. President: May I express a word of deep appreciation to you for having disposed of the Canadian liquor controversy so happily?[1] The Canadians have accepted your proposal and are now arranging with the Treasury mutually satisfactory methods of payment. Without your helpful action the outlook for our future relations with Canada would have been exceedingly gloomy. I am immensely relieved and profoundly grateful to you.

Now that the atmosphere is cleared, I am wondering whether you will find it possible to consider definite plans for your visit to Ottawa in June. As matters now stand, the Governor General knows only that you "hope" to be in Ottawa on the morning of June 8th, but that, owing to the uncertainty of Congress, you cannot make any commitments for this date.

If Congress will not have adjourned in time for you to carry out the program for the 8th, would you care to consider a later date in June?

If there is anything I can do to be of help in this connection, please let me know.

And again ever so many thanks for your help in the liquor cases.

Faithfully yours,

William Phillips

[PSF:Canada:CT]

[1] See Moore to Roosevelt, March 20, 1936, above.

Jesse Isidor Straus, Ambassador to France, to Roosevelt

Paris, May 15, 1936

Personal

Dear Mr. President: Yesterday I received your letter of May 4th and I am a little uncertain as to its meaning and your desires.[1] Do you wish me to come back in August or September, or was it your intention, in writing me, that you would prefer that I do not go home earlier when many other chiefs of mission are away from their posts? Of course, if you want me home at any time to participate in the campaign, I am yours to command. However, it had not been my intention, unless I could be of use in the campaign, to go home at all this summer. I had planned to take a three weeks' cruise to Scandanavia, leaving Paris on August 1st and returning on August 22nd. Beyond that I had made no plans. However, your suggestion that if I go home, I go home at the end of August or the beginning of September, would not prevent my taking the cruise, and, awaiting a clarification of your wishes, I have provisionally reserved accommodations on September 2nd.

From all I hear, the campaign this summer is not going to be a fight, it is going to be a rout. I was rather amused to receive recently a copy of *The Argonaut,* a weekly paper published in San Francisco, of which I had never before heard and in which there is a virulent attack on Landon which states that if he were to be elected the Methodist Church would dominate the country, and going back into the history of the political efforts of the Methodist Church over a period of years.

I saw Breck Long when he passed through Paris and yesterday Grenville Emmet was in town for the day and called on me and wanted to get some information about the probability of devaluation in France because he feels that Holland will promptly have to go off gold if France devalues. They are doing their best here to prevent devaluation. It is bound to come, in my opinion, sooner or later. It may come de facto through an embargo on gold or a restriction on exchange transactions, because I believe they are afraid to do as Belgium did and make a de jure cut. Why, now that the elections are over, I really do not know because industry is suffering and they need Americans who, of course, find it too expensive to spend much time in France.

I think the Blum Cabinet is going to be very much less radical than the name of his party would indicate and I should not be surprised if something akin to your New Deal were to eventuate. Blum is credited with being a very able man. I have met him only a few times and do not know him very well, but he may turn out to be the courageous leader that France has so long lacked.

A remark made by Madame Cerruti, wife of the Italian Ambassador here, to my wife the day before yesterday may be of interest to you. She said that the French are fools, that they are driving Italy into Germany's arms.

I am enclosing, as of possible interest to you, notes of a chat I had with Laval a few days ago, and a paraphrase of a telegram sent to the State Department yesterday.

Mrs. Straus joins me in kindest regards to you and to Mrs. Roosevelt.[2]

Cordially,

Jesse Isidor Straus

[PPF 283:TS]

---

[1] Printed in *Personal Letters, 1928–1945*, I, 585–586. Roosevelt referred to the expected early arrival home of Dodd and to Bingham's plans to come in June. He thought it would be best if Straus came back a little later than the others, so that they would not all be absent from their posts at the same time.

[2] Roosevelt replied June 8, 1936 (*ibid.*, pp. 593–594), that he should remain in Europe during the campaign and to take the vacation he had planned.

[*Enclosure 1*] Jesse Isador Straus to Roosevelt

Paris, May 13, 1936

I called on M. Pierre Laval at his office, 120 Avenue des Champs-Elysées, this morning, by appointment, at 11:30. I told him that I had asked for an opportunity to speak with him because I wanted to get his views as to the elections and as to the outlook. I told him that I wrote to the President an occasional confidential letter and that if he spoke to me frankly, he had no need to worry about any disclosure.

He said that the vote to the left was due to three things: his decree laws which affected pensioners, functionaries and small merchants and was a protest vote against the right, a vote which, in another election, might conceivably swing the other way; that no doubt much Soviet money had been spent here, but that France is neither Soviet nor Fascist; that the small merchants are in France a great number, had enjoyed prosperity, were now in a bad way and wanted a change.

As to Blum, he could not understand how he could promise large expenditures for relief of the unemployed, restoration of pension and pay cuts, armaments, balanced budget, and maintenance of the franc; that even in politics two and two still make four and not six. He regards Blum as a clever man, but thought his continuance in office would depend on the success of his government, restoration of prosperity, in fact, on the prompt results of his policy. His speech last Sunday before the Socialist meeting dealt only in generalities and proposed no concrete plan. M. Laval, in reply to my question as to whether he foresaw a New Deal, said that Blum is the creature and prisoner of his party; that, due to parliamentary methods and processes, he could not as Prime Minister do as President Roosevelt had done; that parliament does not give time to see the fruition of plans, as they had not with him, but upset a government on short notice; that that was the weakness of a responsible government. He thinks Blum may be his own Minister for Foreign Affairs and if not he, Paul-Boncour. I asked about the possibility of Herriot and he replied that Herriot had remained in Lyon, was sulking because he failed of reelection on the first ballot in a constituency for which he had so long labored. He characterized Herriot as the Russian representative in France.

Laval, in reply to my question as to Communist participation in the new Government, replied that he did not believe they would assume any responsibility and that in any case they had no man of outstanding ability who could contribute anything.

M. Laval stated that his own plans for a better relationship with Italy had been frustrated; that the Italian and French armies jointly could have assured peace in Europe and that the Hoare-Laval plan, which would have avoided the Italo-Abyssinian war, would have made Hitler hesitate, but even with respect to this arrangement time was not given to await fruition. He asserted that the Hoare-Laval plan would have satisfied Italy, and would not have precipitated some of the problems that now trouble Europe. I asked him why France had not in March been mobilized. He said that Hitler had no doubt counted on the possibility but had realized that no one wanted war and French mobilization would have meant war; that Hitler could not have taken a back step and that mobilization would have meant a European conflagration.

M. Laval rather gave me the impression, though he did not specifically so state, that Russia and France jointly were a barrier to German aggression; that France is neither at heart Soviet nor Fascist, but that between them they had the pincers on Germany. I rather gathered that at the moment he does not in his heart deprecate the signing of the Franco-Soviet treaty, but that France would have to be on its guard against Soviet influence—just why he did not make clear.

M. Laval gave me the impression that devaluation must sooner or later come.

In talking of Herriot and the possibility that he might be Foreign Minister, M. Laval referred to debts and seemed to agree, as he has never in our talks done before, that sooner or later some basis of settlement must be found. I mentioned that, of course, he would sooner or later return to power, and that I hoped that I would still be here and able with him to negotiate a settlement advantageous to both countries. He referred to the better relations between the two countries, mentioned incidentally the commercial accord, and asked whether there is much anti-French feeling in the U.S.A. I replied that much of the press, particularly Hearst's, was still very antagonistic, but that in my opinion a tender from France of a desire to negotiate debt settlement would remove much anti-French feeling, and be of benefit to both countries.

Jesse Isidor Straus

[PPF 283:T]

[*Enclosure 2*] Jesse Isidor Straus to Cordell Hull

Paris, May 14, 1936

Strictly Confidential

[*Telegram*] From a strictly reliable and confidential source, the Embassy learns tonight that M. Leon Blum, head of the Socialist party, has instructed a member of his Party's Executive Committee to prepare a complete report on French war debts to the United States. According to the Embassy's informant, Ambassador Laboulaye is returning from Washington in the near future and will be called into consultation. In addition, Herriot, in view of the precarious position of France in foreign politics, is said to have exerted strong pressure on Blum to take some action towards the settlement of the debts. Blum is believed to have said that, inasmuch as he had never voted against paying war debts, his record enabled him to reopen the matter. The Embassy's informant, who has been in close touch with Barthod, secretary to Herriot in his capacity as Mayor of Lyon, was told that Blum, as soon as he becomes Premier in the Front Populaire Government, will make a statement of foreign policy before the Chamber of Deputies, at the reconvening of Parliament in June, which will contain a reference to the desirability of settling France's war debt to the United States in some form or other. This might take the shape of a discussion of a solution of the matter in a small way and a gesture towards debt payment might possibly be made on June 15 by the French Government.

The Embassy has also heard that Sarraut has gone over entirely to Blum and that a tentative or provisional arrangement has been arrived at between the Socialists and Radical-Socialists under which the latter will be given the three defense ministries (Sarraut, either Colonies or Navy; Daladier, War; and Cot, Air).[1] By this arrangement the Radical-Socialists would consent to sacrificing Interior, Agriculture, National Education, Commerce, and Labor to the Socialists. This arrangement has been facilitated by the seemingly final decision of the Communist Party and the Confederation Generale du Travail not to take part in a Popular Front cabinet. Herriot is being strongly urged to accept the Ministry of Foreign Affairs, since Chautemps[2] will not tolerate Paul-Boncour in that post at any cost. Herriot has not refused; should he accept the Foreign Office, Paul-Boncour would be named minister without portfolio and permanent delegate to the League of Nations.

Flandin's health is very bad and he will soon have to have his arm operated upon. In so far as the possibility of any combination between the Alliance Democratique and the Popular Front is concerned, he may be considered out of the running.[3]

Straus

[PPF 283:T]

[1] Albert Sarraut, Édouard Daladier, Pierre Cot.
[2] Camille Chautemps.
[3] Printed in part and in paraphrase in *Foreign Relations, 1936,* I, 582.

Rabbi Stephen S. Wise, National Chairman, United Palestine Appeal, to Roosevelt

New York, N.Y., May 18, 1936

Personal

Dear Mr. President: Judge Mack and I and others among your friends have been greatly disturbed for a number of weeks over the situation in Palestine.[1] There has been continued killing of Jews by Arabs, and, as the High Commissioner, Sir Arthur Wauchope, has said again and again, Jews have borne themselves with exemplary patience and self restraint.

The gravity of the situation is bound up with the national Arab strike in Palestine. We are somewhat in the dark with regard to the situation, and I have thought that, in view of our long-sustained interest in Palestine, in view of President Wilson's and Colonel House's really large part in the negotiations that culminated in the issuance of the Balfour Declaration, November 1917, and in view of your own oft generously expressed sympathy with our cause, you might be good enough to send for the British Ambassador, and ask him to get from his Government a full report on the situation.

It is causing much concern to Jews throughout the world, and most especially to American Jews, who have come to have a very considerable interest in Palestine in the form of settlers and of heavy investments in the larger agricultural and industrial undertakings which have contributed much to the economic upbuilding of the land and to the material and other benefits accruing to the Arab people.[2]

Yours,

Stephen S. Wise

[OF 700:TS]

[1] Julian W. Mack, a judge of the United States Circuit Court, had long been active in the Zionist movement and in various Jewish organizations.
[2] Answered June 8, 1936, below.

Press Conference, Executive Offices of the White House, May 19, 1936, 4:07 P.M.

[*Excerpt*] Q: Have you any comment on the Chinese silver agreement?[1]

The President: Yes. I think the accomplishment there has been a very, very fine illustration of what can be done by people getting together and sitting around a table and trying to work things out in a peaceful way to help each other.

This agreement, I think, is going to help China to put into effect a national currency system which, from all that we can gather, is sound and will do a great deal to stabilize their own internal currency problems.

Of course, from our own point of view, it is always a gain to us to have the currency of a great nation, like China, placed on a more stable basis. It means that their purchasing power and selling power both will, through stabilization, increase trade both ways. Besides which they tell us that it is going to help them internally, in their internal domestic trade relations.

The conferences have been very delightful on both sides. I have had the pleasure of meeting the Chinese members over here and I think they are leaving on Thursday with mutual satisfaction on both sides. They told me that the reception of the news of the statement given out in Nanking has been very favorable.

[President's Press Conferences:T]

[1] See press release quoted in Hull to Johnson, May 19, 1936, *Foreign Relations, 1936,* IV, 482–483.

Roosevelt to Senator James F. Byrnes of South Carolina

[Washington] May 20, 1936

My dear Senator Byrnes: I have delayed reply to your letter of May 2, 1936,[1] with reference to imports of Japanese cotton textiles in the expectation that we should be able to make announcement of definite action in this matter.

As you know, I have long been interested and concerned with the problems of the cotton textile industry. On April 26, 1935, I appointed a Cabinet Committee to make a survey of the conditions and problems of the cotton textile industry. With reference to the problems presented by imports, it was the recommendation of this Committee that we seek some arrangement whereby shipments would be voluntarily limited to reasonable amounts by Japanese exporters themselves.

In accordance with this recommended procedure, conversations were held with representatives of the Japanese Government, and on December 21, 1935, we received through the Japanese Ambassador the assurance of the Japanese exporters that they would voluntarily restrict shipments to the United States to moderate levels. It was the opinion of the Japanese Government in view of this assurance that there was little likelihood of a repetition of such abnormal increases in the exports of cotton textiles to the United States as had occurred during the first six months of 1935. Unfortunately, as the statistics for the first three months of 1936 became available, it appeared that these expectations had not been well founded inasmuch as imports showed a considerable increase in these months. These facts were promptly brought to the attention of the Japanese Ambassador by the Department of State as soon as the January figures were available.

Conversations have continued on this subject and I am now able to inform you that it is expected that a more adequate, definite and satisfactory undertaking for the voluntary limitation of exports of cotton textiles to the United States may be received from the Japanese exporters. A few minor details remain to be ironed out but it is to be expected that within a few days we shall be able to announce the conclusion of these negotiations.

I believe that you will agree that it is wholly desirable to reach a solution of the problem presented by imports of Japanese cotton textiles through mutual agreement if possible rather than by unilateral action, which tends to lead to commercial ill will and retaliation. We have sought, therefore, to explore fully the possibilities of voluntary arrangements before resorting to other possible forms of action.

Sincerely yours,

[OF 61-T:CT]

---

[1] Byrnes said that he had forwarded to Secretary of Agriculture Wallace a number of letters from cotton manufacturers concerning the great increase in importations of Japanese cotton goods (OF 61-T). He asked that a quota be fixed or duties increased. The reply here made was drafted by Hull; in his covering letter of May 20, 1936 (OF 61-T), he said that negotiations with the Japanese had not been completed but if agreement was not reached, action would be taken in accordance with the finding of the Tariff Commission. This, Hull added, was the procedure approved by Roosevelt at the May 7 Cabinet meeting.

Roosevelt to Anthony J. Drexel Biddle, Jr., Minister to Norway, Oslo

[Washington] May 20, 1936

Dear Tony: That is an extraordinarily interesting chart and is a wholly new approach.[1]

I am looking forward to seeing you both very soon.

Always sincerely,

[PSF:Norway:CT]

[1] Referring to Biddle's letter of May 7, 1936, above.

Press Conference, Executive Offices of the White House, May 22, 1936, 10:55 A.M.

[*Excerpt*) Q: There has been some suggestion that the increase in the tariff on the imports of Japanese cotton runs somewhat counter to the policy of lowering tariff barriers.

The President: I don't think it has anything to do with it. They are two totally different subjects. The possibility of lowering tariff barriers by agreement and without substantially hurting any important American industry remains substantially what it was. In this case we have a situation where an important American industry was being hurt in one branch of that industry. We tried to reach an agreement, which was the obvious thing to do first, a gentlemen's agreement to limit the exports to this country in that particular line of goods. We did not get the agreement so we took the only other step, which was to act on the report of the Tariff Commission.

[President's Press Conferences:T]

Roosevelt to Henry Morgenthau, Jr., Secretary of the Treasury

[Washington] May 22, 1936

Memorandum for the Secretary of the Treasury: Please confer with the Secretary of State and the Attorney General and try to find an immediate method of carrying out the law. I am convinced that we have to act. It may be possible to make the action apply to Germany only.

F.D.R.

[*Notation*:T] File re proposed Treasury decision giving notice of imposition of countervailing duties on certain imports from Germany under Sec. 303 of Tariff Act of 1930—containing:

Memo. to Secy. Morgenthau from Herman Oliphant 5/20/36, advising of difficulty in withholding definite ruling; (President's notation on this memo: "Pick up. Early April I asked Atty. Gen. for opinion—He handed me papers back four weeks later & asked not to have to give opinion—but that if required he would have to rule with Treasury."

Memo. for the A.G. from Golden W. Bell, Asst. Sol. Gen., 4/30/36.

Let. to Pres. from Secy. Morgenthau. Pres. notation: "A.G. for report & recommendation, F.D.R. 4/16/36," advising of decision he has before him—sees no alternative but to sign; memo. from Mr. Oliphant 4/15/36 attached.

Mimeo. copy of confidential rpt. to Exec. Comm. on Commercial Policy from Subcommittee on countervailing duties in relation to currency problems, 3/28/36.

Copy of let. from Secy. of State to Secy. of Treas. 4/2/36.

Let. to Golden W. Bell from Francis B. Sayre, 5/4/36, enclosing memo. "Policy Aspects of Proposed Treasury Action under Sec. 303."[1]

[OF 614-A:T]

---

[1] These enclosures were returned to Morgenthau. Under section 303 of the 1930 Tariff Act, the Treasury Department was required to levy a countervailing duty on any import produced under an export bounty, the amount of the duty to equal the bounty. The German government's currency policies raised the question whether the 1930 act applied; Treasury took the view that it did while State did not. The former view eventually prevailed and on July 11, 1936, Morgenthau ordered countervailing duties placed on German imports. On Aug. 4, 1936, Germany removed her bounties on exports to the United States and our countervailing duties were withdrawn on Aug. 10, 1936 (New York *Times,* June 5, 1936, p. 1; Blum, *From the Morgenthau Diaries,* pp. 149–155).

Roosevelt to Rudolph Forster, Executive Clerk, White House Offices

Washington, May 23, 1936

Memo for R.F.: Will you speak to Judge Moore about Foreign Service Officers staying more than three or four years in the Department?

F.D.R.

[*Notation*:T] Memorandum for the President. Judge Moore advises that he finds that the law is rigid on the point that when a foreign service officer is brought into the Department, his term in the Department is limited to four years. Really limited to 3 yrs but in special cases may be extended 1 yr—making 4 years absolute limit.

The Judge added that in a few cases when foreign service officers brought into the Department had finished their four-year term, they had resigned from the foreign service and become officials of the Department. (He cited the case of Wallace Murray, Chief of the Division of Near Eastern Affairs.) And, in some cases—not many—the President had later reappointed these officials to the foreign service, adding that, of course, this could only be done by action of the President.[1]

R.F.

[OF 20:T]

[1] A memorandum on this subject by Assistant Secretary of State Carr, May 26, 1936, is with this note. See Roosevelt to Moore, May 27, 1936, below.

Press Conference, Executive Offices of the White House, May 26, 1936, 4 P.M.

[*Excerpt*] Q: Your visit with Ambassador Daniels—any news in connection with that?[1]

The President: No. We talked about all sorts of things. He told me one very interesting piece of news which I cannot tell you. Maybe you can get it from him or the State Department. It is a piece of history that happened down in Mexico very lately. I cannot even give you a hint.

Q: Did you discuss with Secretary Hull Leo Sack's comment on the Governor of Maryland?[2]

The President: You mean the Costa Rica thing? I read it in the paper. I can talk to you off the record on that. It is something that is well worth remembering and it is the sort of thing I can talk to you off the record about.

You know, it is a curious and interesting fact, one that you all know of, that when a Britisher or a Frenchman or a German or an Italian comes to this country, even if they are not in agreement with the existing party in control of their own country, they never run down their own country. That is a very interesting thing about a foreigner. You take a conservative Englishman, when he comes to this country, "Oh, yes; we are getting along all right. I don't agree with the party in power but we are working this thing through all right." And you get the same thing from the Frenchman.

You who have been abroad know the other side of the picture, about Americans of various kinds, the more important American. He talks and he is nearly always running down his own country. It is an American habit we have.

So, on this particular episode of Governor Nice, it is carrying on a normal American habit of going to foreign parts and telling what a rotten place the United States is. (Laughter)

Mr. Early: The Governor said he had been misquoted.

The President: The Governor said he had been misquoted. However, I am talking in general terms and off the record because it is one of those American characteristics that will probably take a good many generations to get over. I suppose we are not old enough to have collected the amount of patriotism that sticks up for your own country in foreign lands.

[President's Press Conferences:T]

[1] Daniels had called on the President earlier in the afternoon, from 1 to 2 P.M. (PPF 1-0).

[2] Harry W. Nice, Republican governor of Maryland, had given an interview to the press in Costa Rica that was strongly critical of President Roosevelt and the Administration. Leo Sack, minister to Costa Rica, rebuked Nice in a letter which he made public. Nice apologized to Sack, saying that although he had been correctly quoted, he had not thought that his remarks would give offense (New York Times, May 25, 1936, p. 9).

Cordell Hull, Secretary of State, to Roosevelt

Washington, May 26, 1936

My dear Mr. President: I enclose herewith a draft letter which you may wish to send in reply to Rabbi Wise's letter on the Palestine situation, which is also returned herewith.[1]

Our information indicates that the British authorities are doing their utmost to preserve order in Palestine and that they have been most prompt in meeting the requests of our Consul General in Jerusalem for protection of American nationals and interests. Confidential reports which we have received indicate that the British task has probably been made more difficult by the financial support which the Arab general strike has received from sources outside Palestine.

In view of all the circumstances I do not think it would help the situation in any way if we pressed the British Government at this time. We are, of course, watching the situation carefully and are constantly bearing in mind the extent of American interests in Palestine. In this connection I think you will be interested to know that on May 23, 1936, we sent a telegram of instructions to the Consul General at Jerusalem, a paraphrase of which I enclose.[2]

Faithfully yours,

Cordell Hull

[OF 700:TS]

[1] The reply to Wise's letter of May 18 (above) was sent June 8, 1936 (below).
[2] Printed in *Foreign Relations, 1936,* III, 442–443.

George Lansbury, Member of Parliament, to Roosevelt

New York City, 26.5.36

My dear Mr President: Please allow me to send this note of thanks & much appreciation for your kindness in seeing & talking with me today.

I will do my best to send, or rather get others to send a "peg" across the ocean, suitable for a "hook up"—no cut & dried scheme but simply, some gesture, that may make possible a meeting of chiefs.

All of us owe it to the youth & early manhood of the world, to do what is needed to put an end to war. Again many thanks for your kindness.[1]

Y[rs] truly

George Lansbury

[OF 394:AS]

[1] Lansbury had arrived in the United States on April 21, 1936, to speak at the National Peace Conference. A leading British pacifist, he had recently resigned as head of the Labor party in protest at the party's acquiescence in the imposition of sanctions on Italy. To assure peace he urged the convening of an international conference to provide the "have-not nations" with equal access to the world's natural resources (New York *Times,* April 22, p. 3; April 23, 1936, p. 14). Both Bingham and Lindsay requested that Roosevelt see Lansbury and he talked with the President for fifteen minutes on May 26 (Phillips to McIntyre, April 16, May 8, 1936, OF 48).

Roosevelt to Antonio C. Gonzalez, Minister to Ecuador, Quito

[Washington] May 27, 1936

My dear Mr. Gonzalez: I have received and have read with much interest your letter of May 15.[1] I am glad to learn of your favorable impressions of what may be accomplished at the Inter-American Conference. I myself believe that if the republics of this continent avail themselves of the opportunities presented, much can be realized to our common benefit.

In view of the probable postponement of the holding of the Conference until the late autumn, I have not as yet given any consideration to the appointment of the delegation. When the time comes for me to reach a decision in this regard, I shall be glad to bear your request in mind.

Believe me, Yours very sincerely,

[OF 621:CT]

[1] Gonzalez had asked to be included among the official delegates at the coming conference (OF 621). Others nominated included Oswald Garrison Villard, whose candidacy was supported by Senator George W. Norris and Secretary of Agriculture Wallace, among others (Norris to Roosevelt, April 22, 1936; Wallace to Roosevelt, April 29, 1936, OF 1970), and just as violently opposed by Representative John Dockweiler of California (Dockweiler to McIntyre, June 20, 1936, OF 1970). Dockweiler objected to the appointment of Villard because of the latter's criticism of his stand in favor of a larger Army and Navy. For a list of the delegates as announced Dec. 1, 1936, see Hull, *Memoirs,* I, 494.

Roosevelt to R. Walton Moore, Assistant Secretary of State

Washington, May 27, 1936

Memorandum for Hon. R. Walton Moore: I think we should have a definite rule that hereafter the President will not reappoint to the Foreign Service any former officers of the Foreign Service who have resigned and become officials of the Department.[1]

Furthermore, I think we should discourage appointing any Foreign Service officers as officials of the Department. They can be detailed to the Department for not to exceed three years with a maximum one year extension.

F.D.R.

[OF 20:CT]

[1] See Roosevelt to Forster, May 23, 1936, above.

Roosevelt to Cordell Hull, Secretary of State

Washington, May 28, 1936

Memorandum for the Secretary of State: This is a most interesting reply from the British Government.[1] I think there is no objection to a general statement between now and November, but I do not think it should be more than a general statement. In other words, we do not want to involve ourselves in the next few months in controversy over specific details which would narrow the field to specific commodities. It is, however, a very useful beginning.

F.D.R.

[OF 20:CT]

[1] Bingham to Hull, May 26, 1936 (*Foreign Relations, 1936*, I, 663–666), quoting in full the British government's memorandum on Hull's proposal for a reciprocal trade treaty with Britain. The British message rejected Hull's arguments for a treaty, upholding the British bilateral agreements idea, and the quota system, two "obstacles" to international trade Hull had long opposed. The memorandum did concede, however, that the hampering of trade by currency exchange restrictions, which created "frozen assets" in the countries traded with, was an obstacle that it would be desirable to remove. Hull's memoranda of his talks with Ambassador Lindsay on this subject, between January and April 1936, are printed *ibid.*, pp. 629ff.

Roosevelt to Alexander W. Weddell, Ambassador to Argentina, Buenos Aires

[Washington] June 4, 1936

My dear Mr. Ambassador: My cousin, Mrs. Robbins, is going to Buenos Aires in a week. As you know, she is the widow of Warren Robbins, our late Minister to Canada, and she is well versed in all matters relating to diplomatic matters, usage, etc. When the conference in Buenos Aires[1] is held later in the year it is the thought of Sumner Welles that she should be attached in some capacity to the American delegation. In the meantime, she will be in Buenos Aires, and being an Argentinean by birth, although, of course, now an American citizen, she may be able to help you in such ways as you may deem advisable between now and the time the regular set up of the delegation is made.[2]

My best wishes to you.

Very sincerely yours,

[OF 467:CT]

[1] The Inter-American Peace Conference.

[2] Mrs. Robbins (Irene de Bruyn, of Buenos Aires) had lived away from Argentina for many of the years since her marriage to Warren Delano Robbins in 1910. Weddell replied July 15, 1936 (PPF 1012), that he thought Mrs. Robbins would be useful as a member of the delegation. Her appointment as a special assistant to the delegation was announced Oct. 31, 1936 (New York *Times,* Nov. 1, 1936, II, p. 6).

Henry A. Wallace, Secretary of Agriculture, to Roosevelt

Washington, June 5, 1936

Dear Mr. President: I wonder if your attention has been called to the figures as set forth in the enclosed.[1] You will note that the United States has lost trade to Germany, Japan and other nations in Guatemala, Honduras, Nicaragua, Costa Rica, El Salvador and Panama. The increase of the German and Japanese trade is very striking. In view of our interest in the Pan American situation, I wonder if the trend revealed by these figures is not worth pondering upon at some length.

Respectfully yours,

H. A. Wallace

315

[*Notation:*A] Sec State to read & return
[OF 1:TS]

[1] A table of statistics from *Business Week,* May 16, 1936, p. 12, showing the amount of trade of the principal exporting nations with South and Central American countries.

Roosevelt to Rabbi Stephen S. Wise, New York

[Washington] June 8, 1936

Strictly Confidential

My dear Dr. Wise: I have received your letter of May 18, 1936, expressing your concern and that of other friends regarding the present situation in Palestine.[1]

We are, of course, following developments there with the closest attention and our Consul General in Jerusalem, who is an officer thoroughly experienced in Near Eastern affairs, has been most active in taking steps with the local authorities with a view to obtaining protection for American nationals. He assures us that the Mandatory authorities are taking proper measures for security and that they have been notably prompt in giving attention to his requests for the protection of American citizens and American property. In this connection you are of course aware that substantial military reinforcements have been brought into the country and that other steps have been taken to keep the situation under control.

You may be sure that we shall continue to watch the situation closely and that we shall not fail to take such action as may seem helpful and proper in seeing that American interests in Palestine are adequately protected.[2]

Sincerely yours,

[OF 700:CT]

[1] Above.
[2] See Hull to Roosevelt, July 27, 1936, below.

Edouard Herriot, President, Chamber of Deputies, to Roosevelt

Paris, June 11, 1936

Translation

My dear President: Mr. Monick, whom you know very well, comes to you charged by the French Government with a confidential mission.[1] He will explain its purpose to you and will give you precise information on the gravity of the European situation. I do not need to tell you how greatly I desire his success. More than ever, I believe, as I have always thought and said, an accord between the United States and France is an element essential to the stability of the world and to peace. The present situation reminds me of the precious interviews that you did me the honor to grant me (in the past).

Accept, my dear President, with my respects to Mrs. Roosevelt, the faithful expression of my affectionate devotion.[2]

Herriot

[PSF:France:T]

[1] Emmanuel Monick, French financial attaché in London, had been sent to the United States to prepare the way for a tripartite stabilization agreement among France, Great Britain, and the United States. Herriot had persuaded Blum to take action on the French debt even before Blum had taken office as Premier on June 4, 1936 (Straus to Hull, May 19, 1936, *Foreign Relations, 1936,* I, 583–585). His dispute with Jean Tannery, governor of the Bank of France, over devaluation of the franc, brought him favorably to Blum's attention, and Monick was eventually able to persuade Blum that devaluation was needed (Blum, *From the Morgenthau Diaries,* pp. 155–159).

[2] Answered July 6, 1936, below.

Cordell Hull, Secretary of State, to Roosevelt

Washington, June 12, 1936

My dear Mr. President: On May 9, 1936, we instructed Mr. Engert, the Minister Resident at Addis Ababa, to give us, after careful investigation, the benefit of his best judgment as to whether it could be said that there was no longer any recognized military opposition to the Italian forces in Ethiopia.[1] It was explained to Mr. Engert that this information was desired for use in considering the possible revocation of the proclamation of October 5, 1935, placing an embargo on the shipment of arms, ammunition and implements of war to Italy and Ethiopia.

On May 17 Mr. Engert reported that it could hardly be said that the war had definitely ended although the Italian Government was most anxious to create such an impression.[2] In this connection Mr. Engert pointed out that some of the Italian footholds in the North were by no means secure and that penetration of Italian troops into the Southern area was bound to be hazardous and slow. On the other hand, he expressed the opinion that organized military operation in the modern sense was unlikely to develop on a large scale. At the same time he pointed out that there were still a number of Ethiopian leaders in the field with guerilla bands but it was impossible to estimate their strength. Under these circumstances Mr. Engert suggested that action in the matter be deferred until the situation had become more clarified.

On June 4, 1936, instructions were sent to Mr. Engert requesting such further reports from time to time with respect to the military situation as might help throw light upon the subject discussed above.[3] On the following day Mr. Engert replied that Italian forces could not be said to be in complete control anywhere South of the Ninth Parallel and West of the Fortieth Meridian except along the Djibouti-Addis Ababa railway.[4] He added that there appeared to be no Italian troops South of the Blue Nile and that the Westernmost point so far occupied in Central Ethiopia was the town of Ambo, some fifty-five miles West of Addis Ababa. Mr. Engert stated, moreover, that the Italians had made no effort to penetrate into vast areas in the Southwest of the country and that the Italian authorities had been unable to accede to the request of the Belgian Minister for the evacuation of eight Europeans located on coffee plantations only fourteen miles by road from one of the railway stations not far from Addis Ababa. The Minister Resident also stated that his repeated inquiries concerning the welfare of American missionaries in the Southern and Southwestern part of the country had always been met with the reply that the Italian authorities had no information concerning the situation in that area and that they were not prepared to send any troops there.

From the foregoing description it would appear that the Italians are not in control of the area marked in purple on the enclosed map.[5] It will be observed that this area amounts to approximately one-third of the territory of Ethiopia.

Mr. Engert reports the receipt of information from some of the Western provinces indicating that local chieftains have set up governments in those areas and are keeping reasonably good order. Disarming of the natives has apparently been slow and unsatisfactory. For example, Mr.

Engert was informed by Marshal Badoglio[6] that only 400 rifles had been collected in Addis Ababa. Inasmuch as nearly every Ethiopian was accustomed to carrying a rifle of some sort the number collected at the capital is obviously extremely small. The proportion of rifles collected in the provinces is doubtless even smaller and reports are received that Italian convoys between Addis Ababa and Dessye continue to be attacked.

Mr. Engert points out that he does not wish to convey the impression that properly constituted political entities exist and govern portions of the country in the name of the Emperor or that any large organized forces are in the field even in those areas where no Italian soldiers have so far penetrated. He observes, however, that certain obvious difficulties are just beginning for the Italians and that even if they are left by other Powers in undisturbed possession it may be six months or more before they will be able properly to garrison the whole country.

I learn informally that the War Department has no reports which throw any additional light upon the military situation in Ethiopia.

In view of the uncertainties of the situation and pending further clarification thereof we are of the opinion that it would be desirable to refrain from taking any action with respect to the revocation of the proclamation of October 5, 1935, establishing an embargo upon the shipments of arms to Italy and Ethiopia, until I report to you further.

Faithfully yours,

Cordell Hull

[PSF:Ethiopia:TS]

[1] Printed in *Foreign Relations, 1936,* III, 194–195.
[2] *Ibid.,* p. 196.
[3] *Ibid.,* p. 205.
[4] *Ibid.,* pp. 205–206.
[5] The map, enclosed with Hull's letter, is an enlargement of one printed in the September 1935 issue of *National Geographic Magazine;* it shows the extent of Ethiopian territory prior to the Italian invasion of October 1935.
[6] Marshal Pietro Badoglio was in command of the Italian forces in the Ethiopian campaign.

Lincoln MacVeagh, Minister to Greece, to Roosevelt

Athens, June 13, 1936

Dear Franklin: I have received your letter and wish to assure you that I wouldn't think of asking for home leave this year, unless it was your wish that I return.[1] The general European situation does not clear up. Rather it seems to be becoming more complicated, and armaments are growing at an alarming rate. Furthermore, Greece has a lot of local trouble of her own in which our people may at any time be involved, and the Department has taken away my two secretaries, old hands and experts in Near Eastern problems, and given me in exchange only a youngster in his twenties, who is going to be a very good man indeed, I believe, but who at present lacks experience. Professionally, in regard to the job you have given me, and which I try to do my best with, it seems to me therefore that I should stick around subject to your decision as to whether I could be of better use elsewhere.

As far as my personal contacts are concerned, these are by this time pretty wide among the scattered half-million or so of the Greek Americans, who have astonished me by the interest they seem to take in who represents our country here. They and I seem to find it easy to think along the same lines, on many subjects, and that goes for thinking along Roosevelt lines. I believe there are few Greek Americans who are not Roosevelt men, or unaware of the fact, which means much to them, that your administration is responsible for conducting Greek-American affairs with sympathy and understanding.

The "non-partisan" government which recently gave way to the "King's own," as we might call it, was naturally a timid one and little action, if any, was taken by it in regard to a multitude of questions, some of them of considerable local importance.[2] The present Premier is accordingly swamped with administrative arrears. But his policy for the next few months before the general elections is gradually taking shape. It appears that he will stall on the question of the foreign debt, in spite of the claims of the English bondholders that Greece can well afford to pay more than 35% of the interest. He will also, it seems do nothing about the German clearing, which has resulted in Greece's accumulating a dangerously large credit in blocked reichsmarks. But he is actively working to strengthen the country's military defences, and increasing the naval forces, and is continuing the King's conciliatory policy toward the Veniselist revolters of last year. Preparedness and unity would thus seem to be his watchwords. As he told me himself, his Government, with probably only a short life ahead of it, has to deal with a thoroughly disorganized country and must not try to do too much at once if it wishes to achieve results.[3]

A sign of the disorganization caused by the events of last year has been the number of labor difficulties which the country has had to face these past months. The Greeks are naturally individualists and resist regimentation of any kind. But much misery exists in the industrial centres, and years of governmental indifference capped by many months of governmental weakness have provided Communistic agitators with their chance. Starting with local strikes in particular industries into which the Communists have been boring for some time, trouble finally flamed out in Macedonia last month in the form of a general strike. There was mob violence and shooting by the police, and a number of "martyrs" were made. I was in Salonika the day the trouble started, and immediately thereafter travelled through the entire region affected. That a strong government was at last in power became evident from the prompt use of the armed forces to quell disturbances. But in conversation with the Prime Minister when I returned to Athens, it did not seem to me that he realized the serious nature of the underlying causes of the trouble. He was inclined to regard the whole thing as political, and due to an alliance between the Liberal Party and the Communists to make difficulties for the Government. His published utterances since that time confirm my impression, since he denies that there exists any danger to the social order in Greece. The lesson of the general strike would seem to be, however, that there is a very real danger of this nature which can only be met effectively by measures to alleviate the wretched condition of the workers in such places as Salonika and Cavalla. The Americans in Macedonia and Thrace are unanimous in taking this point of view and the British Consul General at Salonika, with whom I talked at length, feels the same way. Since then, there have been further troubles in Volo and Patras, but Salonika, a growing city of over 250,000 inhabitants where many textile and other factory hands receive a mere pittance per day, is the chief danger-spot. There can be no doubt but that the Communists regard it as a promising center. During the general strike the progress of the uprising was commented on in broadcasts from Moscow. Indeed, the place has present possibilities of becoming the Barcelona of Greece, if not also of the Near East generally, and unless the Greeks develop a constructive social program soon, it will almost surely do so. The Greeks have this advantage, if they will only forget their petty politics for a time, that it takes little to make their people contented, and a modicum of interest in their welfare on the part of their own government can overbalance much in the way of promises of foreign agitators.

On account of its size and its strategic position, the development of Communism in Salonika is a matter of importance not only for Greece.

We have a very active and intelligent Consul there, James H. Keeley, whose reports I find admirable. In fact, like his opposite number, George Allen, in Patras, he keeps me informed of everything that goes on, as if he were a member of the Legation staff itself.

In foreign affairs there seem to be some big decisions coming in the near future. The French Minister has just been summoned to Paris and tells me that the new French Foreign Minister plans to see every one of his Chiefs of Mission in Europe personally before he goes to Geneva. The French Minister is confident that the Blum Government will prove definitely Anglophile and Sanctionist. We shall see. Today's press reports that d'Ormesson and Pertinax, two of the best known editorial writers on Foreign Affairs in France, are now emphasizing the dangers of a German-Italian-Polish entente. Of course, we all have long been aware of these, but the emphasis in the French press does seem to be new. Is the French nation as a whole going to wake up at last to the facts, which its General Staff makes no bones about, that the one enemy it has to fear is Germany and that England and France have a common frontier on the Rhine? Meanwhile Greece is much impressed by Mussolini's de facto conquest of Abyssinia, and is trying to be very polite indeed to the Italians, while noting almost pathetically every rumor as to the immensity of England's efforts in rearmament. The Greeks fear Italian ruthlessness, which was exhibited in Corfu not so many years ago, and they are familiar with a certain Italian point of view which regards small Mediterranean nations as having no right to exist. She is under the spell of the British Navy, but desperately afraid of the Italian air force, as well she may be. And she knows that Italy's real army is still in Italy, that the Straits of Otranto are held in an Italian vice, that Albania is being rapidly developed in a manner perfectly adapted for service as an Italian bridge-head in the Balkans on the flank of Yugoslavia, that Malta is no longer of any use to the British, who have not yet developed Cyprus and possess a doubtful friend in Egypt, that the Dodecanese Islands are fully equipped to form an Italian base in the Aegean on the flank of Turkey, and that Bulgaria is a possible Italian ally, and militarily stronger than either Greece or Rumania. All these facts would, as you may imagine, make her position intensely difficult in the case of a European conflict in which Italy and England were on opposite sides. No one here expresses the idea that Mussolini actually intends himself to start such a conflict. But there are grave doubts as to the limits of his imperial ambitions, and a very general fear of some spark, probably in Central Europe, setting off the whole fireworks as soon as Germany is prepared.

Ever yours affectionately,

Lincoln MacVeagh

[PSF:Greece:TS]

[1] Roosevelt had written May 23, 1936 (*Personal Letters, 1928–1945,* I, 592), to tell MacVeagh not to return to take part in the coming campaign; he did not want to have all the ministers and ambassadors at home at one time in case anything should "blow up." MacVeagh did, however, come home in August after he had been informed by G. Hall Roosevelt that the President had reconsidered (MacVeagh to Roosevelt, July 22, 1936, PSF:Greece).

[2] The parliamentary elections of Jan. 26, 1936, had created a deadlock with the Venizelos Liberal party holding 142 seats, the Communists 15, and the various other opposition parties 143.

[3] Metaxas' collaboration with the parliamentary commission ended Aug. 4, 1936, when he dismissed parliament and became dictator.

Governor Herbert H. Lehman of New York to Roosevelt

Albany, June 15th, 1936

Not official

My dear Mr. President: You will recall that some months ago I wrote to you enlisting your good offices in reducing to a minimum the difficulties of obtaining visas in Germany for emigration to the United States of those would-be emigrants who are entitled, by reason of good character and other circumstances, to admission.[1] At that time you advised me that you had taken the matter up with the Department of State and that difficulties would be reduced to a minimum in cases of people worthy of admission to our country.[2]

I am sending you herewith correspondence just received from Mr. Felix Warburg to which is a letter attached from Sir Herbert Samuel which you will find self-explanatory.[3]

I am certain that, as in the past, every effort will be made to make possible the obtaining of visas for those who, in the opinion of our authorities, will make worthy citizens of the United States.[4]

With kind personal regards, I am, Very sincerely yours,

Herbert H. Lehman

[*Notation*:A:LeHand] State Department for preparation of reply—
[OF 133:TS]

[1] Nov. 1, 1935, above.
[2] Nov. 13, 1935, above.
[3] Warburg to Lehman, June 5; Samuel to Warburg, May 27, 1936. Samuel, a leading British Liberal and former High Commissioner to Palestine (1920–1925), sent Warburg a summary of a report on the Hilfsverein, a Jewish agency for assisting Jews to get out of Germany. The report indicated that American consulates in Germany were understaffed and flooded with applications for visas. Samuel had talked with Roosevelt at the White House on Feb. 1, 1936 (PPF 1-0). In his letter he referred to this meeting: "I recall what was said in America with regard to the desire of the President that the rules should not be enforced too rigidly by the American Consuls in Germany."
[4] Answered July 2, 1936, below.

Breckinridge Long, Ambassador to Italy, to Roosevelt

Rochester, Minn., June 15, 1936

Dictated from bed in Columbia Hospital

My dear Chief: I expect I have let you down for a while. My presence at Philadelphia is now impossible, and active participation in the Campaign will not be possible until after Labor Day.[1] They took most of my stomach away from me, but all the trouble has been eliminated. It was just an old ulcer that had been irritating the whole stomach and that whole nervous area for years. Now it is gone, and I will be in better health and in stronger physical condition.

I am sorry that it will lessen my activities on your behalf for the time being, but the old head will still work, and there will be no reason why I cannot appear from time to time at Headquarters and do what may be possible in the way of consultation after the next two or three weeks.

There was one phase of the consequence of my resignation which I wanted to present to you along with several other things before I came to the hospital. My belief is that the appointment of a successor will be authentic recognition of the Government of Italy by its new title including "Emperor of Ethiopia" with the consequent recognition of that status.[2] Personally I see no reason why it should not be done—from the practical point of view. It will have to be done some day unless there is a bigger war about it. However, that is a matter of policy for you to decide. You have my resignation whenever you want to use it. The only thing is that I hope never to see Italy again and hope you will not ask me to go back there. I had so much physical suffering on that scene that I really hope I never set foot in the land again.

In my one conversation with you I neglected to give you a message from Jesse Straus and hoped to do so before I got sick. Jesse said that he expected to continue in Europe this summer and to take a cruise to the North Capes; that he had not considered coming home and helping in the Campaign because he did not feel he could be of any great assistance—but he wanted me to tell you that he was sure that you knew him well enough to feel that all you had to do was to make a suggestion and he would gladly do anything that you wanted him to do.[3] He hesitated to write to you on the subject and asked me to convey it orally. I am sorry I forgot, but my conversation with you was quite short and there seemed so many things to talk about that I didn't have time for that and several other things.

As to the Campaign—Please do not let our fellows get over-confident and take chances. I am perfectly confident of your reelection, but I like to see an organization working as if the candidate was "running scared." I mean no betrayal of a lack of confidence but simply a thorough intensity that will not overlook a single bet.

In about three weeks they let me get away from here, and I hope to go to Nantucket to my summer home. From there I shall get to Headquarters occasionally, but it may be a long time before I see you. Whenever you accept my resignation you may take back the commission which I have been honored to hold and under the authority of which I have faithfully tried to serve you.[4]

Affectionately and respectfully,

Breckinridge Long

[PSF:Italy:TS]

[1] The Democratic National Convention was convened in Philadelphia on June 23, 1936, and closed June 27.

[2] The State Department was reluctant to accredit Long's successor, William Phillips, to the "King of Italy and Emperor of Ethiopia," thus giving recognition to territory seized by force. The Italian government finally agreed to receive Phillips as accredited to the King of Italy only (Phillips, *Ventures in Diplomacy,* pp. 178–179).

[3] Straus, fatally ill with cancer, collapsed in Paris during the Bastille Day celebrations and returned home shortly afterward. He died Oct. 4, 1936, at his home in Mt. Kisco, New York.

[4] Answered June 18, 1936, below.

Roosevelt to Cordell Hull, Secretary of State

Washington, June 16, 1936

Memorandum for the Secretary of State: I have received one or two memoranda in regard to proposed International Expositions, stating that it would cost the State Department about $10,000 in each case to extend invitations to foreign governments to participate.

Why are these invitations so expensive? It works out at an average of about $200.00 per invitation.[1]

F.D.R.

[OF 20:CT]

[1] Hull explained in his reply (June 17, 1936, OF 20), that the expense was not involved in the issuance of the invitations (in this case to the coming international expositions in San Francisco and New York) but in the obligations the United States had to assume after the invitations were accepted. Funds were required "to appoint a Commissioner General, to employ his staff, to provide suitable offices at the exposition grounds, to furnish entertainment and by this medium to assist in arrangements for foreign participation and to extend appropriate courtesies."

Cordell Hull, Secretary of State, to Roosevelt

[Washington] June 17, 1936

Memorandum for the President: The attached data contains suggested platform provisions by some of us in the State Department.

Copies of these are today being handed to Senator Wagner.[1]

Hull

[PSF:Democratic Platform:TS]

[1] Senator Robert F. Wagner was chairman of the resolutions committee of the Democratic National Convention. Hull had not been asked to submit a foreign policy statement but he assumed that the several suggestions he had sent to the President had been turned over to the platform committee, and that he would be shown the final draft when he went to Philadelphia for the convention (June 23–27). There he found "no arrangement had been made" to show him the platform draft, and when it was made public he was "dumbfounded" to find that his recommendations had been ignored (Hull, *Memoirs,* I, 485–486). Others in the Administration had, however, been asked for suggestions, including Josephus Daniels. Daniels conferred with State Department officials and submitted a foreign policy plank embodying (in briefer space) the same ideas and in much the same language as the draft printed below (Daniels to Roosevelt, June 19, 1936, PSF:Democratic Platform). See the foreign policy section of the platform, June 25, 1936, below.

[*Enclosure*] State Department Draft of a Foreign Policy Statement for the Democratic Platform

June 17 [1936]

I. We have for three years pursued a constructive foreign policy dedicated to the promotion of American interests at home and abroad. At no time have our relations with foreign powers been more cordial or more friendly. We pledge ourselves to a continuance of this policy.

We reaffirm our opposition to war as a mode of settling international disputes, and continue strenuously to advocate the pacific settlement of international differences through conciliation or judicial process. We stand for a vigorous reassertion of the principles of international morality. We believe in the sanctity of international covenants and firmly advocate, both in theory and in practice, the policy of the "good neighbor" in all international relations.

We have followed and are determined to follow a policy of strict neutrality in foreign wars. In order to deal constructively with this problem, we have materially strengthened our neutrality legislation and will continue our efforts further to strengthen it. We realize, however, that only through world peace can America's vital interests be adequately safeguarded. And this Government has therefore, while continuing strictly to adhere to the traditional policy of refraining from entering into any political entanglement, striven at all times to keep alive the spirit of peace. It has constantly emphasized the doctrine of the Kellogg Pact. It has sought at every stage to promote peace through reduction or limitation of armaments, through the control of traffic in arms, and through the taking of profits out of war. Furthermore, realizing that lasting peace cannot be had without economic stability, we have constantly sought to build for peace by promoting fair and friendly economic relationships.

We have cooperated consistently with other nations in the promotion of the welfare of women and children in all lands; in efforts to control the manufacture of and traffic in opium and other dangerous drugs; in the furtherance of public health; with the agencies devoted to the study and discussion of basic economic and financial problems; and with the activities of the International Labor Office, seeking to improve the conditions of labor throughout the world.

II. We have confirmed by our actions the dedication of this nation to the policy of the "good neighbor," and we have promoted relations of confidence, friendship, and helpful cooperation with and among other American Republics. Suspicion and hostility in the Western Hemisphere towards the United States have vanished. Believing, as we do, that the permanent security of the United States will be better assured by the maintenance of the principles of international justice and fair dealing than by the sole force of arms, this Government has proclaimed the principle of non-intervention in the internal affairs of other sovereign nations.

At Montevideo we cooperated wholeheartedly with the other Republics of the Western Hemisphere in formulating and applying this principle. On our part we have abrogated the Platt Amendment from our Treaty with Cuba, withdrawn our forces of occupation from Haiti, and negotiated new treaties with Panama, which, while fully safeguarding our rights to protect and operate the Canal, eliminate those provisions of our earlier treaty to which warranted exception has been taken by the people of Panama.

The President's suggestion for an Inter-American Conference to be held this year, unanimously welcomed by the American Republics, has aroused general confidence that in that Conference the American nations will find the way to insure the maintenance of peace on this continent.

We will carry on the policy of the "good neighbor," encouraging increased trade and stimulating all means of intercourse with our American neighbors to our mutual advantage.

III. The reciprocal trade agreements program was adopted as an indispensable agency for dealing with an unparalleled emergency. Its central policy is based upon mutually profitable trade and fair and friendly trade methods. It is an economic undertaking which transcends party lines. It has demonstrated its capacity for coping with the vast crop of dangerous economic and political difficulties growing out of the unprecedented depression. It has proved effective in removing excessive trade barriers in an increasing number of countries, in safeguarding our trade from discriminations abroad, in expanding exports, in stimulating employment and in promoting good will. Its method involves procedures with regard to public notice, public hearings, and conferences no different from those employed by Congressional Committees and by such semi-judicial bodies as the Tariff Commission, the Federal Trade Commission, and the Interstate Commerce Commission. Its operation does not contemplate nor result in harmful, unreasonable, or excessive imports.

The national welfare imperatively requires the completion of the great emergency undertaking of the reciprocity agreement agency.

The only alternative which can be offered in good faith is a direct return to Smoot-Hawleyism, which represented a suicidal attempt at economic self-containment or isolation, caused vicious retaliation and discrimination by foreign countries against our trade, operated to wreck farm prices, to send millions of farmers headlong into bankruptcy, and to throw many millions of wage earners out of employment.

The trade agreements program is the sole practicable way of repairing these ravages of super-protectionism and other forms of economic warfare. It is one of the chief means through which reemployment can be provided for labor employed in transportation, in shipping, in our ports, and in our factories, and by which the American farmer can have restored to him a foreign market for his surplus crops. During the period that lies immediately ahead, its cumulative and widening effects will constitute the greatest single force in the world making for stable prosperity and peace. Our people will not be misled into preventing the reciprocal trade agreements program from completing its vital emergency task, but will brand narrow partisan attacks upon it as a betrayal of the interests of American farmers and American wage-earners.

[PSF:Democratic Platform:T]

Sumner Welles, Assistant Secretary of State, to Roosevelt

Washington, June 17, 1936

My dear Mr. President: I am glad to be able to tell you that as a result of continued conversations during the past winter and due particularly to the helpful cooperation of the Mexican Ambassador here, the Mexican Government has now agreed to the dispatch by the Vatican of a special representative to Mexico in order that he may endeavor to secure unity among the Mexican bishops and at the same time take the necessary steps to reestablish some discipline among the Mexican priests.

Monsignor Piani,[1] for many years Apostolic Delegate to the Philippines, was selected for this mission and has already left for Mexico. It was agreed that no publicity whatever should be attendant upon his mission and that he himself should neither make any statements to the press in the United States or Mexico, nor engage directly or indirectly, in conversation with the members of the Mexican hierarchy, in discussions of Mexican political affairs.

The Mexican Ambassador, who is now in Mexico City, told me that he himself would receive the Delegate in that capital and would do what he could to insure the success of his mission. Furthermore, it is the tacit understanding that if this mission proves successful, it will pave the way for an agreement by the Mexican Government that a permanent Apostolic Delegate of Mexican nationality be appointed to reside in Mexico City.

The Apostolic Delegate in Washington, Monsignor Cicognani,[2] asked me to see him before he left for Rome last Saturday, and requested me to convey to you in the name of the Vatican, and in his own name, an expression of very sincere gratitude for the effective and understanding assistance you had rendered in the attainment of this initial step. Father Burke was present at the interview.

I assume from what Father Burke said to me that these facts will be communicated confidentially to the members of the hierarchy in this country.

Believe me, Faithfully yours,

Sumner Welles

[PSF:Mexico:TS]

[1] Guglielmo Piani.
[2] Amleto G. Cicognani.

Roosevelt to Breckinridge Long, Ambassador to Italy, Rochester, Minnesota

[Washington] June 18, 1936

Dear Breck: I have followed your progress at the Mayo's, first with alarm and later with deep satisfaction that the operation was wholly successful and that they found no permanent trouble. Everyone says that you will be better than ever after you have regained your strength.

You must be sure to devote plenty of time to the period of recuperation, and you are fortunate in being able to go to Nantucket.

I do not need to tell you how proud I am of the splendid record you made in Rome, in the midst of trying and difficult situations—and I cannot blame you for not wanting to go back to a place where you had so much physical suffering.

If it is all right with you, I will consider that you resign and that it is accepted a short time after the adjournment of the Congress. As you probably know, I have asked Bill Phillips to go to Rome as Ambassador, and I am hoping that we can straighten out the problem of the King's title by using a series of "etc.'s."

You are right about the campaign. I am telling all our friends that they have a serious task. When you feel wholly well again it will help, I know, for you to go into a number of places and, in the meantime, perhaps you can write some articles that would be useful. Try your hand at it.

You are a grand fellow—and you know my devotion to you.[1]

As ever yours,

[PSF:Italy:CT]

[1] Answered June 23, 1936, below.

Henry M. Kannee to Marvin H. McIntyre, Assistant Secretary to the President

Washington, 6/18 [1936]

As instructed by the President I told Congressman Buchanan:[1]

"That this is just why I think it would be a good thing—if it does not hold things up—to get a Joint Resolution through. The possession has not been disputed by Great Britain and if Congress appropriates this money probably England will not raise any questions."

Congressman Buchanan replied:

"I will get a Resolution through tomorrow and I am going to put in there 'for Administration of the Islands of the United States.' That will be the assertion of ownership by Congress itself."[2]

K.

[OF 6-V:T]

[1] According to Kannee's accompanying memorandum to McIntyre of the same date, Buchanan had telephoned: "The President sent up here an item of $35,000 for administration of 3 islands in the Pacific (Jarvis, Howland and Baker). It seems their possession might be disputed with Great Britain and I want to find out whether that is so important that the President wants me to try to get a Joint Resolution through Congress for it."

[2] Buchanan introduced H.J.R. 639 providing for an appropriation of $35,000 for the initial expenses of administration; this resolution was passed, and approved June 22, 1936 (*Cong. Rec.*, vol. 80, pp. 10211, 10464, 10895; 49 *Stat.* 1896).

Press Conference, Executive Offices of the White House, June 19, 1936, 10:40 A.M.

[*Excerpt*] Q: Do you have any plans for rescinding the Neutrality Act?

The President: You will have to ask the State Department about that.

Q: The State Department said to ask you. (Laughter)

The President: I don't think we have got to the public statement phase, either one of us.

Q: Do you consider the war as over?

The President: Of course I cannot talk about the Ethiopian matter on the record, but I can give you a hint, off the record, just for your information.

Our own Neutrality Statute seems to be fairly clear that when the President finds that a state of war exists he shall—I think it uses the word "shall"—issue a proclamation.

If you will remember last October—of course there was no declaration of war—but almost as soon as there had been a battle and people were killed, regular troops in action on both sides, we found that a state of war existed. I think we were the first nation to do it.

Now, the converse of that would apply in the case of rescinding a neutrality proclamation and actually it becomes a question of fact, has the conflict stopped? Of course, Abyssinia is somewhat a difficult country about which to establish facts. It is a very large country. The Italian Army have occupied, or the Italian Administration has occupied, about two-thirds of the country but not the other third and it is a little difficult to establish all the facts.

We are working on the question of fact at the present time, and if at any time we believe that a state of war has ceased to exist, obviously a proclamation would issue.

Mr. Early: Why not let them use that without attribution to you, instead of off the record?

The President: I think it is all right. You can use that without attribution, without attributing it to me.

Q: Have you any idea as to when the facts will be sufficiently well known?

The President: I should think fairly soon. I don't think the next twenty-four hours or anything like that, but the reports are coming in every day.[1]

[President's Press Conferences:T]

[1] Roosevelt announced revocation of the proclamations of Oct. 5, 1935, and Feb. 29, 1936, relating respectively to travel by Americans on Italian and Ethiopian ships, and the export of arms and munitions to those countries, on June 20, 1936. The statement is printed in *Public Papers,* V, 225, and appeared in the newspapers of June 21.

Roosevelt to William Phillips, Under Secretary of State

Washington, June 20, 1936

Memorandum for the Under Secretary of State: Breck Long asks that his resignation be accepted as of such date as we decide on. I would suggest perhaps a week after the adjournment of the Congress.[1]

F.D.R.

[PPF 434:CT]

[1] See Hull to Roosevelt, July 6, 1936, below.

Breckinridge Long, Ambassador to Italy, to Roosevelt

Rochester, Minnesota, June 23, 1936

My dear Chief: It is with real pleasure I receive your letter of June 18.[1] You are a good friend as well as being a great Chief.

As this is probably the last communication I shall make to you in my capacity as your Ambassador to Italy, I will devote it to a two-fold purpose; first, I am glad you are sending Billie Phillips. I am sure he will do well there. In doing so I hope you will not quibble about the credentials that he will carry. It can be a quiet and innocuous way to effect recognition. Personally I advocate recognition. If we do not do it, England and the Governments of Europe will do so, and England will try to use her benevolent act as a lever with which to pry open again the door of Italian trade. They talk a lot about principles, but these European statesmen are very practical gentlemen. What they want is trade and extension of business. We are now in a position to obtain a great deal of the trade that formerly went to England, and I trust that you will not consider in too generous a light the attitude which the British will profess they will take. It will only be a matter of a short time one way or another until they recognize the status in Ethiopia. We might as well do it first, and I am very glad to see that you have already revoked the Neutrality Proclamation.[2] So I strongly urge that you send Billie with regular credentials and not enter into any fine-spun arguments on the theory of recognition, which themselves, as a matter of fact, will indicate our desire not to recognize.

Secondly, I want you to be advised of a letter I have received. I think it is quite personal, and I think you probably will desire to keep it confidential. It is such an unusual letter that I wanted to show it to you but had not an opportunity, for it was received just shortly before I had to leave Washington to come here. It is from Cardinal Pacelli, the Papal Secretary of State, and came through the open mail. I enclose you a copy.[3] It is quite unique in that it was written by the Minister of Foreign Affairs of one State to an Ambassador accredited to another Government. However, the purpose in showing it to you is to reveal to you something of the character of the relationship which your Ambassador in Rome established with the Vatican authorities. Through this and several other contacts most intimate in the Vatican circle and amongst the most highly placed in the world there existed a relationship "off the record" which might have been placed to practical advantage in case the European war became a reality.

And so I close my official relationship—with a recommendation which I consider to be to our own practical advantage—and with a revelation of an unofficial relationship with the authorities of the Vatican which is not of record anywhere but of which I think you should be advised.

With every good wish and expressions of affectionate regard, I am Most sincerely, your friend and servant,

Breckinridge Long[4]

[PSF:Italy:TS]

[1] Above.

[2] June 20, 1936; the statement is printed in *Public Papers*, V, 225.

[3] In his letter of May 12 Pacelli extended his wishes for Long's recovery. Pacelli (who succeeded Pius XI in 1939) was a guest of the Roosevelts in Hyde Park on Nov. 5, 1936 (New York *Times*, Nov. 6, 1936, p. 7).

[4] Answered July 2, 1936, below.

Stephen T. Early, Assistant Secretary to the President, to Henry M. Kannee, Assistant to Marvin H. McIntyre

Washington, June 24, 1936

Memorandum for Mr. Kannee: Assistant Secretary of State Moore called to say that he has just returned from Philadelphia and has several messages for the President, one from Norman Davis. He would like a five minute appointment tomorrow, if possible. I made him confess that these messages are not very hot, but he still insists that he would like to see the President, if possible.

If it is convenient, that is, if there is time, let him in. Otherwise, postpone it on account of the pressure of work, speech, etc.[1]

Stephen Early

[OF 20:T]

[1] Moore saw the President for twenty minutes the next day (PPF 1-0); the messages are not further identified.

Roosevelt to Governor James M. Curley of Massachusetts, Boston

[Washington] June 25, 1936

My dear Governor Curley: I am glad to acknowledge the receipt of your letter of May twenty-second regarding cotton textile imports and a copy of your radio address of April ninth, which you enclosed therewith.[1] I appreciate your interest. I wish to assure you that the situation in the cotton textile industry has long received the Administration's careful and sympathetic consideration.

In regard to your definite suggestions, you are doubtless aware that the President's power is limited by the Act of 1930. He can raise or lower the rates in that law, upon the findings of the Tariff Commission, by not more than 50 per cent, in order to equalize the difference between domestic costs and the costs of production in the chief competing country; or he can, upon the findings of the Tariff Commission, have the duty assessed upon the American selling price without any change in the rate of duty. But he can do neither except after an investigation by the Tariff Commission, and upon its finding that one or the other of these courses of action is necessary to adjust cost differences.

I am requesting the Tariff Commission to send you a copy of its report on cotton cloth and also its report on Japanese trade, especially in relation to the United States. These reports give evidence of completeness and accuracy. It was on their findings that I proclaimed the increase in duty on cotton cloth. That proclamation has been in effect less than a week. It would be futile to order another investigation until a period has elapsed long enough to be regarded by the Courts as representative. At the end of such a period, if conditions then appear to warrant it, you may rest assured that I shall order another investigation.

Very sincerely yours,

[OF 61-T:CT]

[1] Curley said (OF 61-T) that even with the 42 per cent increase in the duty on cotton textiles recently announced, the duty would still fail to level the difference created by the 40 cents a day Japanese wage. (Curley's speech is not present.) He urged adoption of a duty equal to American production costs plus 10 per cent. This would mean a "tremendous increase" in the New England cotton industry. A reply drafted by the State Department was signed by Roosevelt but was not sent; instead, the Tariff Commission was asked to revise it. The President thought the government's case could be strengthened by including a reference to presidential action already taken (Early to Forster, June 23, 1936; Forster to O'Brien, June 23, 1936, OF 61-T). The main part of the original letter included this paragraph, quoted here because it represents Hull's tariff belief in essence:

"If I were convinced that this country could profitably dispense with foreign trade, or that imports could be restricted to commodities not produced in this country without risking the loss of foreign markets for American goods, the problem would be a comparatively easy one. I can assure you that there are people in every section of the country who would like to have a prohibitive tariff against imports of the particular commodity in which they are interested. The program of this Administration, however, is based upon the conviction that full and durable prosperity in the United States depends in an important measure upon the maintenance of mutually profitable trade between nations. Nor does this contemplate unduly large or harmful imports of foreign goods into this country. Under these circumstances I am sure you will recognize that it would be inconsistent to single out particular commodities as the beneficiaries of extreme tariff protection."

Returning the Tariff Commission draft (the one here printed), Chairman Robert O'Brien wrote: "There is no use in bringing in the international trade discussion which would be very unpopular in the textile centers at this time. Nor do I see any danger in the implicit promise in the last sentence. 'If conditions warrant it,' we ought to make an investigation with or without Presidential direction" (to Early, June 25, 1936, OF 61-T).

From the 1936 Democratic Party Platform

[June 25, 1936][1]

Foreign Policy

[*Excerpt*] In our relationship with other nations, this Government will continue to extend the policy of the Good Neighbor. We reaffirm our opposition to war as an instrument of national policy, and declare that disputes between nations should be settled by peaceful means. We shall continue to observe a true neutrality in the disputes of others; to be prepared, resolutely to resist aggression against ourselves; to work for peace and to take the profits out of war; to guard against being drawn, by political commitments, international banking or private trading, into any war which may develop anywhere.

We shall continue to foster the increase in our foreign trade which has been achieved by this administration; to seek by mutual agreement the lowering of those tariff barriers, quotas and embargoes which have been raised against our exports of agricultural and industrial products; but continue as in the past to give adequate protection to our farmers and manufacturers against unfair competition or the dumping on our shores of commodities and goods produced abroad by cheap labor or subsidized by foreign governments.[2]

[1] The date of the approval of the platform by the convention.

[2] From the text as printed in the Democratic party handbook, *The Campaign Book of the Democratic Party: Candidates and Issues, 1936* (New York, 1936), pp. 5–6. The platform may also be found in Kirk H. Porter and Donald Bruce Johnson, eds., *National Party Platforms, 1840–1956* (Urbana: University of Illinois, 1956), pp. 360–363. A draft entitled, "Tentative Platform Draft" is in PSF:Democratic Party Platform. Samuel Rosenman says the original draft was composed in the White House the night of June 21 by himself and Stanley High on the basis of suggestions previously assembled by Senator Robert F. Wagner and suggestions sent to the President. William C. Bullitt appears to have been responsible for the foreign policy section; this section was inserted on June 22 when High and Rosenman made further revisions (Samuel I. Rosenman, *Working with Roosevelt*, New York: Harper, 1952, pp. 100–103).

Roosevelt to George K. Briggs, Boston

[Washington] June 26, 1936

Dear Liverpool: Many thanks for the latest installment from your grand old uncle.[1] He is pessimistic about world affairs but he is not the only one. I hope he feels happy in being in this country.

I look forward to seeing you this summer.

As ever yours,

[PPF 402:CT]

[1] Briggs, in a letter to Roosevelt of June 19, 1936 (PPF 402), enclosed one he had received from his uncle, Sinclair Kennedy, dated June 17, 1936. Kennedy quoted from a letter he had received from Thomas H. Laby, a professor of physics at Melbourne

University. As secretary of the Round Table Group in Australia, Laby had visited London and had talked with many well-informed Englishmen. His conclusions were that British and French politics were bankrupt, that English thinking on international relations was unrealistic, and that war was imminent.

Grenville T. Emmet, Minister to The Netherlands, to Roosevelt

The Hague, Netherlands, June 30, 1936

Dear Mr. President: I merely wish to send you my heartiest congratulations on the splendid speech accepting your renomination as President which you delivered last night in Philadelphia.[1] It seemed to me to hit just the right note and to arouse the energy and enthusiasm of your supporters to a point where they will repeat their performance of 1932 and reëlect you comfortably.

I am looking forward to sailing from here the middle of August, arriving in New York about August 20th and spending four weeks there at National Headquarters doing what I can to help the campaign. If there is any work you wish me to do, any people that I can see, any help or assistance I can give, please command me.

Everything is going well here. You may be interested to hear that the other day, when I saw Dr. Colijn,[2] he expressed himself very vehemently in favor of the policy of your Administration towards negotiating foreign trade agreements with other countries. He said it had done more than anything since the war to free the foreign trade of the nations of the world from the artificial shackles and restrictions that had been placed upon it and were stifling it. He condemned the plank in the Republican Platform which blamed your Administration for negotiating these trade treaties and promised a change in policy in that respect.

Pauline[3] sends her love to Eleanor and we both join in wishing you complete and entire success in the coming campaign.

Looking forward to seeing you in August, believe me to be,

As ever, Faithfully yours,

Grenville T. Emmet

[PSF:Netherlands:TS]

[1] Actually June 27.
[2] The Dutch Prime Minister.
[3] Emmet's wife.

Walter Runciman, President, British Board of Trade, to Roosevelt

[London] 30th June, 1936.

My dear Mr Roosevelt, I was deeply touched by the cordiality of your letter which Arthur Murray delivered to me a few days ago.[1] I have pondered over its invitation and its kindness impresses me all the more because you wrote to me with your own hand at a time of condensed political pressure.

I can imagine no greater satisfaction than to exchange thoughts with you at this critical period in the history of our two countries. For me to visit America, however, before November would be inconvenient, but later on, say, at the end of 1936, I would enjoy more than I can say the opportunity of gleaning your reflections—not in a council chamber, but at your hospitable table.

I am copying your example at an early date and am about to leave our capital for four weeks in my schooner.[2]

Believe me to be, Yours very sincerely,

Walter Runciman

[PPF 4322:AS]

[1] May 4, 1936, above.
[2] See Murray to Roosevelt, Nov. 26, 1936, below.

Roosevelt to Representative Wesley E. Disney of Oklahoma

[Washington, July 1, 1936]

My dear Mr. Disney: I have your letter of June 19, 1936, suggesting that the subject relating to the conservation of petroleum resources be included on the agenda of the forthcoming inter-American conference which is to be held in Buenos Aires, Argentina.[1]

I know how interested you are in this matter, but in view of the fact that the suggestions of this Government have already been submitted to the Committee on Program,[2] and the fact that the Project of Program has been submitted to the twenty-one American Republics by the Governing Board of the Pan American Union, it would not seem feasible to have this subject included at this time for discussion at the conference.[3]

Sincerely yours,

[*Notation*:A] July 1, 1936.
[OF 1970:CT]

[1] Disney said, in part (OF 1970): "If the other nations represented in the Conference should take parallel action, they would prevent the dissipation of a product which is of increasing importance in time of peace and of foremost importance should war arise. Furthermore, if we could agree with them upon concerted and cooperative action, we would avoid needless and wasteful conflict, increase their public revenues and add to their national wealth."

[2] See Hull to the Argentinian ambassador, May 2, 1936, in *Foreign Relations, 1936*, V, 16–17.

[3] Drafted by Under Secretary of State Phillips.

Memorandum by Roosevelt

Washington, July 2, 1936

This was handed to me by Monsieur Monique, in the presence of William Phillips, Under Secretary of State, at the White House on Tuesday, June 23, 1936.[1]

F.D.R.

[PSF:France:T]

[1] The meeting of Roosevelt and Emmanuel Monick, French financial attaché in London, is described in a memorandum by Phillips, June 23, 1936 (*Foreign Relations, 1936*, I, 539–541), and in Blum, *From the Morgenthau Diaries*, pp. 155–159. The Monick visit broke the ground for the tripartite stabilization agreement between France, Great Britain, and the United States adopted Sept. 25, 1936 (*Public Papers*, V, 376–378). Correspondence on the agreement is printed in *Foreign Relations, 1936*, I, 535–536.

[Enclosure]

At this time of economic disorders in the world which drive nations to isolation, social troubles and perhaps more serious conflicts, it would be impossible for the American dollar to be fixed while the currencies of other nations would be left free to move.

This would bring the United States back to the situation of 1932.

Under such circumstances, the only practical thing to do is to promote monetary peace and, as a first step, to establish more stable relations between the Pound Sterling, the Dollar and the Franc.

Such an understanding between the United States, Great Britain and France would naturally be left open to other nations, provided that they do not resort to the practice of economic dumping and agree to cooperate in the promotion of international trade and thus toward the restoration of prosperity and peace throughout the world.

[PSF:France:T]

Roosevelt to Governor Herbert H. Lehman of New York, Albany

[Washington] July 2, 1936

My dear Governor Lehman: I have your letter of June 15, 1936,[1] with its enclosed letter of June 5, 1936, from Mr. Felix Warburg, with which there was also transmitted Sir Herbert Samuel's letter to Mr. Warburg of May 27, 1936, and its accompanying memorandum, with reference to the question of the immigration of German Jews into the United States.

The general question of the attitude of American consular officers in Germany to the visa applications of the groups of persons covered by your letter was touched upon in some detail in my letter to you of November 13, 1935,[2] and I expressed to you at that time my earnest desire that all consideration and justice should continue to be shown to these immigrants.

As regards the two specific questions raised in the enclosures to your letter, I have consulted the Department of State and I am informed that the situation in regard to the points which have been raised is briefly as follows:

It is true that there has been an abnormally great increase in the number of German Jewish visa applicants at the American Consulate General at Stuttgart during recent months which has necessitated short delays in the handling of individual cases. This situation has been met in the following manner. The Stuttgart personnel has very recently been increased by the additional employment of two clerks and by the transfer to that office of two additional consular officers. Furthermore, effective June 1st, the previous division of duties of the United States Public Health surgeon and the immigrant inspector, who are assigned as technical advisers in visa cases, between Stuttgart and Vienna has been abolished. The full time of these two officials is consequently now given to their Stuttgart duties and immigration visas are now being issued on

341

all working days during each month instead of only during a certain portion of each month as was the case prior to June 1st. This would seem to obviate the necessity of the expenditure of Government funds at this time for the opening up of additional consulates in Germany as regards the issuance of immigration visas.

As to the second question, concerning the weight given by examining officers at the Consulate General at Hamburg to affidavits of support from more distant relatives and friends as compared with such affidavits from close relatives such as a husband, wife, parent, son or daughter, I am informed that the situation is as follows.

Intending immigrants may present any evidence they desire, to establish their admissibility into the United States and to obtain visas, and the consuls are required to consider carefully and judicially all evidence submitted. If an applicant will rely upon another person for support, the willingness and ability of that person to support the applicant must be shown. A promise of support made by a close relative will naturally be given more weight than one from a distant relative upon whom there may be no legal or moral obligation to support the applicant and whose feeling of responsibility toward the applicant will not ordinarily be as great as in the case of a close relative. Consequently, while the promise made by a father to support his child, or by a child to support his father, may be readily accepted, such a promise made by a distant relative may be subject to questioning as to the probability of its being kept. The Department of State holds that in such cases the consular officer may properly take into consideration the past conduct, toward the applicant, of the person promising his support as indicating a recognition of responsibility and interest, such as previous contributions to support and previous associations and interest in the welfare of the applicant, and require an explanation of the reasons for undertaking the applicant's support. A favorable decision is reached when the preponderance of evidence supports a conclusion that the person promising the applicant's support will be likely to take steps to prevent the applicant from becoming a public charge. All consular officers operate under circular instructions from the Department of State which have been issued along the lines indicated.

I believe that the Department of State and its consular officers abroad are continuing to make every effort to carry out the immigration duties placed upon them in a considerate and humane manner. They are issuing considerably more immigration visas to German Jewish applicants at the present time than was the case last year or in recent previous years.

I wish to assure you of my sympathetic interest in the question which you have brought to my attention and of my appreciation of your action in bringing these matters to my attention.[3]

Very sincerely yours,

[OF 133:CT]

[1] Above.
[2] Above.
[3] Drafted by the State Department. See Hull to Roosevelt, July 27, 1936, below.

Roosevelt to Breckinridge Long, Ambassador to Italy, Rochester, Minnesota

[Washington] July 2, 1936

Dear Breck: Many thanks for yours of June twenty-third.[1] I do hope that you will soon be able to move to Nantucket.

That is an awfully nice letter from the Cardinal.

I am telling Bill[2] that when the agrément goes through with Rome your resignation and his appointment can be announced.

Take it easy for a month or six weeks and then when you are feeling wholly fit come down here and we will work on plans for the campaign.[3]

As ever yours,

[PSF:Italy:CT]

[1] Above.
[2] William Phillips.
[3] Long had drafted a speech for Roosevelt at his request; this, however, was not used (Long to Early, Sept. 22, 1936, PPF 434; PPF 1820). Long accompanied the Roosevelt party on the western campaign tour, Oct. 8–17, 1936, but references to foreign policy were confined to two or three statements on the importance of foreign trade and of friendly relations with Canada (*Public Papers,* V, 413–516). Roosevelt thanked Long afterward for the "splendid help you gave me on our western trip" (Oct. 23, 1936, PPF 434).

Arthur Murray to Roosevelt

An Cala, Isle of Seil, Argyll, July 5, 1936

My dear Franklin, When in London recently I went to see my friend W.R.[1]

I had a talk with him in the sense of your conversation with me, and handed to him the letter which you wrote him. He was much touched that you should write him, and with the contents and cordiality of your letter.[2] He has now sent me a letter from himself to you, and I send it on to you herewith.

Thank you so much for your letter of June 5th.[3] We had such a happy visit to you—and so interesting; and we are not going to forget your very kind invitation to come back very soon.

We read with great pleasure and enthusiasm your Philadelphia speech[4] —of a piece with your great Inaugural Address of March 4, 1933. You have a hectic time in the electoral domain ahead of you, and then— another 4 years swimming in your pool at the White House!

The Government here appears to be drifting this way and that, but I doubt whether any previous Government in Great Britain has been faced with so many complex and ever-changing problems in European affairs, largely the heritage of the Lloyd George régime and of his refusal to work with the United States towards the establishment of a real peace based on just and economic grounds. To-day, nothing is static, and the existence of 3 Dictatorships in Europe adds to the difficulty of framing and pursuing a fixed policy. Generally speaking the only policy in this country which appeals to the majority of people is to make the country secure against any eventuality that may arise. The times in which we live are well exemplified by the fact that a British Government can address a questionnaire to the German Government and the latter can treat it as if it were of no account at all, to be answered just *when* it suits the German Government. *Tempora mutantur!* I can imagine how Edward Grey[5] would have taken such a proceeding! Very sadly do we miss his steadying voice in European affairs to-day. I shall always remember how in the last year of his life—the first year of your Presidentship— he used to express to me his great admiration for you. He is a friend that I miss very much.

The rumours of Baldwin's tiredness have been much exaggerated. And it is only a minority that wishes to get rid of him. His present determination is to "see out" the Coronation.

With every good wish
yours very sincerely

Arthur Murray

[PPF 435:AS]

[1] Walter Leslie Runciman, president of the British Board of Trade.
[2] Roosevelt to Runciman, May 4, 1936, above.

[3] This (PPF 435) was a brief note of farewell as the Murrays sailed for home from Canada; Roosevelt also said that he hoped to meet Murray in Canada later in the summer.

[4] Accepting nomination for the presidency, June 27, 1936 (*Public Papers,* V, 230–236).

[5] Sir Edward Grey, British Foreign Secretary, 1905–1916, and close friend of Murray.

Roosevelt to Leon Blum, President, Council of Ministers, Paris

[Washington] July 6, 1936

My dear Mr. Blum: I write to thank you for your letter of June 13 relative to the confidential mission of Mr. Emmanuel Monick, and to assure you that I listened attentively to the message he brought.[1] Please accept my sincere best wishes for the success of your ministry.

Very sincerely yours,

[PSF:France:CT]

[1] Blum merely said that Monick would ask for a strictly confidential interview and that it would be his (Blum's) solicitude to maintain the closest collaboration with Roosevelt.

Roosevelt to Édouard Herriot, President of the Chamber of Deputies, Paris

[Washington] July 6, 1936

My dear Mr. Herriot: I read your letter of June 11[1] with deep interest. I was very happy to receive Mr. Monick and value highly my talk with him, which brought to mind the pleasant conversations which I was privileged to have with you in the spring of 1933. Mrs. Roosevelt joins me in best wishes for your health and happiness.

Very sincerely yours,

[PSF:France:CT]

[1] Above.

Cordell Hull, Secretary of State, to Roosevelt

Washington, July 6, 1936

My dear Mr. President: The Embassy at Rome has telegraphed that the formal consent of the King of Italy to the appointment of Mr. Phillips as American Ambassador to Italy has been given, and that the agrément may now be considered as granted.

I should be grateful if you would inform me whether you have accepted Mr. Long's resignation, or if not, when you propose to do so. I should also appreciate it if you would let me know when you propose to designate Mr. Phillips as Ambassador. Mr. Phillips is on leave and will be absent from Washington until August 1.

Faithfully yours,

Cordell Hull

[*Notation*:AS] C.H. 7/25—OK—any day you say. FDR[1]
[OF 233:TS]

---

[1] Long's resignation was effective July 31, 1936. He was succeeded by William Phillips on Aug. 4, 1936. From 1940 to 1944 Long was Assistant Secretary of State. He died in 1958.

Arthur Sweetser, Director, The Secretariat, League of Nations, to Roosevelt

[New York] July 6, 1936

Dear Mr. President: I am so sorry my two brief visits to Washington happened to occur when you were away;[1] I had anticipated taking advantage of your very kind suggestion that I come in to see you on my return home. May I, however, in default of that and in view of the present dangerous international situation, set down briefly three points which I think will interest you?

First, the international situation is the worst I have known it since the War. It gets more rather than less dangerous almost daily. The lines are getting constantly tighter between the democratic states and the dictator-authoritarian. And it is not a matter of continents, for Asia rivals Europe. It is not excluded, of course, that, in some way now unforeseen, we will turn the corner, for Italy may become "satisfied" by Ethiopia, Germany may be kept in line by the tightening alarms about her, and

Japan may be fully occupied in China. But the economic situation in all three countries is bad; it may leave the dictator-cliques no alternative to an eruption. Dangerously enough, too, they do not fear but rather subconsciously, I think, favor war to prove themselves, while the great democracies are so genuinely pacifist as to have led Goebbels this morning to the amazing charge that they are "cowardly." For the first time, I, who have been optimistic for years, see no break in the clouds and only a policy of anxious vigilance, of recognition that an explosion, even if we could stay out, would dislocate our whole immense domestic effort, and of watchfulness to take advantage of every opportunity, however small, to exert our influence in the other direction.

Secondly and paradoxically enough, the League of Nations, despite all reverses, seems firmer today than ever before. League people, taking the long perspective on history, have ceased being alarmed for its future; they appreciate that, in the end, it must come; feel that the historian writing fifty years from now may give quite a different interpretation to the extraordinary first attempt of sanctions in the Abyssinian dispute from what we in temporary discouragement today give. The League has something so essentially necessary and sound in it that it is sure to keep on in one form or another, even if there were another war. The only question is as to what form, with what changes. My guess is that not much will be done, for some of the reform talk is a sincere effort by the Small Powers to get the Great Powers to take their responsibilities while still more is an attempt by the latter to shift those responsibilities to the League. What is surprising is that many believers in peace turn their batteries not on the enemies of peace but on the institution which is fighting their fight. There is a lot of faintheadedness in this world when some one shows a big enough gun.

Finally, you may have seen that several little Powers, notably Scandinavia and Holland, turned in their distress last week towards us, talking of changing, widening, universalizing the League particularly to facilitate our relations with it. I do not know if they will press this in September—or if they should. Domestically, it might be the worst of times during the campaign; internationally, however, the situation might be so urgent that conceivably we might not find it undesirable to restate our general philosophy.

It is marvelous to be home again. I anticipate a splendid summer. I shall be in New York all this week, at the Hotel Gotham; at Plymouth, Manter's Point, the following month, then Chicago and the Yosemite in late August before sailing again September 5. I have no need to add,

I am sure, that if at any time or in any way I can be of the slightest service, I am 100% at your disposal wherever and whenever desired.[2]

Again with deepest appreciation of your note, I am

Yours most respectfully,

Arthur Sweetser

[PPF 506:TS]

[1] Roosevelt was away from Washington, June 8–15, and June 27–30, 1936; Sweetser had arrived from Geneva on June 7 to spend his summer holiday in this country. He finally saw Roosevelt on Sept. 8, 1936, just before he returned to Geneva.

[2] Answered July 10, 1936, below.

Sumner Welles, Assistant Secretary of State, to Roosevelt

Washington, July 8, 1936

My dear Mr. President: You have agreed to receive tomorrow, Thursday, morning, at eleven o'clock, the Ambassador of Peru and the Minister of Ecuador in order that they may advise you officially of the agreement reached by the two Governments they represent for the settlement of their boundary dispute by your arbitration.[1]

I am enclosing a brief memorandum giving you the background of the dispute.[2] The agreement provides for the settlement of the last really dangerous boundary controversy existing on this Continent, and it clears the atmosphere for the approaching Inter-American Conference. I have asked Steve Early to give all appropriate publicity to the visit that will be paid you tomorrow morning.

Believe me, Faithfully yours,

Sumner Welles

[PSF:Peru:TS]

[1] Ambassador Manuel de Freyre y Santander and Minister Colón Alfaro. The dispute was formally submitted to a Washington conference of delegates of the two countries that opened Sept. 30, 1936, but the matter was not settled until 1944. Roosevelt's welcoming speech to the delegates is printed in *Public Papers,* V, 394–396.

[2] A two-page summary of the Ponce-Castro Oyanguren protocol of 1924 that provided for the eventual submission of the boundary dispute to the President of the United States. See the section, "Boundary dispute between Ecuador and Peru," in *Foreign Relations, 1934,* IV, 457–466, in which is printed the 1924 protocol (pp. 459–460).

Francis B. Sayre, Chairman, Executive Committee on Commercial Policy, to Roosevelt

[Washington] July 8, 1936

My dear Mr. President: I refer to your memorandum of June 1, 1936, transmitting certain figures and conclusions given to you by Mr. Frank Garvan of the Chemical Foundation regarding the international creditor position and the balance of payments of the United States. You requested that these figures and conclusions be checked.[1]

In response to your request the Executive Committee on Commercial Policy requested Mr. Leo Pasvolsky of the Department of State to prepare an analysis of Mr. Garvan's presentation. There is attached to this letter a copy of Mr. Pasvolsky's memorandum, which analyses Mr. Garvan's figures and conclusions with great care.[2]

This memorandum points out that the "thumb-nail sketch of our creditor status" is another of numerous attempts recently made in various quarters to misrepresent the international creditor-debtor position of the United States by understating this country's foreign assets and by over-stating its liabilities to foreigners. This result is accomplished by computing our long-term investments abroad upon different bases of valuation than those used for foreign long-term investments in this country, by including a huge additional unidentified and unexplained sum in the total estimate of foreign investments in the United States and by exaggerating the excess of foreign short-term funds in the United States over similar American funds abroad.

With reference to the statements entitled "Balance of Payments . . . Commodities Only" the memorandum herewith attached indicates the misleading impression that is created by isolating the items relating to only some international operations in a balance of payments discussion without reference to the other items to which they are necessarily related.

Faithfully yours,

Francis B. Sayre

[OF 1746:CT]

[1] This memorandum reads, in its entirety: "Will you please have these figures and conclusions checked? They were given me by Mr. Frank Garvan of the Chemical Foundation" (OF 1746). Francis P. Garvan, an old friend of Roosevelt, had had lunch with him and Henry Wallace at the White House on May 29, 1936. Garvan, while Alien Property Custodian in 1919, had bought up some 4,500 German chemical and

industrial patents seized by the Custodian's office in 1917–18, and with these had set up Chemical Foundation, Inc., with himself as president. In 1924 the government sued to dissolve the corporation but in 1926 the Supreme Court held in its favor.

[2] Not present; described by a file reference (June 1, 1936, PPF 1985), as "Balance of Payments, 4 months ended 4/30/36—Commodities Only, based on Dept. of Commerce reports, with notations," and, "Balance of Payments, 3 months ended 3/31/36—Thumbnail sketch of Our Creditor Status."

Roosevelt to Daniel C. Roper, Secretary of Commerce

Washington, July 10, 1936

Memorandum for the Secretary of Commerce: This analysis of Frank Garvan's Chemical Foundation propaganda is interesting. The Secretary of State suggests that the Department of Commerce take the lead in putting out the necessary publicity on this general subject. I agree. Will you take charge of it?[1]

F.D.R.

[OF 1746:CT]

[1] The reference is to the preceding letter; see Forster to Early, Aug. 4, 1936, below.

Roosevelt to Arthur Sweetser, New York

[Washington] July 10, 1936

My dear Arthur: I am sorry that absence from the city prevented me from seeing you on the occasion of your two brief visits here; but I want you to know how much I appreciate your kind letter of July sixth.[1]

I have read with very great interest your views on the international situation as you have observed it from the vantage ground of Geneva, particularly your observations regarding the future of the League of Nations and with respect to the attitude of small nations toward it. All in all you give me a view of the general international situation which I am exceedingly glad to have.[2]

Very sincerely yours,

[PPF 506:CT]

[1] Above. Sweetser saw Roosevelt briefly just before he sailed for Europe on Sept. 8, 1936 (PPF 1-0). Some kind of plan for world peace was apparently discussed at this

meeting for he refers to this in letters to Roosevelt and McIntyre of Sept. 10, 1936 (PPF 506).

[2] Drafted by William D. Hassett.

Norman Armour, Minister to Canada, to Roosevelt

Ottawa, Canada, July 25, 1936

My dear Mr. President: It is unnecessary for me to tell you with what pleasure and keen anticipation we are awaiting your arrival in Quebec. It is a particular pleasure to me to feel that this is the second time that I have been stationed in a country which has been honored by a visit from you. This time, however, I promise not to choose the occasion of your arrival for an attack of dengue fever!

The arrangements for your reception at Quebec are all completed and they will, I hope, meet with your approval. I am enclosing the programme, as furnished me by the Canadian Government. This gives the order of ceremonies from the time of the arrival of your train (10 a.m. Quebec Time) at the station at Quebec until your departure at 6 p.m.[1]

You will note that four short addresses of welcome are on the programme; the Governor General, the Prime Minister, the Prime Minister of Quebec and the Mayor of Quebec. I understand that these addresses are to be limited to three or five minutes. They ask me to assure you, however, that they hope you will not feel called upon to restrict your remarks: that the time—11.05—given for the departure is entirely elastic.

There is also enclosed a list of those who will be on the platform when you arrive. Our diplomatic Corps here is limited to three representatives: the French, Japanese and American, in addition to the British High Commissioner.

As of possible use in your talks with the Governor General and the Prime Minister, I am also enclosing a memorandum on the Trade Agreement between Canada and the United States. This memorandum, prepared by the office of the Commercial Attaché, undertakes to show in concise form the results of the Agreement to date and will, I think, be of interest to you. Also, I am sure you will be gratified at the really excellent results it has already secured for the trade of both countries. It occurs to me that some of the information in it may also be of use to you after you return to Washington.

The present plan is for all of us—Americans as well as Canadians—to await your arrival at Quebec. I shall be at the station with the Counselor

351

of Legation, Mr. Palmer; the Commercial Attaché, Colonel Bankhead (brother of the Speaker and the Senator); our Consul at Quebec, Mr. Randolph; and Richard Southgate, from the State Department.[2]

If, however, you feel that it would be of use to you, or you would care to have any one of us join your train at St. Andrews and come up with you it can, of course, be very easily arranged. Mr. McIntyre has only to send me a telegram.

I am, my dear Mr. President, with high regard, Faithfully yours,

Norman Armour

P.S. Since the above was written, Richard Southgate has arrived from the Department and in talking the matter over we both feel that a paragraph or two in French, added to the remarks you propose to make, would have a fine effect in the Province of Quebec. This is particularly true in view of the fact that the Lieutenant Governor of the Province, Mr. Patenaude, and the Mayor of Quebec, Mr. Gregoire,[3] will probably speak in French. May I therefore take the liberty of sending to you, under separate cover, a proposed paragraph or two for your approval in case you think well of the idea? I recall what a splendid effect your addressing the Haitians in French had when you were in Cap Haitien, and feel sure that it would have an even wider appeal here.[4]

[Speech File:TS]

[1] This and the other enclosures mentioned below are present.
[2] Ely E. Palmer, Henry M. Bankhead, John Randolph. Southgate was chief of the Division of Protocol and Conferences.
[3] Esioff L. Patenaude; J. E. Gregoire.
[4] See Armour to McIntyre, July 28, 1936, below.

Cordell Hull, Secretary of State, to Roosevelt

Washington, July 27, 1936

My dear Mr. President: In Judge Moore's absence I have received your memorandum of July 21, 1936,[1] addressed to him and enclosing correspondence regarding the concern of Jewish leaders with respect to the reported proposal of the British Government to suspend Jewish immigration into Palestine.

As you know, for several months the Arabs have been on a general strike in Palestine and have engaged in widespread attacks, not only against individual Jews and Jewish property but against the constituted British authorities. The Arab leaders have insisted upon the suspension of Jewish immigration and a prohibition against further sale of land to Jews. The British Government some time ago announced that it proposed to send to Palestine a Royal Commission of Inquiry to make a thorough investigation of the situation and report the facts. Upon the basis of these facts future British policy in Palestine, within the terms of the Mandate, would presumably be based. The British have made it clear, however, that they will not send the Commission to Palestine until the Arabs cease their attacks and bring an end to the general strike. The Arabs, on the other hand, have refused to take these steps until Jewish immigration is suspended. It is presumably with a view to ending this deadlock that the British Government is now considering suspending, temporarily, Jewish immigration into Palestine. It is assumed that once such immigration is suspended the Arabs would cease their attacks and the Royal Commission of Inquiry could then proceed with its undertaking.

As you know, our Consul General at Jerusalem has been most active during recent months in demanding protection for the approximately 10,000 American nationals in Palestine. On one occasion his representations were strengthened by our Embassy at London. Under the circumstances it would seem to be unwise for us to insist that the British follow a particular course of action in their present difficulties. They might very well respond that if we insisted upon their following a particular course they could not assume responsibility for the protection of our nationals in Palestine. Obviously their position there is extremely difficult since they must endeavor to hold a balance between two factions of the population. Any interference from the outside would only make their task more difficult and would aid in no way in the solution of their problem.

It seems to me that the situation might be met by asking Mr. Bingham, entirely personally and unofficially, to mention to Mr. Eden the concern of Jewish circles in the United States at the reported proposal to suspend Jewish immigration into Palestine. I believe that Mr. Bingham, in such a conversation, should stress the fact that he is not presuming in any way to interfere with British policy in Palestine or to offer advice thereon, since it is recognized that the administration of that country is wholly a British responsibility. He might add that he is bringing to the attention of Mr. Eden the fact that Jewish circles here are deeply concerned in this matter merely for such consideration as it may merit. I am sending

Mr. Bingham instructions in this sense and asking him to be particularly careful to point out that he is speaking entirely in a personal capacity and not on behalf of this Government.[2]

I am returning herewith the letter and enclosures sent to you by Mr. Rosenman.[3]

Faithfully yours,

Cordell Hull

[PSF:Great Britain:TS]

[1] No copy of the memorandum has been found in the Roosevelt papers; the enclosures, however, were returned by Hull and are printed below.

[2] See Hull to Bingham, July 27, 1936, and Bingham's reply, July 28, 1936, in *Foreign Relations, 1936*, III, 444, 445.

[3] See Hull to Roosevelt, Aug. 1, 1936, below.

[*Enclosure 1*] Samuel I. Rosenman to Roosevelt

New York, July 16th, 1936

Dear Mr. President: Mr. Simon Rifkind, who, you know, is Senator Wagner's partner and was formerly his secretary in Washington, phoned me yesterday and read me the inclosed cable which he received from London. In view of the fact that the Senator was on the high seas on his way to Europe, he was at a loss as to how to proceed, and, so, he called me.

I do not know whether Frankfurter has communicated with you concerning this matter or not; and I do not know whether you would wish the State Department to do anything at all in the matter. Naturally a great deal seems to be involved, if the cable is correct, so that I am much interested.

I am sending it to you, knowing that you will want to do what you think is proper and possible in the premises.

We are having a grand rest. Missy is developing into quite a bass fisherman. She had one on her line yesterday, and I have never seen her as excited since the night that Walsh beat Shouse as permanent chairman of the 1932 convention.

We all hope that you get more tuna than she does bass. With love from Dorothy and Missy,[1]

Yours most cordially,

Sam

[1] Mrs. Rosenman and Marguerite LeHand.

[Enclosure 2] Will Rosenblatt to Simon H. Rifkind, New York

[undated]

[Cablegram] Serious situation here concerning Palestine. British Cabinet near decision to suspend Jewish immigration Palestine, tho suspension means yielding to Arab violence. Suspension would last during investigation and report Royal Enquiry Commission but suspension means stopping only avenue escape German Polish Jews; furthermore suspension might prove difficult to lift and might provoke Jewish reprisals Palestine with disastrous consequences after continued admirable Jewish restraint. Conferring with Stephen Wise in London who, with Frankfurter, here helping Weizmann.[1] Expect you, Wagner possibly Bulkley, other leaders urge administration make informal representations London against proposed suspension. Such representations would strengthen British Government impression that Anglo-American relations might be injured. Persuaded White House would sympathetically respond to your appeal. We, including Wise, leaving everything America to you. American Jewry, including Wise, would gratefully remember your Wagner's intervention.

Will Rosenblatt

[Notation:A] Hon Samuel Rosenman   Blue Mountain Lake   N.Y.
[PSF:Great Britain:T]

[1] Chaim Weizmann, president of the Jewish Agency for Palestine.

[Enclosure 3] S. H. Rifkind to Samuel I. Rosenman

[undated]

I have just heard from Morris Rothenberg of the Z.O.A. to the effect that he had received a cablegram from Wise suggesting that he (Rothenberg) communicate with me with respect to the Palestine immigration situation. That should confirm the official character of the cablegram, copy of which is herewith being transmitted to you.

I believe that it is of the utmost importance that the matter be made known to the President as I know that his response to these matters is much more warm-hearted than that of some of his official family.

Cordially,

R.

[PSF:Great Britain:TS]

Cordell Hull, Secretary of State, to Roosevelt, Campobello, N.B.

[Washington] 28 July 1936

[*Radiogram*] The Embassy in Madrid reported this morning that plans have been completed to evacuate foreigners to Alicante or Valencia on Thursday morning.[1] The city remains quiet. The USS *Oklahoma* is near Bilbao prepared to evacuate Americans if necessary. Ambassador Bowers has been instructed to join the *Cayuga* and sail along the north coast of Spain as far as Vigo stopping at ports enroute where Americans might have escaped to the coast.[2] The Ambassador will discuss the situation with American consular officers at places visited and will be in communication with me by means of the *Cayuga's* radio. It is also hoped that either the *Oklahoma* or the *Cayuga* will be able to establish radio communication with the American Embassy in Madrid.[3] The Consul at Gibraltar reports that in a battle between rebel and government forces in the south government troops were repulsed.

Cordell Hull

[OF 422-C:T]

[1] Eric C. Wendelin, third secretary at Madrid, reported this to Hull in a dispatch of July 28, 1936, printed in *Foreign Relations, 1936,* II, 649. Hull had cabled Roosevelt (in Nova Scotian waters) on July 2 (OF 422-C) recommending that American vessels in Spanish waters be prepared to take on American nationals in Spain. He said that the *Oklahoma* had been ordered to Cherbourg and the *Quincy* to Gibraltar.

[2] The Coast Guard cutter *Cayuga* arrived at San Sebastián on July 26 and took off Bowers, his family, members of the Embassy staff and others (New York *Times,* July 27, 1936, p. 1). Bowers proceeded to St. Jean de Luz aboard the *Cayuga,* picking up refugees. See Bowers to Hull, and Hull to William W. Corcoran, consul at Vigo, July 27, 1936, in *Foreign Relations, 1936,* II, 648, 648–649.

[3] Bowers' reason for going first to St. Jean de Luz was that radio contact could be established there with Washington, but by July 30 he was able to send messages directly from the *Cayuga* to Washington (Bowers to Hull, received July 30, 1936, *ibid.*, pp. 653–654).

Norman Armour, Minister to Canada, to Marvin H. McIntyre, Assistant Secretary to the President

Ottawa, Canada, July 28, 1936

Dear Mr. McIntyre: Mr. Southgate brought up with him a copy of the draft of the President's remarks for Quebec which Mr. Hull submitted to the President under date of July 7th last.[1]

After reading it, it occurs to me that in addition to these remarks the President might like to have one or two suggestions based on the local situation here. It seems to me that speaking on Canadian soil in one of the British Dominions the President might like to be more specific with regard to our relations not only with Canada but with the British Empire and that a word from him on this angle of world relations would have a very good effect at this time and it would come so naturally in a speech delivered at Quebec that undue significance would not be attached to it.

In any case, I have drafted one or two paragraphs which I thought you might wish to submit to the President for any use he might wish to make of them.[2]

Of course I realize that he has probably recast the remarks sent over from the State Department and it may be these suggestions of mine are already embodied in the remarks he proposes to make.

I also felt that some reference to King George's death would perhaps be in order. The universal sympathy expressed throughout the United States, and particularly the President's own messages of sympathy, did more, I believe to bring Canada even closer to the United States than anything that has happened in years. In addition to one or two sentences referring to the King's death in my own draft I have added the President's own message to the Prince of Wales, the present King, sent after the King's death.[3] It is so beautifully worded that it would seem to me difficult to improve on this language in any reference the President might care to make and I thought he might, therefore, wish to paraphrase this telegram and use it in his remarks instead of the language I have suggested.

I hope that the President will not feel that I am meddling too much in something that is not perhaps my affair but I suppose there is a good wastebasket handy even in Campobello!

I spoke this morning with Colonel Starling[4] who tells me that he is going over all the arrangements. Everything seems to be in good order and I feel sure that there will be no hitch: on the contrary, that all things will go off in fine shape. Certainly, all of Canada is looking forward to the visit with great anticipation, as we all are.

Very sincerely yours,

Norman Armour

P.S. I am also enclosing the few sentences in French, to which I referred in my letter yesterday, which I thought the President might like to use in his remarks to the Premier of Quebec, Mr. Godbout,[5] and the Mayor of Quebec, Mr. Gregoire. (Yesterday, I said by mistake that Mr. Patenaude, the Lieutenant Governor, would speak.) You will note from the enclosed revised programme that the four speakers are, in addition to the President, the Governor General, the Prime Minister, the Premier of Quebec and the Mayor.[6] I thought the President in opening his remarks would wish to address a few words first to the Governor General and then to the Prime Minister, Mr. King; after which he could, in French, use the enclosed remarks addressed to the Premier of Quebec and the Mayor.[7]

[Speech File:TS]

---

[1] The draft brought by Southgate (chief of the State Department Division of Protocol and Conferences) was by Under Secretary of State Phillips. It was not used verbatim but its ideas and occasional phrases appear in the final draft (Speech File). The speech as delivered is printed in *Public Papers,* V, 276–279.

[2] The drafts are present. The two paragraphs (used in part) on King George's death and U.S.–Canadian relations are referred to below.

[3] Jan. 20, 1936, printed *ibid.,* p. 65.

[4] Edmund W. Starling, head of the Secret Service.

[5] Adélard Godbout.

[6] "Luncheon List and Table Plan, July 31st, 1936." Also present is a three-page mimeographed itinerary entitled, "Motor car arrangements on the occasion of the visit of the President of the United States to Quebec, July 31st, 1936."

[7] Armour's two-page French draft, extensively revised by Roosevelt, is present, and appears in the speech as delivered. Armour wrote again on August 5 (PSF:Canada): "I hope you feel, as we all do, that your visit to Quebec was an unqualified success. I have heard only the most favorable comments from Canadians of all groups: the visit itself and your remarks on Dufferin Terrace have made a profound impression on Canada." See Roosevelt to Houston, Aug. 5, 1936, below.

Cordell Hull, Secretary of State, to Roosevelt

Washington, August 1, 1936

Highly Confidential

My dear Mr. President: In continuation of my letter of July 27, 1936,[1] regarding the reported proposal of the British Government to suspend Jewish immigration into Palestine, I think you would wish to know that Ambassador Bingham mentioned the subject to Mr. Eden on July 28.[2] The Ambassador was, as you will recall, instructed to inform Mr. Eden, entirely personally and unofficially, of the deep concern in influential Jewish circles in the United States over the possible consequences of suspending Jewish immigration into Palestine.

Ambassador Bingham has reported that Mr. Eden thanked him for the information but gave no indication as to what the policy of his Government would be.

I have today asked Mr. Bingham whether we are correct in assuming that the recent announcement of the membership and of the terms of reference of the Royal Commission of Inquiry to ascertain the underlying causes of the disturbances that have broken out in Palestine indicates that the British Government has abandoned, at least for the time being, any plan it may have had to suspend Jewish immigration into Palestine temporarily. I shall of course inform you as soon as Mr. Bingham's reply is received.[3]

Faithfully yours,

Cordell Hull

[PSF:Great Britain:TS]

[1] Above.
[2] See Bingham's dispatch of this date in *Foreign Relations, 1936,* III, 445.
[3] See Phillips to Roosevelt, Aug. 6, 1936, below.

Chester C. Davis, Board of Governors, Federal Reserve System, to Roosevelt

Washington, August 3, 1936

Dear Mr. President: I have the honor to submit the accompanying report of observations and conversations relating to international trade and agricultural policies obtained during a visit from March 30 to May

21 in England, Holland, Germany, Sweden, Denmark, Czechoslovakia, Austria, Hungary, Italy and France.[1] I made this trip as Administrator of the Agricultural Adjustment Administration, in obedience to your letter of March 10, 1936.[2]

Western European countries that may become involved in war are pushing for national self-sufficiency in food and feed just as far as their resources will permit. They have restricted imports through tariffs, quotas, embargoes, and exchange controls, accepting the higher costs that go with the curtailment of normal imports, as a necessary price for a greater degree of economic preparedness for war.

Yet the hope that sometime they can work back to a freer system of general trade was expressed to me by responsible leaders in every country visited. No one has an idea as to when the way will be cleared. European economists generally, and many leading statesmen, deplore the excessive nationalism in which their countries are caught or into which they are being drawn. They approve in principle the policies which the American Government seeks to apply to international trade.

Where nations seek to control or direct trade in special bilateral channels instead of permitting it to move freely under generalized agreements, their spokesmen claim and will proceed to prove that it is because:

(1) Other nations whose trade is most important to them have adopted controls that compel them to act similarly, or

(2) Controls are necessary to build up domestic production of materials essential in case of war.

These control measures have had an important bearing on the decline in our agricultural exports to Europe. They will doubtless continue for a long time to come to affect adversely our European market. But this is not to say that the situation can not be improved, that all of our export products are equally affected by these import control measures in European countries.

The chief reason back of the import controls seems to me to be the untenable balance of payments situation. That is to say, there are certain countries which, because of their balance of payments situation, have been forced to adopt a rigid control over foreign exchange. Not to do so would have resulted in a further diminution, if not disappearance, of the already extremely small reserves of gold. While such controls may be explained and, in fact, condoned in a period of grave emergency during the world depression, there is some reason to hope that they may be gradually abandoned under conditions of improved international economic relations. I came back convinced that the United States, through an enlightened trade policy, can contribute substantially to this result.

The controls over imports that have been imposed primarily because of the desire to attain self-sufficiency in the event of war are more difficult to deal with. The problem varies with the commodities. For example, European countries can come closer to meeting their own requirements with respect to a commodity like wheat than they can with respect to a commodity like cotton. So far as the former is concerned, it appears that the wheat acreage of most of the continental European countries is now at a level which in years of average weather will yield a supply sufficient for domestic requirements. These countries can not raise cotton within their own borders. They have to rely upon substitute fibers, which can probably be produced only to a limited extent, or upon artificial fibers, which are considerably more expensive than cotton and for which they must, in any case, have a raw material source of supply.

So far as the practicability of European self-sufficiency is concerned, our other agricultural export products lie somewhere between wheat and cotton. While import restrictions based upon a desire for self-sufficiency are more difficult to deal with, the situation is not hopeless even with respect to these. A fundamental question is whether the world is to have peace or war. This will, of course, be determined, in part, by factors beyond the control and influence of the United States. But it is my opinion that the United States can, through its commercial policy, contribute definitely toward the forces making for peace.

I, therefore, returned from Europe convinced that it will be possible to increase our agricultural exports slowly from the extremely low levels that were reached during the world depression. Reciprocal trade agreements with other nations which work in the direction of increasing the total volume of our international trade—imports, as well as exports— promise a greater degree of improvement than alternatives now generally in use in Europe.

I could find no reason to conclude that general export subsidies would build up our export volume suddenly or considerably under present conditions. Export subsidies may be useful at times to meet special problems with special crops but under existing conditions dependence on that principle as a major part of our farm program can only lead to disaster. I am convinced that the joint policy of exclusion of imports and subsidized exports is utterly contradictory and unworkable. Other nations can exclude too. In fact, under systems of exchange control and specific import quotas, the exclusion is in effect before the subsidized goods leave our shore.

Unless we buy proportionately as we expand our sales, we can not "jimmy" increased exports into the European market no matter how much we subsidize, or apply other high pressure systems to induce them to take more of our goods.

The trade controls that have been established in European countries include water-tight quotas; strict government or semi-official monopolies through which all trade is routed by law; licenses for all business operations; definite allocation among private firms of business growing out of barter trades between nations; and equally definite control of the allocation of exchange be used in private firms in buying goods from abroad. In some countries no man can import or export without first securing the official permission of some government bureau or monopoly. Some countries insist on an actual balancing off of imports with exports, nation by nation.

I was particularly interested to observe how the system of selective imports and exports controlled by a government agency which conducts bilateral bargaining country by country, is working out in the several European nations that have adopted it. My interest was especially keen because this policy is precisely the opposite from the policy of generalized most-favored-nation treatment which has been followed by the United States. Observation of results in Europe convinced me that to adopt the system in the United States would be to copy extreme European nationalism at its worst.

In the first place, government barter, government selection of imports and exports, has resulted in decreased, not in increased, international trade. In the second place, the European example shows that if the United States should set up a government agency to select the exports which may be bartered from this country, and the imports which may come in, that very moment it would start down the path which, in Europe, has led step by step to the most complete governmental regimentation of business, internal as well as external, the modern world has seen.

But beyond this, it must be noted that a system of bilateral balancing with European countries would be particularly disadvantageous to American agricultural exports. The fact is that we ship a great deal more to almost every European country than we import from those countries. It is also a fact that the greater part of our exports to Europe are agricultural products. Now, the European experience has shown that bilateral balancing tends to reduce trade between two countries to the level of the smallest segment. Consequently, it seems to me that such a policy could only mean a reduction in our agricultural exports.

All developments in international trade policy in Europe must be considered in the light of the ever-present possibility of European war. Armaments, training for war, military internal improvements—in short, wholesale militarization—constitute the European public works project which dwarfs everything else going on over there. There was much talk of building up reserves of cereals and other storable farm products that would be important in case of war. This may bring on an abnormal demand for exportable crops. War itself would stimulate this demand. These developments might increase our markets for certain products temporarily but they are far from a long-time solution of our export problem.

The position with respect to the future of our agricultural exports may be summed up briefly in this way. There has been a definite curtailment in the total outlet, the extent of which varies from product to product, due to increased European production. At the same time, it is beginning to be evident that complete self-sufficiency is virtually impossible for practically every one of the European countries which has been an important market for our products. There still remains a very substantial potential outlet for most of the items of which we produce an export supply. Whether we will take advantage of these potential outlets will depend largely on the extent to which we are willing to accept more European goods and services in payment. European capital that is flowing into the United States is seeking safety and investment, and is not available for purchase of commodities as long as foreign nations can fill their needs elsewhere by trade balances. I believe it is possible to follow a policy which would result in bringing back a substantial part of our former export trade. But I do not see any possibility that this can be done to the extent that will make it unnecessary to make important production readjustments within the United States.

Because this reorganization of our domestic agriculture to meet a curtailed outlet abroad is so difficult and far reaching, it is important that in our negotiations with other countries every effort be made to see that agriculture gets as large a share as possible in the concessions we obtain. As a practical matter this means that special stress should be placed upon the negotiations with the industrialized countries of Europe.

I believe that there are sound reasons for favoring agricultural over industrial exports wherever possible. Among these reasons is the fact that the urge for self-sufficiency is much more deep-seated with respect to agricultural than with respect to industrial products. Secondly, the nations which buy our manufactured goods are for the most part industrialized only to a small extent and are quite willing to accept manufactured goods from this country in exchange for shipping to us certain raw materials which we need and do not produce. Finally, it may be observed that factory mass production enables some lines of domestic manufacturers to put better goods in the world markets at lower prices than other countries—automobiles for example. This advantage does not exist generally in the case of our agricultural exports.

These are a few reasons why, left to itself, international trade might see a continuously falling percentage of our export trade supplied from the American farms. Yet American agriculture was developed on a market in which exports played a more important part than has been the case with our manufacturing industries in general.

Even if our government in its foreign trade negotiations strives—as I am confident it will—for every practical and obtainable advantage for agricultural exports, the obligation and necessity will still rest on American agriculture, with normal yields, to make and maintain difficult and far-reaching adjustments.

Respectfully submitted,

Chester C. Davis

[OF 1-K:TS]

[1] A typed document of about 25,000 words, consisting of reports of conversations with officials and agriculture and food industry people in all the major European countries.

[2] Davis became a member of the board of governors of the Federal Reserve System on June 25, 1936.

Rudolph Forster, Executive Clerk, White House Offices, to Stephen T. Early, Assistant Secretary to the President

Washington, August 4, 1936

Memo. for STE: Acting Secretary of Commerce Draper called this morning and said that the President had sent a memorandum to Secretary Roper, asking him to issue a statement relative to the creditor-debtor position of the United States.[1]

The Department has prepared the attached statement, which Mr. Draper said had been checked over and over again very carefully, and he hoped to be able to announce it at his press conference at 11:30 Wednesday morning (5th); but before doing so, he would like to have word from the President or from you that its release at that time was in accordance with the President's wishes. He said the Department thought the sooner the statement was made the more timely it would be, but he wanted to be sure that the President agreed.

Can you have a wire flash or a telephone message sent me tomorrow morning, if possible before 11:30?[2]

R.F.

[OF 1746:T]

[1] July 10, 1936, above.
[2] Answered Aug. 5, 1936 (OF 1746). Early said that before any such statement was given out, the President wanted the approval of the Federal Reserve Board, the Secretary of the Treasury, the Secretary of State, and the Central Statistical Board. He added that there had been a crossing of wires in past instances and for that reason the President insisted on unanimous agreement on figures. The statement was issued Aug. 13, 1936; it appeared in the New York *Times* of Aug. 14, 1936 (p. 25). Francis Garvan (see Sayre to Roosevelt, July 8, 1936, above) protested the accuracy of the statement and was answered by Secretary of Commerce Roper on Oct. 8, 1936 (New York *Times,* Oct. 9, 1936, p. 19). Roosevelt's contact with Garvan came to an end over this episode.

[*Enclosure*] Statement of Ernest G. Draper, Acting Secretary of Commerce, Relative to the Creditor-Debtor Position of the United States

August 3, 1936

In view of numerous statements recently made which tend to misrepresent the creditor-debtor position of the United States, I wish to call attention to certain items in the report on *The Balance of International Payments of the United States in 1935,* which was officially released Monday by the Bureau of Foreign and Domestic Commerce.

One form of misrepresentation which has been widely disseminated is based upon the use of dissimilar methods of evaluating corresponding classes of long-term investments abroad and foreign investments in the United States. Certain estimates which have been given wide publicity include a huge unidentified and unexplained sum in the total estimate of foreign investments in the United States. In other cases the excess of foreign short-term funds in the United States over similar American funds abroad has been grossly exaggerated in spite of the fact that actual data pertaining to these items on an annual basis are available.

The Finance Division of the Bureau of Foreign and Domestic Commerce has recently completed a comprehensive study of foreign investments in the United States. The results, which include carefully checked estimates covering items for which no complete data were available, showed that total long-term investments in the United States at the end of 1935 aggregated slightly more than $5,000,000,000. Total long-term investments of Americans in foreign countries aggregate approximately $12,600,000,000. Foreign owned bank balances and other short-term funds in this country owed to foreigners as reported by American banks amounted at the end of 1935 to approximately $1,200,000,000, while corresponding short-term banking assets held abroad by American banks aggregated $850,000,000. The United States at the end of 1935 was therefore a net creditor on long-term investment account of approximately $7,600,000,000, and a net debtor on short-term account of about $350,000,000. The creditor-debtor position of the United States at the end of 1935 may be briefly summarized as follows:

Foreign dollar bonds in hands of United States
citizens..................................... $ 4,800,000,000
   Direct investments abroad.....................   7,800,000,000
   American-owned bank balances and other short-
term credits abroad reported by banks and brokers   850,000,000
     Total..................................... $13,450,000,000
   Foreign holdings of American
securities and other foreign
investments in the United States $5,000,000,000
   Foreign-owned bank-balances and
other short-term funds reported by
banks and brokers owed to
foreigners....................... 1,200,000,000
     Total.....................................   6,200,000,000
     Net Creditor Position.....................   7,250,000,000

If account be taken of the fact that at the end of 1935 outstanding credits extended by American manufacturers and exporters materially exceeded corresponding credits extended by foreign concerns to American customers, the net creditor position of the United States at the end of last year was several hundred million dollars in excess of the figure shown in the table.

In these figures all corresponding long-term assets and liabilities are computed on comparable bases. The investments of American concerns in plants and properties abroad which are directly controlled by the former, and the corresponding interests of foreign concerns in this country, are shown at book values. All bonds and preferred stocks are reported at par, while miscellaneous (non-controlling) holdings of common stocks are shown on the only basis practicable, namely, at market values.

Since American holdings of foreign bonds—of which various issues are in default—constitute a much more important factor in total United States investments abroad than do foreign holdings of American bonds in total foreign investments in this country, it has been objected that the reported figures exaggerate the net creditor position of the United States. It has also been contended that the reported value of American direct investments abroad is in fact exaggerated because of losses and "write-downs" which resulted from the world-wide depression. It is undoubtedly true that if actual liquidity were considered as a criterion, the value of American long-term assets abroad would be more seriously affected than foreign assets in the United States. Any basis of valuation is, however, open to dispute, and it is therefore appropriate that we take cognizance of a more single test of a country's creditor-debtor position, namely, the actual flow of income from the respective groups of investments.

In its annual bulletin on the balance of international payments, the Finance Division of the Bureau of Foreign and Domestic Commerce reports the following itemized summary of the interest and dividend items in the country's 1935 balances.

Receipts:

Interest on American holdings of foreign bonds	$188,000,000
Income from American-owned direct investments abroad	320,000,000
Earnings on American-owned short-term investments abroad	13,000,000
Total	$521,000,000

Payments:

Interest on foreign-held American bonds	22,000,000
Income to foreigners from direct investments in the United States	35,000,000
Dividends on foreign-held American stocks	63,000,000
Income to foreigners from other long-term investments in the United States	25,000,000
Payments to foreigners on short-term investments in the United States	1,000,000
Total	$146,000,000

It is thus apparent that the actual receipts by the United States on its private investments abroad in 1935 exceeded corresponding payments by this country to residents of foreign countries on their investments in this country by a ratio of approximately $3\frac{1}{2}$ to 1. Since the income on the short-term funds is comparatively small, this ratio remains virtually the same if the respective interest and dividend figures are confined to stocks, bonds and other long-term investments. The importance of these figures as an index of the country's long-term creditor-debtor position is emphasized by the fact that the reported interest and dividend figures are largely the result of actual computations based on the holdings of individual issues or the financial statements of individual companies. The income figures as computed are in large part independent of the data pertaining to the value of the investments and can not be viewed as subject to appreciable margins of error.

[OF 1746:T]

Roosevelt to Herbert S. Houston, New York

Hyde Park, N.Y., August 5, 1936

Personal

Dear Herbert: I do wish you could have been in Quebec with me last Friday. The whole day was an inspiration and I think has done much permanently to cement Canadian-American solidarity.

I am glad you spoke at the Institute of Public Affairs—and for what you said. For two years, however, I have been given the feeling that in conducting the Institute the Liberty League element has been given the best of the breaks and the best of the publicity. I do not know whose fault this is but it is certainly not that of the administration.[1]

As ever yours,

[PPF 2856:CT]

[1] Houston, member of the American Committee of the International Chamber of Commerce and active in organizations devoted to the bettering of international relations, wrote frequently to Roosevelt. This note is in reply to Houston's letter of July 31, 1936 (PPF 2856), in which he congratulated the President on his Quebec speech. He enclosed a copy of a speech he had made on July 10, 1936, before the Institute of Public Affairs at the University of Virginia, *Economic Justice as the Basis of World Peace* (Charlottesville, Va., 1936). The speech urged as a means of securing peace the sharing of essential raw materials among the nations of the world.

William Phillips, Under Secretary of State, to Roosevelt

Washington, August 6, 1936

Highly Confidential

My dear Mr. President: As you will recall from the Secretary's letter of August 1, 1936,[1] Ambassador Bingham was asked whether we were correct in assuming that the recent announcement of the membership and of the terms of reference of the Royal Commission of Inquiry to ascertain the underlying causes of the disturbances that have broken out in Palestine indicates that the British Government has abandoned, at least for the time being, any plan it may have had to suspend Jewish immigration into Palestine temporarily. Mr. Bingham has now replied to this query. A copy of his telegram is enclosed.

Faithfully yours,

William Phillips

[PSF:Great Britain:TS]

[1] Above.

[*Enclosure*] Robert W. Bingham, Ambassador to Great Britain, to Cordell Hull, Secretary of State

London, August 5, 1936

Personal for the Secretary

[*Telegram*] Your 293, August 1, noon. In the House of Commons on July 22nd in reply to a direct question whether the Secretary of State for the Colonies would assure the House that no change in the declared policy of the Government with respect to immigration of Jews into Palestine would take place until after the Royal Commission had reported, Mr. Ormsby-Gore[1] said inter alia:

As regards, however, the suggestion that there should be a temporary suspension of immigration while the commission is carrying out its inquiry, I am not at present in a position to make any statement as to the intentions of His Majesty's Government beyond saying that their decision will be taken in due course on the merits of the case and that there is no question of it being influenced by violence or attempts at intimidating.

On July 30th the Secretary of State for the Colonies was asked in the House of Commons whether he could give an assurance that there would be no restriction of Jewish immigration into Palestine pending the investigation and report of the Royal Commission. Mr. Ormsby-Gore in reply invited the attention of the questioner to the reply given on July 22nd and said that in that reply he had made it clear that he could not give a definite reply and that "the matter has not been and will not be decided."

Confidential. With reference to these statements in the House of Commons the matter was taken up informally this afternoon at the Foreign Office which confirmed the statement of the Colonial Secretary that no decision has been made.

Bingham

[PSF:Great Britain:M]

[1] William G. A. Ormsby-Gore, Colonial Secretary.

André Roosevelt to Roosevelt

Villa Hilda, Ambato, Ecuador, August 6th 36.

My dear Franklin: Just two months after your letter was mailed it reached me here.[1] We have been out of touch with civilization during the last six weeks, sojourning in the jungle of Santo Domingo de los Colorados where we were able to practically finish the picture, which we shall show you in the White House—of course.

On my way back to Ambato I stopped at Quito where I met Dr Alfredo E. Cuhne who is the head of the Direccion General del Servico Informativo de la Jefatura Suprema, otherwise speaking the Secret Service of Ecuador. He made an engagement with me and the following is an accurate résumé of what transpired—

We know that you are friendly towards the Ecuadorians since you have expressed yourself in public and in private to that effect; we also know that you are on friendly terms with the President of the United States; as a mutual friend would you present to the President something in the utmost confidence? I want you to understand that only two persons in this country know of the proposal that I am going to make—those two are Dr Paez, the President of Ecuador and myself. It is, moreover, at the request of Dr Paez[2] that I am taking this step.

At present there are forty thousand Japanese in Peru whose interests necessaraly ally them with that country. The Japanese have acquired extensive oil interests, oil tanks etc in Peru. This country (Ecuador) has good reasons to suppose that there exists an arrangement between Peru and Japan. In case of war between Ecuador and Peru, the latter country will receive every assistance from Japan (money, officers, ships, etc). Peru will then occupy the Islands of Galapagos, with the direct or indirect help of Japan, and later, the Islands will be transferred to Japan.

Now, let me assure you of one thing; we will never willingly allow any power to gain control over the Galapagos group but, since we are aware of the strategic value of these islands to your country which has always befriended us, we are ready to come to an understanding convenient for you and for us.

If President Roosevelt will let us know through you his views in this matter we will then be in a better position to negotiate through the regular channels. We are taking this unofficial manner of reaching the President because we are afraid of the slightest leak which would lead to very serious complications, and we feel that as far as you are concerned we can trust you implicitly.

That is the gist of what D[r] Cuhne told me, but in order to be absolutely certain that I have not misquoted him, I sent this letter to him for approval. It has been returned to me in its present form after being corrected by D[r] Paez himself.

May I add that it is my heartfelt desire that something worth while may ensue both for the United States and Ecuador as a result of this communication.

I can be reached for the next 30 days at the above address at Ambato.[3] With kindest regards and congratulations upon your brilliant renomination, I am,

Yours faithfully,

André Roosevelt

[PPF 3389:AS]

[1] May 28, 1936, in reply to André Roosevelt's letter of May 11, 1936 (PPF 3389), reporting that the expedition led by him and Cyril von Baumann to the headwaters of the Amazon in Ecuador was about to leave Quito. André was the grandson of Silas Weir Roosevelt (a brother of the senior Theodore Roosevelt) and thus a distant cousin of President Franklin D. Roosevelt. The film he made was shown at the White House on about April 22 or 23, 1937 (Kannee to Fleishman, April 26, 1937, PPF 3389).

[2] Federico Páez.

[3] See Welles to Roosevelt, Aug. 28, 1936, below.

Roosevelt to Breckinridge Long, Nantucket, Massachusetts

[Washington, August 10, 1936]

My dear Mr. Ambassador: I have recieved your resignation as American Ambassador to Rome, to take effect July 31, 1936; and, in accepting it with great reluctance, I wish to express not only my deep regret that for considerations of health you are obliged to resign, but also my most sincere appreciation of your splendid work in Rome. The distinguished and outstanding services which you have rendered as American Ambassador to Italy deserve the highest commendation of your country.

May I take this occasion to congratulate you on the work you have done and to express my sincere wishes for your speedy recovery in health.[1]

Very sincerely yours,

[OF 447:CT]

[1] Drafted in the State Department (Hull to Roosevelt, Aug. 7, 1936, OF 447).

Roosevelt to Leo S. Rowe, Director General, Pan American Union, Washington

[Washington] August 10, 1936

My dear Doctor Rowe: It is most reassuring to learn from your letter of August third that the "Good Neighbor" policy has brought about changes in the attitude of the Latin American governments and peoples towards the United States. I have read with great interest the memorandum you submitted based upon your observations during the last three years.[1] It is a great satisfaction to learn of the feeling of confidence evidenced by the people of Latin America toward the purposes and policies of this government. I am indeed grateful to you for giving me the benefit of your experienced observations.[2]

Very sincerely yours,

[OF 480:CT]

[1] Rowe enclosed with his letter a memorandum of July 31, 1936, entitled, "The Attitude of Latin American Nations toward the United States." In this he said that in the previous three years he had noticed a marked change in the attitude of Latin American governments toward the United States. "Not only has the undercurrent of distrust disappeared but there is noticeable everywhere a strong and earnest desire to enter into closer cooperative relations with the United States."

[2] Drafted by William D. Hassett.

Mary E. Woolley, President, Mount Holyoke College, to Roosevelt

South Hadley, Massachusetts, August 10, 1936

Dear Mr. President: Your suggested meeting of the Heads of the Seven Great Powers has been constantly in my mind since Saturday. Are you sure that it is too "Idealistic" to be practicable? Might not its unusual character make an appeal which a less dramatic proposition could not make? Human nature in general, as well as Mussolini and Hitler, has a weakness for the dramatic![1]

I have just signed an appeal to you to call a conference of the nations signatory to the Paris Pact. If your suggestion seems to you not feasible, is not the "next best" an attempt to bring the signatory Powers together to consider a ten years' truce, stopping increase of armaments and giving opportunity for the world to cool off? A Truce in the present state of prejudice, passion, and fear seems the only way out. I have a reputation of being a "hopeless optimist," but I must confess that the present world outlook subjects that optimism to a severe test. Surely something must be done and done quickly, if the world is to be saved from "going on the downfall."

Your wish to have me radio on the subject of the "good neighbor" policy and what the Administration is doing to further it pleases me. I infer that you will have sent to me definite information and facts on which such a talk may be based.

I greatly enjoyed my luncheon with you and Mrs. Roosevelt and appreciate your thoughtfulness in adding me to your program.[2]

With many good wishes for your trip, Very sincerely yours,

Mary E. Woolley

[PPF 537:TS]

[1] Roosevelt had presumably discussed this with Miss Woolley when they had lunch together at Hyde Park on Saturday, August 8. The appointment was confidential (it is not noted in the appointments list) and no mention of the proposal appeared in the press until the New York *Times* published a long and circumstantial account of it by Arthur Krock on Aug. 26, 1936 (p. 1). This is no doubt what the President was referring to in his letter to Dodd of Aug. 5, 1936, when he asked Dodd to try to find out Hitler's reaction to a proposal for a general limitation of armaments (*Personal Letters, 1928–1945,* I, 605–606). See Early to McIntyre, Aug. 26, 1936, below.

[2] Roosevelt sent this letter to Mary Dewson, head of the Women's Division of the Democratic National Committee, with this note: "Will you be sure to follow this up?"

(Aug. 24, 1936, PPF 537). On September 5, Miss Dewson announced that Miss Woolley was departing from her lifelong allegiance to the Republican party to support Roosevelt, largely because of his record in international relations. On Sept. 15, 1936, she joined Hull and others in speaking at a dinner of the Good Neighbor League, an organization promoting Roosevelt's reelection (New York *Times,* Sept. 16, 1936, p. 1).

Press Conference, Executive Offices of the White House, August 11, 1936, 3:50 P.M.

[*Excerpt*] Q: Mr. President, in connection with your conference yesterday with Secretary Swanson and Admiral Standley, is there anything new to be said on the re-establishment of an European Naval Squadron?[1]

The President: I will talk off the record. I can't imagine why and how any of you people get excited about that. There has never been a discussion of the establishment of an European naval squadron except in the press. The Navy Department never had any thought about it and neither did I.

Q: Secretary Hull said he was not unmindful of it.

The President: That's probably a polite way of telling the Press there is no story . . .

Q: Is the new St. Lawrence waterway treaty being drafted to meet the objections of the Canadian Government?

The President: No; nothing new on it.

Q: It was announced in Ottawa the night before last that one was now before the State Department and it was certain of passage before the next session of Congress.

The President: That's a new one . . .

Q: Was there any particular phase of foreign affairs which prompted you at this time to make a speech on foreign affairs?

The President: I think the only reason you can advance is that I haven't talked on foreign affairs since San Diego on the fourth of October, 1935. They are about due for it . . .[2]

Q: Have there been any reports at all from the French Government with reference to the possibility of our taking part in the non-intervention pact with reference to the Spanish situation?

The President: Not that I know of. I had seen everything up to last night; nothing then.

Q: There is a dispatch from Paris saying they have been keeping close touch with the Embassy here and there is a matter—

The President: I talked to Phillips last night and he didn't mention it . . .

Q: Could you outline the attitude of the United States toward this non-intervention French program and what steps are to be taken toward American neutrality?

The President: I said I haven't heard anything from the French Government. On the other thing, hasn't the State Department given out something today on the sale of airplanes?

Q: No, sir.

The President: They may have something for you . . .

Q: Mr. President, did you talk to the Governor General of Canada about coast air defenses?

The President: No. I can truthfully say, "No."

[President's Press Conferences:T]

[1] There is no information in the Roosevelt papers on what was taken up at this conference; however, the Washington correspondent of the New York *Times* (Aug. 11, 1936, p. 2) said that they had discussed "the advisability of re-establishing a European squadron in view of the struggle in Spain." On August 5 the President had directed that Coast Guard vessels in European waters (there because of the Spanish crisis) should operate as part of the Navy (Roosevelt to Morgenthau, Aug. 5, 1936; and to Swanson, same date, OF 18).

[2] See speech of Aug. 14, 1936, below.

Olive E. Clapper, Secretary, People's Mandate to Governments to End War Committee, to Roosevelt

Washington, D.C., August 11, 1936

My dear Mr. President: I am writing to ask you to receive a delegation from the People's Mandate Committee while you are at Hyde Park. The delegation will consist of members of the Mandate Committee and other distinguished women from the Eastern States.

We represent people throughout the country who believe that constructive action by our government to end war is a paramount issue in the coming national election. A delegation from the Middle Western States presented our point of view to Governor Landon in Topeka a few days ago. A similar delegation from the Eastern States will interview him at Lake Chautauqua. We are anxious to have the opportunity to put our convictions before you.

We shall greatly appreciate it if you will receive our representatives at any time that is convenient for you between August 17 to 22, inclusive, at Hyde Park, before you start on your drought control tour. We shall be grateful for an immediate reply.

Most respectfully yours,

Olive E. Clapper

[*Notation*:A:LeHand] Mac   I think I should see these people only 15 minutes & arrange it for the 24[th][1]

[OF 394:TS]

[1] The delegation, headed by its president, Mary E. Woolley, was received by the President on Sunday, August 23, after he had returned from morning church services in Hyde Park (PPF 1-0). He endorsed their objective, the securing of 50,000,000 signatures throughout the world to a petition urging all governments to reduce armaments and to renounce war (New York *Times*, Aug. 24, 1936, p. 1). His talk to the group was not taken down stenographically; the *Times* said he had told the delegates that real peace could be achieved only "as the great bulk of citizens of all countries impress their desire on their governments." The *Times* also said Roosevelt had met the group in a friendly spirit but disagreed with them in his belief that peace could be safeguarded for the nation only through maintaining a strong defense.

Senator Elmer A. Benson of Minnesota and Others to Roosevelt, Great Lakes Exposition

Washington, D.C., Aug. 14 [1936]

[*Telegram*] In view of our neutrality legislation the clear interest of Congress and the expressed will of the people of this country, we wish to go on record urging every possible effort on the part of the government to prevent shipment of war supplies to Spain. We urge that you make a statement to this effect in your Chautauqua address.

Senators Elmer A. Benson, Gerald P. Nye; Congressmen Fred Biermann, Guy Gillette, Fred Hildebrandt, Herman P. Kopplemann, Henry C. Luckey, Louis Ludlow, Byron N. Scott, and Fred Sisson.[1]

[OF 1561:T]

[1] Benson was a Farmer-Laborite, Nye a member of the progressive wing of the Republican party, and the others were Democrats. According to Ickes (*Diary*, I, 663), Nye had told Ickes that he would come out for Roosevelt after the Chautauqua speech on the basis of his peace efforts in his first Administration. Ickes was eager that Nye

would do this because he was "very influential with the peace people." On August 17 Nye telegraphed Moore (Moore Papers) that he only then had had a chance to read the speech. He thought it a "fine expression of splendid resolve" to maintain a neutrality that could be much strengthened by making the present neutrality legislation permanent and by adding a stringent cash and carry provision respecting trade with nations at war.

On the same day Ickes telephoned Nye at Yellowstone and urged him to come out for Roosevelt. Nye did not do so, however, and Ickes then arranged a meeting between Nye and Roosevelt at Hyde Park on August 21 (*Diary,* I, 663). Ickes says he talked with Roosevelt on the telephone just before the Nye appointment and told him he believed he could get Nye to make a statement for him on the basis of his Chautauqua speech (*ibid.,* p. 665). Nye, however, announced on October 1 that he would take no part in the campaign nationally (New York *Times,* Oct. 2, 1936, p. 9).

Speech by Roosevelt, Chautauqua, New York, August 14, 1936, 8 P.M.

Dr. Bestor, ladies and gentlemen: I am always appreciative of that well-remembered and splendid salute.[1] As many of you who are here tonight know, I formed the excellent habit of coming to Chautauqua more than twenty years ago. And it was after my Inauguration in 1933 that I promised Dr. Bestor that during the next four years I would come to Chautauqua again and here I am.[2]

A few days ago some of my friends of the Press asked me the subject of this talk tonight, and I replied that for two good reasons I wanted to discuss the subject of peace: First, because it is eminently appropriate in Chautauqua and, secondly, because in the hurly-burly of domestic politics it is important that our people should not overlook problems and issues which, though they lie beyond our borders, may, and probably will, have a vital influence on the United States of the future.

Many people who have visited me in Washington in the past few months may have been surprised when I have told them that personally and because of my own daily contacts with all manner of difficult problems I am more concerned and less cheerful about international world conditions than about our immediate domestic prospects.[3]

And I say this to you not as a confirmed pessimist but as one who still hopes that envy, hatred and malice among nations have reached their peak and will be succeeded by a new tide of peace and good will—I say this as one who has participated in many of the decisions of peace and war during and after the World War; as one who has traveled much, as one who has spent a goodly portion of every twenty-four hours in the study of foreign relations.

Long before I returned to Washington as President of the United States, I had made up my mind that pending what might be called a more opportune time on other continents, the United States could best serve the cause of a peaceful humanity by setting an example. And that is why on the 4th of March, 1933, I made the following declaration:

In the field of world policy I would dedicate this Nation to the policy of the good neighbor—the neighbor who resolutely respects himself and because he does so, respects the rights of others—the neighbor who respects his obligations and respects the sanctity of agreements in and with a world of neighbors.[4]

That declaration represented my purpose then, it represents my purpose now, but it represents more than a purpose now, for it stands for a practice. To a measurable degree the practice has succeeded; and the whole world now knows that the United States cherishes no predatory ambitions. We are strong: but less powerful nations know that they need not fear our strength. We seek no conquest: we stand for peace.

In the whole world of the western hemisphere our good neighbor policy has produced results that are especially heartening.

The noblest monument to peace, the noblest monument to economic and social friendship in all the world is not a monument in bronze or stone, it is the boundary that unites the United States and Canada— 3000 miles of friendship with no barbed wire, no gun, no soldiers, and no passports on the whole frontier.

What made it?[5]

Mutual trust—and to extend the same sort of mutual trust throughout the Americas was our aim.

The American Republics to the south of us have been ready always to cooperate with the United States on a basis of equality and mutual respect, but before we inaugurated the good neighbor policy there was among them resentment and fear, because certain administrations in Washington had slighted their national pride and their sovereign rights.

In pursuance of the good neighbor policy, and because in my younger days I had learned many lessons in the hard school of experience, I stated that the United States was opposed definitely to armed intervention.

And so, in these four years, we have negotiated a Pan-American Convention embodying the principle of non-intervention.[6] We have abandoned the Platt Amendment that gave us the right to intervene in the internal affairs of the Republic of Cuba.[7] We have withdrawn

American Marines from Haiti.[8] We have signed a new Treaty which places our relations with Panama on a mutually satisfactory basis.[9] We have undertaken a series of trade agreements with other American countries to our mutual commercial profit. And finally, at the request of two neighboring Republics, I hope to give assistance in the final settlement of the last serious boundary dispute between any of the American nations.[10]

Yes, throughout the Americas the spirit of the good neighbor is a practical and living fact. The twenty-one American Republics are not only living together in friendship and in peace; they are united in the determination so to remain.

And to give substance to this determination a conference will meet on December 31st—December 1st—of this year at the Capital of our great southern neighbor, Argentina, and it is, I know, the hope of all Chiefs of State of the Americas that this will result in measures which will banish wars forever from this vast portion of the earth.

I have always thought that peace, like charity, begins at home; and that's why we have begun at home, here in North and South and Central America. But peace in the western world is not all we seek.[11]

It is our hope that knowledge of the practical application of the good neighbor policy in this hemisphere will be borne home to our neighbors across the seas.[12]

For ourselves we are on good terms with them—terms in most cases of straightforward friendship, and peaceful understanding.

But, of necessity, we are deeply concerned about tendencies of recent years among many of the nations of other continents. It is a bitter experience—a bitter experience to us—when the spirit of agreements to which we are a party is not lived up to. It is an even more bitter experience for the whole company of nations to witness not only the spirit but the letter of international agreements violated with impunity and without regard to the simple principles of honor. Permanent friendships among nations as between men can be sustained only by scrupulous respect for the pledged word.

And in spite of all this we have sought steadfastly to assist international movements to prevent war. We cooperated to the bitter end—and it was a bitter end—in the work of the General Disarmament Conference. When it failed we sought a separate treaty to deal with the manufacture of arms and the international traffic in arms. That proposal also came to nought. We participated—again to the bitter end—in a conference to continue Naval limitations, and when it became evident that no general treaty could be signed because of the objections of certain other nations, we concluded with Great Britain and France a conditional treaty of qualitative limitation which, much to my regret, already shows signs of ineffectiveness.

We shun political commitments which might entangle us in foreign wars; we avoid connection with the political activities of the League of Nations; but I am glad to say that we have cooperated whole-heartedly in the social and humanitarian work at Geneva. Thus we are a part of the world effort to control traffic in narcotics, to improve international health, to help child welfare, to eliminate double taxation and to better working conditions and laboring hours throughout the world.

No, we are not isolationists except insofar as we seek to isolate ourselves from war. Yet we must remember that so long as war exists on earth there will be some danger even to the nation that most ardently desires peace, danger that it also may be drawn into war.

I have seen war. I have seen war on land and sea. I have seen blood running from the wounded. I have seen men coughing out their gassed lungs. I have seen the dead in the mud. I have seen cities destroyed. I have seen two hundred limping, exhausted men come out of line—the survivors of a regiment of one thousand that went forward forty-eight hours before. I have seen children starving. I have seen the agony of mothers and wives. I hate war.[13]

Yes, I have passed unnumbered hours and I shall pass unnumbered hours thinking and planning how war may be kept from the United States of America.

I wish I could keep war from all nations; but that is beyond my power. I can at least make certain that no act of the United States helps to produce or to promote war. I can at least make clear that the conscience of America revolts against war and that any nation that provokes war forfeits the sympathy of the people of the United States.

There are many causes that produce war. There are ancient hatreds, turbulent frontiers, the "legacy of old forgotten, far off things, and battles long ago." There are new-born fanaticisms, convictions on the part of certain peoples that they have become the unique depositories of ultimate truth and right.

A dark old world was devastated by wars between conflicting religions. A dark modern world faces wars between conflicting economic and political fanaticisms in which are intertwined race hatreds. To bring it home to us, it is as if within the territorial limits of the United States, forty-eight nations, forty-eight forms of government, forty-eight customs barriers, forty-eight languages, forty-eight eternal and different verities, were spending their time and their substance in a frenzy of effort to make themselves strong enough to conquer their neighbors or strong enough to defend themselves against their neighbors.

In one field, that of economic barriers, the American policy may be, I hope, of some assistance in discouraging the economic source of war and therefore a contribution towards the peace of the world. The trade agreements which we are making are not only finding outlets for the products of American fields and American factories but they are also pointing the way to the elimination of embargoes, quotas and other devices that place such pressure on nations not possessing great natural resources that to those nations the price of peace sometimes seems less terrible than the price of war.

We do not maintain that a more liberal international trade will stop war but we do fear that without a more liberal international trade, war is a natural sequence.

The Congress of the United States, as you know, has given me certain authority to provide safe-guards of American neutrality in case of war.

The President of the United States, who, under our Constitution, is vested with primary authority to conduct our international relations, thus has been given new weapons with which to maintain American neutrality.

Nevertheless—and I speak from long experience—the effective maintenance of American neutrality depends today, as in the past, on the wisdom and the determination of whoever at the moment occupy the offices of President and Secretary of State.

It is clear that our present policy and the measures passed by the Congress would in the event of a war on some other continent reduce war profits which would otherwise accrue to American citizens. Industrial and agricultural production for a war market may give immense fortunes to a few; but for the nation as a whole we know that it produces disaster. It was the prospect of war profits that made our farmers in the west plow up prairie land that ought never to have been plowed, but should have been left for grazing cattle. And today we are reaping the harvest of those war profits in the dust storms that have devastated those war plowed fields.

It was the prospect of war profits that caused the extension of monopoly and unjustified expansion of industry and a price level so high that the normal relationships between debtor and creditor were destroyed.

Nevertheless, if war should break out again in another continent, let us not blink the fact that we would find in this country thousands of Americans[14] who, seeking immediate riches—fool's gold—would attempt to break down or evade our neutrality.

They would tell you—and, unfortunately, their views would get wide publicity, by methods that you can understand as readily as I do—that if they could produce and ship this and that and the other article to belligerent nations, the unemployed of America would all find work. They would tell you that if they could extend credit to warring nations that credit would be used in the United States to build homes and factories and pay our debts. They would tell you that America once more would capture the trade of the world.

My friends, it would be hard to resist that clamor; it would be hard for many Americans, I fear, to look beyond—to realize the inevitable penalties, the inevitable day of reckoning that comes from a false prosperity. To resist the clamor of that greed, if war should come, would require the unswerving support of all Americans who love peace.

And so if we face the choice of profits or peace, this Nation will answer—this Nation must answer—"we choose peace." And it is the duty of all of us, each and every one of us, men, women and children, to encourage such a body of public opinion throughout this Nation that the answer will be clear and for all practical purposes unanimous.

With that wise and experienced man who is our Secretary of State, whose statesmanship has met with such wide approval, I have thought and worked long and hard on the problem of keeping the United States at peace. But all the wisdom of America is not to be found in the White House or the Department of State; we need the meditation, we need the prayer, and we need the positive support of the people of America who go along with us in seeking peace.

No matter how well we are supported by neutrality laws, we must remember that no laws can be provided to cover every contingency, for it is impossible to imagine how every future event may shape itself. In spite of every possible forethought, international relations involve of necessity a vast uncharted area. In that area safe sailing will depend on the knowledge and the experience and the wisdom of those who direct our foreign policy. Peace will depend on their day to day decisions.

And at this late date, many years after, with the wisdom which is so easy after the event and so difficult before the event, we find it possible to trace the tragic series of small decisions that led Europe into the great war in 1914 and eventually engulfed us and many other nations.

We can keep out of war if those who watch and decide have a sufficiently detailed understanding of international affairs to make certain that the small decisions of each day do not lead toward war and if, at the same time, they possess the courage to say "no" to those who selfishly or unwisely would get us into war.

Of all the nations in the world today we are in many ways most singularly blessed. Our closest neighbors are good neighbors. And if there are remoter nations that wish us not good but ill, they know that we are strong; they know that we can and will defend ourselves and defend our neighborhood.[15]

They know we seek to dominate no other nation, that we ask no territorial expansion, that we oppose imperialism, and that we desire reduction in world armaments.

We believe in democracy; we believe in freedom; and we believe in peace. And so we offer to every nation of the world the handclasp of the good neighbor. Let those who wish our friendship look us in the eye and take our hand.[16]

[RL Recordings]

[1] The waving of handkerchiefs, traditional at Chautauqua. This sentence was added by Roosevelt in reading the speech.

[2] Arthur E. Bestor, Sr., president of Chautauqua Institution since 1915, had invited Roosevelt to speak to a Chautauqua assembly in 1934 and 1935 and he had promised to do so sometime during his Administration (Bestor to Roosevelt, July 3, 1936, PPF 1687). Earlier appearances of Roosevelt before Chautauqua audiences had been in 1917, 1919, and 1929.

[3] These first three paragraphs were added by Roosevelt to his revision of the original draft (Speech File) that William C. Bullitt had prepared (Rosenman, *Working with Roosevelt*, p. 108). An abbreviated and much revised version of the 15-page Bullitt draft is present (Speech File); this version appears to have been very hastily typed in the White House but certainly not by one of the White House typists. Possibly Bullitt was given the task of "boiling down" his own first draft; however, see Rosenman, *ibid.* Of the forty-one paragraphs of the first draft, nineteen, much revised and condensed, appear in the second. This second draft, with numerous revisions in Roosevelt's hand, was sent to William Phillips. Phillips returned it with a note saying that he had taken the liberty of making a few penciled suggestions, and that the speech seemed to fit the needs of the audience (Phillips to Roosevelt, Aug. 13, 1936, Speech File).

Some of these suggestions were adopted and are noted below. The reading copy was typed directly from this much marked-up draft. (The State Department had supplied material on the Spanish revolution as it affected American neutrality, and the Commerce Department had sent a memorandum on foreign trade but none of this material was used.) Other texts in the Roosevelt papers are the mimeographed press release of the reading copy, with the stenographer's notes of changes made by Roosevelt when he read the speech; the typescript showing these changes; and the recording of the broadcast. The text here printed is that of the recording and thus varies in a number of places from the press release of the reading copy; cf. New York *Times,* Aug. 15, 1936, p. 4 (Rosenman in his *Public Papers,* V, 285–292, follows the press release.)

[4] The inaugural speech, printed *ibid.,* II, 11–16.

[5] This sentence was added when the speech was read.

[6] The Convention on Rights and Duties of States, adopted at the Montevideo Conference in December 1933.

[7] By treaty with Cuba signed June 9, 1934.

[8] In August 1934.

[9] Signed March 2, 1936; ratified July 25, 1939.

[10] The Chaco War between Bolivia and Paraguay was ended by a truce signed June 12, 1935, but the peace conference dragged on until 1939.

[11] In the first draft this sentence read: "But peace in the western world is far better than no peace." In the second draft this read: "But peace in the western world is not all that we seek, even though peace in the western world be far better than no peace at all." Phillips questioned this and Roosevelt changed it to the form here printed.

[12] In the second draft this sentence was followed by a paragraph pointing to American policy in the Philippines as evidence of national good will; this was an adaptation of a longer paragraph in the first draft. Phillips questioned this paragraph also and Roosevelt crossed it out.

[13] "I hate war" was Bullitt's phrase; see Rosenman, *Working with Roosevelt,* p. 108.

[14] Originally "millions of Americans" but Phillips questioned it and Roosevelt changed it.

[15] On the margin Phillips wrote: "There is something threatening about this. Coming at the end it seems to change the tone of the speech." Roosevelt crossed out Phillips' comment.

[16] Originally, "Our friendship is not without value," was the concluding sentence. This was crossed out by Roosevelt.

Emil Ludwig to Roosevelt

Paris 15.8.36

Mr. President: in December last year you kindly invited me to write you occasionally my impressions on Europe.[1] I have not as yet done this. To-day, allow me to do this in sending you the enclosed paper.

Yours very sincerely

Emil Ludwig

(Ascona. Locarno. Switzerland)

[*Notation:*A] Judge Moore   Will you Prep. reply to this? P.[2]
[PPF 3884:AS]

[1] Ludwig, in the United States on a lecture tour in the fall of 1935, was at the White House on Dec. 6, 1935 (White House Social Appointments). Henry Goddard Leach,

editor of the *Forum*, had previously suggested that Roosevelt allow Ludwig to write a biographical article about him to be published in the *Forum* (Leach to Roosevelt, Dec. 12, 1935, PPF 324). Apparently permission was not given for Leach's letter was not answered.

[2] Sept. 17, 1936, below.

[*Enclosure*] Europe, August 1936

Looking at Europe coldly and logically we see war approaching in the course of a year; but as things do not always work logically, it might tarry two years. Up to that date the general deceit of governements[1] tries to conceal their true intentions: Italy is deceiving France in avowing her friendship in order to have a freer hand in the Mediteranean, and at the same time she tries to scare France by sending help to Spain.

France is deceiving Checo-Slowackia with assurances of assistance, which are repelled by the half of her citizens. England is deceiving Germany with her readiness for treaties. Russia is not working against an individual opponent, but she hopes that her system will be victorious everywhere, after the war. Germany deceives all round, in daring to stammer peace declarations, while she is fanatically preparing war.

Germany alone, among all Great Powers, has aggressive ends; this corresponds to her militant character, her longing for revenge her inferiority-complex, and her ad hoc race theory, as she cannot invade her two half French speaking neighbours Belgium and Switzerland without having a French war declaration she must first break out towards the East. Here she might come to an under standing at the cost of the Baltic Stater, which powerless and mistable Poland that at the moment has no real leader, but it cannot compromise with Checo-Slowackia this country is, therefore in the focus of danger.

The Little Entente is based to-day on the two men Benesch and Titulescu, two of the cleverst Europeans.[2] Benesch has no strong cooperators behind him, but a number of opposing parties, and in Roumania the weak and reactionary king is only forced by the European prestige of his minister to hold him. Should he fall—as it almost happened in July—then Roumania might join the German bloc. This would be probable as also the Jugoslavs have great sympathies to join. An attentate on Titulescu's life might dissolve the whole Little Entente.

This is complicated by the lack of clearness in the treaties. The members of the Little Entente are not clearly forced to help one another if France does not march; Roumania and Jugo-Slavia need only help the Checs if Hungary marches, and the Russian help is quite uncertain. But France will perhaps not march at all as long as it is not attacked. This is the popular opinion, although M. Delbos yesterday assured me the contrary.[3] In 1934, Marshal Pétain said to me "Il n'y à pas de Président de Conseil à Paris qui pourrait mobiliser sans que la France soit attaquée." When now asking Léon Blum if this was the voice of France I was given the answer: "I think it is no more."

Italy, wholly unmilitant by nature, is morally satisfied by the easy victory over the blacks, it might therefore be one of this war's greatest consequences that it leads Italy to remain neutral at least in the beginning of the World war. As fascist pretentions have asserted themselves. After the two "victories" 1918 and 36 Mussolini has no need to prove to his people that they are a nation of heros. Who knows how clear and sceptical his opinion of his fellow-countrymen is, cannot assume that he will try a knock-out game with England in the Mediteranean. His help to the Spanish rebels can only be intended to weaken France, not aggrevate England. But his slyness does not permit any conclusion as to which side he will take. Culture and education invariably lead him to the Latin side. His position seems firm for a long time coming, attentates against his life improbable as long as he is not involved in a European war. In Rome the experience will soon be made that for the next ten years, Abessinia will cost Italy a lot and bring her nothing.

In England the want of armaments and allies and also of Psychology in treating Mussolini and the German character has brought about two most desastrous political mistake. Mussolini standing before a map of Europe, once drastically demonstrated to me his coasts and his dependence on English politics. By an iron ultimatin of England in September 35 he might have been called to order, as Hitler might have in 36. The English are wrong in supposing their own familiar democratic reactions in the hearts and brains of adventurers who like somnambules will risk anything up to the moment they are shouted at; then they awake and bend to force. Not to save Abessinia, whose sovereign governed badly, was a slave-holder and a cad like William II, but to protect the power of the League, not to save the Rhineland from being fortified, but to break Hitler's dangerous self-adoration. Europe under England's lead should have stood up against Italy and Germany.

To-day, anti-German feeling prevales among English Government men, but none have the courage to avow this. Churchill and Chamberlain sometimes do so in Parliament, but they do not seem probable Government candidates. Perhaps, however, England is trying to deceive

Germany with its amical inclination, in order to gain two years time for arming. The great German hope, when war breaks out to have England, if not on their side, at least not against them, will surely not be fulfilled. England will not come to a binding alliance with France in peace-time, but she will never forsake France in a coming German-French war, because her own position is lost if she does. Through continual flirting and spying between London and Paris, great political moments like that of the occupation of the Rhineland have been lost to Europe and to Peace.

In Germany Hitler's power is stabilised and the growing discontent of a great part of the people is a silent undercurrent, not organised, and not yet self concious. A change can only come through Hitler's death. Attentates from Nazi ranks, are more probable here than in Italy.

A blow of the Reichswehr which a year ago seemed possible, is now quite improbable. Like all vainglorious demagogues who talk war, Hitler is driven into it like William II., although he would like to avoid it. One week after the Rhineland occupation Hitler said to the widow of his friend the architect Trost in Muenchen: "Ich hab' mächtig Blut geschwitzt (my heart was in my trousers). But now they will only talk it to pieces."

No need to talk about the "war-camp" Germany only a hint that the most obedient people of the world is at the same time the best organised, and for both reasons absolutely sure of victory. Schools and universities have done more in this direction than gun factories. The consciousness of an elect race, the will to sacrifice, the courage to die have been grafted on to the tree that Bismarck planted to the war machine of 1914 is now added the impulse of revenge, only directed westwards. It is a mistake to believe that the Germans will be satisfied by political success, (colonies) without having a war. They don't want land, but the satisfaction of being victorious over France. Not only the enthusiastic Nazis, the workmen too, will willingly return to war, the Radio is preparing them daily. They will however be the first to frater-nise, in the course of a war with their French and Russian enemies, and so carry mutiny into the German front! In this way, the coming war will dissolve into a civil war in which the classes will club together across national frontiers. But this can only develop during the war. As in Europe no country—except the small ones of Austria and Hungary—want expansion but as all want to defend their actual possessions the brillantly organized military power in the centre has natural advantage over all its smaler neighbours, who will give in to anything—even the breach of traties—as long as their own territories are not broken in to. That war should come about through dangerous conflicts in the inner politic of a nation, like in Austria 1914, is not probable, even not in France, shaken as it is by inner troubles, because pacifism seems to have become the state-religion of the French. Blum, much to honest a man to be able to hold himself in the political atmosphere of to-day told me on August 12 that he would hold the Conference of Five, but would conclude no treaties without Russia and the Little Entente. But he also emphatically said that he abhorred Mussolini more than Hitler. The party-man seems stronger in this word than the states-man, because there is no danger for France from Italy, but all her danger lies in Germany.

All eyes are turned to America. Clever heads unite in the idea that America cannot remain neutral in the coming war, which would mean a victory of the German-Japanese alliance. This should be prevented by America. If the Americans see the danger, they should continue ever and again to repeat their resolve to defend democracy as the President did on this splendid document at New Year. If however, America continues to declare that she will keep aloof from Europe, war will break out all the sooner. For as America is the only country the Germans are afraid of, since her almost legendary appearance on the battlefields of 1918, this turning away is the very thing the Germans (and Japanese) are praying for. In the moment, America should try to prevent treaties signed in a conference of the 5 Powers without cooperation of Russia and the Little Entente. At the conference of the Locarno powers Germany will promise everything and might attain Air and other treaties to back her position when she begins her attack to the East.

A new possibility for American influence appears: Herriot who spoke about you, Mr. President, with the greatest respect, as also Titulescu, sees the only way to save France and Europe in the cooperation with the United States. He believes the paying of a part of the French debt to be possible, unter the actual reign of the Front Populaire, but he is not sure of Blum's readiness. Delbos told me, he voted in December 1932 for the payment of the debts, but he now hides himself behind the minister of Finance, when I asked him to repeat this now. Herriot, however, said: "Si on m'envoyait à Washington, j'arrangerais les dettes encore aujourd'hui."

Emil Ludwig

[PPF 3884:T]

[1] Spelling, here and below, as in the original.
[2] Eduard Beneš, president of Czechoslovakia, and Nicolae Titulescu, Rumanian Foreign Minister.
[3] Yvon Delbos, French Foreign Minister.

Jesse Isador Straus, Ambassador to France, to Roosevelt

Mt. Kisco, New York, August 18, 1936

My dear Mr. President: When I left Paris at the beginning of the month, I had hoped to return about the first of October. Upon arriving at home, however, my physicians informed me that I was in a very run-down condition and that I must have a complete rest for six months.[1] In view of the fact that there is much work to be done in Paris at the moment, I feel that it is imperative to keep the Embassy staff at its full complement. I, therefore, tender my resignation, to be accepted immediately or at your pleasure.

Needless to say, I give up my post with regret. The three and a half years that I have held it have been filled with enjoyable, interesting, and instructive experiences. The career foreign service officers who were associated with me have won my gratitude and affection. They gave me the most able and intelligent assistance that I could have desired, and I wish particularly to commend them to you, as I relinquish my responsibility.

Though my official association with your administration is, I fear, thus ended, my interest in the campaign will continue unabated, and I only wish I were well enough to take an active part, as I did in 1932. However, all the indications are favorable and the country will give its appreciation of your courage, initiative, and foresight.[2]

Very sincerely yours,

Jesse Isador Straus

[PSF:France:TS]

[1] Straus died of cancer on Oct. 4, 1936.
[2] Answered Aug. 25, 1936 (*Personal Letters, 1928–1945*, I, 609–610).

Oswald Garrison Villard to Roosevelt

Thomaston, Conn., August 18, 1936

Dear Mr. President: Thank you from the bottom of my heart for your noble utterance at Chautauqua, quite the finest peace speech that has been voiced by any man in high position. It will do an enormous amount of good, and I am particularly grateful to you for the slap at Hitler and Mussolini. Also for what you say as to neutrality and the fact that it ultimately comes down to the question whether the President and the Secretary of State want to preserve neutrality and keep us out of war, or not. When you say that "we can keep out of war if they (our officials) possess the courage to say 'no' to those who would selfishly or unwisely let us go to war" I think you prove my contention that Woodrow Wilson could have kept us out of the war in 1917 had he had the backbone, the courage and the desire. But I do not want to stir up sleeping dogs, merely to add this word of gratitude to the multitudes you must have received.

I took the liberty of sending to Secretary Hull the other day some recommendations for statements to be made by you during this campaign. You have covered several of them in this one speech, including the fixing of the date of the Pan-American Peace Conference. But there are one or two others about which I should very much like to talk to you if you can sandwich me in the next time you are at Hyde Park.[1]

Most sincerely yours,

Oswald Garrison Villard

[PPF 2178:TS]

[1] Villard had known Roosevelt since 1913, and as editor of *The Nation* had been highly critical of his foreign policy. Assistant Secretary of State Moore wrote to Bullitt on Aug. 18, 1936 (Moore Papers), that all the comments on the speech he had seen and heard continued to be highly favorable. Among others who congratulated the President on the speech were Nicholas Murray Butler and Edward M. House, in letters both dated Aug. 15, 1936 (PPF 445; PPF 222).

William E. Dodd, Ambassador to Germany, to Roosevelt

Berlin, August 19th, 1936

Dear Mr. President: Your re-election on a safe margin is about the most important thing in the world and this is recognized here. Democracy everywhere may fail if it fails with us. So you must know how much concerned I am. Today the Minister of the Netherlands revealed to me the great interest of his people in your continued success. He said that information had come to him the last few days that the German

Party leaders had captivated our former Ambassador Schurman,[1] who has been in Berlin nearly a month; and he added: Schurman is being used to stimulate Republican opposition among Germans in America with the expectation of his being returned here as Ambassador. Judge Moore can give you the details in case it is worth while.[2]

My hope is that your second term may enable you to solve the unemployment problem perhaps by leaving it to states, cities and counties, the Federal Government supervising and granting a certain proportion of needed money. The greatest problem is to save our country from erosion, dust storms and floods. This can be done but it will require a real free press which will give our people information as to blunders of the past and the necessity of scientific management. If these things are not done the next generation is apt to have one third of the country a desert. You have certainly awakened people to the cause of troubles.

But a free press and genuine education are necessary. I think your re-election on a large margin might enable you to start press reform, perhaps enable you to help start real newspapers at strategic points. Many able young journalists are ready to set up papers of their own if they could have a fair chance. With this I think we ought to have a Department of Education in Washington whose chief would reform gradually state institutions, and see to it that real teachers of the truth about our past be employed in high schools and feel themselves actually free. You know how many states, even the District of Columbia, have been trying to deny freedom to teachers. It would be a difficult thing, but a genuine national leadership in this realm and direction would have constructive and conspicuous influence in a decade.

As to the second paragraph of your letter[3] I may say that animosity here is such that one may not easily get a quiet answer to such an inquiry as you suggest. I had a talk with Dr. Schacht on the 18th. A hint of the subject mentioned brought a repetition of the present German demand for expansion and colonies. The telegram which I sent on that day was probably handed to you.[4] There is a chance of such a ten year pact in the case of French and British ability to prevent Spain from becoming a dependency of Italy. Schacht did suggest that you call a world conference next winter (I never intimated of course your inquiry). His idea was, however, not so much for peace as to enable him to save Germany from economic disaster. He insisted, though, on your demanding return of German colonies. When I said that was England's business, he said: "Oh, England is losing her position and power every day."

During the next few weeks I shall watch every opportunity to make an opening in the direction you mention.[5]

With best wishes, sincerely yours,

William E. Dodd

[*Notation*:A] Typed by my daughter—strictly confidential
[PSF:Germany:TS]

[1] Jacob Gould Schurman, ambassador to Germany from 1925 to 1930.

[2] See immediately below.

[3] This is in reply to Roosevelt's letter of Aug. 5, 1936 (*Personal Letters, 1928–1945,* I, 605–606), asking Dodd what would happen if Hitler were secretly asked (by Roosevelt) "to outline the limit of German foreign objectives" during a ten-year period, and to say whether or not he would be in sympathy with a general armaments limitation proposal.

[4] To Hull, printed in *Foreign Relations, 1936,* I, 335.

[5] Roosevelt did not reply to this nor to Dodd's next few letters in which he recurred to the subject of Roosevelt's August 5 letter.

R. Walton Moore, Assistant Secretary of State, to Roosevelt

Washington, August 21, 1936

Dear Mr. President: I would not send you the enclosures except for Dr. Dodd's evident desire to have you know about his predecessor's performance in Germany.

The Department hears only praise of the work done by our officials in Spain in taking care of American citizens and property, and I do not believe there will be any dispraise of the note to the Minister of Uruguay, which was the result of a great deal of careful consideration.[1]

I hope you are enjoying more comfortable weather at Hyde Park than now prevails in Washington, where it is wretchedly hot.

Yours very sincerely,

R. Walton Moore

[PSF:Germany:TS]

[1] Not present.

[*Enclosure*] William E. Dodd, Ambassador to Germany, to R. Walton Moore

[Berlin] Aug. 13, 1936

Dear Judge: I enclose copy of our daily Press summary marking one item which might interest Secretary Hull, even the President.[1] The former Ambassador was here a month last autumn. We showed him every courtesy as we have done this time.

But he was too free last fall in trying to "get in with" high party officials and propagandists, i.e. for a former Ambassador. This time he is here as a guest of the Partei-Government, has a house, a huge car and a chauffeur at public expense. He is cultivated by Hitler and other members of the triumvirate every day and he makes speeches which seem to "correct" careful and non-partisan attitudes of our Embassy and Consulate. And last night he was a guest of Hitler at a dinner (Hitler has never given such a dinner before) to which English, Italian and Balkan State diplomats were invited. French and other ambassadors not invited. The French Ambassador told me yesterday. We were not, though we were known to be entertaining other people (Germans & Americans). It is considered as a scheme to unite Germany, Italy and certain Balkan states. Why should our Ambassador here, 1924–30, be making speeches and playing such a rôle? I refer to Schurmann. It may lead to embarrassments.

Yours sincerely,

William E. Dodd

[PSF:Germany:AS]

---

[1] This item reads: "Schurman—according to *Press-Bericht,* our former Ambassador, in an interview with *N.S. Korrespondenz,* said 'Only a Germany with equal rights, and sovereign, can arrive at agreement with the two great European states which fought and struggled in particularly close union against the Reich.'"

Press Conference, Hyde Park, August 21, 1936, 4:30 P.M.

[*Excerpt*] Q: Mr. President, this foreign situation looks rather alarming. Have you any reports on that?

The President: Nothing, except what I read in the morning paper.

Q: Any move on the part of this country in following Great Britain in placing an embargo?

The President: I will have to talk about it off the record.

Q: Can we use it for background?

The President: No, you can't. That's the problem and I don't know what to do about it. Frankly, I don't know why the State Department shouldn't tell you a little more about that thing they discussed with you two weeks ago.[1] You will remember that I spilled the beans on them at that time and they gave you a story. That story was true as far as it went but they didn't tell you the exact language that was used. They didn't do it because they didn't want to give the name of the company. I don't know of any reason why they shouldn't give it to you now, so I am suggesting that you shoot through a query to Washington. I think that is the most practical way of handling it. "Can't the State Department be a little more specific in regard to the letter that was sent to an American manufacturing firm or firms?" They don't have to give up the name of the company but it is about the American shipment of munitions to Spain.[2]

Mr. McIntyre: Do you suggest they use this?

The President: I suggest they query the State Department in Washington; I haven't got a copy of it here.

Mr. McIntyre: Couldn't I get hold of Bill Phillips or somebody and ask him if they can't give it to us?

Q: I would like to break it out of here.

Mr. McIntyre: I frankly think it ought to come from the State Department.

The President: You can't break it out from here because, not having a copy of it I can't tell you the language and it is one of those things where you have to follow the language, word for word. But it is damn good and it went out two weeks ago.

[President's Press Conferences:T]

[1] See press conference of Aug. 11, 1936, above.

[2] The Glenn L. Martin Company of Baltimore had inquired about United States policy on the sale of airplanes to the Spanish government. In a letter to the Martin Company of Aug. 10, 1936, Under Secretary of State Phillips called attention to the American policy of nonintervention that had been emphasized by the Montevideo Treaty of 1933 and had been incorporated in the neutrality acts. He said the proposed sale would not be in accordance with this policy. The letter was made public by the State Department on Aug. 22, 1936 (probably in consequence of this press conference), and was published by the New York *Times* in its issue of Aug. 23, 1936, p. 3. It is also printed in *Foreign Relations, 1936,* II, 475–476.

Roosevelt to Oswald Garrison Villard, Thomaston, Connecticut

[Washington] August 24, 1936

Dear Oswald: Thank you for that nice note of yours.[1] You are right in part about President Wilson. The difficulty is that in those days most people were thinking in terms of the old international law which is now completely disappeared. From the point of view of hindsight, we might have kept out, but at the time we were following the precedents of several centuries.

I do hope to see you at Hyde Park after I get back from these next two trips. Will you give Mr. McIntyre a ring at Poughkeepsie about September nineteenth?[2]

As ever yours,

[PPF 2178:CT]

[1] Aug. 18, 1936, above.

[2] Villard saw Roosevelt at Hyde Park on September 23. From August 25 to September 5 Roosevelt was in the western drought area, conferring with state and federal officials on emergency and remedial measures. From September 8 to 11 he was on a trip to North Carolina; on September 10 he addressed the Green Pastures Rally at Charlotte, N.C.

Claude G. Bowers, Ambassador to Spain, to Roosevelt

Hendeye,[1] August 26, 1936

Dear Mr. President: Probably you have seen the telegrams I have sent the Department regularly,[2] but you may be interested in something on the background and real significance of the struggle in progress here. Nine tenths of the press reports are false. I have never seen, not even during the World War such persistent and outrageous propoganda.

There is no possible justification for the rebellion in anything done by the legal, legitimate Government, voted in overwhelmingly a few months ago. Azana is probably the only great statesman in Spain. He is a republican, and a democrat, with no sympathy with doctrines we call "subversive." He is a real patriot and his purpose has been to change Spain from a 16th Century state into a modern European State and to end feudalism which has persisted here. Knowing that without drastic reforms as to labor and the peasants communism or worse would ultimately come, he has sponsored plans for placing peasants on the lands on small farms, and for giving labor a living wage and civilized conditions under which to work. He has no desire to interfere with the Catholic religion as a religion, and church services have never been interfered with, but he stands for a seperation of the church and state and the creation of a public school system. In mentality, in genius, I think him one of the outstanding statesmen of Europe and certainly he is the most enlightened and constructive statesman Spain has produced in fifty years. But he has been hated with fierce hate by the Church because of his public school policy, his expulsion of the Jesuits. And hated by the aristocracy because he proposes to make the huge absentee landlords part with a portion of their lands to create a small farm system. And hated by the nobility because he is recognized as the sustaining pillar of the republic.

He lead the liberal forces in the late elections and won.[3] He served for a time as Prime Minister and then went to the Presidency to the applause of both Rights and Lefts. He was the one man all the Lefts could accept, and the more intelligent of the Rights thought him a barricade against extremes. All he has done since returning to power is this: He has put about 70,000 peasant families on the land, has returned to the enforcement of the church laws laid down in the Constitution, and has started the construction of 7,000 school buildings. That is all he has done.

In his Government there is not even a sociolist. All Ministers are stout Republicans of his party and that of Barrio.[4]

So there is no provocation for the rebellion. Count Romanones,[5] with whom you may be acquainted, seven times Prime Minister of the King, and nine times Minister of State, had an estate next to the place I had in Feunterrebia and I saw him daily in the first days of the Rebellion. On the second day he told me that the organizing for the rebellion began the day after the election when it became clear that the people are against reaction. There is no doubt of that. On that day he told me the organization was so perfect the fight would "speedily be ended." I asked him how long. He replied "in four days or five days at the utmost." Ten days later I reminded him of what he had said and he made this very significant reply: "We counted on the Navy and were disappointed. We thought the Basques would be with us and they are against us. But the most serious thing of all is we did not count on the general rising of the people."

The fact is the people of all classes, under the nobility and moneyed aristocracy are fighting with a superhuman courage and heroism never equalled in the history of Spain. This is true in every village. These people are convinced they are fighting for liberty and life, and they would rather die fighting than give up.

Romanones did not add another miscalculation of the rebels. They counted on the army. That was stupid. Most of the privates are from the peasants and the workers. Many of the army are republicans. In barracks after barracks it was found at the last moment the rebel officers could not count on the soldiers and rather than permit them to support the Government they were locked in the barracks. Many escaped. Many were shot by officers, trying to escape. Many are in the armed forces of the republic.

Because of this, the rebels have been driven to the appalling device of bringing over from Africa the Moors and the Foreign Legion. The latter is an organization of criminals of all nations. In Spain criminals for long have been given their choice between prison and the Foreign Legion. Both these and the Moors are as savages and nine tenths of the atrocities committed in the Asturian revolt of October 1934 were committed by these and not by the miners as the world press would have you think. But the effect of bringing these people in has been to intensify the ardor of the republicans.

The rebel armies then are composed as follows: First a small part of the regular army. Second, the Moors and the Foreign Legion. Third the facists. Fourth the Carlists—religionists. And there is no harmony among them. I have this from all the war correspondents who have been with Mola's[6] army. They hate each other and are operating in most instances seperately.

Should the rebels win there will be, according to the plan ascribed to Franco and Mola, a military dictatorship with advisory council. The program is to end parliamentary government, to suspend all constitutional guarantees ending freedom of speech and liberty of the press, to end the public school program, to restore all the old privileges to the Church, to recall the Jesuits, to repeal all labor laws passed by the Azana regime, to make it a crime for workers to strike, to end all agrarian reforms, to expell the small peasant farmers and restore the land to the absentee landlords. And they add "possibly a plebecite on the restoration of the monarchy." Now the military men have no wish for the monarchy, but this is given out as a bait to the religious fanatics of Navarre. Bluntly it is to put Spain back again into the 16th century and hold her there by bayonets. The final result would be communism.

The average person, viewing things superficially and with little knowledge of history or of peoples, tells you the military will win. They have not been winning. And others are convinced that an army composed in large part of foreigners and Moors cannot put down a people. I am sure of it. Will Duranty[7] who is here shares this view with me. That the rebel chiefs are not so sure is shown by the fact that while all the political leaders of the Left are in Spain and hard at work, most of the Rightists are out of Spain, and all the nobility is trying to get out. Azana is working day and night at the palace. Barrio is the Lloyd George of the time, going constantly from town to town, animating the people, and turning factories into munition plants. Fernando de los Rios[8] is on a mission to Paris. Prieto[9] is writing and speaking. Largo Cabellero[10] is supporting the Government strongly at Madrid. But Lerreux is safe in Portugal as is Gil Robles.[11] Santiago Alba[12] is safe in France as are many of the nobility.

It is a ruthless war, a life and death struggle, but the Government is acting within the law. The court martials have been held weeks after rebel generals and officers have been taken, and these trials have been conducted with scrupulous regard to the rights of the accused. In cases of conviction and execution, they have been treated with every consideration. Priests of their choice are summoned. Most of the executions by the Government have been of officers of the army caught in rebellion. The rebels execute Civil Governors when they take a town and leaders of Left parties are shot without trial. Packard of the United Press tells me of an incident near Tolosa, which he witnessed. Twelve loyalists in a motor truck who had lost their way drove into the rebel camp. Fifteen minutes later Packard heard a volley. They had been stood up and shot without any pretense at a trial.

There have been some outrageous things ascribed to the "Government" or the communists. Now here is the strange thing: The communists, under rigid discipline, are supporting the Government loyally. They are not looting or shooting in the streets. They are under drastic orders not to molest private property and to do nothing except on direct orders from the Government. They are living up to these orders. Their organ in Madrid is proposing shooting for thieves. The people who are killing and stealing and breaking in, are the Syndicalists and Anarchists. These were bitter enemies of the Government before the rebellion began. And these constitute Azana's problem.

These are my private views. The possibilities of this crisis precipitating a European war are really grave. Germany and Italy have been openly, brazenly, against the Government and I refer to the Italian and German Ambassadors. France and the French Ambassador are as openly with the Government and against the rebels. I have found the diplomatic corps generally with the rebels. It is not due to instructions from their Governments. Most of these gentlemen are weak sisters, bridge and golf players, snobs, enemies of democracy, toadies to rank and fortune. Their personal friends, and mine, are among the nobility and aristocracy of Spain and many of these are in jail. They see no further than that. They are constantly seeking an opportunity, under the lead of the Argentine Ambassador,[13] for nine years Ambassador to the Vatican, to deal a blow to the Government. My own staff is right—with one exception. Johnson,[14] the Counsellor, I have had to brush aside because of his hysteria and blatant advocacy of the rebel cause. Eddie Flynn may have told you about him.[15] I shall discuss him bluntly on my return with the Department. Flynn heard him propose to me that we have a joint office in Irun with the German and Italian Embassies!!

The Argentine who is dean called a meeting to consider offering mediation. That would have been a public proclamation of the equal status of the Government and the rebels and was intended as such. I was surprised to find Sir Henry Chilton, the British Ambassador, a nice fellow who strikes his predecessor Sir George Grahame about the ankles intellectually, in favor of it. I called his attention to the implications of such action and his First Secretary who was present agreed with me and Chilton then telephoned his Government. He was told he might attend but was to say nothing. I thought it unwise to attend since the press might get the story and publish the names of those attending. I wired my impressions to Hull and asked for instructions to stay away and got them. Chilton attended as an observer only and yesterday the London *Times* had the story and had him present as one of the sponsors. So many took my view that nothing was actually done. Then the Argentine called another meeting to offer services in arranging an exchange of prisoners. This without a suggestion from either side. The trick here, is, that nobles and members of the aristocracy who are open rebels and have financed the rebellion are in jail, and the purpose really is, according to admissions in private, to get them out. But there are none of the Government people of any consequence in jail. I thought it probable that the Government would decline a one sided proposition which would turn active enemies loose within their lines and again did not attend, notifying Hull who sends his approval. My firm conviction is this: We must not become involved by any kind of meddling with the domestic quarrel of Spain. We must confine ourselves rigidly to getting Americans out and looking after American interests exclusively. I am asking for instruction where I have the slightest doubt.

I had gone to Feunterrebia to rest three weeks before sailing for home the first of August and while there put the finishing touches on my preparations for the campaign. I am ready for the campaign now. But it would be exceedingly bad to leave my post for politics so long as the situation here remains as it is. It would be used against the Administration. I really think the thing will be over soon.

My relations with all elements here have been of the best, and I am sure that the best way to keep on good terms with all is to attend to our business and stand aloof from all suggestions of interference by the corps.

This letter is choppy but I am writing to the music of cannon and bomb explosions and of machine guns in a battle now on just across the border.

Sincerely,

Claude G. Bowers

I have written you with a frankness in which I do not indulge with others. Of course my sympathy is with the Government. The rebels are of the same element as that opposing your Administration. But do not be alarmed lest I talk as freely as I write you in confidence . . .[16]

[PSF:Spain:TS]

[1] Bowers' eccentric spelling has been retained, here and below.

[2] A number of these are printed in *Foreign Relations, 1936,* II, 437ff; see also Bowers, *My Mission to Spain: Watching the Rehearsal for World War II* (New York: Simon and Schuster, 1954), chap. XVII.

[3] Azaña was elected president of the Spanish Republic on May 10, 1936.

[4] Diego Martínez Barrio was speaker of the Cortes.

[5] Alvaro de F. de Torres (Count Romanones) was a royalist and Rightist politician.

[6] Emilio Mola Vidal commanded Franco's armies in northern Spain before his death in 1937.

[7] Walter Duranty, Moscow correspondent of the New York *Times,* 1921–1935, is apparently meant.

[8] Los Ríos, Minister of Foreign Affairs and later ambassador to the United States.

[9] Indalecio Prieto y Tuero, formerly in the Azaña cabinet.

[10] Largo Caballero, Minister of Labor, later Premier.

[11] Rightists, Gil Robles being the Rightist leader in the Cortes.

[12] President of the Cortes.

[13] Daniel García-Mansilla; Bowers discusses his activities in telegrams to Hull, in *Foreign Relations, 1936,* II, 488, 497, 509, and in his book, *My Mission to Spain,* 291ff.

[14] Hallett Johnson, counselor of embassy.

[15] Presumably Edward J. Flynn, Democratic party leader of Bronx County, who had been in Europe during the summer.

[16] (Omitted is a reference to a member of Bowers' staff.) Roosevelt replied Sept. 16, 1936 (*Personal Letters, 1928–1945,* I, 614–615), that he agreed with Bowers' decision not to return home; he also said Bowers was "absolutely right" in what he said about American neutrality.

Stephen T. Early, Assistant Secretary to the President, to Marvin H. McIntyre, Assistant Secretary to the President, Presidential Train, Chicago

Washington, D.C., Aug. 26, 1936

[*Telegram*] New York *Times* under Krock's signature today says President giving serious consideration if reelected to inviting heads several nations to confer for purpose of insuring world peace and if proposal carried out President would ask King Edward, Stalin, Mussolini, Hitler, Lebrun, Representatives of China, Japan and others to meet him. Says further that President has outlined his ideas to friends. Hull and I in response to many inquiries stated we knew nothing, never heard of proposal and expressed surprise story being cabled and published throughout world. Hull urges for international reasons that President decline all comment.[1]

Stephen Early

[OF 394:T]

[1] Krock's article also stated that the President believed that if reelected in the face of the strong opposition confronting him he would be in a stronger position than any previous president to further the cause of world peace. He was not sure that he would go through with the idea of a conference even if reelected, wrote Krock, "but the concept has fascinated him; he returns to it often; and it would not be difficult to convince him that he has made a new discovery in world leadership for what he considers the greatest cause of mankind." The New York *Times* Washington dispatch of August 26, described official and diplomatic reaction to the proposal as shocked and skeptical; Krock commented that what particularly disturbed the State Department was that the idea sounded so like Roosevelt (Aug. 26, p. 1; Aug. 28, 1936, p. 16).

McIntyre answered Early's telegram from Chicago where he was en route with the President to a drought conference in Des Moines: "The President says you and Secretary have done just right" (OF 394). Roosevelt then authorized Secretary of Agriculture Wallace (with him on the presidential train) to tell reporters: "The President has not seen the story and does not know just what was in it, so he can't deny it. But he said that I could tell you that there has been nothing in any shape, manner or form looking toward any meeting of the sort described" (New York *Times,* Aug. 27, 1936, p. 4). Letters sent to the White House on the subject were sent to the State Department where they were answered with a form reply, which concluded: "As you may have noted, the accuracy of this information was subsequently denied for the President, who is, however, deeply concerned with the problem of war and peace as is attested by his recent speech at Chautauqua, New York, a copy of which I enclose (Moore to McIntyre, Sept. 17, 1936, OF 394).

Frank Kingdon, President, University of Newark, to Roosevelt

Newark, New Jersey, August 26, 1936

Dear Mr. President: The New York *Times* of this morning carries a statement so full of meaning for the present distressed world that I cannot refrain from commenting on it from the point of view of one who believes that the perpetuation of international peace is the paramount need of the contemporary world.[1]

Decisive social issues in all countries are now being faced. In a sense, the whole pattern of society is in the process of reexamination. This itself is arousing so many passions within nations that the air is charged with an almost irrational emotionalism. The very instability thus engendered demands that the wider area of international relations be steadied at some center of equilibrium. The nations can and will find methods of social settlement, even though they come to them through harassing internal experiences, if they can be released from the international insecurity that now adds to their bewilderment. Without peace, there probably will be either no social adjustment at all, or else a plunge into reaction. Every nation needs international peace for the sake of its own rational settlement of its own problems.

There is another consideration worth pondering. The young men and women of our country have come to maturity in a situation that has given them no inspiration and little hope. They are in danger of a cynicism that will leave them without any moral meaning for their lives. They need a cause to waken their ideals. In spite of all the gibes of subsequent years, President Wilson did uncover among the peoples a tremendous latent devotion to peace. It is still there, and favorably inspired, it can transform the outlook of youth and become a force for inaugurating a brighter world community.

To dare much is to risk much. If you undertake a meeting of the powers of the world you may end in spectacular failure. I, however, have a certain confidence in audacity. Somebody must match the new physical world order with a sweep of the social imagination that will control

402

it for humane ends. The techniques of conference among the nations are still tentative. Skill can come only through experiment. I sincerely hope that the conventional timidities of cautious men will not deter you from following courageously the line of your present intention.

Many more considerations cry for utterance but since I am sure they are a part of your own thinking, please allow me to subscribe myself,
Yours respectfully,

Frank Kingdon[2]

[PPF 3880:TS]

[1] See above.
[2] Answered Sept. 2, 1936, below.

Sumner Welles, Assistant Secretary of State, to Roosevelt

Washington, August 28, 1936

My dear Mr. President: Bill Phillips gave me your memorandum of August 19 the day he left the Department.[1]

You will remember that I had already spoken to you of the information given to me by the Minister of Ecuador regarding the conversations which Mr. André Roosevelt had been having in Ecuador. In accordance with your instructions, I have written a personal and confidential letter to our Minister in Quito[2] asking him to see Mr. André Roosevelt at the earliest opportunity and to tell him that the Government of Ecuador had already been informed upon several occasions during the past three years that the Government of the United States would not only not consider, but would not even discuss, the purchase of the Galapagos Islands.

I further requested Mr. Gonzalez to tell Mr. Roosevelt that the circulation of rumors at this time that this Government was discussing such a possibility would be seriously prejudicial to our interests, inasmuch as you would soon be called upon to act as arbitrator in the Ecuadoran-Peruvian boundary dispute, and that if the Peruvian press commenced to publish stories that the United States was making a deal with Ecuador for the sale of the Islands, public opinion in Peru would at once jump to the conclusion that your arbitral decision would be partial to Ecuador.

Finally, Mr. Roosevelt was to be requested to cease any and all discussions of the matter.

Mr. Gonzalez will report to me as soon as he has had his talk with Mr. Roosevelt. I would suggest that you defer your reply to Mr. Roosevelt until I hear from Mr. Gonzalez.

With regard to points 1 and 3 of your memorandum, I feel that the suggestion contained therein is the only procedure which will both safeguard our national interests and at the same time avoid the charge that we are undertaking territorial expansion on this continent. It is a proposal which should be suggested by Ecuador herself at the regular Pan American Conference to be held in Peru in 1938 and I think that a proposal of this character would be enthusiastically supported by the other republics of the continent at that time.[3]

Believe me, Faithfully yours,

Sumner Welles

[PPF 3389:TS]

[1] Printed in *Personal Letters, 1928–1945*, I, 607–608, asking what he should reply to André Roosevelt's letter of Aug. 6, 1936, above.

[2] Antonio C. Gonzalez. He had reported to Hull on Jan. 13, 1936 (*Foreign Relations, 1936*, V, 533–534), that Japanese submarines had been taking soundings in the waters around the Galápagos Islands.

[3] The idea of acquiring the Galápagos Islands recurred a number of times later. In a letter to Hull of April 1, 1944, Roosevelt referred to his efforts to have the Galápagos made an international park: "I have been at this for six or seven years and I would die happy if the State Department could accomplish something on it!" (OF 4017).

Statement by Roosevelt on the Bombing of the U.S.S. *Kane*

[Rapid City, South Dakota, August 30, 1936][1]

The President has received dispatches relating to the dropping of bombs in the vicinity of the U.S.S. *Kane* about 38 miles off the Spanish coast by an unidentified plane.[2] He has talked with the Secretary of State on the telephone and representations will be immediately made to the Spanish Government and the Spanish Rebels.[3]

Any further information will be given out by the Secretary of State. The President is in constant touch with Washington.

The U.S.S. *Kane* (destroyer), with other American ships, has been engaged in evacuating American citizens from Spanish ports.

[Statements File:T]

[1] Roosevelt was en route to Salt Lake City to attend the funeral of Secretary of War George Dern.

[2] Early (in Washington) had telephoned two dispatches from the captain of the *Kane*, both dated Aug. 30, 1936 (Statements File).

[3] See Hull to Wendelin, Aug. 30 and 31, 1936, in *Foreign Relations, 1936*, II, 687–688, 688–689.

William E. Dodd, Ambassador to Germany, to R. Walton Moore, Assistant Secretary of State

Berlin, August 31st, 1936

Dear Judge Moore: *If you think it worth while you might show this letter to the President.*[1] It is my summary of things as they appear to me in Europe.

The German people seem to be now 60% behind the Führer; but they are 75% desperately afraid of a European war. Dr. Schacht insists before the dictators that war would ruin all countries involved; but he is overruled and compelled to meet expenses of unprecedented armament.[2] In order to do this he was trying in Paris last week to find a way to buy cotton, copper and other war materials. The French Ambassador[3] here acknowledged this to me August 29th. The idea is to get American exports to France and then have the needed materials re-exported to German manufacturers. This was done by American airplane companies for Italy through Germany last autumn, as you know.

The Führer is so set in his course against Russia that he will not participate in any world conference if the French-Russian treaty is not renounced by France. This I think was also urged by Schacht in Paris. German officials say frankly that there can be no conference if Russians have anything to do with it. Schacht called upon the Russians through the Press yesterday as he returned to stop all propaganda—the very same day Goebbels was in Venice conferring with the Italian Propaganda Minister; and we know the Nazis have maintained highly expensive propaganda agents and groups in Spain for two years. The Propaganda chief for dissemination of "enlightenment" to other countries now has more than 500 clerks in his Berlin office.

The German journalists have not mentioned the world-wide newspaper story that President Roosevelt had asked for a conference of world leaders for peace.[4] A Foreign Office official laughed when one of our staff people asked him discreetly if the Germans had heard of the matter. How could the Führer leave his country with a thousand armed guards-

405

men? There is no prospect of a peace agreement except upon the basis of a solid Fascist-Nazi European front. The French Ambassador, himself half-Fascist, a shareholder in the largest iron-ore mines in Lorraine and a member of the Comité de Forges, and very uneasy, said yesterday: If the Schacht negotiations fail war is almost certain to come next year. I think from the tone of the conversation, Schacht is trying to persuade the French to go Fascist in order to avoid war; and a special leader of Fascist Poland is now working for the same thing in Paris. That would mean Spanish surrender and British helplessness. Such a drift I have felt and sadly prophesied since the autumn of 1934.

A very able and prominent American, talking with Mussolini two weeks ago reported to me: "Mussolini said 'no use for you to go to Vienna, nothing is decided there; I and Hitler tell them what to do; you might stop in Prague, but Berlin is the only other place for you to visit.'" A Vienna correspondent of long residence told me yesterday that our Ministry there is of no more use at all; Austria is not annexed but both Nazi and Catholic elements have surrendered with Schusnigg.[5] Even Messersmith admitted personally to him that nothing could be done in Vienna. And we learn that Schusnigg was with Hitler a week ago and Mussolini expected to be with him soon. Hungary is in about the same position as Austria, in addition, strong anti-Semitic feeling and territorial claims which have been used by Nazi propaganda; Roumania's present change of chief official is due to urgent pressure to make a co-operative treaty with Germany; and I expect the Minister of Czechoslovakia, now in Prague, to report a proposed treaty with, if not surrender to, Germany when he returns. It would not be called that to be sure. As you probably know Mussolini started Franco on his revolt against the Spanish Government July 17th and sent much assistance. Germany supported the same policy and sent many airplanes to Revolutionists up to last week. The neutrality promises were made when these powers felt certain of Fascist dictatorship in Spain.

Europe is, therefore, fast moving in the direction I have feared a long time. France, I am told by Government official from Paris, may get rid of Blum in December, if he does not devaluate, or if his devaluation brings charges of betrayal of promises from the French people.[6] Will there follow a dictatorship? Doriot,[7] paid by Fascists in France and by industrialists, with great appeal to the working classes, is now the most prominent opposition leader. England's armament goes on at a terrific rate, but there is no real safety without co-operation with the United States; and that can not be arranged. Moreover, there is increasing activity from London, as in Berlin, against the re-election of President

Roosevelt. A competent American journalist told me last week that Lord Beaverbrook and a large number of London investors in United States securities, especially utilities, were very active in New York in fighting the Administration. There is a "deal" between the Beaverbrook and Hearst Press associations for the same purpose. This supports the accounts I gave you a week ago about what is being done here by Propaganda people. They have been urging Kermit Roosevelt, thought to be against his distant cousin, to attend the grand Partei Tag show in Nürnberg, September 8–15. Kermit is reported to be in Switzerland where Schurman is supposed to be. A correspondent of the United Press was in London a little while ago. He wrote an account to America of what came to him about London business men against Roosevelt. His chief over there telegraphed him refusal to print and a rebuke for telling the story, especially as he had said the British government was opposed to such conduct. Hearst as you know is now in Italy with Mussolini to whom he secured great loans, McAdoo helping, from California a few years ago. All of these activities, among many others already given public attention, point to the possibility of Fascism in our country. We have not yet ascertained whether London and New York have made recent loans to Rome, as reported two weeks ago.

Our country has certainly permitted "interests" to abuse our system; and we have Tammany Hall in New York and a worse thing in Chicago. If you have time to read chapters XVII and XVIII of my Wilson book[8] you will see why many high officials in Europe criticize us. But the democratic spirit is as real with us now as at any time since 1865. If Roosevelt is defeated it would be a serious set-back which would greatly affect the countries of Europe where democracy is already being abandoned altogether. If we yield in part how much worse our system would be—and over here the historic democracies of Switzerland, Holland and Sweden are almost trembling with fear.

I have been a little surprised at the failure of the Balkan Ministers here since my return. They all formerly talked freely and hoped to see a loose union of their little countries, settling their boundary disputes among themselves. Now they are silent or show such a fear of Germany that they must give up outside relationships—every-thing depends on the Führer.

More interesting to the President, perhaps, is the fact that Latin-American Ministers here: Brazil, Argentine, Chile, Colombia and Nicaragua are frankly Fascist, although they speak highly of the present United States policy toward them. They all seem to wish Europe to go Nazi or Fascist; all attend the Partei Tag propaganda event which the representatives of the democratic countries decline to attend. Perhaps this may interest Secretary Hull too.

In conclusion I ought to say that our service people, diplomatic and consular, have indicated their Fascist favor toward German-Italian domination of Spain; they have even indicated their opposition to their President. This is not saying they ought to favor Communism. It is only saying that they have in the last six months swung back into the ranks of privileged capitalists. This adds troublesome elements to my work here for we must have absolutely non-partisan reports and telegrams. Is the western world going to give up the human system of Locke, Adam Smith and Jefferson who labored so hard to secure it? The present campaign is, I fear, the most important we have had since the Civil War, and there will be millions of dollars spent to defeat Roosevelt. If he could only manage to hold his majority of 1932!

With sincere personal regards,

William E. Dodd

[*Notation*:A:Dodd] Typed by my daughter so entirely confidential [PSF:Germany:TS]

[1] Moore underscored this sentence and wrote "p. 4" on the margin opposite it; in the original, page 4 is the part on anti-Roosevelt activity in London.

[2] Dodd and Schacht had talked in Berlin on Aug. 18, 1936; see Dodd, *Diary,* pp. 344–345.

[3] André François-Poncet.

[4] New York *Times,* Aug. 26, 1936, p. 1.

[5] Kurt von Schuschnigg, Austrian Chancellor following the death of Dollfuss in 1934.

[6] Blum remained as Premier until June 1937.

[7] Jacques Doriot, a leader of the Dissident Communists in France, one of the splinter parties making up the Popular Front in 1936.

[8] *Woodrow Wilson and His Work* (New York: Doubleday, 1920). Dodd sent Roosevelt a copy of the revised edition (New York: Peter Smith, 1932) on July 11, 1932, with an inscription to Roosevelt as "the fourth great dreamer of American presidential leaders," the other three being Jefferson, Lincoln, and Wilson. The chapters referred to are "Political Sabotage" and "The Breaking of Woodrow Wilson."

Norman Thomas, Socialist Party Candidate for the Presidency, to Roosevelt, Green River, Wyoming

New York, N.Y., Aug. 31, 1936

[*Telegram*] Dear Mr. President: This morning's papers announce that you consider the Spanish Civil War and its possible consequences in our foreign relations as your greatest worry.[1] Last week's papers announced that the State Department had informed the official government of Spain duly and democratically elected that it would insist on the right of American ships and American exporters to land supplies of all sorts in Spanish ports held by rebels unless the Madrid Government should be able to establish a complete blockade.[2] There may be a basis for this in international law, but in fact it makes Americans potential allies in the Fascist triumph which endangers the peace of the whole world. In America there has been abundant precedent for a refusal by our State Department to permit shipments of supplies to rebels in Latin American countries who take up arms against a duly constituted and democratically elected government. I do not urge that this principle should be made absolute and final in international law. I do urge that it has had value and that it is a principle which might well be applied now in the Spanish situation. The Spanish war is not a war between nations with both of which America is on terms of peace. It is not an uprising of the exploited masses against autocracy. It is a singularly cruel and dangerous military revolt engineered by the economic royalists of Spain. What its success will mean to any genuine democracy in Western Europe I need not tell you, neither need I urge upon your consideration the difficulty which every American Government will find in keeping clear of new World War. Hence I urge you to reverse the ruling of the Department of State so as to discourage rather than to encourage exports of supplies useful in war to ports held by the Spanish rebels. I also urge you to issue a public statement appealing to the business interests of the United States to refrain from this kind of trade with rebels who have not even established recognition as belligerents in Europe and whose rebellion threatens the peace of the world. The policy I am urging ought to be an American policy not a football of campaign policy. I am therefore sending a copy of this letter to Governor Landon, Mr. Lemke and Mr. Browder[3] in the hope that each of them will endorse the policy which I am urging upon you and which I shall take the liberty of urging upon the public. It goes without saying that time is all important, hence my request for very prompt action.[4]

Respectfully yours,

Norman Thomas

[OF 422-C:T]

[1] The New York *Times,* Aug. 31, 1936, p. 1, carried a story by Charles W. Hurd, filed from Rapid City, S.D., on August 30, about the President's reaction to the bombing of

the destroyer *Kane*. Hurd said that Roosevelt had "recently" said that the Spanish situation was his greatest worry. He made no such assertion in any of his July or August press conferences, or in his speeches of that period, and the occasion of this remark has not been identified.

[2] The State Department's action is reported in the New York *Times,* Aug. 27, 1936, p. 3, and in Wendelin to Hull, Aug. 21, 1936, and Hull to Wendelin, Aug. 25, 1936, in *Foreign Relations, 1936,* II, 679, 682–683.

[3] The other 1936 presidential nominees: Governor Alfred M. Landon, Republican party; Rep. William Lemke, Union party; and Earl Browder, Communist party.

[4] An extract from Thomas' letter was published in the New York *Times,* Sept. 1, 1936, p. 12. No reply has been found.

Henry Morgenthau, Jr., Secretary of the Treasury, to Roosevelt, Laramie, Wyoming

Washington, D.C., Aug. 31 [1936]

[*Telegram*] President Roosevelt: Think you will be interested in Associated Press report this morning indicating that the Mexican Government decided August thirtieth to increase the amount of silver in circulation and in required reserves against notes.[1] Step by the Mexican Government seems to constitute an important development in the restoration of monetary use of silver. The following reported changes would require substantial increases in the use of silver: one peso notes introduced in 1935 are to be withdrawn and replaced with silver pesos of old .720 fineness. Five peso notes now in circulation are to be replaced by silver certificates redeemable as will be all note issues of the Bank of Mexico in silver coin or bar silver at twelve grams approximately two fifths ounce per peso. For small coins now in circulation new coins containing more silver are to be substituted. Further important information will be forwarded as received.[2]

Henry Morgenthau, Jr.

[OF 229:T]

[1] Printed in the New York *Times,* Aug. 31, 1936, p. 2.
[2] Answered below.

Roosevelt to Henry Morgenthau, Jr., Secretary of the Treasury

[Salt Lake City] 9/1 [1936]

[*Telegram*] Good old Mexico.[1]

FDR

[OF 229:T]

[1] See above.

Roosevelt to Joseph C. Grew, Ambassador to Japan, Tokyo

Aboard the Presidential Special, September 2, 1936

My dear Joe: This will introduce Mr. Henry F. Misselwitz, one of our "old guard" newspaper men.

He has a very interesting idea and wants to have an opportunity of talking to you about it.[1]

Very sincerely yours,

[PPF 3845:CT]

[1] Misselwitz, foreign news editor of the United Press Associations, had written to Roosevelt Aug. 19, 1936 (PPF 3845), to remind him of their talk at the White House in June. Misselwitz had proposed the holding of a Japanese-American World Series and Roosevelt had "grasped the significance at once" of the idea as a means of improving relations between the United States and Japan.

Roosevelt to Frank Kingdon, President, University of Newark, Newark, New Jersey

Aboard the Presidential Special, September 2, 1936

Personal

My dear Dr. Kingdon: I read with much interest your letter to me of August 26th.[1] It was an inspiration and I am wondering if some time before so very long we could not arrange for an opportunity to talk things over. I agree with you with reference to the danger of the situation as it affects our youth. It is a problem that should have the attention of all of us.

Very sincerely yours,

[PPF 3880:CT]

¹ Above.

Robert W. Bingham, Ambassador to Great Britain, to Roosevelt

[London] September 4, 1936

Dear Mr. President: Following your request to me to return home for a few weeks prior to the election, I secured passage long ago on the *Berengaria* sailing on Sept. 23rd, expecting to sail from New York returning on Nov. 4th. It goes without saying that I want very much to do whatever you wish me to do, and I am retaining my space awaiting further instructions from you.

However, the situation in Spain, as you know, is very grave, and carries with it dangerous and menacing possibilities. In addition, there is grave reason to apprehend a blow-up in France. A weak France means a strong Germany. A serious outbreak there might mean immediate hostile action by Germany. This country cannot be defended from the Channel. England must fight to save the Channel ports, and France and Belgium must be England's front line.

The Government and the intelligent and well-informed people here realize this. It is quite true there has been much pro-German sentiment, but this has been steadily diminishing, and it is an attitude not shared by the people to whom I have referred above. There is a pro-German cabal led by Lord Lothian and actively fostered by the Waldorf Astors. This carries with it the *Times,* as the Waldorf Astors have more influence with Geoffrey Dawson than John Astor has, who is the real proprietor of the *Times.*

Members of the Government and the best-informed and most influential people here are more anxious and apprehensive than I have ever seen them before. The whole situation leads me to the conclusion that I ought not to leave my post now, unless there is a decided change for the better in the near future, which does not seem probable.

I submit my opinion on this subject to you for your consideration, prepared, of course, to take whatever course you deem desirable.[1]
Sincerely yours,

Robert W. Bingham

[PSF:Great Britain:TS]

[1] The President, in his reply of September 14, agreed that Bingham should remain in London (*Personal Letters, 1928–1945,* I, 614).

Roosevelt to Nicholas Murray Butler, President, Columbia University, New York

[Washington] September 8, 1936

My dear Dr. Butler: I thank you most heartily for your letter of August fifteenth.[1] I am not sure that your kind comments on my speech at Chautauqua are deserved, but at least I said exactly what I thought and felt.

If a calamity such as you foresee should fall upon mankind, we must make sure that this Nation shall not become involved.

In the days to come I shall need your counsel and help, and that of all other Americans who really care for peace.

Very sincerely yours,

[PPF 445:CT]

[1] PPF 445.

Roosevelt to R. Walton Moore, Assistant Secretary of State

Washington, September 8, 1936

Confidential

Memorandum for Judge Moore: I wish you would speak with Cordell about this Schurman matter. I am inclined to think that the German government should know of our disapproval. When distinguished foreigners come here, the Secretary of State and the President see them only with the full approval and knowledge of their Embassy or Legation.

F.D.R.

[*Notation*:AS] Sept 8   The Sy thinks & I agree that we should not act RWM[1]

[Moore Papers:TS]

---

[1] See Dodd to Roosevelt, Aug. 19, 1936, above. Moore wrote to Dodd on September 8 (Moore Papers) that although the Administration disapproved of the actions of the German government and of the activities of people like Schurman, all that could be done was to get all possible evidence showing that the German authorities were trying to influence American sentiment, "since should that fact be made apparent it would really help us in the campaign."

Claude G. Bowers, Ambassador to Spain, to Roosevelt

Hendaye, September 9, 1936

Dear Mr. President: I am inclosing a copy of a despatch that may be of interest to you. Since it was written del Vayo[1] has formally informed the diplomats still in Madrid that the present Government will do precisely what I indicate in this note, and for the very reason I assign.

There is no doubt now that the plane that tried to bomb the *Kane* was a rebel plane. The statement of the Government in prompt reply to our protest is most convincing to me, and the Captain of the *Kane* tells me today that he is convinced the plane was of Italian make. That settles it. I do not think it was deliberately the intent to aim at us; the *Kane* has a little of the appearance of a Government boat. However while we have received every possible courtesy and consideration from the Government, we have had some little difficulty occasionally from the facists[2] who cultivate the best facist manner.

My course in reference to the meddling of the Diplomatic Corps has been entirely vindicated by events. Of course the Government turned down the proposition regarding prisoners since it was clearly proposed to furnish the rebels with propoganda. Most of the diplomatic corps have been outrageously pro-rebel. This is due, first to the aggressive bullying tactics of the three facist states, Germany, Italy especially and Portugal. Second to the inevitable snobbery of diplomats of the professional variety who are always against the masses of the people. Third to the fact that the nobility here and the moneyed aristocracy are cultivated by most of the corps to the point of sycophancy.

In the beginning I was amazed with the intense pro-rebel proclivities of Sir Henry Chilton, the British Ambassador, since the fight is glaringly one against political democracy. He measures up to his predecessor, Sir George Grahame intellectually and in political sagacity about to the ankles. He is a nice, colorless, drawing room diplomat and rather weak. He was first astounded and then frightened when I told him I would not attend a meeting for the purpose of making a public offer of mediation because it naturally would be resented by the Government as a public proclamation that the corps places Government and the rebels on an equal legal footing. Becoming alarmed, over his whole-hearted acquiesence in a purely pro-rebel propoganda plan, he hastily telephoned Whitehall for instructions and was told to keep out. But recently there has been a decided change in the British slant. There can be no doubt, I think, that there is a bargain between General Franco and Italy for the former in case of victory to give Italy all sorts of advantages on the Medeterrenian.

By staying entirely out, by refusing to convert our Embassy into an asylum for rebels and enemies of the regime as practically all the others have, we stand better, I am sure, than any other country and we have had no trouble at all. The British at first admitted numerous titled Spaniards on the ground that they were remotely related to the British Royal family, but soon after this was done London sent instructions to stop it.

The fight at Irun was epic.[3] Never such astonishing heroism. The fishermen, miners, peasants, untrained in arms, repulsed with deadly losses the trained Foreign Legion for six days and on the day before the fall they wiped out columns of the Foreign Legion. They failed on the last day because of the exhaustion of their amunition, and even then they stood with antique heroism at their posts to await certain death rather than surrender.

This failure of amunition indicates one of two things;—either that France has not been sending them amunition, or that at the critical moment France deserted her ally. The France of the Spanish fight is the France of the Abyssinian war.

I think the fall of Irun in its effect on the war has been much exaggerated. It took a week for trained soldiers of the most desperate character, with all the instrumentalities of war, tanks, machine guns, cannon, war ships and planes to take a little town of 12,000 people. To reason that because they finally took Irun they can now take Madrid with its million people and huge defending force seems far fetched. Meanwhile the rebels are about to lose Cordoba, Granada, Zaragoza; and they really are making no progress in the mountains about Madrid. The trouble is that they do not have enough men, since the moment they take a town and move the soldiers on to the next, the town they had taken rises and becomes Government territory again. It seems to me that they can only win by having enough soldiers to keep a regiment or so in the towns they take. Floyd Gibbons[4] and the *Herald-Tribune* man who have been in Seville tell me that Franco's army cannot number more than 17,000 men. I have heard that of Mola variously estimated at between 20,000 and forty thousand. I think the latter figure much exaggerated. Gibbons does not think that they have been able to bring more than 5,000 Moors and Foreign Legion soldiers over from Africa, and it is said that because of the increasing uneasiness in Morocco it is thought impossible to further decrease the army there.

You probably see our despatches but I am sending you personally such observations as occur to me.

Gibbons says your reelection is as certain as the rising of the sun tomorrow morning.

Sincerely,

Claude G. Bowers

[PSF:Spain:TS]

[1] Julio Alvarez del Vayo, Minister of State.
[2] Bowers' misspellings, here and below, as in the original.
[3] Irún was captured Sept. 4, 1936.
[4] Correspondent for the Chicago *Tribune*.

[*Enclosure*] Claude G. Bowers to Cordell Hull, Secretary of State

Hendaye, France, September 7, 1936

Subject: Observations on the Government of Caballero.

Sir: I have the honor to report that in my opinion the bald announcement of the appointment of Largo Caballero[1] as Prime Minister has a sinister sound, but from another point of view it may be the solution of the problem of ending the outrages of the syndicalists and anarchists in Madrid and elsewhere. For weeks before the rebellion, conservatives looked forward with satisfaction to a Government presided over by Prieto.[2] This seemingly strange infatuation of the most reactionary for the socialist orator was due to the conviction that no moderate of the type of Azana or Barrio could safely resort to drastic methods in putting these people down. It was thought that the immediate effect of an attempt by Azana, or any moderate, would be to rally all the proletariat against the Government, but that the strong arm could be used by a socialist like Prieto with safety, without creating the fear that the repression was aimed at the working classes or the peasants.

I have frequently heard this point of view expressed by ultra-conservatives of the old regime in my own house.

However, in view of the split between Caballero and Prieto, the extremists following the former and the moderate socialists the latter, it became apparent that the creation of a Prieto Government would probably be most obnoxious to the followers of Caballero in the Socialist Party. In fact, when on assuming the Presidency, Azana offered the Premiership to Prieto, it was declined on that very ground.

No one on the side of the Republic is in a stronger position to put down the lawlessness of the syndicalists and anarchists, and to bring the popular militia under strict discipline than Caballero.

Does he wish to do it?

For a long while he sought to bring the syndicalists into his organization in a unification of all the proletariat elements. It was on this proposition, along with a few others, that Caballero and Prieto split. But Caballero made no progress, and he is said to have looked with increasing alarm on the utter lawlessness of the syndicalists because, as he said, it tended to discredit the whole proletarian program. Perhaps the climax came when he attended a national syndicalist convention at Zaragosa, in a final effort to coax them in. Here he was constantly interrupted with insults and all but mobbed. There is no doubt that he has had no sympathy with the anarchistic proceedings of the syndicalists in Madrid since the beginning of the rebellion. If he is convinced, as he easily may be, that the excesses of these people are discrediting the cause he represents, he would probably take pleasure in applying the lash of authority. And he alone perhaps is in a position where he can do so and retain the support of the greater part of the workers.

Character of Caballero. It would be a mistake in anticipating probable events to put Largo Caballero down as a lawless, anarchistic demagogue. I never have heard his personal honesty questioned. No amount of money could buy him, and no honors could bribe him. His personal habits are beyond reproach. He lives simply and is not found about the cafes. He works constantly and in his own home. For years a follower of Pablo Iglesias,[3] an evolutionary socialist, at one time a servant of the King, and Minister of Labor in the Ministry of Azana from 1931 to 1933, he became embittered by the savagery of the methods in the suppression of the Asturian revolt of October 1934. Imprisoned for a year and a half, an ingrowing resentment drove him more and more to the extreme Left, and the evolutionary socialist gave way to the revolutionary socialist. For months before the rebellion he gave me the impression of being entirely communistic, though his speeches in the elections of February were singularly free from demagogy or extreme statements.

Some weeks before the rebellion an acquaintance of mine, who enjoys intimate relations with the extremists told me that these were having trouble with Caballero, and would like to brush him aside but for the fact that he had become a "legend," a personification of the cause of the workers in the minds of the masses, and consequently was beyond their capacity to ignore. These extremists, according to my informant, would mention some plan in his presence without a comment from him, and then they would work out all the details of the plan and finally present it to him for his approval. He would look up at them with an amazed expression and quietly reply: "I would not think of such a thing. The Spanish people are not Russians." After the removal of President Alcala Zamora[4] these extremists determined to make Caballero President. He treated their suggestions with indifference, showing no interest. At length, when they thought they had mustered sufficient votes, they went to him: "It is all arranged," they told him. "But no time can be wasted. You can be elected but you must instantly give us permission to go ahead."

He looked up at them with an annoyed expression: "I never have thought of such a thing. I would not think of considering it. My election would be the signal for a civil war. No." I submit this to show the contradictory and strange character of this man.

Prieto. The fact that Prieto has consented to enter a Government under Largo Caballero is rather promising. His influence will be on the side of moderation. The most brilliant orator of his party, good-natured, humane, and possessed of a comfortable fortune measured by Spanish standards, he is an evolutionary socialist. His inclusion in the Ministry of Caballero means a unification of the Frente Popular which for a time seriously was threatened.

Minister of State. The new Minister of State, Alvarez del Vayo, I know

418

personally. Before the revolution of April, 1931, he was the most brilliant political journalist in Spain, and at the time of that revolution was President of the Press Association. He was made Ambassador to Mexico, where he was very acceptable, and while there was known intimately by Josephus Daniels, who formed a very high opinion of him and who can, if desired, give you his impressions. On his return from Mexico he called upon me with a note from Daniels. He is a man of most pleasing appearance, and his manners are those of a cultured gentleman, and a man of the world. He speaks English perfectly. Although he belongs to the left-wing of the socialists, he did not impress me as a fanatic. His brother-in-law, however, Luis Araquistain, whom I have also met, and former Ambassador to Germany, makes a very unfavorable impression upon me, though this may be due in part to a rather pompous and supercilious personality. These two who married sisters, who are Swiss, are in the Cortes, and have been accepted as the two closest advisors of Caballero. Sr. del Vayo appeared to me to be friendly to the United States and rather familiar with our politics, but some years ago Araquistain wrote an anti-American book called *The Yankee Peril*. From my one conversation with him I gathered that he had greatly moderated his views because of our new South American policy. I may add, for I have always found this important in the case of a radical, that Sr. del Vayo has a sense of humor.

Minister of Finance. I also know personally the new Minister of Finance, Juan Negrin,[5] also a socialist, who is the Secretary of the University of Madrid. He is a man of broad culture, very pleasing personality, and no mean ability. He can be described as one of Spain's "intellectuals." I do not know that he has any special qualifications for the post he has taken over, though he probably is an economist.

The Communist Members. Perhaps the most disturbing feature of the new Government is the assignment of the two communists in it to the posts of Minister of Agriculture and of Public Instruction. It is not probable that either will have much to do during the period of the rebellion, and in the event that the Government prevails, this Government will no doubt make way for another, since the purpose of this is to include every party in the Frente Popular. To maintain a communist in the Department of Public Instruction would mean the conversion of the schools into an agency of communistic propaganda.

Quite as interesting is the assignment of the post of Minister of Agriculture to a communist.

Apropos of this, some time ago Louis Fischer, who writes for the *New*

Statesman in London, and *The Nation* in New York, . . . called on me while in Madrid. It was at the time Azana was pushing his land reforms with great speed, resulting in the placing of 70,000 peasant families on small farms in four months. Fischer asked me what I thought of the Azana plan, and he asked the question in a manner indicating disapproval. I replied that since the great problem in Spain is to solve the living problem of the peasants, I supposed that he, Fischer, would approve. "But," he said, "the trouble is that Azana will thus form a middle class of small property owners and won't this hold back the Revolution?" The remark was illuminating, but I made no reply.

The real significance of the change in Government remains to be judged by events. I think it means at this time a more vigorous prosecution of the war against the rebels. The method adopted may throw light on the real meaning of the change. In the sense that Azana, who is a man of great intellect and powers of persuasion, will now have frequent opportunities of dealing directly with men like Caballero, it may have a moderating effect upon the extremists and may make for a more vigorous suppression of syndicalist lawlessness in Madrid and elsewhere.

Respectfully yours,

Claude G. Bowers

[PSF:Spain:CT]

[1] Francisco Largo Caballero, Socialist Spanish labor leader, was known as the "Spanish Lenin" and was implicated in the revolt of the Asturian miners in 1934. He became Premier and Minister of War, Sept. 4, 1936.

[2] Indalecio Prieto y Tuero, Minister of Air and Marine in the Largo Caballero government.

[3] Iglesias was the first Socialist deputy in the Cortes, 1910–1925.

[4] In the spring of 1936; Azaña succeeded him.

[5] Negrín succeeded Largo Caballero as Premier in May 1937 and continued in office until the fall of the government in March 1939.

Cordell Hull, Secretary of State, to Roosevelt

[Washington] September 11, 1936

My dear Mr. President: The Ambassador of Spain[1] has informed the Department of the desire of his Government to appoint as his successor at Washington His Excellency Señor Don Fernando de los Rios, and inquires if this appointment would be agreeable to this Government.

Señor de los Rios was for twenty years a professor of political science at the University of Granada, and more recently has been professor of jurisprudence and Rector of the University of Madrid. He was one of the intellectuals instrumental in bringing about the formation of the Spanish Republic.

In the Azana Cabinet, Señor de los Rios has held the portfolios of Minister of Justice, Minister of Public Instruction and Minister of Foreign Affairs. He is a Socialist Member of Parliament but belongs to the Right Wing of the Socialist Party.

I do not believe that the present difficulties in Spain should in any way affect the decision as to the acceptability of Señor de los Rios as Ambassador of the present Spanish Government, as we have continued to maintain normal relations with the Madrid Government. If you concur in this opinion, I shall inform Ambassador Calderón that Señor de los Rios is acceptable to this Government.

The present Spanish Ambassador has informed me that he has submitted his resignation to the Government at Madrid and has expressed the wish that he may have an opportunity of making his adieus to you personally before his departure from Washington.

I shall be gratified if this courtesy, which you have been so good as to extend to other retiring Ambassadors, could be granted to Ambassador Calderón. He has stated that he intends to take no part in the present struggle in Spain, and will not go to Spain upon his departure from the United States. I believe, therefore, that in order to maintain an appearance of absolute impartiality, it would be particularly desirable for you to receive the retiring Ambassador if it would be convenient for you to do so.

Faithfully yours,

Cordell Hull

[*Notation*:A] CH   de los Rios OK   FDR
[OF 422:CT]

[1] Luis Felipe Calderón was ambassador from March to September 1936.

Roosevelt to Marvin H. McIntyre, Assistant Secretary to the President

Washington, September 11, 1936

Memo for Mac: Tell Secretary Hull that the President hesitates about receiving Calderón because he resigned in protest against the present Government. I doubt very much the wisdom of my receiving him.[1]

F.D.R.

[OF 422:T]

[1] This memorandum refers to the letter above. Calderón was, however, received on October 19 (PPF 1-0).

Roosevelt to Samuel R. Fuller, Jr., New York

[Washington] September 12, 1936

Dear Dick: I am glad to know that you are off again for another trip to various places in Europe. I hope you will be able to see our friends again. I do not think that any formal letters are necessary but you may show this to our Embassy people just by way of check-up.

I hope you will have a delightful time.[1]

As ever yours,

[PPF 2616:CT]

[1] This note was in reply to Fuller's letter of Sept. 8, 1936 (PPF 2616), saying that he was to visit England, Holland, and possibly Germany on a quick business trip and that he was at the President's disposal.

Roosevelt to the Right Reverend George Craig Stewart, Bishop of Chicago, Chicago

[Washington] September 12, 1936

Dear Bishop Stewart: It is fitting that the Chicago-Lambeth Quadrilateral should celebrate its fiftieth anniversary by extending an invitation to the Bishops of the Western World to attend and to set for discussion the subject of "The Western Hemisphere and the Peace of the World."[1]

The Government of the United States has declared the policy of "the good neighbor" in its international relations. This policy has the virtue of explaining itself; surely I do not need to attempt to explain the source of its inspiration to any Christian fellowship, nor offer apology for making much of it in extending greetings to a conference of the Bishops of all the Americas of the church that nurtured me.

The history of mankind teaches that if peoples are to be free, economically and politically, they must preserve the independence and sovereignty of their state; but if peoples are to be free spiritually, how can they better achieve and preserve such freedom than to contemplate the world in the spirit and purpose of the good neighbor.

Once a great people undertook to live unto themselves in the things of the spirit and of them a great historian wrote:

"Alone in the universe, the self-styled pride of the Greeks was not disturbed by the comparison of foreign merit; and it is no wonder if they fainted in the race, since they had neither competitors to urge their speed, nor judges to crown their victory."

Buenos Aires, Santiago, Rio de Janeiro are now nearer to Montreal and Chicago than Boston was to Philadelphia when the Constitution of the United States was framed. Only since yesterday, it seems the Hemisphere has become a vast neighborhood. May I suggest, that in the re-orientation of this neighborhood of the Western World, the Bishops face new and challenging responsibility and opportunities.

The spokesmen for religion—by virtue of the Gospel which is their text—are ambassadors of the Good Neighbor ideal. I doubt if there was ever a time so much as today when the voice of religion needed to be heard preaching that doctrine—a doctrine which can unify men and nations now, in so many places, so sorely divided.

Will you please convey my greetings to the Bishops in attendance at this significant gathering.[2]

Very sincerely yours,

[PPF 3876:CT]   •

[1] The Quadrilateral of 1886 was a statement of four basic propositions for reuniting the Christian church. The fiftieth anniversary of this Quadrilateral was to be celebrated at Chicago, Oct. 12–19, 1936, by a Pan-American conference of the Anglican and Episcopal clergy, and Bishop Stewart had written to Roosevelt on June 24, 1936, to request a "word of greeting" from him to the conference, "not only because you are our most eminent layman in the Episcopal Church, but also because as President of the United States you have yourself done so much to hold the Western Hemisphere together" (PPF 3876).

[2] This letter (drafted by Stanley High) was read to the conference on Oct. 15, 1936.

Roosevelt to Stephen T. Early, Assistant Secretary to the President

Washington, September 14, 1936

Memo for S.T.E.: I want to use this in the Press Conference this week if I can. Will you speak to me about it?

[OF 184:T]

[*Enclosure*] Possible Declaration or Press Statement

For consideration September 19 to 21, on the eve of the meeting of the Assembly of the League of Nations.

Statesmen of many of the nations of the world are coming together in Geneva today to consider many of the important issues in international life. Their discussions will cover the general field of international relations, the problems of economic reconstruction, and very possibly the political questions underlying the vexed question of armaments. While this government is not participating in these discussions, it is following them with keen interest and an eager hope that the statesmen engaged in them may find ways of contributing to world peace and of reversing the present dangerous currents which this country rightly regards with deep apprehension.

For its part, this Government stands ever ready to participate in any effort which promises to contribute towards either a reduction of the armaments which now threaten world peace, or the removal of the economic barriers which stifle world trade.[1]

[OF 184:T]

[1] No use was made of the proposed statement.

Press Conference, Executive Offices of the White House, September 15, 1936, 4:15 P.M.

[*Excerpt*] Q: Can you tell us anything about your campaign plans for next month?

The President: Well, I can tell you as far as we have gone, and it is wholly negative. I had, quite frankly, in the last month been thinking about a trip to the Coast and I had gone so far as to get timetables out and see how many days and nights it would take. But I don't know, frankly, whether I will be able to go to the Coast or not. I want to, if I can, but I am not sure whether it will be advisable for me to be so far away from first base for four days. Now, don't say there is an European situation—a war scare—in this but the fact remains—you had better use this as background—the fact does remain that I ought not to be, at the present time, if it is a question of leaving tomorrow or next week, I probably ought not to be four days away from Washington. How things will shape up by the first of October, I don't know. I have an awful lot of things here. And, in the second place, on the general world situation, I don't know how it is going to be around the first of October. The trip was planned and may still be carried out but I have deferred a decision until I see how things are the first part of October.

Q: Assuming you do not go to the Coast?

The President: I haven't got to the next step . . .

Q: Mr. President, have you any plans to visit Rio de Janeiro before—

The President: No. Fred, the wish on your part is father to the thought. No. I will tell you what I probably will do and that is after the 3rd of November I am going to try to get on a boat somewhere and take ten days to two weeks' holiday. But that again depends on the general world situation.

Q: Either way?

The President: Any way.

Q: Would that be down to the South American conference?

The President: No; probably the Bahamas. It may be that fishing ground we haven't gone to yet.

Q: Off the coast of Mexico?

The President: Fred[1] and I haven't caught tarpon yet.

[President's Press Conferences:T]

[1] Fred Storm of the United Press.

R. Walton Moore, Assistant Secretary of State, to Roosevelt

Washington, September 15, 1936

Dear Mr. President: A few minutes after I sent you this morning the letter in which Dr. Dodd indicates that there may be European propaganda against you,[1] there came into my office Constantine Brown,[2] who is just back from Europe, where he has been writing letters to the American newspapers for the McClure Syndicate, and he told me an amazing story which he had from Richard Waldorf, President of that Syndicate, the story being in substance as follows:

London financiers, during your Administration, have invested about $3,000,000,000 here, mainly in the stock of the power companies, the insurance companies and the chain store companies. The investors have become apprehensive and are now exerting all the influence they can command to accomplish your defeat. Lord Beaverbrook and Hearst are identified with this effort. They are an important factor of an American group composed of about seventy-five men, who largely control national advertising, and pressure is being brought to bear on newspapers that cannot exist without such advertising. Beaverbrook has recently sold, or is under contract to sell to Hearst, an enormous quantity of Canadian print paper, and has taken in payment stock in the Hearst companies. The propagandists not only manage to bring to bear pressure on newspapers, but on the insurance companies and chain stores and the power companies. The propaganda plan goes to the extent of making its agents the clerks in chain stores.

Brown, who is a very alert and fair-minded man, has not invented this story, but gives it to me as he has it from Waldorf, and I believe I should pass it on to you, particularly in view of the fact that you are to see important insurance men today. I have not intimated to Brown that you might like to see him, but possibly you may wish to do so. He is not only full of fear about the supposed propagandist scheme that is said to have its origin in London, but he would be able to tell you of very interesting conversations with Blum and other European statesmen, with reference not only to conditions on the other side, but their view of conditions here.

Yours very sincerely,

R. Walton Moore

[PSF:Moore:TS]

---

[1] Aug. 31, 1936, above.

[2] Brown, a Washington journalist, had been educated in Germany and had had a long journalistic career in London. He was co-author with Drew Pearson of *The American Diplomatic Game* (New York: Doubleday, 1935).

Roosevelt to Fred J. Freestone, Chairman, National Seaway Council, Washington

[Washington] September 16, 1936

My dear Mr. Freestone: I have received your letter of this date in which you advise that the National Seaway Council gives unqualified and active support to the St. Lawrence Seaway Project.[1] Your statement that "the peace of the world will ultimately be determined by the capacity of great neighboring Nations to cooperate in the constructive development and use of their frontiers," is particularly timely and I am glad indeed that you give it such emphasis.

I subscribe wholeheartedly to this declaration of the Seaway Council and to all other particulars set forth in your letter. It is my very earnest hope that negotiations for the St. Lawrence Project may be carried forward within the coming year to a successful and final conclusion.

Very sincerely yours,

[PPF 3898:CT]

[1] The letter recapitulated the history of the seaway proposal and the arguments for its undertaking. This, with a letter from Alfred Landon, Republican candidate for the Presidency, also endorsing the project, and with Roosevelt's reply, were published in a folder issued by the Seaway Association; a copy is with the correspondence (PPF 3898).

Claude G. Bowers, Ambassador to Spain, to Roosevelt

San Jean de Luz, September 16, 1936

Dear Mr. President: I am inclosing a copy of my despatch to the Department on Fernando de los Rios whose name, I understand, has been submitted as a possible Ambassador. He is one of the finest figures in Spain, a personal friend of mine, and, what is more significant, a great admirer of yours. The press reports are still packed with propoganda,[1] and the international phase in the Spanish situation continues to stand out like a flaming torch in the Diplomatic Corps. We are wise in standing aloof from these many meetings, most of which unquestionably are called and engineered under the guidance of the facist states. Last night I listened to the daily "news" announcements from the rebel station brazenly maintained in Portugal, and I heard the lowest propoganda I have heard yet—the ridiculous story that the "reds" in leaving San Sebastian, had forced "the daughters of leading families to go with them." Portugal has done everything but declare war. The Italian Ambassador is working to bring about international complications. The whole thing would be ghastly but for the absurdity of the scenes at these meetings. Now that Sir George Grahame has gone, there is not a man in the corps who in political matters is not a mere child, and it is pitiful to observe how these very ordinary men sit with mouths open drinking in, as from an inspired source, the crude propoganda of the Italian. When one reflects on the possibility that European Governments may determine policies on this very elemental conflict on the advice of such men one wonders how old Europe can escape war, pestilence and famine long. By staying out we are protecting our neutrality in the best manner.

The neutrality of France is peculiar. The rebel forces have propoganda headquarters here, with our friend Yrujo[2] in charge, and everyone knows it. Just how France's consent to this can be justified is a puzzle. I am absolutely positive that for some time France has refused to permit war material to enter Spain. But there is abundant evidence that Italy is sending material all the time. The Big Bad Man with a Gun and an Inflated Chest and Loud Voice appears to be the master of Europe in all these controversies from Abyssinia to Spain. England which began with decided pro-rebel learnings finally has shifted, no doubt on the conviction that Italy's support has been purchased by the rebels with the promise of land and war advantages in the Medeterranian—all aimed at depriving England of her old mastery of that sea. Meanwhile, Blum's shift has aroused the ire of the masses behind the Frente Popular in France and there are grave possibilities of serious trouble in France if the war goes against the Government here.

I have not heard from Farley for weeks and have only the papers to go on regarding the campaign at home.

Sincerely,

Claude G. Bowers

[PSF:Spain:TS]

---

[1] Misspellings, here and below, as in the original.

[2] Luis Martínez Yrujo, former counselor of the Spanish Embassy in Washington. His resignation was forced by the Azaña government because of his pro-Franco activities.

[*Enclosure*] Claude G. Bowers to Cordell Hull, Secretary of State

Saint-Jean-de-Luz, France, Sept. 15, 1936

Sir: I have the honor to report that in my opinion the proposed naming of Fernando de los Rios as Ambassador to the United States is complimentary to us, since he is, perhaps, one of the half dozen most cultured men in Spain. He is the nephew and protégé of his famous uncle, Francisco Giner de los Rios who began the fight, single-handed, forty years ago, for the establishment of training schools for teachers and public high schools. For this crime he served more than once in jail, but at the time of his death his fine service was generally recognized, and he was accorded honors in the Spanish Pantheon under the monarchy. He was no doubt one of the two or three greatest educators in Spanish history.

The nephew was for some years a professor in the University of Granada, and for years since, in the University of Madrid. As such, he has delivered series of lectures in various leading American Universities— Columbia, the University of Chicago, the University of California, etc.

Having actually lived for weeks in all sections of the United States, he has a more intelligent conception of America than any other Spaniard, and a broader insight into our life than any European statesman of whom I can think. I have been in the library of his modest scholar's apartment, and I was astonished at the number of American books, all well worn with use, dealing with history, politics, economics and sociology. Incidentally I found two of my own.

Like his uncle, profoundly interested in the lifting of the status of the masses, he has been concerned with politics since youth. He is a republican, an evolutionary socialist, which means that he is as moderate as was Ramsay MacDonald in the days of the latter's leadership of the Labor Party in England.

He was one of the founders of the Republic and one of the few signers of the Pact of San Sebastian, which launched the revolution of 1931. He was, among these, the one man who recognized at a glance the political genius of Azana, and it was he who brought Azana into public life, taking him with him to San Sebastian for the signing of the Pact and later taking him into the Ministry of the Interior for the formation of the provisional government.

Fernando de los Rios was first made Minister of Justice, and then of Public Instruction, and then he became Minister of State, in which capacity I had dealings with him of an official character. He was Minister at the time of our trouble with the Americans of Palma, and he was most active and sympathetic in helping to solve the problem.

In that capacity, and in social intercourse (for I suppose he is among Spanish statesmen my best friend, unless it is Madariaga), I found him amazingly familiar with our political history and philosophy, and most sympathetic toward both.

It was he who engineered the recognition of Russia. I asked him at the time why the same governmental regime that had refused recognition in the first two and a half years of the Republic had finally reversed itself. He replied that at first the Russians thought the conditions ripe in Spain for the spreading of Communism here, and that they were most active in trying to bring this about. He said that the Spanish temperament is incompatible with Communism, and that so long as the Russians were seeking to prevent the establishment of a democratic republic they had to be considered as enemies. "Now," he continued, "they recognize their failure, and we no longer look upon them as dangerous. We need their trade and so we have reversed our original policy."

I have found him from the beginning intensely interested in the policies of Roosevelt, about which he has talked with me many times. He once said to me that he thought Roosevelt is making the most significant experiment being made anywhere in the world—that of trying to make democracy so serve the mass of the people as to destroy the appeal of both communism and fascism. He said then that if Roosevelt succeeds, his work will have a tremendous effect on Europe. He reads everything he can find on the Rooseveltian policies.

Personally he is a man of great charm, a thorough gentleman, so recognized by his political enemies of the Right. These regret his radicalism but such is their admiration for the motives and intellect of the man that they are able to set aside their political prejudices in passing upon his character as a man. This is very rare in Spain.

To illustrate: During the last Cortes, dominated entirely by the extreme Right, when party feeling was running hot, de los Rios spoke in the Cortes on the general subject of education in Spain, and not only was he heard for more than an hour with the closest attention, but at the conclusion he was given an ovation, and the common comment was that few such speeches had been heard in the Cortes in many years. He is an orator of the thoughtful sort. He has art in expression, but the thought predominates. He may best be described perhaps as the greatest of the academic orators of Spain.

I doubt if Spain has sent to the United States in our time any envoy so intelligently familiar with our institutions and purposes or one so sympathetic toward our people as a whole.

Respectfully yours,

Claude G. Bowers

[PSF:Spain:CT]

Roosevelt to Emil Ludwig, Paris

[Washington] September 17, 1936

My dear Mr. Ludwig: I am writing to thank you for your note of August 15th, and the memorandum therewith, which presents in such a vivid and interesting fashion your view of the European situation.[1] I shall often find myself reflecting on the thoughts and impressions of a great historian who has the opportunity of observing at close range the manner in which history is now being made.[2]

With very deep appreciation of your kindness in complying with my request, I am, Yours very sincerely,

[PPF 3884:CT]

[1] Above.
[2] Drafted by Assistant Secretary of State Moore.

Cordell Hull, Secretary of State, to Roosevelt

Washington, September 18, 1936

Personal and Confidential

My dear Mr. President: The attached memorandum deals with an important question which I am informed has already been brought to your attention by the Navy Department and on which there is a difference of opinion between that Department and the Department of State.[1]

Under the recently enacted neutrality statute, this Department is required to issue licenses for the export of arms unless the issuance thereof "would be in violation of this act or any law of the United States or a treaty to which the United States is a party in which cases such licenses shall not be issued."

The Douglas Aircraft Company, said to be the largest manufacturer of aircraft in this country, has applied for a license to export one of its commercial flying boats. The Navy Department, in interposing objection to the issuances of the desired license, relies upon the Espionage Act of June 15, 1917, which makes it a criminal offense to deliver or transmit to a foreign nation any instrument, appliance, et cetera, "with intent or reason to believe it is to be used to the injury of the United States or to the advantage of a foreign nation." The Department of State thinks that the restriction thus provided applies only to articles involving "military secrets of interest to the National Defense" and the War Department concurs in this view, but the view of the Navy Department is to the contrary and it considers that the license asked for should not be issued. So far as I can understand the case, the exportation of a Douglas airplane of the type in question to a foreign nation would not reveal any military secret.

Should the Navy Department hold to its present attitude this Department, as you can easily perceive, will be placed in a difficult position. Furthermore, I should perhaps point out that, if the Douglas Aircraft Company and other aircraft manufacturers in this country are refused licenses for the exportation of planes which do not involve military secrets, they will probably construct and operate plants elsewhere and, if not, foreign purchasers will obtain aircraft from foreign manufacturers.

The Navy Department has been informed that I am communicating with you.

Faithfully yours,

Cordell Hull

[OF 1561:TS]

[1] The memorandum was from Joseph C. Green, chief of the Office of Arms and Munitions Control in the State Department, to Hull, Sept. 17, 1936 (OF 1561). Green said that the State and War departments agreed that articles for export relating to the national defense would come under the export ban only if they were manufactured or developed exclusively for the use of the War and Navy departments, or if either had used or continued to use these articles, or had contracted to procure them. The Navy view was that even these exceptions violated the Espionage Act of 1917. The point at issue was the proposal of the Douglas Aircraft Company to sell some of its DF Flying Boats to Russia and Japan, the company maintaining that these were not essential to national defense. Green said the State Department could find no legal justification in the Espionage Act for refusing to issue export licenses to Douglas. See Roosevelt to Swanson, Sept. 22, 1936, below.

Roosevelt to General Jorge Ubico, President of the Republic of Guatemala, Guatemala City

[Washington] September 19, 1936

My dear Mr. President: Your letter of September 7 last offering me your felicitations upon the address I delivered at Chautauqua last month has afforded me very real satisfaction.[1] It is indeed heartening for me to know that the objectives I sought to point out, and the policy I proposed in order to further the attainment of world peace, have met with so generous an expression of support as that which Your Excellency has conveyed to me.

Your letter has done much to strengthen my conviction that the Presidents and the peoples of the American Republics are afforded a signal opportunity at the approaching Conference for the Maintenance of Peace to be held on December 1 next at Buenos Aires to advance the cause of permanent peace on this continent, and thus assist by their example, in the attainment of the conditions which engender peace throughout the rest of the world.

Let me thank you as well for the gratifying expressions, which you were good enough to include in your letter, concerning the policy of my Government in its dealings with its sister republics of this continent.[2]

With the assurances of my highest and most distinguished consideration, believe me, my dear Mr. President,

Yours most sincerely,

[OF 439:CT]

[1] Ubico said the speech constituted "a Magna Charta for the entire world at large and in a special manner for the American Community" (OF 439).
[2] Drafted by Sumner Welles.

William E. Dodd, Ambassador to Germany, to Roosevelt

[Berlin] Sept. 21, 1936

Dear Mr. President: In spite of the newspaper misrepresentations of what you hoped might be done for world peace, I indirectly raised the question with the most sympathetic representative of the Government in the Foreign Office here—sympathetic as to possible peace movements.[1] He said Germany would participate in any conference in which the

United States played a role. He even said Hitler would agree to abandon air attacks in next war, if it came, provided other greater nations did the same. You know Hitler frequently declares himself against war. But the Secretary did not think Hitler would attend any conference outside of Germany. He did think he would yield to presence of Russian delegates in case the United States participated.

However, there are grave doubts. My reason for entertaining them will be found in the copy of a memorandum I am sending Secretary Hull in to-day's pouch.[2] I am also enclosing a clipping or two from this morning's German papers.[3] One of them is headed: The Greatest Army Maneuvre since 1914 which seems to me a half-acknowledgement here of Germany's beginning the Great War. If this were the first thing of the sort I would not enclose it. Since March 1935 representatives of all countries have been urged to attend meetings of the Partei where great military performances were made the major affairs. I was in Meiningen ten days ago and the hotel manager told us of the great aircraft attacks and defenses scheduled a week later. The enclosed clipping shows in some respects what was done.

Nothing is clearer here than the general Government belief that the Balkan zone must be subordinated to Hitler. Former Foreign Office people, who really meant to be co-operative in peace movements, are no longer in their positions; or, if so, they have changed their attitudes like von Neurath who is now maneuvering in that area to extend German power over Austria, Czechoslovakia, Hungary and Roumania. Goebbels in Venice two weeks ago is now in Greece and Göring is head of the greatest war aircraft in the world.

Not without interest has been the assistance of our great corporations: Du Ponts, Standard Oil, U.S. Steel and others, even though they can not take earnings out of the country. Many war flying machines have been sold to Göring's organization through Krupps. Our military attaché sent a cable last December showing that people in Ohio, who had agreed not to send 100 aircraft to Italy, had sent a hundred or more to Mussolini through Krupps—an allied company here. You see, therefore, some of the reasons for my doubts. Hope I am wrong.

Yours sincerely,

William E. Dodd

[*Notation*:A] The police of Berlin are being drilled same as other soldiers, also S.S. and S.A. men, about three million.

[PSF:Germany:AS]

---

[1] Hans Dieckhoff, Secretary of State of the Foreign Office. Dodd describes his interview in his *Diary*, pp. 351–353.

[2] Not present.

[3] Not present.

Roosevelt to Claude A. Swanson, Secretary of the Navy

Washington, September 22, 1936

Confidential

Memorandum for the Secretary of the Navy: On the face of things the State Department seems to be right in its interpretation of the Espionage Act of June 15, 1917. In relation to the case in point, please let me know specifically whether "military secrets of interest to the national defense" are involved.[1]

F.D.R.

[OF 1561:CT]

---

[1] This memorandum refers to Hull to Roosevelt, Sept. 18, 1936, above. The Navy Department refused to yield to the State Department view and Hull then asked that Roosevelt either decide the question or refer it to the Attorney General (Hull to Roosevelt, Oct. 19, 1936, OF 1561). See Roosevelt to Cummings, Oct. 20, 1936, below.

Claude G. Bowers, Ambassador to Spain, to Cordell Hull, Secretary of State

Saint-Jean-de-Luz, France, September 23, 1936

Personal

Dear Mr. Secretary: It occurs to me that some personal observations on the Spanish situation in regard to the international phase may not be unwelcome. I notice that del Vayo, Spanish Minister of State, now in Geneva, may demand that the League of Nations take action to stop the supplying of the rebels with arms, ammunition, and men by Portugal, especially, and Italy and Germany. It is my deliberate opinion that all the decencies are on the side of this demand.

For some weeks now there has been nothing to indicate that France is not rigidly enforcing its neutrality. There is every indication that the fascist Powers are violating their pledge and furnishing arms, ammunition and men. More and more the controversy here is taking the form of an international fascist conspiracy to destroy the democracy of Spain under the pretext of saving it from communism. This is being carried forward quite openly and with true fascist arrogance.

I am informed by Knickerbocker of the Hearst press, John Whittaker of the New York *Herald-Tribune,* and Floyd Gibbons, who recently returned from a survey of the miltary situation in the south, that when in Seville they saw night after night in a cafe, German aviators who are accompanied by German mechanicians. They admit they are not giving this important news to the public, and explain their silence by saying that the publication of this fact would result in their expulsion, if not in their arrest. They tell me that the rebels are using German bombing planes and Italian pursuit planes.

The offence of Portugal is especially glaring. Night after night I listen in on the radio, and the rebel radio station in Lisbon nightly pours the most poisonous propaganda into Spain and Europe. It is more unscrupulous in its lying than the Spanish rebel station in Seville. Thus, when the Basques, who are moderates, not socialistic and certainly not communistic, acted on orders from Madrid and removed the prisoners in San Sebastian to Bilbao to save them from a possible massacre by the anarchistic minority, the Lisbon radio announced that "the reds when they left San Sebastian forced the young women of the best families to go with them." The implication is both false and infamous. Naturally, in Portugal which is under the iron hand of a dictator, this station could not operate thus without the consent, if not under the orders of the military dictator there.

In this connection the correspondent of the London *News-Observer* who has been in Lisbon says that the principal hotel there is the headquarters of the rebel junta, and in charge of a brother of General Franco and Gil Robles. These assume the airs of properly accredited diplomats to Portugal. They not only give out information to the press, but they issue passports and visas which are recognized by the Portuguese officials on the frontier. Meanwhile, Albernoz,[1] the Spanish Ambassador there, former Minister of State, an Azana Republican, and the greatest living authority on mediaeval Spain, is utterly ignored, is almost a prisoner in his house and surrounded by spies. I cite this as an illustration of how all the established rules governing the relations of nations are ignored. Under normal conditions the action of Portugal would be tantamount to a declaration of war.[2]

On top of all this the Portuguese dictator[3] has announced the formation of a new army legion purporting to be for the purpose of protecting the country against communism. It is my impression, shared by many others, that this legion is organized for the service of the Spanish rebels if conditions require later on.

The radio announcements from Milan and Rome are quite as much rebel propaganda as those from Portugal. In brief, the fascist States are pooling their interest and making common cause against the constitutional Government of Spain, and the democratic States are rigidly observing their neutrality. This means that the rebels are getting arms, ammunition, etc., and that the legal Government is being refused this material.

In the early stages of the struggle here there is no doubt that France furnished or sold planes and war material to the Government. But more than three weeks ago it cut off these supplies, and I have not heard of a single instance since of such material crossing the border. This week two cars filled with arms and ammunition, and headed for Spain, were stopped by French soldiers, and the material confiscated. It seems, therefore, that the present attitude of France is entirely in the interest of the rebels.

Another illustration of the strange change in French attitude: Here in Saint-Jean-de-Luz[4] the rebels quite openly maintain headquarters in the Villa Nacha Enea on the Avenue Larrequy, where rebel agents, including Irujo, erstwhile Counselor in Washington, are in charge, receiving the press and issuing passes into Spain. This is winked at by neutral France. In the early stages of the war the French Government forced Gil Robles to leave Biarritz, on the ground that he was using French territory as a propaganda base.

I have been astonished by the shift of Herbette, the French Ambassador.[5] He is a socialist, a member of Blum's party, and was formerly Ambassador to Russia. He has been rather open in his partiality for the Lefts for three years, and in the first weeks of the war, he was so openly hostile to the rebels that he became the pet aversion of the rebel sympathizers. He gave out a statement to the press denouncing the rebel shelling of San Sebastian. He was denounced in the rebel papers, and people here boasted that when the rebels took Fuenterrabia they would destroy his house there. Two weeks ago he called on me and I was amazed to hear his cynical comments about the Government and his not unfriendly attitude toward the rebels.

There can be no doubt that the French Government is not a little alarmed by the situation in France. It seems possible if not probable that it fears that a triumph for the Government here will encourage the extreme elements of the Popular Front in France, which is far more numerous than the same element of the Popular Front in Spain, to attempt to take over the Government in France. This fear is predicated on the theory, not without foundation, that the rebellion has weakened the authority of democrats like Azana and increased the power of the extremists. The shift in the French Government is causing uneasiness and unrest among the French Popular Front and anything may happen here in the event that the fortunes of war go against the Spanish Government.

One hears here among the members of the Spanish nobility and aristocracy that Rosenberg,[6] the new Russian Ambassador in Madrid, is running things in the capital. I know of nothing tangible with which to sustain this theory. Rosenberg received much popular acclaim when he presented his credentials in Madrid but this is natural and to some extent any diplomat presenting credentials in the time of trouble for the Government would get acclaim. But unless Rosenberg lied to Wendelin, his influence is being thrown against the anarchists and syndicalists who have been breaking into houses and indulging in private executions. The communists in fact have been under rigid discipline and they have been supporting the constituted authorities. It was the communist paper that ran editorials demanding the death penalty for looting, and breaking into houses. This week it ran an editorial leader denouncing all who support these criminal practices as traitors.

But should the coalition of the fascist States against the legal Government of Spain become more flagrant and open, it is not beyond the possibilities that Russia may be drawn into the fight, and this would open the way for the feared European war to determine whether Europe shall be all fascist or all communist.

Meanwhile, the British, who in the beginning were not very considerate of the Government and its troubles, have moved toward an honest neutrality. In the first stages the Embassy in Madrid gave refuge to Spanish rebels on the ground that these were remotely connected with the British royal family. But these have since been expelled and orders issued from London that no more be admitted. This has led to some ugly comments against the British by the refugees in these parts. When Ogilvie Forbes, the British Chargé d'Affaires in Madrid, ordered some of these Spaniards out of the Embassy, the wife of Merry del Val, former monarchist Ambassador in London, made the welkin ring, I am told, at social functions, declaring Forbes' action "infamous" and saying that "when we come in we will take care of him." For some time Merry del Val was here acting as a sort of diplomat, and seeing some of the diplomats here, but I did not see him. He has now gone to London where he is carrying on.

No one has questioned the absolute neutrality of the United States. It is appreciated in Madrid and the rebels do not complain. We are about the only Mission that has not given refuge to the rebels. Those of South America have been especially obnoxious in this respect, and I ascribe it to the fact that the average South American is very partial to the nobility and aristocracy. Mexico has been more favorable to the Government. Our non-participation in the all-too-many conferences of the Diplomatic Corps here, for reasons I gave the Department, has without exception proven wise.[7] This meddling has met with rebuffs and the consequent humiliation of the Corps. As a result of these rebuffs and humiliations, the diplomats here are now less prone to meddle without previous instructions from their home Governments.

I think we should continue our present policy without deviation. This is a serious European quarrel in which we have no proper part.

With regards and best wishes, Sincerely yours,

Claude G. Bowers

P.S. If you think the President would be interested, pass this on to him.

[PSF:Spain:T:Copy]

[1] Sánchez Albornozá y Mendiuña.
[2] Portugal's unneutral attitude is described in dispatches from Lisbon in *Foreign Relations, 1936*, II, 456–457, 485–487. Portugal severed diplomatic relations with the Azaña government on Oct. 23, 1936.
[3] Antonio de Oliveira Salazar.
[4] The diplomatic corps, in summer residence at San Sebastián, found itself beleaguered there and moved across the border to this French seaside resort.
[5] Jean Herbette.
[6] Marcel Rosenberg.
[7] See Bowers, *My Mission to Spain*, pp. 291ff, and his telegrams to Hull in *Foreign Relations, 1936*, II, 488, 497, 509, 511.

Press Conference, Hyde Park, September 25, 1936, 12:05 P.M.

[*Excerpt*] Q: Is that situation over there as intense as it was a few months ago?

The President: I can only answer that off the record. In other words, I can't give it to you as anything but off the record and strictly off the record. About this French franc situation: Everybody is working on it. You can't even let that cat out of the bag. It will probably break from the other side because our French friends are apt to talk out loud before our other friends do. But they have to break the story over there. It is for the advantage of the situation to have it come from France instead of from London or Washington.[1]

Q: It came out this morning.

Q: In the paper this morning there was a story about the franc and someone said that large gold shipments to this country had been made.[2] The story out of Washington said it would not do any harm but the story from Paris dealt quite lengthily with the franc situation.

The President: It only dealt with it to the extent that they let the cat out of the bag that they are awfully worried.

Mr. McIntyre: Can't we express it that it is not as tense as it was a month ago?

The President: That does not sound right.

Mr. McIntyre: I mean off the record.

The President: That is off the record. Also, again off the record, all these things involve something. If France does something, it involves going to the French Parliament, and you know what that means at this particular stage of the game. The French Parliament always riles up and if the Blum Government stands or falls, we have to be careful not to say things over here that backlash over there. I have been sitting up nights—I sat up last night until about one o'clock (indicating telegrams piled on his desk), so it has not been a complete holiday.

Q: Is the situation out in the Far East giving you any cause for concern?

The President: There again I can't talk except off the record. Just for your information, there has been a rather interesting development the past month in the Far East. It was about two months ago that the Cantonese revolt blew up and the Cantonese armies disbanded. Since then, for the first time in ten years, there has been a definite rapprochement between the Cantonese and the Nanking group. In other words, the tendency has been for them to unite. And further west, in the provinces out there, they are thinking more in terms of an integrated China and they are working with the Kai-Shek Government. Of course those poor devils haven't anything to fight Japan with but it looks as if they were gradually uniting with the idea of saying to Japan, "Are you going to stop and where are you going to stop? If you don't stop, we will have to fight to protect our country." Meanwhile, the Japs have gone up the Yangtze six hundred miles with ships and troops. They have

440

practically got Shanghai and the thing looks as if it might break, but not necessarily this week or next week. It is heading up toward resistance on the part of China but you can't tell when that will happen.

Q: The Japanese seem to be taking ports where the revenues come in.

The President: It is one of those situations, Fred,[3] where you can't tell from one day to the next.

Q: Entirely off the record, because I could not quite understand the dispatch we had this morning from Paris on the franc: Our man wrote the story in a manner which would indicate that the French Government could devalue the franc without calling Parliament. Would that be an assumption of temporal powers?

The President: As far as I know, they would use the powers given them by the last Parliament which, as I understand it, included the right to embargo shipment of gold, but they would have to go to Parliament for the right to take the franc off the fixed gold point, the point at which it is fixed at the present time by law.

Q: There would have to be an affirmation by Parliament?

The President: Yes, before they could change the gold point of the franc, the gold content of the franc. But they could take the first step, such as the embargo, without calling Parliament. Then, of course, there are so many different figures. There is not only the rate between the dollar and the franc and the dollar and the pound but there is what they call the "cross-rate," being a triangular thing and only an Einstein can understand it. You cannot just say that the dollar will have this relationship to the franc and that relationship to the pound unless you know the relationship of the pound to the franc, what that is going to be, otherwise you might be out of luck.

Of course, absolutely off the record, this is more or less in line with what happened in London in 1933. It is a very interesting thing to go back and read those papers because what they wanted us to do—the gold bloc that the French Government was playing with—was to es-tablish a fixed rate, the pound with the gold bloc and the gold bloc with each other.

The pound was then about 4.10 or 4.20. They wanted us to come in and we discovered subsequently that the British had perfectly defi-nitely in mind that they wanted the pound at 3.50 and the effect, if I had gone ahead with that agreement proposed in London, would have been, through that cross-rate I am talking about to get a 3.50 pound which, of course, would have absolutely wrecked our level of values in this country and we would have had to go in on a 40-cent dollar or something like that and we would have been bound, if we had gone in.

Q: You gave us a pretty good press conference at Campobello.[4]

The President: So what we are doing, we feel that the British price level and our price level around approximately $5 is pretty good. The British, of course, always haggle and say, "Let us go back to $4.86," but around $5, approximately, is a pretty—gives a pretty good natural level of prices, both in Great Britain and here.

If we can bring the French into that without destroying that British-American level, we will have accomplished something that means un-official stabilization with the right, of course, to every country at any time, if their domestic level is affected adversely, to change on twenty-four hours notice. In other words, we are not tied.

Q: A flexible managed stabilization?

The President: A flexible managed stabilization and subject to renegotiation and change on the part of any one country on twenty-four hours' notice.

You see, the British Government and our Government are keeping our rate of exchange pretty even and if the French can work out something along the same line, you can get three nations working toward the same objectives and cooperation without anything that ties the hands of any individual nation in the case of a national emergency.

Q: Still off the record, the reports from France indicate that there might be some violent opposition to a plan along those lines.

The President: They hope not, because, in the present condition of all France, it is awfully ticklish. In fact, the easiest way of telling you what happened is by comparison. Suppose Brother Hoover had remained President until April, 1936, carrying on his policies of the previous four years; in other words, hadn't taken any steps towards social security or helping the farmer or cutting out child labor and shortening hours, etc., and old-age pension. Had that been the case, we would have been a country this past April very similar to the country that Blum found when he came in. The French for 25 or 30 years had never done a thing in the way of social legislation. Blum started in and he jumped right into the middle of a strike the first week he was in office. Well, they demanded a 48-hour week or something like that and he put through legislation that did provide for shorter hours in industry. Then they demanded a one-week's holiday with pay and then they demanded, immediately, a commission to set up an old-age pension plan. Well, all of those Blum got through but, query, was it too late?

In other words, suppose I had come in in April, 1936, and the country had been going on for three years without any of the type of legislation we had, would it have been too late last April for me to go in and start all of those new things?

And I think if Blum—of course I cannot say anything to even intimate that I am in favor of Blum—but if Blum can be kept there for a while he may be able to do certain things that almost every nation in the world has done. We did not start until three years ago. The question is, "Has he the time before there is a serious outbreak?" Of course they are terribly upset in France. The thing that may hold them together is the fact that if the Spanish rebellion goes through, they will be surrounded by Germany, Italy and Spain and that may solidify the French and prevent an outbreak.

Q: So far as the devaluation of the franc is concerned, their hands are being virtually forced. They haven't any alternative.

The President: Yes. Every two or three weeks there is another drive and every time there is a drive against the franc we get another 20 or 30 or 40 millions of gold from them. Of course there is an end to it. They have to stop some day. They were up to about 4 billions, as I remember it, about $4\frac{1}{2}$ billions of gold and I think they are down now to close to one billion. They ought not to go much lower, and we would not mind letting them have some gold. (Laughter)

[President's Press Conferences]

[1] Negotiations on a tripartite stabilization agreement had been going on for several months in greatest secrecy (*Foreign Relations*, I, 535–565).

[2] The New York *Times,* Sept. 25, 1936, p. 1, carried an article headed, "France Now Ready to Devalue Franc; Britain and U.S. Aid." First official notice of French devaluation was made by Morgenthau on September 25 (*Public Papers*, V, 376–378).

[3] J. Fred Storm of the United Press.

[4] On June 30, 1933. No transcript of this press conference has been found in the Roosevelt papers but it was reported in the New York *Times,* July 1, 1933, p. 1.

Roosevelt to Robert Mayer, President, American Cotton Shippers Association, Dallas, Texas

Hyde Park, New York, September 25, 1936

My dear Mr. Mayer: I am indeed grateful to you for your telegram of September twenty-first and have considered very carefully all that you said concerning our commercial relationship with Russia. I am delighted to have the benefit of your observations particularly so since they represent the point of view of our cotton merchants.[1]

Very sincerely yours,

[OF 220-A:CT]

[1] Mayer said his association approved the Administration's policy of resuming trade relations with the Soviet Union and rejected Hearst's attacks on it. "It is most astonishing that Mr. Hearst who is using all his influence to ruin our internat'l trade by prohibiting imports of any commodity and who constantly is objecting to any cooperation with other countries in solving world problems should be so anxious to have us interfere in the internal affairs of other countries thru a policy of non-recognition of an established govt. because we do not agree with its policies or operations" (OF 220-A).

Cordell Hull, Secretary of State, to Roosevelt

Washington, September 26, 1936

My dear Mr. President: During the present conflict in Spain every effort has been made to evacuate from that country all Americans who have been willing to leave. In taking this action we have been actuated not only by a desire to ensure the safety of our nationals but have wished also by removing all American nationals to reduce insofar as possible the likelihood of incidents which might involve us in the struggle. In carrying out this policy we have found it necessary in view of the reluctance of many Americans to avail themselves of the facilities provided for their evacuation to announce on several occasions that those Americans who remained in Spain did so on their own responsibility and at their own risk.

In inquiring, however, into the reasons which induced Americans to remain in Spain in spite of such warnings it was found that a few of these Americans though anxious to comply with the wishes of their government were unable to do so because they were without funds to leave the country or to support themselves outside of Spain. It did not seem to us possible to abandon such Americans to the perils of civil war merely because of their financial disabilities. We, therefore, took up their cases with the American Red Cross which most generously undertook to supply funds for their evacuation from Spain and repatriation to the United States even though the use of the society's funds for such purposes is entirely contrary to its established policy. The Red Cross is, however, unable to supply funds for the maintenance of these persons in this country until such time as they may be able to find means of support.

The number of these cases cannot be stated definitely as new cases may come to light from time to time nor can the extent of their needs be stated exactly as the possibilities of their obtaining relief through private sources will in some cases probably be determinable only after their arrival in this country. In some cases it may be necessary only to provide transportation to their former homes, in other cases it may be necessary to provide for their support for some time. In any event it is not expected that their total number will greatly exceed thirty nor the necessary expenses amount to more than a few thousand dollars.

The provision of means for the relief of these people is now becoming a matter of some urgency as a few of them have already been evacuated and are now on their way to the United States, some to New York and some to gulf ports. It is feared that the regulations governing the relief organizations of the States and municipalities are such that these people, not having maintained their domicile in the United States, will be held ineligible for local relief. It is felt, therefore, that the Federal Government should make some provision for their relief in order that these American citizens who have returned to the United States at the wish of their Government may not find themselves upon their arrival in a situation which they may well consider even more precarious than that which they have been urged to leave. May I not, therefore, ask you, Mr. President, to take whatever steps may be within your power to have Federal funds made available in one way or another for at least the temporary relief of these people? The Department of State will, of course, be very glad to cooperate with any agency which you may designate to deal with this matter.[1]

Faithfully yours,

Cordell Hull

[OF 422-C:TS]

[1] Answered Oct. 6, 1936, below.

Henry Morgenthau, Jr., Secretary of the Treasury, to Roosevelt

Washington, September 29, 1936

My dear Mr. President: The following is an oral message from the Chancellor of the Exchequer which Mr. Mallet, Chargé d'Affaires of the British Embassy,[1] brought in to me today:

The Chancellor of the Exchequer fully shares the satisfaction felt by Mr. Morgenthau and also by the President and the Secretary of State at the conclusion of the recent discussions in regard to the French monetary measures.

An operation which might have caused a disastrous disturbance has been converted by the co-operation of the three Governments into an instrument for the initiation of a new international confidence.[2]

The Chancellor is delighted at this happy result and he trusts that the effort so fortunately directed will prove to be only the prelude to a better understanding and more friendly relations between the nations of the world.

Respectfully yours,

H. Morgenthau, Jr.

[OF 203:TS]

[1] V. A. L. Mallet, counsellor of embassy.

[2] This reference is to Russian efforts to sell 1,200,000 pound sterling at the best price it would bring in an attempt to undermine the Tripartite Agreement. The attempt was blocked when Morgenthau directed the New York Federal Reserve Bank to buy the offered sterling at the market price (Blum, *From the Morgenthau Diaries,* pp. 173–176).

R. Walton Moore, Assistant Secretary of State, to Roosevelt

[Washington] October 2, 1936

Dear Mr. President: As you may have occasion to make some further reference to the matter of foreign loans since the World War to which you alluded in your speech last night at Pittsburgh,[1] I am handing you two parts of the report of the hearing on the Resolution introduced by Senator Johnson of California in 1930, and have indicated on the covers of the volumes the pages where loans made through some of our international bankers are listed and the accruals to them in the way of commissions and otherwise. After the committee hearing Senator Johnson, who was much wrought up by the evidence of rascally methods used in some of the transactions, made an elaborate speech in the Senate discussing the whole business.[2] If you do say anything about the matter again, would it not be well for you to make a particular reference to Johnson, who, I take it for granted, favors your reelection and is said to be still the strongest man in California?[3] You will recall that the State Department from the beginning of the Harding Administration to the end of the Hoover Administration, whenever apprized by the bankers of their purpose to negotiate loans and float bonds here, made a practice of saying that they found no objection to what was proposed; that the attitude of the State Department, while not included in the advertisements, was widely known, and that it undoubtedly led thousands of small investors to put their money in securities, many of which have become worthless. The Department's practice was from time to time vehemently criticized by Senator Glass and perhaps others. It is, of course, conceivable that any talk on that point might stir the resentment of former Secretary Stimson, but I have no idea that he will vote for you under any circumstances. He is simply quiet.

Yours very sincerely,

[Moore Papers:CT]

[1] Printed in *Public Papers,* V, 401–408.

[2] Senator Hiram Johnson introduced S.R. 19, calling for an investigation by the Senate Finance Committee of the sale of foreign bonds and other securities in this country, on Dec. 9, 1931, not in 1930. The resolution was approved the next day, and hearings under Senator Reed Smoot were begun on Dec. 18, 1931 (*Cong. Rec.,* vol. 75, pp. 213–214, 271). The hearings extended until Feb. 10, 1932, and were published as *Hearings Before the Committee on Finance, U.S. Senate, 72nd Congress, First Session, Pursuant to S. Res. 19* (Washington, 1931–1932). On March 15, 1932, Johnson summed up the Committee's findings in the Senate (*Cong. Rec.,* vol. 75, pp. 6052–6062). The information thus made public was later used to gain support for Johnson's amendment to the Federal Securities Act of 1933 to establish a Foreign Bond Holders Corporation, and the Johnson Act of 1934, which forbade loans to nations in default on their obligations to the United States.

[3] Roosevelt did not again refer to foreign loans in his 1936 campaign speeches.

Press Conference, Executive Offices of the White House, October 6, 1936, 4:20 P.M.

[*Excerpt*] Q: Anything on the international currency situation?

The President: Only what you read in the papers. This is off the record—you had better ask the State Department whether they have anything from Switzerland about the reduction of quotas. I understand they did have something on Swiss quotas.[1]

Q: Secretary Morgenthau said he would recommend the continuing of the stabilization (fund) but would not want to comment on the power to continue to deflate the dollar. He said that was up to you.

The President: You are premature. Not right yet . . .

Q: On the international situation, could we do away with the power to devalue further until Great Britain went on a gold standard such as ours, within a bracket?

The President: That is a pretty hypothetical question, but I should say, offhand, that in order to retain our primary purpose, what has always been the primary purpose, which is to retain our domestic values, that it should be in the Government emergency powers to prevent the destruction of domestic values through unexpected action on the part of another nation or nations. I don't know whether—I think that is about as clear as it can be made. In other words, action would only be used in case of some unexpected world convulsion.

Q: As I understand it, their market is fixed by the free gold market in London?

The President: Very much, yes.

Q: We have a very narrow range?

The President: Yes.

Q: I was wondering whether, as long as they are on the free gold market—

The President: (Interposing) Of course one answer to that is that controlling such a very large amount of gold ourselves, we have quite an influence on the prices in the free gold market.

[President's Press Conferences:T]

[1] Acting under the Tripartite Agreement of Sept. 25, 1936, Switzerland had devalued on September 30 (New York *Times*, Sept. 30, 1936, p. 7).

Roosevelt to Cordell Hull, Secretary of State

[Washington] October 6, 1936

My dear Mr. Secretary: I have taken up with the Works Progress Administration the question which you raise in your letter of September twenty-sixth,[1] as to whether there is any way in which we might make provision for those Americans who have been evacuated from Spain during the present conflict and who, upon arrival in this country, find themselves without resources.

While there is no way in which special funds can be set aside for this group, it is possible that many of them would be able to qualify on the basis of need for employment under the Works Program or benefits extended through the Resettlement Administration.

It is suggested, therefore, that you furnish the Works Progress Administration with information regarding those persons who have returned to this country from Spain and who appear to be in need. Mr. Hopkins will then, through the usual channels, determine whether they are eligible for the Works Program or for assistance from the Resettlement Administration.

Very sincerely yours,

[OF 422-C:CT]

[1] Above.

Robert W. Bingham, Ambassador to Great Britain, to Roosevelt

[London] October 7, 1936

Dear Mr. President: I am enclosing copies of a letter I have received from the Imperial Policy Group, and of my reply, which I hope will have your approval.

This group represents the extreme financial and industrial element here, and I regard this gesture as interesting and significant.

It took the tragedy in Spain and the danger of a blow-up in France, to bring this group to its senses sufficiently to bring the British government into the monetary agreement which you have recently effected, and which, in my judgment, has done more to relieve tension in Europe and give hope for a measure of stability in France, than anything else which has been done. I know it has been obvious to you, as it has to me, that a working agreement between ourselves and the British would inevitably bring in France, and as inevitably bring in at least Belgium, Holland, the Scandinavian countries and probably Switzerland.

The British have taken persistently a short-sighted view, preferring to reap the advantage of their depreciated pound, regardless of the danger to them which this involved. It is this same element which so far has prevented the British government from making a proper trade agreement with us, and I have tried to drive this thought home in my reply to the letter which I have received.

On this phase of the situation I have made progress here, and their own apprehensions and dangers are tending to bring them around to a wiser attitude, as shown by this letter, and by recent public statements by members of the Cabinet.[1]

Sincerely yours,

Robert W. Bingham

[OF 491:TS]

[1] Answered Oct. 27, 1936, below.

[*Enclosure 1*] Kenneth de Courcy, the Imperial Policy Group, to Robert W. Bingham

London [October 2, 1936]

Dear Mr. Bingham: You may recollect that from the early part of this year to the close of the last Parliamentary Session, a small unofficial Foreign Affairs Mission, representing the fifty-five members of both Houses of Parliament who belong to this Group, toured Europe on several occasions to study the foreign situation. I can tell you privately that the Mission actually visited the British Diplomatic Posts in most of the important capitals, and also had conversations with various foreign statesmen—Ribbentrop, Benes, Schuschnigg, Mussolini and others.

One of our main conclusions was the great necessity of withdrawing from Europe as far as possible, and coming closer to the United States. This, of course, is becoming of greater importance every day, because quite clearly our path must lie alongside the United States, and as far away as possible from Europe in the future.

The actual members of the Mission were the Earl of Mansfield, Mr. A. R. Wise, M.P., and myself. After some thought, we have come to the conclusion that it would be very desirable for two of us, I think Mr. Wise and myself, to go to the United States in the early fall of 1937, or possibly in the spring, whichever is best, to make a series of speeches emphasizing the necessity for the closest possible Anglo-American understanding.

I am given to understand that there is an organization called the "Town Hall" in most parts of the United States, which particularly studies Foreign Affairs, among other things.[1]

Unfortunately, I have no means whatever, apart from begging your kindly help, of getting into direct touch with any authority or quarters who could perhaps invite us for such a lecture tour.

My colleagues and I feel it is of such profound importance that every effort should be made to build up Anglo-American relationships that we are more than anxious to undertake this trip. I wonder whether there is any way in which you could very kindly help me to get in touch with those who might be able to deal with the matter from that stage onwards.

I think we should be in a position to give audiences in the States a very considerable amount of information that might interest them, and I also think from an international point of view much good might be done.

I should be so grateful if you could let me know what quarter I had best approach.

Believe me, Your Excellency, Yours sincerely,

(Signed) Kenneth de Courcy

[OF 491:T]

---

[1] The League for Political Education was at this time sponsoring "America's Town Meeting of the Air," a series of radio broadcasts under the chairmanship of George V. Denny, Jr., for discussion of current issues.

[Enclosure 2] Robert W. Bingham to Kenneth de Courcy

London, October 5, 1936

My dear Mr. de Courcy: I have received your letter of October 2nd and read with great interest your observations on the conclusions which the Imperial Policy Group has reached as a result of their journeyings on the Continent. May I suggest, in reply to your questions, that it should prove equally valuable if a similar tour of inquiry were undertaken by your Parliamentary group in the United States, so that they could learn at first hand the American situation and the American point of view. In particular, I feel that such a trip would be of interest to them in revealing the opportunity offered by the American Government's policy of liberalizing international trade as the most immediate and practical means of cooperation between our two countries.

If you concur in my suggestion, and representatives of the Imperial Policy Group undertake such a visit to the United States, I am sure that you will come in contact with those bodies and organizations with whom you will be particularly interested in exchanging views on Anglo-American cooperation, about which we are all vitally concerned.

I should be very glad to give you any assistance I may be able to render in this connection.

Yours sincerely,

Robert W. Bingham

[OF 491:T]

Speech by Roosevelt, St. Paul, Minnesota, October 9, 1936

[*Excerpt*] I am happy in the strengthening of this movement at home.[1] But, my friends, let us remember that the same spirit of cooperation is an essential part of our relations with the other nations of the world. It is this realistic factual appreciation of the benefits of cooperation that lies behind our consistent and successful efforts to reestablish foreign markets for our farm products.

You will remember back three and a half years, in the spring of 1933 our American foreign trade had fallen off to about a third of its former value. That was what I inherited.

Let us go back to fundamentals some more. The very word "trade" means articles of commerce flowing in two directions. It is not a one-way street. And at last we have come to understand this in our domestic trade within our own borders. For instance, no single state can produce either crops or merchandise and continue indefinitely to sell them to other states for money alone. Eventually, they have to be paid for in other products as well.

Foreign trade is just like that. There cannot be a revival of foreign exports without a revival of foreign imports—unless, of course, we do as we did between 1920 and 1930—lend our money to foreign nations to enable them to buy our own farm and industrial products.

But I have a suspicion that America has learned her lesson once and for all about that kind of frenzied finance.

The Secretary of State of the United States has spoken in Minnesota, the day before yesterday, clearly and unequivocally in regard to the trade agreements that have been made with fourteen foreign countries for mutual trade advantage.[2] He pointed out to you the chapter and verse of the statistical record which shows what these agreements have accomplished to increase the trade and income not only of the industrial workers but of the farmers of the Nation. It was not a question of winning or losing any treaty. Mutual advantage has been the successful objective; and our exports during the first half of this year, as compared with last year, have increased by one hundred and thirty-two million dollars.

And to our good neighbors in Canada on the north, the twenty-four million dollars of our increased exports during the first six months have included not only exports of manufactured articles but also agricultural products. American industry and American agriculture are both benefitting by increased general trade and, my friends, the figures prove it.

I wish every American—city dweller and farmer alike—could fasten this home truth in his memory: When the nations of the world, including America, had jacked their tariffs to the highest point and enacted embargoes and imposed quotas—in those days farm prices throughout the world were at their lowest, and world trade had almost ceased to exist.

But, today, under the leadership of the United States, other nations of the world are coming to recognize that home truth. Back in 1932, although there was a tariff on wheat of forty-two cents a bushel, you all know that the wheat which you produced up here in the Northwest was selling as low as thirty cents a bushel. There were no farm imports then to worry about; but low prices were plenty to worry about.

Within the past two weeks, just as an example, splendid progress has been made in giving a greater stability to foreign exchange. Within that same time there have been lifted many quotas and embargoes including those on important American agricultural export products.

But, my friends, the increasing restoration of trade, the increase in industry, the increase in employment, they serve more than a mere economic end. For three years we have had faith that it would turn us and other nations away from the paths of economic strife which lead to war and toward economic cooperation which leads to international peace.

Peace cannot be attained in this old world of ours just by getting sentimental about it. Peace depends upon the acceptance of the principle and practice of the good neighbor. That practice is founded on the Golden Rule and must be fortified by cooperation of every kind between nations.

Peace makes money; peace saves money for everybody. A prosperous world, just the opposite to a bankrupt world—a prosperous world has no permanent room in it for dictatorship or war. And so, in striving for peace, I am confident that the American people seek it with their hearts and with their heads as well. Enlightened self interest is justification for what we do.

So, my friends, confident in the practical wisdom of the ends we seek, with full faith that it will serve in a practical way for peace on earth and good will between men and nations, we are going in the years to come to continue on our way.[3]

[Speech File:T]

[1] Roosevelt had been discussing farm cooperatives.

[2] Hull's speech at Minneapolis on Oct. 7, 1936; printed in New York *Times,* Oct. 8, 1936, p. 10.

[3] This excerpt represents Roosevelt's fullest expression during the campaign of his ideas on foreign policy. (The entire speech is printed in *Public Papers,* V, 418–423.) The emphasis throughout the campaign was upon the close connection between reciprocal trade and world peace; improvement in agriculture was tied to the success of reciprocity. See these parts of his speeches of October 10 (Omaha), 11 (Fort Warren, Wyoming), 13 (Wichita), 17 (Niagara Falls), and 21 (Boston), *ibid.,* pp. 434–435, 440–441, 462–463, 507–508, 520. He summed up his ideas on peace in his Madison Square Garden speech on October 31 (*ibid.,* pp. 566–573).

Roosevelt to Judge William Denman, United States Circuit Court of Appeals, San Francisco

Aboard Presidential Special, October 16, 1936

Dear Bill: Thank you for your note and the information.[1] I wish much I could get to the Coast but the official reason is the whole truth—so many things are going on outside our borders that I do not want to be four days away from Washington or to be away from there more than the eight days this trip takes.[2]

I hope you will get some Congressional action on Courts this fall.

Always sincerely,

[PPF 336:CT]

[1] Denman's letter of Sept. 27, 1936, on the need of additional judges for the United States Circuit Court of Appeals in California, was sent to the Attorney General (Roosevelt to Cummings, Oct. 19, 1936, PPF 336).

[2] Roosevelt's absences from Washington during the previous three months included his cruise along the New England coast and Canadian visit from July 11 to August 15; visiting drought areas from August 25 to September 6; and participating in the Harvard Tercentenary program and visiting Hyde Park, September 17 to 30.

William E. Dodd, Ambassador to Germany, to Roosevelt

Berlin, October 19, 1936

Personal

Dear Mr. President: I congratulate you on what I think will be your second great popular majority. You have therefore another four years, and I fear your problems are going to be as difficult as those of Woodrow Wilson in 1917.

I. According to your request of early August,[1] I have had three talks with officials here who see the Fuehrer often and who seem to know his purposes. The first of these talks was with Dr. Schacht, who fears war here the most. I wrote you that he was a little hopeful, but that Hitler could not participate.[2] On the 16th of September I saw Secretary Dieckhoff, brother-in-law of von Ribbentrop, one of the favorites of the Fuehrer, now Ambassador in London. Incidentally, the *Times* story was mentioned.[3] He was of the same attitude as Schacht, only less committal. On the 15th of October I saw Minister von Neurath, head of the Foreign Office here, and the subject of German-British relations was discussed. When I asked whether Germany would really participate in the oft-proposed Locarno conference, he said: "In case England satisfies the Italian demands." This led to a reference to the imminent danger of war here, and I asked whether Hitler would agree to participate in a peace conference of the greater Powers. He said: "Only in case the main points are agreed to beforehand." This I took to mean a previous promise to Italy and Germany of colonies and condemnation of Russia. I asked whether the Fuehrer intended to send the Russian Ambassador home. He said no, but added: "The Russian position here is getting to be so embarrassing that I think he will go home"—no successor to be appointed. This last he did not say, but made me believe.

These interviews and the statements rather definitely made seem to me to mean no approval of a peace conference unless Germany and Italy are granted about all they want. And events in Europe since last December all point the same way: Hitler and Mussolini intend to control all Europe. If that be agreed to beforehand, a peace conference is quite possible; but what sort of peace? Anyone who knows the sophomoric and egotistic mentalities of these men and their chief supporters can hardly fail to forecast the coming state of European civilization. Is there any way democratic countries can save the civilization which dates back to Luther, Erasmus, the Hollanders and the English?

Our country made democracy possible for Europe between 1776 and 1815, the population 3,000,000 to 8,000,000. It was a "miracle" which made the French Revolution possible, and then all western Europe became substantially democratic before 1860. The war of 1914–18 would have subjected Europe to a single dictatorship but for the intervention of our country: Our one aim to save democracy. The blunders all greater nations have made since 1920 surpass anything recorded in modern history. Now we see clearly what is before us. Can our country of 130,000,000 people and more real wealth than all western Europe do anything? Our people say no; and the Senate says the Constitution authorizes one-third of their members to defeat any policy the President might persuade men to accept: their treatment of Wilson's programme.

II. Much as I believe in peace as our best policy, I cannot avoid the fears which Wilson emphasized more than once in conversations with me, August 15, 1915 and later: the breakdown of democracy in all Europe will be a disaster to the people. But what can you do? At the present moment more than a hundred American corporations have subsidiaries here or cooperative understandings. The Du Ponts have three allies in Germany that are aiding in the armament business. Their chief ally is the I. G. Farben Company, a part of the Government which gives 200,000 marks a year to one propaganda organization operating on American opinion. Standard Oil Company (New York sub-company) sent $2,000,000 here in December 1933 and has made $500,000 a year helping Germans make Ersatz gas for war purposes; but Standard Oil cannot take any of its earnings out of the country except in goods. They do little of this, report their earnings at home, but do not explain the facts. The International Harvester Company president told me their business here rose 33% a year (arms manufacture, I believe), but they could take nothing out. Even our airplanes people have secret arrangement with Krupps. General Motor Company and Ford do enormous businesses here through their subsidiaries and take no profits out. I mention these facts because they complicate things and add to war dangers. If you wish proof of this story, talk with our Commercial Attaché here, Douglas Miller, in the United States till early December.[4]

Whether our people can prevent another world war is certainly a grave question. Yet no real democratic President can fail to realize the consequences of a world war to us. There is, however, increasing evidence here, in Rome, Paris and London that we may not have a war soon. Germany and Italy, with the greatest war equipments any people have ever had, are cooperating in such a way that their dictators may do what they wish. You saw what happened last winter when Mussolini agreed publicly to support Hitler's Rhine move. Everybody recognizes the helplessness of France when Italy and Germany sent men, airplanes and arms to the Spanish revolutionists from July to October. And the second week in September Hitler, Goebbels and Rosenberg delivered offensive attacks upon democracies. If you or the English monarch delivered such an attack on neighboring powers serious results would almost surely follow among one's constituents. The democratic peoples in Europe made no protests, not even Russia. Of course, the cruel dictatorship in Moscow could hardly look for international support. At the present moment small European democracies: Czechoslovakia, Sweden, Denmark, Holland and Switzerland, according to their representatives, are contemplating some such declarations as ungrateful Belgium made the other day. These Ministers say the League of Nations and the World Court have no more value; one sees readily why small powers resort to armed neutrality.

With so many democracies nervous, even fearful of annexations, and England and France helpless as a result of their foolish decisions since 1930, why may not Hitler annex strategic parts of the Balkan area and Mussolini seize islands in the Mediterranean without war? Spain is to be a protectorate of Italy, perhaps Egypt annexed. High officials here say Germany is to have colonies in the Far East with Italian-Japanese approval. One thing is certain: these dictators mean to dominate Europe and there is a fair chance of their doing it without war.

One serious difficulty is mentioned here by men like Dr. Schacht, and that is the enormous debt situation. According to best possible figures here, Germany owes her own people 45 billion marks, only 18 billions publicly acknowledged by the Reichsbank. Debts to outside countries certainly amount to something like fifteen billion marks—with interest unpaid to many creditors. This debt situation is known to enough people to cause much uneasiness. If crops were to fail by half for a single year, there would be starvation to millions of people unless international credit could be had. The barrier system forbids imports even of foodstuffs. This dilemma is duplicated in Italy. So loans and commercial concessions may become most vital matters. Of course Germany rarely has a drouth; but five successive years of excellent crops suggest always the possibility of a short harvest. Hitler said a few days ago that a twenty percent shortage would be a calamity of the first order. A few days later Hess (intimate counsellor of Hitler) said: "Do not forget that cannon are better than butter."

The second dilemma will come when German roads from Berlin to all frontiers (roads so built that all crossings are under or above and speed said to be 200 miles per hour) and the German armaments are completed. That will mean three to four millions of unemployed. At present Germany has only one million unemployed. Four or five millions of unemployed would be more serious here than twenty millions with us. A debt here of 60 billion marks is far more serious in comparison to German income than 60 billion dollars with us.

A dictator of sophomoric psychology would probably go to war to avoid possible difficulties, even with his submissive people. Of course successful threats, such as we have witnessed the last year or two, might bring annexations and postponement of war; but these cannot solve serious economic situations. And here comes one more opportunity of the United States to cooperate with European democracies. The stabilization matter suggests much, and increasing cooperation with the United States suggests more.[5] But can our people ever recognize the importance of lowering tariffs for cooperating countries? Wilson's second method of bringing about world peace was freer trade. His first one was naturally the guarantee by larger powers of the borders and rights of smaller ones. Both of these have been violated almost regularly since 1920 and consequently there has been no real League of Nations.

This long story may not be altogether right; but it represents the best information I have been able to gather. One thing is certain: all well-informed people here, even distinguished Germans, think modern civilization is in grave danger, and they repeat their opinions to me: the cooperation of the United States with European democracies is the only hope we have. How can you lead our people to a correct understanding of things when they allowed a minority of the Senate (contrary to the intentions of the writers of our Constitution) to defeat Wilson's marvellous democratic foreign agreements in 1919, even if the Treaty of Versailles was bad? Certainly it was nothing like the treaty of Brest-Litovsk the year before. If you could only get the great nations to see things as they are and apply their coercive power to any leader who wishes to go back to the fifteenth century morals! That would be what Henry IV of France tried to do, what Jefferson hoped for in 1807 and what Wilson almost accomplished in 1918–19.[6]

Sincerely yours,

William E. Dodd[7]

[PSF:Germany:TS]

[1] Roosevelt's letter of Aug. 5, 1936 (*Personal Letters, 1928–1945,* I, 605–606).
[2] See Dodd's letter of August 19, above, and his *Diary,* pp. 344–345.
[3] See *ibid.,* pp. 351–353, and Early to McIntyre, Aug. 26, 1936, above.

[4] Miller arrived in the United States on October 23 but apparently Roosevelt did not talk with him.

[5] The monetary stabilization agreement between the United States, France, and Great Britain, signed Sept. 25, 1936.

[6] As late as Jan. 27, 1937, Schacht urged on Ambassador Joseph E. Davies "the hope that President Roosevelt would call a peace conference in Washington" (Dodd, *Diary*, pp. 380–381).

[7] Answered Nov. 9, 1936 (*Personal Letters, 1928–1945*, I, 625–626). Roosevelt referred to his coming visit to Buenos Aires and said it would have little practical effect in Europe, "but at least the forces of example will help if the knowledge of it can be spread down to the masses of the people in Germany and Italy."

Roosevelt to Homer S. Cummings, Attorney General

Washington, October 20, 1936

Memorandum for the Attorney General: Will you be good enough to look into this whole problem personally? It is a difficult question. Will you let me have your recommendation?[1]

F.D.R.

[OF 1561:CT]

[1] Roosevelt enclosed a memorandum from Hull of Oct. 19, 1936, and a letter from W. H. Standley, Chief of Naval Operations, Sept. 24, 1936 (OF 1561). Standley said the Navy Department opposed granting an export license for sale of the Douglas DF flying boat because it was of definite military value as a patrol plane and would at once be copied by other nations. Hull, who had previously stated his Department's view that the plane was a commercial plane and therefore not subject to the Espionage Act, asked for a decision from the President. See Roosevelt to Early and McIntyre, Nov. 18, 1936, below.

S. R. Fuller, Jr., to Roosevelt

New York, 22 October 1936

Dear Mr. President: Subject: Germany. Reference: (a) My letter, 10 October 1936; (b) Our conversation, 20 October 1936.[1]

Supplementing the above references, may the liberty be taken, please, of adding some personal impressions and thoughts with the belief that they are within the scope of the work you so kindly gave me while on my last European trip? As you instructed, interviews were had with the Secretary of State and the Secretary of the Treasury.

It seems logical to believe that the German military party has gained and Schacht lost through the tripartite stabilization announcement. Schacht apparently had no foreknowledge of the matter.

May it not be true, therefore, that the militarists are now convinced that negotiations are useless; that the Tri-partite Powers are in practical alliance against Germany, as witnessed by the conclusion of the tri-partite arrangement without asking Germany beforehand whether she would come in; and that the time for drastic action is now—not later when England will be ready and France perhaps more a unit?

Schacht last spring (see Reference a) made certain propositions then satisfactory to Germany which today are predicated practically upon the announcement that the present stabilization between the dollar and the pound remain for a year. As a peace move, therefore, might it not be well to ask the British if they would be agreeable to such an announcement, provided Schacht would do today what he agreed to me last April? If the British answer affirmatively, then might not Schacht be approached?

Could not the British be approached through the same channel utilized so successfully for the tri-partite agreement? If you desire it, I would be glad to see Schacht. Would not the attempt be worth while? I believe success might follow. Hitler told me last spring that Germany must protect herself. He further said that she must have raw materials and exchange. He would negotiate for both; but his implications were plain: he would get them in other ways if he must.

If Germany could be brought within the stabilization fold, might not this be sufficient to permit Hitler to go before his people enabled safely to devalue? The tri-partite arrangements saved France—perhaps from revolution. Might not similar action toward Germany further prolong peace?

It is trusted from the depths of my heart that the European information gained will be of some little service to you. Call upon me, please, if you want me.

With warmest regard always, and again thanking you for the great honor of being permitted to make my trips as your friend, believe me always,

Faithfully yours,

S. R. Fuller, Jr.

[PPF 2616:TS]

[1] Fuller's letter, which includes a report of his talk with Prime Minister Colijn of the Netherlands on Sept. 25, 1936, was sent to Miss LeHand under cover of a note of Oct. 20, 1936 (PPF 2616). His conversation with Roosevelt occurred on October 19, not 20 (PPF 1-0).

Marvin H. McIntyre, Assistant Secretary to the President, to Representative Fred J. Sisson of New York

[Washington, October 22, 1936]

Dear Fred: I have referred your letter of October 14, 1936, with reference to a letter which was allegedly sent by Premier Mussolini to the President sometime during the trouble in Ethiopia, to the Department of State.[1] I now have a reply from the Department, saying that there is no record of any such letter ever having been received by the President from the Prime Minister of Italy.

For your information, however, Signor Mussolini in a conversation in May with a member of our Embassy staff, expressed appreciation of the position of neutrality taken by this Government during the Ethiopian crisis and, on June 23, the leading Rome newspaper, the *Messagero*, in an inspired editorial, acknowledged with gratitude the American attitude of strict neutrality and pointed out that the United States had resisted all pressure to subscribe to embargoes on metals and oils.[2]

Sincerely yours,

Marvin H. McIntyre

[OF 233:CT]

[1] Sisson had asked (OF 233) for a copy of a letter Mussolini was supposed to have sent Roosevelt, congratulating him on the government's refusal to apply oil sanctions against Italy. Sisson said that Italian party workers in his heavily Italian district were anxious to use the Mussolini letter to oppose political charges that the Administration had attempted to hinder Italy's Ethiopian campaign. So far as is known the only letters sent by Mussolini to Roosevelt in his first Administration were those of April 24, 1933 (above), and Nov. 19, 1936 (below). Luigi Criscuolo, a New York investment banker, wrote to Roosevelt on Oct. 26, 1936 (OF 233-A), to say that unless the impression was changed that the Administration was anti-Italian many Italian-Americans would vote Republican. He urged the President to declare himself in favor of recognition of Italian sovereignty over Ethiopia. His letter was briefly acknowledged by McIntyre, Oct. 27, 1936 (OF 233-A).

[2] Drafted in the State Department.

Roosevelt to Robert W. Bingham, Ambassador to Great Britain, London

[Washington] October 27, 1936

My dear Ambassador Bingham: I am glad to have your judgment that the recent monetary agreement has done so much to relieve tension in Europe, and your report of progress in bringing important elements of British opinion around to a broader attitude toward international trade.[1]

I approve your cordial reply to the group which approached you on possible methods of promoting Anglo-American understanding. As to the methods which the group may follow, they must know that unofficial foreign missions of any kind cannot be assured an unmixed welcome by press and public in so far as they are regarded as propaganda missions. This Government has carefully withheld official sponsorship from various American good will and business missions to other countries and regions, although we have allowed our representatives abroad to facilitate their journeys and contacts. The limitations on official identification with a foreign private mission would of course be somewhat greater, but I concur heartily in your personally encouraging any "tour of inquiry" which elements in a position to influence favorably British economic policy toward the United States may desire to take.

It is very important that Great Britain take timely action to associate itself definitely in the leadership of the movement toward more liberal trade conditions so essential at the present time.[2]

Very sincerely yours,

[OF 491:CT]

[1] See Bingham to Roosevelt, Oct. 7, 1936, above.
[2] Drafted in the State Department.

William C. Bullitt, Ambassador to France, to Roosevelt

Paris, October 28, 1936

Personal and Confidential

Dear Mr. President: Max Van Horn, the Belgian industrialist who, as you know, is an intimate friend of Van Zeeland and Neville Chamberlain, and as nearly as we could discover was sent to America recently by the British and Belgian Governments to feel out the question of war debts, came to Paris yesterday from Brussels and gave me an ear full on that subject.[1]

I listened. He said that he had said to Neville Chamberlain that he felt there might be a chance that Great Britain could make a settlement with the United States on the basis of 25% of the present debt, the great reduction to be concealed by spreading out the payments over a long period of years. He alleged that Neville Chamberlain had indicated that Great Britain might possibly be ready to settle on a 20% basis.

He said that Chamberlain had stated to him once again that he positively would never agree to an absolutely definite stabilization until the matter of war debts had been settled and that Chamberlain had said further that Great Britain was soon going to begin a campaign in the United States to try to bring the United States to a greater "appreciation of the British point of view."

Van Horn stated that this campaign would be begun by a series of articles by a professor whose name, I think, was Robinson.

He went on to say that he had given Van Zeeland all the details of his conversation with Chamberlain and that Van Zeeland had felt that settlement on the basis of 20% would be "somewhat too high for Belgium." He asked me for my views.

I replied that the Government of the United States had been and would be prepared to consider any offer made officially through official channels but that in view of unfortunate past experience we, I believed, would not discuss any hypothetical or unofficial proposals.

Van Horn seemed somewhat disappointed that I did not show any more interest than this in his remarks and I derived the impression that you would receive soon from various quarters, feelers and semi-official proposals.

I think we should flatly refuse to discuss anything but a straight out-and-out offer.

The French and the Italians are both exceedingly anxious to borrow money in the United States now and will wish to make some sort of settlement in order to escape from the Johnson Act and open the American money market with the underlying thought that war is on the horizon; that the loans will never have to be paid because of war and that they can get a great deal of money for one or two comparatively small payments. We can not, of course, refuse a reasonable offer but I believe we should not accept anything less than a thoroughly reasonable offer. I believe that it is definitely in the national interest for us to have the capital which has now accumulated in the United States invested in the United States rather than loaned abroad to be lost in a new war. In other words, thanks to the Johnson Act, the debts unpaid are proving to be of considerable value to us.

You should receive this letter on Election Day and I will say now Congratulations and the Lord be with you.

Yours affectionately,

Bill

[PSF:France:TS]

[1] Belgium had made no payments on her war debt to the United States since 1932 and by the end of 1936 owed $4,642,453 (State Department, *Press Releases,* June 20, 1936, p. 621; Dec. 19, 1936, pp. 524–525).

Claude G. Bowers, Ambassador to Spain, to Roosevelt

San Jean de Luz, October 29, 1936

Dear Mr President: I am inclosing a copy of my despatch to Hull since the reference to Japan, and the further proof—if any were necessary—of the active participation of Italy in the war here may be worth your knowing.

By the time this reaches you, you will have received the vindication of the American people. There has never been any doubt of it since the first of September. I have suffered quite a lot from the bitter disappointment of not being able personally to participate, but have consoled myself with the knowledge that it was unnecessary, and with the fact that I had been of weekly service from September of last year until in April through my material to Jim.[1]

I see that the enemy did not want to miss one of the old Federalist tricks against Jefferson which I have set forth in the latest book,[2] and that in the last days you, like Tom, were accused of aiming at the overthrow of religion. Of course you have been a communist just as he was a jacobin all along. I certainly should have sent you a copy of the book but I had none over here. I hope you like it. I think I have rendered a real service to clear thinking in smashing the Liberty League attempt to have Jefferson, Hamilton and John Marshall marching, arm in arm, behind the banner of reaction. Jefferson and Marshall were as remote from one another as Brandies and Cardoza from McReynolds and Sutherland. I hope you liked the book.

Let me anticipate the telegram I expect to send congratulating you on a victory which is as significant in our times as was Jeffersons in 1800, and Jacksons in 1832—and considering the times and the magnitude of the problems, more significant than either.

Sincerely,

Claude G. Bowers

Since writing the despatch the Government has assumed the offensive successfully this week and no doubt the planes and tanks are of Russian origin. But this only after notice was given that if Germany and Italy are permitted to continue in their policy, Russia would act on her rights under international law to sell to the legal Government.

[PSF:Spain:TS]

[1] James A. Farley.
[2] *Jefferson in Power* (Boston: Houghton, Mifflin, 1936).

[*Enclosure*] Claude G. Bowers to Cordell Hull, Secretary of State, and William Phillips, Under Secretary of State

Saint-Jean-de-Luz, France, October 30, 1936

Confidential for the Secretary and Under Secretary

Sir: I have the honor to report that the Japanese Minister called upon me yesterday afternoon to say that after his arrival here six weeks ago, and after talking with all the members of the diplomatic corps, he became convinced that the United States is probably the only nation that is strictly adhering to an honest neutrality. Learning in his talk with me that we were refusing to convert our Embassy into a refuge for Spaniards engaged in the war, he had instructed his Chargé d'Affaires in Madrid to follow a like course. The purpose of his call yesterday was to say that after he had informed his Government that the United States is strictly neutral, and that scarcely any country is, he was instructed by Tokyo to follow in every instance whatever course that should be taken by us.

I have observed with some curiosity for six weeks that the Japanese Minister has shown an unusual interest in our course and that he has acted precisely as we have in every instance, or I might have suspected some ulterior motive, though he did not appear to be prying into our future intentions. He said that the United States and Japan are similarly situated in that we are both remote from the scene of the conflict, and are in a position to be absolutely neutral.

I am giving you this information on the chance that you may have your own opinion as to the significance of this unusual expression of solidarity with us. Personally I am positive that the Minister was entirely sincere.

II. The rebellion which was to have triumphed in "four days or five at the utmost" is now in progress after three and a half months. Caught unprepared in the beginning, with the professional soldiery seizing the barracks and the instrumentalities of war, the Government would have gone down as speedily as Franco expected but for the very remarkable rising of the people.

This has necessitated the bringing of armies of the Foreign Legion and the Moors from Africa and these constitute the greater part of the so-called "nationalist army." These are rough but effective soldiers, and they are perfectly equipped with tanks and airplanes from Germany and Italy. In addition, the rebels have the most able generals and the greater discipline that goes with a professional army. But such has been and is the stubborn resistance of the people that I am not at all persuaded that the fall of Madrid will mean the termination of the war. That Madrid will fall seems inevitable from information received from Colonel Fuqua and from the observations made to me by reputable correspondents who have just come from the capital, but they cannot believe that without these, and despite the fact that the defenders will greatly outnumber the rebels, the Government can hold the town. The highest figure I can get from correspondents who have been with the attacking forces is that they do not number more than 20,000.

III. The non-intervention pact is nothing more than a device conceived by France to excuse herself from selling arms to the legal Government. The violations of this pact by Portugal, Germany, and Italy are notorious. The denials made by these Powers are grotesquely false. A dozen press correspondents have told me of the German and Italian planes. Webb Miller, European head of the United Press, told me of meeting numbers of Italian officers in Seville with whom he had been associated in Abyssinia. And yesterday three correspondents, Minifie of the *Herald-Tribune,* Gorrell of the *United Press,* and the correspondent of the London *News-Chronicle,*[1] arrested and then released by the insurgents, all told me that when they were captured they saw an astonishing number of small Italian tanks in operation, and that all were operated by Italian soldiers who could not speak Spanish.

466

The counter-charge that Russia has been supplying arms to the Government I cannot verify from any source thus far. I have invariably asked the war correspondents if they have seen anything of the sort and they all give a negative answer. But it is possible that the insurgents really believe this story. There is some justification for this assumption in the fact that Minifie and Gorrell were interrogated at the insurgent head-quarters on that very point and they had to reply that they had seen nothing of the sort.

It is reasonable assumption that now that Russia has denounced the utterly dishonest pact, that she may make an effort to send arms and planes, but up to the time of the denunciation of the pact she apparently had observed it herself as far as arms and ammunition or war material are concerned.[2]

IV. The Eden proposition to the Government for an "exchange of hostages" requires some clarification. There are some thousands of prisoners in Madrid. These I think are undoubtedly enemies of the regime, and are held as potential enemies and not as hostages. General Mola made the blunder recently of publicly announcing that there are thousands of rebels in Madrid, and these he called "my fifth column." He said publicly that when the attack on Madrid begins these will come out and fight. I personally have no doubt of it.

Under these circumstances the Government has been feverishly seeking these enemies of the regime bent on the overthrow of the Government and putting them under lock and key. No Government in the world, I suppose, would do less.

But I have yet to learn where the prisoners of the rebels are held. It has been my information from war correspondents that the rebels take no prisoners. They shoot them. Minifie, Gorrell and Weaver (the British correspondent) told me of the fate of guards assigned by the war department as their escort. These threw up their hands and surrendered as prisoners of war. With their hands up they were shot down with a pistol and after they fell their bodies were riddled with musket bullets.

I asked Sir Henry Chilton, British Ambassador, at my house the other day what prisoners held by the rebels Eden wished to exchange for those held in Madrid. He did not know. I asked him if he knew of any such prisoners in any numbers. He said he did not.

I am sure the Government's promise to give every protection to the Madrid prisoners was made in good faith, but if there is a prolonged fight for Madrid there is a danger that the anarchists and the syndicalists, indifferent to Government orders, should attempt to storm the prisons and kill the prisoners. Much may depend upon the rapidity with which the insurgents take complete possession of the town, after it becomes clear that they actually will take it.

V. In view of the problematical aftermath of the fall of Madrid, I would call your attention to the fact that the Government, the real Government, voted in, has been constantly harassed by the syndicalists and anarchists since the elections in February. Up until the beginning of the rebellion there were not enough anarchists in Madrid to make any impression. The syndicalists were decidedly in the minority among the workers. The socialist union, which was conservative within bounds, vastly outnumbered the syndicalist union. And yet strikes were called and enforced over the protest of the socialists by the syndicalists, and the socialists were threatened with assassination by the syndicalist members if they did not conform. Thus there was at least one strike forced by a majority.

At that time it is my understanding that the Government, composed entirely of democratic republicans, contemplated putting the syndicalists down by force. This, however, would mean the shooting of workers and the political effect was feared. It was a question whether the moderate socialists might not in the hysteria of the shooting be driven further to the left.

These are the people who have made it impossible for the Government of Azana to conduct the war on a strictly democratic basis. When Largo Caballero was made premier it was with the thought that he might be able to discipline and control this syndicalist and anarchist element. He has brought some little semblance of order out of chaos. But I have received some significant information from Minifie, Gorrell and Weaver, who have been in Madrid for almost two months.

They tell me that the syndicalists and anarchists assume all power; that they are all armed but that they refuse to go to the front; and that not long ago it was under serious consideration to disarm these people if it meant, as seemed probable, fighting in the streets. This project was finally abandoned on the ground that it would throw the city into turmoil in the face of the approaching enemy.

With the fall of Madrid, it is possible that these extremists who have made a mess of things may be eliminated, and that the Government, established elsewhere, may continue the war along democratic or moderately socialistic lines. If not, I look for anarchy in spots, and for different cities and sections, recognizing no central authority, to prepare for independent defences.

Should the Azana Government succeed in regaining authority, the fight of the legal Government can continue. Otherwise the prevention of anarchy and the preservation of Spain will rest with force—the form of Franco's soldiers.

In view of the fact which looms like a mountain above a plain that the primary purpose of the rebellion was to destroy democracy in this country, and that this would have failed without the assistance of foreign troops and other nations, I would suggest—thinking of terms of history—that we jump to no precipitate conclusions, and especially, since on yesterday the Government forces took the offensive in several places and succeeded in their objective.

Respectfully yours,

Claude G. Bowers

[PSF:Spain:CT]

[1] James Minifie, Henry T. Gorrell, and Denis Weaver.
[2] The Non-intervention Pact.

Press Conference, Executive Offices of the White House, November 6, 1936, 10:40 A.M.

[*Excerpt*] The President: Yes. And the only other news you may want to know is this possible South American trip but I haven't got anything to add. I still don't know whether I shall go and I won't make up my mind until probably the middle of next week.[1]

There are two alternatives, the first being to take the cruiser on the 17th—I have forgotten whether it is the 17th or 18th, from Charleston and go down into the Caribbean for two and a half weeks, playing around and fishing. That trip would probably mean going down to the Windward and Leeward Islands to Trinidad, fishing on the way and then from there going across to the Central American coast and fishing there, and probably coming back and landing in Pensacola or Mobile or New Orleans, somewhere on the Gulf and then taking the train back to Washington. That is Plan No. 1.

Q: Is that on the way back or down?

The President: It makes a circle. Going down the islands on the eastern side of the Caribbean as far as Trinidad and then go west over to the Central American Coast and then going up the Central American Coast through the Gulf of Mexico to one of the southern ports. That is Plan No. 1.

Plan No. 2 is much faster speeding. Leave the same day, same place, and go straight down to Trinidad and get fuel oil there and then go straight to Buenos Aires, with probably one stop somewhere in Brazil to get fuel oil. That has not been worked out. Spend one day there and come back—the day being December 1.

Q: That is the opening day?[2]

The President: Yes.

Q: That would not call for a speech, would it?

The President: Yes.

Q: What time would that bring you back to Washington?

The President: About the 13th of December.

Q: You wouldn't go to Warm Springs?

The President: No. I would have to cut out Warm Springs.

Q: In either case?

The President: No. 1 Plan, I'd be back earlier. If I do No. 2 Plan, landing in Pensacola or Mobile or New Orleans, I'd probably go to Warm Springs for two or three days on the way up.

Q: Would you care to indicate what would govern your decision?

The President: Oh, general Government business is the easiest way of putting it.

Q: Did you say where you were landing on your second trip?

The President: No. I'd come back, probably, to Charleston . . .

Q: Will there be a speeding up of the trade agreements?

The President: I don't know enough about it. There are, you know, six or eight in process of either negotiations or discussion.

Q: Yes, sir.

The President: We will just go ahead with those . . .

Q: Can we expect anything this afternoon, after you talk to the members of the Cabinet, about the shipping situation?

The President: I don't think so. I don't know whether I will talk to the Cabinet. It is a special thing.

Q: When you go to Buenos Aires, did you say who will go with you on the same ship?

The President: No. If I do go, I will go on a cruiser. There will be very little room for any other people than my own staff and, of course, I will have to take along the Aides and the Navy people, et cetera. There won't be anybody connected with the Conference. To do it in that time—in about 26 days—will mean some all-high speeding. It would be a record trip, so far as speed goes, down and back. Average about 24 or 5 knots, which no other ship has ever done . . .

Q: Will the Jusserand Memorial be much of a speech?[3]

The President: No; about five minutes. And, when that is done, I think I won't make another speech for a long, long time.

Q: What cruiser are you going to take?

The President: The *Indianapolis* with the *Chester* acting as escort. That is where you (the Press Association representatives) will live.

Q: I hope we get some liberty down in Trinidad.

The President: That's a good place. The liberty in Trinidad will be short. The stop would be six or seven hours; long enough to take fuel on.

Q: If you go there, will you deliver the opening address?

The President: I merely participate, with the others, in the opening. I don't open it. In other words, there are twenty-one republics, all equal.

Q: Do you expect to remain here in Washington until before sailing?

The President: Yes. I don't think there are any other plans except this awful problem of mail.

[President's Press Conferences:T]

[1] Roosevelt left Washington on November 17 and boarded the *Indianapolis* in Charleston, S.C., the next day, arriving in Rio de Janeiro on November 27. There he addressed a joint session of the Brazilian Congress and Supreme Court. He addressed the opening session of the Inter-American Conference for the Maintenance of Peace on December 1 and on December 3 spoke at a luncheon given for him in Montevideo by President Gabriel Terra of Uruguay. The Buenos Aires address is printed below; all the speeches are printed in *Public Papers*, V, 597–615. Roosevelt was back in Washington on Dec. 15, 1936.

[2] Of the Inter-American Peace Conference.

[3] Roosevelt dedicated the Jusserand Memorial in Rock Creek Park in Washington on Nov. 7, 1936; his remarks are printed in *Public Papers*, V, 584–585.

William C. Bullitt, Ambassador to France, to Roosevelt

Paris, November 8, 1936

Personal and Confidential

Dear Mr. President: I am as happy as a proud father about the election! But you know that already, and I will not burden you any more with my emotions but will tell you about the reactions of the French.

The wave of enthusiasm in France which greeted your election was really phenomenal. No American President ever received such a tornado of praise. I enclose herewith the translations of articles which Herriot and Claudel wrote.[1]

Blum came personally to express his congratulations. That is unheard of. If you could have seen the manner of his coming, it would have done you good. At least you would have laughed. He entered the front door, flung his broad-brimmed black hat to the butler, his coat to a footman, leaped the three steps to the point where I was standing, seized me and kissed me violently! I staggered slightly; but having been kissed by Stalin, I am now immune to any form of osculation, and I listened without batting an eye to as genuine an outpouring of enthusiasm as I have ever heard.

You have, of course, received from de Laboulaye the resolution adopted by the Chamber of Deputies and the resolution of the town of Lannoy which claims to be the home of your ancestors. How many cities was it that claimed Homer?

The cause of this outburst is that the French regard you as a national leader who has succeeded in giving the lower classes a greater proportion of the national income without disturbing any of the ancient liberties. The French are all praying for such a man. Blum, himself, said to me that he felt his position had been greatly strengthened because he is attempting in his way to do what you have done in America. In addition, the French all feel that you have a genuine understanding of French civilization and a genuine liking for France, and that you will somehow manage to keep Europe from plunging again into war.

In every conversation that I have had, either with members of the French Government or the opposition, or ambassadors and ministers, or French statesmen who happen to be outside the government, like Herriot, I have attempted to elicit some statement of some constructive project for the prevention of war. I have never encountered such complete hopelessness. There is no feeling of crisis because no one believes that war is imminent; but there is a universal belief that Europe is drifting toward war and that no man on the continent has imagination enough to devise any method of reconciliation.

Every minister of a small European state who has yet called on me has expressed the hope that you might intervene, saying that if you did not, his country would certainly be destroyed by the inevitable conflict. I have asked how you could intervene, what you could do to prevent war, how you could be certain that anything you did would not produce a fiasco similar to the London Economic Conference. The reply invariably has been that no one in Europe can think of any way in which you can intervene effectively—but you might be able to think of some way yourself.

You are, in other words, beginning to occupy the miracle man position. And I am strongly reminded of the sort of hope that for a time was reposed in Woodrow Wilson. I wish I could talk out with you some evening in the White House the possibilities and impossibilities.

You would, I am sure, get nothing whatever from an unprepared conference of chiefs of state or prime ministers or foreign secretaries. The mess would be greater, because the conflict of interests would be greater, than at the London Economic Conference. On the other hand, I am not at all sure that you may not be able to do something which may have at least a fair chance of success.

You will remember in 1932, after your election but before your Inauguration, I had conversations with Schleicher and Neurath in Berlin and with Herriot and Boncour in Paris. It looked at that time as if something could be done to draw France and Germany together. You will remember also that all four of the gentlemen mentioned above felt that the essential thing would be quiet pressure and assistance from the United States acting through the American Ambassadors in Berlin and Paris.

In spite of the explosions of Mussolini, the nub of the problem of European peace is still—as it has been for so long—reconciliation between France and Germany. Ever since Hitler came into power everyone in France has assumed that reconciliation is impossible, and when I passed through Berlin last May, Neurath said to me that he felt there were fewer chances of reconciliation than ever before.

I don't believe that this is true. The essential thing the Germans must have, is the development of their economic relations with Central Europe and the Balkans. The French (or at least Blum and Delbos) have no objection to this. Indeed, it is perfectly obvious that whether the French want it or not, it will come to pass. It is in the logic of economic facts, for example, that Rumania should exchange her wheat and oil for German machines and construction material. Similarly, the Germans need the products of Yugoslavia, Hungary, Bulgaria and Turkey, and those countries need German products. No one can invent any legitimate reason for trying to prevent this German economic development. The reason why so many people are afraid of it is because they fear that economic domination will lead to political domination and the realization of the old Berlin-to-Bagdad bloc.

473

I do not believe that political domination must necessarily follow economic domination and I believe that it may be possible to get together the French and the Germans on the basis of an economic agreement which would give the Germans a chance to develop Central Europe and the Balkans economically: provided such an agreement should be accompanied by an agreement with regard to limitation of armaments and a general revival of a feeling of European unity.

That sounds like a large order. It is a large order; but the events in Spain have made most people in most European countries realize that there is such a thing as European civilization which reposes on certain very old civilized principles that may be destroyed by war or Bolshevism. I do not mean that people are anxious to start a crusade against Bolshevism or that anyone (even Germany) intends to invade the Soviet Union, but I do mean that there is beginning to be a feeling that if the nations of Western Europe do not hang together, they will all hang separately.

If we can assist diplomatically in laying the basis for a reconciliation between France and Germany, I think we should help. If we get anywhere diplomatically and see a fair chance of success, you could then come forward with some tremendous public announcement. But I feel emphatically that you should not let yourself be persuaded to make some great gesture until you have prepared the ground with great care.

How can we prepare the ground? You can, of course, do much in any conversations you may have with the French and German Ambassadors in Washington and I shall be, I think, in a position to do whatever you want me to do here; at least so long as the present government remains in office. I have been astonished by the frankness with which Blum and Delbos have treated me and I have, of course, had a very confidential relationship with Leger for many years.

When Dodd leaves Berlin I think you should select your man for that post with extreme care. As Hitler does not speak anything but German any Ambassador of ours there who does not speak German perfectly will be useless. That qualification rules out most of the men who have been mentioned for the post. (Incidentally, Joe Davies' German is, I understand, lousy.) I wish I had someone better to suggest, but I can think of no one better than Hugh Wilson, who has been for many years our Minister in Berne. His German is perfect and in spite of the fact that his connections are largely Republican and that his wife especially is no lover of the Democratic Party or you or myself, I can not think of anyone else who could begin to establish the really intimate and confidential relationship we need with the bosses in Berlin, which will be essential if we are to accomplish anything.[2]

At the same time, I think you should signalize the arrival of Wilson or whoever replaces Dodd, by beginning at once to rebuild the Blücher Palace as the center of our activities in Berlin. As you know, we have owned the Blücher Palace for years and expected to house in it not only the Ambassador but also all the officers of the Embassy and Consulate General. As Dodd wanted to save money, he didn't want to take on any such establishment and held up the matter. Our Berlin establishment at the present moment would be an excellent one for Honduras. It is not a good stage setting for dealings with gentlemen who conceive of themselves as Parsifal and young Siegfried. And whether we like it or not, the Pure Fool and Goering are the bosses of Germany.

It is perhaps silly for me even to attempt to make suggestions of this sort in a letter. A discussion of all the whys and wherefores is so necessary that I may simply succeed in making you believe that I have lost whatever mind I ever possessed. However, it won't be useless if I can make you realize how intensely many people in Europe want you to do something about the European situation; and how inordinately difficult it is to do anything constructive, and how necessary to prepare the way. After all, it wouldn't have happened without John the Baptist.

I have lots of news to write you; but this letter is already so long that I shall only put in a few lines of it.

You probably saw the telegram in which I said that Blum had told me that he intended to replace de Laboulaye.[3]

What actually happened was this: Blum said that he would like to see me at once and asked me to come to his own apartment on the Isle St. Louis. I did and he said he had a highly indiscreet question to ask me. He said he had wished to withdraw de Laboulaye last Spring and his predecessors had wished to replace de Laboulaye for more than a year, and de Laboulaye had wished to be replaced. But Jesse Straus had informed him, as well as his predecessors, that it was absolutely essential to the interests of France that de Laboulaye should be kept in Washington so long as you were President, because he was such an intimate friend of yours that you would regard his removal as a personal affront. He wished to know if this was really the case because, while he would leave de Laboulaye in Washington if it were the case, he had received in the past week letters from three different men, all of whom he regarded as entirely reliable, informing him that both de Laboulaye and Madame de Laboulaye had made statements about him and the present government of France which were, to say the least, disloyal. He said that he did not wish to go into personal details which were most unpleasant, but did wish to tell me that he had been informed that de Laboulaye had said that he, Blum, was incompetent, that the present government could last only a short time, and that it was really not worth while to take up serious matters with the present government.

I replied that de Laboulaye had never made any such statements to me and that I thought he had conducted himself very satisfactorily as a career ambassador; that he was a very good friend of yours and that Madame de Laboulaye was a very good friend of Mrs. Roosevelt; but that I felt that you would not consider it a personal affront if de Laboulaye should be replaced. (Incidentally, de Laboulaye said to me the day I left Washington that he was sure I would be asked this question and asked me please to reply as I did. He said that he was most anxious to bring out his daughter in Paris and would welcome being placed *en disponibilité* in Paris for a certain period.)

Putsi Haenfstengel blew into Paris a couple of days ago and I had a talk with him night before last. He said that Goering will be made Reichskanzler with Hitler retaining the superior position of Fuehrer. He prophesied that Rosenberg (the fellow who runs the anti-Russian propaganda and the plans for expansion to the East) will disappear from circulation during the next twelve months. He predicted that the rise of Goering would bring a very strong movement in Germany for rapprochement with the Soviet Union which would be opposed only by Hitler because of his religious conviction that the Bolsheviks are the children of Hell. Goering will be supported by the Reichswehr, the industrialists and Schacht.

Wiley and his wife came down to visit me for election night. Wiley is thoroughly pleased with Antwerp and doesn't want to go as Counselor of Embassy to London.

I have, thank God, now completed all the obligatory speeches that I have to make. The last one was at the American Students and Artists Center, which is under the aegis of Dean Beekman of our noble church. The Latin Quarter religious audience has a somewhat peculiar odor of sanctity. While I was speaking, Offie[4] was seated next to a very strange looking lady who kept pulling out of her pocket a quart bottle of Pernod and taking enormous swigs, while announcing to the lady on her right that when I had finished speaking, she intended to brain me with the bottle. The lady on her right, in whispers, argued with her that this would not be seemly. Finally, the absinthe drinking lady screeched out, "Can't you understand I'm in love with him?"!

Anne[5] is firmly and happily established in an American school. I can not tell you what a difference it makes to me to be able to have her with me. She is growing to be a really lovely person.

Good luck to you for your trip to South America and for all the years to come.

Yours affectionately,

Bill

[*Notation*:A:FDR] File Personal confidential
[PSF:France:TS]

[1] Present.
[2] Wilson's appointment as ambassador to Germany was confirmed by the Senate on Jan. 13, 1938.
[3] Not found in the Roosevelt papers.
[4] Carmel Offie, third secretary in the Embassy.
[5] Bullitt's daughter.

Roosevelt to R. Walton Moore, Acting Secretary of State

Washington, November 10, 1936

Memorandum for Hon. R. Walton Moore: Please tell the Chilean Ambassador that the importance of saving even twenty-four hours is so great that on this trip I must return immediately from Buenos Aires—but that I very much hope to be able to go down the west coast next year.[1]

F.D.R.

[OF 429:CT]

[1] The ambassador, Manuel Trucco, had invited Roosevelt to visit Chile (Moore to Roosevelt, Nov. 7, 1936, OF 429).

R. Walton Moore, Assistant Secretary of State, to Roosevelt

Washington, November 10, 1936

Dear Mr. President: The enclosed memoranda give the information I requested yesterday of our Western European Division and Near Eastern Division.

The one that deals with Spain you will probably wish to look at before the Spanish Ambassador calls this morning. The other pertains to the Ethiopian matter.

I have had it suggested to the Spanish Ambassador that he may wish to be very reticent in talking to the press after he sees you.

I think you will like to know that we have taken pretty effective steps to protect the secrecy of our codes, so far as concerns the Department itself, by guarding the distribution and safekeeping of confidential communications, and we are starting a similar effort to insure the same thing in our foreign offices.

Yours very sincerely,

R. Walton Moore

[PSF:Spain:TS]

[*Enclosure*] John H. Morgan, Division of Western European Affairs, Department of State, to R. Walton Moore

November 10, 1936

Memorandum

Mr. Moore: For many years the summer capital of Spain has been at San Sebastian on the North coast. The Foreign Office and other Ministries send delegations to San Sebastian and the Diplomatic Corps moves as a body to that city leaving only skeleton staffs in Madrid. Ambassador Bowers was at San Sebastian when the revolt broke out and remained there for some days until the situation became untenable and he was evacuated aboard the coast guard cutter *Cayuga*. For some two weeks Ambassador Bowers traveled up and down the North coast aboard the *Cayuga* picking up Americans who wished to leave Spain. When this task was completed Ambassador Bowers set up his office at St. Jean de Luz since conditions remained impossible in San Sebastian. In the meantime all the other Ambassadors who had been at San Sebastian had established themselves either in San Jean or the neighboring town of Hendaye. None of these Ambassadors have since returned to Madrid except the Mexican Ambassador whose Government has been an ardent supporter of the Madrid Government and has sent that Government very large stores of munitions and other supplies. Like the Embassies of the other principal powers our Embassy in Madrid has been conducted during the rebellion by a Chargé d'Affaires. The conduct

478

of our Embassy has been competent and our relations friendly. It is not believed, therefore, that anything will have been gained by directing Ambassador Bowers to leave the Diplomatic Corps in St. Jean and proceed to Madrid.

2. In addition to the American Embassy at Madrid we had in continental Spain a Consulate General at Barcelona, a Consular Agency in Tarragona and Consulates at Valencia, Malaga, Seville, Vigo and Bilbao. Outside continental Spain we had Consulates in the Canary Islands at Las Palmas and Tenerife. All these offices are still open with the exception of the Consulates at Bilbao and Malaga and the Consular Agency at Tarragona. The insurgents are firmly in control and conditions are quiet in the Canary Islands and also in the Vigo and Seville districts. In both Bilbao and Malaga internal conditions appear to be chaotic. These cities are subject to fairly frequent bombardment from the air and from the sea but pending the termination of the campaign against Madrid no serious attempt has been made by the insurgents to capture them. Conditions are now reasonably quiet in Tarragona but as our agent, a private business man, seemed to be in danger as the result of his efforts to protect American property he was authorized to leave Spain. There have been no military operations in the vicinity of Valencia which is now the official seat of the Spanish Government. The July revolt of the insurgents was put down in Barcelona within 24 hours and the city has remained quiet from the military point of view since then, except for an unsuccessful expedition from the city against the Island of Mallorca which is held by the insurgents, and an ineffectual bombardment of the coast north of the city by a rebel cruiser about ten days ago.

3. It is estimated that there may be still in Spain about 250 American nationals. Those remaining are either persons having close family ties in Spain or persons who feel that they must remain to watch over their interests at all costs or who have no source of income outside of Spain and do not therefore wish to leave the country.

4. The efforts of our officers in Spain were primarily devoted to evacuating our nationals to points of safety. At the same time they took all possible steps to protect American property by notifying the Spanish authorities of the whereabouts and nature of property belonging to the American nationals and provided these nationals with certificates and seals to be pasted on windows and doors, as a notice to persons who might otherwise be disposed to molest the property. Our Embassy at Madrid and our Consuls in their several jurisdictions also notified the appropriate authorities that this Government could not admit that

American private property, whether actually in the hands of American nationals or abandoned by them temporarily because of conditions over which they had no control, might be interfered with with impunity. Our officers further informed these authorities that the American Government would, of course, look to the Government of Spain for indemnification for any delinquency in this respect and that in the event of requisition of American property for the necessities of war or otherwise the American Government would insist that provision be made for prompt and full compensation to the owners. In response to these representations our offices received both from the national and local governments assurances that American property would be respected and full payment made for such property as it might prove necessary to requisition.

Due to the almost complete disruption of the usual commercial means of communication resulting from the civil war, our consular and diplomatic officers have for the last four months, provided practically the sole dependable means of contact between the American owners of commercial and industrial property in Spain and their managers and representatives in that country. Our officers have not only followed with the closest attention, for the guidance of the Department and the information of American business, the measures taken by the Spanish Government in regard to commerce and industry, but have also under most difficult and in many cases dangerous conditions located the representatives of American companies, reported on their welfare, assisted certain of them to leave Spain, transmitted their reports to their principals and conveyed to them the latter's instructions, advised them as to the procedure to be followed in the event of requisition of their property by the constituted authorities, and taken steps to prevent irresponsible and unauthorized seizures.

5. The total value of American property in Spain is roughly estimated at about 80 million dollars of which about 64 million dollars is accounted for by the property of the National Telephone Company of Spain which is owned by the International Telephone and Telegraph Company of New York. Aside from real estate the remaining 16 million dollars is accounted for by stocks of merchandise in warehouses or shops, the most important being cotton stocks worth about 800 thousand dollars, the assets of banking organizations and plants for the manufacture of motor cars, shoe machinery, automobile tires, cork products, sulphur products, olive oil and a number of miscellaneous products.

6. Our Chargé d'Affaires in Madrid and our consular officers in those cities under the control of the Government have been uniformly success-

ful in maintaining cordial relations with the successive Cabinet officers and civil and military governments. The cordiality of our relations with these officials has been of great value to us in the protection of American lives and property. Similarly our Consuls in rebel territory have maintained friendly relations on an informal basis with the insurgent authorities in control in their districts. When contact with the Commander of the insurgent forces has been necessary for the protection of American nationals we have made our approach informally through the American Consul at Seville which in the early stages of the revolt was the headquarters of the rebel forces. Although Seville has ceased to be the headquarters of the insurgents the local Commander has continued to cooperate informally with our Consul and has forwarded our representations immediately to General Franco. It appears from the information available to us that the British have endeavored in their relations both with the insurgents and with the Madrid Government to follow a policy of neutrality parallel to our own.

7. The information received from our Embassy in the case is that in the event of Franco's success the first European countries to recognize his government will be Germany, Italy and Portugal. San Sebastian and Guatemala have already recognized Franco and it is not improbable that such countries as Brazil, Chile and Argentina will recognize Franco at about the same time as they are recognized by Germany and Italy. Mexico will probably withhold recognition as long as possible.

8. Our latest information indicates that both Great Britain and France are following a cautious policy and will not reach a decision with regard to the possibility of recognizing Franco until the situation becomes more clear.

JHM

[PSF:Spain:TS]

Roosevelt to Carrie Chapman Catt, New Rochelle, New York

[Washington] November 12, 1936

Dear Mrs. Catt: Though you tell me not to write, I must tell you how grateful I am.[1] I do hope to go—leaving next Tuesday. The only thing that might keep me here would be the shipping strike or trouble in Europe. In Buenos Aires we have a real opportunity to continue the good example.

Always sincerely,

[PPF 3177:CT]

[1] Mrs. Catt's letter has not been found in the Roosevelt papers.

Press Conference, Executive Offices of the White House, November 13, 1936, 10:50 A.M.

[*Excerpt*] Q: Have you been invited to attend a London conference?

The President: Not that I know of.

Q: A report from London is that you accepted an invitation.

The President: No.

Q: Are you framing what you call "anti-war legislation"?

The President: No, I am not framing a thing. (Laughter) Or anybody. (Laughter)

Q: Are you going to ask for any legislation?

The President: I am not in a framing mood at all . . .

Q: Mr. President, can you tell us what Governor Eccles and Mr. Landis had to say about the securities market?[1]

The President: I cannot tell you anything more than what they said about the securities market. They are much better at language, when it comes to talking about margins and bidding and selling stocks, than I am. I think probably the important thing was what they told me about this very large foreign buying and of course foreign buying, when it gets to a certain point, is a dangerous thing because those same securities can be sold very quickly in case anything happens on the other side. It corresponds to what they call "hot money." You cannot tell when it will go out on you. That is always a disturbing factor in foreign exchange and in the general credit situation.[2]

Q: Mr. President, is there any precaution you can take against that?

The President: I think you can guess that the thing is being studied; they have just begun to study it . . .

Q: Anything in the S.E.C. or Federal Reserve laws which would bar foreign buying in the American market?

The President: I don't think there is.

Q: Do you think there is need for it?

The President: I think it would probably take legislation.

Q: That is for control?

482

The President: Yes.

Q: Is that a possibility, that legislation?

The President: All I can tell you is that we have just begun to study it. The Federal Reserve Board has begun to study it and I have asked the Treasury Department to begin to study it when the Secretary gets back next week. So it is in the early stages of study . . .

Q: On the foreign money in the stock market, would it require new legislation?

The President: I think it would probably take legislation.

Q: Have you any estimate of how much new foreign money has come in recently?

The President: No. I believe the Federal Reserve Board has given out some statistics on that.

Q: It shows in their statement of gold coming in.

The President: Yes.

Q: Have you any idea of the character of the legislation?

The President: Not at all. Literally, we haven't done anything more than agreed that it is a subject that ought to be studied and the statement of Eccles to me that he thought it would require legislation . . .

Q: On these foreign securities: Doesn't the Secretary of the Treasury have the right to stop the export of gold, even if they do sell those securities?

The President: Yes.

Q: Has Secretary Roper told you his plan for the unemployment census?

The President: No. We won't take that up until I get back, probably.

Q: Mr. President, what has been said the last day or two on the subject of securities would tend to give the impression that there is some fear of a runaway stock market.

The President: I don't think that was one of the factors.

Q: But the impression is given by what is being said.

The President: I don't know. Nobody has ever talked that phase with me at all.

Q: Purely the exchange factor?

The President: The exchange and the fact—I suppose the easiest way to put it is this: that currencies of European nations and gold reserves have been affected in the past, as we all know, by certain private groups. For instance, all you have to do on that is to look back on the attacks made, for instance, on the franc over the past three or four years. There would be a concerted drive by what might be called private syndicates— simultaneous attacks on currencies which, of course, upset not only the particular currency that was being attacked but also the exchange rate between those currencies and other currencies and then, being a triangular thing, it affects the exchange rate of those other currencies among themselves. It is a disturbing factor. Well, that particular factor seems to have been taken care of by the gentlemen's agreement and that kind of attack on currencies is fairly well under control.

Of course, the obvious thing is to see what other kind of a topheavy situation might exist that, for one reason or another, would cause the same effect as the attacks on gold, or on gold currencies. The accumulation of very large security holdings in any one nation, subject to withdrawal at a moment's notice, is a dangerous factor in the world and it is being looked at from that point of view, as a potential danger not only to our currency and our exchange but to everybody else's currency and exchange.

Q: The stock market itself is a secondary thing?

The President: Yes, yes. Somebody ought to write a story some day—I don't believe anybody over here could do it—on the expert attacks on the franc and the lira and the guilder and the pound—and the pound, you can smash the pound, if you like. It is a very interesting story if one can find the inside facts with respect to the attacks that were made on those things in the past four years.

Q: Who is doing it?

The President: There are all kinds of rumors. That is why the thing should be studied and written up.

[President's Press Conferences:T]

[1] Marriner Eccles, chairman, board of governors, Federal Reserve System, was at the White House on November 12, and James M. Landis, chairman of the Securities and Exchange Commission, was there on the day before (PPF 1-0).

[2] In commenting on this press conference, the New York *Times,* in its Nov. 14, 1936, issue (p. 1), noted that some $7,000,000 in foreign money had poured into the United States in recent months for investment in securities. Roosevelt and others (said the *Times*) feared that this "hot money," so-called because it could be withdrawn at any time, would upset the Tripartite Agreement in its first months of activity.

Robert W. Bingham, Ambassador to Great Britain, to Roosevelt

London, November 13, 1936

Dear Mr. President: I am sure you would be gratified if you could know how warmly and even enthusiastically your triumphant re-election

has been received here. The British press service is so bad and so insuffi-
cient, so far as the United States is concerned, and there are so many
blind bigots of Americans who come here, there was a belief in some
quarters that Landon would win, and in others that it would be a close
race. I think this had its effect on the government here, leading it to
temporize until after the election. Unfortunately, this is customary with
the British at any time, since it is their habit to temporize and try to
compromise, and that is why they fumble and muddle so often.

I am glad to say I am on record not only verbally, but in writing,
with the Prime Minister and Anthony Eden and other members of the
government, and with influential people outside of the government, as
to the result of the election, telling them months ago the issue of the
election was certain; weeks before, that Landon would not carry as many
as ten states, and three weeks before November 3rd, he would have less
than eight states.[1] I told them this because I wanted to give them a
correct impression and because I wanted them to conduct their negotiations with us on the basis of a certainty instead of an uncertainty.

I was told by Eden before the election that the Prime Minister would
make a more definite statement on international trade than had yet been
made, when he made his speech at the Lord Mayor's Banquet on
November 9th. Shortly before the 9th, but after the election, Mr. Baldwin told me this himself, and further told me what he intended to say
about the mad armament race in Europe. He spoke firmly and strongly
about the latter, and did go further in committing his government to
the principle of the restoration of international trade than any one has
done heretofore.

However, he referred to the strictly bilateral agreement just completed
with Italy, and predicted a successful result along the same lines for the
negotiations pending with Argentina. With these two agreements in
effect, I think they will consider themselves in a better position to trade
with us. Their real difficulty lies in the fact that the government is too
largely influenced by the City, and these money-changers are nearly,
if not quite as blind, as our own.

Speaking generally, there is a wide-spread, persistent, increasing feeling
here that it is to their interest to cultivate better relations with the United
States. Unfortunately, so far this has taken the form of propaganda only,
and has not yet reached a point where they are willing to make a fair
and mutually profitable agreement with us, although it is probable they
will come to that in time.

It is certainly a time when those of us who represent our country's
interests here must keep our feet on the ground and our heads clear,

because, while some of their propaganda is crude, much of it is subtle and cunning. They are still fumbling, with no really definite and capable leadership. Their aircraft program has broken down badly and has involved not only mismanagement, but some graft. While not panicky, they are jittery. I have known these people for many years, and I have never seen them as nervous as they are now.

What is really in the back of their minds is to try to work out something which will not cost them anything, or at least very little, by which they can tap American credit when the storm breaks upon them, which they all believe will come, and I think they will try to play the game along with us until they become convinced it is quite hopeless. The sooner they reach this conclusion and make up their minds that they have no chance with us except in a fair, open and cooperative and mutually profitable undertaking, the better off they will be.

They have set the stage for Neville Chamberlain to succeed Mr. Baldwin, and if they carry this out they will be making a great mistake, in my opinion. I think their best choice will be Sir Samuel Hoare, and possibly even a better man, except he is too young, according to their habits, would be W. S. Morrison,[2] who has recently succeeded Walter Elliott as Minister of Agriculture, Elliott remaining in the Cabinet as Minister for Scotland. At this time, however, all signs point to the election of Neville Chamberlain, who lives and breathes only in the atmosphere of the money-changers of the City.[3]

Now another great cause of alarm and anxiety has come to them about the King. His conduct has caused wide spread resentment, and the most loyal people here state unreservedly that he has damaged the prestige of the Monarchy itself, and they are very apprehensive of the results if he follows the course he has so far pursued.

On the whole case, however, they are more inclined now to treat with us intelligently and reasonably and fairly than they have been since I have been here as Ambassador, and within a reasonably short time it seems probable to me that you will be able to go as far with them as you think is consistent with our interests.[4]

Sincerely yours,

Robert W. Bingham

[Notation:A:FDR] File Personal
[PSF:Great Britain:TS]

[1] Landon carried Maine and Vermont.

[2] Member of Parliament since 1929 and Minister of Agriculture and Fisheries from 1936 to 1939.

---

[3] Chamberlain, Chancellor of the Exchequer since 1931, became Prime Minister May 28, 1937.

[4] See Bingham to Roosevelt, Jan. 5, 1937, below.

Thomas J. Watson, President, International Business Machines Corporation, to Roosevelt

New York, November 13th, 1936

Dear Mr. President: Dr. James T. Shotwell and I have been working together on international affairs, through the Carnegie Endowment for International Peace and the International Chamber of Commerce, for a good many years.[1] We believe that plans for world peace must be based on sound international economics and that the United States must play an important part in the development of sound political economy.

We are enclosing a memorandum with the thought that possibly you might deem it feasible to make some indirect or veiled reference to this subject in your speech in Rio de Janeiro. The job is bigger than any organization in existence today, but it is not too big for an organization led by you, to work out plans to save civilization. If our preliminary thoughts appeal to you, upon your return Dr. Shotwell and I will be at your service.

With all best wishes for a pleasant trip and a safe return, I am

Sincerely yours,

T. J. Watson

[Notation:A:LeHand] Trip[2]
[PPF 2489:TS]

[1] Shotwell, professor of history at Columbia, was also director of the Division of Economics and History of the Carnegie Endowment for International Peace.

[2] This notation means that the correspondence was taken along on Roosevelt's trip to Buenos Aires.

[Enclosure] James T. Shotwell and Thomas J. Watson to Roosevelt

Recovery is now assured, so far as the United States is concerned. But world-recovery is held back by the haunting fear of insecurity, which distorts peace-time economic life and destroys the basis of confidence on which credit rests. It is a psychological rather than a real situation, however, and would yield to leadership, if constructive policies can be substituted for negative attitudes. Such policies would naturally have to concentrate upon the erection of an adequate machinery for international peace, to match that for war which is so largely the cause of anxiety and fear today.

The suggestions which follow rest upon the history of both failures and successes in the efforts of recent years. They call for a World Organization, simple in outline, but capable of adjustment to all the varying forces of a dynamic world. That this organization does not exist at present will be clear from the following sketch of possible future developments.

It is proposed that there be at least four separate bodies, one of which would be the League of Nations, duly modified to fit alongside the others. To emphasize their autonomous character, these bodies might bear some such name as: The House for International Planning; The House for Economic Relations; The House for Political Relations; and the World Court. They would be distinct in scope and purpose. Membership could be had in any one without involvement in any other.

The House for International Planning would cover all those varied interests which the Germans group under the term Kultur. It would build on one of the least developed but fundamentally important sections of the present League, the Organization for Intellectual Cooperation, and would embrace all the varied activities of that body and its affiliates. It would deal with what the European nations have termed Moral Disarmament. It would provide for the study of international relations and organization and all such matters as come within the purview of the social and political sciences, especially technical questions arising from the effect of the scientific advance and mechanization. It would also work to preserve the catholicity of culture in the sciences, arts and letters. It would furnish a focal point for thought and discussion. While there are a number of bodies that partially deal with these subjects at present, such as the Institute of Pacific Relations, the International Studies Conference and the Permanent Commission of Arts and Letters, none of these deal with the problem as a whole, and all of these worth while could be articulated into a world organization of this type.

The House for Economic Relations is already half built. The International Labor Organization is adequately dealing with all industrial and labor problems. The other half, however, is hardly even begun. For the Financial and Economic Section of the League has never been made adequate to its task. Trade and finance, the two most international things in the life of nations, should have a place by themselves. Around it similar interests would naturally cluster, such as communications, transit and humanitarian interests, where those are not specifically dealt with by the I.L.O.

The House for Political Relations would be all of the present League that has to deal with diplomacy and war. This body will probably develop into regional groupings, and, for the present at least, the United States would not be a member of it. It is unnecessary to elaborate this point further. Everyone agrees that the League of Nations as it stands today is inadequate for its task. The remedies, however, which have been proposed are equally inadequate; because, for the most part, they simply call for more of the same thing. The League is to be either more universal, or supplied with more effective sanctions, or both. The proposals look to greater police power for the suppression of war instead of turning to its prevention by greater effort to deal with causes.

The World Court and the provisions for arbitration whether by Court or Commissions, would no longer be open to the charge of being a mere appanage of the League of Nations if that League were only a section of the quadruple body which is here envisaged as a World Organization.

Thomas J. Watson
James T. Shotwell

[PPF 2489:T]

Stephen T. Early, Assistant Secretary to the President, to Marguerite A. LeHand, Private Secretary to the President

Washington, November 13, 1936

Memorandum for Miss LeHand: A Mr. Clarence E. Pickett wrote Mrs. Roosevelt, asking her good offices in obtaining from the President a letter to Reverend Dr. Harry Emerson Fosdick, Pastor of the Riverside Church in New York, endorsing an appeal which is to be made from the Christian pulpits of the United States during November in behalf of suffering Christian refugees from Germany.[1]

We referred the matter to the State Department and today received from Acting Secretary Moore the following memorandum:

It is the opinion of the Department of State that it would not be appropriate for the President to support an appeal for assistance for one particular class of refugees or for refugees from one particular country. The President has, in the past, carefully refrained from taking such action in behalf of any single interested group.

In view of these circumstances it is believed that Dr. Fosdick should be advised not to make the request which he contemplated making and that the situation should be explained to him or Mr. Pickett, preferably by telephone rather than by letter.

If the President approves we will handle as suggested by Acting Secretary Moore.

S.E.

[*Notation*:AS] S.T.E.   OK   FDR

[OF 133:TS]

[1] Pickett, executive secretary of the American Friends Service Committee, had written to Mrs. Roosevelt on Nov. 7, 1936, enclosing drafts of a proposed exchange of letters between him and the President (OF 133). Fosdick proposed that an appeal be made to Christian congregations in behalf of the some 15,000 German Christian refugees; the letter prepared for the President's signature would have endorsed this appeal.

Roosevelt to President Getulio Vargas of Brazil, Rio de Janeiro

[Washington] November 16, 1936

[*Telegram*] I thank Your Excellency and Madame Vargas for your cordial invitation to visit Rio de Janeiro as the guest of the Republic in the event that I find it possible to go to South America on the occasion of the opening of the Inter-American Conference for the Maintenance of Peace at Buenos Aires.[1] If, as I hope, circumstances permit me to accept your kind invitation, I probably would sail on November 18th and arrive at Rio de Janeiro on Friday, November 27th. It would afford me the greatest pleasure to have the opportunity to experience a direct contact with the people of the Republic of Brazil for whom my fellow citizens hold feelings of sincere friendship and admiration. If Your Excellency will allow me to delay for three or four days, I shall be in a position to send a definite reply within that period to your gracious invitation.[2]

Accept, Excellency, the assurance of my highest consideration and personal esteem.

[OF 11:M]

[1] Nov. 10, 1936 (OF 11).

[2] Actually no delay occurred. A second telegram was sent to Vargas by Roosevelt on the same day, saying that he accepted the invitation but regretted that Mrs. Roosevelt would not be able to accompany him (OF 11). Hull had approved the opening date of the conference, Dec. 1, 1936, on Aug. 11, 1936 (Hull to Saavedra Lamas, Aug. 11, 1936, *Foreign Relations, 1936,* V, 23–24), and it had been known for some time that Roosevelt would attend. In another telegram of November 16, the President accepted an invitation from President Justo of the Argentine Republic to visit Buenos Aires (OF 11). Both replies were drafted in the State Department.

Robert P. Skinner to Roosevelt

Paris, France, November 17, 1936

Dear Mr. President: At various times since the conclusion of the Great War I have attempted to draw attention to certain commercial arrangements which we succeeded in making with Great Britain early in 1916, arrangements which, had they been made two years earlier, would have saved our people millions of dollars and, at the same time, greatly reduced the friction between the two Governments, with which you are familiar.[1] Unfortunately, I have thus far made no practical headway in obtaining consideration of this important matter in influential circles, and I, therefore, address myself to you in the hope that my present observations, based upon personal experience, may be of some assistance to you in dealing with a subject likely to figure conspicuously in the work of your next administration.

As you are aware, nearly all discussion of neutrality legislation nowadays revolves around the idea of *preventing* shipments of goods as a means of keeping us out of the war. This may be necessary, as respects shipments to actual belligerents, but does not take into consideration the rights and necessities of neutral powers. We may be sure that, in any future war, as in every past war, our exporters of cotton, manufactured goods and what not, will clamor for the right to forward their wares at least to neutral destinations, and we may be equally sure that, unless we take anticipatory action now, this right will be denied as it was during the Great War.

I am proposing, therefore, that we endeavor *now* to obtain from Great Britain a convention based upon what was actually arranged unilaterally in 1916, but going somewhat farther in certain directions, as a reasonably sure means of protecting our trade with neutral powers within those limitations that every reasonable person must agree are proper. There is this probability to be considered: Legislation in Congress is likely to be obtainable with difficulty and perhaps not at all and when enacted will doubtless be an ordinance of self-denial only. Such a treaty as I now have in mind would be worked out through diplomatic channels and should not arouse opposition either in business circles or in the Senate. It is unlikely, also, that Great Britain would hesitate long before accepting an arrangement which actually took effect in 1916 and proved to be most helpful in practice.

The plan I have in mind I urged upon our Ambassador in London during the last war. As you are aware, Mr. Page[2] was not very useful in dealing with our practical troubles but, eventually, I obtained the approval of Mr. Lansing[3] and managed to place the idea before Lord Robert Cecil, then Minister of Blockade. Lord Robert Cecil was so impressed with the suggestion that he caused it to be embodied in an Order in Council. I attach copies of correspondence with him showing what was actually done, correspondence which proves conclusively that the British Government of the day was willing to adopt any plan that was feasible and likely to reduce friction.[4]

With these rather tiresome explanations out of the way, I submit herewith a rough draft of a possible convention, to which other powers could subscribe if disposed to do so. Naturally, I am always at your disposition to discuss any points of detail which may require elucidation. The language of the suggested convention runs as follows:

Draft Convention

Being desirous of lightening as far as possible the burdens falling upon trade and commerce in the event of war, and of facilitating the free movement of goods to neutral countries within the limits of their normal requirements, the two contracting powers have agreed as follows:

1. Should either contracting party become involved in war, the other being a neutral, the belligerent power undertakes to set up at the capital of the neutral power or in such commercial centers as may be expedient, an office or offices equipped to consider and pass upon the history of all proposed exportations to neutral destinations, and if such exportations are found to be in fact intended for a neutral destination and no other, and in quantities within the normal requirements of the contemplated

destination, the office or offices will thereupon issue a certificate to accompany the goods; and when goods are thus covered by a certificate declaratory of the facts above indicated, they shall be assured free passage to destination and shall not be detained or interfered with by any naval or military measures of the belligerent power.

2. It is likewise agreed that should one of the contracting parties being a belligerent set up in the territory of the other, being a neutral, an office as provided in the preceding paragraph, the neutral power shall likewise establish an organization for the reception and examination of the papers relating to proposed exports of goods to neutral destinations and when convinced of their trustworthiness shall issue a certificate to this effect which, on being submitted to the control office of the belligerent power, shall be accepted as conclusive as to the facts alleged.

3. It is further agreed that neither party, being a belligerent, shall apply to the goods of the other party any prohibition or restrictive measure not in effect on the date of shipment by sea of such goods.

4. It is further agreed that if ships of the one contracting party are detained by the other contracting party, being a belligerent, and are subsequently released, having been found innocent of any contra-convention of international law, compensation shall be paid to the owner of the detained ship equal to losses sustained.

5. It is further agreed that either party, being a belligerent, will seek to enforce no prohibitive or restrictive action against the goods of the other which does not apply equally to the goods of the party seeking to impose the prohibition or restriction.

I am persuaded, Mr. President, that if the foregoing suggestions can be embodied in a convention with Great Britain, we shall have done something to mitigate the rigors of any future war and shall have succeeded in preventing much of the irritation and dangerous controversy which characterized our relations with Great Britain during the first part of the last war.

Believe me, dear Mr. President, Sincerely yours,

Robert P. Skinner

[OF 502:TS]

[1] Skinner, who had retired as ambassador to Turkey on Feb. 29, 1936, had served as consul general in London from 1914 to 1924.

[2] Walter Hines Page.

[3] Robert Lansing.

[4] Copies of Cecil's letter to Skinner, Feb. 9, 1916, with a memorandum of their conversation, same date, and Cecil's secretary's letter of Feb. 5, 1916, arranging the appointment, are present.

Roosevelt to R. Walton Moore, Acting Secretary of State

Washington, November 17, 1936

Memorandum for the Acting Secretary of State: Confirming my conversation with you yesterday,[1] will you be good enough to arrange to have Mr. Hickerson, Mr. Basil Manly and Mr. Frank Walsh visit Norman Armour in Ottawa and have some very unofficial preliminary conversations with the Prime Minister in regard to the St. Lawrence Treaty?[2]

If there is any publicity from Ottawa, it can well and truthfully be said that there is nothing official but that it is merely a social visit in which, of course, it has been natural to talk about the future of the St. Lawrence Waterway and the hydroelectric development which goes with it.[3]

F.D.R.

Copy to: Mr. Manly, Mr. Walsh
[OF 156:CT]

[1] Presumably at the Cabinet meeting.

[2] Walsh, chairman of the New York State Power Authority, had written to Roosevelt Nov. 12, 1936 (OF 156), suggesting that he direct the State Department to begin immediate preparations for renewal of treaty discussions with Canada. He enclosed a memorandum suggesting that opposition to the treaty be met by conversations with Canadian seaway experts and by bringing up to date the 1934 report on the project. John D. Hickerson, assistant chief of the Division of Western European Affairs of the State Department, was the liaison officer in the negotiations. Basil Manly was vice chairman of the Federal Power Commission.

[3] See Walsh to Roosevelt, Dec. 12, 1936, below.

Roosevelt to Stephen T. Early and Marvin H. McIntyre

Washington, November 18, 1936

Memorandum for S.T.E., Mac: If this thing comes up while I am away, see if you can work out something. I think the Navy has got to go along with the War Department and the State Department.

F.D.R.

[OF 1561:T]

[*Enclosure*] R. Walton Moore, Acting Secretary of State, and Harry H. Woodring, Secretary of War, to Roosevelt

[Washington] November 11, 1936

The President called into consultation at the White House yesterday the Acting Secretary of State, the Secretary of War, the Secretary of the Navy, and the Acting Attorney General.[1] The subject discussed was the restriction on the exportation of arms, ammunition and implements of war—with particular reference to airplanes—under the provisions of the Espionage Act of June 15, 1917.

It is our understanding that the President definitely decided:

1. That the War and Navy Departments should henceforth adopt in full the War Department's interpretation of the pertinent section of the Espionage Act and should follow the War Department's procedure in dealing with proposed exportations; specifically:

(a) That the War and Navy Departments should not express objection to the exportation of any article which does not fall within the categories adopted by the War Department as follows: (a) Articles, the whole or any features of which, have been or are being developed or manufactured by or for the War Department or the Navy Department or with the participation of either of those Departments; and (b) Articles, the whole or any features of which, have been used or are being used by the War Department or the Navy Department or which either Department has contracted to procure.

(b) That when the War and Navy Departments express objection to the exportation of articles relating to the National Defense, they should do so only on the ground of military secrecy.

2. That the Department of State should issue an export license pursuant to the pending application of the Douglas Aircraft Corporation for a license to export DF flying boats to the Union of Soviet Socialist Republics.

3. That for the time being all new types of military planes should be considered as military secrets for at least a period of one year after the delivery of the second plane of such new types; that the War and Navy Departments, perhaps in cooperation with the Department of State, should undertake a study to determine whether or not that minimum period of one year should at a later date be reduced; and that

495

arrangements should be made which would permit manufacturers to negotiate for foreign sale before the actual exportation is permitted.[2]

R. Walton Moore
Harry H. Woodring

[OF 1561:TS]

[1] Stanley Reed.
[2] See press conference, Dec. 29, 1936, below.

Benito Mussolini, Prime Minister of Italy, to Roosevelt

My dear Mr President,

In the last three years I have often remembered our exchange of letters of 1933,[1] and regretted that the course of events has not allowed the first contacts then established between ourselves to be pursued with the continuity wich was in our intention.

It is therefore with the deepest satisfaction that I avail myself of the occasion presented by your triumphal reelection to the Presidency, to convey to you my warmest congratulations for this expression of universal approval that your great work has met with.

I also desire to express to you my very sincere wishes for the even-greater prosperity, which—I am sure—the United States will achieve under your enlightened guidance.

Hoping that our relations, now re-established, may not undergo any further interruption, I am, my dear Mr President

Very sincerely yours

Mussolini[2]

Roma 19 Novembre 1936—XV
[PSF:Italy:AS]

[1] April 24 and May 14, above.
[2] No reply was made until July 29, 1937 (*Foreign Relations, 1937,* I, 662–664). Roosevelt said he had delayed replying in the hope that the world situation would become more favorable for a discussion of world peace. This, unfortunately, had not come to pass but he urged renewed consideration of the reduction of world trade barriers and of armament reduction.

R. Walton Moore, Acting Secretary of State, to Roosevelt

Washington, November 21, 1936

Dear Mr. President: This is a tabloid report on our Department's relation to the state of the union. I am glad to tell you that because of the friendly and whole-hearted cooperation of the people here, the machine seems to be working very smoothly. I do not suffer any sense of fatigue, although my working day begins before nine o'clock in the morning, and runs until after dark, with an intermission of only five or ten minutes for a sandwich and cup of tea brought to my desk. In fact I am glad that you have given me the first opportunity to exert myself to the limit since the hard years when I was trying to persuade courts and commissions that railroad corporations were entitled to the same sort of justice that is accorded natural persons. When the situation is again normal, I fear that I shall feel almost at a loss to know what to do with myself.

Some steps recently taken I think will tend to make better conditions. I have reference to your Executive Order about the marriage business;[1] a plan to require periodical physical examinations of the Foreign Service people, many of whom serve in bad climates; the protection here and abroad of the secrecy of our codes, and a better supervision of what goes on in the various divisions and offices of the Department, a matter which strange to say has heretofore received almost no attention. Under your permission, Mr. Carr[2] and I have had a very satisfactory talk with Mr. Bell,[3] and I hope that his conclusion as to appropriations for the Department will be favorable. What is asked is not more than needed under present conditions, and hardly takes into account un-expected happenings abroad, such as the Spanish War, which necessitate unusual expense, and of course, although we hope for the contrary, there may be much more of that sort of thing.

Referring to your suggestion that thought should be given to the appointment of a successor to Governor Murphy,[4] the only man I have heard much mentioned is Governor Winant,[5] but the other day someone suggested that Frank Sayre[6] might be considered, and I am telling you this without ever a word on the subject having passed between Sayre and myself. He is certainly very able, conscientious and zealous. By the way, I had him out to my house in Virginia last Sunday, along with several other people, among them Mr. John L. Lewis and his wife. Lewis is my neighbor, because of now living in Alexandria, and I find him very attractive.

You requested me some time to mention to you Jenkins, who is our Consul General in Berlin. I know him and have no doubt whatever that he and Cochran would serve well in Ministerial posts.[7] Yesterday, after we had received assurances from Moscow, Joe Davies' appointment was announced by the White House, and Monday morning he is to come here to be sworn in, accompanied by some of the ladies of his family, and thus I may have the opportunity of meeting the new Mrs. Davies. We have brought about improvements in the residence that he will occupy at Moscow, he standing the cost.

The only worry that I have at this moment is about our representatives in Madrid and Barcelona, and yesterday I sent a cable to Mr. Bowers, urging that he let us have his definite recommendations as to whether or not it is wise for them to remain at their posts any longer.[8] I think the answer should be in the negative, since anyone at Madrid is now in danger of a violent death, and pretty soon will be in danger of death by starvation.

I hope you will not regard this as an egotistical letter. I despise the egotist, who is a man without sense enough to recognize that he is only one of several hundred million people now living, and only one of countless trillions that have lived. I never think of that character without thinking of the Chanticleer. You will remember that Rostand in that play described the young rooster that had got into the early habit of going to the barnyard at daybreak and crowing until the sun rose. He thought he was the sunrise king until one morning he overslept and got to the barnyard after sunrise, when of course his feathers fell.

I trust that in spite of the ordeal at Rio and Buenos Aires you will return to Washington thoroughly rested and that then some plan can be devised of relieving you of seeing so many people and considering so many matters not of major importance. I rather think the plan of a few Executive Assistants would be a good beginning.

Many of the foreign Ambassadors drop in, and I am surprised to find that they know so much less than we about what is going on abroad. Suvich got his first information of the recognition by Italy and Germany of the Spanish insurgents from the statements in our newspapers.[9] I can tell you that all of them who talk to me speak of you with the greatest astonishment and admiration.

With the warmest best wishes for you always, I am

Yours very sincerely,

R. Walton Moore

[PSF:State Department:TS]

[1] Executive order 7497, issued Nov. 17, 1936, barred the marriage of Foreign Service officers to aliens without permission of the State Department.

[2] Assistant Secretary of State Wilbur J. Carr.

[3] Acting Director of the Budget Daniel W. Bell.

[4] Frank Murphy had recently resigned as governor general of the Philippines.

[5] John G. Winant, former governor of New Hampshire.

[6] Assistant Secretary of State; Paul V. McNutt was eventually named.

[7] Douglas Jenkins, Sr.; H. Merle Cochran, first secretary at Paris.

[8] Printed in *Foreign Relations, 1936*, II, 766–767.

[9] Fulvio Suvich, Italian ambassador.

William C. Bullitt, Ambassador to France, to Roosevelt

Paris, November 24, 1936

Personal and Confidential

Dear Mr. President: The appended memorandum will give you the gist of a conversation I had with Monick but will not give you the odour of it. It is a subtle, and not altogether pleasant, odour which pervades every conversation I have in Paris whether with Frenchmen, Englishmen, Belgians, or Czechs. It is the emanation of a violent nervous desire to get us into the next war.

Everyone in France, including Blum and the British Ambassador, is convinced that war is about to arrive. Herriot, Claudel, and the more nervous representatives of the smaller countries, are convinced that war will come next Spring or Summer. Everyone is convinced that war will come by the Spring or Summer of 1938.

As you will see from the memorandum, I refused to listen to the details of Monick's scheme, and I have since refused to receive his project from a third party. I suspect that it involves not simply a debt settlement but also some vast scheme for economic and financial collaboration of the United States with England and France, designed to get us into close political collaboration as well.

We shall have to watch every agreement or other commitment with extreme care if we are to avoid slipping into a position from which there will be no retreat. I think that henceforth we should not accept any "proposal in principle." We ought to be willing to discuss specific detailed proposals but nothing else.

It will be difficult for me to make you realize the degree to which French Cabinet Ministers and representatives of all the countries of Europe in Paris talk as if they had within them the same phonograph record—playing the theme, "War is inevitable and Europe is doomed to destruction unless President Roosevelt intervenes."

Invariably I reply by asking how you can intervene effectively. Invariably the reply is, "We don't know, but the President must have some idea." Invariably I answer that I am reminded of the situation at the close of a Greek tragedy, when the difficulties become too vast to be handled by man and the *deus ex machina* appears to set everything right. I then remark that you are not a *deus* and that you have no authority to bend the rulers of Europe to your will, and that you are not going to send the American Navy and American soldiers to Europe.

Invariably the reply is, "That is quite right. There is no reason why you should send your armed forces again to Europe; but————."

Thereupon the conversation begins again; and once more it becomes obvious that our money, ships and men are the things that are wanted.

As the situation grows worse, you will hear much flattery about your moral prestige and your duty to western civilization.

The pressure of one sort and another will not be easy to handle.

I am informed reliably that the Muscovites themselves are about to begin a new drive to attempt to get our good will and that they will inaugurate it by covering Joe Davies with tons of the very best butter. They are disturbed by the recent Japanese-German agreement[1] and are beginning to realize how foolish they were to give us the kick in the face which they delivered so light-heartedly when they made the American communists the stars of the Comintern Congress in the summer of 1935.

Incidentally, I am informed that they are reinaugurating the propaganda, which they started at that time, to the effect that neither you nor the American Government cared in the least whether or not they directed the American Communist Party from Moscow; but that the protest we made at that time was due entirely to my ill temper. I understand that they have been attempting to get *The Nation* and *The New Republic* of New York to commence this line of attack on me and to start a campaign for close cooperation between the "democracies" of the United States and the Soviet Union!

I hope that you have instructed Joe Davies to be exceedingly cordial to the Bolsheviks but also to be absolutely adamant on the point of Russian interference in our internal affairs through control of the American Communist Party from Moscow. In the period ahead, we can not let either Mussolini, Hitler, or Stalin organize and direct groups of American citizens.

The war in Spain, as you know, has become an incognito war between the Soviet Union and Italy. The Spanish Ambassador here admitted to me a couple of days ago that the entire air force of the Madrid Government is composed of Russian pilots and Russian planes. He boasted that some of the Russian pursuit planes in Madrid had a speed of 510 kilometers per hour and admitted that the only hope of the Madrid Government was in the Russian planes and Russian arms. On the other hand, Franco's forces actually at the fighting front are composed almost entirely of Moors, and Italian and German aviators. Reports are that the German aviators are much better than the Italian. My own impression is that Mussolini has decided to put through Franco whatever the cost may be. I think that the cost will be very high.

I would not be surprised if Mussolini should be compelled to enlist a couple of Italian Army Corps in the Spanish Foreign Legion. I believe that before the Spanish Civil War is over it may bring Europe to the very edge of war. I believe, however, that war will not spring directly out of it. A situation may arise from it, however, which will give Hitler a chance to make some move against Czechoslovakia.

Czechoslovakia, clearly is the next item on Hitler's menu.

If Hitler should send forces into Czechoslovakia the position of France, as well as Czechoslovakia, would become tragic. (No military man with whom I have talked believes that the Soviet air force can bring any effective aid to Czechoslovakia.) The French would have to decide whether or not to carry out the obligations of their treaty of alliance with Czechoslovakia.

The Quai d'Orsay would be all for carrying out those obligations but I am inclined to believe that the greater part of the country would be dead against carrying them out.

The Belgian Ambassador here is an able man of long experience. He said to me a few days ago that he was certain France would not march in support of Czechoslovakia. He predicted that France would first ask Belgium and England what they would do. He said that he was certain both his own country and England would refuse to do anything; that the French would then be faced with the problem of attacking Germany alone, unsupported, or allowing Czechoslovakia to be swallowed and denying their pledged word. He added that he was certain the French, under the circumstances, would not march.

I have, however, discussed the same eventuality with a number of Frenchmen, and they say that France would march, knowing perfectly well that, when France began to be beaten by Germany, England would have to come in on the side of France.

My own guess is that there would be a hair's breadth decision, and that no one can predict with certainty as to whether or not France would march in support of Czechoslovakia.

I do not want to worry you with more of this sort of speculation. The tragic fact is that no one in Europe today is putting any constructive energy whatsoever behind the idea of preserving peace. Everyone is spending every ounce of energy on preparing instruments of war. The nub of the situation remains the hostility between France and Germany. As I wrote you before, I see no sign of rapproachement. I should like to see us in a position to do what we can to help in Berlin and Paris if there should be a chance that they may come together. I shall keep my ears as wide open as possible, as well as my nostrils, to try to detect any faint trace of peace and shall let you know at once if I feel that there is anything we can do without involving ourselves in the horrors to come.

What those horrors will be, you can imagine. Pierre Cot, the French Air Minister, said to me a few days ago that, while he was going on building airplanes as fast as he could, he felt that the airplane race between France and Germany had now reached the point of absolute idiocy. He already had in his air force sufficient planes to destroy Berlin and Essen instantly. Goering already had enough planes to destroy Paris instantly. Neither of them had any means of defense against those planes. The destruction of cities and populations was inevitable. Incidentally, the French Government recently considered a proposal to supply the population of Paris with gas masks. It was found that the cost would be two billion francs. It was decided to let the population take its chances.

In all this intellectual chaos and impending doom, the underlying truth is that the development of the airplane has made Europe an absurdity. Last year, flying from Munich to Venice, I crossed Austria in fifteen minutes. When you and I were children, it took that long to drive from the Place de la Concorde to the Bois de Boulogne. These dinky little European states can not live in an airplane civilization. Today they have the alternative of submerging their national hatreds and national prides sufficiently to unify the continent or of destroying themselves completely and handing Europe over to the Bolsheviks. There is as yet no sign that there may be an outbreak of common sense.

I hope you are having a grand trip to South America. My love and blessings.

Yours affectionately,

Bill

[PSF:France:TS]

---

[1] The anti-Comintern pact signed Nov. 25, 1936; for the text see *Foreign Relations, 1936,* I, 400–401.

[*Enclosure*] William C. Bullitt to Roosevelt

Memorandum for the President: Your cable saying that I was right arrived at the right minute.[1] Less than twenty-four hours later Monick called to see me. As I had your cable I could answer him categorically.

Monick began by saying that he understood I was taking steps to reopen the matter of the French debt to the United States.[2]

I asked him to stop right there, and said that I had not taken any steps whatsoever to open the matter, and that I would not take any steps whatsoever.

I told him how Madame Claudel had telephoned asking me to come to see Claudel urgently; how Claudel had then proposed that he (Monick) should go to talk with you in Buenos Aires; and how I had squashed the idea.

I explained that Claudel had then asked me if I felt there was anything inadvisable in his continuing his newspaper campaign for payment of the debts and that I had replied that I saw nothing against it. Claudel had then said that he felt it advisable to get the cooperation of Madame Tabouis, who was at the moment the cleverest journalist in Paris, and had stated to me that he had intended to ask Monick to see Madame Tabouis.[3] I informed Monick Madame Tabouis had then repeated to me what Claudel had said to her, and that I had warned her that if she began a campaign in her paper that there was every likelihood that the impression would be created that I had started the campaign. I felt it was advisable, therefore, that any campaign should be started in another quarter and that, in any event, I would have nothing to do with the campaign.

I had explained to Madame Tabouis that while the American Government would be glad to consider any definite offer, we would not participate in any way in cooking up an offer; that we would not play French internal politics and that so far as I was concerned I desired to be left out of any consultations as to what should and what should not be done.

I should, of course, be glad to serve as a channel of communication if Monsieur Blum desired to make an official offer of a debt settlement to me.

I then said to Monick that you were entirely unwilling to enter into any secret and semi-official schemings such as those which he had conducted with Jimmy Warburg which had resulted in Daladier's attack on Herriot while Herriot was in mid-ocean.[4]

He replied, "Bon. That clears the ground. Now I should like to tell you exactly what I consider are the only possible principles on which we could pay the debts."

I replied that I did not wish to discuss any scheme. He said that there were merely certain principles he would like to state. Before doing so he would like to ask the question whether or not you desired the debts to be paid and whether or not, from your point of view, it would be inopportune at the present time to open the question of the debts.

I replied that, of course, you wanted the debts to be paid and added that I saw no reason why the present time should be inopportune.

Monick said that he had asked this question because he had been in communication with the British on the question of reopening the debt negotiations and the British had informed him that they had received the impression from Washington that you would be averse to considering any debt offer at this time.

I replied that I thought this was a mistaken impression.

Monick then said that he would go on to state his principles which would be of a general nature.

(1) Any debt settlement with the United States must be made by France and England simultaneously.

I asked him "Why?" He replied that inasmuch as France owed large debts to England as well as to the United States, it was impossible for France to make a settlement which did not include a settlement with England as well. He therefore proposed to keep the British informed of every action which the French might take.

(2) He then said that his next principle was that no debt settlement should be of such a nature as to destroy the monetary equilibrium between France, Great Britain and the United States as established by the recent monetary accords.

(3) His third principle was that any debt settlement made should be one which would not add to restrictions on international trade, but would tend to remove barriers to international trade in line with the policy which you and the Secretary of State had inaugurated.

I replied that while these principles sounded impeccable I had no idea what he meant by them in detail and that the details were the important thing. Any sort of document could be drawn out of general principles. The Treaty of Versailles had been drawn from Wilson's Fourteen Points. He must remember in preparing any proposal, that the detailed proposal would be considered by Congress on its merits in relation to the interests of the United States, and not on the basis of general principles.

(4) That brought him to his final point. He wanted to know whether or not, if a definite proposal should be made by the French Ambassador in Washington to you or by Blum to me, and if you should find such a proposal acceptable, you could submit it to Congress for Congressional consideration or whether it would be necessary for the French Government to send a commission to Washington to appear before Congress to discuss the matter. He said that, in his opinion, any such commission would give rise to interminable trouble.

I replied that I was unfamiliar with the details of the matter to which he referred but that I did not see why, if you approved of a proposal, you could not transmit it direct to Congress without the intervention of a French commission.

I then added that there were certain factors of American public opinion which he doubtless had in his mind, as he was so familiar with the United States, but to which he should give attention.

(1) That at the time of the French, Belgian and British defaults the United States had been in the most serious financial situation; (2) that the stoppage of the payments had been an actual financial blow; (3) the blow to American confidence in European good faith had been even greater; (4) the defaults had produced a feeling throughout the whole United States that those countries of Europe which pretended to be our best friends would use us to the limit when we had something to give them and would treat us with the most callous indifference and dishonesty when it suited them to do so; (5) that there was now an important section of public opinion in the United States which believed that the debts *unpaid* were of great value to the United States, because (thanks to the Johnson Act), nations in default could not borrow in the United States. As a result, American capital today was remaining at home and not leaving in floods for European countries. If any nation should make a debt settlement, it would at once be able to borrow in the American money market.

For example: Italy today was in great need of capital. If Italy should have sense enough to make a debt settlement with the United States, it could float loans in the United States to the amount perhaps of a billion dollars, and could use a small portion of these loans to pay the United States its annual debt obligations and finally default on loans. If there should be war, such a default would be inevitable. The defaulted debts today were a guarantee that this could not happen.

Furthermore, the fact that the debts were unpaid made it almost certain that the United States could not be swept into a war of European and not of American interest.

I then added that he must get out of his mind once and for all any idea which he might have that the United States would send troops or battleships to Europe.

He replied that he understood this perfectly. But in this crisis of democracy, just because the United States was unwilling to participate with physical means in the European situation, we had all the more duty to participate morally, financially, and economically in the maintenance of peace in Europe. He himself was convinced that there was a possibility of maintaining peace in Europe if the Germans could be given an economic position which would enable them to live and develop; that this could not be done without the assistance and cooperation of the United States. If this were not done, there would be war in Europe which would end in Bolshevism from one end of the continent to the other.

I replied that so far as duty was concerned, we had amply discharged any obligations we had to Europe by our military assistance in the past war and by our loans from government to government for the reconstruction of Europe after the armistice—all of which had been defaulted—that we felt no sense of obligation whatever; that we had, however, an interest in the preservation of civilization.

Monick then said that he felt an agreement on the debts might be made the first step toward collaboration with England, France and the United States for the preservation of European peace and pacification of the continent.

I said that it seemed to me the nub of European peace was still reconciliation between France and Germany.

He said that it unquestionably was; but that he was opposed to any direct negotiations between France and Germany.

I asked him how he expected to get anywhere if that were his attitude.

Monick dodged this question and finally concluded by saying that we must reach a debt settlement at once and this Spring have another World Economic Conference.

I replied that any World Conference held today would unquestionably produce just the same results as the Economic Conference in London; that the ground was totally unprepared; that every nation in Europe was engaged in demonstrating that its pledged word was worthless; and that I felt no Economic Conference should be called until agreement had been reached by previous negotiation and that a Conference should be called merely to record the results with pomp and circumstance.

As he was leaving, Monick stated that he intended to press the matter, and that he would see to it that any proposal made to us should be made officially either by Blum to me or by the French Ambassador in Washington to you.

W.C.B.

[PSF:France:TS]

[1] No copy has been found.

[2] Possibly in consequence of Bullitt's talk before the Agence Économique et Financiere in Paris on Nov. 11, 1936, although all he said was that the United States was ready at any time to renew debt discussions with France and to submit any reasonable debt payment proposal to the Congress (New York *Times,* Nov. 12, 1936, p. 42). On November 19 Morgenthau denied Paris reports that debt repayment proposals had been brought to his attention (*ibid.,* Nov. 20, 1936, p. 16).

[3] Geneviève Tabouis, who wrote frequently under her pseudonym of "Cassandra."

[4] In 1933, when en route to Washington to confer with Roosevelt.

R. Walton Moore, Acting Secretary of State, to Roosevelt

Washington, November 25, 1936

Dear Mr. President: I shall not bother you about problems of importance that are coming along here, but am writing simply to mention a few items that might have been mentioned in my letter of November 21st.[1]

We have asked London to keep us advised of the appointment by any other country of representatives at the Coronation, with the thought that you may wish to appoint representatives as soon as one or two other nations have acted. I notice that a Wisconsin Congressman has gone into the newspapers to give his reasons why we should not be represented at the Coronation, and it is stated he will offer a resolution on the subject when Congress convenes.[2] Fairly early action by you will tend to end that sort of foolishness. It seems to be against precedent to include our Ambassador, and thus it will be entirely proper to designate the three other gentlemen you have in mind, and name your son as their Secretary.[3]

Some time ago you spoke of transferring Mr. Atherton from London,[4] and if this is to be done before the Coronation, I suppose there should not be very much delay. I have thought of Herschel Johnson, the present

First Secretary there, and when you return I would like to find an opportunity to introduce him to you, as he is now on leave here. He is a Georgia man who was educated at Harvard, was Chief of the Mexican Division when I entered the Department, and has always been a Democrat. I have a very good opinion of him.[5] Bullitt, since suggesting John Wiley, who is now at Antwerp, has written me that Wiley prefers to remain as Consul General at that place, and I think he should be kept there for a while, just as I think Pierrepont Moffatt should be kept in Australia to the end of a two year period.

The Department's Foreign Service School has been revived, and is now engaged in instructing the young men who have been admitted to the career service, but have not yet received assignments. From what some of the young men tell me, I think the school is conducted in a pretty satisfactory way, but that it could perhaps be made of more value if supervised by such a man as Howland Shaw.[6]

There come to me some very interesting letters from our people abroad, among them Phillips, Dodd, Messersmith and Nicholson,[7] all rejoicing over the result of the election and most of them containing pretty doleful predictions of a large scale war—predictions with which I do not find myself in agreement.

Before this reaches you, I hope that our officials at Madrid and Barcelona will have gotten away from those dangerous places.[8] We are handling that matter in a very definite manner, so as to avoid their continual exposure to real danger of being killed, and the howl of criticism to which we would be subjected should that occur. I do not understand how any good ground of objection can be found to the action taken, particularly in view of the fact that Wendelin, at Valencia, will be in close contact with the officials of the Spanish Government, which is now at that place. So far as American property is concerned, most of it, against our protest, was some time ago taken over, by the Spanish Government, both at Madrid and Barcelona.

As I said to you before you left Washington, and now venture to repeat, I hope it may be possible for you to do something for former Senator Brookhart.[9] I understand there is a vacancy on the Board of Tax Appeals, and two vacancies on the Interstate Commerce Commission, but I am not mentioning these at Brookhart's instance, for I have not seen or heard from him since you left Washington. I came to know him quite well while he was Senator, soon after I entered the House, and had an opportunity to form an estimate of him. He has always been disliked by very conservative people, and there are others who dislike him because he is of the very distinct rough and ready Western type. There can be no doubt that he possesses more than ordinary ability, and is very earnest and fearless in trying to serve the real public interest. As he dropped into my office frequently during the campaign, before and after his trip to the West, I came to understand how strongly, and I think effectively, he was striving in Iowa, Minnesota, and elsewhere, to promote your reelection.

It is regrettable that now that everyone is so anxious for the success of the Buenos Aires Conference that the Mexican Legislature has enacted, and it is said President Cárdenas is about to sign, an expropriation law which should really be called a confiscation law. When it becomes effective, the American owners of every kind of property in Mexico will be in peril of having their property taken over on the basis of its assessed value, and with no certainty as to whether they will be paid even that. In advance of the Act being signed, I have requested Mr. Daniels to discuss the matter confidentially with the President,[10] with a view to ascertaining what can be done at least to have a fairer measure enacted. The thing as now written is unthinkably bad, and a menace to the proper sort of relations between our Government and the Government of Mexico. But in saying this I forget about my promise at the outset not to trouble you with matters of importance.

With earnest best wishes for you in every way, I am

Yours very sincerely,

R. Walton Moore

P.S. Since the above was dictated, the Spanish Ambassador has come in, and in the course of his talk about the general situation he said that yesterday he had been in telephone communication with Madrid, and was aware of the dangerous situation there, and thought we had taken a sensible course in getting our people out. Incidentally he said that more than a thousand women and children, to say nothing of men, had suffered death from bombing. Wendelin hopes that tomorrow morning he will be started for Valencia with about fifty Americans besides his staff. He will locate at Valencia, where he will be in immediate touch with the Spanish Government, and there will be one of our warships there to take charge of such of the Americans as desire to leave Spain. I have informed Secretary Hull very fully about what has been done, and the compelling reasons for it.

Having heard that Prime Minister King's engagements will probably prevent him from seeing our representatives, should that be desired, until early next month, the visit of Messrs. Hickerson, Walsh, Olds and Manly has been postponed to December 5th.[11]

R.W.M.

[*Notation*:A:FDR] File Pers
[PSF:State:TS]

[1] Above.

[2] Raymond J. Cannon, a Democratic representative from Milwaukee (New York *Times*, Nov. 18, 1936, p. 3). Cannon urged that American representation at the coronation of Edward VIII be canceled because the British had defaulted on their war debt.

[3] Moore had written Roosevelt on Nov. 12, 1936 (PSF:Great Britain), suggesting that the American mission to the coronation should consist of three members and a secretary. Roosevelt, in his reply (*Personal Letters, 1928–1945*, I, 629), Nov. 14, 1936, suggested that James W. Gerard, Ambassador Bingham, Rear Admiral Hugh Rodman, and James Roosevelt, as secretary, attend the ceremony. General John Pershing was eventually substituted for Bingham but only Gerard attended the coronation in May 1937.

[4] At this time consul general.

[5] Johnson was named counselor of embassy in London, July 8, 1937, and Atherton became American minister to Bulgaria, July 13, 1937.

[6] G. Howland Shaw, chief of the Foreign Service Personnel Division of the State Department.

[7] Meredith Nicholson, American minister to Venezuela since 1935.

[8] Moore had telegraphed Roosevelt, Nov. 23, 1936, while the latter was on his way to South America, that he had instructed Wendelin, chargé in Madrid, to evacuate all American nationals who so desired from Madrid under Embassy protection (*Foreign Relations, 1936*, II, 773).

[9] Smith W. Brookhart of Iowa, an independent Republican, was defeated for nomination to the Senate in 1936 after having served there from 1927 to 1933.

[10] Moore to Daniels, Nov. 23, 1936, and Daniels' reply, Nov. 28, 1936, in *Foreign Relations, 1936*, V, 723–725, 725–728.

[11] John D. Hickerson, assistant chief, Division of Western European Affairs, Department of State; Frank P. Walsh, chairman, New York State Power Authority; Leland Olds, executive secretary, New York State Power Authority; and Basil Manly, vice-chairman, Federal Power Commission. See Walsh to Roosevelt, Dec. 12, 1936, below.

Arthur Murray to Roosevelt

[London] Nov. 26th, 1936

Personal

My dear Franklin: Your triumphant personal victory was mightily refreshing to liberal thought wherever it exists. You must badly have needed a holiday, and I much hope that this will find you greatly refreshed as a result of your sea-voyage.

I am very glad indeed to be able to tell you that the "Walter Runciman" matter has now worked out "according to plan." He asks me to say to

510

you that he is much looking forward to accepting, in January, your kind invitation to pay a personal visit to you, assuming that nothing happens in the meantime on "the home front" to prevent him getting away.

In order to avoid prior publicity and the appearance of an official visit it was necessary to provide a good private reason and "cover" for his crossing the Atlantic. Accordingly, after discussion, we agreed that I should take John Tweedsmuir (an old friend of us both, as I know he is of yours) into our confidence and ask him to invite *Cornwall* (the word Tweedsmuir and I have used in our cable communications as meaning Walter Runciman) to come out to Ottawa to see Canada in the winter time. This Tweedsmuir did by cable a few days ago.

Confidentially I have told Tweedsmuir of the circumstances that gave rise to your invitation to Cornwall, and have also said to him that I was telling you that I had done so.

According to present arrangements Cornwall will sail in the *Caledonia*, Anchor Line, on January 8th, and will arrive at Government House, Ottawa, about January 18th.

Would you very kindly cable me to let me know that you have received this letter, and whether a date about January 25th would suit you for Cornwall to visit you.[1]

I know you will like him—a very old friend of mine; and one of the best, straightest-minded fellows that ever stepped the earth. You have in common with him "all the things of the sea." He owns the Isle of Eigg, and has a big yacht!

To other things—I am sending you an etching and watercolour (of a First Rate of 120 Guns) which used to belong to my Father. There is tremendous "life" in it, and I think you will like it.

I have been busy on our joint genealogical tree! I find that we have the same descent, on your Mother's side, from 1296 (earliest recorded) to about 1450, and then branch off, you from the elder, my family from the fourth son! But curiously enough there was an interlocking marriage between the branches some 60 years later! When I have completed the whole "Tree" I will send you a copy of it.

Faith and I are going to Monte-Carlo on Dec. 16th for 3 weeks. I shall have to try and remember your lucky number!

With every good wish
yours very sincerely

Arthur Murray

[PPF 435:AS]

---

[1] Murray cabled Roosevelt about dates for Runciman's visit to Washington on Dec. 18, 22, and 23, 1936 (according to a file note of Dec. 31, 1936, PPF 435; the cables are missing). On Dec. 22, 1936, Roosevelt cabled to Murray: "Delighted see Cornwall as suggested. Merry Christmas you both" (PPF 435). On Dec. 26, 1936, Murray wrote to Roosevelt to say that Runciman's plans had changed and that he would not be able to visit Ottawa but that he would see Roosevelt in Washington on Jan. 23, 1937.

R. Walton Moore, Acting Secretary of State, to Roosevelt

Washington, November 27, 1936

Dear Mr. President: Perhaps you may care to glance through the enclosed letters from Messersmith.[1] The one dated November 9th I find particularly interesting. Some of the statements in it tend to confirm my impression, which you may rightly say is of little value, that there is not going to be a European war on an extensive scale in the near future. For many reasons, Mussolini does not wish to bring on a war, and is now in a better position than ever to exert a restraining influence on Hitler. Every month of delay by leaders who have the warlike inclination is favorable, because that affords Great Britain the opportunity to build up her Air Force and strengthen her Navy. Russia is becoming so very strong, in preparation for the possibility of war, that I doubt whether either Germany or Japan, both together, will venture to strike at her. Much it seems to me rather encouraging might be said along this line, and in addition there is the fact, which is full of encouragement, that the peoples everywhere are now expressing their hate of war, and debating what can be done to prevent it. And besides this, in the next few days your voice for peace is to sound out through the world as no other voice ever has.[2] Perhaps the fine weather and the pleasing appearance of everything in Washington this morning make me too hopeful, but even when the weather is gloomy, I am an incurable optimist about the war business.

The communications I have sent you evidence what is a cold fact, namely, that we have taken the wise course in Spain, which seems to have nearly everybody's approval. I am extremely fond of Claude Bowers, and am sorry that in this instance, at rather long distance from Madrid,[3] he has viewed the situation in an unduly theoretical and political manner, and without sufficient concern as to the serious trouble to us that would result from a lot of Americans in Madrid being killed. Wendelin, who is young and adventurous, now seems to agree very definitely that we have done the correct thing. I assumed a heavy responsibility in making the decision, and the case had so many ramifications that it was simply impossible for me, at this distance, to present it in detail to the Secretary and expect him to be able to reach a speedy conclusion. All that I can say is that after the most careful and deliberate consideration of which I was capable, action was taken, of which there now appears to be little complaint.

I trust that this morning you feel as well as I feel, and that all of your great hopes and expectations will be fully realized.

With earnest best wishes for your health, happiness and success, I am

Yours very sincerely,

R. Walton Moore

The Polish Ambassador came in a few minutes ago to disclaim for his Government any connections whatever with the German-Japanese agreement.[4]

I am sorry to see the press reports that President Cardenas has signed the new Mexican expropriation (it might properly be called confiscation) law.[5] In Mexico that action is coupled with the threat of very extensive strikes—

R.W.M.

[PSF:State Department:TS]

[1] To Hull, Nov. 6, and to Moore, Nov. 9, 16, 1936, on the European situation in general.

[2] Plans for broadcasts of the Buenos Aires conference proceedings, Roosevelt's major addresses, and daily commentary by H. V. Kaltenborn and others are described in a letter of Harry C. Butcher, vice-president of the Columbia Broadcasting System, to Early, Nov. 17, 1936 (OF 256).

[3] Bowers had been in San Jean de Luz, on the southwest coast of France, since shortly after the outbreak of the civil war.

[4] Moore's memorandum of his conversation with Potocki and the text of the agreement are printed in *Foreign Relations, 1936*, I, 400–401.

[5] Signed November 23; the text is printed *ibid.*, V, 720–723. See Daniels to Roosevelt, Dec. 22, 1936, below.

Edmundo de Miranda Jordão, President, Brazilian Bar Association, to Roosevelt, on Board the U.S.S. *Indianapolis*

Rio de Janeiro, 27 de November de 1936

O Instituto da Ordem dos Advogados Brasileiros (Brazilian Bar Association) at its meeting in this city last night, upon motion of its President unanimously adopted a resolution extending to you our sincere and hearty welcome upon your arrival in Rio de Janeiro. Our Association, founded in 1843 under the auspices of Dom Pedro II, then Emperor of Brazil, is very gratified in having the honor to greet such a distinguished member of our profession from our sister Republic in North America. We assure you of our whole hearted approval of your good neighbor policy among the Republics of this hemisphere and in this message to you we express our sincere wish that the Peace Conference to be held in Buenos Aires may be a further star of successful accomplishment in the interest of humanity in your long and useful public career.

With highest esteem and consideration, we have the honor to be, Sir, Very respectfully yours,

Edmundo de Miranda Jordão
Alvaro de Souza Macedo, 1st Secretary

[PPF 4190:TS]

Roosevelt to Edmundo de Miranda Jordão, President, Brazilian Bar Association, Rio de Janeiro

Aboard U.S.S. *Indianapolis,* November 28, 1936

Dear Snr. Miranda Jordão: Upon my return to the U.S.S. *Indianapolis* last evening, I received with much pleasure indeed your letter conveying the unanimously adopted Resolution of the Brazilian Bar Association, extending me a sincere and hearty welcome to Rio de Janeiro.[1]

My welcome to Brazil was most sincere and hearty. As the opening day of the Inter-American Conference nears, it was indicative of the quickening tempo of the good neighbor policy throughout the Americas.

I am deeply grateful for the kind sentiments you express and wish you would convey my thanks to the members of your distinguished Association at the first opportunity.

With best wishes to yourself and the members of the Brazilian Bar Association, I remain,

Very sincerely yours,

[PPF 4190:CT]

[1] Above.

Statement by Roosevelt at the University of Buenos Aires

[November 30, 1936]

The spokesman for the University said: "It is with great pleasure that I place in your hand the degree of Doctor of Laws of the University of Buenos Aires. It is the highest degree that the University can offer."[1]

He then talked of the good feeling that exists between our two countries, and, in testimony of the great esteem in which he was held, conferred the degree.

The President: "Please tell the Director and his associates how very happy I am and how very deeply I am honored by the giving of this degree. And especially so because I am a son of the oldest American university—Harvard, and that I look forward to this as being a symbol of a closer association between the universities of the United States and the universities of the Argentine Republic. I am very sorry that I cannot stay here long enough to see the university and to take part in some of its discussions. Thank you very much. Sometime I am going to come here and see you again. I hope to see you all in Washington. Thank you very much."

Pan American Union, Members of Association of the River Plate Instituto Cultural Argentina Norte Americano: The members were presented to the President, who greeted them cordially and said that he had heard about the fine work that this Association is doing and observed that the more exchange of cultural facilities we can get between us the better it will be. He then jokingly remarked that there was one thing that he was sure of and that is that we will have to improve the steamship facilities. He then went on to say that this sort of exchange of students is very interesting. The Institute then presented a special volume containing the signatures of thousands of persons, which is a form of homage that is paid in these countries.

Dr. and Mrs. Romulos Naon, former Ambassador to Washington, were presented to the President and he chatted with them cordially for a few moments.

Also the Robbins family (the deBruin family also were presented and were cordially greeted).[2]

"You have seen this tremendous demonstration in the streets. This is an expression of the sentiments that we feel for you and of our greatest esteem."

The President: "I have always heard about the splendid work of this group and wish that we had in the United States something that would

515

correspond to this in the United States. When I started the New Deal I hoped that it would be that sort of thing—an adequate group of trained social workers.

"I hope very much that we will be able to send some of our people down here to learn from what you have accomplished. I spoke to Mr. Hopkins[3] about it just before I left. He is the head of our work of that kind in the United States."[4]

[PPF 4211:T]

[1] The degree was conferred late in the afternoon of November 30, the day Roosevelt arrived in Buenos Aires. The diploma, dated Nov. 28, 1936, is in the Roosevelt Library.
[2] The widow of Warren Delano Robbins, Roosevelt's cousin, was Irene deBruin Robbins, of a Buenos Aires family.
[3] Harry L. Hopkins, Works Progress Administrator.
[4] This text is that of a typescript presumably prepared as a press release.

Speech by Roosevelt before the Inter-American Conference for the Maintenance of Peace, Buenos Aires, December 1, 1936

Your Excellency, President Justo, Members of the American Family of Nations, my Friends:[1]

On the happy occasion of the convening of this conference I address you thus, because members of a family need no introduction or formalities when, in pursuance of excellent custom, they meet together for their common good.

As a family we appreciate the hospitality of our host, President Justo, and the Government and the people of Argentina; and all of us are happy that to our friend Dr. Saavedra Lamas has come the well deserved award of the Nobel Prize for great service in the cause of world peace.[2]

Three years ago the American family met in nearby Montevideo, the great capital of the Republic of Uruguay. They were dark days. A shattering depression, unparalleled in its intensity, held us with the rest of the world in its grip. And on our own continent a tragic war was raging between two of our sister Republics.

And yet at that conference there was born, not only hope for our common future, but a greater measure of mutual trust between the American democracies than had ever existed before. In this Western Hemisphere the night of fear has been dispelled. Many of the intolerable burdens of economic depression have been lightened, and due in no small part to our common efforts, every nation of this hemisphere is today at peace with its neighbors.

This is no conference to form alliances, to divide the spoils of war, to partition countries, to deal with human beings as though they were pawns in a game of chance. Our purpose, under happy auspices, is to secure the continuance of the blessings of peace.

Three years ago, recognizing that a crisis was being thrust upon the New World, with splendid unanimity our twenty-one Republics set an example to the whole world by proclaiming a new spirit, a new day in the affairs of this hemisphere.

And while the succeeding period has justified in full measure all that was said and done at Montevideo, it has unfortunately emphasized the seriousness of threats to peace among other nations. Events elsewhere have served only to strengthen our horror of war and all that war means. The men and women and children of the Americas know that warfare in this day and age—warfare means today more than mere clash of armies: they see the destruction of cities and of farms—they foresee that children and grandchildren, if they survive, will stagger for long years not only under the burden of poverty, but also amid the threat of broken society and the destruction of constitutional government.

And I am profoundly convinced that the plain people everywhere in the civilized world—not only here in the Americas but everywhere else—wish to live in peace one with another. And still leaders and governments resort to war. Truly, if the genius of mankind that has invented the weapons of death cannot discover the means of preserving peace, civilization as we know it lives in an evil day.

But we cannot now, especially in view of our common purpose, accept any defeatist attitude. We have learned by hard experience that peace is not to be had for the mere asking; that peace, like other great privileges, can be obtained only by hard and consistent effort. And so we are here to dedicate ourselves and our countries to that work.

You who assemble today carry with you in your deliberations the hopes of millions of human beings in other less fortunate lands. Beyond the ocean we see continents rent asunder by old hatreds and new fanaticism. We hear the demand that injustice and inequality be corrected by resorting to the sword and not by resorting to reason and peaceful justice. We hear the cry that new markets can be achieved only through conquest. We read that the sanctity of treaties between nations is disregarded.

We know, too, that vast armaments are rising on every side and that the work of creating them employs men and women by the millions. It is natural, however, for us to conclude that such employment is false employment, that it builds no permanent structures, creates no consumers goods for the maintenance of a lasting prosperity. We know that nations guilty of these follies inevitably face the day either when their weapons of destruction must be used against their neighbors or when an unsound economy like a house of cards will fall apart.

In either case, even though the Americas become involved in no war, we must suffer too. The madness of a great war in other parts of the world would affect us and threaten our good in a hundred ways. And the economic collapse of any nation or nations must of necessity harm our own prosperity.

Can we, the Republics of the New World, help the Old World to avert the catastrophe that impends? Yes, I am confident that we can.

First, it is our duty by every honorable means to prevent any future war among ourselves. This can best be done through the strengthening of the processes of constitutional democratic government—to make these processes conform to the modern need for unity and efficiency, and at the same time, preserve the individual liberties of our citizens. By so doing, the people of our nations, unlike the people of many nations who live under other forms of government, can and will insist on their intention to live in peace. Thus will democratic government be justified throughout the world.

In this determination to live at peace among ourselves we in the Americas make it at the same time clear that we stand shoulder to shoulder in our final determination that others who, driven by war madness or land hunger might seek to commit acts of aggression against us, will find a hemisphere wholly prepared to consult together for our mutual safety and our mutual good. And I repeat what I said in speaking before the Congress and the Supreme Court of Brazil, "Each one of us has learned the glories of independence. Let each one of us learn the glories of interdependence."

Secondly, and in addition to the perfecting of the mechanisms of peace, we can strive even more strongly than in the past to prevent the creation of those conditions which give rise to war. Lack of social or political justice within the borders of any nation is always cause for concern. Through democratic processes we can strive to achieve for the Americas the highest possible standard of living conditions for all our people. Men and women blessed with political freedom, willing to work, able to find work, rich enough to maintain their families and to educate their children, contented with their lot in life and on terms of friendship with their neighbors, they will defend themselves to the utmost but will never consent to take up arms for a war of conquest.

And interwoven with these problems is the further self-evident fact that the welfare and the prosperity of each of our nations depends in large part on the benefits derived from commerce among ourselves and with other nations, for our present civilization rests on the basis of an international exchange of commodities. Every nation of the world has felt the evil effects of recent efforts to erect trade barriers of every known kind. Every individual citizen has suffered from them. And it is no accident that the nations of the world that have carried this process furthest are those which proclaim most loudly that they require war as an instrument of their policy. It is no accident that attempts to be self-sufficient have led to falling standards for their people and to ever increasing loss of the democratic ideals in a mad race to pile armament on armament. And it is no accident that because of these suicidal policies and the suffering attending them, many of their people have come unfortunately to believe—to believe with despair—that the price of war seems less than the price of peace.

This state of affairs, my friends, we must refuse to accept with every instinct of defense, with every exhortation of enthusiastic hope, with every use of mind and skill.

I cannot refrain here from reiterating my gratification that in this, as in so many other achievements, the American Republics have given a salutary example to the world. The resolution adopted at the Inter-American Conference at Montevideo endorsing the principles of liberal trade policies has shone forth like a beacon in the storm of economic madness which has been sweeping over the entire world during these later years. True, if the principles there embodied find still wider application in your deliberations, it will be a notable contribution to the cause of peace. For my own part I have done all in my power to sustain the consistent efforts of my Secretary of State in negotiating agreements for reciprocal trade, and even though the individual results may seem small, the total of them is significant. These policies in recent weeks have received the approval of the people of the United States, and they have, I am sure, the sympathy of the other nations here assembled.

There are many other causes for war—among them, long festering feuds, unsettled frontiers, territorial rivalries. But these sources of danger which still exist in the Americas, I am thankful to say, are not only few in number, but already on the way to peaceful adjudication. While the settlement of such controversies may necessarily involve adjustments at home or in our relations with our neighbors which may appear to involve material sacrifice, let no man or woman forget that there is no profit in war. Yes, sacrifices in the cause of peace are infinitesimal compared with the holocaust of war.

Peace comes from the spirit, and must be grounded in faith. In seeking peace, perhaps we can best begin by proudly affirming the faith of the Americas; the faith in freedom and its fulfillment which has proved a mighty fortress beyond reach of successful attack in half the world.

That faith arises from a common hope and a common design given us by our fathers in differing form, but with a single aim—freedom and security of the individual, which has become the foundation of our peace.

If then, by making war in our midst impossible, and if within ourselves and among ourselves we can give greater freedom and fulfillment to the individual lives of our citizens, the democratic form of representative government will have justified the high hopes of the liberating fathers. Democracy is still the hope of the world. If we in our generation can continue its successful application in the Americas, it will spread and supersede other methods by which men are governed and which seem to most of us to run counter to our ideals of human liberty and human progress.

Three centuries of history—three centuries sowed the seeds which grew into our nations; the fourth century saw those nations become equal and free and brought us to a common system of constitutional government; the fifth century is giving to us a common meeting ground of mutual help and understanding. Our hemisphere has at last come of age. We are here assembled to show its unity to the world. We took from our ancestors a great dream. We here offer it back as a great unified reality.

And finally, in expressing our faith of the Western World, let us affirm:

That we maintain and defend the democratic form of constitutional representative government.

That through such government we can more greatly provide a wider distribution of culture, of education, of thought and of free expression.

That through it we can obtain a greater security of life for our citizens and a more equal opportunity for them to prosper.

That through it we can best foster commerce and the exchange of art and science between nations; that through it we can avoid the rivalry of armament, avert hatred and encourage good will and true justice.

And that through it we offer hope for peace and a more abundant life to the peoples of the whole world.

But this faith—this faith of the Western World will not be complete if we fail to affirm our faith in God. In the whole history of mankind, far back into the dim past before man knew how to record thoughts or events, the human race has been distinguished from other forms of life by the existence—the fact—of religion. Periodic attempts to deny God have always and will always come to naught.

In the constitutions and in the practice of our nations is the right of freedom of religion. But this ideal, these words presuppose a belief and a trust in God.

The faith of the Americas, therefore, lies in the spirit. The system, the sisterhood of the Americas is impregnable so long as her nations maintain that spirit.

In that faith and spirit we will have peace over the Western World. In that faith and spirit we will all watch and guard our hemisphere. In that faith and spirit may we also, with God's help, offer hope to our brethren overseas.

[RL Recordings]

[1] This speech was given before the Conference at its opening session in the building of the Argentinian Chamber of Deputies at 6 P.M. (Buenos Aires time). President Roosevelt's address followed that of President Justo of Argentina, who welcomed him and the delegates. The address is printed also in Rosenman, *Public Papers,* V, 604–610; it is reprinted here because it is Roosevelt's final major foreign policy statement of his first administration. The text here printed is that of the radio broadcast recording in the Roosevelt Library. A comparison of the broadcast with the press release issued in Buenos Aires (also in the Roosevelt Library) indicates that the President made but few departures from the prepared text, and none of these variations is significant. In addition to the Buenos Aires press release the Library has a copy of the State Department press release of the speech issued in Washington. This varies in a number of words and phrases from the Buenos Aires release and was doubtless prepared earlier. Rosenman's text closely follows the Buenos Aires release. No drafts of the speech are present; Rosenman notes in his book *Working with Roosevelt,* p. 140, that "the material and drafts . . . were prepared in the State Department." The reading copy is in the possession of James Roosevelt, who accompanied his father on the South American trip.

Punctuation and capitalization in the text as here printed are that of the Buenos Aires press release except where President Roosevelt plainly changed the punctuation in reading the speech.

[2] Carlos Saavedra Lamas, Argentinian Minister of Foreign Affairs, had received the Nobel peace prize on Nov. 24, 1936, for his part in bringing to a close the Chaco war between Bolivia and Paraguay, mentioned by Roosevelt in the paragraph following.

Reply by Roosevelt to a Toast by President Augustín Justo of Argentina, at Dinner, December 1, 1936, Buenos Aires

Your Excellency: In acknowledging Your Excellency's gracious courtesy,[1] let me offer my heartfelt thanks, not only for the hospitality which has been shown here, but for the deep understanding of our point of view, which you, Mr. President, have just manifested. It is always a great experience for nations to meet as they have done today; it is greater still, when they meet, to find that they thoroughly understand one another. I am heartily in agreement with Your Excellency in what you have said and I feel sure that your words will re-echo throughout this Continent.

This is a fitting occasion to express my deep thanks to the Government of the Argentine Republic, and, especially, to the people of the Republic, for the honor they have paid me. Let me accept it not for myself but for the people of the United States as a tribute of fellowship fron one nation to another, and as a mark of devotion to the great ideal which all of us are here to serve. Rarely have I been as moved and touched as by my experiences of yesterday and today. It seems to me as though everyone, from the great statesmen of your country to the little children who play in your gardens, have combined to say, "Welcome—we are friends." Friends we are; friends we shall always be. I shall treasure these days as a link in the great chain of intercourse which binds our countries and as a poignant memory in my heart.

The Conference for the Maintenance of Peace has opened. As Your Excellency has said, it is rare in history that such a conference opens without hate, without rancor, without difference; with no desire on the part of any one or of any country to triumph; inspired only by the desire of all to cement our family relationship. Its success is forecast by the attitude you have just expressed in behalf of the Argentine people in announcing the Republic's willingness to continue her collaboration without reservation of any kind in the work of continental brotherhood and solidarity. That has been one of the great glories of the Argentine Republic. Joined in now by all of her sister Republics, we can and we must achieve a triumphant realization of a long cherished hope.

If we can give tangible form and substance to our will to peace, to justice, and to fair play, we shall have accomplished a memorable thing in this hour when the world is torn by hatreds. Buenos Aires will stand out with an even greater lustre; to her glories as an ancient and famous City, she will add the splendour of being a Capital of Peace.

Let me return the toast! I raise my glass to Your Excellency and Señora de Justo; to your health and happiness; to your splendid work in strengthening the work of justice in the Republic and the ties of friendship and unity throughout the Continent. Let me also express the earnest hope that you, Mr. President, and Señora de Justo may give the people of the United States the honor and the privilege of visiting their country, where both Government and people will endeavor to reciprocate in kind the magnificent hospitality we have so splendidly received.[2]

[Speech File:T]

[1]Justo's remarks at the dinner, given by him at the Casa Rosada in Buenos Aires following the opening session of the Conference, are printed in the *Bulletin* of the Pan American Union for January 1937, pp. 26–28.

[2]Roosevelt's reply to Justo is printed also *ibid.,* pp. 28–29. It is not clear whether his reply was extemporaneous or was drafted in advance. On Dec. 19, 1936, Elsie Brown, managing editor of the Pan American Union *Bulletin,* sent Early her own translation of Roosevelt's remarks as printed in a Buenos Aires newspaper (OF 480). Her copy differs somewhat from the printed version; Miss Brown's letter bears a notation that a corrected copy of the President's remarks was sent to her on Jan. 9, 1937; this was the version published in the *Bulletin.* The three principal addresses made by Roosevelt in South America: before the Brazilian Congress in Rio de Janeiro on November 27; before the Inter-American Conference in Buenos Aires on December 1 (printed above); and at Montevideo on Dec. 3, 1936, are published in *Public Papers,* V, 597–602, 604–610, 612–615, in the Pan American Union *Bulletin* January 1937, pp. 2–14, and in the press generally. These three speeches were issued in an elaborately bound edition by the Government Printing Office in 1937; copies of this edition were sent by Roosevelt to the members of the United States delegation at the conference, to members of the Cabinet, and to a number of Latin American chiefs of state. Roosevelt also spoke informally at a dinner given by President Vargas of Brazil on November 27, and at a luncheon for President Justo of Argentina on December 2; these remarks are printed in *Public Papers,* V, 602–603, 610–612

Remarks by Roosevelt at Luncheon for President Augustín Justo of Argentina, American Embassy, Buenos Aires, December 2, 1936

The President said: An otherwise very delightful occasion makes me quite sad because within two hours I shall be going away and I am very, very sorry that I have to go away, because I cannot imagine a more delightful three days than I have had here and yet, Mr. President, I do not feel as if I knew Argentina yet because to come only to Buenos Aires is to know only a part of this great nation. One hundred and six years ago my grandfather came to Argentina.[1] It has taken me more than a century to follow in his footsteps and I am very certain that if I live it will not be another century before I come back. There is one matter which I should like to take this opportunity of saying and because it is a matter that affects both of our nations, I might say an official matter, I will read a very short statement.

Every nation has the right and the duty to adopt such measures as may be necessary, in the interest of its own citizens, in order to prevent the entrance into its territory from abroad of contagious or infectious diseases prejudicial to human, animal, or plant life. But it is equally clear that quarantine or sanitary regulations should neither be used as disguised tariff measures nor should they be ever applied except in accordance with strict justice.

About a year ago, the Argentine Government and the Government of the United States negotiated a sanitary convention which had for its purpose the removal of an inequitable situation which had arisen as a result of the all embracing character of legislation adopted by the Congress of the United States. The ratification of this Convention would make it possible for Patagonia, a sheep raising area, where the hoof and mouth disease has not existed, and which territory is separated by natural barriers from the cattle raising regions of the Republic, to be relieved from the sanitary embargoes now placed upon it. This Convention, which I had the honor of submitting to the Senate of the United States last year, affects in no wise existing tariff rates. It is intended solely to remove an obvious inequity resulting from an unnecessarily wide application of a sanitary embargo. The ratification of this Convention by the Senate of the United States would eliminate an injustice without detriment or prejudice of any kind to the legitimate interests of the cattle industry of the United States, and without relaxing in the least full sanitary protection of our own livestock. I intend to present these facts clearly to the attention of the members of the Senate of the United States, with the hope that our Senate may give its consent to the ratification of the simple instrument of justice.

May I further say that I trust that conversations may soon be undertaken between us in order to ascertain the bases which exist for the negotiation of a trade agreement between our two countries, which may prove to be mutually profitable to both the people of the Argentine Republic and the people of the United States.

So may I take this last opportunity—I wish there were many more—of thanking you and the good people of Argentina for the very wonderful reception that you have given me, and on behalf of my son[2] and the members of my party to extend to you our profound thanks for all that you have done for us and, as I said last night, I am counting on a visit from you, Mr. President, and Señora de Justo in Washington just as soon as you can.[3]

[Speech File:M]

[1] Warren Delano (1809–1898).
[2] James had accompanied his father.
[3] The luncheon was at 12:15 P.M. and Roosevelt sailed on the *Indianapolis* about two hours later.

Roosevelt to Eleazar Videla, Minister of Marine, Buenos Aires

U.S.S. *Indianapolis,* Montevideo, Uruguay
3 December, 1936

Dear Mr. Minister: I want you to know before I get too far away how much I appreciated the many things which you personally did to bring to me and my whole party the feeling of warmth and the genuineness of our welcome by the people of your Country. We were all greatly impressed by the well executed maneuvers and fine appearance of the officers and men of the Argentine Navy. May I offer my congratulations to you and to them.

With my warm personal regards to you, Sincerely,

[PPF 4188:CT]

Josephus Daniels, Ambassador to Mexico, to Roosevelt

México, December 4, 1936

Dear Franklin: The best part of your address at Buenos Aires was its climax in the sentence beginning: "But this faith of the western world will not be complete if we fail to affirm our faith in God."[1] That appeal to Christian faith entered deep into the hearts of the people of the world (I have heard many expressions of its grateful reception here) and will make a far stronger impression than the papers indicate.

In this connection I am venturing to suggest that at your inauguration you invite Cardinal Mundelein to offer prayer before you deliver the inaugural address. However, if you think it more fitting to have a minister or priest from your own State, I suggest that you invite Cardinal Hayes.[2] I am moved to make this suggestion because the great loyalty to their party and their principles caused the large body of Catholic voters to turn a deaf ear to the pleas of Mr. Carmody of the Knights of Columbus, Bishop Kelley of Oklahoma, Father Coughlin and Al Smith to oppose your reëlection because you had declined to support the Borah resolution to authorize a Congressional investigation into the religious conditions in Mexico. At one time I feared that the resentment toward the religious limitation here might enable them to stampede a large Catholic vote against you. I think that tide ebbed rapidly after the address by Cardinal Mundelein at Notre Dame. The vote showed that the attempt failed.

You will know better than I whether this suggestion is wise, and I submit my "hunch" for your consideration without any feeling that my judgment is as good as yours.

I expect to be in Washington on December 21st and 22nd and am writing to Marvin McIntyre to arrange an engagement when I can talk to you about one or two important matters.[3]

With my affectionate regards to you and Mrs. Roosevelt, in which my wife joins, I am,

Faithfully yours,

Josephus Daniels

[PSF:Mexico:TS]

[1] The speech, Dec. 1, 1936, is printed in *Public Papers,* V, 604–610.
[2] At the January 20 inauguration, the Reverend Ze Barney T. Phillips, chaplain of the Senate, gave the invocation, and Monsignor John A. Ryan of Catholic University gave the benediction.
[3] Daniels saw Roosevelt on December 21.

William E. Dodd, Ambassador to Germany, to Roosevelt

Berlin, December 7, 1936

Dear Mr. President: Your addresses in Latin America have occasioned a great deal of discussion here.[1] The German people of the better informed classes are most favorable toward your propositions as to peace. Some university people, in the presence of officials, now as in October–November 1935, criticize the regime here, especially its militarism, which they think will plunge them into a war more disastrous to Germany than that of 1914–18. The Spanish struggle, with Germans supporting Franco, gives much trouble even to high army officials; but Hitler and Mussolini think they will come into control of Spain and still further frighten England and France.

Under these circumstances, I spoke quite freely on the fifth of December with the Assistant Secretary of State here, Dr. Dieckhoff.[2] After his indications of grave concern about war dangers, I asked him what Germany would do if the American Conference now in session asked them to join a world peace and disarmament conference. He indicated more interest than Dr. Schacht or Von Neurath did some months ago when I touched upon the same subject (see my telegram of the fifth).[3] This led me to speak freely about the grave danger of present German armaments and German-Italian-Spanish relations. He then said, in a round-about way, that he thought the Foreign Office would favor such a conference and would support gradual disarmament proposition. His greatest doubt was as to Mussolini's attitude.

From what information I can get, there is a rising doubt here as to Hitler's success in his Italian, Japanese, Spanish procedure. High army generals were positively opposed to the recognition of Franco, and rumors circulate that Hitler fears now that he will not succeed this time as on former occasions—since December 1935. I enclose a news clipping which shows how Party chiefs are preaching to the people the Führer's status with God Almighty. This Gross speech is the third of its kind, i.e., Gross[4] is the third Party man of high position who talks this way to teachers, writers and church people. It is the method of rallying simple souls to the idea that Hitler must always succeed.

There is no doubt that democratic countries in Europe would welcome a call for a world conference. Their representatives here stress this matter every time I see them—always confidential. What Hitler will say no one can say, certainly not Foreign Office officials. But if the Fascists do not conquer Spain, I am convinced there will be a silent popular demand here for international cooperation. Decided success of Mussolini in dominating Spain would not greatly please Hitler unless he could take what he plans to take from the Danube and Polish zones. No one can say what is the Führer's plan at the present moment. He is here every day now conferring with Party people who have been preaching such sermons as are revealed in the enclosed clipping. England is engaged in a quarrel about the King's marriage; France is divided sharply as to her policy; Russia is proclaiming her solid front against anybody that starts a war in the Balkan or Baltic areas; and all the smaller democracies are hopeless. It is my feeling that Hitler is simply waiting for his best opportunity to seize what he wants.

In case both North and South America agree to accept your ideas, there might be a world conference—and Germany might assent to representation if the Führer listens to the officials indicated above and actually fears, as the intelligent people do, that he might not win a war before 1938. Certainly the debt situation is bad. A half or two-thirds crop next year would be a most serious matter. There have been five or six good crop yields and these never rise above 80% of the needs of the country. With a debt about equal to the total yearly income, with new unemployment when arming begins to decline and a single bad crop, the economic situation might give a chance for a real international agreement, might.[5]

Sincerely yours,

William E. Dodd

[PSF:Germany:TS]

[1] Dodd noted in his *Diary* (Nov. 29, 1936, p. 367), that the German press people were greatly angered by the Rio de Janeiro speech and no German newspaper had mentioned it.

[2] Reported at length *ibid.*, pp. 367–369.

[3] Neither this telegram nor the clipping mentioned below have been found in the Roosevelt papers.

[4] Walther Gross.

[5] Roosevelt replied on Jan. 9, 1937 (*Personal Letters, 1928–1945*, I, 648–649), that the difficulty about any world conference was that delegates never had any authority and had to refer everything to their governments.

William C. Bullitt, Ambassador to France, to Roosevelt

Paris, December 7, 1936

Personal and Confidential

Dear Mr. President: Jim Farley has just passed through Paris. I took him to the dog races but did not lead him any further into the paths of iniquity so that, if he returns to you a changed man, you must blame the result on Ralph Strassburger and not on me.[1] It was a delight to see him.

In talking with Jim, I tried to convince him (and I believe I did) that the situation in Europe today is too serious for him to suggest the planting of dubs in diplomatic posts in order to repay them for contributions to the campaign fund. Jim said that he agreed with me, and we went on to discuss how it might be possible for you to get rid of some of the men who are not fit to hold their present jobs as chiefs of mission in the present world crisis.

In the course of our discussion, it occurred to me and I suggested to Jim and now suggest to you, and shall suggest to Judge Moore, that it might be advisable for you to order him (Judge Moore) as soon as you get back from South America, to issue at once a circular instruction to all chiefs of mission reading as follows:

"Chiefs of mission are reminded that owing to the change in the date of Inauguration, their resignations should be in the hands of the President not later than January 15, 1937."[2]

(Offie[3] suggests that, as a result of this letter, I am likely to receive the only one of such instructions issued. Anyhow, I hereby submit my resignation.)

I suggest an instruction of this kind from Judge Moore to the chiefs of mission because I have no doubt that there are a number of men whom you wish to replace, but that you will find it highly unpleasant to ask for their resignations. If the reminder is sent out as a circular instruction by the Department of State, no one can resent receiving it because it would be addressed to all chiefs of mission without distinction. Then you would be able to get rid of misfits by a polite and hearty letter of thanks and praise.

I should like to pour into your ear a vast number of ideas with respect to men that are not fitted for their present jobs; but it looks as if I should not have an opportunity to see you. I shall restrain myself, therefore, and make merely one suggestion.

If there is a chance to maintain peace in Europe during your next Administration, that chance lies in the small possibility that it may be possible to draw the French Government and the German Government closer together.

Blum, lunching with me alone a few days ago, said that he hoped to be able to inaugurate soon a movement for reconciliation with Germany based on the reduction of economic barriers, financial and economic collaboration and reduction of armaments. He said that he felt the active support and collaboration of the United States would be essential in any attempt to bring France and Germany together.

Another conversation on the same lines was one in which Delbos,[4] the Papal Nuncio,[5] and others participated. They said that Hitler two weeks ago had sent to Paris his "super-Ribbentrop," von Lersner,[6] to say to the French Government, and to the leading French politicians outside the Government, that Hitler still desired most ardently to reach agreement with France. Von Lersner stated that Hitler felt the two countries were so far apart that they could not be brought together without the friendly assistance of the United States. He added that Hitler felt that Luther was not in close touch with our Government and that he should be replaced by someone closer to his intimate circle.

I have managed to establish entirely confidential relations with Blum and Delbos and can see them privately whenever I wish.[7] (I am having lunch with Blum privately twice this week.) It should be possible for our ambassador in Berlin to establish the same sort of relationship with the heads of the Nazi Government in Berlin. It would be difficult but it could be done. If we had an Ambassador who could do that in Berlin, he and I could at least be of some assistance in bringing France and Germany together—nothing much is needed except some verbal assistance in erasing the lies each believes about the other—and in any event, we should be able to keep you fully informed with regard to the most intimate inner details of the European situation.

Dodd has many admirable and likeable qualities, but he is almost ideally ill-equipped for his present job. He hates the Nazis too much to be able to do anything with them or get anything out of them. We need in Berlin someone who can at least be civil to the Nazis and speaks German perfectly. The latter qualification is an absolute necessity as Hitler speaks only German and, unless I am mistaken, Goering speaks only German.

As I wrote you before, I can not think of any American so well qualified as Hugh Wilson for the Berlin job. He speaks perfect German and is on good terms with the Germans without being in the faintest degree pro-German or pro-Nazi. Unless you have someone up your sleeve, I think that you ought to send Wilson to Berlin.[8]

I spare you the dozen other suggestions which I should make if I were with you tonight.

Good luck and every good wish.

Yours affectionately,

Bill

[PSF:France:TS]

[1] Strassburger, publisher of the Norristown (Pa.) *Times-Herald,* owned racing stables in England and France. He had held minor diplomatic posts under Republican administrations.

[2] See Roosevelt to Moore, Dec. 19, 1936, in *Personal Letters, 1928–1945,* I, 641.
[3] Carmel Offie, third secretary at Paris.
[4] Yvon Delbos, French Foreign Minister.
[5] Valerio Valeri.
[6] Baron Kurt von Lersner.
[7] Bullitt's conversations with Blum and Finance Minister Vincent Auriol on war debts are reported in his dispatches to Hull of Dec. 1 and 10, 1936, in *Foreign Relations, 1936,* I, 586–587, 587–588.
[8] Assistant Secretary of State Hugh Wilson succeeded Dodd in December 1937.

Roosevelt to President Getulio Vargas of Brazil, Rio de Janeiro

[Aboard U.S.S. *Indianapolis,* December 8, 1936]

[*Radiogram*] As we leave Brazilian waters I want to thank you for your very kind message[1] and once again tell you how much I appreciate this opportunity, brief as it has been, to greet you and the citizens of Brazil. We have enjoyed every minute of our trip including some very excellent fishing at Cape Frio. We all send to you and Madame Vargas our warmest greetings.

[OF 11:T]

[1] Dec. 5, 1936 (OF 11), congratulating Roosevelt on the "successful realization your grandoise and humane idea of the gathering of the Inter-American Conference for the maintenance of peace."

Roosevelt to Hoffman Philip, Ambassador to Chile, Santiago

U.S.S. *Indianapolis,* Passage,
Montevideo to Port of Spain, 9 December, 1936

Dear Hoffman: In the crowded hours in Rio de Janeiro, Buenos Aires and Montevideo I did not have an opportunity either to thank you for your letter or to write President Allessandri.[1] I am enclosing a note for you to give him—and you can tell him that I am really planning for a visit to the West Coast in 1937 and 1938.[2] My difficulty of course was that if I had gone to Santiago on this trip, I should have had to stop also in Peru and Ecuador and possibly Colombia—the whole length of the cruise being increased by about a week. As you know, it is almost impossible for me to be away from Washington at any one time for more than four weeks as there is no person who can sign necessary documents in my absence.

I think the Buenos Aires Conference is going well and there is no question that the solidarity of thought and action is gaining ground every day.

Most sincerely,

[OF 429:CT]

[1]Philip had written from Santiago, Nov. 12, 1936, that Alessandri regretted that Roosevelt had not planned to go to the Buenos Aires Conference via the west coast of South America, the shorter of the two routes (OF 429). He urged Roosevelt to send Alessandri a "friendly word from Buenos Aires."
[2]Below.

Roosevelt to President Arturo Alessandri of Chile, Santiago

U.S.S. *Indianapolis,* Passage,
Montevideo to Port of Spain, 9 December 1936

My dear President Allessandri: On my return voyage from Buenos Aires I want to send you a message of greeting and also to tell you how deeply sorry I am that I could not have come to visit you in Santiago. I know you will understand the necessity of my immediate return to Washington, but I hope very much that during my second term as President I will be able to visit you. I have, as you know, special family ties with Chile.[1]

My family and I were deeply distressed to hear of your very great personal loss and again we send you our heartfelt sympathy.[2]

With my respects and warm personal regards, I am,

Very sincerely yours,

[OF 429:CT]

[1] A remote ancestor of Roosevelt, Captain Amasa Delano, had spent some time in Chile in 1800, and in 1817 published his *Narrative of Voyages and Travels in the Northern and Southern Hemispheres* (Boston: E. G. House, printer). Other members of Delano's family played a part in Chile's war of independence and eventually settled there, where their

descendants still live (William Phillips to Roosevelt, May 15, 1934, PPF 1683). Roosevelt had earlier presented (on June 16, 1934) a copy of the Delano book to the University of Santiago, Chile, whose copy had disappeared (PPF 1683).

[2] Señora Alessandri had died earlier in the year.

Roosevelt to Robert G. Caldwell, Minister to Portugal, Lisbon

U.S.S. *Indianapolis,* Passage,
Montevideo to Port of Spain, 9 December 1936

My dear Caldwell: Many thanks for your note which followed me all the way to Buenos Aires.[1] You must be having a fairly strenuous time just now with the Spanish situation so close at hand. Things in Europe keep us worried.

Most sincerely,

[OF 509:CT]

[1] Nov. 4, 1936 (OF 509), congratulating him on his reelection.

Roosevelt to Francis W. Hirst, *The Atheneum,* London

U.S.S. *Indianapolis,* Passage,
Montevideo to Port of Spain, 9 December, 1936

My dear Mr. Hirst: I am grateful to you for your note which followed me all the way to Buenos Aires.[1]

The situation in the Americas is distinctly good and I wish that I could feel the same way about the future on your side of the water.

I hope that you and Mrs. Hirst will be coming over here again this coming year. It would be delightful to see you.

Very sincerely yours,

[PPF 1147:CT]

[1] Nov. 7, 1936 (PPF 1147); Hirst said Roosevelt's reelection had filled English liberals and free traders "with a new hope of an economic appeasement for the world." Hirst was an English economist and author, much interested in the American governmental system. He and his wife had visited Hyde Park as friends of the President's mother.

Roosevelt to Arthur Sweetser, Director, Information Section, League of Nations, Geneva

U.S.S. *Indianapolis,* Passage,
Montevideo to Port of Spain, 9 December, 1936

My dear Arthur: It has been good to get your note—which incidentally, followed me all the way to Buenos Aires.[1]

Things in the Americas are in every way most hopeful and I hope there will be at least some moral repercussions in Europe.

Write me from time to time. It is always good to get your news and to have your thought on the situation from the Geneva end.

Always sincerely,

[PPF 506:CT]

[1] Nov. 4, 1936 (PPF 506), congratulating Roosevelt on the election.

Roosevelt to Carlos Vay Ferrlia, Rector, University of the Republic of Uruguay, Montevideo

U.S.S. *Indianapolis,* Passage,
Montevideo to Port of Spain, 10 December, 1936

Dear Dr. Ferrlia: I feel deeply honored in having conferred upon me the degree of "Doctor Honorario" by the University of the Republic of Uruguay and I wish you would express to your associates my great appreciation of their kindness.

I hope that the degree with which you have honored me will be a symbol of a closer association between the universities of North America and those of Uruguay and South America.[1]

With every good wish for your own continued success,

Very sincerely yours,

[PPF 4207:CT]

[1] The diploma, dated Dec. 3, 1936, is in the Roosevelt Library.

Roosevelt to James Harvey Rogers, Yale University, New Haven

U.S.S. *Indianapolis,* Passage,
Montevideo to Port of Spain, 10 December, 1936

My dear Jim: Yours of November 17th reached me in Buenos Aires and am glad to have the memorandum on the silver matter.[1] I had not heard of that particular Chinese problem before but I will take it up with Henry[2] as soon as I get back.

I do hope to see you in Washington some of these days soon.

Very sincerely yours,

[PPF 3038:CT]

[1] Rogers (PPF 3038) said that the Chinese government wished to have considerable amounts of silver dollars minted in the United States for circulation in areas of China where the new paper currency was not being well received. However, the Treasury Department had thus far refused to mint coins of less than 90 per cent fineness, and Rogers thought this was unfortunate in view of our national silver policy. With this correspondence is a memorandum of Dec. 22, 1936, from Wayne C. Taylor, special adviser on foreign trade, to the effect that the Chinese would use silver dollars of 72 per cent fineness, and samples of these had been furnished them by the United States Mint.

[2] Henry Morgenthau, Jr.

Frank P. Walsh, Chairman, Power Authority of the State of New York, to Roosevelt

New York City, December 12, 1936

Dear Mr. President: In accordance with your instructions to the Acting Secretary of State before your departure,[1] Mr. Manly and I went to Ottawa, accompanied by Mr. Hickerson and Mr. Olds on December 4, 1936, for conversations with the Prime Minister.

As a result of the good offices of the American Minister, Mr. Armour, of whose ability and helpfulness I cannot speak too highly, arrangements had been made which assured very favorable auspices for our conference.[2]

The Prime Minister very kindly invited us to dine with him and the members of his Cabinet at his official residence on the evening of our arrival. The Cabinet members present included the Ministers of Finance, Justice, Public Works and Transport, the Postmaster General and the

Under Secretary of State for External Affairs. Following the dinner we had a frank and informal discussion of the problem of finding an approach to agreement on the joint undertaking of the Great Lakes-St. Lawrence development on a comprehensive basis.

The discussion was participated in by all present, the Prime Minister calling upon each member of his Cabinet for an expression of his views. Of especial importance, I felt, were the remarks of Prime Minister Mackenzie King, as well as those of the Ministers of Finance and Transport and the Under Secretary of State for External Affairs. Without exception the views expressed were quite encouraging.

In a preliminary afternoon conference with Mr. Armour it was decided to take the general approach suggested in your message to the Detroit Seaway Conference of March 11, 1936,[3] as the basis for discussion, emphasizing (a) the desirability of a new approach in which existing plans are adapted to the mutual interests and respective needs of the two countries; (b) the importance of the project in carrying on the tradition of amity which has bound the two countries together for more than a century; (c) the possibility of drafting a treaty under which each country will be able to utilize its share of the great common resource when such use becomes desirable or necessary to its economic progress; and (d) the growing need for power in both New York State and the Province of Ontario.

We presented a broad picture of the possibility of including the seaway and the development of additional power both at Niagara and in the International Rapids Section of the St. Lawrence River in a single treaty in which the interests of both parties in the entire basin would be conserved and the needs of both met as they arose.

Although the remarks of all those present were recognized as purely exploratory, the reaction of the Canadian officials indicated the possibility of an understanding of a concrete character. The significant reactions of the Prime Minister and his Cabinet may be briefly noted as follows:

1. They were definitely interested in the new approach, with its conception of a comprehensive plan for utilization of the Great Lakes–St. Lawrence basin to meet the needs of the two countries.

2. They felt that consideration must be given to the fact that the waterway would offer competition to the railroads, which are at present a financial burden to the country, but acknowledged that, with the growth of traffic in the seven-year construction period, this might not prove an insuperable obstacle.

3. They referred to the attitude of Ontario and Quebec, especially that of the Premier of Ontario,[4] as a problem but considered that the new plan, with its treatment of the power problems of all concerned in a comprehensive manner, offered a basis for asking the Provinces to reconsider their position.

4. They indicated that changes in the details of existing treaties must be handled in such a way as to prevent Canadian public opinion from believing that advantages in the 1932 treaty were being sacrificed.

5. They indicated that Canada would not take an uncompromising position in the matter of reconsideration of the single stage plan with its large potential saving in the cost of developing the International Rapids of the St. Lawrence.

6. They were interested in discussing the possibility of including a plan for power interchange between the two countries in order to meet the requirements of both more economically.

7. The Prime Minister announced he would confer with the Premiers of Ontario and Quebec with reference to the suggestions of our conference.

On the following morning, at the request of the Prime Minister, we again discussed the matter in greater detail with Dr. Skelton, Under Secretary of State for External Affairs, and the experts of the several governmental departments immediately concerned with the development, answering the numerous questions which they raised. This discussion followed the general lines of the previous evening. Many points were developed more precisely, as follows:

1. The President's Detroit message suggested a new approach which the Canadians were interested in exploring further;

2. Modification of such terms of the old treaty, as those limiting the Chicago Diversion and prescribing the employment of Canadian labor, presented a difficult problem;

3. The Canadian engineers had an open mind on the question of accepting a single stage plan in the International Rapids Section;

4. Ontario's unwillingness to commit herself to paying the Dominion her share of the cost of joint works, in accordance with the 1932 agreement, presented a problem in terms of financing the navigation development in the Lachine Section;

5. The Province of Ontario is vitally interested in securing more power at Niagara and will be influenced by a clear understanding that the United States will not collaborate to this end unless Canada agrees to the St. Lawrence development;

6. The experts would discuss with the Prime Minister the results of the conferences in order to determine whether a workable basis for further procedure had been developed.

Throughout both conferences there was an underlying note of serious consideration rather than of mere formality and there appeared to be a genuine desire to find a substantial basis upon which the two countries could cooperate in the development of the Great Lakes–St. Lawrence basin along the lines set forth in the President's message to the Detroit Conference, which was read in full to the conferees. The expectation of further conferences was also apparent.

In the light of the foregoing we are working on the draft of a suggested treaty which will take account of our interests, as well as the views of the Canadian Ministers and other officials, as expressed in the conferences. I think we have progressed far enough to discover that such a treaty, drawn in the form of a planned use of the resources of the entire basin, including both Niagara and the St. Lawrence, can be reasonably simple.

Although I do not minimize the difficulties in the situation, nevertheless, it is my conviction that it is not out of the realm of possibility that proposals may be presented so adapted to Canadian interests that a workable agreement may be reached for presentation to the Senate early at the coming session of Congress.[5]

With great respect, Sincerely,

Frank P. Walsh

[OF 156:TS]

[1] Roosevelt to Moore, Nov. 17, 1936, above.

[2] Armour's report to Hull, Dec. 7, 1936 (*Foreign Relations, 1936,* I, 845–846), outlines the discussions in Ottawa on Dec. 4–5, 1936. There is also a memorandum by Hickerson, Dec. 14, 1936 (PSF:St. Lawrence Waterway), which summarizes the talks.

[3] Printed in *Public Papers,* V, 117–121.

[4] Mitchell F. Hepburn, Liberal Premier of Ontario, 1934–1942; he continued to oppose the St. Lawrence project while in office.

[5] Answered Dec. 19, 1936, below.

Roosevelt to Dr. Francisco Castillo Nájera, President, First Commission, Inter-American Conference, Buenos Aires

USS *Indianapolis,* 13 December [1936]

[*Radiogram*] I thank you for your very gracious message.[1] This excellent result of the unceasing effort on the part of the members of the Commission on the organization of peace in the Inter-American Conference will be an inspiration to all the peoples of the Americas.

The Conference is justifying the highest hopes of all of us.

Good neighbors we are, good neighbors we shall remain.

Through you I send my warmest greetings.

[OF 1970:CT]

[1] Not present.

R. Walton Moore, Acting Secretary of State, to Roosevelt

Washington, December 15, 1936

My dear Mr. President: The attached memorandum lists some of the matters which, speaking for the State Department, you may wish to consider in connection with your legislative program and otherwise. They are barely mentioned, and I am not now troubling you with any elaboration, but I am prepared to do that whenever you desire.

Yours very sincerely,

R. Walton Moore

Enclosed is a letter from Bullitt that came in after the above was dictated. R.W.M.

[PSF:State:TS]

[*Enclosure 1*] R. Walton Moore to Roosevelt

December 15, 1936

1. The Work of the Executive Office. Some time ago the President referred to the possible expediency of attaching persons to his office who

might relieve him of some of the incessant work which he has been performing. They might, for example, meet or receive communications from people desiring to see the President, and either dispose of the questions they have in mind or head them in some other direction. They might give an assurance to individuals that in a short time they would be satisfactorily advised. There are many things they would be able to do in order to very materially cut down demands on the President's time. It was suggested that a start could be made by selecting three very intelligent and active men who would be able to contact with the Departments and Agencies of the Government in performing their duties, and my own belief is that this would be better than to initiate the plan in a more ambitious way. I have talked with Louis Brownlow, who expects to embody a more complete plan in the proposed legislation to reorganize governmental work so as to avoid duplications, etc.[1] But inasmuch as that kind of legislation may not be enacted for some time, I would personally like to see a step immediately taken to afford the President a measure of relief. Brownlow and I have talked a little about men who could be counted on for efficient work. Of course the staff would keep the President closely advised of its activities to the extent necessary. I do not think the annual salary should be less than $10,000, and it will be necessary to provide a few stenographic clerks.

2. Space for the Work of the Department of State. I doubt whether any Department of the Government is now so lacking in space necessary for the proper and efficient conduct of its business. During this administration increase of the force has been required, not only because of the normal expansion of the work, but because of new activities—the Trade Agreement program, the provision of a Munitions Office, the provision of an office to consider all questions relative to the Philippines, etc. It has been necessary to house in the Winder Building two of the Divisions of the Department, the Treaty Division and the Visa Division. Several of the divisions and offices are now so crowded that besides the discomfort created there is some actual waste of effort. For example anyone making an inspection of the very important Division of Communications and Records, which handles outgoing and incoming messages, and among other things is charged with protecting the secrecy of our codes, or the Division of Accounts, which is very important, would see at a glance what is meant by the crowding together of a lot of people in something like half the space that is reasonably necessary. There are photographs showing the condition in those and other places, and it is safe to say that no one dissents from the view that I am expressing. The

simple truth is that the entire building should be used by the State Department by some arrangement being made that would locate the War Department work elsewhere. I do not know what use is to be made of the old Interior Department, or how much space may be available in the new Interior Department building, but it is obvious that something should be done without delay if possible. The other day I had a letter from an official of the Interior Department speaking of the construction of a new State Department building, but that is not only a far off idea, but in my own judgment the work of the State Department should be continued in the building where it is now carried on, and if so I believe no further accommodations will be needed in the next twenty-five or fifty years.

3. Amalgamation of Foreign Services. It seems to me very obvious that there should be an amalgamation of certain of the foreign services. Apparently many disinterested observers and investigators entertain the opinion that there is undesirable duplication and unwarranted expense in failing to coordinate with the main foreign service of the State Department the services now maintained by the Departments of Commerce, Treasury and Agriculture. The other departments would not suffer by this step being taken, which seems to be altogether logical and practical. If no authority for this now exists, it seems to me that it should be included in the legislation that Mr. Brownlow proposes. Very recently I have had a communication from Mr. Bullitt on this subject, and have approved his suggestion that he communicate directly with Secretary Roper, sending the President a copy of his letter. One point I may mention is that my experience during the last few weeks leads me to believe that our officials in the foreign field are, as a rule, stronger and more capable than I once believed. They are certainly as strong and capable as special representatives of the other Departments, whose work largely overlaps the work of our officials.

4. Provision for Foreign Buildings. I am very strongly of the opinion that there should be a lump sum appropriation of say $5,000,000 to be expended during a period of say five years in the construction and repair of buildings abroad to house our employees. At this time the total rent payments are considerable, and in a few places repairs are needed. When I was in the House of Representatives and a member of the Committee on Foreign Affairs there was a lump sum appropriation authorized of $10,000,000, but that is nearly exhausted and hereafter, unless there is another such appropriation authorized, recourse will have to be had to Congress in special cases, a process that will be a nuisance to everybody.

The expenditure of the former appropriation has been entrusted to the Foreign Buildings Commission, composed of representatives of the State, Commerce and Treasury Departments, and the Chairmen of the two Foreign Committees of Congress, and I am satisfied that the expenditures have been very carefully guarded and in the main judiciously made. I think it is simply common sense to continue the policy that was adopted several years ago, and which has had beneficial results. Incidentally, if legislation should be enacted authorizing a lump sum appropriation, I think the Commission should be given larger powers so as to enable it to sell or exchange buildings. At this time we have a problem at Berlin, where we own and are carrying without any return the costly Bluecher Palace. There is a diversity of opinion as to what should be done, but most of those who have inspected the Palace strongly believe that it should be sold and the proceeds used in adequate construction somewhere else in the city. That is Dr. Dodd's opinion, and only last night Representative Bloom,[2] of New York, very emphatically expressed the same opinion. I think that Mr. Phillips reached that conclusion after looking the building over. There are two or three people who think that the building should be placed in condition at a cost of approximately $750,000.

5. Renewal of the Tariff Act. It is to be determined whether legislation for this purpose should be initiated at once, on the theory that it will meet little opposition, and if this course is taken, then in advance of the meeting of Congress Senators Harrison and Robinson and Representative Doughton should be consulted. If there is to be anticipated a serious fight, then perhaps it might be well to postpone the matter until Mr. Hull's return. Recently the Customs Court has thrown out a suit brought to test the constitutionality of the present Act, but other litigation of that character is coming on. Nevertheless it is thought that the validity of the Act will be sustained, and personally I am more sanguine than I was prior to the election.[3]

6. Treaties. At any time I will be prepared to report to the President on the Canadian attitude relative to the St. Lawrence Waterways Treaty, as ascertained by the conferences at Ottawa this month between the Canadian authorities and the representatives of our Government named by the President. Mr. Hickerson, who is, I think, perhaps more familiar with all of the details than anyone else, seems to believe that the President may regard it as unwise to bring the treaty to the attention of the Senate during the coming session. While I was in favor of asking the Senate to ratify the World Court Convention during the last Congress, I now do not believe that effort should be renewed. To do so would

of course bring on a very sharp controversy and even if the Convention were ratified, it does not seem to me that that would have much effect either in the way of advantage to our Government or in its bearing upon the cause of world peace. There are doubtless officials of this Department who entertain the contrary view, and at this moment I cannot speak for the Secretary. The President will probably wish to draw the attention of the Senate to the United States–Argentine Sanitary Convention.

I have furnished Senator Pittman a full list of pending or prospective treaties, so far as now known, and that list will be plussed by treaties negotiated at the Pan American Conference.

7. Neutrality. This of course is a subject of major importance, which is under constant study in this Department, and Congress will have to deal with the present Statute prior to June 1st. All of my thought strengthens my conviction that all of our domestic legislation should be discretionary, since it is utterly impossible to forecast what will be the nature and extent of any future war, and that accordingly the Executive should have a very free hand. It may be very doubtful whether Congress could be persuaded to divest of its mandatory character the embargo provision respecting arms, ammunition and implements of war, but I do believe that if the matter is properly handled the present statute can be so amended and enlarged as to make all of the other provisions discretionary. Senator Pittman was here a short time ago. At his invitation I talked with him very briefly and inconclusively. I think it would be most helpful, as a first step, for the President to fix a time to see Pittman when he comes back this month, and have a full talk with him, as I am pretty sure he can be persuaded to take the discretionary view.[4] As Chairman of the Senate Committee, and personally popular with its members, he has great influence, and he and Robinson working together could very nearly do exactly what they desire. It would be well to dissuade Chairman McReynolds from going forward in the House until after the Senate has acted, since I am confident that the House will approve any bill passed by the Senate with the President's approval. At the President's convenience it might be well for him, before seeing Pittman, even before Mr. Hull returns, to give Mr. Hackworth and myself the opportunity of suggesting what we think Congress should do.[5]

I regret that the word "neutrality" was ever used, and has gotten so fixed in the public mind. It would have been much better to call our domestic legislation peace legislation. In the extensive discussion of the subject with the Senate Committee in its private sessions, members were constantly suggesting that this or that provision would not be real neutrality, because it would give a little more advantage to one belligerent than the other, which is undoubtedly true, because in practice the scales always tip one way or the other, but it is now too late to change the label.

8. Miscellaneous. The President will probably wish to select pretty quickly a successor to Mr. Murphy, the Philippine Governor General.

He will wish to decide when to designate his representatives at the British Coronation, but about that I have already communicated with him.

The President will also wish to decide if and when he will transfer Atherton from London. The man some of us have had in mind to succeed him is Herschel Johnson, now on the London staff, and as he is in this country, I can arrange to have the President see him and size him up, should that be desired.

The Executive Order relative to the marriage of our Foreign Service Officers seems to meet general approval. Perhaps I have already told the President that in two cases, and there is a third pending, I permitted the marriage of two officials who had contracted their engagements before the order was issued, which was a possibility [we] had in mind at the time the President signed the order.[6]

I think some pretty fine work has recently been done towards protecting the secrecy of our codes, and also some good work in bringing about a closer supervision of the divisions and offices of the Department, in analogy to what any business corporation would do in conducting its activities.

I am now attempting to effect a revision and codification of the mass of diplomatic and consular regulations, so as to save the time of officials here and in the field, in ascertaining what is required in specific cases. I think I can give the assurance that in all of the administrative improvements attempted to be made, no hostility or controversy has been created. Care has been taken to do everything in a tactful and quiet manner.

I might write almost endlessly about various matters that have come along on the basis of questions arising in the Department and presented by our officials abroad and conversations with many of the foreign representatives here, and perhaps now and then some of these things may be of interest to the President.

R. Walton Moore

[Notation:A] Very interesting
[PSF:State:TS]

---

[1] Brownlow was chairman of the Committee on Administrative Management.

[2] Rep. Sol Bloom's interest in the matter arose from the fact that he was second-ranking member of the House Foreign Affairs Committee.

[3] The Trade Agreements Act of June 12, 1934, was extended to June 12, 1940, by the act approved March 1, 1937 (50 *Stat.* 24).

[4] Moore, Pittman, and McReynolds talked with Roosevelt for over an hour on Dec. 30, 1936 (PPF 1-0).

[5] Moore saw the President at the White House on Dec. 16, 21, 26, and 28, 1936, but apparently not with Hackworth, legal adviser to the State Department (PPF 1-0).

[6] The executive order of Nov. 17, 1936, forbidding marriage of Foreign Service officers to aliens without consent of the State Department.

[*Enclosure 2*] William C. Bullitt, Ambassador to France, to R. Walton Moore

Paris, December 8, 1936

Personal and Confidential

Dear Judge Moore: I want to make a suggestion to you which I believe will be of real assistance to the President.

When Jim Farley was here the other day, I tried to convince him that he should refrain from urging the President to appoint to diplomatic posts incompetents who had contributed to the campaign fund. I tried to explain to him the extreme gravity of the situation both in Europe and the Far East and tried to impress on him the fact that an intelligent Foreign Service is the first line of defense of the United States—or at least the first line of defense against involvement in war.

Jim, as usual, was quick to see the point, and went on to say that he felt there were many chiefs of mission today who were thoroughly incompetent and that there were a number the President would be glad to get rid of, but he felt the President would hesitate to ask for their resignations. I agreed with his statement and a solution suddenly occurred to me.

There used to be, as you know, a thoroughly healthy custom that all chiefs of mission should resign at the close of each Presidential term, in order to give the President a completely free hand with regard to reappointments. The custom still exists but I fear there are a number of incompetent chiefs of mission who will not resign. The change in the date of Inauguration seems to me to give you, as Acting Secretary of State, an excellent opportunity to relieve the President of the burden of asking for resignations by issuing the following circular instruction to all chiefs of mission:

"Chiefs of Mission are reminded that owing to the change in the date of Inauguration their resignations should be in the hands of the President not later than January 15, 1937."

I am writing to the President by the same pouch that will bring you this letter to make the same suggestion to him.[1] As the instruction would be addressed to all chiefs of mission, no individual chief of mission could in any way feel injured by its receipt. On receipt of the resignations, the President would then be in the happy position of being able to get rid of incompetents and other undesirables by writing them a polite note of thanks and praise.

If the suggestion appeals to you, I hope you will take it up with the President shortly after his return from South America as there will not be much time for the receipt of the resignations before January 15th.

I think you will find that a number of the chiefs of mission who are now conversant with the old custom will submit their resignations as a matter of course, but there will be a number, and those the less desirable, who will not. Incidentally, I submit my resignation here and now.

Before I left Washington the President said to me that he hoped I would come back for Christmas but of course, I shall not unless I receive an order from him to do so. I may take advantage of Anne's[2] Christmas holidays to visit the French colonies in Africa by airplane.

The Naval Attaché has an excellent new plane which carries five passengers and as the Christmas season usually brings a lull in political activity in France, I shall probably take the plane on December 18th for a brief visit to Tunis, Algiers and Morocco, returning about January 1st. All those colonies are within my official bailiwick, and such a visit would make an excellent impression, so that, if I go, I shall not feel I am playing truant. If the situation here continues to be tense, I shall, of course, remain in Paris.

My love to you and a Merry Christmas and the Happiest of New Years.

Yours devotedly,

William C. Bullitt

P.S. It was delightful to hear your voice. You sounded as if you were growing younger at an alarming rate. Love. W.C.B.

[PSF:State:TS]

[1] Dec. 7, 1936, above.
[2] Bullitt's daughter, in school in France.

Robert W. Bingham, Ambassador to Great Britain, to Roosevelt

London, December 18, 1936

Dear Mr. President: I was distressed to hear of the death of your old friend Gus because I know you will miss him with all of his devotion and loyalty.[1]

The British have passed through their crisis successfully and I have no doubt they are better off for the present and for the future than they could have hoped to be with the former King. Mr. Baldwin handled the difficult situation admirably and has regained much, if not all, of the prestige he has lost in the last year. There was a real danger in the situation due to the possibility of a "King's Party" against the Government. This was fomented by the two press lords, Rothermere and Beaverbrook, who, as you know, are the Hearsts of this country. However, fortunately, their influence here is about as small as Hearst's is in our country. On the other hand, I have it on definite and unimpeachable authority that a group was forming in the War Office under the leadership of Duff Cooper, the head of the War Office, and that about fifty War Office officials had joined. The movement was spreading but to his credit, be it said, it was stopped by the former King himself. It means, however, that they will probably get rid of Duff Cooper in the near future.

Sir George Paish, whom you know, is at the Brevoort House in New York and is eager to see you.[2] He tells me that he is going to Ottawa to urge Mackenzie King to refuse to renew the Ottawa Agreement. He believes, further, that if Mr. Baldwin retires after the Coronation and is succeeded by Neville Chamberlain the latter will be unable to hold the Conservative majority in the House of Commons and that another general election is likely to occur next Autumn.

Some time ago a group of members of the House of Commons called on me and told me they had formed an organization to promote a better understanding with the United States and to show personal courtesies to visiting Americans, especially Government officials and members of our Congress. They stated that they wished to give a dinner for me at the House of Commons, which was done last Tuesday night. Sir Austen Chamberlain presided and the Prime Minister proposed a toast to me, which was seconded by Mr. Attlee, the leader of the Opposition. The Liberal Party was also represented. In the course of his speech, Mr. Baldwin referred to his first visit to the United States, forty-six years ago, but the significant statement that he made was that on his second visit he had secured a debt settlement with the United States which he wished to state emphatically he had never regretted for one moment. Both in official and unofficial circles there is an ever-increasing desire to cultivate better relations with the United States and they are becoming more and more anxious about the debt situation. When approached on this subject, I have persistently stated that I am not authorized to discuss this matter officially or unofficially. I merely refer officials to the repeated statements by the United States Government that debtors will be given an opportunity to discuss the matter with the United States Government when they desire to do so. The real basis of this movement, which has been accumulating here for some time, is their desire to regain access to American credit in view of the dangers which menace them. As an indication of their present attitude on general principles—we were having a great deal of trouble for a long period with their rubber control, headed by a pig-headed man named Sir John Campbell. I had Ray Atherton take a representative of the Foreign Office with him and he had a last interview with Campbell, which was in September. Growing out of Campbell's conduct at this time and later, the Foreign Office has undertaken to have him removed and has informed me this will be done.

Their frame of mind towards a trade agreement has improved and Walter Runciman has asked me to see him today, which I shall do.

I hope now to see you on the seventh or eighth of January when I can give you a fuller report of the situation here.

Sincerely yours,

Robert W. Bingham

P.S. Since writing the above, I have seen Walter Runciman and had a long and on the whole satisfactory talk with him. He said that in the preliminary discussions on the subject of a trade agreement which had taken place our technical representatives—of whom he had no criticism, but who were ardent as their own representatives are—had begun on a basis which was in violation of the British obligations under the Ottawa Agreement. He said, however, that he believed that it would be possible to work out such an agreement as you and Mackenzie King had effected as between the United States and Canada and that he hoped this could and would be done.

I enclose two clippings, one from *The Times* referring to the dinner at the House of Commons, and the other from *The Spectator,* which is doubtless the most influential of the weeklies here, referring to the war debts.[3]

[PSF:Great Britain:TS]

[1] Gus Gennerich, Roosevelt's personal attendant, who had been with him for years and of whom he was very fond, had died on Dec. 1, 1936.

[2] Paish was at one time joint editor of the *Statist* and during World War I was adviser to the Chancellor of the Exchequer and the Treasury on financial and economic matters.

[3] Present.

Roosevelt to Frank P. Walsh, Chairman, Power Authority of the State of New York

[Washington] December 19, 1936

Dear Frank: I find your letter of the twelfth on my return and I am delighted that progress is being made.[1] Keep me in touch.

I hope to see you soon.

Always sincerely,

[OF 156:CT]

[1] Above. See Walsh to Roosevelt, Jan. 13, 1937, below.

Fred Morris Dearing, Ambassador to Peru, to Roosevelt

Lima, December 19, 1936

Personal

Dear Mr. President: [*Excerpt*] Here are two more stamps for you—surcharges which, I am told, are somewhat rare. And here is a set of new issues which were just placed in circulation yesterday, December 18th. I hope you will find them interesting additions to your collection.

We have watched your trip to Buenos Aires and return with the most intense interest. I have poached upon your remarks, both at Rio de Janeiro and at Buenos Aires, for speeches I have had to make in closing American schools here for the summer vacations, hoping thus to give a further extension to your great initiative.

The reaction to the Conference here in Peru has been quite extraordinary. At first, political difficulties within the country made it hard for Peru to keep its mind on what was taking place. But the moment the situation became easier, all eyes were turned towards Buenos Aires and the papers have been filled every day with long and detailed reports, the texts of the more important speeches, and really most intelligent comment upon the meaning of the Conference's deliberations.

The character of the public reaction has never been higher. Something very deep and very fundamental in the nature of these people has at last been reached and touched, and that is going to give color to all they do throughout the rest of their lives. One has the distinct sensation that they are seeing things and possibilities and meanings they have never seen before; and these new visions are giving them a new courage and putting a light in their minds and eyes which will carry them far along towards that better existence for which we are all working.

The European tradition is strong in this part of the world, but one can almost see a new orientation taking place from day to day as the center of interest shifts to our own country, and in a most notable degree to yourself. There has been a tremendous disillusionment on account of what is taking place in the dictatorships in Europe and in Asia, and a more liberal and democratic existence which now becomes so imminent and great a reality, and which is too precious a thing to lose, absorbs all minds. Peruvians feel—but in no over-weening way, that Europe can now learn something from our Western world. An article I read this morning with regard to French and other European propaganda, brings this out very clearly . . .[1]

Yours very sincerely,

Fred Morris Dearing

[PPF 1210:TS]

[1] Answered Jan. 11, 1937, below.

William C. Bullitt, Ambassador to France, to Roosevelt

Paris, December 20, 1936

Personal and Confidential

Dear Mr. President: It was grand to hear your voice over the telephone. I heard you as clearly as if you had been in the next room and it took me exactly two minutes to get through from the Embassy to the White House. That is the result of the installation of direct telephone communication between Paris and New York. If by any chance you should ever wish to call me, tell the telephone operator at the White House to put the call through to France direct, not via England.

I have written you so often in the past few weeks that, in spite of the fact that you said you still liked to get letters from me, I hesitate to keep on writing; but I should like to make one suggestion to you which may possibly prove to be important.

I am more convinced every day that the only chance of preserving peace in Europe lies in the possibility that the French and the Germans may reach some basis of understanding. The new element which has created this possibility is the fact that the bombing plane has been developed to such a pitch of efficiency that the French Government knows the Germans can destroy the city of Paris in 24 hours and the German Government knows the French can destroy Essen and all the towns of the Ruhr in 24 hours. There is beginning to be a general realization, therefore, that war will mean such horrible suffering that it will end in general revolution, and that the only winners will be Stalin and Company.

For different reasons, the British, Italians and Russians are all opposed to Franco-German reconciliation. The only great Power which favors it genuinely is the United States. Poland desires it ardently and so do all the small countries of Europe, except Hungary and Bulgaria.

You will have seen from my recent cables that I have attempted to do what I could, in a quiet way and without involving the United States in the least, to encourage the idea of Franco-German rapprochement. I think it might be most useful if, when you see de Laboulaye and Luther, you should stress the idea that peace in Europe is purely a question of Franco-German reconciliation; that the modern bombing plane has confronted Europe with the alternative of unification or destruction and that we ardently desire to see France and Germany reconciled.

If, on some occasion, you should have an opportunity to say to Ronald Lindsay that we should be shocked if we should find that England was not genuinely doing everything possible to promote Franco-German rapprochement, it might be very helpful.

The British, of course, will say that they favor it and will do everything possible to sabotage it. But they may be less active if they think your eye is on them.

Delbos again this morning reiterated to me his remarks about Great Britain's absolute opposition to any concessions to Germany in the matter of colonies. As he pointed out yesterday to me, it was the frown of Britain which prevented France from following up Schacht's conversations with Blum.

Inasmuch as we can not involve ourselves directly in European politics, inasmuch as Great Britain, Italy, and the Soviet Union will do everything possible to prevent Franco-German rapprochement and inasmuch as the French and the Germans fear and suspect each other deeply, the chances are slim, but I feel that there is nevertheless a chance—the only chance.

If the Franco-German conversations should make some progress, there may come a moment when you could make a general declaration which would be most helpful. Meanwhile, I feel that the less we say about Europe the better. Above all, I hope that you will not let anyone persuade you into launching some scheme without previous consultation in the first instance with the French Government, and in the second, with the German and the British.

We can and should avoid the mistake that Hoover made when he launched his moratorium proposal without consulting the French in advance.[1] That sort of thing produces over all Europe a sense that we are apt to do uncertain and unexpected things. Hitler and Mussolini have given the whole Continent the jitters by their unexpected explosions—we ought to be steady and should, I think, move only on firm ground after preparation and consultation.

During the past few days, I have taken the liberty of saying to Delbos, Bonnet and Monick that I knew you would never involve the United States in general commitments by the acceptance of proposals in the form of general principles. I enclose herewith a most secret document which will show you the reason for these declarations of mine. It is the memorandum on debt settlement which Monick prepared for the French Government.[2]

You will perceive that he proposes to get us to accept certain general principles which would in fact involve us in the whole European tangle up to the hilt. He gave me the document himself under pledge of strict secrecy and I am sending it to no one except yourself. He elaborated on the ideas in the document and made it entirely clear that he hoped, via such a debt settlement, to get us to promise enormous economic and financial aid to France and Germany, and to involve ourselves in all the economic difficulties of Europe. Furthermore, he wished the scheme to be sprung on the Germans by a united front of England, France and the United States. I can not imagine a better way for us to start toward involvement in the next war than by accepting his proposal.

I do not know whether or not my conversations here in the past few days have killed the idea but I suspect that it will be brought up in one form or another at a later date.

I have been working unbelievably hard since I reached Paris, but I hope to get a bit of rest this week by spending Christmas in Algiers. The work is, of course, fascinating; but there is so much of it that one gets too tired to enjoy anything. When I come back after Christmas, I think I shall imitate you and inaugurate regular afternoon swims.

I wish to Heaven I could swim with you today. There is so much to talk about and all of it is interesting—tragically interesting.

My love to you and a Merry Christmas and a Happy New Year to Mrs. Roosevelt and all the family.

Yours affectionately,

Bill

P.S. You will receive from Mme. Jusserand a grand New Year's present.[3] The dear old lady just showed it to me. Do send her a cable on New Years day. B.

[PSF:France:TS]

[1] Hoover's war debt moratorium proposal of 1931.
[2] Not present.
[3] Mme. Jules Jusserand sent Roosevelt a handsomely bound set of her husband's *Literary History of the English People* (Paris, 1904). In her inscription she said that the gift represented her appreciation of Roosevelt's speech of Nov. 7, 1936, dedicating the Jusserand Memorial in Rock Creek Park in Washington (printed in *Public Papers,* V, 584–585). Roosevelt had sent her the reading copy of his address in token of his long friendship.

Josephus Daniels, Ambassador to Mexico, to Roosevelt

Washington, December 22, 1936

Dear Franklin: There were so many things to talk about when I saw you on Monday, I do not recall that I emphasized as much as I intended the invitation sent you by President Cardenas to visit Mexico at the conclusion of Congress. You would be received by the President and the people of Mexico with more, if possible, warmth and enthusiasm than you received in your history-making trip to South America. President Cardenas feels, as I told you, that your policy of giving a better

chance to the average man has had a helpful influence in the same direction in his and all other Pan American countries.[1]
  Faithfully,

Josephus Daniels

[PSF:Mexico:TS]

[1] See Roosevelt to Moore, Jan. 16, 1937, below.

James Clement Dunn, Chief, Division of Western European Affairs, State Department, to Marvin H. McIntyre, Assistant Secretary to the President

Washington, December 22, 1936

  Dear Colonel McIntyre: I am enclosing as of possible interest to the President a copy of a despatch which we have received from the American Consul at Quebec entitled "The Use of French by President Roosevelt."
  Sincerely yours,

James Clement Dunn

[PSF:Canada:TS]

[Enclosure] John Randolph, Consul at Quebec, to the United States Legation, Ottawa

Quebec, December 10, 1936

The Use of French by President Roosevelt

  President Roosevelt's use of the French language in a part of his speech on the occasion of his visit to Quebec on July 30, 1936,[1] was received very favorably by the people of Quebec City and French Canada generally not only at the time but also since then, there having been frequent further mention thereof during the past months. To hear the President of the United States, when in Quebec, speak their own language was both pleasing and flattering to French-Canadians and in contrast to the attitude of some English-Canadians of Ontario who are alleged to object to two official languages for Canada.

The latest local reference to the President's use of French at Quebec appeared in *L'Action Catholique* of December 7, 1936, in an editorial, which called attention to a report that President Roosevelt had again used French successfully in his conversation at Buenos Aires on December 1, 1936, with the President of Argentine Republic.

The editorial (the French text of which is attached) reads in translation as follows:

Roosevelt and French

The voyage of Roosevelt to Buenos Aires is interesting for more than one reason. It admits of a thousand lessons. Here is one which is not without flavor, as the Orangemen of Toronto would say.

It was asked how the President of the United States and the President of the Argentine Republic were able to converse with each other. A brief despatch informed American newspapers that the two personages used the second language of all educated people: the French language.

Commenting on this incident *The Independent* of Fall River writes:

At Quebec Roosevelt received an ovation when he responded to Mayor Gregoire in French; at Buenos Aires he found himself quite at ease in conversing amicably with President Justo, by again using the French language, which the President of Argentine likewise speaks, because he is a distinguished person.

Roosevelt arrived at Buenos Aires, crowned with the glory of a victory unsurpassed since the election of George Washington, but it is certain that at Quebec and at Buenos Aires his knowledge of the French language was of more service to him than the glory of his re-election.

During the course of life the practical utility of the French language manifests itself many times. Often the knowledge of this language will be the fundamental reason for a rapid advancement and the grounds for success impossible without it. In every case it will be always the mark and the proof of intellectual superiority, which will give to those possessing this knowledge an advantage over those who are without it, and it would be a crime and folly, if, through apathy, lack of judgment, laziness and meanness, we should deprive our children of this advantage, when so many others spend millions of dollars to acquire it.

We wager that the gesture of Roosevelt and the comments of the Franco-American confrere will convert the Ontario fanatics, the number of whom fortunately diminishes from year to year.

[PSF:Canada:T]

[1] Actually July 31; the speech is printed in *Public Papers,* V, 276–279.

Roosevelt to Carlos Saavedra Lamas, President, Inter-American Conference for the Maintenance of Peace, Buenos Aires

The White House, December 23, 1936

[*Telegram*] I wish to thank you for your telegram of December twenty-second,[1] expressing pursuant to the resolution approved by the Conference the gratification of American nations at the approaching sesquicentennial of the Federal Constitution of the United States. This sentiment collectively and individually extended by the American Republics is deeply appreciated.

May I at this time send my heartiest congratulations on the splendid achievements of the Conference over which you have so ably presided. The high hopes we all had that the Conference would result in a very definite contribution to the cause of peace have been well fulfilled.

Will you be good enough to extend to the members of the 21 delegations my warm greetings and my good wishes for a Happy Christmas and a prosperous New Year.[2]

Franklin D. Roosevelt

[OF 1970:T]

[1] Not present.
[2] Drafted by Willard L. Beaulac, assistant chief, Division of Latin American Affairs.

R. Walton Moore, Acting Secretary of State, to Roosevelt

Washington, December 24, 1936

Dear Mr. President: In connection with the suggestion that all chiefs of missions should hand in their resignations, a question has arisen that I think you will wish to consider.[1] It does not refer to persons outside of the career service, but only to those who belonged to that service.

Should a career chief resign who has been in the service for at least thirty years, or reached the age of sixty-five years, having had a service of at least fifteen years, upon his resignation being accepted he would have the benefit during the rest of his life of a pretty generous retirement allowance. But a person who has not served thirty years, or reached the age of sixty-five years with fifteen years of service, upon his resignation being accepted, would not be entitled to retirement annuities, but only entitled to the return of the amount paid into the foreign service retirement fund with interest at four per cent.

Attached is a memorandum showing the two categories into which the career chiefs at this time fall.[2]

Should a career chief's resignation be accepted, the President would have authority to reinstate him to the classified Foreign Service. This is provided for by Section 12 of the Act,[3] copy of which is herewith enclosed. I do not believe, and Mr. Hackworth concurs in that view, that the reinstatement appointments would have to be approved by the Senate, but apparently others, who, however, are not lawyers, take a different view. Should the latter view be held correct, the President would probably find the Senate willing to confirm his nominations. You will notice the last sentence of Section 12, which limits the number of reinstatements, but at this moment seven reinstatements to Class I would be permissible.

In the event you determine to request all the chiefs to resign, I think the following form would be suitable:

To _____: You are reminded that the date of the Presidential Inauguration has been changed to January 20th. According to a custom formerly observed, and in order to regularize procedure, your resignation should be placed at the disposal of the President, through the Secretary of State, not later than January 15, 1937.

The foregoing is being sent to all chiefs of missions.

Acting Secretary of State

Whenever necessary the communication would be sent by wire, in order to insure a reply before January 15th.

Yours very sincerely,

R. Walton Moore

P.S. Colonel McIntyre thinks I can see you about two or three important matters Saturday morning, and if so, I will have an opportunity for a word or so with you about the matter to which this letter relates.[4]

R.W.M.

[PSF:State:TS]

[1] See Roosevelt to Moore, Dec. 19, 1936, in *Personal Letters, 1928–1945,* I, 641, suggesting that a note be sent to all chiefs of mission reminding them of the custom that resignations be offered at the close of the presidential term.

[2] This memorandum was sent by Thomas M. Wilson, chief of the Division of Foreign

Service Personnel, to Moore, Dec. 17, 1936 (PSF:State Department). It pointed out that career officers who were chiefs of mission abroad would lose their retirement rights if they broke their service by retiring at the end of a presidential term.

[3] Act approved Feb. 23, 1931 (46 *Stat.* 1207).

[4] Moore saw the President for half an hour on Saturday, December 26. See Roosevelt's reply, below.

Roosevelt to R. Walton Moore, Acting Secretary of State

Washington, December 28, 1936

Confidential

Memorandum for the Acting Secretary of State: In regard to resignations of Chiefs of Mission, it seems best to do nothing further in regard to the career men but the non-career Chiefs should, of course, submit their resignations as has always been done in the past.

FDR

[PSF:State:T]

Roosevelt to Marvin H. McIntyre, Assistant Secretary to the President

Washington, December 28, 1936

Memo for Mac: Call up Pershing and Rodman[1] and ask them if they would do me the honor of going as members of the Special Embassy of three to the Coronation of King George VI; that it means leaving here about May first, in order to be there on May 12th, and, for their own confidential information, the third member will be former Ambassador Gerard, and if they will go the President will announce it soon.[2]

F.D.R.

[OF 48-I:T]

[1] General John J. Pershing and Admiral Hugh Rodman.
[2] Gerard's appointment was announced Jan. 25, 1937 (New York *Times,* Jan. 26, 1937, p. 22). See Roosevelt to Swanson, Jan. 7, 1937, below.

R. Walton Moore, Acting Secretary of State, to Roosevelt

Washington, December 28, 1936

Dear Mr. President: Complying with your request for a statement of what was accomplished at the Buenos Aires Conference I am handing you a memorandum prepared by the Latin American Division. I am also enclosing a press release by the Pan American Union. For convenient reference there is further enclosed a copy of Secretary Hull's closing address.[1]

Were I venturing an opinion on the work of the conference, without minimizing the specific agreements, I would not hesitate to say that the greatest item on the program was your speech which has heartened the advocates of peace everywhere and I hope started a stronger tide of sentiment against war. Of course you would not say this but the newspapers are free to do so.

Very sincerely,

R. Walton Moore

[OF 1970:TS]

[1] All the enclosures are present; the memorandum only is here printed. Roosevelt used the material in preparing his annual message to Congress of Jan. 6, 1937 (*Public Papers*, V, 634–642). Hull's closing address of Dec. 23, 1936, together with his other addresses at the Conference, is printed in *Addresses and Statements by the Honorable Cordell Hull, In Connection with His Trip to South America to attend the Inter-American Conference for the Maintenance of Peace held at Buenos Aires, Argentina, December 1–23, 1936* (Washington, 1937), pp. 34–43.

[*Enclosure*] Results of the Buenos Aires Conference

It may be said that the broad aims of the Conference were:

1. The strengthening of existing peace machinery and the adoption of new instruments for the maintenance of peace and the elimination of causes leading to war;

2. The adoption of measures to be brought into effect for the protection of the interests of the American Republics in the event of war outside the Western Hemisphere;

3. The strengthening of the respect for and observance of international treaties and international law;

4. The reaffirmation of the principles of liberal trade policies as effective aids to the maintenance of peace;

5. A broadening of the intellectual and cultural relations among American Republics as a part of the general peace program.

The principal measures adopted by the Conference have been made public and it is apparent to all that the general aims of the Conference as set forth have been amply achieved.

Among the specific results of the Conference the following are important:

The existing machinery for the maintenance of peace in this hemisphere has been coordinated and made more effective. The efficiency of the peace pacts already in existence has been enhanced by provisions for consultation and by other measures designed to assist the parties in carrying out their obligations under those pacts.

The national security of each American Republic has now become the common interest of all. Any threat by a non-American power to the peace of any Republic would become the collective concern of all others. The fear of intervention by one American Republic in the domestic affairs of any other has been removed.

The basis has been laid for a common and solidary policy of neutrality.

The movement toward eliminating the economic causes of war by reducing the obstacles to trade and by insuring equality of treatment, has been carried one step further. A stronger basis has been laid for the reestablishment of flourishing and untrammeled trade between nations—a necessary adjunct and aid to world peace.

In the intellectual field, provisions have been made for the exchange of professors and students and for scientific and artistic cooperation. In the field of communications, additional facilities have been created for the construction of an Inter-American Highway. These measures cannot fail of effect in drawing still closer the bonds of friendship which characterize the relations of the American Republics today.

While the conventions and declarations adopted by the Conference in themselves constitute great gains, there are broader achievements of the Conference which must not be overlooked. In a world unhappily thinking in terms of war, the representatives of twenty-one nations have sat down at a common table and earnestly discussed measures for maintaining peace. At a time when the relations of so many great nations are characterized by distrust and fear, the representatives of the neighbor countries of America have met in an atmosphere of complete confidence and understanding. Such an example cannot but have a wholesome effect upon the rest of the world.

[OF 1970:T]

Memorandum to Stephen T. Early, Assistant Secretary to the President

Washington, Dec. 28, 1936

Give to the President on Tuesday for his press conference.

[OF 476:T]

[*Enclosure*]

Confidential

Liberia is the only independent country in Africa today. A group of Polish farmers recently settled there, and a short while ago Poland suddenly announced the need for colonies! Germany only last week reiterated its need for colonial raw materials under some sort of mandate and one of its most urgent requirements is rubber. Liberia is perfectly suited for rubber growing. Firestone has some 60,000 acres under cultivation and prosperous Liberian farmers have some 4,000 or 5,000.

Liberia is an experiment in negro self-government started and often aided by the United States and American philanthropic societies. The Liberians have constantly had to contend with political and financial difficulties and it is a miracle that this country still exists. British colonies on one side and French on the other have gobbled up Liberian territory in the past until now only about one-half of the original area is left.

In the past few years a considerable amount of prejudicial propaganda against the country has appeared in European books and press, comparing this poor and slowly developing country with European standards! If a fair comparison were made with certain hinterland areas under the rule of great colonial powers, Liberia would stand out pretty well.[1]

[OF 476:T]

---

[1] This memorandum was prepared in the State Department; see press conference following. Also enclosed was a 2,000-word review of Liberian history from the organization of the American Colonization Society in 1816 to the recognition by the United States of the Barclay administration in 1935.

Press Conference, Executive Offices of the White House, December 29, 1936, 4:05 P.M.

[*Excerpt*] The President: If anybody wants to write a feature story on Liberia, I have a memorandum from the State Department which is quite interesting.[1] I did not know very much about it—as much about it before I read it as I do now. It is quite interesting. I am not having any copies made but I will let Mac take it out to the Press Room if any are interested to read it over and write a story. The occasion for it is recognition of the new Liberian Government by Great Britain. You know, they went through a good many vicissitudes and we sent McBride over there and he tried to untangle it and then we sent Governor Winship over there and he tried it.[2] They put in a good many reforms and they are paying their debts and the thing is going quite nicely.

Q: Over in the State Department, we found over a period of thirty-five years, that whenever the State Department has some story they want to cover up, they usually put out a Liberian story (laughter) and, Mr. President, this story was given to us last week when they were keeping quiet the story that the *Erie* was fired upon.[3] I am wondering what story they are trying to cover up now. (Laughter)

The President: I have had it for about a week. It is probably the same story. I am not trying to cover up by that. I am probably the only person who did not see it. However, you can check . . .

Q: Can you say whether you are giving any consideration to legislation that would strengthen the Arms Embargo Act, particularly in the case of Civil War?

The President: Obviously, there should be a further discretion vested in the President with the appropriate penalties to take care of internal strife. I leave out the words "Civil War" for the perfectly obvious reason which is illustrative of why no Act can possibly take into consideration every future contingency.

In other words, ask yourself the question, Fred,[4] what is a civil war and you see how impossible it is to define it.

The Confederate States, as I remember it, most of them seceded from the Union in the winter of 1861. Most of them had seceded some time before Sumter. Well, what was the status then? Was it a civil war?

Then, in the late April of 1861, Sumter was fired on. Hostilities were confined at that time to Charleston Harbor. Was there a civil war going on? I don't know. In the North, they called it a Rebellion; in the South, they called it a War Between the States.

For a good many years we fought in this country a series of wars with the Redskins. They were recognized as wars because of the fact that special decorations were given to people who fought in them. They were the Indian Wars. Was that a civil war in the United States or not?

Further back, there was a Whiskey Rebellion, soon after the Revolution. Was that a civil war? I don't know.

In other words, civil war means anything or nothing and the circumstances and the particular case must be decided on by somebody who has authority 365 days of the year. That is about the easiest answer.

Of course it seems obvious that today, in this particular case in Spain, there are two organized groups of armies and the normal person trying to define the Spanish situation would normally call that particular situation a Civil War. There isn't much question about that.

In this particular case of the sale of these planes and engines, it is perhaps a rather good example of the need of some power in the Executive.[5] It is, furthermore, an example of cooperation by business. As the State Department has told you, they have had a number of applications from American citizens and firms to sell munitions to the belligerents in Spain, one side or the other, and the State Department told them, they specifically and definitely requested them not to engage in the transaction on two grounds, the first that it was contrary to the Government policy and secondly that it was endangering, even if only to a slight degree, of our desire to be neutral in this unfortunate happening in Spain.

Well, these companies went along with the request of the Government. There is the 90 per cent of business that is honest, I mean ethically honest; there is the 90 per cent we are always pointing at with pride. And then one man does what amounts to a perfectly legal but thoroughly unpatriotic act. He represents the 10 per cent or less of business that does not live up to the best standards.[6]

Excuse the homily, but I feel quite deeply about it.

Q: Supposing that the Government would not grant this license, or whatever you call it, for the exportation of those munitions?

The President: We have to under the law. The law says we must issue them.

Q: There are some persons who say that you have discretion under the law and that it could be refused?

The President: Couldn't do it. Absolutely not a chance. The law says that this Committee in the State Department shall grant the license.

Q: A mandamus could be obtained?

The President: Of course, there is the other phase of the case. If legislation is passed extending even the present Neutrality Act to civil wars and I find, by an executive finding, that a Civil War exists in the same way that I would under the present Act that a war between two nations exists, and that Act should become law within the next two weeks and after Congress meets, we could then clamp down on this particular shipment under this particular contract or commission.

That immediately raises the question as to whether this particular individual could go to the court of claims and seek damages for the profits which he otherwise would claim he could have made.

The best way of answering that is to ask you to read the Supreme Court's decision in the Neutrality case the other day.[7] There is an intimation in there, while it is only an intimation—nobody can guess what the Supreme Court would rule in a case like that—but the intimation is there to the effect that it being an act contrary to the request of the Government, and the conduct of foreign affairs being in the Executive, that the Courts would not grant reimbursement to this individual for a loss of what he otherwise would have made as being contrary to public policy. But, as I say, you cannot tell until the case is decided.

Q: This manufacturer who obtained this license was quoted today as saying that his planes were not to be used for military purposes at all and he claims he had a perfectly valid right and that he would provide employment for 1500 skilled workmen. He says they are not to be used for war purposes at all.

The President: Of course that particular plea was made in 1914 and 1915 and 1916, just the same way. They said that the export of machine guns would give work to Americans. It does not mean it is the right thing to do.

[President's Press Conferences:T]

[1] Above.

[2] Harry A. McBride, a veteran of the Foreign Service, at this time assistant to the Secretary of State; Blanton Winship was governor of Puerto Rico.

[3] The gunboat *Erie* had recently completed a cruise along the north coast of Spain, evacuating American nationals. No mention of this incident appeared in the newspapers.

[4] Fred Essary of the Baltimore *Sun.*

[5] Robert Cuse, president of the Vimalert Company, had obtained export licenses for the sale of almost $3,000,000 worth of airplanes and parts to the Loyalists. Moore explained to Bullitt in a dispatch of Dec. 29, 1936, that the Neutrality Act applied

to wars between nations only, and did not specifically forbid the export of arms and munitions to parties in civil strife (*Foreign Relations, 1936,* II, 618–620).

[6] Roosevelt referred to Cuse. The *Times* report of this press conference (Dec. 30, 1936, p. 1) commented on the President's annoyance.

[7] The Court, on Dec. 21, 1936, upheld the constitutionality of the joint resolution of May 28, 1934, empowering the President to ban arm sales to Bolivia and Paraguay.

Norman Thomas, Chairman, Public Affairs Committee of the Socialist Party, to Roosevelt

New York City, December 29, 1936

Dear Mr. President: It is with concern that I read newspaper stories to the effect that in the interest of neutrality, and in part at the suggestion of certain European nations, you contemplate asking Congress for immediate legislation to make it impossible for the Spanish Government to buy any military supplies whatsoever in the United States.[1]

The Socialist Party has long been an advocate of very drastic laws against supplying belligerent nations or prospective belligerents with the means of war. Exceptions to this rule, we have felt, should be permitted only by solemn act of the body authorized to declare war.

It is true that necessarily the sale of implements of war to the Spanish Government at this juncture means that some Americans are making a profit out of another nation's civil war, but nevertheless in vital respects the situation that now confronts the United States is very different from that created by a war between nations.

The Spanish Government is a duly constituted, democratically elected government, recognized by the United States. It is fighting against a military, fascist revolt. The effective rebel soldiers are mercenaries and foreigners, and they are well supplied with the most modern weapons of war by their friends among the European Powers. It is the legitimate democratic government which, despite the gallantry of the Spanish workers and other Loyalists, has been almost strangled by "non-intervention" agreements in Europe which have worked mostly to the advantage of the rebels.

The Powers which now request American cooperation in non-intervention have not, so far as the public is aware, consulted the United States upon the terms of their agreement or the way in which it is enforced. Apparently they offer no assurances whatsoever that they will stop the continuing stream of supplies to the rebels whose victory would menace the peace of the world by the encouragement it would give to fascist aggression. The victory of the Spanish Loyalists will have no such ill effects. That victory would have been won long ere this except for foreign aid—and this includes, according to report, the aid of British capitalist interests in Spain—to the rebels.

As you well know there has been precedent on this hemisphere for refusal to permit American citizens to furnish rebels against a democratically elected government with arms while allowing that government to make necessary purchases. I do not assume that that precedent is infallible and should always be binding. It has on occasion worked well. Is it not suggestive in the case of Spain?

Back in August the State Department gave a certain amount of aid to the rebels by ruling that supplies might be shipped to Spanish ports in rebel hands without fear of search and seizure by the Loyalist navy unless and until an effective blockade should be established. Although the rebels did not buy arms in this country, the State Department's interpretation of international law worked to their advantage. Now it is proposed still further to help them against a democratically elected government by the enactment of new domestic law in this country.

It is not a simple world wherein a principle useful to keep the United States out of international war must be automatically and inexorably applied in civil insurrection under circumstances where there is no danger of dragging this country into war. Let it be remembered that under no circumstances are we asking that the United States Navy, directly or indirectly, be used to guarantee delivery of the supplies the recognized Spanish Government has bought.

In the long run it is not peace for the world, or even for America, which will be served by applying to the Spanish rebellion a general principle which should be asserted more rigorously than is yet the case in Congressional legislation concerning neutrality in international war. We plead for recognition of the possibly disastrous effect of your action in disarming the Spanish Government in the face of well armed and ruthless rebel armies.[2]

Believe me, Respectfully yours,

Norman Thomas

[OF 422-C:TS]

[1] See New York *Times,* Dec. 29, 1936, p. 1.
[2] Answered Jan. 25, 1937, below.

Press Conference, Executive Offices of the White House, January 5, 1937, 4:20 P.M.

(Assistant Secretary of State Moore and Senator Pittman were present at this Conference.)

[*Excerpt*] Q: Anything on the neutrality legislation about to be proposed tomorrow?

The President: No. Some of you have already talked to the Acting Secretary of State on it and the next news, I imagine, will come through the Chairman of the Foreign Relations Committee of the Senate . . .[1]

Q: Does the Resolution which Senator Pittman wanted to introduce in the Senate, asking an embargo on munitions and arms to both Loyalists and Rebels in Spain, have your approval?

The President: I think you will have to get that from Senator Pittman. He is going out in a few minutes and I do not think he will give it to you when he goes out. (Laughter) . . .

Q: Coming back a moment to neutrality, is it your intention to have neutrality legislation concerning the civil war apply exclusively in this case to Spain, or is that a general policy?

The President: You will have to wait until you see Senator Pittman's Resolution.

Q: Will that be in accord with your views?

The President: You are just twenty-four hours too early.[2]

[President's Press Conferences:T]

---

[1] Acting Secretary of State Moore and Senator Pittman had conferred with Roosevelt (at Pittman's request) after the Cabinet meeting of Jan. 5, 1937 (Forster to Moore, Jan. 5, 1937, OF 1561).

[2] The Cuse affair (see press conference of Dec. 29, 1936, above), led to demands for amendment of the Neutrality Act. On Jan. 6, 1937, Pittman introduced S.J.R. 3 to prohibit the export of arms and munitions to Spain, and asked unanimous consent to consider it without reference to committee. Debate on the resolution was suspended during the morning session so that the Senate could hear the President deliver his annual message to the Congress; in this he asked immediate consideration of the neutrality legislation. The resolution's lengthy statement of aims drew objection from Senators Borah, Nye, and Vandenberg, and Pittman thereupon withdrew this. S.J.R. 3 was then passed by the Senate by a voice vote of 81 to 0, with 12 abstentions. In the House McReynolds introduced a similar resolution (H.J.R. 80) but this was sent to committee and the House took up the Senate measure. Here Maverick took the position that Nye and others had taken in the Senate, that the resolution was an unneutral act taken after the fact of civil war had been established. S.J.R. 3 was, however, approved by the House on the same day by a vote of 406 to 1, with 22 abstentions, and the President approved it on Jan. 8, 1937 (*Cong. Rec.*, vol. 81, pp. 71, 73–75, 76–80, 90–99; 50 *Stat.*

3). The message to Congress is printed in *Public Papers*, V, 634–642. Before the law became effective, the Cuse shipment left New York; the new law, however, provided that export licenses previously granted for export of war materials to Spain were invalid.

Robert W. Bingham, Ambassador to Great Britain, to Roosevelt

London, January 5, 1937

Dear Mr. President: I was of course eager to see you and to go home, but I know I need not assure you that I am not only willing but eager to carry out your wishes in this or in any other matter.[1]

So far as the internal situation here is concerned, the British have passed through their dynastic crisis successfully. I have no doubt they are much better off for the present and for the future than would have been possible under the previous regime. The present King is the most stable and reliable of the four brothers and the young Queen is all they could wish for in character and fitness for her position. Her parents were near neighbors of mine during the years when I spent the shooting seasons in Scotland and we are old friends. Indeed, I have known the whole family well for a long time.

The Duke of Windsor was surrounded by a pro-German cabal and many people here suspected that Mrs. Simpson was actually in German pay. I think this is unlikely and that her strong pro-German attitude was the result of flattering propaganda. However, the whole crowd has been cleared out. The Court has become respectable again, and the situation from the dynastic end is immeasurably improved.

My wife is sailing on the *Aquitania* tomorrow to look after some family matters, especially one happy event of great importance since we are expecting a new grandchild this month.

As she is going to Washington, I have asked her to deliver this letter to Mrs. Roosevelt, for delivery to you, and also another letter which I am preparing and expect to finish today dealing with the general situation here.[2]

I know you need no advice from me or anyone on this subject, but I cannot refrain from telling you how vitally necessary I believe a wide measure of discretion is for you in dealing with the question of neutrality. When you last discussed this subject with me, you told me of your statement to a group of Congressmen suggesting the possibility of a hostile landing, for example by the Japanese on Canadian or Mexican territory. That should have been enough, it seems to me, to convince any reasonable person with any knowledge of the subject. The recent situation in Spain perhaps may be regarded as fortunate since it may have clarified the basic necessities of neutrality legislation to some of those whose minds were still in a fog on the subject. Fundamentally, it is impossible to anticipate and to provide for all the contingencies which might arise. This being true, I have no doubt the widest possible latitude should be left to the discretion of the President.

Anthony Eden committed himself definitely to me more than a year ago on the subject of a trade agreement between our country and Great Britain. Mr. Baldwin committed himself on principle several months ago and told me of an announcement which he would make and did make at the Lord Mayor's banquet early in November. Quite recently, I have sent over a report of a conference I had with Walter Runciman, who for the first time definitely committed himself to the principle of an agreement along the lines of your agreement with Canada. This statement would not have come from Runciman without the approval of the financial and commercial influences in the Government, which had hitherto been holding out on us, so that this marks concrete progress towards some form of trade agreement.

In addition, both in and out of the Government, these people are becoming more and more anxious about the debt situation, but their financial element still hopes for a proposal from you instead of taking advantage of the opportunity you have given them to go to you. In the end, in my judgement, they will go to you with some form of proposal, especially if their outlook becomes darker, as it well may.

The spirit of peace and concord which you have created in the whole Western Hemisphere is really the one bright and shining light in an otherwise dark and unhappy world.

With every good wish for you and Mrs. Roosevelt, As ever,

Sincerely yours,

Robert W. Bingham

[PSF:Great Britain:TS]

[1] Bingham had proposed a visit home to confer with Roosevelt but Hull pointed out that since 1933 he had had 337 days of home leave and should remain in London (Bingham to Roosevelt, Dec. 4, 1936; Hull to Roosevelt, Dec. 18, 1936, PSF:Great Britain).

[2] Below.

Robert W. Bingham, Ambassador to Great Britain, to Roosevelt

[London] Jan. 5, '37.

Dear Mr. President: England turns the corner of the new year congratulating herself upon the manner, economically and politically, in which she has come through 1936; and the outlook for 1937 is bright for the prosperity of the Empire, provided war is avoided, and not unfavorable for the maintenance of peace in Europe. Meanwhile England is pushing her rearmament program as fast as she can, for she is confronted by two mighty autocracies—Russia and Germany, the latter in treaty understanding with Japan, the great autocracy of the Far East. While Belgium and France under ordinary circumstances may be considered as democratic allies of England, the internal position of these two countries makes the value of their assistance problematical. In spite of the terms of the Anglo-Italian declaration published today, Italy remains unreliable.[1]

I venture to recall that since the Spring of 1934 it has been my thesis that events must eventually force the British to come to us, and I believe we should realize that we are now actually in the midst of a British drive, the object of which is to persuade the United States, as the great democratic country of the West, that the frontier of democracy lies somewhere in the North Sea; that England, the outpost of democracy in Europe, is a small island containing over forty-five million people without raw materials and dependent upon the United States and the British Dominions for war materials and foodstuffs.

The methods of British propaganda are not hidden. Outstanding figures in politics and finance are constantly visiting the United States. Committees exist in Parliament today to study cooperation with the United States and to influence American visitors in this country. Parliamentary groups are planning visits, not only to the Eastern States, but through the Middle West as well. A press meeting at the English-speaking Union has been called for next week to examine monthly, weekly, and even daily exchanges of information by publications and broadcasts for the better understanding between the two countries. Official orders have been given in the British Army and Navy that good relations with their American opposite numbers at home and abroad must be established and maintained. Similarly, the attitude of government officials in their daily contacts with the Embassy and the public and private hospitality in England is marked with a progressive and almost bewildering friendliness that cannot pass unnoticed.

Furthermore, a large part of the foreign news appearing in the United States press, not only about England but concerning Europe generally, is sent by American correspondents stationed in London. These men are largely dependent upon English sources for much of their interpretative comment. This reporting of foreign news interpreted by British sources is bound to have an effect on American thought, as is also the foreign interpretative broadcasts, which, for reasons of language, generally emanate from British sources.

Due in large measure to the Buenos Aires Conference, it is increasingly clear to the United States how far we are prepared to go to cooperate for peace in the Western Hemisphere, but I feel that we should be equally clear in our minds as to how far we are prepared to go in working for peace outside of North and South America. Our recent neutrality legislation clearly indicates the trend of American thoughts and fears.

If, in the light of our increasing experiences, our neutrality legislation may be passed in a form that is not mandatory but leaving the discretionary power in the hands of the President and the Secretary of State, I feel we shall have indicated as great a contribution to peace in Europe as we can envisage without raising false hopes on this side of the Atlantic. For the rest, our contributions to peace must be in the economic field as has been so frequently indicated by the Administration.

I find a tendency here to claim that the position of the world today is so abnormal one cannot attempt to correct it by the normal processes looking to the restoration of international trade and finance. We should not be influenced by this line of argument, but continue to urge those measures we can defend as restoring the economic bases of peace.

Sincerely yours,

Robert W. Bingham

[PSF:Great Britain:TS]

[1] The so-called Anglo-Italian "Gentleman's Agreement" of Jan. 2, 1937, a brief document recognizing mutual interests in the Mediterranean, agreeing to maintain the status quo there, and agreeing to discourage all activities liable to impair good relations. See Stephen Heald, ed., *Documents on International Affairs, 1937* (London: Oxford University, 1939), p. 87.

Roosevelt to Claude A. Swanson, Secretary of the Navy

[Washington] January 7, 1937

Personal and Confidential

Memorandum for the Secretary of the Navy: Instead of sending Gerard alone, I am sending a delegation of three as Special Ambassadors to the Coronation. Gerard, Pershing and Rodman.[1] This makes it the most distinguished delegation I could find and Rodman is a particularly excellent choice because he was such a friend of King George V, and was with the Grand Fleet as you know.[2]

F.D.R.

[OF 48-I:CT]

[1] James W. Gerard, Gen. John J. Pershing, and Rear Admiral Hugh Rodman.
[2] This memorandum is in reply to Swanson's letter of Dec. 28, 1936 (OF 48-I), recommending the appointment of Rear Admiral A. Andrews to be naval aide to Ambassador Gerard.

John Cudahy, Ambassador to Poland, to Roosevelt

Warsaw, Poland, January 7, 1937

Confidential

My dear Mr. President: This is the first opportunity I have had to congratulate you very genuinely upon your great work in South America. I am certain the effect of your visit will be far-reaching as far as the American hemisphere is concerned. Your speech at Buenos Aires created a profound impression in Europe but I must tell you very frankly that now, scarcely two weeks later, its influence has been largely dissipated. The people of this continent are concerned primarily with their own troubles and above all they have a very realistic approach.

There is a tenacious belief in diplomatic circles that you contemplate some sort of move toward the pacification of Europe and only a few days ago there appeared a story in the Polish press that you were coming over here to preside over an international conference. I know this is entirely without foundation yet I can not resist writing you again that, in my opinion, any intervention without some specific remedy for the difficulties over here would not only be unavailing but would be a mistake from the viewpoint of American prestige.

I do not know what we can do. The outstanding menace to peace, of course, is Hitler. No one knows where he is going; probably he, himself, does not know, and this accounts for the lack of direction and apparent vacillation in the foreign policy of Great Britain and the continent.

My sources of information convince me that Great Britain will be prepared for eventualities in the summer of 1937 and this should change the atmosphere considerably. Until then, it is my belief that the British hope to hold Germany by conciliatory measures.

I do not like to clutter your very much over-cluttered desk with letters but I do want to impress upon you the futility of attempting any gesture toward Europe at this time unless this be based upon realistic remedies for the relief of existing troubles.

Very respectfully yours,

John Cudahy

[PSF:Poland:TS]

Press Conference, Executive Offices of the White House, January 8, 1937, 10:55 A.M.

[*Excerpt*] The President: I told you the other day[1] that I would give you the formal announcement about the two battleships, but because it came up in the Budget Conference yesterday afternoon, I thought it would be better to keep it and not release the battleship story until the Budget story is out of the way. It is only a matter of a couple of hours because the Budget will be up there at twelve o'clock today.

This is the memorandum given to me:

In accordance with the provisions of the Navy Appropriation Act of June 3, 1936, I have directed the Navy Department to proceed with the construction of two replacement Capital Ships. The keels of these ships may be laid in conformity with existing treaties at any time after January 1. Three of our battleships, the *Arkansas, Texas* and *New York,* will be more than 26 years old before these ships can be completed. If we are not to reduce our Navy by obsolescence, the replacement of capital ships can no longer be deferred.

The last Congress made an initial appropriation for "Two Capital ships, as replacement of over-age Capital ships, to be undertaken only in the event that the President determines as a fact that Capital-ship-replacement construction is commenced by any of the other signatory powers to the Treaty for the Limitation and Reduction of Naval Armaments signed at London, April 22, 1930."[2]

That Treaty prohibited the United States, the British Commonwealth of Nations and Japan from laying the keel of any battleship prior to January 1, 1937, and this restriction has been observed.

However, the laying of the keel does not mark the actual commencement of the construction of a ship. Prior to laying the keel, contracts have to be made and material assembled so that it will be some time before the actual keel is laid and, in fact, some time before the actual contract is let.

On July twenty-ninth, last year, the First Lord of the Admiralty, Sir Samuel Hoare, announced that the orders for two battleships of the 1936 program had been let. The keels, as I remember it from the press story, were laid the other day.

Q: On January third.

The President: On January third.

Q: How many, two?

The President: Two. And, in addition to those two British battleships, France laid the keel of the capital ship *Jean Bart* on December 12, 1936, and there are eight other capital ships under construction besides them, three in France, two in Italy and three in Germany.

I guess that is all except, of course, that I would like to express my very deep regret that it was impossible last year to obtain an agreement which would further limit battleship construction. It is true that this is replacement construction, but we had hoped that the date of replacement could have been deferred for another term so as to avoid the building of these new ships. However, agreement could not be reached although the United States Delegation did everything in their power to get an extension of new building, replacement building, agreed to by the other nations, but it did not go through. That is much to our regret and I think that is all we can say.

Q: What does a capital ship, completely equipped, cost now?

The President: I don't know.

Q: Is the fifty million figure approximately right?

The President: Approximately right. We haven't anything final from the other side but, as I remember it, the news story from England said that their ships would cost fifty to fifty-five million dollars each.

Q: Any existing funds available to start these ships?

The President: Only the general lump sum for construction and the item for continuing with the work—letting the contracts—is in the Budget that goes up at noon.

Q: Mr. President, when these two obsolete ships are taken out of the line, is there any purpose for which they can be used, training or any-thing?

The President: I cannot answer you except by a case that at the present time we have one obsolete battleship, off of which they have taken the guns. It is either—I think it is the *Wyoming*. She is not considered a battleship because her armor has been taken off and her guns have been taken off. She is used for the midshipmen's cruise every year.

Q: I think two of the old battleships, the *Texas* and the *Arkansas,* have also been taken out of the line within the last six weeks or two months and detailed to training service.

The President: Oh, we have been using the *Arkansas* for midshipmen also, but they are still considered a part of the sixteen battleships allowed under the old treaty.

Q: Would you say that the world naval armament race is now on?

The President: No.

Q: Has there been any decision as to fourteen or sixteen-inch guns or will there be any before April first when the time element expires for Japan to decide?

The President: That I cannot tell you. I do not know. I think so, though.

Q: Do you anticipate any difficulty of getting bids on these battleships because of the Walsh-Healey Act?[3]

The President: I do not believe there will be; I hope not.

Q: What if they refuse?

The President: You have to build them in the navy yards.

Q: Any estimate as to when the ships will be commissioned?

The President: I won't know that until the bids come in. One of them, of course, will have to be built in the navy yard anyway.

Q: Mr. President, three of our battleships are much older than any of the others. Has any thought been given as to when we will build their replacements?

The President: No; haven't got as far as thinking along that line. The hope is that we never will.

Q: Have the two new battleships been designed? Is the design com-plete?

The President: No, only rough sketches.

Q: Can you tell us any of the characteristics that will probably be in them?

The President: No.

Q: Any names been decided on for the new ships?

The President: No. You are about two years ahead of time, Fred[4] . . .

Q: In view of this new situation in China,[5] do you expect to ask for an embargo on the shipment of goods to China?

The President: That raises the question of the fact of the rebellion. I have not thought of anything else at the present time except this Spanish Resolution.

Q: One more point about the battleship question: In the discussion in the Budget, it says the Naval estimates of 1938 involve no expansion whatsoever over what it was planned before it was known that the treaty would not be renewed. How does that fit in?

The President: I do not quite understand. Do you mean there is nothing further planned?

Q: It says, "The Naval estimates for 1938 have been prepared on the basis of our Naval needs as covered by plans evolved under conditions obtaining under the Washington and London treaties. They involve no expansion whatever over what has been planned before it was known that these treaties were not going to be renewed."

The President: I guess Dan Bell forgot to put in the "if" clause. We would not be building them if the other fellows were not.

Q: Are you going to sign the Resolution today?[6]

The President: The State Department is supposed to have all the documents ready for me. Just as soon as it comes down here.

Q: This morning?

The President: No, but we will get it out as fast as we can and notify all the Collectors of Customs, et cetera.

Q: Thank you, Mr. President.

[President's Press Conferences:T]

[1] At the January 5 press conference, above.

[2] The full text of this statement was issued as a press release and is printed in *Public Papers*, V, 658–659.

[3] The Government Contracts Act approved June 30, 1936 (49 *Stat.* 2036), requiring prevailing wages and working conditions on government contracts.

[4] Fred Essary of the Baltimore *Sun.*

[5] The Communist-led army revolt in Shensi and Kansu provinces against the Nationalist government.

[6] S.J.R. 3, banning export of arms and munitions to Spain, approved Jan. 8, 1937.

Stanley High, Chairman, The Good Neighbor League, to Roosevelt

New York, N.Y., Jan. 8, 1937

Memorandum to the President: Mr. Walter Van Kirk is head of the National Peace Conference—which co-ordinates the work of 30 peace organizations. He is one of the most practical peace people I know.

Through these organizations he has prepared a statement endorsing the Reciprocal Trade Agreements. This statement has already been signed by approximately 1000 leading college presidents, economists, business men and (a very few) prominent clergymen.

This statement is for release a week from Monday, January 18th. Mr. Van Kirk would like to present it to you before its release—though without any tie-up between the presentation and the news story.

I believe that because of the importance of the men signing the statement and—even more—because of the groups back of Mr. Van Kirk this might be a good thing.[1]

Stanley High

[*Notation*:A:LeHand] STE   I suppose we had better do it—it will only take a few minutes   FDR

[OF 2020:TS]

---

[1] The statement, in the form of a letter to the President, was dated Jan. 14, 1937. (The original was sent to the State Department and was not returned to the White House.) As released to the press it was dated Jan. 17, 1937. Two copies of the press release are with the letter here printed; it appeared in the New York *Times* of Jan. 18, 1937, p. 19. The statement gave unqualified support to the trade agreements program and urged extension of the Trade Agreements Act. Van Kirk gave the letter to the President on January 22 who replied February 8, expressing his appreciation of the support Van Kirk's group was giving (OF 2020). The National Peace Conference issued a second press release on Jan. 24, 1937, proposing a number of economic measures to be adopted by the Administration in the interest of world peace (New York *Times*, Jan. 25, 1937, p. 3).

Roosevelt to R. Walton Moore, Acting Secretary of State

Washington, January 9, 1937

Private

My dear Mr. Secretary: As I have told you, I should personally like to nominate Cordell Hull for the Nobel Prize to be awarded December

10, 1937—but I hesitate to do so because of my position as the head of the Executive branch of the Government and of the fact that Cordell serves as the number one man in the Cabinet.[1]

I think it would be a fine thing if somebody not in the Government service at this time could make the nomination, but such a person would have to qualify under the terms of the enclosed notice.[2] If Nicholas Murray Butler or Newton Baker or Henry Stimson are members of the Institute of International Law and would care to make the nomination, it would be a very fitting thing.

Perhaps you would be good enough to take it up with one or more of them, and I have no objection if you care to show them this letter.[3]

Always sincerely,

Franklin D. Roosevelt

[PSF:Moore Papers:TS]

[1] In a memorandum to Moore of Dec. 28, 1936 (*Personal Letters, 1928–1945*, I, 642), Roosevelt had asked if it would be proper for him to nominate Hull for the 1937 Nobel peace prize and had asked Moore to consult with the persons named.
[2] Not present.
[3] Answered Jan. 14, 1937, below.

R. Walton Moore, Acting Secretary of State, to Roosevelt

Washington, January 9, 1937

Dear Mr. President: Since I recovered from my muddle-headed misnomer of Bill Bullitt,[1] I tried this morning to do some thinking on neutrality legislation, and the enclosure is the result. Since the memorandum was dictated, I have gone over it with Messrs. Sayre, Hackworth, and with Mr. Savage,[2] who has been for a year studying the neutrality question here, and I believe that it meets their general approval. I would not bother you with it at this time, except that I believe you will wish to reach your conclusions at an early date with reference to the legislation you will approve.

Yours very sincerely,

R. Walton Moore

[PSF:Neutrality:TS]

[1] Moore had talked with Roosevelt the day before (PPF 1-0); presumably this refers to something said then.
[2] Carleton Savage, assistant to Hunter Miller, historical adviser to the State Department.

[*Enclosure*] Suggestions with Reference to Neutrality Legislation

It will have to be determined whether to amend the present law or to substitute for it a new law, except a re-enactment of the license section.

Aside from the point just mentioned, my general view as to what would be possible and perhaps satisfactory is as follows:

1. I think it may be assumed that there will be insistence on maintaining the mandatory embargo provision relative to the shipment of arms, ammunition and implements of war to both or all belligerents when the President finds that there is a state of international war.

2. I think that the President should be authorized, when he finds that civil strife is threatened or in progress in any country and in his opinion the public safety so requires (I am adopting this language from one of the cases recently cited by the Supreme Court) to apply the provisions of the Joint Resolution approved January 31, 1922,[1] to such country.

3. I think that the President should be authorized, when an international war or civil strife is threatened or in progress and in his opinion the public safety so requires, to do all or any of the following things:

(a) Forbid or restrict the export from the United States to both or all of the belligerents any or all articles not included in the description "arms, ammunition and implements of war," with the proviso that such articles may be transported in foreign vessels if the consignor in every case shall have certified under oath that neither he nor any other citizen of the United States retains or has any right, title or interest in the articles shipped.

(b) Forbid the flotation in the United States of loans to belligerents and forbid or restrict commercial credits under such regulations as may be prescribed.

(c) Forbid or restrict under such regulations as may be prescribed travel by nationals of the United States on vessels belonging to or in which belligerents may have an interest.

(d) Forbid or restrict under the prescribed regulations the operation of commercial vessels of the United States in zones that, in the opinion of the President, are dangerous and

(e) Forbid the enlistment of nationals of the United States in the services of any belligerent wherever the nationals may be at the time.

In making these suggestions, of course, I have all the time had in mind that, in the actual drafting, a great deal of elaboration will be necessary and I have also constantly tried to think of what I believe to be the attitude of the Senate Committee.

There is attached to the memorandum a paper that shows the provisions of the Act of January 31, 1922, which is referred to under the above heading "2."

R.W.M.

[PSF:Neutrality:TS]

---

[1] Prohibiting the export from the United States of arms and munitions to certain countries (42 *Stat.* 361).

[*Enclosure*] Proposed Amendments to Joint Resolution of January 31, 1922

[Omit the part struck through and insert the part in brackets].

That whenever the President finds that in any ~~American~~ [foreign] country, ~~or in any country in which the United States exercises extraterritorial jurisdiction,~~ conditions of domestic violence exist, which are or may be promoted by the use of arms ~~or munitions~~ [, ammunition, or implements] of war procured from the United States, and makes proclamation thereof, it shall be unlawful to export, except under such limitations and exceptions as the President prescribes, any arms ~~or munitions~~ [ammunition, or implements] of war from any place in the United States to such country until otherwise ordered by the President or by Congress.

Sec. 2. Whoever exports any arms ~~or munitions~~ [, ammunition, or implements] of war in violation of section 1 shall, on conviction, be punished by fine not exceeding $10,000, or by imprisonment not exceeding two years, or both.

[PSF:Neutrality:CT]

Roosevelt to Fred Morris Dearing, Ambassador to Peru, Lima

[Washington] January 11, 1937

Dear Fred: Many thanks for your interesting letter.[1] I do hope that things will continue quiet in Lima. It is very important in these days to have no serious violence in this hemisphere.

Ever so many thanks for those interesting stamps.

Always sincerely yours,

[PPF 1210:CT]

[1] Dec. 19, 1936, above.

Roosevelt to Charles R. Crane, Palm Springs, California

[Washington] January 11, 1937

Dear Mr. Crane: Many thanks for your very interesting letter—especially the information about radios in China.[1] Certain of our friends in Germany and Italy should note this.

I had a wonderful rest on my trip to South America and I am going to take things more easily in the next four years than during my first term.

Always sincerely,

[PPF 462:CT]

[1] Crane, in a letter of Dec. 31, 1936 (PPF 462), said he had learned that the Chinese government had made wide distribution of cheap radios throughout the country, and that the people had been learning enough of the Mandarin dialect to understand the messages sent out every day from Nanking. This and the Japanese aggressions had unified China as never before and the total result was exactly the opposite of what the Japanese had been trying to accomplish.

Frederic R. Coudert to Roosevelt

[New York] January 13, 1937

My dear Frank: You doubtless know, from the newspapers and otherwise, of the visit of Mr. Walter Runciman to New York, which is entirely unofficial and personal.[1] He is now on the *Caledonia* en route to New

York and expects to arrive about the 18th or 19th of this month. Owing to family connection through marriage, he has asked me to act as honorary host during his stay in this city, which will be, I take it, for about a week. I am doing what I can to carry out his wishes and to make his visit as quiet and free from publicity as possible, and, in consequence, all invitations to speak, etc. have been declined on his behalf.

Mr. Runciman does intend, I know, going to Washington, and he will doubtless have the pleasure of seeing you and discussing matters of common interest. I have no doubt that through your own unfailing forethought everything has been or will be arranged so that this "mere commercial traveler," as he calls himself, may have an opportunity of seeing you in as unostentatious a fashion as may be possible. I am sure that such a meeting would be very pleasant to you both, and of importance to Anglo-American relations.

I take this opportunity of sending you, as always, my best wishes and congratulations upon the admirable fashion in which the "Skipper" has sailed the Ship of State through the troubled waters.[2]

Believe me, Very faithfully yours,

Frederic R. Coudert

[PPF 269:TS]

[1] Runciman, as head of the British Board of Trade, was to discuss British-American trade policies with Hull and other officials in Washington. So many rumors about the Runciman visit had appeared that on Jan. 6, 1937, Ambassador Lindsay informed McIntyre that the London Foreign Office would issue a statement January 8 to the effect that the visit was private and personal and that no political importance should be attached to it (PPF 4322). A statement appearing in the press on January 9 merely noted that Runciman's visit would be informal and that it was not known whether he would take up "governmental questions" (New York *Times,* Jan. 9, 1937, p. 2).

[2] Answered Jan. 16, 1937, below.

Frank P. Walsh, Chairman, New York State Power Authority, to Roosevelt

[Washington] January 13, 1937

Memorandum to the President in re: St. Lawrence Treaty: Yesterday, January 12, representatives of the National Seaway Council had an extended conference with Senator Pittman. In the course of the discussion the Senator stated that there were three factors of utmost importance to the successful handling of the St. Lawrence Treaty. These were:

1. That it be submitted by February 1. That if it could be submitted early it would be possible to get it through with very little delay. That the Foreign Relations Committee has as yet very little before it but expects within a month to be deluged with elaborate neutrality legislation which would probably interfere with efforts to expedite the St. Lawrence Treaty.

2. That the treaty have a new face, but cover approximately the same ground as the existing treaty. That it must have a new face in order to enable some who formerly voted against the treaty to switch to the favorable side without seeming inconsistent. That it must be substantially the same as the old treaty in order to warrant the contention that it was unnecessary to hold extensive hearings.

3. That he must have definite assurance of favorable action in Canada before the treaty is actually submitted to the Senate. That this is important because one of the first questions which will be raised will be whether, if it is ratified here, it can be ratified in Canada.

In connection with Senator Pittman's remarks it seems to me that early attention should be given to the importance of preparations for facilitating consideration of the treaty when it reaches the Senate.

In 1934 Senator Pittman did splendid work in leading the fight for ratification but complained that he was somewhat handicapped by having the plan of action brought to his attention almost simultaneously with the message of the President requesting the Senate to consider the treaty.

Our experience in that year suggests the advantage of having the Chairman of the Foreign Relations Committee kept informed in advance, so far as possible, of plans and progress. There are also points in the redrafting of the treaty at which consultation with him might prove valuable in the way of insuring the knocking off of rough spots which might stand in the way of Senate approval.

For this reason it might be considered advisable to discuss plans with Senator Pittman at an early date. A suggestion might also be made to the State Department that close cooperation with Senator Pittman is desirable.[1]

F.P.W.

[OF 156:T]

[1] The National Seaway Council was made up of representatives of Great Lakes and St. Lawrence valley business and civic groups interested in promoting the seaway. An unsigned memorandum of Dec. 31, 1936 (OF 156), apparently originating with the Council, reported that the project was in a strong position in the Senate and that 17

of the 23 members of the Foreign Relations Committee favored a new treaty with Canada. The memorandum warned, however, that delay would jeopardize ratification.

On January 12, 1937, Walsh and the President met at the White House with Hickerson, Olds, Manly, Armour, and Assistant Secretary of State Moore. The result of this conference was that Roosevelt recommended that certain measures be taken, including a visit by Prime Minister King to Washington in February "on personal invitation" of the President. He also urged that those present do what was necessary to bring the treaty before the Senate early in March (memorandum by Walsh, Feb. 18, 1937, OF 156). The day after Walsh's January 12 meeting with Roosevelt, he sent a note to McIntyre (OF 156) informing the latter that the President had said he would write a note to Lehman about the St. Lawrence situation. Walsh explained that it was important that he (Walsh) talk to Lehman as soon as possible but that he preferred that the governor hear first from Roosevelt. See below.

Roosevelt to Governor Herbert H. Lehman of New York, Albany

[Washington] January 14, 1937

Dear Herbert: I think you will be glad to know that the St. Lawrence situation is coming to a head again. Informal negotiations are now going forward with Canada and I hope that within six weeks or two months they can be made formal and result in a modified treaty. This being so, I hope the New York State Authority can continue as it is very valuable to us in Washington in the work it does and the information it supplies.[1]

As ever yours,

[OF 156:CT]

[1] A copy of this letter was sent to the chairman of the New York State Power Authority (McIntyre to Walsh, Jan. 14, 1937, OF 156).

R. Walton Moore, Acting Secretary of State, to Roosevelt

Washington, January 14, 1937

Dear Mr. President: In compliance with your suggestion[1] I communicated with Dr. Nicholas Murray Butler, Mr. Newton D. Baker and Mr. Henry L. Stimson. Attached is a letter I have received this morning from Dr. Butler.[2] It seems to me that it would be well for you to write to Anthony Biddle, indicating that when he hears that Dr. Butler has made

the nomination you desire to have your interest in the matter manifested.[3]

Yours very sincerely,

R. Walton Moore

P.S. Since the above was dictated, a letter has come in from Mr. Baker,
which I enclose along with your letter to me and also a copy of Mr.
Baker's letter to the Nobel Committee.[4]

I am thanking Dr. Butler and Mr. Baker for their kindness.

R.W.M.

[PSF:State:TS]

[1] Roosevelt to Moore, Jan. 9, 1937, above.
[2] Jan. 13, 1937, saying that he could think of no more deserving a recipient than
Hull and that he would write to the Nobel committee.
[3] See Roosevelt to Biddle, Jan. 19, 1937, below.
[4] Baker to Moore, Jan. 13, 1937, enclosing Baker's letter to the Nobel committee, Jan.
13, 1937.

Press Conference, Executive Offices of the White House, January 15, 1937, 10:45 A.M.

[*Excerpt*] Q: Mr. President, can you tell us about any prospects of a
new St. Lawrence Treaty, or whether any consideration has been given
to including the Niagara Falls power and improvement work in it?

The President: I read a story this morning and, of course, it is just
one of those things. The story is a factual story that goes about ninety
percent further than there is any justification for. What has happened
is this: Perfectly informally we have been talking with the Canadian
Government in regard to the possibility of discussing the question of
the St. Lawrence. Now that, literally, is as far as we have got and there
isn't another thing. It is the question of the St. Lawrence—I am not
referring to specific treaties—and the question of the St. Lawrence, of
course, includes any one of the treaties, such as the Great Lakes, and
it includes the question of Niagara Falls. It is the whole thing. You can
call it the area from the headlakes of Superior—from Duluth down to
the Montreal tidewater. That is as far as anybody has got. I could not
write anything more than that because there isn't anything more to say.

Q: Then there is not likely to be any treaty submitted at this session of Congress?

The President: I honestly haven't got any idea. In other words, we are talking about whether we will have conversations . . .

Q: Do you care to say anything about the story that you are calling an economic conference with France and Great Britain?

The President: Of course there is not a word of truth in it. I don't know how a thing like that gets started. Sir Walter Runciman is coming over here. He has been planning to come over here on a holiday—I think the thing was planned two or three months ago—and when he comes here he will come to see me. But he is over here on a holiday and he is coming to see me as a personal friend and that is all there is to it.

[President's Press Conferences:T]

Henry Morgenthau, Jr., Secretary of the Treasury, to Roosevelt

Washington, January 15, 1937

My dear Mr. President: I am inclosing herewith extract from Cochran's cable of January 12 reporting a conversation with Schacht whom he met at the meeting of the directors of the Bank of International Settlements.[1]

Respectfully,

H. Morgenthau Jr.

[PSF:Germany:TS]

[1] Schacht, as president of the Reichsbank, was an ex officio director of the Bank for International Settlements.

[Enclosure] H. Merle Cochran, First Secretary, American Embassy, Paris, to Henry Morgenthau, Jr.

Extract

I had a separate conversation with Schacht. He made reference to his article in Foreign Affairs on the question of colonies for Germany.[1]

I asked whether he had made any progress in this regard with the French and the British. The French attitude, he said, after his visit to Paris late last summer, was satisfactory; the Germans had found it entirely possible to have direct conversations with the French. The British, he said, had not yet given a definite or formal answer to Germany's plea for raw material resources although he had been most discouraged by Eden's attitude and the British rebuff to the French approach on this subject after Schacht's visit to Paris. Schacht reminded me of the Hitler Government's sincere offers for disarmament and peace. One after another of these offers, he said, including that of limiting the army to 300,000 men had either been totally ignored or had been refused. He told me he thought they might be making their last offer in the outstanding offer for peace in return for colonies. Great Britain and the world, he said, should understand that the Hitler Government is firmly established, and if there is any attempt to humble Germany the German people will be solidly behind it.

Schacht said again that it is not possible to have world peace without German peace. He emphasized the efforts and aims of the United States toward peace: He expressed the hope that the United States would not let slip the opportunity which he says is now ours, particularly the President's, to take the lead in solving the outstanding questions of Europe, and primarily Germany's problems.

The idea of a Washington conference was mentioned by Schacht; I asked him why in Washington, and he replied that the United States has now the world's leadership and the wealth to make it effective so that other nations should be called to Washington for conference and discussion. I asked Schacht whether he had been told the scheme which had been suggested to me that day by one of my earnest Central Bank friends; i.e., for Germany to borrow from the United States to buy neutral territory from England and for the latter to apply the proceeds of the sale upon British war debt to us. This suggestion was made by Yahagita (Japan). The reply of Schacht was that he was not suggesting the measures that should be taken; however, he hopes that we would take advantage of Runciman's visit and that of another distinguished Britisher—Niemeyer,[2] I assume—to indicate to the British that we are interested in a final and happy liquidation of the problems facing Germany.

Schacht's Basel representative, Heschler, told me that the atmosphere created by press accusations of German activities in Morocco had disgusted Schacht.[3] This subject was discussed at length by Schacht and

Norman. According to Heschler, Schacht told him (Heschler) that the whole press story was a pure fabrication, that Germany had sold certain supplies to France and the latter could not pay in cash; consequently there was some activity in France shipping to Germany in a barter for such supplies, ores, and other materials which could be obtained in Spanish Morocco. The affair was no more than that. Niemeyer remarked, in discussing the article of Schacht's in *Foreign Affairs,* that the two raw materials which are needed most by Germany, rubber and wool, are not commercially available in the colonies which Schacht is seeking.

February 8 has been set as the date for the next meeting of the B.I.S.

[PSF:Germany:T]

[1]"Germany's Colonial Demands," *Foreign Affairs,* XV (January 1937), 223–234. Ambassador Dodd told Hitler on Jan. 11, 1937, that he had read Schacht's article and thought it "very able" and in the main he agreed with all he said (*Diary,* p. 379).

[2]Presumably Sir Otto E. Niemeyer, British financial expert, member of the Joint Exchequer Board of Great Britain and Ireland.

[3]Late in 1936 reports of German troop landings in Spanish Morocco, and rumors of German-built fortifications and air and submarine bases there, were regarded in France as evidence that Germany and Italy were trying to cut France off from her African colonies. Berlin branded the reports as French fabrications (New York *Times,* Jan. 10, 1937, p. 1).

Roosevelt to Frederic R. Coudert, New York

[Washington] January 16, 1937

Dear Fred: We are looking forward to have Mr. and Mrs. Runciman as our guests in the White House. I understand that they are to come down here on Saturday, January twenty-third, to stay over Sunday.

If they get to the White House soon after luncheon on the twenty-third, I will be able to have some free time to talk with him that day and Sunday.

I do hope to see you one of these days soon and to tell you of some of my problems.[1]

As ever yours,

[PPF 269:CT]

[1]This note was in reply to Coudert's letter of Jan. 13, 1937, above. The Runcimans were at the White House the week end of January 23–25; on January 24 Runciman conferred with Hull and Roosevelt on trade agreements (New York *Times,* Jan. 27, 1937,

p. 7). At his January 26 press conference Roosevelt said further talks would be necessary to see if a basis for future negotiations existed; he also said their conversation had touched on other matters. In a letter to LeHand of Jan. 22, 1937, Stanley High said that the Runciman visit was reported to be "part of an effort to bring about Anglo-American cooperation for the rehabilitation of German economy" (PPF 4322).

Runciman also talked with Assistant Secretary of State Sayre on trade agreements; see *Foreign Relations, 1937,* II, 6–8. Ambassador Lindsay said British press reports of the talks were unduly optimistic (Early to Roosevelt, Jan. 26, 1937, PPF 4322), and both the State Department and the British Foreign Office minimized the results achieved (New York *Times,* Jan. 27, 1937, p. 7). Roosevelt later wrote to Arthur Murray (who had suggested the Runciman visit) that he and Runciman were just getting to know each other well enough to talk freely when the visit came to an end. He said neither was particularly optimistic but that the talks had helped (Feb. 25, 1937, PPF 435).

Roosevelt to R. Walton Moore, Assistant Secretary of State

[Washington] January 16, 1937

Memorandum for Assistant Secretary Moore: I have read with some surprise the memorandum of December 30th, sent to you from the Division of Mexican Affairs.[1] It does not represent the policy of the government.

First, the Ambassador to Mexico states that the statement on February first concerning President Cardenas' attitude is not verbally correct.[2]

Secondly, the statement at the bottom of page 1 and at the top of page 2 that the United States cannot acquiesce in the expropriation of lands of Americans unless compensation based on the actual loss to the owner is paid, represents perhaps a policy of many years ago but certainly not the policy of today.[3]

Finally, the suggested instructions to the Ambassador at the foot of the page are also wholly out of line with present policy.[4]

I think our policy can best be stated as follows:

In the matter of expropriation of American owned property of any kind in any foreign country the United States expects prompt and effective compensation to be paid to the owners on not less than the same basis that payments are made to the nationals of the country making the expropriation.

Please inform the Division of Mexican Affairs and all other Divisions of the State Department of this policy.[5]

[PSF:Mexico:CT]

[1] Prepared by R. C. Tanis, acting chief of the division, and addressed to Moore, printed in *Foreign Relations, 1937,* V, 602–603. The copy with the letter here printed bears a notation by Moore that he had asked Daniels to consider the policy statement proposed by Tanis (quoted below in n. 4) and to talk with the President about it. Daniels did so at the White House on January 11 (PPF 1-0).

[2] Not further identified.

[3] "Some time ago we took the position in instructions sent to Ambassador Daniels that the Department cannot acquiesce in the expropriation of lands belonging to American citizens unless prompt and effective compensation based upon the actual loss to the owner is to be paid" (Tanis to Moore, cited in n. 1).

[4] These instructions read: "The President cannot regard without deep concern the continuance of a policy in Mexico which amounts virtually to confiscation of American-owned lands. While the President would have no objection to a settlement of the specific case of the Yaqui Valley problem along the lines of a plan acceptable to the American landowners in that area, he sincerely hopes that not as a favor but as a matter of right from now on there may be a cessation of expropriations of American-owned lands in Mexico unless prompt and effective compensation based upon the actual loss to the owners of such lands is to be paid. The President also anticipates that arrangements will shortly be made by the Mexican Government for the effective compensation of American citizens who have already been deprived of their property."

[5] Cárdenas' administration had greatly moderated its anti-clerical attitude of 1934–35, and Daniels reported to Hull in a dispatch of March 28, 1936 (*Foreign Relations, 1936,* V, 774), that conditions were much improved. The Mexican land expropriation law was, however, still a matter of contention. On Dec. 16, 1936, Daniels reported to Hull (*ibid.,* pp. 709–715), that Cárdenas had offered Roosevelt any settlement he desired in the Yaquí Valley land controversy (involving many American landowners) "to save him from embarrassment and difficulty in the United States."

Roosevelt to Virginia C. Gildersleeve, Dean, Barnard College, Columbia University, New York

[Washington] January 18, 1937

Dear Dean Gildersleeve: The Inter-American Conference for the Maintenance of Peace which was held at Buenos Aires last month marks a very definite advance toward assuring peace in the new world. Further, it gave evidence, which should be of real value to a troubled world, that nations may meet in an atmosphere of confidence and good will to seek just solutions for their common problems. The concrete steps taken to increase intellectual cooperation among the American Republics and to strengthen a public opinion in favor of peace must be placed high among effective measures to counteract international fear and suspicion.[1]

Very sincerely yours,

[PPF 3289:CT]

[1] Roosevelt had been invited to attend a Pan-American dinner to be held at Barnard College on January 22; when he could not accept the invitation, he was asked to send a message to Dean Gildersleeve to be read on the occasion (Carolina Marcial-Dorado to Early, Jan. 13, 1937, PPF 3289). This reply was drafted by Welles (Welles to Early, Jan. 16, 1937, PPF 3289).

Roosevelt to Anthony J. Drexel Biddle, Jr., Minister to Norway, Oslo

[Washington] January 19, 1937

Dear Tony: I am enclosing some correspondence which tells its own story.[1] I really believe that Secretary Hull is more entitled to the Nobel Peace Prize than any other person this year. He was so big and generous last year that he eliminated himself and supported the award to Carlos Saavedra Lamas. Dr. Lamas, of course, well merited the Prize because of his work in the Assembly of the League of Nations but, so far as untiring efforts for peace on this Continent are concerned, Secretary Hull has been for three whole years the guiding spirit—beginning with Montevideo in 1933 and culminating this year at Buenos Aires. It was his splendid spirit and, at the same time, his energy which has made possible the great Inter-American contribution to world peace.

My personal preference would have been to nominate Secretary Hull myself, as I am entitled to do as the head of the Government; I am afraid, however, that the Committee might feel that I was pushing my own Secretary of State and that the nomination should come from sources which are wholly non-partisan.

Perhaps you can informally explain this thought of mine and, at the same time, that quite aside from my Administration or official position and as one who long before assuming the Presidency maintained an active interest in international peace, I very strongly believe that Secretary Hull, at this time, stands far above any other individual whom I can think of who is worthy of the bestowal of the Nobel Peace Prize.[2]

Always sincerely,

[PPF 335:CT]

[1] Copies of letters from Butler and Moore; see Moore to Roosevelt, Jan. 14, 1937, above.

[2] Biddle replied Feb. 17, 1937 (PSF:Norway), that the letters of recommendation had been received by the Nobel committee. He enclosed copies of a cablegram and a letter from Senator Gerald P. Nye to the committee, both of Jan. 29, 1937. In the letter Nye

said, "One does not need draw on his imagination to enthuse over the will which has moved Secretary Hull in his activities, nor does one doubt the profound desire which has been his for better international understanding. This, I can say even as one who had not always agreed with his direction, yet his purpose has ever been high and noble . . ."

Roosevelt to Norman Thomas, Chairman, Public Affairs Committee of the Socialist Party, New York

[Washington] January 25, 1937

My dear Mr. Thomas: I acknowledge the receipt of your letter of December 29, 1936,[1] in which you describe your objections to the policy of discouraging the export of arms from this country to Spain for the use of the Spanish Government.

The Department of State, with my entire approval, soon after the beginning of the civil war in Spain, took a definite stand on the subject of the export of arms to that country—a stand which was in entire conformity with our well-established policy of non-intervention and with the spirit of the recent neutrality acts. On August 7, 1936, the Acting Secretary of State sent an instruction to all representatives of this Government in Spain in which he said in part:

. . . in conformity with its well-established policy of non-interference with internal affairs in other countries, either in time of peace or in the event of civil strife, this Government will, of course, scrupulously refrain from any interference whatsoever in the unfortunate Spanish situation. We believe that American citizens, both at home and abroad, are patriotically observing this well-recognized American policy.[2]

You will observe that this stand was taken some weeks before the non-intervention pact among the several European nations came into effect and while the policy of those nations toward the Spanish conflict was still uncertain and undetermined. No suggestion was made to us by any European country in regard to the attitude which we should adopt at that time nor have there been any subsequent suggestions of such a nature. Our stand was taken as a completely independent measure which arose naturally and inevitably from our policy of non-intervention and from the spirit of the recent neutrality laws.

It is true that these laws referred only to wars between nations and that our policy in this hemisphere has frequently been to permit the export of arms to established governments, while denying them to insurgent groups. In dealing with civil strife in this hemisphere, however, we have been acting under a law—the Joint Resolution of January 31, 1922—the underlying principle of which has been embodied since 1928 in a Convention which we entered into with many of our neighbors to the South.

This Joint Resolution is not applicable to exports of arms to Europe and in this case we have felt bound to hold to the strict impartiality envisaged by our more recent neutrality acts. Furthermore, the very circumstances which you set forth so fully in your letter must make it clear that the civil conflict in Spain involves so many non-Spanish elements and has such wide international implications that a policy of attempting to discriminate between the parties would be dangerous in the extreme. Not only would we, by permitting unchecked the flow of arms to one party in the conflict, be involving ourselves directly in that European strife from which our people desire so deeply to remain aloof, but we would be deliberately encouraging those nations which would be glad of this pretext to continue their assistance to one side or the other in Spain and aggravating those disagreements among the European nations which are a constant menace to the peace of the world.[3]

Very sincerely yours,

[OF 422-C:CT]

[1] Above.

[2] The entire dispatch is printed in *Foreign Relations, 1936,* II, 471.

[3] Drafted by Assistant Secretary of State Moore (Moore to Roosevelt, Jan. 7, 1937, OF 422-C). Although this letter does not come within the chronological period of Roosevelt's first term, it is included in this volume to avoid breaking his exchange of correspondence with Norman Thomas on a major issue of foreign relations arising during the first Administration.

Index for Volumes I–III

Abbink, John, I: 626

Académie Diplomatique Internationale, II: 575; location, I: 331–332; II: 327–328, 329, 375–376

Acheson, Dean G., I: 263, 264; letters of, I: 251, 253; letters to, I: 270, 431; favors currency stabilization agreement, I: 253, 266; opposes inflation policy, I: 414; and foreign security holders organization, I: 417; attitude toward British war debt, I: 422

Adair, J. Leroy, I: 226

Adams, Alva B., I: 311; II: 418; and Waterway Treaty, II: 20, 23, 371; favors World Court, II: 353

Adams, Charles F., I: 348, 463

Adams, James T.: letter to, II: 83

Adler, Cyrus, II: 404

Agadir crisis (1911), III: 297

Agence Économique et financière, II: 548; III: 507

Agnew, W. D.: letter of, II: 104

Agricultural Adjustment Act (1933), I: 61; and wheat production, I: 147; and sugar production, I: 181–182; II: 86; presidential authority under, I: 436; II: 131

Agricultural Adjustment Administration: and foreign trade, I: 441, 450; III: 70; and tobacco prices, II: 416

Agriculture, Department of, I: 455, 556; II: 331

Agriculture, Secretary of, *Henry A. Wallace,* I: 454; III: 349; letters of, I: 186, 281, 466; II: 405; III: 38, 315; letters to, II: 224, 409, 508, 555; III: 8, 123, 124; and sugar quotas, I: 262; at Annapolis conference, I: 268; drafts tariff memorandum, I: 271–272; and sugar agreement, I: 414–415; and Roerich peace pact, I: 423; differs with Peek, I: 483, 521; and report of Executive Committee on Commercial Policy, I: 544; talks with FDR, I: 571, 578; and shipping subsidies, II: 185–186; and wartime economic controls, II: 311; and cotton exports, II: 365, 405, 409, 425; and foreign trade credit, II: 582; recommends repeal of whale oil tax, II: 603;

at press conference, III: 72; drafts FDR letter and speech, III: 98, 116; and Japanese cotton exports, III: 307; supports Villard as Inter-American Conference delegate, III: 313; denies FDR has peace plan, III: 401

Ailman, Mildred A., III: 232

Aitken, William M. (Lord Beaverbrook), I: 579; III: 407, 426

Alaska, II: 443

Alba, Santiago, II: 277; III: 398

Albania: and Italy, I: 258, 284–287; and Balkan Pact, II: 97; and Greece, II: 303; and U.S., II: 512

Albernoz, Sanchez, III: 436

Albert I, of Belgium: letter of, I: 280; letter to, I: 198; FDR visit with (1919), I: 176; and Morris, I: 288, 412

Aldrich, Winthrop, I: 359

Alessandri Palma, Arturo, III: 531, 532

Aleutian Islands, II: 323, 443

Alexander I, of Yugoslavia, II: 235, 303

Alfaro, Colon, III: 348

Alfieri, Dino, I: 257

Alfonso XIII, of Spain, I: 261

Alien Property Custodian, II: 37, 518

All American Cables Inc., I: 648

Allen, Frederick H., II: 376; letters of, II: 327, 367; III: 156; letters to, I: 331; II: 329, 374, 575; III: 166

Allen, George, III: 322

Allen, Jay, II: 279, 280

Allinson, Brent, II: 587

Aloisi, Pompeo, I: 284; II: 613

Álvarez del Yayo, Julio, III: 414, 418–419, 435

Amberjack II, I: 248, 250, 251, 283

American Academy of Arts and Letters, II: 49, 50, 151

American Association of University Women, I: 223; II: 353

American Bankers Association, II: 119

American Bar Association, II: 348

American Bemberg Corporation, I: 175

American Chamber of Commerce (Madrid), I: 528